*Everyman's Thesaurus
of English Words
and Phrases*

Everyman's Thesaurus of English Words and Phrases

**Revised from PETER ROGET
by D. C. BROWNING**
MA (GLASGOW), BA, B. LITT (OXON)

SPHERE REFERENCE

First published in Great Britain in the *Everyman* edition by
J. M. Dent and Sons Ltd 1952
This edition compiled by D. C. Browning
Last revised edition 1971
Revisions copyright © J. M. Dent and Sons Ltd 1971
Published by Sphere Books Ltd 1981
27 Wrights Lane, London W8 5TZ
Reprinted 1982, 1983, 1984 (twice), 1985 (twice), 1986, 1987

TRADE
MARK

Set in Photon Times by Fleetlines Ltd,
Southend-on Sea, Essex

Printed and bound in Great Britain by
Collins, Glasgow

INTRODUCTION

It is just a hundred years since Roget's *Thesaurus of English Words and Phrases* was first published. In the course of that century of unprecedented development and change our language and vocabulary have undergone modifications and additions which have been dealt with from time to time in previous revisions of the work. But a new generation has grown up since the last recension, and the time seemed ripe for a more complete overhaul which would make it thoroughly up to date. Accordingly, the opportunity has been taken, in preparing this new single-volume edition, of giving the work as complete a revision as was possible, short of doing the whole compilation afresh. Every paragraph has been carefully reviewed, over 10,000 words and phrases have been added, and the articles have been 'tidied up' so that all additions follow the logical order which agrees with the original plan.

In the course of its century of use Roget's *Thesaurus* has come to be as widely accepted and as indispensable to writers as a dictionary and its system and arrangement have become so familiar that any radical alteration of them would lessen the value of the book to those who know their way about it from constant use. For that reason no attempt has been made to modify the main scheme which Roget originally laid down, and except for a few very minor alterations of numbering where the order had become confused the arrangement is the same as in previous editions. Within this scheme the articles have been greatly amplified and expanded, some of the pages containing up to a hundred fresh insertions.

The list of contents at the beginning sets out the plan of classification, and indicates the general divisions of the book. Readers who are interested in the detailed subdivisions of the classification will find them in the different paragraph headings, and the general principles of the work are explained in Roget's original Introduction, now printed at the end of the volume.

Technical Terms.

In giving some account of the additions which have been made, it is natural to start off with those technical terms which have been coined to fit modern scientific, political, and cultural developments. The wide range of the subjects covered is shown by these typical examples taken at random: *air-condition, airgraph, allergy, antibiotic, Appleton layer, bathysphere, Dadaism, deviationist, diarchy, displaced person, electrolysis, existentialism, fifth column, Gallup poll, geriatrics, Heaviside layer, hydroponics, intercom, ionosphere, iron curtain, libido, liquidate, parapsychology, psychotherapist, quisling, radar, robot, rotor, stratosphere, surrealism, telekinesis, television, troposphere, weather station.*

Aviation.

Along with the previous section may be grouped the very numerous terms which deal with recent developments in aviation and aerial warfare. These represent new types of aircraft: *autogiro, flying fortress, flying wing, jet aircraft, stratocruiser, stratoliner;* new types of weapon: *atom bomb, buzz-bomb, doodlebug, flying bomb, guided missile, V1, V2;* new names for personnel: *group-captain, wing-commander, squadron-leader, flight-lieutenant;* and for their evolutions: *air lift, bunt.* Finally there are words for the yet untried adventure of interplanetary voyaging: *astronautics, spacecraft, space ship, space travel.*

Everyday Neologisms.

In addition to words marking scientific advance there are also, of course, many neologisms reflecting change or fashion in everyday affairs, such as *baby-sitter, bingle, blurb, bottle-neck, bottle party, bulldozer, cannibalize, cartophily, embus, exclosure, frogman, green belt, infrastructure, jive, lumberjacket, nylons, phillumenist, play-pen, plug* (repeat), *prefab, pullover, quiz, screen* (test), *stockpile, totalizator, zipper.*

Slang Terms.

New slang terms form a considerable proportion of our additions, and among them will be noted a large number of service, particularly Air Force, coinages; the newest arm seems to have eclipsed the Navy in fertility of etymological invention. A few of the more recent terms are: *blah, browned off, bunce, chokka, dippy, erk, flap* (fuss), *flat out, flicks* (cinema), *gen, good show, hush-hush, It, Joe Soap, loopy, mike* (microphone), *never-never system, oodles, popsy, scarper, scatty, shemozzle, smashing, sprog, toffee-nose, twerp, whodunit,* and such phrases as *get cracking, get weaving, gone for a Burton, in a spin, it's in the bag, a piece of cake, shoot down in flames, step on it, tear off a strip, couldn't care less.*

Americanisms.

So many of our slang and other new words are borrowed from across the Atlantic that they demand a separate paragraph. A number of the commoner Americanisms had already been incorporated in the work, but fresh additions include *attaboy, bobbysoxer, boloney, bonehead, bughouse, burp, calaboose, chipper, come-back, cutie, didoes, doll up, faze, floosy, 'fraid-cat, G-man, gander* (look), *goo, grip-sack, haywire, hick, high-hat, hoodlum, hooey, hophead, jeep, jinx, josh, juke box, mazuma, mortician, motel, oomph, once-over, pan* (face), *pep, pinch-hitter, punk, rube, scram, screwball, simoleons, simp, smog, snoop, soup-and-fish, spondulics, stand-in, stooge, stuffed shirt, teenager, tuxedo, upstage, wisecrack, wop, yegg,* along with phrases like *cut no ice, hit the hay, out of kilter, stick one's neck out, take a run-out powder, give the frozen mitt.*

Scotticisms.

The opportunity has also been taken to insert a few of the terms in most common use north of the Tweed or wherever there are colonies of Scots. Only the most familiar words have been inserted, such as *ben, brae, callant, canny, clachan, clarts, dander, dunt, fash, flyte, glaur, gowk, havers, hoots, jalouse, kenspeckle, kittle, kyle, kyte, lum, ooss, pech, ploy, quaich, scunner, shilpit, shoogle, siller, skelp, skirl, smeddum, smirr, snowk, sonsy, speer, stot* (bounce), *stour, stramash, thole, thrapple, thowless, tirrivee, wean* (child), *wersh, wheesht.*

Nouns of Assemblage.

Among the more interesting old-fashioned additions may be mentioned the collection of nouns of assemblage in paragraph 72. In addition to the familiar *flock, herd, drove, pack,* there are listed the distinctive terms *sounder* (of swine), *skulk* (of foxes), *pride* (of lions), *charm* (of finches), *flush* (of mallards), *gaggle* (of geese), and *wedge* (of swans). To old patrons of the work this list should make up for the omission of the tedious and pointless catalogue of different methods of divination, from aeromancy to sciomancy, which was formerly given as a footnote under *Prediction* (511).

Changes and Excisions.

Very few changes have been made in the original grouping. The list of types of *tobacco-pipe* has been transferred from the *Air-pipe* paragraph to the *Tobacco* section, where it will naturally be more in keeping. The account of religious terms towards the end of the book has been rearranged so that *dissenters* and *nonconformists* are not grouped with *idolaters, fire-worshippers,* and other *heathens* under the comprehensive but hardly explicit heading of *Heterodoxy.* A number of foreign words and phrases have been omitted, particularly the more out-of-the-way Latin phrases, which are no longer so popular as in the days when Classics and culture were synonymous. Finally, many words like *caisson, chaperon, château,* which were formerly italicized as foreign are now printed in ordinary characters, having been accepted as English.

The Index

The opportunity has been taken of arranging the alphabetization of the references according to the up-to-date 'nothing-before-something' system set out in the pamphlet on Alphabetical Arrangement published by the British Standards Institution. By this system phrases are inserted in order after their initial word, and hyphened words are reckoned as two except when the initial component is merely a prefix. Every attempt has been made to render the index as complete as possible, and the process of hunting the required word in the body of the work has been further simplified by the insertion of numerous cross-references in those cases where one paragraph is closely related to others.

NOTE

Since the first publication of the single-volume edition in Everymans's Reference Library in 1952 several reprints and a substantial revision in 1962 have taken account of recent developments in English vocabulary.

Two hundred words or meanings have been inserted in their appropriate places throughout the various sections, and corresponding references have been added to the index. In 1955 separate sections were allotted to *Aircraft, Cinema* and *Radio*. The revision of 1962 reflected progress in space travel, radio, transport and jazz music, with such words as *astronaut, lunik, orbital; newscast, teleprompter, transistor; clearway, speedway, traffic warden; bebop, rock-and-roll, skiffle.* Also included were examples of terms coined for types of pompous circumlocution (e.g. *officialese, gobbledygook)*, and modern slang.

D. C. Browning having relinquished his editorship, the publishers' staff have continued the process of updating with numerous words in the same sections, and have added many more hitherto omitted from other sections. The present edition of the *Thesaurus* continues to record the neologisms of recent years in the *push-button* age, among them *bent, hippy, junkie, mini-, teach-in, whizz-kid* and everyday phrases such as *cliff-hanging, hive-off, industrial action, lean over backwards, steady as she goes,* and *at the end of the day.*

1971

CONTENTS

*Everyman's Thesaurus
of English Words
and Phrases*

CLASS I
WORDS EXPRESSING ABSTRACT RELATIONS

SECTION I—EXISTENCE

1°. *Being in the Abstract*

1 Existence *(Substantives)*, being, life, vital principle, entity, ens, essence, quiddity, subsistence; co-existence (120).

Reality, actuality, positiveness, absoluteness, fact, truth (494); actualization.

Presence; existence in space (186).

Science of existence, ontology; existentialism.

(Phrases) The sober reality; hard fact; matter of fact; the whole truth; no joke.

(Verbs) To be, to exist, have being, subsist, live, breathe, stand, abide, remain, stay, obtain, occur, prevail, be so, find itself, take place, eventuate, consist in, lie in; to vegetate, pass the time.

To come into existence, arise, come out, emerge, come forth, appear (448).

To bring into existence, produce, bring forth, discover (161), objectify.

(Adjectives) Existing, being, subsisting, subsistent, in being, in existence, extant, living, breathing, obtaining, prevailing, prevalent, current, afoot.

Real, actual, positive, absolute, essential, substantial, substantive, self - existing, self - existent; undestroyed, tangible, not ideal, not imagined, not suppositious, not potential, virtual, effective, unideal, true, authentic, genuine, mere, objective.

(Adverbs) Actually, really, absolutely, positively, etc., in fact, *de facto, ipso facto.*

(Phrase) In esse; cogito ergo sum.

2 Inexistence *(Substantives)*, non-existence, not-being, nonentity, *nihil,* nil, non-subsistence, nullity, vacuity, blank (4), negativeness, absence (187), removal (185).

Annihilation, abeyance, extinction (162); nirvana.

Philosophy of non-existence, nihilism.

(Phrases) No such thing; Mrs. Harris; 'men in buckram.'

(Verbs) Not to be, not to exist, etc.

To cease to be, pass away, perish, vanish, fade away, dissolve, melt away, disappear (449), to be annihilated, extinct, etc., to die (360), to die out.

(Phrases) To have no being; to have no existence; to be null and void; *non est;* to be no more; 'to leave not a rack behind'; to disappear into thin air; to be brought out of existence.

(Adjectives) Inexistent, non-existent, non-existing, etc., negative, blank, absent.

Unreal, potential, virtual, baseless, unsubstantial (4), imaginary, ideal, vain, fanciful, unpractical, shadowy, fabulous (515), supposititious (514).

Unborn, uncreated, unbegotten, unproduced, unmade.

Annihilated, destroyed, extinct, gone, lost, perished, melted, dissolved, faded, exhausted, vanished, missing, disappeared, departed, extinct, defunct (360).

(Adverbs) Negatively, virtually, etc.

(Phrase) In nubibus.

2°. Being in the Concrete

3 Substantiality *(Substantives)*, hypostasis, person, thing, being, something, existence, entity, reification, corporeity, body, physique, substance, object, article, creature, matter, material, stuff (316), substratum, protoplasm.

Totality of existences, world (318), continuum, plenum.

(Phrase) Something or other.

(Adjectives) Substantive, substantial, personal, bodily, tangible, true, real, concrete, corporal, corporeal, material, objective, hypostatic.

(Verbs) Substantialize, actualize, materialize, reify, embody.

(Adverbs) Substantially, etc., essentially.

———

4 Unsubstantiality *(Substantives)*, insubstantiality, nothingness, nihility, nothing, naught, damn-all, *nihil*, nil, nix, love, zero, cipher, a duck, duck's-egg, pair of spectacles; nonentity, nobody, no one (187).

A shadow, phantom, phantasm, phantasmagoria, dream, mockery, air, thin air, idle dream, pipe dream, castle in Spain (515), idle talk, ignis fatuus, *fata morgana*, mirage.

Void, vacuum, vacuity, vacancy, voidness, vacuousness, inanity, emptiness, hollowness, blank, chasm, gap, hiatus (198); empty space, ether.

(Phrases) Nothing at all; nothing whatever; nothing on earth; nothing under the sun; not a particle.

A man of straw; *vox et praetera nihil;* 'such stuff as dreams are made on.'

(Verbs) To vanish, fade, dissolve, evaporate.

(Adjectives) Unsubstantial, immaterial, void, vacant, vacuous, blank, null, inane, idle, hollow, airy, visionary (515).

3°. Formal Existence

Internal Conditions

5 Intrinsicality *(Substantives)*, in-being, immanence, inherence, inhesion, essence; essentiality, essentialness, subjectiveness, subjectivity, essential part, soul, quintessence, quiddity, gist, pith, core, backbone, marrow, sap, lifeblood; incarnation.

Nature, constitution, character, type, quality (157), temperament, temper, manner, spirit, ethos, habit, humour, grain, endowment, capacity, capability, moods, declensions, features, aspects, specialities, peculiarities (79), particularities, idiosyncrasy, idiocrasy, diagnostics.

(Verbs) To be innate, inborn, etc.

(Phrases) To be in the blood; to be born like that.

External Conditions

6 Extrinsicality *(Substantives)*, extraneousness, objectiveness, objectivity, accident, superficiality, incident.

(Adjectives) Derived from without, objective, extrinsic, extrinsical, extraneous, modal, adventitious, adscititious, incidental, accidental, nonessential, outward (220).

Implanted, engrafted.

(Adverb) Extrinsically, etc.

———

(Adjectives) Derived from within, subjective, intrinsic, intrinsical, inherent, essential, natural, internal, implanted, inborn, innate, inbred, engrained, inherited, immanent, indwelling, radical, constitutional, congenital, connate, hereditary, instinctive, indigenous.

(Phrases) In the grain; in the blood; bred in the bone.

Characteristic, peculiar, qualitative, special, diagnostic (79), invariable.

(Adverbs) Intrinsically, subjectively, substantially, at bottom, *au fond*, at the core.

4°. *Modal Existence*

Absolute

7 State *(Substantives)*, condition, category, class, kind, estate, lot, case, constitution, habitude, diathesis, mood, temper, morale.

Frame, fabric, structure, texture, contexture (329), conformation, organism.

Mode, modality, schesis, form, shape (240), figure, cut, cast, mould, stamp, set, fit, tone, tenor, trim, turn, guise, fashion, aspect, complexion, style, manner, character, kind, get-up, set-up, format, *genre.*

(Verbs) To be in a state, to be in condition, to be on a footing, etc.

To do, fare; to have, possess, enjoy, etc., a state, condition, etc.

To bring into a state, etc. (144).

(Adjectives) Conditional, modal, formal, structural, organic, textual.

(Phrases) As the matter stands; as things are; such being the case.

(Adverb) Conditionally, etc.

Relative

8 Circumstance *(Substantives)*, situation, phase, position, posture, attitude, place, point, bearings, terms, fare, regime, footing, standing, status, predicament, contingency, occasion, juncture, conjuncture, emergency, exigence, exigency, crisis, pinch, impasse, pass, push, plight, fix.

(Phrases) How the land lies; how the wind blows; how the cat jumps.

(Adjectives) Circumstantial; given, conditional, provisional, modal, critical, contingent, incidental (6, 151), circumstanced, placed.

(Verb Phrases) To bow before the storm; to take things as they come; to cut one's coat according to the cloth.

(Adverbs) In or under the circumstances, conditions, etc.; thus, so; in such a case, contingency, etc.; accordingly, such being the case; since, sith, seeing that, as matters stand, as things go.

Conditionally, provided, if, an if, if so, if so be, if it be so, if it so prove, or turn out, or happen; in the event of, provisionally, unless, without.

(Phrases) According to circumstances; as it may happen, or turn out; as the case may be; *pro re nata;* wind and weather permitting; D.V.; rain or shine, sink or swim; at all events; other things being equal; *ceteris paribus.*

SECTION II—RELATION

1°. *Absolute Relation*

9 Relation *(Substantives)*, relationship, bearing, reference, standing, concern, cognation, correlation (12), analogy, affinity, homology, alliance, homogeneity, connection, association, approximation, similarity (17), filiation, affiliation, etc. (11, 166), interest, habitude; relativity.

Relevancy, pertinency, fitness, etc. (646, 23).

Aspect, point of view, comparison (464); ratio, proportion.

Link, tie (45), homologue.

10 Want or absence of relation.

Irrelation *(Substantives)*, disconnection, dissociation, disassociation, misrelation, independence, isolation (44), multifariousness, disproportion; commensurability, irrelevancy; heterogeneity, irreconcilableness (24), impertinence.

(Verbs) To have no relation with, or to, to have nothing to do with, to have no business there, not to concern, not to admit of comparison.

(Verbs) To be related, have a relation, etc., to relate to, refer to, have reference to, bear upon, regard, concern, touch, affect, have to do with, pertain to, belong to, appertain to, answer to, interest.

To bring into relation with, correlate, associate, connect, affiliate, link (43), bring near (197), homologize; to bring to bear upon.

(Phrase) To draw a parallel with.

(Adjectives) Relative, correlative, cognate, relating to, relative to, relevant, in relation with, referable to, pertinent (23), germane, belonging to, pat, to the point, apposite, to the purpose, apropos, *ad rem*, just the thing, quite the thing; pertaining to, appertaining to, appurtenant, affiliated, allied, related, implicated, connected, associated, *en rapport*, in touch with, bound up with, homological, homologous.

Approximate, approximative, approximating, proportional, proportionate, proportionable, allusive, comparable, like, similar (17).

(Adverbs) Relatively, thereof, as to, about, connecting, concerning, touching, anent, as relates to, with relation to, relating to, as respects, with respect to, in respect of, respecting, as regards, with regard to, regarding, in the matter of, with reference to, according to, while speaking of, apropos of, in connection with, inasmuch as, whereas, in consideration of, in point of, as far as, on the part of, on the score of, under the head of, *in re*; pertinently, etc. (23).

To isolate, separate, detach, disconnect, segregate (44).

(Adjectives) Irrelative, irrespective, unrelated, without reference, etc., to, arbitrary, episodic, remote, farfetched, forced, out of place, out of tune (414), inharmonious, malapropos, irrelevant, foreign to, alien, impertinent, inapposite, extraneous to, strange to, stranger to, independent, paranthetical, incidental, outlandish, exotic, unallied, unconnected, disconnected, unconcerned, adrift, detached, isolated, insular.

Not comparable, incomensurable, inapplicable (24), irreconcilable, heterogeneous (83), uncomfortable.

(Phrases) Foreign to the purpose; nothing to the purpose; having nothing to do with; *nihil ad rem*; neither here nor there; beside the mark; *à propos des bottes*; dragged in by the scruff of the neck.

(Adverbs) Parenthetically, by the way, by the by, *obiter dicta, en passant,* incidentally, irrespectively, irrelevantly, etc.

----

11 Relations of kindred.

Consanguinity *(Substantives)*, relationship, kindred, blood, parentage (166), filiation, affiliation, lineage, agnation, connection, alliance, family connection, family tie, nepotism.

A kinsman, kinswoman, kinsfolk, kith and kin, relation, relative, friend, sibling, one's people, clan, connection, one's own flesh and blood, brother, sister, father, mother, uncle, aunt, nephew, niece, stepfather, etc., brother-in-law, etc., guid-brother, etc., cousin, cousin-german; first, second cousin; cousin once, twice, etc., removed; grand- or great-grandfather, etc., great-uncle, etc., a near relation, a blood-relation, a distant relation or relative, congener, collateral.

Family, issue, fraternity, sisterhood, brotherhood, parentage, cousinhood, etc.; race, stock, generation, sept, clan, tribe, strain.

(Verbs) To be related, to have or claim relationship with.

(Adjectives) Related, akin, consanguineous, congeneric, family, kindred, affiliated, allied, collateral, sib, agnate, agnatic, fraternal, of the same blood, nearly or close related, remotely or distantly related.

(Phrase) Blood is thicker than water.

12 Double relation.

Reciprocalness *(Substantives)*, reciprocity, mutuality, correlation, correlativeness, interdependence, interchange, interaction, reciprocation, etc. (148), alternation (149), barter (794).

(Verbs) To reciprocate, alternate, interchange, interact, exchange, counterchange, interdepend.

(Adjectives) Reciprocal, mutual, common, correlative, alternate, alternative; interchangeable, interdependent, international.

(Adverbs) Reciprocally, mutually, etc.

(Phrases) Mutatis mutandis; each other; vice versa; turn and turn about.

13 Identity *(Substantives)*, sameness, oneness, coincidence, coalescence, convertibility; selfness, self, ego, oneself, number one; identification, monotony; equality (27), tautology (104).

Synonym; facsimile (21), counterpart (17).

(Verbs) To be identical, to be the same, etc., to coincide, to coalesce.

To render the same.

To recognize the identity of, to identify, recognize.

(Adjectives) Identical, identic, same, self, selfsame, very same, no other, ilk, one and the same, ditto, unaltered, coincident, coinciding, co-essential, coalescing, coalescent, indistinguishable, tantamount, equivalent, equipollent, convertible, much the same.

(Adverbs) All one, all the same, *ibidem*, ibid, identically, likewise.

(Phrases) Semper idem; toujours la même chose; *alter ego*; on all fours; much of a muchness.

14 Non-coincidence.

Contrariety *(Substantives)*, contrast, foil, set-off, antithesis, contradiction, opposition, oppositeness, antagonism (179, 708), distinction (15).

Inversion, reversion (218).

The opposite, the reverse, inverse, converse, antonym, the antipodes (237).

(Phrases) The reverse of the medal; the other side of the shield; the tables being turned.

(Verbs) To be contrary, etc., to contrast with, contradict, contravene, oppose, negate, antagonize, invert, reverse, turn the tables, to militate against.

(Adjectives) Contrary, opposite, counter, converse, reverse, antithetical, opposed, antipodean, antagonistic, opposing, conflicting, inconsistent, contradictory, contrarious, contrariant, negative.

(Phrases) Differing *toto caelo*; diametrically opposite; as black to white; light to darkness; fire to water; worlds apart; poles asunder.

(Adverbs) Contrarily, contrariously, contrariwise, *per contra,* oppositely, *vice versa*, on the contrary, *tout au contraire*, quite the contrary, no such thing.

15 Difference *(Substantives)*, variance, variation, variety, diversity, modification, allotropy, shade of difference, nuance; deviation, divergence, divarication (291), disagreement (24), dissimilarity (18), disparity (28).

Distinction, contradistinction, differentiation, discrimination (465); a nice or fine or subtle distinction.

(Phrases) A very different thing; a *tertium quid*; a horse of a different colour; another pair of shoes.

(Verbs) To be different, etc., to differ, vary, mismatch, contrast, differ *toto caelo*.

To render different, etc., to vary, change, modify, varify, diversify, etc. (140).

To distinguish, differentiate, severalize (465), split hairs, discriminate.

(Adjectives) Different, differing, disparate, heterogeneous, heteromorphic, allotropic, varying, distinguishable, discriminative, varied, modified, diversified, deviating, diverging, devious, disagreeing (24), various, divers, all manner of, multifarious, multiform, variform (81), variegated (440), diacritical.

Other, another, other-guess, not the same.

Unmatched, widely apart, changed (140).

(Phrase) As different as chalk is from cheese.

(Adverbs) Differently, variously, otherwise.

2°. Continuous Relation

16 Uniformity *(Substantives)*, homogeneity, homogeneousness, consistency, connaturality, conformity (82), homology, accordance, agreement (23), regularity (58), routine, monotony, constancy.

(Verbs) To be uniform, etc., to accord with, harmonize with, hang together, go together.

16ᴀ Absence or want of uniformity.

Non-uniformity *(Substantives)*, variety, multiformity (81), diversity, unevenness, irregularity, unconformity (83).

(Adjectives) Multiform, multifarious, various (81), diversified, inconsistent, of various kinds.

To become uniform, conform with, fall in with, follow suit.

To render uniform, to assimilate, level, smooth (255).

(Adjectives) Uniform, homogeneous, homologous, of a piece, of a kind, consistent, connatural, monotonous, even, unvarying, flat, level, constant.

(Adverbs) Uniformly, uniformly with, conformably (82), consistently with, in unison with, in harmony with, in conformity with, according to (23).

Regularly, at regular intervals, invariably, constantly, always, without exception.

(Phrases) In a rut (or groove); *ab uno disce omnes*; 'forty feeding like one.'

3°. Partial Relation

17 Similarity *(Substantives)*, resemblance, likeness, similitude, affinity, semblance, approximation, parallelism (216), analogy, brotherhood, family likeness; alliteration, head-rhyme, rhyme, pun, assonance, repetition (104), reproduction.

An analogue, copy (21), the like, facsimile, match, double, pendant, fellow, pair, mate, twin, *alter ego*, parallel, counterpart, brother, sister; simile, metaphor (521), resemblance, imitation (19).

(Phrases) One's second self; *Arcades ambo*; birds of a feather; *et hoc genus omne*; a chip of the old block; the very spit (and image) of.

(Verbs) To be similar, like, resembling, etc., to look like, resemble, bear resemblance, favour, approximate, parallel, match, imitate, take

18 Dissimilarity *(Substantives)*, unlikeness, dissimilitude, diversity, divergence, difference (15), novelty (123), originality (515), disparity (28).

(Verbs) To be unlike, etc., to vary (15, 20).

To render unlike, to diversify (140).

(Phrase) To strike out something new.

(Adjectives) Dissimilar, unlike, disparate, of a different kind, class, etc. (75); diversified, novel, new (123), unmatched, unique, unprecedented (83).

(Phrases) Nothing of the kind; far from it; cast in a different mould; as different as chalk is from cheese.

(Adverb) Otherwise.

after (19), represent, simulate, personate, savour of, have a flavour of, favour, feature.

To render similar, assimilate, approximate, reproduce, bring near, copy, plagiarize.

(Adjectives) Similar, like, alike, resembling, twin, analogous, analogical, parallel, allied to, of a piece, such as, connatural, congener, matching, conformable, on all fours with.

Near, something like, suchlike, mock, pseudo, simulating, representing, approximating, a show of, a kind of, a sort of.

Exact, accurate, true, faithful, close, speaking, lifelike, breathing.

(Phrases) True to nature; to the life; for all the world like; like as two peas; *comme deux gouttes d'eau*; cast in the same mould; like father, like son.

(Adverbs) As if, so to speak, as it were, quasi, as if it were, just as, after, in the fashion or manner of, *à la.*

19 Imitation *(Substantives)*, assimilation, copying, transcription, transcribing, following, repetition (104), duplication, reduplication, quotation, reproduction.

Mockery, mocking, mimicry, mimicking, echoing, reflection, simulation, counterfeiting, plagiarism, forgery, fake, fakement, acting, personation, impersonation, representation (554), copy (21), parody, paraphrase, travesty, burlesque, semblance, mimesis.

An imitator, mimic, impersonator, echo, cuckoo, parrot, ape, monkey, mocking-bird.

Plagiary, plagiarist, forger, counterfeiter.

(Phrase) O imitatores, servum pecus.

(Verbs) To imitate, copy, plagiarize, forge, fake, reproduce, photograph, repeat (104), echo, re-echo, transcribe, match, parallel, emulate, do like, take off, hit off, reflect, mirror, model after (554).

To mock, mimic, ape, simulate, personate, impersonate (554), act, represent, adumbrate, counterfeit, parody, travesty, caricature, burlesque.

(Phrases) To take or catch a likeness; to take after; to follow or tread in the steps of, or in the footsteps of; to take a leaf out of another's book; to follow suit; to go with the stream; to be in the fashion.

(Adjectives) Imitated, copied, matched, repeated, paralleled, mock, mimic, parodied, etc., modelled after, moulded on, paraphrastic, imitative, mimetic, slavish, mechanical, synthetic, second-hand, imitable.

(Adverbs) Literally, verbatim, to the letter, *literatim, sic, totidem verbis,* so to speak, in so many words, word for word, *mot à mot* (562).

20 Non-imitation *(Substantives)*, originality, inventiveness, novelty.

(Adjectives) Unimitated, uncopied, unmatched, unparalleled, inimitable, unique, original, novel.

(Verb) To originate.

Variation *(Substantives)*, alteration, modification, difference (15), change (140), deviation (279), divergence (291); moods and tenses.

(Verbs) To vary, modify, change, alter, diversify (140).

(Phrase) To stear clear of.

(Adjectives) Varied, modified, diversified, etc.

(Adverbs) Variously, in all manner of ways.

21 Result of imitation.
Copy *(Substantives)*, facsimile, counterpart, effigies, effigy, form, likeness, similitude, semblance, reflex,

22 Thing copied.
Prototype *(Substantives)*, original, model, pattern, standard, type, scale, scantling, archetype, protoplast,

portrait, photograph (556), photostat, microfilm, enlargement, miniature, study, cast, autotype, electrotype, imitation, replica, representation, adumbration.

Duplicate, transcript, transcription, repetition (104), réchauffé, reflection, shadow, record, recording.

Rough copy, fair copy, revise, carbon copy, tracing, rubbing, squeeze, draft or draught, proof, pull, reprint.

Counterfeit, parody, caricature, burlesque, travesty, paraphrase, forgery.

antitype, module, exemplar, example, ensample, protoplast, paradigm, fugleman, lay figure.

Text, copy, design, plan, blueprint, keynote.

Mould, matrix, last, plasm, proplasm, mint, die, seal, stamp, negative.

(Verbs) To set a copy, to set an example.

_____

(Phrases) A second edition; a twice-told tale.

4°. *General Relation*

23 Agreement *(Substantives)*, accord, accordance, unison, uniformity, harmony, union, concord, concert, concordance (714), cognation, conformity, conformance (82), consonance, consentaneousness, consensus, consistency, congruity, congruence, congeniality, correspondence keeping, parallelism.

Fitness, pertinence, suitableness, adaptation, meetness, patness, relevancy, aptness, aptitude, coaptation, propriety, apposition, appositeness, reconcilableness, applicability, applicableness, admissibility, commensurability, compatibility, adaptability.

Adaptation, adjustment, graduation, accommodation, reconciliation, reconcilement, concurrence (178), consent (488), co-operation (709).

(Verbs) To be accordant, to agree, accord (714), correspond, tally, jibe, respond, harmonize, match, suit, fit, befit, hit, fall in with, chime in with, quadrate with, square with, cancel with, comport with, assimilate, unite with.

To render accordant, to adapt, accommodate, adjust, reconcile, fadge, dovetail, dress, square, regulate, comport, graduate, gradate, grade.

(Phrases) To become one; to fit like a glove; to suit one to a T.

(Adjectives) Agreeing, accordant, concordant, consonant, congruous, consentaneous, consentient, corresponding, correspondent, congenial,

24 Disagreement *(Substantives)*, discord, discordance, dissonance, disharmony, dissidence, discrepancy, unconformity, disconformity, nonconformity, incongruity, incongruence, *mésalliance*, discongruity, jarring, clashing, jostling (713), inconsistency, inconsonance, disparity, disproportion, disproportionateness, variance, divergence, jar, misfit.

Unfitness, repugnance, unsuitableness, unsuitability, unaptness, ineptitude, inaptness, impropriety, inapplicability, inadmissibility, irreconcilableness, irreconcilability, incommensurability, inconcinnity, incompatibility, inadaptability, interference, intrusion, irrelation (10).

(Verbs) To disagree, belie, clash, jar, oppose (708), interfere, jostle (713), intrude.

(Phrase) To have no business there.

(Adjectives) Disagreeing, discordant, discrepant, jarring, clashing, repugnant, incompatible, irreconcilable, intransigent, inconsistent with, uncomfortable, incongruous, disproportionate, disproportioned, unproportioned, inharmonious, inconsonant, mismatched, misjoined, misjudged, unconsonant, incommensurable, incommensurate, divergent (291).

Unapt, inapt, inept, inappropriate, improper, unsuited, unsuitable, inapposite, inapplicable, irrelevant, not pertinent, impertinent, malapropos, ill-timed, intrusive, clumsy, unfit,

harmonizing, harmonious with, tallying with, conformable with, in accordance with, in harmony with, in unison with, in keeping with, squaring with, quadrating with, falling in with, of one mind, of a piece, consistent with, compatible, reconcilable with, commensurate.

Apt, apposite, pertinent, germane, relating to, pat, bearing upon (9), applicable, relevant, fit, fitting, suitable, happy, felicitous, proper, meet, appropriate, suiting, befitting, becoming, seasonable, deft, accommodating, topical.

(Phrases) The cap fits; to the point; to the purpose; *rem acu tetigisti*; at home; in one's element.

unfitting, unbefitting, unbecoming, misplaced, forced, unseasonable, far-fetched, inadmissible, uncongenial, ill-assorted, ill-sorted, repugnant to, unaccommodating, irreducible.

(Phrases) Out of season; out of character; out of keeping; out of joint; out of tune; out of place; out of one's element; at odds; a fish out of water.

(Adverbs) Discordantly, etc.; at variance with, in defiance of, in contempt of, in spite of, despite.

SECTION III —QUANTITY

1°. *Simple Quantity*

25 Absolute quantity.

Quantity *(Substantives)*, magnitude (192), amplitude, size, mass, amount, volume, area, quantum, measure, substance.

Science of quantity, mathematics.

Definite or finite quantity, handful, mouthful, spoonful, bucketful, pailful, etc.; stock, batch, lot.

(Adjective) Quantitative.
(Phrase) To the tune of.

----

26 Relative quantity.

Degree *(Substantives)*, grade, gradation, extent, measure, ratio, stint, standard, height, pitch, reach, sweep, radius, amplitude, magnitude, water, calibre, range, scope, shade, tenor, compass, sphere, rank, station, standing, rate, way, sort.

Point, mark, stage, step, position, slot, peg; term (71).

Intensity, might, fullness, strength (31), conversion (144), limit (233).

(Adjectives) Comparative, gradual, shading off.

(Adverbs) By degrees, gradually, *gradatim*, inasmuch, *pro tanto*, however, howsoever, step by step, rung by rung, bit by bit, little by little, by inches, inch by inch, by slow degrees, by little and little, in some degree, to some extent.

2°. *Comparative Quantity*

27 sameness of quantity or degree.

Equality *(Substantives)*, parity, coextension, evenness, equipoise, level, balance, equivalence, equipollence, equilibrium, poise, equiponderance, par, quits.

Equalization, equation, equilibration, co-ordination, adjustment, symmetry.

28 Difference of quantity or degree.

Inequality *(Substantives)*, disparity, imparity, imbalance, odds, handicap, bisque, difference (15), unevenness.

Preponderance, preponderation, inclination of the balance, advantage, prevalence, partiality.

Superiority (33), a casting vote; inferiority (34).

A drawn game or battle, a dead heat, a draw, a tie.

A match, peer, compeer, equal, mate, fellow, brother (17), equivalent, makeweight.

(Phrases) A distinction without a difference; a photo finish.

(Verbs) To be equal, etc., to equal, match, come up to, keep pace with; come to, amount to, balance, cope with.

To render equal, equalize, level, balance, equate, aequiparate, trim, dress, adjust, fit, accommodate, poise, square; to readjust, equipoise, equilibrate, set against.

(Phrases) To be or lie on a level with; to come to the same thing.

To strike a balance; to establish or restore equality; to stretch on the bed of Procrustes; to cry quits.

(Verbs) To be unequal, etc., to preponderate, outweigh, outbalance, overbalance, prevail, countervail, predominate, overmatch, outmatch (33).

To fall short of, to want (304), not to come up to.

(Phrases) To have or give the advantage; to turn the scale; to kick the beam; to topple over.

(Adjectives) Unequal, uneven, disparate, partial, unbalanced, overbalanced, top-heavy, lopsided, preponderating, outweighing, prevailing.

(Phrases) More than a match for, above par; below par; *haud passibus aequis.*

———

(Adjectives) Equal, even, quit, level, coequal, co-ordinate, equivalent, synonymous, tantamount, convertible, equipollent, equiponderant, equiponderous, square.

Rendered equal, equalized, equated, drawn, poised, levelled, balanced, symmetrical, trimmed, dressed.

(Phrases) On a par with; on a level with; much of a muchness; as broad as it is long; as good as; all the same; all one; six of one and half a dozen of the other; not a pin to choose between them; tarred with the same brush; diamond cut diamond.

(Adverbs) *Pari passu,* equally, symmetrically, *ad eundem,* practically, to all intents and purposes, neck and neck.

29 Mean *(Substantives)* medium, intermedium, compromise, average, norm, balance, middle (68), *via media, juste milieu.*

Neutrality, mediocrity, middle course, shuffling.

(Phrases) The golden mean; the average man; the man in the street.

(Verbs) To compromise, pair off, cancel out.

(Phrases) To sit on the fence; split the difference; strike a balance; take the average; reduce to a mean; to take a safe course.

(Adjectives) Mean, intermediate, middle, median, normal, average, mediocre, middling, ordinary (82), neutral.

(Adverb phrases) On an average; in the long run; half-way; taking the one with the other; taking all things together; in round numbers.

30 Compensation *(Substantives),* equation, commutation, compromise (774), indemnification, neutralization, nullification, counteraction (179), recoil (277), atonement (952).

A set-off, offset, makeweight, counterpoise, ballast, indemnity, hush-money, amends, equivalent.

(Phrases) Measure for measure; give and take; *quid pro quo;* tit for tat.

(Verbs) To compensate, make up for, indemnity, countervail, counterpoise, balance, compromise, outbalance, overbalance, counterbalance, counteract, set off, hedge, redeem, neutralize (27), cover.

(Phrases) To make good; split the difference; fill up; make amends.

(Adjectives) Compensating, compensatory, countervailing, etc., equivalent, equipollent (27).

(Phrase) In the opposite scale.

(Adverbs) However, yet, but, still, all the same, for all that, nevertheless, none the less, notwithstanding, be that as it may, on the other hand, although, though, albeit, *per contra*.

(Phrases) As broad as it's long; taking one thing with another; it is an ill wind that blows nobody any good.

Quantity by Comparison with a Standard

31 Greatness *(Substantives)*, largeness, magnitude, size (192), multitude (102), fullness, vastness, immensity, enormity, infinity (105), intensity (26), importance (642), strength.

A large quantity, deal, power, world, macrocosm, mass, heap (72), pile, sight, pot, volume, peck, bushel, load, stack, cart-load, wagon-load, truck-load, ship-load, cargo, lot, flood, spring tide, mobs, bags, oodles, abundance (639), wholesale, store (636).

The greater part (50).

(Verbs) To be great, etc., run high, soar, tower, transcend, rise, carry to a great height (305).

(Phrases) To know no bounds; to break the record.

(Adjectives) Great, gross, large, considerable, big, ample, above par, huge, full, saturated, plenary, deep, signal, extensive, sound, passing, goodly, famous, noteworthy, noble, heavy, precious, mighty (157), arch, sad, piteous, arrant, red-hot, downright, utter, uttermost, crass, lamentable, consummate, rank, thorough-paced, thorough-going, sovereign, unparalleled, matchless, unapproached, extraordinary, intense, extreme, pronounced, unsurpassed, unsurpassable.

Vast, immense, enormous, towering, inordinate, severe, excessive, monstrous, shocking, extravagant, exorbitant, outrageous, whacking, thumping, glaring, flagrant, preposterous, egregious, overgrown, stupendous, monumental, prodigious, marked, pointed, remarkable, astonishing, surprising (870), incredible, marvellous, transcendent,

32 Smallness *(Substantives)*, littleness, minuteness (193), tenuity, scantness, scantiness, slenderness, meanness, mediocrity, insignificance (643), paucity, fewness (103).

A small quantity, modicum, atom, particle, molecule, corpuscle, microcosm, jot, iota, dot, speck, mote, gleam, scintilla, spark, ace, minutiae, thought, idea, suspicion, *soupçon*, whit, tittle, shade, shadow, touch, cast, taste, grain, scruple, spice, sprinkling, drop, droplet, driblet, globule, minim, dash, smack, nip. sip, scantling, dole, scrap, mite, slip, snippet, tag, bit, morsel, crumb, paring, shaving (51), trifle, thimbleful, toothful, spoonful, cupful, mouthful, handful, fistful.

Finiteness, a finite quantity.

(Phrases) The shadow of a shade; a drop in a bucket or in the ocean.

(Verbs) To be small, etc., to run low, diminish, shrink, decrease (36), contract (195).

(Phrases) To lie in a nutshell; to pass muster.

(Adjectives) Small, little, wee, scant, inconsiderable, diminutive, minute (193), tiny, minikin, puny, petty, sorry, miserable, shabby, wretched, paltry (643), weak (160), slender, feeble, faint, slight, scrappy, fiddling, trivial, scanty, light, trifling, moderate, low, mean, mediocre, passable, passing, light, sparing.

Below par, below the mark, under the mark, at a low ebb, imperfect, unfinished, partial (651), inappreciable, evanescent, infinitesimal, atomic, homoeopathic.

Mere, simple, sheer, bare.

incomparable, tremendous, terrific, formidable, amazing, phenomenal, superhuman, titanic, immoderate.

Indefinite, boundless, unbounded, unlimited, incalculable, illimitable, immeasurable, infinite, unapproachable, unutterable, indescribable, unspeakable, inexpressible, beyond expression, swingeing, unconscionable, fabulous, uncommon, unusual (83).

Undiminished, unrestricted, unabated, unreduced, unmitigated, unredeemed, untempered.

Absolute, positive, decided, staring, unequivocal, serious, grave, essential, perfect, finished, completed, abundant (639).

(Adverbs) In a great degree, much, muckle, well, considerably, largely, grossly, greatly, very, very much, a deal, not a little, no end, pretty, pretty well, enough, richly, to a large extent, to a great extent, ever so, mainly, ever so much, on a large scale, insomuch, all lengths, wholesale, in a great measure.

In a positive degree, truly (494), positively, verily, really, indeed, actually, in fact, fairly, assuredly, decidedly, surely, clearly, obviously, unequivocally, purely, absolutely, seriously, essentially, fundamentally, radically, downright, in grain, altogether, entirely, completely.

In a comparative degree, comparatively, *pro tanto*, as good as, to say the least, above all, most, of all things, pre-eminently.

(Adverbs) In a small degree, on a small scale, to a small extent, a wee bit, something, somewhat, next to nothing, little, inconsiderably, slightly, so-so, minutely, faintly, feebly, lightly, imperfectly, scantily, shabbily, miserably, wretchedly, sparingly, weakly, slenderly, modestly.

In a limited degree, in a certain degree, to a certain degree or extent, partially, in part, some, somewhat, rather, in some degree, in some-measure, something, simply, only, purely, merely, in a manner, at least, at most, ever so little, thus far, *pro tanto*, next to nothing.

Almost, nearly, well-nigh, all but, short of, not quite, close upon, near the mark.

In an uncertain degree, about, thereabouts, scarcely, hardly, barely, somewhere about, say, more or less, *à peu près*, there or thereabouts.

In no degree, noways, nowise, nohow, in no wise, by no means, not in the least, not at all, not a bit, not a bit of it, not a whit, not a jot, in no respect, by no manner of means, on no account.

(Phrases) As little as may be; after a fashion; in a way.

Within an ace of; on the brink of; next door to; a close shave (or call).

———

In a complete degree, completely (52), altogether, quite, entirely, wholly, totally, *in toto, toto coelo*, utterly, thoroughly, out and out, outright, out and away, fairly, clean, to the full, in every respect, *sous tous les rapports*, in all respects, on all accounts, nicely, perfectly, fully, amply, richly, wholesale, abundantly, consummately, widely, as … as … can be, every inch, *à fond, de fond*, far and wide, over head and ears, to the backbone, through and through, *ne plus ultra*.

In a greater degree, even, yea, *a fortiori*, still more.

In a high degree, highly, deeply, strongly, mighty, mightily, powerfully (157), profoundly, superlatively, ultra, in the extreme, extremely, exceedingly, excessively, comsumedly, sorely, intensely, exquisitely, acutely, soundly, vastly, hugely, immensely, enormously, stupendously, passing, surpassing, supremely, beyond measure, immoderately, monstrously, inordinately, tremendously, over head and ears, extraordinarily, exorbitantly, indefinitely, immeasurably, unspeakably, inexpressibly, ineffably, unutterably, incalculably, infinitely, unsurpassably.

In a marked degree, particularly, remarkably, singularly, uncommonly, unusually, peculiarly, notably, *par excellence*, eminently, pre-eminently, superlatively, signally, famously, egregiously, prominently, glaringly, emphatically, strangely, wonderfully, amazingly, surprisingly, astonishingly, prodigiously, monstrously, incredibly, inconceivably, marvellously, awfully, stupendously.

In a violent degree, violently, severely, furiously, desperately, tremendously, outrageously, extravagantly, confoundedly, deucedly, devilishly, diabolically, with a vengeance, *à outrance*, like mad (173).

In a painful degree, sadly, grievously, woefully, wretchedly, piteously, sorely, lamentably, shockingly, frightfully, dreadfully, fearfully, terribly, horribly.

Quantity by Comparison with a Similar Object

33 Superiority (*Substantives*), majority, supremacy, primacy, advantage, preponderance, excess (641), prevalence, pre-eminence, championship.

Maximum, acme, climax, zenith, summit, utmost height, record, culminating point (210), the height of, lion's share, overweight.

(Phrases) A Triton among the minnows; cock of the walk; *ne plus ultra: summum bonum.*

(Verbs) To be superior, etc.; to exceed, surpass, excel, eclipse, transcend, top, overtop, o'ertop, cap, beat, cut out, outclass, override, outmatch, outbalance, overbalance, overweigh, overshadow, outdo; preponderate, predominate, prevail.

To render larger, magnify (194).

(Phrases) To have the advantage of; to have the upper hand; to bear the palm; to have one cold; to beat hollow; to take the shine out of; to throw into the shade; to be a cut above.

(Adjectives) Superior, greater, major, higher, surpassing, exceeding, excelling, passing, ultra, vaulting, unequalled, unsurpassed, peerless, matchless, transcending, transcendent, unparalleled, without parallel.

34 Inferiority (*Substantives*), minority, subordination, shortcoming (304); deficiency, minimum.

(Verbs) To be less, inferior, etc., to fall or come short of, not to pass (304); to want, be wanting.

To become smaller, to render smaller (195); to subordinate.

(Phrases) To be thrown into the shade; to hide one's diminished head; to give a person best; to play second fiddle.

(Adjectives) Inferior, deficient, smaller, minor, less, lesser, lower, sub, subordinate, subaltern, secondary, second-rate, second-best.

Least, smallest, wee-est, minutest, etc., lowest.

(Phrases) Weighed in the balance and found wanting; not fit to hold a candle to.

(Adverbs) Less, under or below the mark, below par, at the bottom of the scale, at a low ebb, short of, at a disadvantage.

———

Supreme, greatest, utmost, paramount, pre-eminent, foremost, crowning, sovereign, culminating, superlative, topmost, top-hole, highest, first-rate, champion, A1, the last word, the limit.

(Phrases) Facile princeps; nulli secundus; primus inter pares.

(Adverbs) Beyond, more, over and above the mark, above par, over and above, at the top of the scale, at its height.

In a superior degree, eminently, pre-eminently, egregiously, prominently, superlatively, supremely, above all, of all things, principally, especially, particularly, peculiarly, *par excellence, a fortiori.*

Changes in Quantity

35 Increase *(Substantives)*, augmentation, enlargement, extension, dilatation (194), increment, accretion, development, rise, growth, swell, swelling, expansion, aggrandizement, aggravation, rise, exacerbation, spread, climax, exaggeration, diffusion (73), flood-tide; accession (37).

(Verbs) To increase, augment, enlarge, amplify, extend, dilate, swell, wax, expand, grow, stretch, shoot up, mushroom, rise, run up, sprout, burgeon, advance, spread, gather head, aggrandize, add, superadd, raise, heighten, strengthen, greaten, exalt, enhance, magnify, redouble, aggravate, exaggerate, exasperate, exacerbate, escalate.

(Phrases) To add fuel to the flame; to pour oil on the flames.

(Adjectives) Increased, augmented, enlarged, etc., undiminished; cumulative; additional (37).

(Adverb) Crescendo.

36 Non-increase.

Decrease *(Substantives)* diminution, depreciation, lessening, reduction, abatement, bating, declension, falling off, dwindling, contraction (195), shrinking, attenuation, extenuation, anticlimax, abridgment, curtailment (201), coarctation, narrowing; deduction (38).

Subsidence, wane, ebb, decrement.

(Verbs) To decrease, diminish, lessen, dwindle, decay, crumble, shrink, contract, shrivel, fall off, fall away, waste, wear, wane, ebb, subside, decline, languish, wear off, run low, grow downward.

To abridge, reduce, curtail, cut down, pare down, subtract, shorten, cut short, dock (201), bate, abate, fritter away, attenuate, extenuate, lower, weaken, dwarf; to mitigate (174), to throw in the shade.

(Phrase) To hide its diminished head.

(Adjectives) Decreased, diminished, lessened, etc., shorn, short by, decreasing, on the wane.

(Adverbs) *Diminuendo, decrescendo.*

3°. Conjunctive Quantity

37 Addition *(Substantives)* adjection, introduction, superinduction, annexation, superposition, superaddition, subjunction, supervention, increment, accession, superfetation, corollary, reinforcement, supplement, accompaniment (88), interposition (228), insertion (300).

(Verbs) To add, annex, affix, superadd, supplement, reinforce, subjoin, superpose, throw in, clap on, tack to, append, tag, engraft, saddle on, saddle with, superinduce, introduce, work in, interleave, extra-illustrate, grangerize.

To become added, to accrue, advene, supervene.

(Phrase) To swell the ranks of.

(Adjectives) Added, annexed, etc., additional, supplementary, supplemental, suppletory, subjunctive,

38 Non-addition.

Subduction *(Substantives)*, subtraction, abstraction, deduction, deducement, retrenchment, removal, elimination, ablation (789), purgation, curtailment, etc. (36), garbling, mutilation, truncation, abscission, excision, amputation, detruncation, sublation, castration, apocope.

Subtrahend, minuend; decrement, discount.

(Verbs) To subduct, exclude, deduct, subtract, abscind, retrench, remove, withdraw, eliminate, bate, detract, deduce, take away, deprive of, curtail (36), garble, truncate, mutilate, eviscerate, exenterate, detruncate, castrate, spay, geld, purge, amputate, cut off, excise, cut out, dock, lop, prune, pare, dress, clip, thin, shear, decimate, abrade (330).

adscititious, additive, accessory, cumulative.

(Adverbs) Additionally, in addition, more, *plus*, extra, and, also, likewise, too, furthermore, forby, item, and also, and eke, else, besides, to boot, etcetera, and so forth, into the bargain, over and above, moreover.

With, together with, withal, along with, including, inclusive, as well as, not to mention, to say nothing of; jointly, conjointly (43).

39 Thing added.

Adjunct *(Substantives)*, additament, addition, affix, appendage, annex, suffix, postfix, inflexion, augment, increment, augmentation, accessory, item, garnish, sauce, supplement, extra, bonus (810), adjective, addendum, complement, corollary, continuation, increment, reinforcement, pendant, apanage.

Sequel (65), postscript, codicil, envoy, rider, corollary, heel-piece, tag, tab, skirt, flap, lappet, trappings, tail, tailpiece (67), queue, train, suite, cortège, accompaniment (88).

(Phrase) More last words.

_____

(Adjectives) Subtracted, deducted, etc., subtractive.

(Adverbs) In deduction, etc., less, *minus*, without, except, excepting, with the exception of, but for, barring, save, exclusive of, save and except (83).

_____

40 Thing remaining.

Remainder *(Substantives)*, residue, remains, remnant, the rest, relics, leavings, heel-tap, odds and ends, cheese-parings, candle-ends, off-scourings, orts.

Residuum, *caput mortuum*, dregs, refuse (645), scum, recrement (653), ashes, dross, cinders, slag, sediment, silt, alluvium, stubble; slough, exuviae, result, educt.

Surplus, overplus, surplusage, superfluity, excess (641), balance, complement, fag-end, stump, butt, rump, wreck, wreckage, ruins, skeleton.

(Verbs) To remain, be left, be left behind, exceed, survive.

(Adjectives) Remaining, left, left behind, residual, exuvial, residuary, sedimentary, outstanding, net, cast off, odd, over, unconsumed, surviving, outlying.

Superfluous, over and above, exceeding, redundant (641), supernumerary.

41 Forming a whole without coherence.

Mixture *(Substantives)*, admixture, commixture, commixtion, intermixture, alloyage, marriage, miscegenation.

Impregnation, infusion, infiltration, diffusion, suffusion, interspersion, transfusion, seasoning, sprinkling, interlarding, interpolation, interposition (228), intrusion; adulteration, sophistication.

Thing mixed, a touch, spice, tinge, tincture, dash, smack, sprinkling, seasoning, infusion, suspicion, *soupçon*, shade, bit, portion, dose.

Compound resulting from mixture, blend, alloy, amalgam, magma, *mélange*, half and half, hybrid, *tertium quid*, miscellany, medley,

42 Freedom from mixture.

Simpleness *(Substantives)*, singleness, purity, clearness, homogeneity.

Purification (652), elimination, sifting, winnowing.

(Verbs) To render simple, simplify, sift, winnow, bolt, screen, sort, eliminate; to separate, disjoin (44).

To purify (652).

(Adjectives) Simple, uniform, of a piece, homogeneous, single, pure, clear, sheer, blank, neat, absolute, elemental, elementary; unmixed, unmingled, untinged, unblended, uncombined, uncompounded, undecomposed, unadulterated, unsophisticated, undiluted, straight.

Free from, exempt from.

(Phrase) Pure and simple.

_____

pastiche, pasticcio, patchwork, odds and ends; farrago, jumble (59), mess, salad, sauce, hash, hodge-podge or hotchpotch or hotchpot, mash, mish-mash, job lot, omnium gatherum, gallimaufry, olla podrida, olio, salmagundi, pot-pourri, Noah's ark, cauldron, marquetry, mosaic (440), complex.

A cross, hybrid, mongrel, half-breed, Eurasian, mulatto, quadroon, octoroon, sambo.

(Phrases) A mingled yarn; a scratch team.

(Verbs) To mix, commix, immix, intermix, associate, join (43), mingle, commingle, intermingle, bemingle, interlard, intersperse, interpose, interpolate (228); shuffle together, hash up, huddle together, deal, pound together, stir up, knead, brew, jumble (59); impregnate with.

To be mixed, to get among, to be entangled with.

To instil, imbue, infuse, infiltrate, dash, tinge, tincture, season, sprinkle, besprinkle, suffuse, transfuse, attemper, medicate, blend, alloy, amalgamate, compound (48), adulterate, sophisticate, infect, cross, intercross, interbreed, interblend.

(Adjectives) Mixed, mingled, intermixed, etc., motley, miscellaneous, promiscuous; complex, composite, mixed up with, half-and-half, linsey-woolsey, mongrel, heterogeneous; miscible.

43 Junction *(Substantives)*, joining, joinder, union, connection, connecting, hook-up, conjunction, conjugation, annexion, annexation, annexment, attachment, compagination, astriction, ligation, alligation, colligation, fastening, linking, accouplement, coupling, matrimony (903), grafting; infibulation, inosculation, symphysis, anastomosis, association (72), concatenation, communication, approach (197).

Joint, join, juncture, pivot, hinge, suture, articulation, commissure, mitre, seam, stitch, meeting, reunion, mortise.

Closeness, firmness, tightness, compactness, attachment, communication.

(Verbs) To join, conjoin, unite, connect, associate, put together, embody, re-embody, hold together, lump together, pack, fix together, attach, affix, saddle on, fasten, bind, secure, make fast, grapple, moor, clench (or clinch), catch, tie, pinion, strap, sew, lace, string, stitch, tack, knit, tat, crochet, knot, button, buckle, hitch, lash, truss, bandage, braid, splice, swathe, gird, tether, picket, harness, inspan, bridge over.

Chain, enchain, shackle, pinion, fetter, manacle, handcuff, lock, latch,

44 Disjunction *(Substantives)*, disconnection, disunity, disunion, disassociation, disengagement, abstraction, abstractedness, isolation, insularity, oasis, separateness, severalness, severality.

Separation, parting, detachment, divorce, sejunction, seposition, segregation, insulation, diduction, discerption, elision, caesura, division, subdivision, break, fracture, rupture, dismemberment, disintegration, dislocation, luxation, severance, disseverance, severing, fission, scission, rescission, abscission, laceration, dilaceration, wrenching, abruption, disruption, avulsion, divulsion, tearing asunder, section, cutting, resection, cleavage, fissure, breach, rent, split, crack, slit, tear, rip, dispersion (73), incision, dissection, vivisection anatomy.

Anatomist, prosector.

(Phrase) Disjecta membra.

(Verbs) To be disjoined, separated, etc., to come off, fall off, get loose, fall to pieces.

To disjoin, disconnect, disunite, part, dispart, detach, separate, space, space out, cut off, rescind, segregate, insulate, dissociate, isolate, disengage, set apart, liberate, loose, set free (750), unloose, unfasten, untie, unbind,

belay, brace, hook, clap, together, leash, couple, link, yoke, bracket, hang together, pin, nail, bolt, hasp, clasp, clamp, screw, rivet, solder, weld, impact, wedge, rabbet, mortise, mitre, jam, dovetail, enchase, engraft, interlink, inosculate, entwine, enlace, interlace, intertwine, intertwist, interweave, interlock.

To be joined, etc., to hang or hold together, cohere (46).

(Adjectives) Joined, conjoined, coupled, etc., bound up together, conjunct, corporate, compact.

Firm, fast, close, tight, taut, secure, set, fixed, impacted, jammed, locked, etc., intervolved, intertwined, inseparable, indissoluble, inseverable, untearable.

(Phrases) Hand in hand; rolled into one.

(Adverbs) Conjointly, jointly, etc.

With, along with, together with, in conjunction with.

Fast, firmly, closely, etc.

———

disband, unfix, unlace, unclasp, undo, unbutton, unbuckle, unchain, unfetter, untack, unharness, ungird, unpack, unbolt, unlatch, unlock, unlink, uncouple, unpin, unclinch, unscrew, unhook, unrivet, untwist, unshackle, unyoke, unknit, unsolder, ravel out, unravel, disentagle, unpick, unglue, switch off, shut off.

Sunder, divide, subdivide, divorce, sever, dissever, abscind, cut, scissor, incide, incise, snip, nib, cleave, rive, slit, split, split in twain, splinter, chip, crack, snap, burst, rend, break or tear asunder, shiver, crunch, chop, cut up, rip up, hack, hew, slash, whittle, haggle, hackle, discind, tear, lacerate, mangle, mince, gash, hash, knap.

Dissect, cut up, carve, slice, castrate, detruncate, anatomize; take, pull, or pick to pieces; unseam, tear to tatters, tear piecemeal, divellicate, disintegrate; dismember, disembowel, eviscerate, disbranch, dislocate, joint, disjoint, behead, mince, break up, crunch, gride, comminute (330), vivisect.

(Phrase) To tear limb from limb.

(Adjectives) Disjoined, disconnected, etc., snippety, disjointed, multipartite, abstract, disjunctive, isolated, insular, separate, discrete, apart, asunder, loose, free, liberated, disengaged, unattached, unannexed, distinct, unassociated, unconnected, adrift, straggling, dispersed, disbanded, segregated.

Cut off, rescinded, etc., rift, reft.

Capable of being cut, scissile, fissile, discerptible.

(Adverbs) Separately, etc., one by one, severally, apiece, apart, adrift, asunder; in the abstract, abstractedly.

45 Connecting medium.

Vinculum *(Substantives)*, link, connective, connection, junction (43), conjunction, copula, intermedium, hyphen, bridge, stepping-stone, isthmus, span, girder.

Bond, filament, fibre (205), hair, cordage, cord, thread, string, packthread, twine, twist, whipcord, tape, ferret, raffia, line, snood, ribbon, riband, rope, cable, hawser, painter, halyard, guy, guy-rope, wire, chain.

Fastening, tie, tendril, tendon, ligament, ligature, strap, tackle, rigging, traces, harness, yoke, band, withe, withy, brace, bandage, roller, fillet, thong, braid, inkle, girth, cinch, cestus, girdle, garter, halter, noose, lasso, lariat, surcingle, knot, running-knot, slip-knot, reef-knot, sailor's knot, grannyknot, etc.

Pin, corking-pin, safety-pin, nail, brad, tack, skewer, staple, clamp, vice, bracket, cramp, screw, button, buckle, brooch, clasp, slide, clip, hasp, hinge, hank, bolt, catch, latch, latchet, tag, hook, tooth, hook and eye, lock, locket, holdfast, padlock, rivet, anchor, grappling-iron, stake, post, gyve, shackle (752).

Cement, adhesive, mucilage, glue, gum, paste, size, goo, solder, lute, putty, bird-lime, mortar, stucco, plaster, grout.

46 Coherence *(Substantives)*, cohehesion, adherence, adhesion, accretion, concretion, agglutination, conglutination, aggregation, consolidation, set, cementation, soldering, welding, grouting.

Sticking, clinging, adhesiveness, stickiness, gumminess, gummosity, glutinosity (352), cohesiveness, density (321), in separability, inseparableness, tenaciousness, tenacity.

Clot, concrete, cake, lump, conglomerate (321).

(Verbs) To cohere, adhere, stick, cling, cleave, hold, take hold of, hold fast, hug, grow or hang together, twine round.

To concrete, curdle, cake.

To glue, agglutinate, conglutinate, agglomerate, consolidate, solidify (321); cement, lute, paste, gum, grout, stick, solder, weld.

(Phrases) To stick like a leech; to stick like wax; to cling like ivy, like a bur, like a limpet.

(Adjectives) Cohesive, adhesive, cohering, tenacious, sticky, tacky, glutinous, gluey, gooey, gummy, viscous (352), agglutinatory.

United, unseparated, sessile, inseparable, inextricable, infrangible (321).

47 Want of adhesion.

Incoherence *(Substantives)*, non-adhesion, immiscibility, looseness, laxity, slackness, relaxation, freedom, disjunction.

(Phrases) A rope of sand; *disjecta membra.*

(Verbs) To loosen, make loose, slacken, relax, unglue, unsolder, etc., detach, untwist, unravel, unroll (44, 313), to comminute (330)

(Adjectives) Incoherent, immiscible, detached, non-adhesive, loose, slack, lax, relaxed, baggy.

Segregated, flapping, streaming, dishevelled, unincorporated, unconsolidated, uncombined.

(Phrase) Like grains of sand.

———

48 Combination *(Substantives)*, union, unification, synthesis, incorporation, amalgamation, coalescence, crasis, fusion, embodiment, conflation, absorption, blending, centralization; mixture (41).

Compound, composition, amalgam, impregnation, decompound, decomposite, resultant.

(Verbs) To combine, unite, unify, incorporate, amalgamate, synthesize, embody, unify, re-embody, blend, merge, fuse, absorb, melt into one, consolidate, coalesce, centralize; to impregnate, to put together, to lump together.

(Adjectives) Combined, compound, composite, coalescent, synthetic, synthetical, impregnated with, engrained.

49 Decomposition *(Substantives)*, analysis, resolution, dissolution, disintegration, catalysis, electrolysis, corruption (653), dispersion (73), disjunction (44).

(Verbs) To decompose, rot, disembody, analyse, electrolyse, decompound, resolve, take to pieces, separate into its elements, dissect, unravel (313), break up.

(Adjectives) Decomposed, etc., catalytic, analytic, analytical, corrupted, dissolved.

———

4°. *Concrete Quantity*

50 Whole *(Substantives)*, totality, integrity, integrality, allness, entireness, entirety, *ensemble*, collectiveness, individuality, unity (87), indivisibility, indiscerptibility, indissolubility; embodiment, integration.

All, the whole, total, aggregate, integer, gross amount, sum, sum total, *tout ensemble*, upshot, trunk, hull, skeleton, hulk, lump, heap (72).

The principal part, bulk, mass, tissue, staple, body, compages, the main, the greater part, major part.

(Phrases) The whole caboodle; the whole boiling.

(Verbs) To form or constitute a whole, to integrate, embody, aggregate, amass (72), to total, amount to, come to.

(Adjectives) Whole, total, integral, entire, one, unbroken, uncut, undivided, seamless, individual, unsevered, unclipped, uncropped, unshorn, undiminished, undemolished, undissolved, unbruised, undestroyed, indivisible, indissoluble, indissolvable, indiscerptible.

Wholesale, sweeping.

(Adverbs) Wholly, altogether, totally, entirely, all, all in all, as a whole, wholesale, in the aggregate, in the mass, *en masse*, in the lump, *en bloc*, on the whole, *in toto*, in the gross, *in extenso*, in the bulk, to the full, throughout, every inch.

(Phrases) The long and short of it; nearly or almost all; root and branch; lock, stock, and barrel; hook, line, and sinker; in the long run; in the main; neck and crop; from end to end; from beginning to end; from first to last; from head to foot; from top to toe; fore and aft; from alpha to omega.

51 Part *(Substantives)*, portion, item, division, subdivision, section, chapter, verse, extract, passage, gobbet, sector, segment, fraction, fragment, frustum, detachment, piece, bit, lump, chunk, dollop, scrap, whit, swatch, morsel, mouthful, scantling, cantle, cantlet, slip, crumb (32), fritter, rag, tag, shred, tatter, splinter, snatch, cut, cutting, snip, snippet, snick, collop, slice, chip, chipping, shiver, sliver, matchwood, spillikin, smithereens, driblet, clipping, paring, shaving, debris, odds and ends, oddments, sundries, detritus, lamina, shadow, flotsam and jetsam, pickings.

Parcel, share, instalment, contingent, compartment, department, dividend, dose, particular, article, clause, paragraph.

Member, limb, lobe, lobule, arm, branch, scion, bough, joint, link, ramification (256), twig, bush, spray, sprig, offshoot, leaf, leaflet, stump, stub, butt, rump, torso.

(Verbs) To part, divide, subdivide, break (44); to partition, parcel out, portion, apportion (786), to ramify, branch, branch out.

(Adjectives) Part, fractional, fragmentary, scrappy, lobular, sectional, aliquot, divided, multifid, partitioned, isomeric.

(Adverbs) Partly, in part, partially, piecemeal, in detail, part by part, by driblets, bit by bit, little by little, by inches, inch by inch, foot by foot, drop by drop, in snatches, by fits and starts.

---

52 Completeness *(Substantives)*, entirety, fullness, impletion, completion (729), perfection (650), solidity, stop-gap, makeweight, padding, filling up, integration, absoluteness, sufficiency; complement, supplement (39).

Fill, load, bumper, brimmer, bellyful, skinful.

53 Incompleteness *(Substantives)*, deficiency, defectiveness, shortcoming (304), unreadiness, defalcation, failure, imperfection (651), hollowness, patchiness.

Part wanting, omission, defect, break, deficit, ullage, caret, lacuna, hiatus (198).

(Verbs) To be complete, etc., suffice (639).

To render complete or whole, to complete, exhaust, perfect, finish, make up, fill up, charge, load, replenish, make good, piece out, eke out.

(Phrases) To give the finishing touch; to supply deficiencies; to go to all lengths; to go the whole hog; to thrash out.

(Adjectives) Complete, entire, whole (50), absolute, perfect, full, plenary, solid, undivided, with all its parts, supplementary, adscititious, thorough, exhaustive, radical, sweeping, searching; consummate, thorough-paced, regular, sheer, unmitigated, unqualified.

Crammed, saturated, brimful, chock-full.

(Adverbs) Completely, entirely, to the full, outright, wholly, totally, thoroughly (31), *in toto, toto caelo*, in all respects.

(Phrases) To the top of one's bent; up to the ears; *à fond*; from first to last; from beginning to end; *ab ovo usque ad mala*.

(Verbs) To be incomplete, etc., to fail, fall short (304).

To dock, lop, mutilate, garble, truncate, castrate (38).

(Adjectives) Incomplete, unfinished, imperfect, defective, deficient, wanting, failing, short by, hollow, meagre, insufficient, half-baked, perfunctory, sketchy, scrappy, patchy.

Mutilated, garbled, docked, lopped, truncated; proceeding, in progress.

(Phrase) Cetera desunt.

-----

54 Composition *(Substantives)*, make-up, constitution, constituency, crasis.

Inclusion, admission, comprehension, reception.

(Verbs) To be composed of, to consist of, be made of, formed of, made up of, be resolved into.

To contain, include, hold, comprehend, take in, admit, embrace, involve, implicate.

To compose, constitute, form, make, make up, fill up, build up, put together, embody.

To enter into the composition of, to be or form part of (51), to merge in, be merged in.

(Adjectives) Comprehending, containing, including, comprising, etc.

Component, constituent, formative, forming, constituting, composing, etc., belonging to, appertaining to, inclusive.

-----

56 Component *(Substantives)* component part, integral part, element, constituent, ingredient, member,

55 Exclusion *(Substantives)*, nonadmission, omission, exception, rejection, proscription, repudiation, exile, banishment, excommunication.

Separation, segregation, elimination, seposition.

(Verbs) To be excluded from, etc., to be out of it.

To exclude, shut out, bar, leave out, omit, reject, repudiate, neglect, blackball; lay, put, or set apart or aside; segregate, pass over, throw overboard, slur over, neglect (460), excommunicate, banish, expatriate, extradite, deport, ostracize, relegate, rusticate, send down (297), rule out.

To eliminate, weed, winnow, screen, bar, separate (44), strike off.

(Phrase) 'Include me out.'

(Adjectives) Excluding, omitting, etc., exclusive.

Excluded, omitted, etc., unrecounted, inadmissible.

(Adverbs) Except, save, bar, barring, excepting.

57 Extraneousness *(Substantives)*, extrinsicality (5), exteriority (220).

limb (51), part and parcel, contents (190), appurtenance, feature, personnel.

———

(Adjectives) Extraneous, foreign, alien, tramontane, ultramontane, interloping.

(Adverbs) Abroad, in foreign parts, overseas.

A foreign body, alien, stranger, intruder, outsider, incomer, interloper, foreigner, dago, wop, *novus homo*, parvenu, immigrant, newcomer, new chum, pommy, greenhorn, tenderfoot.

SECTION IV—ORDER

1°. *Order in General*

58 Order (*Substantives*), regularity, orderliness, tidiness, uniformity, even tenor, symmetry.

Gradation, progression, pedigree, line, descent, subordination, course, series (69), array, routine.

Method, disposition, arrangement, system, economy, discipline, pattern, plan.

Rank, station, hierarchy, place, status, stand, scale, step, stage, period, term (71), footing; rank and file, pecking order.

(*Verbs*) To be or become in order, to form, fall in, arrange itself, place itself, range itself, fall into its place, fall into rank.

(*Adjectives*) Orderly, regular, in order, arranged, etc. (60), in its proper place, correct, tidy, shipshape, trim, *en règle*, well regulated, methodical, business-like, uniform, symmetrical, systematic, unconfused, undisturbed, untangled, unruffled, unravelled, still, etc. (265).

(*Phrases*) In apple-pie order; Bristol fashion.

(*Adverbs*) Systematically, methodically, etc., in turn, in its turn.

Step by step, by regular steps, gradations, stages, periods, or intervals, periodically (138).

At stated periods (138), *gradatim, seriatim.*

(*Phrase*) Like clockwork.

———

59 Absence, or want of Order, etc.
Disorder (*Substantives*), irregularity, asymmetry, anomaly, confusion, confusedness, disarray, untidiness, jumble, huddle, litter, lumber, farrago, mess, hash, clutter, pie, muddle, mix-up, upset, hotchpotch, hugger-mugger, anarchy, anarchism, imbroglio, chaos, tohubohu, omnium gatherum(72),derangement(61).

Complexness, complexity, complication, intricacy, intricateness, implication, perplexity, involution, ravelling, tangle, entanglement, snarl, knot, coil, skein, sleave, network, labyrinth, Gordian knot, jungle.

Turmoil, *mêlée*, tumult, ferment, stew, fermentation, pudder, pother, riot, uproar, bobbery, rough-house, rumpus, scramble, fracas, vortex, whirlpool, maelstrom, hurly-burly, bear-garden, Babel, Saturnalia, Donnybrook, pandemonium.

Tumultuousness, riotousness, inquietude (173), derangement (61), topsyturvydom (218).

(*Phrases*) Wheels within wheels; confusion worse confounded; most admired disorder; *concordia discors*; hell broke loose.

A pretty kettle of fish; a fine state of things; a how-d'ye-do; the fat in the fire; a bull in a china shop; the devil to pay.

The cart before the horse; hysteron proteron.

(*Verbs*) To be out of order, irregular, disorderly, etc., to ferment.

To derange, put out of order (61).

(Phrases) To be at cross-purposes; to make hay of.

(Adjectives) Disorderly, orderless, out of order, disordered, misplaced, out of place, deranged, disarranged (61), irregular, desultory, anomalous, untidy, sloppy, slovenly, tousled, straggling, unarranged, immethodical, unsymmetrical, unsystematic, unmethodical, undigested, unsorted, unclassified, unclassed, asymmetrical.

Disjointed, out of joint, out of gear, out of kilter, confused, tangled, involved, intricate, complicated, inextricable, irreducible.

Mixed, scattered, promiscuous, indiscriminate, casual.

Tumultuous, turbulent, riotous, troublous, tumultuary (173), rough-and-tumble.

(Adverbs) Irregularly, etc., by fits and snatches, pell-mell; higgledy-piggledy, hugger-mugger; at sixes and sevens; helter-skelter, harum-scarum, anyhow.

60 Reduction to Order.

Arrangement *(Substantives)*, disposal, disposition, collocation, allocation, distribution, sorting, assortment, allotment, apportionment, marshalling, alignment, taxis, taxonomy, gradation, organization, ordination; plan (626).

Analysis, sifting, screening, classification.

Result of arrangement, digest, synopsis, analysis, table, register (551).

Instrument for sorting, sieve, riddle, screen (260).

(Verbs) To order, reduce to order, bring into order, introduce order into.

To arrange, dispose, place, form; to put, set, place, etc., in order; to set out, collocate, pack, marshal, range, align (or aline), rank, group, parcel out, allot, distribute, assort, sort, sift, riddle.

To class, classify, categorize, file, string, thread, tabulate, pigeon-hole, catalogue, index, register, take stock.

To methodize, digest, regulate, size, grade, gradate, graduate, alphabetize, co-ordinate, systematize, organize, settle, fix, rearrange.

To unravel (246), disentangle, ravel, card, disembroil.

(Phrases) To put or set to rights; to assign places to.

(Adjectives) Arranged, methodical (58), embattled, in battle array.

(Phrase) A place for everything, and everything in its place.

61 Subversion of Order, bringing into disorder.

Derangement *(Substantives)*, disarrangement, misarrangement, displacement, misplacement, dislocation, discomposure, disturbance, bedevilment, disorganization, perturbation, shuffling, rumpling, embroilment, corrugation (258), inversion (218), jumble, muddle, disorder (59).

(Verbs) To derange, disarrange, misarrange, misplace, mislay, discompose, disorder, embroil, unsettle, disturb, confuse, perturb, jumble, tumble, huddle, shuffle, muddle, toss, hustle, fumble; to bring, put, or throw into disorder, trouble, confusion, etc., break the ranks, upset.

To unhinge, put out of joint, dislocate, turn over, invert; turn topsy-turvy; turn inside out (218), bedevil, throw out of gear.

To complicate, involve, perplex, tangle, entangle, embrangle (or imbrangle), ravel, ruffle, tousle, rumple, dishevel, muss, litter, scatter, make a mess of, monkey with, make hay of.

(Adjectives) Deranged, etc., disordered (59).

2°. Consecutive Order

62 Precedence *(Substantives)*, coming before, antecedence, antecedency, anteposition, priority (116), anteriority, the *pas*, the lead.

Superiority (33), precession (280).

(Verbs) To precede, come before, lead, introduce, usher in.

To place before; to prefix, affix, premise, prelude, preface, prologize.

(Phrases) To have the *pas*; to take the lead; to have the start; set the fashion; to open the ball.

(Adjectives) Preceding, precedent, antecedent, anterior, prior, previous, before, ahead of, leading.

Former, foregoing; coming or going before; precursory, precursive, prevenient, inaugural, prodromal, prodromic, preliminary, aforesaid, said, aforementioned, prefatory, introductory, prelusive, prelusory, proemial, preparatory, preambulatory.

(Adverbs) In advance, ahead, in front of, before, in the van (234).

---

64 Precursor *(Substantives)*, antecedent, precedent, predecessor, forerunner, pioneer, outrider, avant-courier, leader, bell-wether, herald, harbinger.

Prelude, preamble, preface, foreword, prologue, prodrome, protasis, prolusion, overture, premise, proem, prolepsis, prolegomena, prefix, introduction, heading, advertisement, frontispiece, groundwork (673).

(Adjectives) Precursory, prefatory (62).

---

66 Beginning *(Substantives)*, commencement, opening, outset, incipience, inception, inchoation, initiative, overture, exordium, introduction (64), inauguration début, onset, brunt, alpha.

Origin, source, rise, conception, birth, infancy, bud, embryo, germ, egg, rudiment, *incunabula*, start, cradle, starting-point, starting-post (293); dawn, morning (125).

63 Sequence *(Substantives)*, coming after, consecution, succession, posteriority (117), secondariness; following (281).

Continuation, order of succession, successiveness; alternation (138).

Subordination, inferiority (34).

(Phrase) Proxime accessit.

(Verbs) To succeed, come after, follow, come next, ensue, come on, tread close upon; to alternate.

To place after, to suffix, append.

(Phrases) To be in the wake or trail of; to tread on the heels of; to step into the shoes of; to assume the mantle of.

(Adjectives) Succeeding, coming after, following, subsequent, ensuing, sequent, sequacious, consequent, next; consecutive, amoebean, alternate (138).

Latter, posterior.

(Adverbs) After, subsequently, since, behind, in the wake of, in the train of, at the tail of, in the rear of (234).

---

65 Sequel *(Substantives)*, after-part, aftermath, suffix, successor, tail, runner-up, queue, train, wake, trail, rear, retinue, suite, appendix (39), postscript, epilogue, peroration, excursus, after-piece, tailpiece, tag, colophon, afterthought, second thoughts, *arrière pensée*, codicil, continuation, sequela, apodosis.

(Phrases) More last words; to be continued.

(Adjectives) Subsequent, ensuing (63).

---

67 End *(Substantives)*, close, termination, desinence, conclusion, finish, finis, finale, period, term, terminus, limit, last, omega, extreme, extremity, butt-end, fag-end, stub, tail, nib, tip, after-part, rear (235), colophon, coda, tailpiece, tag, *cul-de-lampe*, peroration, swan-song.

Completion (729), winding-up, *dénouement*, catastrophe, consummation, expiration, expiry, finishing

Van, vanguard, title-page, heading, front (234), fore-part, head (210).

Opening, entrance, entry, inlet, orifice, porch, portal, portico, gateway, door, gate, postern, wicket, threshold, vestibule, mouth, *fauces*, lips.

Alphabet, A B C, rudiments, elements.

(Phrase) The rising of the curtain; the thin end of the wedge.

(Verbs) To begin, commence, inchoate, rise, arise, originate, initiate, open, dawn, set in, take its rise, enter upon, embark on, set out (293), rcommence, undertake (676).

To usher in, lead off, lead the way, take the lead or the initiative; head, stand at the head, stand first, broach, set on foot, set a-going, set abroach, set up, handsel, institute, launch, strike up.

(Phrases) To make a beginning; to cross the Rubicon; to break ground; set the ball in motion; take the initiative; break the ice; fire away; open the ball; kick off; tee up; pipe up.

(Adjectives) Beginning, commencing, arising, initial, initiatory, initiative, inceptive, incipient, proemial, inaugural, inchoate, inchoative, embryonic, primigenial, aboriginal, rudimental, nascent, natal, opening, dawning, entering.

First, foremost, leading, heading, maiden.

Begun, commenced, etc.

(Adverbs) At, or in the beginning, at first blush, first, in the first place, *imprimis*, first and foremost, *in limine*, in the bud, in embryo.

From the beginning, *ab initio, ab ovo*.

stroke, knock-out, K.O., death-blow, *coup de grâce*, upshot, issue, fate, doom, Day of Judgment, doomsday.

(Phrases) The *ne plus ultra*; the fall of the curtain; *'le commencement de la fin.'*

(Verbs) To end, close, finish, expire, terminate, conclude; come or draw to an end, close or stop, be all over, pass away, give out, peter out, run its course; to say one's say, perorate, be through with.

To come last, bring up the rear.

To bring to an end, close, etc., to put a period, etc., to; to make an end of; to close, finish, seal, wind up, complete, achieve (729), crown, determine.

(Phrases) To cut the matter short; to shut up shop.

(Adjectives) Ending, closing, etc., final, terminal, eschatological, desistive, definitive, crowning.

Last, ultimate, penultimate, antepenultimate, hindermost, rear, caudal, conterminal, conterminous.

Ended, closed, terminated, etc., through.

Unbegun, fresh, uncommenced.

(Adverbs) Once for all, in fine, finally, at the end of the day, for good, for good and all.

———

68 Middle *(Substantives)*, midst, mean, medium, happy medium, *via media*, middle term, centre (223), *mezzo termine, juste milieu*, half-way house, hub, nave, navel, omphalos, bull's-eye, nucleus.

Equidistance, equator, diaphragm, midriff; bisection (91).

Intervenience, interjacence, intervention (228), mid-course (628).

(Adjectives) Middle, medial, median, mesial, mean, mid, middlemost, midmost, mediate, intermediate (29), intervenient, interjacent (228), central (222), equidistant, embosomed, merged.

Mediterranean, equatorial.

(Adverbs) In the middle, amid, amidst, midway, amidships, midships, half-way.

(Phrases) In the thick of; *in medias res*.

69 Uninterrupted sequence.

Continuity *(Substantives)*, consecution, consecutiveness, succession, suite, progression, series, train, chain, catenation, concatenation, scale, gradation, course, procession, column, retinue, cortège, cavalcade, rank and file, line of battle, array, pedigree, genealogy, lineage, race.

File, queue, echelon, line, row, rank, range, tier, string, thread, team, tandem, randem, suit, flush, colonnade.

(Verbs) To follow in, form a series, etc.; to fall in.

To arrange in a series, to marshal (60); to string together, file, thread, graduate, tabulate.

(Adjectives) Continuous, sequent, consecutive, progressive, serial, successive, continued, uninterrupted, unbroken, entire, linear, in a line, in a row, etc., gradual, constant, unremitting, unintermitting, evergreen (110).

(Adverbs) Continuously, consecutively, etc., *seriatum*; in a line, row, series, etc., in succession, etc., running, gradually, step by step; uninterruptedly, at a stretch, at one go.

(Phrase) In Indian file.

70 Interrupted sequence.

Discontinuity *(Substantives)*, interruption, pause, period, interregnum, break, interval, interlude, episode, lacuna, cut, gap, fracture, fault, chasm, hiatus (198), caesura, parenthesis, rhapsody, anacoluthon.

Intermission, alternation (138); a broken thread, broken melody.

(Verbs) To be discontinuous, etc.; to alternate, intermit.

To discontinue, pause, interrupt, break, interpose (228); to break in upon, disconnect (44); to break or snap the thread.

(Adjectives) Discontinuous, inconsecutive, broken, interrupted, unsuccessive, desultory, disconnected, unconnected, fitful, spasmodic, sporadic, scattered.

Alternate, every other, intermitting, alternating (138).

(Phrase) Few and far between.

(Adverbs) At intervals, by snatches, *per saltum*, by fits and starts, *longo intervallo*.

———

71 Term *(Substantives)*, rank, station, stage, step, rung, round, degree (26), remove, grade, link, place, peg, mark, point, *pas*, period, pitch, stand, standing, status, footing, range.

(Verbs) To hold, occupy, find, fall into a place, station.

3°. Collective Order

72 Assemblage *(Substantives)*, collection, dozen, collocation, compilation, levy, gathering, ingathering, muster, round-up, colligation, contesseration, *attroupement*, association, concourse, conflux, convergence, meeting, assembly, congregation, at home (892), levee, club, reunion, gaudy, soirée, conversazione, accumulation, cumulation, array, mobilization.

Congress, convocation, convention, *comitium*, committee, quorum, conclave, synod, caucus, conventicle, eisteddfod, mass-meeting.

73 Non-assemblage.

Dispersion *(Substantives)*, scattering, dissemination, diffusion, dissipation, spreading, casting, distribution, apportionment, sprinkling, respersion, circumfusion, interspersion, divergence (291), demobilization.

Odds and ends, waifs and strays, flotsam and jetsam.

(Verbs) To disperse, scatter, sow, disseminate, diffuse, shed, spread, overspread, dispense, disband, disembody, distribute, dispel, cast forth; strew, bestrew, sprinkle, sparge, issue, deal out, utter, resperse, intersperse,

Miscellany, olla podrida, museum, *collectanea,* menagerie (636), Noah's ark, anthology, encyclopaedia, portfolio, file.

A multitude (102), crowd, throng, rabble, mob, press, crush, horde, posse, body, tribe, crew, gang, knot, band, party, swarm, school, shoal, bevy, galaxy, covey, flock, herd, drove, corps, troop, troupe, squad, squadron, phalanx, platoon, company, regiment, battalion, legion, host, army, division.

set abroach, circumfuse; to decentralize, demobilize; to hive-off.

(Phrases) To turn adrift; to scatter to the four winds; to sow broadcast; to spread like wildfire.

(Adjectives) Unassembled, uncollected, dispersed, scattered, diffused, sparse, spread, dispread, widespread, sporadic, cast, broadcast, epidemic, adrift.

(Adverbs) Sparism, here and there, *passim.*

A sounder (of swine), skulk (of foxes), pride (of lions), charm (of finches), flush (of mallards), gaggle (of geese), wedge (of swans).

Clan, brotherhood, fraternity, sisterhood, party (712).

Volley, shower, storm, cloud, flood, deluge.

Group, cluster, clump, set, batch, battery, pencil, lot, pack, budget, assortment, bunch, parcel, packet, package, bundle, fascicle, fascicule, *fasciculus,* faggot, wisp, truss, tuft, rosette, shock, rick, fardel, stack, sheaf, stook, haycock.

Accumulation, congeries, heap, hoard, lump, pile, rouleau, tissue, mass, pyramid, bale, drift, snowball, acervation, cumulation, glomeration, agglomeration, conglobation, conglomeration, conglomerate, coacervation, coagmentation, aggregation, concentration (290), congestion, omnium gatherum.

Collector, tax-gatherer, whip, whipper-in.

(Verbs) To assemble, collect, muster, meet, unite, cluster, swarm, flock, herd, crowd, throng, associate, congregate, conglomerate, concentrate, congest, rendezvous, resort, flock together, get together, reassemble.

To bring, get or gather together, collect, draw together, group, convene, convoke, convocate, collocate, colligate, round up, scrape together, rake up, dredge, bring into a focus, amass, accumulate, heap up, pile, pack, do up, stack, truss, cram, pack together, congest, acervate, coagment, agglomerate, garner up, lump together, make a parcel of; to centralize; to mobilize.

(Phrases) To heap Pelion upon Ossa; to collect in a drag-net.

(Adjectives) Assembled, collected, etc., undispersed, met together, closely packed, dense, crowded, serried, huddled together, teeming, swarming, populous.

(Phrases) Packed like sardines; crowded to suffocation.

74 Place of meeting.

Focus *(Substantives),* point of convergence, corradiation, rendezvous, home, headquarters, club, centre (222), gathering-place, meeting-place, trysting-place, rallying-ground, haunt, howff, resort, museum, repository, depot (636).

4°. *Distributive Order*

75 Class *(Substantives),* division, category, predicament, head, order, section, department, domain, province.

Kind, sort, variety, type, genus, species, family, phylum, race, tribe, caste, sept, clan, *gens,* phratry, breed, kith, sect, set, assortment, feather, stripe, suit, range, run.

Gender, sex, kin, kidney, manner, nature, description, denomination, designation, character, stamp, stuff, *genre.*

(Adjectives) Generic, racial, tribal, etc.

(Verbs) To classify, catalogue (60).

76 Inclusion *(Substantives),* comprehension under a class, reference to a class, admission, comprehension, reception, subsumption.

Inclusion in a compound, composition (54).

(Verbs) To be included in, to come under, to fall under, to range under; to belong, or pertain to, appertain; to range with, to merge in, to be of.

To include, comprise, comprehend, contain, admit, embrace, receive; to enumerate among, reckon among, reckon with, number among, refer to, place under, class with or among, arrange under or with, take into account, subsume.

(Adjectives) Including, inclusive, all-embracing, congener, congeneric, congenerous, *et hoc genus omne,* etcetera.

Included, merged, etc.

(Phrase) Birds of a feather.

77 Exclusion from a class *(Substantives),* rejection, proscription.

Exclusion from a compound (55).

(Verbs) To be excluded from, etc.; to exclude, proscribe, debar, rule out, set apart (55).

(Phrase) To shut the door upon.

(Adjectives) Exclusive, excluding, etc.

———

78 Generality *(Substantives),* universality, catholicism, catholicity.

Every man, every one, everybody, all, all hands.

Miscellaneousness, miscellany, encyclopaedia, generalization, prevalence, drag-net.

(Phrases) The world and his wife; N or M.

(Verbs) To be general, common, or prevalent, to prevail.

To render general, to generalize.

(Adjectives) General, generic, collective, comprehensive, encyclopaedic, panoramic, bird's-eye, sweeping, radical, universal, world-wide, cosmopolitan, catholic, common, oecumenical, transcendental, prevalent, prevailing, all-pervading, epidemic, all-inclusive.

Unspecified, impersonal; every, all.

(Adverbs) Whatever, whatsoever, to a man; generally, universally, on the whole, for the most part.

———

79 Speciality *(Substantives),* particularity, peculiarity, individuality, haecceity, thisness, personality, characteristic, mannerism, idiosyncrasy, trick, gimmick, specificness, specificity, eccentricity, singularity (83).

Version, reading (522).

Particulars, details, items, counts.

I, myself, self, I myself, *moi qui vous parle.*

(Phrases) Argumentum ad hominem; local colour.

(Verbs) To specify, particularize, individualize, realize, specialize, designate, determine.

(Phrases) To descend to particulars; to enter into detail.

(Adjectives) Special, particular, individual, specific, proper, appropriate, personal, private, respective, several, definite, determinate, especial, certain, esoteric, endemic, partial, party, peculiar, characteristic, distinctive, typical, unique, diagnostic, exclusive, *sui generis,* singular, exceptional (83).

This, that, yonder, yon, such and such.

(Adverbs) Specially, specifically, etc., in particular, respectively, personally, individually, *in propria persona.*

Each, apiece, one by one, severally, seriatim, namely, *videlicet,* viz., to wit.

5°. *Order as regards Categories*

80 Rule *(Substantives)*, regularity, uniformity, constancy, standard, model, nature, principle, the order of things, routine, prevelance, practice, usage, custom, use, habit (613), regulation, precept (697), convention, *convenances*.

Form, formula, law, canon, principle, keynote, catchword.

Type, archetype, pattern, precedent, paradigm, the normal, natural, ordinary or model state or condition; norm, control.

(Phrases) A standing order; the bed of Procrustes; laws of the Medes and Persians.

(Adjectives) Regular, uniform, constant (82).

81 Multiformity *(Substantives)*, variety, diversity, multifariousness, allotropy, allotropism.

(Adjectives) Multiform, variform, polymorphic, multifold, manifold, multifarious, multigenerous, omnifarious, omnigenous, heterogeneous, motley, epicene, indiscriminate, desultory, irregular, diversified, allotropic; different (15).

(Phrase) Of all sorts and kinds.

_____

82 Conformity *(Substantives)*, conformance, observance, naturalization, harmony, convention (613).

Example, instance, specimen, sample, ensample, exemplar, exemplification, illustration, pattern (22), object lesson, case in point, quotation, the rule.

(Phrases) The order of the day; the common or ordinary run of things (23); a matter of course.

(Verbs) To conform to rule, be regular, orthodox, etc., to follow, observe, go by, bend to, obey rules; to be guided or regulated by, be wont, etc. (613), to comply or chime in with, to be in harmony with, follow suit; to standardize, naturalize.

To exemplify, illustrate, cite, quote, put a case, produce an instance, set an example.

(Phrases) To go with the crowd; to do in Rome as the Romans do; to follow the fashion; to swim with the stream; to keep one in countenance.

(Adjectives) Conformable to rule, regular, uniform, constant, steady, according to rule, *en règle, de rigueur,* normal, well regulated, formal, canonical, orthodox, conventional, strict, rigid, positive, uncompromising (23).

Ordinary, natural, usual, common, wonted, accustomed, habitual (613), household, average, everyday, current, rife, prevailing, prevalent, established,

83 Unconformity *(Substantives)*, nonconformity, unconventionality, informality, arbitrariness, abnormity, abnormality, anomaly, anomalousness, lawlessness, peculiarity, exclusiveness; infraction, breach, violation, of law or rule; individuality, idiosyncrasy, mannerism, eccentricity, aberration, irregularity, unevenness, variety, singularity, rarity, oddity, oddness, exemption, salvo.

Exception, nondescript, a character, original, nonesuch, monster, monstrosity, prodigy (872), *lusus naturae, rara avis,* freak, curiosity, crank, queer fish; half-caste, half-breed, cross-breed, mongrel, hybrid, mule, mulatto (41), *tertium quid,* hermaphrodite, sport.

Phoenix, chimera, hydra, sphinx, minotaur, griffin, centaur, hippocentaur, hippogriff, basilisk, cockatrice, tragelaph, kraken, dragon, wyvern, roc, sea-serpent, mermaid, merman, cyclops, unicorn.

(Phrases) Out of one's element; a fish out of water; neither one thing nor another; neither fish, flesh, nor fowl, nor good red herring; a law to oneself.

(Verbs) To be unconformable to rule, to be exceptional, etc.; to violate a law or custom, to stretch a point.

(Phrases) To have no business there; to beggar description.

(Adjectives) Unconformable, excep-

received, stereotyped, acknowledged, typical, accepted, recognized, representative, hackneyed, well-known, familiar, vernacular, commonplace, trite, banal, cut and dried, naturalized, orderly, shipshape, run of the mill.

Exemplary, illustrative, in point, of daily or everyday occurrence, in the order of things.

(Phrases) Regular as clockwork; according to Cocker (or Hoyle).

(Adverbs) Conformably, by rule, regularly, etc., agreeably to; in accordance, conformity, or keeping with.

Usually, generally, ordinarily, commonly, for the most part, as usual, *more solito, more suo, pro more*; of course, as a matter of course, *pro forma*.

Always, uniformly (16), invariably, without exception, never otherwise.

For example, for instance, *exempli gratia, inter alia*.

(Phrases) Ab uno disce omnes; ex pede Herculem; ex ungue leonem; birds of a feather.

tional, abnormal, anomalous, anomalistic, out of order, out of place, misplaced, irregular, unorthodox, uneven, arbitrary, informal, aberrant, stray, peculiar, funny, exclusive, unnatural, eccentric, unconventional, Bohemian, beatnik, hippy, yippy.

Unusual, unaccustomed, unwonted, uncommon, rare, singular, unique, curious, odd, extraordinary, strange, *outré*, out of the way, egregious, out of the ordinary, unheard of, queer, quaint, old-fashioned, unfashionable, nondescript, undescribed, unexampled, *sui generis*, unprecedented, unparalleled, unfamiliar, fantastic, newfangled, grotesque, bizarre, weird, eerie, outlandish, exotic, preternatural, unexampled, unrepresentative, uncanny, denaturalized.

Heterogeneous, heteroclite, amorphous, out of the pale of, mongrel, amphibious, epicene, half-blood, hybrid (41), androgynous, betwixt and between.

(Phrases) 'None but himself could be his parallel'; caviare to the general.

(Adverbs) Unconformably, etc.; except, unless, save, barring, beside, without, but for, save and except, let alone, to say nothing of; however, yet, but.

SECTION V—NUMBER

1°. *Number in the Abstract*

84 Number *(Substantives)*, symbol, numeral, figure, cipher, digit, integer, counter, a round number, notation, a formula; series.

Sum, difference, subtrahend, complement, product, factorial, multiplicand, multiplier, multiplicator, coefficient, multiple, least common multiple, dividend, divisor, factor, highest common factor, greatest common measure, quotient, sub-multiple, fraction, vulgar fraction, mixed number, numerator, denominator, decimal, circulating decimal, recurring decimal, repetend, common measure, aliquot part, reciprocal, prime number; permutation, combination, election.

Ratio, proportion, progression (arithmetical, geometrical, harmonical), percentage.

Power, root, exponent, index, function, logarithm, antilogarithm; differential, integral, fluxion, fluent; incommensurable, surd.

(Adjectives) Numeral, complementary, divisible, aliquot, reciprocal, prime, fractional, decimal, factorial, fractional, mixed, incommensurable.

Proportional, exponential, logarithmic, logometric, differential, fluxional, integral.

Positive, negative, rational, irrational, surd, radical, real, imaginary, impossible.

85 Numeration *(Substantives)*, numbering, counting, tale, telling, tally, calling over, recension, enumeration, summation, reckoning, computation, ciphering, calculation, calculus, algorism, dactylonomy, rhabdology.

Arithmetic, analysis, algebra, differential and integral calculus.

Statistics, dead reckoning, muster, poll, census, capitation, roll-call, muster-roll, account, score, recapitulation, demography.

Addition, subtraction, multiplication, division, proportion, rule of three, reduction, involution, evolution, practice, equations, extraction of roots, approximation, interpolation, differentiation, integration. ·

Abacus, logometer, ready-reckoner, slide-rule, sliding-rule, tallies, Napier's bones, calculating machine, tabulator, totalizator, totalizer, tote, cash-register.

(Verbs) To number, count, tell, tally, call over, take an account of, enumerate, muster, poll, run over, recite, recapitulate; sum, sum up, cast up, tell off, score, cipher, compute, calculate, reckon, estimate, figure up, tot up; add, subtract, multiply, divide; amount to.

Check, prove, demonstrate, balance, audit, overhaul, take stock.

(Adjectives) Numerical, arithmetical, logarithmic, numeral, analytic, algebraic, statistical, computable, calculable, commensurable, incommensurable, incommensurate.

86 List *(Substantives)*, catalogue, inventory, schedule, register, census, return, statistics, record (551), account, registry, syllabus, roll, terrier, cadastre, cartulary, tally, file, muster-roll, roster, rota, bead-roll, panel, calendar, index, table, book, ledger, day-book, synopsis, bibliography, contents, invoice, bill of lading, bill of fare, menu, red book, peerage, baronetage, Almanach de Gotha, Debrett, Domesday Book, prospectus, programme, directory, gazetteer, who's who.

Registration, etc. (551).

2°. *Determinate Number*

87 Unity *(Substantives)*, unification, oneness, individuality, singleness, solitariness, solitude, isolation (893), abstraction; monism.

One, unit, ace, monad.

Someone, somebody, no other, none else, an individual; monist.

(Verbs) To be alone, etc.; to isolate (44), insulate, set apart.

To render one, unify.

(Phrase) To dine with Duke Humphrey.

(Adjectives) One, sole, single, individual, apart, alone, lone, isolated, solitary, lonely, lonesome, desolate, dreary, insular, insulated, disparate, discrete, detached; monistic.

Unaccompanied, unattended, *solus*, single-handed, singular, odd, unique, unrepeated, azygous.

Inseverable, irresolvable, indiscerptible, compact.

88 Accompaniment *(Substantives)*, coexistence, concomitance, company, association, companionship, partnership, collaboration, copartnership, coefficiency.

Concomitant, adjunct, context, accessory (39), coefficient, companion, attendant, fellow, associate, consort, spouse, colleague, collaborator, partner, copartner, side-kick, buddy, satellite, escort, hanger-on, parasite, shadow; travelling tutor, chaperon, duenna.

(Verbs) To accompany, chaperon, coexist, attend, associate or be associated with, keep company with, collaborate with, hang on, shadow, wait on, to join, tie together.

(Phrases) To go hand in hand with; to be in the same boat.

(Adjectives) Accompanying, coexisting, attending, attendant, concomi-

(Adverbs) Singly, etc., alone, by itself, *per se*, only, apart, in the singular number, in the abstract, one by one; one at a time.

One and a half, sesqui-.

tant, fellow, twin, joint, associated with, accessory.

(Adverbs) With, withal, together with, along with, in company with, collectively, hand in hand, together, in a body, cheek by jowl, side by side; therewith, herewith, moreover, besides, also, and (37), not to mention.

89 Duality *(Substantives)*, dualism, duplicity, twofoldness, doubleness, biformity; polarity.

Two, deuce, couple, brace, pair, dyad (or duad), twins, Siamese twins, Castor and Pollux, Damon and Pythias, fellows, gemini, yoke, span, file, conjugation, twosome; dualist.

(Verbs) To unite in pairs, to pair, pair off, couple, match, mate, bracket, yoke.

(Adjectives) Two, twain, dual, binary, dualistic, duplex (90), duplicate, dyadic, binomial, twin, tête-à-tête, Janus-headed, bilateral, bicentric, bifocal.

Coupled, bracketed, paired, etc., conjugate.

Both, both the one and the other.

90 Duplication *(Substantives)*, doubling, gemination, reduplication, ingemination, repetition, iteration (104), renewal.

(Verbs) To double, redouble, geminate, reduplicate, repeat, iterate, re-echo, renew (660).

(Adjectives) Double, doubled, redoubled, second.

Biform, bifarious, bifold, bilateral, bifacial, twofold, two-sided, two-faced, duplex, duplicate, ingeminate.

(Adverbs) Twice, once more, over again, *da capo, bis, encore*, anew, as much again, twofold (104, 136).

Secondly, in the second place, again.

91 Division into two parts.

Bisection *(Substantives)*, bipartition, dichotomy, halving, dimidiation, bifurcation, forking, branching, ramification, divarication, splitting, cleaving.

Fork, prong, fold, branch, Y.

Half, moiety, semi-, demi-, hemi-.

(Verbs) To bisect, halve, divide, split, cut in two, cleave, dimidiate, dichotomize.

To separate, fork, bifurcate, branch out, ramify.

(Phrases) To go halves; to go fifty-fifty; to split the difference.

(Adjectives) Bisected, halved, divided, etc., bipartite, bicuspid, bind, bifurcated, bifurcate, cloven, cleft, split, etc.

92 Triality *(Substantives)*, trinity.

Three, triad, triangle, triplet, trey, trio, tern, trinomial, leash, threesome, trefoil, triquetra, *terza rima*, trilogy.

Third power, cube.

(Adjectives) Three, triform, trine, trinal, trinary, ternary, ternal, ternate (93), trinomial, tertiary, tri-.

93 Triplication *(Substantives)*, triplicity, trebleness, trine.

(Verbs) To treble, triple, triplicate, cube.

(Adjectives) Treble, triple, tern, ternary, ternate, triplicate, trigeminal, threefold, third.

(Adverbs) Three times, thrice, threefold, in the third place, thirdly.

94 Division into three parts.

Trisection *(Substantives)*, tripartition, trichotomy; third part, third.

(Verbs) To trisect, divide into three parts.

(Adjectives) Trifid, trisected, tripartite, trichotomous, trisulcate, triform.

95 Quaternity (*Substantives*), four, tetrad, quadruplet, quad, quartet, quaternion, foursome, square, tetragon, tetrahedron, tessara, quadrature; tetralogy.

(*Verbs*) To reduce to a square, to square.

(*Adjectives*) Four, quaternary, quaternal, quadratic, quartile, tetractic, tetra-, quadri.

96 Quadruplication.
(*Verbs*) To multiply by four, quadruplicate, biquadrate.

(*Adjectives*) Fourfold, quadruple, quadruplicate, fourth.

(*Adverbs*) Four times, in the fourth place, fourthly, to the fourth degree.

97 Division into four parts.
Quadrisection (*Substantives*), quadripartition, quartering, a fourth, a quarter.

(*Verbs*) To quarter, to divide into four parts.

(*Adjectives*) Quartered, etc., quadrifid, quadripartite.

98 Five (*Substantives*), cinque, cinqfoil, quint, quincunx, pentad, pentagon, pentahedron, quintuplet, quin, quintet.

(*Adjectives*) Five, quinary, quintuple, fivefold, fifth.

Six, half a dozen, hexad, hexagon, hexahedron, sextet.

(*Adjectives*) Senary, sextuple, sixfold, sixth.

Seven, heptad, heptagon, heptahedron, septet.

(*Adjectives*) Septenary, septuple, sevenfold, seventh.

Eight, octad, octagon, octahedron, octet, ogdoad.

(*Adjectives*) Octonary, octonal, octuple, eightfold, eighth.

Nine, ennead, nonagon, enneagon, enneahedron, novena.

(*Adjectives*) Enneatic, ninefold, ninth.

Ten, decad, decagon, decahedron, decade.

(*Adjectives*) Decimal, denary, decuple, tenfold, tenth.

Twelve, a dozen.

(*Adjectives*) Duodenary, duodecimal, twelfth.

Thirteen, a long dozen, a baker's dozen.

Twenty, a score, icosahedron.

(*Adjectives*) Vigesimal, twentieth.

Forty, twoscore.

(*Adjectives*) Quadragesimal.

Fifty, twoscore and ten.

(*Adjectives*) Quinquagesimal.

Sixty, threescore.

(*Adjectives*) Sexagesimal, sexagenary.

Seventy, threescore and ten.

Eighty, fourscore.

99 Quinquesection, etc.
(*Adjectives*) Quinquefid, quinquarticular, quinquepartite.

Sexpartite.

Septempartite.

Octopartite.

Decimation, tithe.
(*Verb*) To decimate.

Ninety, fourscore and ten.

Hundred, centenary, hecatomb, century. One hundred and forty-four, a gross.

(Verbs) To centuriate.

(Adjectives) Centesimal, centennial, centenary, centurial, centuple, centuplicate, hundredfold, hundredth.

Thousand, chiliad, millennium.

(Adjective) Millesimal.

Myriad, lac, crore.

Million, billion, trillion, etc.

3°. Indeterminate Number

100 More than one.

Plurality *(Substantives)*, a number, a certain number, a few, a wheen, a round number.

(Adjectives) Plural, more than one, upwards of, some, a few, one or two, two or three, umpteen, certain.

(Adverb) Etcetera.

101 Zero *(Substantives)*, nothing (4) nought (or naught), cipher; nobody, *nemo.*

(Adjectives) None, not one, not any, not a soul.

———

102 Multitude *(Substantives)*, numerousness, numerosity, numerality, multiplicity, majority, profusion, legion, host, a great or large number, numbers, array, power, lot, sight, army, sea, galaxy, populousness (72), a hundred, thousand, myriad, million, etc.

A shoal, swarm, draught, bevy, flock, herd, drove, flight, covey, hive, brood, litter, mob, nest, crowd (72).

Increase of number, multiplication, multiple; greater number, majority.

(Verbs) To be numerous, etc., to swarm, teem, crowd, come thick upon, outnumber, multiply, to people.

(Phrase) To swarm like locusts or bees.

103 Fewness *(Substantives)*, paucity, a small number, handful, scantiness, rareness, rarity, thinness.

Diminution of number, reduction, weeding, elimination, thinning; smaller number, minority.

(Verbs) To be few, etc.

To render few, reduce, diminish in number, weed, weed out, prick off, eliminate, thin, thin out, decimate.

(Adjectives) Few, scanty, scant, rare, infrequent, sparse, scattered, hardly or scarcely any, reduced, thinned, etc.

(Phrases) Few and far between; you could count them on the fingers of one hand.

———

(Adjectives) Many, several, a wheen, sundry, divers, various, a great many, very many, full many, ever so many, no end of, numerous, profuse, manifold, multiplied, multitudinous, multiple, multinomial, endless (105), teeming, populous, peopled.

Frequent, repeated, reiterated, outnumbering, thick, crowding, crowded; galore.

(Phrases) Thick as hail; thick as leaves in Vallombrosa; plentiful as blackberries; in profusion; numerous as the sands on the seashore; their name is Legion.

104 Repetition *(Substantives)*, iteration, reiteration, harping, recapitulation, run, recurrence (136), recrudescence, tautology, monotony; cuckoo-note, chimes, repetend, echo, burden of a song, refrain, jingle, renewal, rehearsal, réchauffé, rehash, reproduction (19).

Cuckoo, mocking-bird, mimic, imitator, parrot.

Periodicity (138), frequency (136).

(Phrase) A twice-told tale.

(Verbs) To repeat, iterate, reiterate, recapitulate, renew, reproduce, echo, re-echo, drum, hammer, harp on, plug, rehearse, redouble, recrudesce, reappear, recur, revert, recommence.

(Phrases) Do or say over again; ring the changes on; to harp on the same string; to din or drum in the ear; to go over the same ground; to begin again.

(Adjectives) Repeated, repetitional, repetitionary, repetitive, recurrent, recurring, reiterated, renewed, ever-recurring, thick-coming, monotonous, harping, sing-song, mocking, chiming; above-mentioned, said, aforesaid.

(Phrases) It's that man again; cut and come again; *cramoe repetita*.

(Adverbs) Repeatedly, often (136), again, anew, over again, afresh, ditto, *encore, de novo, da capo, bis* (90).

(Phrases) Toties quoties; again and again; in quick succession, over and over again; ever and anon; time after time; year after year; times out of number; *ad nauseam*.

105 Infinity *(Substantives)*, infiniteness, infinitude.

(Adjectives) Infinite, numberless, innumerable, countless, sumless, untold, unnumbered, unsummed, incalculable, unlimited, limitless, illimitable, immeasurable, unmeasured, measureless, unbounded, boundless, endless, interminable, unfathomable, exhaustless, termless, indefinite, without number, without limit, without end, unending.

(Adverbs) Infinitely, etc., without measure, limit, etc., *ad infinitum*, world without end.

SECTION VI—TIME

1°. *Absolute Time*

106 Duration *(Substantives)*, time, period, term, space, span, spell, season, era, epoch, decade, century, chiliad, age, cycle, aeon.

Intermediate time, while, interval, interim, pendency, intervention, intermission, interregnum, interlude, recess, break, intermittence, respite (265).

Long duration (110).

(Phrases) The enemy; the whirligig of time.

(Verbs) To continue, last, endure, remain, go on; to take, take up, fill or occupy time; to persist, to intervene.

107 Timelessness *(Substantives)*, neverness, absence of time, no time, *dies non*.

Short duration (111).

(Adverbs) Never, ne'er, at no time, on no occasion, at no period, nevermore, *sine die*.

(Phrases) On Tib's eve; at the Greek Calends; *jamais de ma vie*; 'jam every other day.'

———

To pass, pass away, spend, employ, while away or consume time, waste time.

(Adjectives) Continuing, lasting, enduring, remaining, persistent, perpetual, permanent (150).

(Adverbs) While, whilst, so long as, during, pending, till, until, up to, during the time or interval, the whole time or period, all the time or while, in the long run, all along, throughout, from beginning to end (52).

Pending, meantime, meanwhile, in the meantime, in the interim, *ad interim, pendente lite*, from day to day, for a time, for a season, for good, yet, up to this time.

108 Definite duration, or portion of time.

Period *(Substantives)*, second, minute, hour, day, week, fortnight, month, lunation, quarter, year, leap-year, lustrum, quinquennium, decade, lifetime, generation, century, age, millennium, *annus magnus*.

(Adjectives) Hourly, horary; daily, diurnal, quotidian; weekly, hebdomadal, menstrual, monthly, annual, secular, centennial, bicentennial, etc., bissextile, seasonal.

(Adverbs) From day to day, from hour to hour.

Once upon a time; Anno domini, A.D.; Before Christ, B.C.

108A Contingent Duration.
During pleasure, during good behaviour, *quamdiu se bene gesserit*.

110 Long duration.
Diuturnity *(Substantives)*, a long time, an age, a century, an eternity, aeon.

(Phrases) Temporis longinquitas; a month of Sundays.

Durableness, durability, persistence, lastingness, continuance, permanence (150), longevity, survival.

Distance of time, protraction, extension or prolongation of time, delay (133).

(Verbs) To last, endure, stand, remain, continue, abide, tarry, protract, prolong, outlast, outlive, survive; spin out, draw out, eke out, temporize, linger, loiter, lounge (275), wait.

(Phrase) To live to fight another day.

(Adjectives) Durable, of long duration, permanent, enduring, chronic, intransient, intransitive, intransmutable, lasting, abiding, persistent; livelong, longeval, long-lived, macrobiotic, diuturnal, evergreen, perennial, unintermitting, unremitting, perpetual (112).

Protracted, prolonged, spun out, long-winded, surviving, lingering.

(Adverbs) Long, a long time, permanently.

(Phrases) As the day is long; all the

109 Indefinite duration.
Course *(Substantives)*, progress, process, succession, lapse, flow, flux, stream, tract, current, tide, march, step, flight, etc., of time.

Indefinite time, aorist.

(Verbs) To elapse, lapse, flow, run, proceed, roll on, advance, pass, slide, press on, flit, fly, slip, glide, run its course.

(Adjectives) Elapsing, passing, etc.; aoristic.

(Adverbs) In course of time, in due time of season, in process of time, in the fullness of time.

(Phrase) Labuntur anni.

———

111 Short duration.
Transientness *(Substantives)*, transitoriness, impermanence, evanescence, transitiveness, fugitiveness, fugacity, fugaciousness, caducity, mortality, span, shortness, brevity.

Quickness, promptness (132), suddenness, abruptness.

A *coup de main*, bubble, Mayfly, nine days' wonder.

(Verbs) To be transient, etc., to flit, pass away, fly, gallop, vanish, fade, intromit.

(Adjectives) Transitory, transient, transitive, passing, impermanent, evanescent, fleeting, momentary, fugacious, fugitive, flitting, vanishing, shifting, flying, temporary, temporal, makeshift, provisional, provisory, rough and ready, cursory, galloping, short-lived, ephemeral, deciduous, meteoric.

Brief, sudden, quick, prompt, brisk, abrupt, extemporaneous, summary, hasty, precipitate.

(Adverbs) Temporarily, etc., *en passant, in transitu*, extempore.

In a short time, soon, at once, awhile, anon, by and by, briefly, presently, apace, eftsoons, straight, straightaway, quickly, speedily, promptly, presto, slapdash, directly,

day long; all the year round; the live-long day; hour after hour; morning, noon, and night; for good; for many a long day.

---

112 Perpetuity *(Substantives),* eternity, sempiternity, immortality, athanasy, everlastingness, perpetuation.

(Verbs) To last or endure for ever, to have no end: to eternize, perpetuate.

(Adjectives) Perpetual, eternal, everlasting, sempiternal, coeternal; endless, unending, ceaseless, incessant, unceasing, uninterrupted, interminable, having no end, unfading, evergreen, never-fading, amaranthine, ageless, deathless, immortal, undying, never-dying, imperishable, indestructible.

(Adverbs) Always, ever, evermore, aye, for ever, for aye, for evermore, still, perpetually, eternally, etc., in all ages, from age to age.

(Phrases) For ever and a day; *esto perpetua*; for ever and ever; world without end; time without end; *in secula seculorum*; to the end of time; till Doomsday; till hell freezes; to a cinder.

---

114 Estimation, measurement, and record of time.

Chronometry *(Substantives),* chronology, horology, horometry, registry, date, epoch, style, era.

Greenwich, standard, mean, local, solar, sidereal time; summer time, double summer time.

Almanac, calendar, ephemeris, chronicle, annals, register, journal, diary, chronogram, time-book.

Instruments for the measurement of time, clock, watch, stop-watch, repeater, chronograph, chronometer, sextant, timepiece, dial, sun-dial, horologe, pendulum, hour-glass, water-clock, clepsydra; time signal.

Chronographer, chronologer, chronologist, time-keeper, annalist.

(Verbs) To chronicle, to fix or mark the time, date, register, etc., to bear date, to measure time, to beat time, to make time, to time.

(Adjectives) Chronological, chronometrical, chronogrammatical.

(Adverb) O'clock.

immediately, incontinently, forthwith; suddenly, *per saltum,* at one bound.

(Phrases) At short notice; the time being up; before the ink is dry; here to-day and gone to-morrow (149); *sic transit gloria mundi.*

---

113 Point of time.

Instantaneity *(Substantives),* instantaneousness, moment, instant, second, split second, minute, twinkling, trice, flash, breath, span, jiffy, flash of lightning, suddenness (111).

(Verbs) To twinkle, flash, to be instantaneous.

(Adjectives) Instantaneous, push-button, sudden, momentary, extempore.

(Phrases) Quick as thought; quick as a flash; quick as lightning.

(Adverbs) Instantly, momentarily, *subito,* presto, instanter, suddenly, plump, slap, slapdash, in a moment, in an instant, in a second, in no time, in a trice, in a twinkling, at one jump, in a breath, extempore, *per saltum,* in a crack, out of hand.

(Phrases) Before one can say 'Jack Robinson'; in a brace of shakes; between the cup and the lip; on the spur of the moment; in the twinkling of an eye; in a jiffy; in two ticks; on the instant; in less than no time; at one fell swoop; no sooner said than done.

---

115 False estimate of time.

Anachronism *(Substantives),* error in time, prolepsis, metachronism, prochronism, parachronism, anticipation.

Disregard or neglect of time.

(Verbs) To anachronize, misdate, antedate, postdate, overdate, anticipate.

(Adjectives) Anachronistic, anachronous, misdated, undated, overdue, postdated, antedated.

(Phrases) To take no note of time; to prophesy after the event.

2°. Relative Time

1. TIME WITH REFERENCE TO SUCCESSION

116 Priority *(Substantives)*, antecedence, anteriority, precedence, pre-existence.

Precursor, predecessor, prelude, forerunner (64), harbinger, antecedent; the past (122).

(Verbs) To precede, come before, forerun, pre-exist, prelude, usher in, dawn, announce (511), foretell, anticipate, forestall.

(Phrases) To be beforehand; to steal a march upon.

(Adjectives) Prior, previous, preceding, precedent, anterior, antecedent, pre-existent, pre-existing, former, foregoing, aforesaid, said, above-mentioned, prehistoric, antediluvian, pre-Adamite.

Precursory, prelusive, prelusory, proemial, introductory, prefatory (62), prodromal, prodromic.

(Adverbs) Before, prior to, previously, anteriorly, antecedently, aforetime, ere, ere now, erewhile, before now, heretofore, ultimo, yet, beforehand, above, *supra*.

(Phrase) Before the flood.

117 Posteriority *(Substantives)*, succession, sequence, subsequence, supervention, sequel, successor (65), postlude.

(Verbs) To follow, come or go after, succeed, supervene, ensue.

(Phrases) To tread on the heels of; to follow in the footsteps of.

(Adjectives) Subsequent, posterior, following, after, later, succeeding, post-glacial, post-diluvial, post-diluvian, puisne, posthumous, postprandial, post-classical.

(Adverbs) Subsequently, after, afterwards, since, later, later on, at a subsequent or later period, proximo, next, in the sequel, close upon, thereafter, thereupon, whereupon, upon which, eftsoons, below, *infra*.

---

118 The Present Time *(Substantives)*, the existing time, the time being, the present moment, juncture, crisis, epoch, day, hour; the twentieth century.

Age, time of life.

(Verb) To strike while the iron is hot.

(Adjectives) Present, actual, current, existing, that is.

(Adverbs) At this time, moment, etc., now, at present, at this time of day, at the present time, day, etc., to-day, nowadays, instant, already, even now, but now, just now, upon which.

(Phrases) For the time being; for the nonce; *pro hac vice*; on the nail; on the spot; on the spur of the moment; now or never.

119 Time different from the present.

Different Time *(Substantives)*, other time.

Indefinite time, aorist.

(Adjective) Aoristic.

(Adverbs) At that time, moment, etc., then, at which time, etc., on that occasion, upon, in those days.

When, whenever, whensoever, upon which, on which occasions, at another or a different time, etc., otherwhile, otherwhiles, at various times, ever and anon.

(Phrases) Once upon a time; one day; some other time; one of these days.

---

120 Synchronism *(Substantives)*, synchronization, coinstantaneity, co-existence, coincidence, simultaneousness, coevality, contemporaneousness, contemporaneity, concurrence, concomitance.

Having equal times, isochronism.

A contemporary, coeval, coetanean.

(Verbs) To coexist, concur, accompany, synchronize.

(Phrase) To keep pace with.

(Adjectives) Synchronous, synchronal, synchronistic, simultaneous, co-existing, coincident, concomitant, concurrent, coeval, coetaneous, contemporary, contemporaneous, coeternal, isochronous.

(Adverbs) At the same time, simultaneously, etc., together, during the same time, etc., in the interim, in the same breath, in concert, *pari passu*; meantime, meanwhile (106), while, whilst.

121 Prospective time.

Futurity *(Substantives)*, the future, futurition, the approaching time, hereafter, the time to come, posteriority (117), after time, after age, the coming time, the morrow, after days, hours, years, ages; after life, millennium, doomsday, the day of judgment, the crack of doom.

The approach of time, the process of time, advent, time drawing on, the womb of time.

Prospection, anticipation, prospect, perspective, expectation (507), horizon, outlook, look-out.

Heritage, heirs, progeny, issue, posterity, descendants, heir apparent, heir presumptive.

Future existence, future state, post-existence, after-life, beyond.

(Verbs) To look forward, anticipate, forestall (132), have in prospect, keep in view, expect (507).

To impend, hang over, lie over, approach, await, threaten, overhang, draw near, prepare.

(Phrases) Lie in wait for; bide one's time; to wait impatiently; kick one's heels.

To be in the wind; to be cooking; to loom in the future.

(Adjectives) Future, to come, coming, going to happen, approaching, impending, instant, at hand, about to be or happen, next, hanging, awaiting, forthcoming, near, near at hand, imminent, threatening, brewing, preparing, in store, eventual, ulterior, in view, in prospect, prospective, in perspective, in the offing, in the wind, on the cards, that will be, overhanging.

Unborn, in embryo, in the womb of time.

122 Retrospective time.

Preterition *(Substantives)*, the past, past time, *status quo,* days of yore, time gone by, priority (116), former times, old times, the olden time, ancient times, antiquity, antiqueness, lang syne, time immemorial, prehistory.

Archaeology, palaeology, palaeontology, palaeography, archaism, retrospection, retrospect, looking back.

Archaeologist, antiquary, medievalist, palaeographer, palaeologist, Dr. Dryasdust.

Ancestry (166), pre-existence.

(Phrases) The good old days; the golden age; the rust of antiquity.

(Verbs) To pass, be past, lapse, go by, elapse, run out, expire, blow over; to look back, cast the eyes back, retrospect, trace back, dig up, exhume.

(Phrases) To have run its course; to have had its day.

(Adjectives) Past, gone, gone by, over, bygone, foregone, pristine, prehistoric, quondam, lapsed, elapsed, preterlapsed, expired, late, *ci-devant*, run out, blown over, that has been.

Former, foregoing, late, last, latter, recent, overnight, preterperfect, preterpluperfect, forgotten, irrecoverable, out of date.

Looking back, retrospective, retroactive, *ex post facto*; archaeological, etc.

Pre-existing, pre-existent.

(Adverbs) Formerly, of old, erst, whilom, erewhile, before now, time was, ago, over, in the olden time, anciently, in days of yore, long since, retrospectively, ere now, before now, till now, once, once upon a time, hitherto, heretofore, *ultimo*.

(Adverbs) Prospectively, hereafter, by and by, some fine day, one of these days, anon, in future, to-morrow, in course of time, in process of time, sooner or later, *proximo*, in after time.

On the eve of, ere long, at hand, near at hand, on the point of, beforehand, against the time.

After a time, from this time, henceforth, henceforwards, thence, thenceforth, thenceforward, whereupon, upon which.

(Phrases) All in good time; in the fullness of time.

The other day, yesterday, last night, week, month, year, etc.; just now, recently, lately, of late, latterly.

Long ago, a long while or time ago, some time ago.

(Phrases) Once upon a time; from time immemorial; in the memory of man; time out of mind.

Already, yet, at length, at last.

---

2. TIME WITH REFERENCE TO A PARTICULAR PERIOD

123 Newness *(Substantives)*, novelty, recentness, recency, modernity, freshness, greenness, immaturity, youth (127), rawness.

Innovation, renovation (660), renewal.

Nouveau riche, parvenu, upstart, mushroom; latest fashio, *dernier cri.*

(Verbs) Renew, renovate, restore (660), modernize.

(Adjectives) New, novel, recent, fresh, green, evergreen, raw, immature, untrodden, advanced, twentieth-century, modern, modernistic, avant-garde, neoteric, new-born, nascent, new-fashioned, up-to-date, new-fangled, vernal, renovated, brand-new, split-new, virgin.

(Phrases) Fresh as a rose; fresh as a daisy; fresh as paint; just out; spick and span.

(Adverbs) Newly, recently, lately, afresh, anew.

124 Oldness *(Substantives)*, age (128), antiquity, eld, ancientry, primitiveness, maturity, decline, decay, obsolescence; seniority, eldership, primogeniture.

Archaism, relic, antique, fossil, eolith; elder, doyen.

(Verbs) To be or become old, mature, mellow; to age, fade, decay.

(Adjectives) Old, ancient, antique, antiquated, out-of-date, of long standing, time-honoured, venerable, hoary, primitive, diluvian, antediluvian, fossil, palaeozoic, preglacial, palaeolithic, neolithic, primeval, primordial, prime, pre-Adamite, prehistoric, antemundane, archaic, classic, medieval.

Immemorial, inveterate, rooted, traditional.

Senior, elder, eldest, oldest, first-born (128).

Obsolete, obsolescent, out-of-date, stale, time-worn, faded, decayed, effete, declining, played-out, crumbling, decrepit (128), *passé.*

(Phrases) Nothing new under the sun; old as the hills; old as Methuselah; old as Adam; before the Flood; time out of mind; since the year one.

---

125 Morning *(Substantives)*, morn, morrow, forenoon, a.m., prime, dawn, daybreak, dayspring, peep of day, break of day, matins, aurora, first blush of the morning, prime of the morning, twilight, crepuscule, sun-rise, sun-up, cockcrow.

126 Evening *(Substantives)*, eve, e'en, decline of day, close of day, eventide, nightfall, curfew, vespers, evensong, dusk, twilight, gloaming, eleventh hour, sunset, sundown, afternoon, p.m., bedtime, midnight; autumn, Indian summer, St.

Noon, midday, noontide, meridian, fathers, forebears, fathers, ancestors, midsummer.

(Adjectives) Matutinal, auroral, vernal, midsummer.

_____

127 Youth *(Substantives)*, infancy, babyhood, boyhood, juvenility, childhood, youthhood, juniority, juvenescence, adolescence (131), minority, nonage, teens, tender age, bloom, heyday, boyishness, girlishness.

Cradle, nursery, leading strings, pupilage, pupilship, puberty.

(Phrases) Prime of flower of life; the rising generation; salad days; schooldays.

(Adjectives) Young, youthful, juvenile, callow, sappy, beardless, under age, in one's teens, boyish, girlish, junior, younger.

(Phrase) In statu pupillari.

_____

Martin's summer, St. Luke's summer, winter, the fall.

(Phrases) The witching time of night; the dead of night; blindman's holiday.

(Adjectives) Nocturnal, vespertine, autumnal, hiemal, brumal.

128 Age *(Substantives)*, old age, senility, senescence, oldness, longevity, years, anility, grey hairs, climacteric, decrepitude, hoary age, caducity, crow's feet, superannuation, dotage, anecdotage, seniority, green old age, eldership.

(Phrases) The vale of years; decline of life; the sere and yellow leaf; second childhood.

(Adjectives) Aged, old, elderly, senile, matronly, anile, in years, ripe, mellow, grey, grey-headed, hoary, hoar, venerable, timeworn, declining, antiquated, *passé*, rusty, effete, decrepit, superannuated.

Patriarchal, ancestral, primitive, older, elder, senior; eldest, oldest, first-born, bantling, firstling.

(Phrases) With one foot in the grave; marked with crow's feet; advanced in life, or in years; stricken in years; no chicken; long in the tooth; old as the hills.

_____

129 Infant *(Substantives)*, babe, baby, nursling, suckling.

Child, bairn, wean, little one, brat, toddler, kid, chit, urchin, bantling, bratling, papoose, elf, piccaninny.

Youth, boy, lad, laddie, stripling, youngster, teenager, callant, younker, gossoon, nipper, whipster, whipper-snapper, schoolboy, young hopeful, hobbledehoy, cadet, minor.

Girl, lass, lassie, wench, miss, colleen, flapper, bobbysoxer, damsel, maid, maiden, *jeune fille*.

Scion, sapling, seedling, tendril, mushroom, nestling, chicken, larva, chrysalis, tadpole, whelp, cub, pullet, fry, foetus, calf, lamb, lambkin, colt, filly, pup, puppy, foal, kitten.

(Adjectives) Infantine, infantile, puerile, boyish, girlish (127), virginal, childish, baby, babyish, unfledged, new-fledged, kittenish, callow.

(Phrases) In leading-strings; at the breast; in arms; in one's teens; tied to mother's apron-strings.

130 Veteran *(Substantives)*, old man, seer, patriarch, greybeard, gaffer, grandsire, grandam, dowager, matron, crone, beldam, hag, sexagenarian, octogenarian, centenarian, oldster, old-timer, old stager, old buffer, fogy, geezer.

Methuselah, Nestor; elders, forefathers, forebears, fathers, ancestors, ancestry.

(Adjectives) Veteran, aged, old, grey-headed (128).

_____

131 Adolescence *(Substantives)*, puberty, pubescence, majority, adultness, maturity, ripeness, manhood, virility.

A man, adult (373), a woman, matron (374), *parti*; ephebe.

(Phrases) Prime of life; man's estate; flower of age; meridian of life; years of discretion; *toga virilis*.

(Adjectives) Adolescent, pubescent, of age, out of one's teens, grown up, mature, middle-aged, manly, virile, adult.

Womanly, matronly, nubile, marriageable, out.

3. TIME WITH REFERENCE TO AN EFFECT OR PURPOSE

132 Earliness *(Substantives)*, timeliness, punctuality, readiness, promptness (682), promptitude, expedition, quickness, haste, acceleration, hastening, hurry, bustle, precipitation, anticipation, precociousness, precocity.

Suddenness, abruptness (111).

(Phrases) A stitch in time saves nine; the early bird catches the worm.

(Verbs) To be early, to be in time, keep time, be beforehand.

To anticipate, forestall, book, engage, bespeak, reserve.

To expedite, hasten, haste, quicken (274), press, dispatch, accelerate, precipitate, hurry, bustle (684).

(Phrases) To take time by the forelock; to steal a march upon; to be beforehand with; to be pressed for time.

(Adjectives) Early, prime, rathe, timely, timeous, punctual, matutinal, forward, ready, quick, expeditious, precipitate, summary, prompt, premature, precocious, prevenient, anticipatory, pre-emptive.

Sudden, abrupt, unexpected (508), subitaneous, extempore.

(Adverbs) Early, soon, anon, betimes, apace, eft, eftsoons, in time, ere long, presently, shortly, punctually, to the minute, on time, on the dot.

Beforehand, prematurely, before one's time, in anticipation.

Suddenly, abruptly, at once, extempore, instanter.

(Phrases) In good time; at sunrise; with the lark; early days.

On the point of; at short notice; on the spur of the moment; all at once; before you can say 'knife'; no sooner said than done.

133 Lateness *(Substantives)*, tardiness, slowness (275), delay, cunctation, procrastination, deferring, lingering, lagging, etc., postponement, dilatoriness, adjournment, shelving, prorogation, remand, moratorium.

Protraction, prolongation, leeway.

(Phrase) Fabian tactics.

(Verbs) To be late, etc., tarry, wait, stay, bide, take time, dally, dawdle, linger, loiter, lag, bide one's time, shuffle (275, 683).

To stand over, lie over, hang fire.

To put off, defer, delay, leave over, suspend, stave off, postpone, adjourn, carry over, shelve, procrastinate, temporize, stall, filibuster, prolong, protract, draw out, spin out, hold up, prorogue.

(Phrases) To tide it over; to bide one's time; to let the matter stand over; to sleep on it; to kick (or cool) one's heels.

(Adjectives) Late, tardy, slow, dilatory (275), posthumous, backward, unpunctual, procrastinatory, behind-hand, belated, overdue.

Delayed, etc., suspended, pending, in abeyance.

(Adverbs) Late, after time, too late, behind time; at length, at last.

Slowly, leisurely, deliberately.

(Phrases) Late in the day; a day after the fair; at the eleventh hour; after death, the doctor.

————

134 Occasion *(Substantives)*, opportunity, chance, opening, break, show, room, suitable or proper time or season, high time, opportuneness, tempestivity, seasonableness, crisis, turn, juncture, conjuncture.

Spare time, leisure, holiday (685), spare moments, hours, etc., time on one's hands.

(Phrases) Golden (or favourable) opportunity; the nick of time.

(Verbs) To use, make use of, employ, profit by, avail oneself of, lay hold of, embrace, catch, seize, snatch, clutch, pounce upon, grasp, etc., the opportunity.

To give, offer, present, afford, etc., the opportunity.

To time well; to spend or consume time.

(Phrases) To turn the occasion to account; to seize the occasion; to strike the iron while it is hot; to make hay while the sun shines; *carpe diem*; to take the tide at the flood; to furnish a handle for.

(Adjectives) Opportune, timely, well-timed, timeful, timeous, seasonable, happy, lucky, providential, fortunate, favourable, propitious, auspicious, critical.

135 Intempestivity *(Substantives)*, untimeliness, unsuitable time, improper time, unseasonableness, inopportuneness, evil hour.

Hitch, impediment (706), check, *contretemps*.

(Verbs) To be ill-timed, etc., to mistime, intrude, come amiss.

To lose, omit, let slip, let go, neglect, pretermit, allow, or suffer the opportunity of occasion to pass, slip, go by, escape, lapse; to lose time, to fritter away time (683).

(Phrases) To let slip through the fingers; to lock the stable door when the steed is stolen.

(Adjectives) Ill-timed, untimely, untimeous, mistimed, unseasonable, out of season, unpunctual, inopportune, untoward, intrusive, too late (133), too early (132), malapropos, unlucky, inauspicious, unpropitious, unfortunate, unfavourable, unsuited, unsuitable.

(Adverb) Inopportunely, etc.

(Phrases) As ill luck would have it; in evil hour; after meat, mustard; a day before (or after) the fair.

———

(Adverbs) Opportunity, etc., on the spot, in proper or due time or season, high time, for the nonce.

By the way, by the by, *en passant, à propos,* parenthetically.

(Phrases) In the nick of time; on the spur of the moment (612); now or never; at the eleventh hour; time and tide wait for no man.

3°. *Recurrent Time*

136 Frequency *(Substantives)*, oftness, recurrence, repetition (104), recrudescence, reiteration, iteration, run, reappearance, renewal, *ritornello, ritournelle,* burden.

Frequenter, *habitué,* fan, client.

(Verbs) To recur, revert, return, repeat, reiterate, reappear, renew, reword.

To frequent, resort to, visit, attend, haunt, infest.

(Adjectives) Frequent, common, not rare, repeated, reiterated, thick-coming, recurring, recurrent, incessant, everlasting, perpetual, rife; habitual (613).

137 Infrequency *(Substantives)*, rareness, rarity, uncommonness, scarcity, fewness (103), seldomness.

(Verb) To be rare, etc.

(Adjectives) Infrequent, rare, scarce, unfrequent, uncommon, unprecedented, unheard-of.

(Phrase) In short supply.

(Adverbs) Seldom, rarely, scarcely, hardly, scarcely ever, ever, hardly ever, not often, unfrequently.

Once, once for all, once in a way.

(Phrases) Once in a blue moon; angels' visits.

———

(Adverbs) Often, oft, oft-times, not infrequently, frequently, often-times, many times, several times, repeatedly.

Again, anew, afresh, *de novo*, ditto, over again, *da capo*, again and again, over and over, ever and anon, many times over, time after time, time and again, repeatedly (104).

Perpetually, continually, constantly, incessantly, everlastingly, without ceasing.

Sometimes, occasionally, at times, now and then, now and again, from time to time, at intervals, between whiles, once in a while, there are times when.

Most often, for the most part, generally, usually, commonly, most frequently, as often as not.

(Phrases) A number of times; many a time (and oft); times out of number.

138 Regularity of recurrence, punctuality.

Periodicity *(Substantives)*, intermittence, beat, ictus, pulse, pulsation, rhythm, lilt, swing, alternation, alternateness, bout, round, revolution, rotation, turn.

Anniversary, jubilee; silver, golden, wedding; centenary, bicentenary, tercentenary, etc.; feast, festival, birthday.

139 Irregularity of recurrence uncertainty, unpunctuality, fitfulness.

(Adjectives) Irregular, uncertain, unpunctual, capricious, desultory, unrhythmic, unrhythmical, fitful, spasmodic, flickering, casual.

(Adverbs) Irregularly, etc., by snatches, by fits and starts, skippingly, now and then, occasionally.

Regularity of return, rota, cycle, period, stated time, routine.

(Phrase) The swing of the pendulum.

(Verbs) To recur in regular order or succession, to come round, return, revolve, alternate, come in its turn, beat, pulsate, intermit; to regularize.

(Adjectives) Periodic, periodical, recurrent, cyclical, revolving, intermittent, remittent, alternate, every other, alternating, rhythmic, rhythmical, steady, punctual.

Hourly, daily, diurnal, tertian, quotidian, weekly, hebdomadal, fortnightly, bi-monthly, monthly, biannual, annual, yearly, biennial, triennial, centennial.

(Phrase) Regular as clockwork.

(Adverbs) Periodically, at regular intervals, at stated times, at fixed periods, punctually, from day to day.

By turns, in turn, in rotation, alternately, in shifts, off and on, ride and tie, hitch and hike.

SECTION VII—CHANGE

1°. *Simple Change*

140 Difference at different times.

Change *(Substantives)*, alteration, mutation, permutation, variation, modification, modulation, inflexion, mood, qualification, innovation, metastasis, metabolism, deviation, turn, diversion, inversion, reversion, reversal, eversion, subversion (162),

141 Absence of change.

Permanence *(Substantives)*, persistence, endurance, *status quo;* maintenance, preservation, conservation, conservatism, *laissez-faire,* rest, sleep, establishment, truce, suspension, settledness (265), perdurability, stability (150).

bouleversement, upset, organic, change, revolution (146), substitution (147), transposition (148), transit, transition.

Transformation, transmutation, transfiguration, metamorphosis, transmigration, transubstantiation, transmogrification, metempsychosis, avatar.

Vicissitude, flux, unrest (149); change of mind, tergiversation (607).

(Phrase) The wheel of fortune.

(Verbs) To change, alter, vary, modify, modulate, diversify, qualify, tamper with, edit, turn, shift, veer, tack, chop, shuffle, swerve, warp, deviate, turn aside, turn topsy-turvy, upset, invert, reverse, introvert, subvert, evert, turn inside out.

Form, fashion, mould, model, vamp, warp, work a change, superinduce, resume, disturb (61), innovate, reform, remodel, refound, new-model, modernize, revolutionize.

Transform, transume, transmute, transfigure, transmogrify, metamorphose, pass to, leap to, transfer.

(Phrases) To ring the changes; to turn over a new leaf; to introduce new blood; to shuffle the cards; to turn the corner; to wax and wane; to ebb and flow; *tempora mutantur; nous avons changé tout cela.*

(Adjectives) Changed, altered, new-fangled, warped, etc.,; transitional, metamorphic, metabolic, metastatic.

(Adverb) Mutatis mutandis.

(Phrase) The law of the Medes and Persians.

(Verbs) To remain, stay, stop, persist, tarry, hold, last, endure, continue, dwell, bide, abide, maintain, keep, hold on, stand, subsist, live, stand still, outlive, survive.

To let alone, let be.

(Phrases) To keep one's footing; to hold one's ground; to stick to one's guns; to stand fast.

(Adjectives) Persisting, etc., permanent, established, unchanged, unmodified, unrenewed, unaltered, fixed, settled, unvaried, intact, inviolate, persistent, stagnant, rooted, monotonous, unreversed, conservative, unprogressive, undestroyed, unrepelled, unsuppressed, unfailing, stationary (265), stereotyped, perdurable.

(Adverbs) In statu quo, for good, finally, at a stand, at a standstill, *uli possidetis.*

(Phrases) J'y suis, j'y reste; plus cela change, plus cela est la même chose; esto perpetua.

---

142 Change from action to rest.
Cessation *(Substantives)*, discontinuance, desistance, quiescence.

Intermission, remission, suspension, interruption, suspense, stand, halt, closure, stop, stoppage, pause, rest, lull, breathing-space, respite, truce, drop, interregnum, abeyance.

Comma, colon, semicolon, period, full stop.

(Verbs) To discontinue, cease, desist, break off, leave off, hold, stop, pause, rest, drop, lay aside, give up, have done with, stick, hang fire, pull up, give over, shut down, knock off, relinquish (624), surcease.

To come to a stand, or standstill, suspend, cut short, cast off,

143 Continuance in action *(Substantives)*, continuation, perseverance, repetition (104), persistence, run.

(Verbs) To continue, persist, go on, keep on, abide, keep, pursue, hold on, run on, follow on, carry on, keep up, uphold, sustain, perpetuate, persevere, keep it up, stick it, peg away, maintain, maintain one's ground, harp upon, repeat (104), take root.

(Phrases) To keep the pot boiling; to keep the ball rolling.

(Adjectives) Continual, continuous, continuing, etc., uninterrupted, inconvertible, unintermitting, unreversed, unstopped, unrevoked, unvaried, unshifting, perpetual (112).

---

go out, be at an end; intromit, interrupt, arrest, intermit, remit; put an end or stop to.

To pass away, go off, pass off, blow over, die away, wear away, wear off (122).

(Phrases) To shut up shop; to stay one's hand; to rest on one's oars; to rest on one's laurels.

(Interjections) Hold! hold on! stop! enough! avast! *basta!* have done! a truce to! stop it! drop it! cheese it! chuck it! stow it! cut it out!

144 Gradual change to something different.

Conversion *(Substantives)*, reduction, transmutation, resolution, assimilation; chemistry, alchemy; growth, lapse, progress, becoming; naturalization.

Passage, transit, transition, transmigration, flux, shifting, sliding, running into, etc.; phase, conjugations; convertibility.

Laboratory, alembic, crucible (691).

Convert, pervert, vert, turncoat, renegade, apostate.

(Verbs) To be converted into; to become, get, wax, come to turn to, turn into, assume the form of, pass into, slide into, glide into, lapse, shift, run into, fall into, merge into, melt, grow, grow into, open into, resolve itself into, settle into, mature, mellow; assume the form, shape, state, nature, character, etc., of; illapse.

To convert into; to make, render, form, mould, reduce, resolve into; transume (140), fashion, model, remodel, reorganize, shape, modify, transmogrify; assimilate to; reduce to, bring to; refound, re-form, reshape.

(Adjectives) Converted into, become, etc., convertible, transitional.

(Adverbs) Gradually, *gradatim*, by degrees, step by step, by inches, inch by inch, by little and little, by slow degrees, consecutively, seriatim, *in transitu*.

145 Reversion *(Substantives)*, return, reconversion, relapse (661), recidivism, atavism, throwback, reaction, recoil (277), backlash, rebound, ricochet, revulsion, alternation (138), inversion, regression (283).

Reinstatement, re-establishment (660).

(Phrases) The turning-point; the turn of the tide; *status quo ante bellum*.

(Verbs) To revert, turn back, return to, relapse, recoil, rebound, react; to restore (660), to undo, unmake.

(Phrase) To turn the tables (719).

(Adjectives) Reverting, etc., restored, etc., regressive, retrogressive, atavistic, revulsive, reactionary.

(Interjection) As you were!

146 Sudden or violent change.

Revolution *(Substantives)*, counter-revolution, revolt, rebellion (742), transilience, jump, leap, plunge, jerk, start, spasm, convulsion, throe, storm, earthquake, catastrophe, cataclysm (173).

Legerdemain, conjuration, sleight of hand, hocus-pocus (545), harlequinade, witchcraft (992).

A revolutionary, revolutionist, counter-revolutionist, deviationist; the red flag.

(Verbs) To revolutionize, remodel, recast, refashion, reconstruct.

(Adjectives) Revolutionary, radical, extreme, intransigent, catastrophic, cataclysmic.

(Adverbs) Root and branch.

147 Change of one thing for another.

Substitution *(Substantives)*, commutation, supplanting, replacement, supersession, enallage, metonymy, synecdoche, antonomasia.

Thing substituted, substitute (634), succedaneum, makeshift, shift, apology, stand-in, pinch-hitter, locum-tenens, representative, proxy; understudy, deputy (759), vice, double, dummy, changeling, scapegoat, stooge; stop-gap, jury-mast, palimpsest, metaphor (521).

(Phrase) Borrowing of or robbing Peter to pay Paul.

(Verbs) To substitute, put in place of, commute, supplant, cut out, change for, supersede, take over from.

To give place to; to replace.

(Phrases) To serve as a substitute, etc.; to do duty for; to stand in the shoes of; to take the place of.

(Adjectives) Substituted, etc., vicarious, subdititious, makeshift, provisional.

(Adverbs) Instead, in place of, in lieu of, in the room of, *faute de mieux*.

148 Double and mutual change.

Interchange *(Substantives)*, exchange, commutation, intermutation, reciprocation, transposition, permutation, shuffling, castling (at chess), hocus-pocus, interchangeableness, interchangeability.

Reciprocity (12), retaliation (718), barter (794).

(Phrases) A Roland for an Oliver; tit for tat; *quid pro quo*.

(Verbs) To interchange, exchange, bandy, transpose, shuffle, change hands, swap, dicker, permute, reciprocate, commute, counterchange.

(Phrases) To play at puss in the corner; to play musical chairs; to return the compliment; to give and take; you scratch my back, and I'll scratch yours.

(Adjectives) Interchanged, etc., reciprocal, mutual, commutative, interchangeable, intercurrent.

(Adverbs) In exchange, vice versa.

2°. Complex Changes

149 Mutability *(Substantives)*, changeableness, changeability, inconstancy, variableness, mobility, instability, unsteadiness, vacillation, unrest, restlessness, slipperiness, impermanence, fragility, fluctuation, vicissitude, alternation, vibration, oscillation (314), flux, ebbing and flowing, ebbs and flows, ups and downs, fidgets, fidgetiness, fugitiveness, disquiet, disquietude.

A Proteus, chameleon, quicksilver, weathercock, kaleidoscope, harlequin; the moon.

(Phrases) April showers; shifting sands; the wheel of fortune; the Cynthia of the minute.

(Verbs) To fluctuate, vary, waver, flounder, vibrate, flicker, flit, flitter, shift, shuffle, shake, totter, tremble, vacillate, ebb and flow, turn and turn about, change and change about.

150 Immutability *(Substantives)*, stability, unchangeableness, unchangeability, constancy, permanence, persistence (106), invariableness, durability, steadiness (604), immobility, fixedness, stableness, settledness, stabiliment, firmness, stiffness, anchylosis, solidity, aplomb, ballast, incommutability, insusceptibility, irrevocableness.

Rock, pillar, tower, foundation, fixture.

(Phrase) The law of the Medes and Persians.

(Verbs) To be permanent, etc. (265), to stand, stand fast, stand pat, remain.

To settle, establish, stablish, perpetuate, fix, set, stabilitate, retain, keep, hold, make sure, nail, clinch, rivet, fasten (43), settle down, set on its legs.

(Phrases) To build one's house on a rock; to weather the storm.

To fade, pass away like a cloud, shadow, or dream.

(Adjectives) Mutable, changeable, variable, ever-changing, inconstant, impermanent, unsteady, unstable, protean, proteiform, unfixed, fluctuating, vacillating, shifting, versatile, fickle, wavering, flickering, flitting, restless, erratic, unsettled, mobile, fluttering, oscillating, vibratory, vagrant, wayward, desultory, afloat, alternating, plastic, disquiet, alterable, casual, unballasted, volatile, capricious (608).

Frail, tottering, shaking, shaky, trembling, fugitive, ephemeral, transient (111), fading, fragile, deciduous, slippery, unsettled, irresolute (605), rocky, groggy.

Kaleidoscopic, prismatic, iridescent, opalescent, shot.

(Phrases) Unstable as water; changeable as the moon, or as a weathercock; *sic transit gloria mundi*; here to-day and gone tomorrow.

(Adjectives) Immutable, inco... mutable, unchangeable, unaltered, unalterable, not to be changed, constant, permanent, invariable, undeviating, stable, durable (265), perennial (110), valid.

Fixed, steadfast, firm, fast, steady, confirmed, immovable, irremovable, rooted, riveted, stablished, established, incontrovertible, stereotyped, indeclinable, settled, stationary, stagnant.

Moored, anchored, at anchor, on a rock, firmly seated, deep-rooted, ineradicable.

Stranded, aground, stuck fast, high and dry.

Indefeasible, irretrievable, intransmutable, irresoluble, irrevocable, irreversible, inextinguishable, irreducible, indissoluble, indissolvable, indestructible, undying, imperishable, indelible, indeciduous, insusceptible of change.

(Phrases) J'y suis, j'y reste; stet; can the Ethiopian change his skin, or the leopard his spots?

Present events

151 Eventuality *(Substantives)*, event, happening, occurrence, incident, affair, transaction, proceeding, fact, matter of fact, phenomenon, advent.

Business, concern, circumstance, particular, casualty, accident, adventure, passage, crisis, episode, pass, emergency, contingency, consequence (154).

The world, life, things, doings, course of things, the course, tide, steam, current, run, etc., of events.

(Phrases) Stirring events; the ups and downs of life; a chapter of accidents; the cast of the dice (156).

(Verbs) To happen, occur, take place, take effect, come, come of, become of, come about, come off, pass, come to pass, fall, fall out, run, be on foot, fall in, befall, betide, bechance, turn out, go off, prove, eventuate, draw on, turn up, crop up, supervene, survene, issue, arrive, ensue, arise, spring, start, come into existence, fall to one's lot.

Future events

152 Destiny *(Substantives)*, fatality, fate, doom, destination, lot, fortune, star, planet, preordination, predestination, fatalism, inevitableness, kismet, karma, necessity (601), after life, futurity (121).

(Phrases) The decrees of fate; the wheel of fortune.

(Verbs) To impend, hang over, overhang, be in store, loom, threaten, await, come on, approach, stare one in the face, foreordain, preordain, predestine, doom, must be.

(Phrase) To dree one's weird.

(Adjectives) About to happen, impending, coming, destined, imminent, inevitable, ineluctable, inexorable, fated, doomed, devoted.

(Phrases) On the cards; on the knees of the gods.

(Adverbs) Necessarily, inevitably.

(Phrases) What must be, must; *che sarà sarà*; 'It is written'; the die is cast.

To pass off, wear off, blow over.

To experience, meet with, go through, pass through, endure (821), suffer, fare.

(Adjectives) Happening, occurring, etc.; going on, current, incidental, eventful, stirring, bustling.

(Phrase) The plot thickening.

(Adverbs) Eventually, in the event of, on foot, on the *tapis*, as it may happen, happen what may, at all events, sink or swim, come what may.

(Phrases) In the course of things; in the long run; as the world wags.

SECTION VIII—CAUSATION

1°. *Constancy of Sequence in Events*

153 Constant antecedent.

Cause *(Substantives)*, origin, source, principle, element, occasioner, prime mover, *primum mobile*, spring, mainspring, agent, seed, leaven, groundwork, basis (215), fountain, well, fount, fountain-head, spring-head, author (164), parent (166), *fons et origo, raison d'être.*

Pivot, hinge, turning-point, key, lever.

Final cause, proximate cause, immediate cause, ground, reason, the reason why, the why and the wherefore, rationale, occasion, derivation, provenance.

Rudiment, germ, embryo, bud, root, *radix*, radical, etymon, nucleus, seed, ovum, stem, stock, trunk, taproot.

Nest, cradle, womb, *nidus,* birthplace, hot-bed, forcing-bed.

Causality, origination, causation, production (161), aetiology.

Theories of causation, creationism; evolution, Lamarckism, Darwinism, Spencerism, orthogenesis.

(Verbs) To be the cause of, to originate, germinate, give origin to, cause, occasion, give rise to, kindle, suscitate, bring on, bring to pass, give occasion to, produce, bring about, institute, found, lay the foundation of, lie at the root of, procure, draw down, induce, realize, evoke, provoke, elicit, entail, develop, evolve, operate (161).

154 Constant sequent.

Effect *(Substantives)*, consequence, product, result, resultant, resultance, upshot, issue, end (67), fruit, crop, aftermath, harvest, development, outgrowth, derivative, derivation.

Production, produce, work, handiwork, performance, creature, creation, offshoot, fabric, offspring, firstfruits, firstlings, output, *dénouement*, derivation, heredity, evolution (161).

(Verbs) To be the effect, work, fruit, result, etc., of; to be owing to, originate in or from, rise from, take its rise from, arise, spring, proceed, evolve, come of, emanate, come, grow, germinate, bud, sprout, stem, issue, flow, result, follow, accrue, etc., from; come to; to come out of, be derived from, be caused by, depend upon, hinge upon, result from, to be dependent upon, hang upon; to pan out.

(Phrase) To take the consequences.

(Adjectives) Owing to, due to, attributable to, ascribable to, resulting from, through, etc., all along of, hereditary, genetic, derivative.

(Adverbs) Of course, consequently, necessarily, eventually.

(Phrases) Cela va sans dire; thereby hangs a tale.

———

To conduce, contribute, tend to (176); to determine, decide.

(Phrases) To have a hand in; to have a finger in the pie; to open the door to; to be at the bottom of; to sow the seeds of; to turn the scale.

(Adjectives) Caused, occasioned, etc., causal, original, primary, primordial, having a common origin, connate, radical, embryonic, embryotic, in embryo.

Evolutionary, Darwinian; aetiological.

(Phrase) Behind the scenes.

155 Assignment of cause.

Attribution *(Substantives)*, theory, aetiology, ascription, reference to, rationale, accounting for, imputation to, derivation from, filiation, affiliation, genealogy, pedigree, paternity, maternity (166), explanation (522), cause (153).

(Verbs) To attribute, ascribe, impute, refer to, derive from, lay to, point to, charge on, ground on, invest with, assign as cause, trace to, father upon, account for, theorize, ground, etc.

(Phrases) To put the saddle on the right horse; to point out the reason of; to lay at the door of.

(Adjectives) Attributable, imputable, assignable, traceable, ascribable, referable, owing to, derivable from.

Putative, attributed, imputed, etc.

(Adverbs) Hence, thence, therefore, because, from that cause, for that reason, on that account, owing to, thanks to, forasmuch as, whence, *propter hoc*, wherefore, since, inasmuch as.

Why? wherefore? whence? how comes it? how is it? how happens it? how does it happen?

In some way, somehow, somehow or other, in some such way.

(Phrase) Hinc illae lacrimae.

156 Absence of assignable cause.

Chance *(Substantives)*, indetermination, accident, fortune, hazard, hap, haphazard, chance-medley, luck, lot, fate (152), casualty, contingency, adventure, venture, potluck, lucky dip, treasure trove, hit.

A lottery, toss-up, game of chance, *sortes Virgiliance, rouge et noir*, heads or tails, gambling (621), sweepstake.

Possibility, probability, odds, long odds, a near shave, bare chance.

(Phrases) The turn of the cards; a cast or throw of the dice; a pig in a poke; a blind date.

(Verbs) To chance, hap, turn up; to fall to one's lot, to be one's fate (152); to light upon; stumble upon.

To game, gamble, cast lots, raffle, play for.

(Phrases) To take one's chance; to toss up for; to chance one's arm; to take a flyer.

(Adjectives) Casual, fortuitous, random, accidental, adventitious, causeless, incidental, contingent, uncaused, undetermined, indeterminate, suppositional, possible (470); aleatory.

(Adverbs) By chance, by accident, perchance, peradventure, perhaps, maybe, mayhap, haply, possibly.

Casually, etc., at random, at a venture, as it may be, as it may chance, as it may turn up, as it may happen; as chance, luck, fortune, etc., would have it.

2°. *Connection between Cause and Effect*

157 Power *(Substantives)*, potentiality, potency, prepotence, prepotency, prepollence, puissance, strength (159), might, force, energy, metal, dint, right hand, ascendancy, sway, control, almightiness, ability, ableness, competency, efficiency, effectiveness, efficacy, efficaciousness, validity, cogency, en-

158 Impotence *(Substantives)*, inability, disability, disablement, impuissance, weakness (160), imbecility, paralysis, inaptitude, incapacity, incapability, invalidity, inefficacy, inefficiency, inefficaciousness, ineffectualness, disqualification, helplessness, incompetence.

(Phrases) A dead letter; waste

ablement; agency (170), casualty (153), influence (175), authority (737).

Capability, capacity, faculty, quality, attribute, endowment, virtue, gift, property.

Pressure, high pressure, mechanical energy, applied force, motive power.

(*Verbs*) To be powerful, etc., to gain power; to exercise power, sway, etc., to constrain.

To be the property, virtue, attribute, etc., of; to belong to, pertain to, appertain to, to lie or be in one's power.

To give or confer power, to empower, enable, invest, endue, endow, arm, render strong (159).

(*Adjectives*) Powerful, high-powered, potent, puissant, potential, capable, able, equal to, cogent, valid, effective, effectual, efficient, efficacious, adequate, competent.

Forcible, energetic, vigorous, nervous, dynamic, vivid, sturdy, rousing, all-powerful, omnipotent, resistless, irresistible, inextinguishable, sovereign, invincible, unconquerable, indomitable.

(*Adverbs*) Powerfully, etc., by virtue of, in full force.

159 Degree of power.

Strength (*Substantives*), energy (171), power (157), vigour, vitality, force, main force, physical force, brute force, spring, elasticity, tone, tension, tonicity.

Stoutness, sturdiness, lustiness, lustihood, stamina, physique, nerve, muscle, thews, and sinews, backbone, pith, pithiness.

Feats of strength, athletics, gymnastics.

Strengthening, invigoration, bracing, recruital, recruitment, refreshment, refocillation (689).

Science of forces, dynamics, statics.

Adamant, steel, iron, oak, heart of oak.

An athlete, gymnast, acrobat; an Atlas, a Hercules, Sampson, Cyclops, Goliath.

(*Phrases*) A giant refreshed; a tower of strength.

paper; *brutum fulmen*; blank cartridge.

(*Verbs*) To be impotent, powerless, etc.; to collapse, fail, flunk, break down, fizzle out, fold up.

To render powerless, etc., to deprive of power, disable, disenable, incapacitate, disqualify, unfit, invalidate, nullify, deaden, cripple, cramp, paralyse, muzzle, hamstring, bowl over, render weak (160).

(*Phrases*) To go by the board; to end in smoke.

To clip the wings of; spike the guns; to tie a person's hands; to put a spoke in one's wheel; to take the wind out of one's sails.

(*Adjectives*) Powerless, impotent, unable, incapable, incompetent, inadequate, unequal to, inefficient, inefficacious, inept, ineffectual, ineffective, inoperative, nugatory, incapacitated, harmless, imbecile, disqualified, disabled, armless, disarmed, unarmed, weaponless, defenceless; unnerved, paralysed, palsied, disjointed, nerveless, adynamic, unendowed.

(*Phrases*) Laid on the shelf; *hors de combat*; not having a leg to stand on.

160 Weakness (*Substantives*), feebleness, impotence (158), debility, atony, relaxation, helplessness, languor, slackness, enervation, nervousness, faintness, languidness, infirmity, emasculation, effeminacy, feminality, femineity, flaccidity, softness, defencelessness.

Childhood, etc. (127, 129); orphan, chicken.

Declension, loss, failure, etc., of strength, invalidation, delicacy, delicateness, decrepitude, asthenia, neurasthenia, anaemia, bloodlessness, palsy, paralysis, exhaustion, collapse, prostration, faintness, cachexy (or cachexia).

A reed, thread, rope of sand, house of cards; a weakling, sissy, jellyfish.

(*Verbs*) To be weak, etc., to droop, fade, faint, swoon, languish, decline, flag, fail, totter, drop, crock; to go by the board.

(Verbs) To be strong, etc., to be stronger, to overmatch.

To render strong, etc., to give strength, tone, etc., to strengthen, invigorate, brace, buttress, sustain, fortify, harden, case-harden, steel, gird up, screw up, wind up, set up, tone up.

To reinforce, refit, recruit, vivify, restore (660), refect, refocillate (689).

(Phrase) To set on one's legs.

(Adjectives) Strong, mighty, vigorous, stout, robust, sturdy, powerful, puissant, hard, adamantine, invincible, able-bodied, athletic, Herculean, muscular, brawny, sinewy, made of iron, strapping, well-set, well-knit, stalwart, doughty, husky, lusty, hardy, irresistible; strengthening, etc.; invigorative, tonic.

Manly, manlike, masculine, male, virile, manful, full-blooded.

Unweakened, unallayed, unwithered, unshaken, unworn, unexhausted, unrelaxed, undiluted, unwatered, neat.

(Phrases) Made of iron; as strong as a lion, as a horse; in great form; fit as a fiddle.

(Adverbs) Strongly, forcibly, etc., by main force, *vi et armis*, by might and main, tooth and nail, hammer and tongs, for all one is worth.

To render weak, etc., to weaken, enfeeble, debilitate, devitalize, deprive of strength, relax, enervate, unbrace, unman, emasculate, castrate, geld, hamstring, disable, unhinge, cripple, cramp, paralyse, maim, sprain, exhaust, prostrate, blunt the edge of, deaden, dilute, water, water down.

(Adjectives) Weak, feeble, debile, strengthless, nerveless, imbecile, unnerved, relaxed, unstrung, unbraced, enervated, nervous, sinewless, spineless, lustless, effeminate, feminine, womanly, unmanned, emasculated, castrated.

Crippled, maimed, lamed, shattered, broken, frail, fragile, flimsy, gimcrack, halting, shaken, crazy, shaky, paralysed, palsied, paralytic, decrepit, puny, shilpit, drooping, languid, faint, sickly, flagging, dull, slack, limp, spent, effete, weatherbeaten, worn, seedy, exhausted, deadbeat, all in, whacked, done up, languishing, wasted, washy, vincible, untenable, laid low, run down, asthenic, neurasthenic, neurotic, rickety, invertebrate, feckless.

Unstrengthened, unsustained, unsupported, unaided, unassisted, defenceless, indefensible, unfortified, unfriended, fatherless, etc.

(Phrases) On one's last legs; the worse for wear; weak as a child, as a baby, as a kitten, as water; good or fit for nothing.

3°. *Power in Operation*

161 Production *(Substantives)*, creation, formation, construction, fabrication, manufacture, building, architecture, erection, edification, coinage, organization, putting together, establishment, setting up, performance (729), workmanship, output.

Development, breeding, evolution, flowering, genesis, generation, *epigenesis,* procreation, propagation, fecundation, impregnation, gestation, birth, bringing forth, parturition, growth, proliferation.

162 Non-production.

Destruction *(Substantives)*, waste, dissolution, breaking up, disruption, consumption, disorganization, falling to pieces, crumbling, etc.

Fall, downfall, ruin, perdition, crash, smash, havoc, desolation, *bouleversement, débacle,* upset, wreck, shipwreck, cataclysm, extinction, annihilation; doom, destruction of life (360), prang (716, 732).

Demolition, demolishment, overthrow, subversion, suppression, dismantling, cutting up, corrosion,

Theory of development, Mendelism, eugenics.

(*Verbs*) To produce, effect, perform, operate, do, make, form, construct, fabricate, frame, contrive, manufacture, weave, forge, coin, carve, sculp, chisel, build, raise, edify, rear, erect, run up, establish.

To constitute, compose, organize, institute, work out, realize, bring to bear, bring to pass, accomplish, bring off.

To create, generate, engender, beget, bring into being, breed, propagate, proliferate, conceive, bear, procreate, give birth to, bring forth, yield, flower, fructify, hatch, develop, bring up.

To induce, superinduce, suscitate (153).

(*Phrases*) To be brought to bed of; to usher into the world.

(*Adjectives*) Produced, etc., producing, productive of, etc., creative, formative, parturient, pregnant, *enceinte*, genetic; eugenic.

(*Phrase*) In the family way.

163 Reproduction (*Substantives*), renovation, restoration (660), reconstruction, revival, regeneration, revivication, resuscitation, reanimation, resurrection, resurgence, reappearance, palingenesis, reincarnation, multiplication; phoenix.

(*Verbs*) To reproduce, revive, renew, renovate, rebuild, reconstruct, regenerate, revivify, resurrect, resuscitate, reanimate, reincarnate, quicken; come again into life, reappear.

(*Phrase*) To spring up like a mushroom.

(*Adjectives*) Reproduced, etc., renascent, reappearing; hydra-headed.

———

erosion, crushing, upsetting, abolition, abolishment, sacrifice, immolation, holocaust, dilapidation, devastation, *razzia*, ravaging, extermination, eradication, extirpation, rooting out, averruncation, sweeping, etc., death-blow, *coup de grâce*, the crack of doom.

(*Verbs*) To be destroyed, etc., to perish, waste, fall to pieces, break up, crumble, break down, crack.

To destroy, do or make away with, demolish, overturn, upset, throw down, overthrow, overwhelm, subvert, put an end to, uproot, eradicate, extirpate, root out, grub up, break up, pull down, do for, dish, ditch, crumble, smash, crash, crush, quell, quash, squash, squelch, cut up, shatter, shiver, batter, tear or shake to pieces, tear to tatters, pick to pieces, put down, suppress, strike out, throw or knock down, cut down, knock on the head, stifle, dispel, fell, sink, swamp, scuttle, engulf, submerge, wreck, corrode, erode, consume, sacrifice, immolate, burke, blow down, sweep away, erase, expunge, liquidate, wipe out, mow down, blast.

To waste, lay waste, ravage, dilapidate, dismantle, disorganize, devour, swallow up, desolate, devastate, sap, mine, blow up, stifle, dispatch, exterminate, extinguish, quench, annihilate, kill (361), unroot, root out, rout out, averruncate, deracinate.

(*Phrases*) To go to the dogs, or to pot; to go to the devil, or to rack and ruin; to be all over with one.

To lay the axe to the root of; to make short work of; make a clean sweep of; to make mincemeat of; to scatter to the winds; cut up root and branch; knock on the head; to wipe the floor with; to knock into a cocked hat; to sap the foundations of; to nip in the bud; to strike at the root of; to pluck up by the root; to ravage with fire and sword.

(*Adjectives*) Destroyed, done for, dished, etc.; destructive, subversive, pernicious, ruinous, deadly, incendiary, demolitionary.

164 Producer *(Substantives)*, originator, author, artist, creator, prime mover, founder, workman, doer, performer, manufacturer, forger, agent (690), builder, architect, factor.

166 Paternity *(Substantives)*, fatherhood, maternity, motherhood, parentage, parent, father, sire, paterfamilias, pater, dad, daddy, papa, pa; mother, mamma, ma, mummy, mum, dam, materfamilias, mater, procreator, pregenitor, begetter, ancestor, ancestry, forefathers, forebears, grandsire; house parent, stem, trunk, stock, pedigree.

(Adjectives) Paternal, maternal, parental, fatherly, motherly, family, ancestral, patriarchal.

———

168 Productiveness *(Substantives)*, fecundity, fruitfulness, fertility, prolificness; creativeness, inventiveness.

Pregnancy, gestation, pullulation, fructification, multiplication, propagation, procreation.

A milch cow, rabbit, warren, hydra.

(Phrase) A land flowing with milk and honey.

(Verbs) To procreate (161), multiply, teem, pullulate, fructify, proliferate, generate, fertilize, impregnate, conceive.

(Adjectives) Productive, prolific, teeming, fertile, fruitful, luxuriant, fecund, pregnant, great, gravid, *enceinte*, with child, with young.

Procreant, procreative, generative, propagable, life-giving.

165 Destroyer *(Substantives)*, extinguisher, exterminator, assassin (361), executioner (975), ravager, annihilator, subverter, demolisher; iconoclast, vandal.

167 Posterity *(Substantives)*, progeny, breed, issue, offspring, brood, seed, litter, spawn, scion, offset, child, son, daughter, grandchild, grandson, granddaughter, etc., bantling, shoot, sprout, sprig, slip, branch, line, lineage, filiation, family, offshoot, ramification, descendant, heir, heiress, heir apparent, heir presumptive.

Straight descent, sonship, primogeniture, ultimogeniture.

(Adjectives) Filial, daughterly, dutiful, lineal, hereditary.

(Phrase) A chip of the old block; the rising generation.

169 Unproductiveness *(Substantives)*, infertility, barrenness, sterility, unfruitfulness, unprofitableness, infecundity, fruitlessness (645), non-agency.

(Verbs) To be unproductive, etc., to come to nothing.

To render unproductive, sterilize, castrate, spay, pasteurize.

(Adjectives) Unproductive, inoperative, barren, addled, infertile, unprolific, sterile, unfruitful, fallow, fruitless, infecund, issueless, unprofitable (645).

———

170 Agency *(Substantives)*, operation, force, working, strain, function, office, hand, intervention, intercession, interposition, exercise, work, swing, play, causation (153), impelling force, mediation (631), action (680).

Modus operandi, quickening power, maintaining power.

(Verbs) To be in action, to operate, function, work, act, perform, play, support, sustain, strain, maintain, take effect, quicken, strike, strike hard, strike home, bring to bear.

(Phrases) To come into play; to make an impression.

(Adjectives) Acting, operating, etc., operative, practical, efficient, efficacious, effectual, in force.

Acted upon, wrought upon.

171 Physical **Energy** *(Substantives)*, force, power, activity, keenness, intensity, sharpness, pungency, vigour, strength, edge, point, raciness, metal, mettle, vim, dash, fire, punch, go, pep.

Seasoning, mordant, pepper, mustard, cayenne, caviare (392).

Mental energy (604), mental excitation (824), voluntary energy (682).

Exertion, activity, stir, bustle, hustle, agitation, effervescence, fermentation, ferment, ebullition, splutter, perturbation, briskness, voluntary activity (682), quicksilver.

(Verbs) To give energy, energize, stimulate, invigorate, kindle, galvanize, electrify, intensify, excite, exert (173).

(Adjectives) Strong, energetic, emphatic, forcible, forceful, active, keen, vivid, intense, severe, sharp, acute, pungent, poignant, racy, brisk, ebullient, mettlesome, enterprising, go-ahead, double-edged, double-barrelled, double-distilled, drastic, intensive, trenchant.

(Phrases) Fortiter in re; with telling effect; with full steam; at high pressure; flat out.

172 Physical **Inertness** *(Substantives)* inertia, *vis inertiae*, inertion, passiveness, passivity, inactivity, torpor, latency, torpidity, dullness, stagnation, deadness, heaviness, flatness, slackness, tameness, slowness, languor, lentor, quiescence (265), sleep (683), intermission (141).

Mental inertness, indecision (605), placidity (826).

(Verbs) To be inalert, inactive, passive, etc.; to hang fire, smoulder.

(Phrase) To sit on the fence.

(Adjectives) Inert, inactive, passive, torpid, flaccid, limp, lymphatic, sluggish, dull, heavy, flat, slack, tame, slow, supine, slothful, stagnant, blunt, lifeless, dead.

Latent, dormant, smouldering, unexerted, unstrained, uninfluential.

(Adverbs) Inactively, in suspense, in abeyance.

———

173 Violence *(Substantives)*, inclemency, vehemence, might, impetuosity, boisterousness, abruptness, ebullition, turbulence, horseplay, bluster, uproar, shindy, row, riot, rumpus, fierceness, rage, wildness, fury, heat, exacerbation, exasperation, malignity, fit, paroxysm, orgasm, force, brute force, *coup de main,* strain, shock, spasm, convulsion, throe.

Outbreak, burst, outburst, dissilience, discharge, volley, explosion, blow-up, blast, detonation, rush, eruption, displosion, torrent.

Turmoil, tumult, storm, tempest, squall, hurricane, tornado, typhoon, cyclone, earthquake, volcano, thunder-storm.

A rowdy (949), berserk (or berserker), spitfire, fireeater, hellhound, fury, termagant, virago, vixen, hellcat, dragon, demon, tiger, beldam, Tisiphone, Megaera, Alecto, Maenad.

174 **Moderation** *(Substantives)*, gentleness, temperateness, calmness, mildness, composure, sobriety, slowness, tameness, quiet (740), restfulness, reason.

Relaxation, remission, measure, golden mean, mitigation, tranquillization, assuagement, soothing, allaying, etc., contemperation, pacification (723), restraint, check (751), lullaby, sedative, lenitive, demulcent, palliative, opiate, anodyne, balm, opium.

Mental calmness (826).

(Verbs) To be moderate, etc., to keep within bounds or within compass, to settle down, to keep the peace, to sober down, remit, relent.

To moderate, soften, soothe, mitigate, appease, temper, attemper, contemper, mollify, lenify, tame, dull; take off the edge, blunt, obtund, tone down, subdue.

To tranquillize, assuage, appease, lull, cool, compose, still, calm, quiet,

(Verbs) To be violent, etc., to run high, ferment, effervesce, run wild, run riot, run amuck, rush, tear, rush headlong, bluster, rage, rampage, riot, storm, boil, fume, let off steam, foam, wreak, bear down.

To break out, fly out, bounce, go off, explode, displode, fly, fulminate, detonate, blow up, flash, flare, burst, burst out, shock, strain.

To render violent, sharpen, stir up, quicken, excite, incite, stimulate, kindle, lash, suscitate, urge, accelerate, foment, aggravate, exasperate, exacerbate, convulse, infuriate, madden, lash into fury, inflame, let off, discharge.

(Phrases) To break the peace; to see red; to out-herod Herod; add fuel to the flame.

(Adjectives) Violent, vehement, warm, acute, rough, rude, wild, boisterous, impetuous, ungentle, tough, brusque, abrupt, rampant, knock-about, rampageous, bluff, turbulent, blustering, riotous, rowdy, noisy, thundering, obstreperous, uproarious, outrageous, frantic, phrenetic, headstrong, rumbustious, disorderly (59).

hush, quell, sober, pacify, damp, lay, allay, rebate, slacken, smooth, soften, alleviate, rock to sleep, deaden (376), check, restrain, slake, curb, bridle, rein in, hold in, repress, smother, counteract (179).

(Phrases) To pour oil on the waves; to pour balm into; to throw cold water on.

(Adjectives) Moderate, gentle, mild, sober, temperate, measured, reasonable, tempered, calm, unruffled, tranquil, smooth, untroubled; unexciting, unirritating, soft, bland, oily, demulcent, lenitive, cool, quiet, anodyne, hypnotic, sedative, peaceful, peaceable, pacific, lenient, tame, halcyon, restful.

(Phrases) Gentle as a lamb; mild as milk.

(Adverbs) Moderately, gently, temperately, softly, etc.

(Phrases) Softly, softly, catchee monkey; *suaviter in modo; est modus in rebus.*

Savage, fierce, ferocious, fiery, fuming, excited, unquelled, unquenched, unextinguished, unrepressed, unbridled, unruly, boiling, boiling over, furious, outrageous, raging, running riot, storming, hysteric, hysterical, wild, running wild, ungovernable, unappeasable, immitigable, uncontrollable, insuppressible, irrepressible, raging, desperate, mad, rabid, infuriated, exasperated.

Tempestuous, stormy, squally, spasmodic, spastic, paroxysmal, convulsive, galvanic, bursting, explosive, detonating, volcanic, meteoric, seismic.

(Phrases) Fierce as a tiger; all the fat in the fire.

(Adverbs) Violently, etc., by force, by main force, like mad.

(Phrases) By might and main; tooth and nail; *vi et armis*; at the point of the sword, or bayonet.

4°. *Indirect Power*

175 Influence *(Substantives)*, weight, pressure, prevalence, sway, ascendancy (or ascendency), preponderance, predominance, predominancy, dominance, prepotency, importance (642), reign, ableness, capability (157).

Footing, hold, foothold, purchase,

175A Absence of Influence, impotence (158), weakness (160), inertness (172).

(Verb) To have no influence.

(Phrase) To cut no ice.

(Adjective) Uninfluential.

fulcrum, stance, *point d'appui, pou sto, locus standi,* leverage, vantage-ground; aegis, protection, patronage, auspices.

(Phrases) A tower of strength; a host in himself.

(Verbs) To have influence, etc., to have a hold upon, to have a pull, to gain a footing, work upon, take root, take hold, permeate, penetrate, infiltrate, prevail, dominate, predominate, outweigh, overweigh, carry weight, weigh, tell, to bear upon.

(Phrases) To be in the ascendant; to cut some ice; to pull wires; to pull the strings; to set the fashion; to have a voice.

(Adjectives) Influential, valid, weighty, prevailing, prevalent, dominant, regnant, predominating, predominant, prepotent, ascendant, rife.

(Adverb) With telling effect.

176 Tendency *(Substantives),* aptness, proneness, proclivity, conduciveness, bent, bias, quality, inclination, trend, propensity, predisposition, leaning, drift, conducement, temperament, idiosyncrasy, vein, humour, mood.

(Verbs) To tend, contribute, conduce, lead, dispose, incline, trend, verge, bend to, affect, carry, promote, redound, to, subserve to (644), bid fair to, make for, gravitate towards.

(Adjectives) Tending, contributing, conducing, conducive, working towards, calculated to, disposing, inclining, bending, leading, carrying to, subservient, subsidiary (644, 707); apt, liable, prone, disposed, predisposed.

(Adverbs) For, whither, in a fair way to.

177 Liability *(Substantives),* subjection to, dependence on, exposure to, contingency, possibility (156), susceptivity, susceptibility.

(Verbs) To be liable, etc., incur, to lay oneself open to, lie under, expose oneself to, stand a chance, to open a door to.

(Phrase) To stick one's neck out.

(Adjectives) Liable, apt, prone, subject, open to, incident to, exposed to, dependent on; answerable, accountable, responsible.

Contingent, incidental, possible, casual.

(Phrases) Within range of; at the mercy of.

5°. *Combinations of Causes*

178 Concurrence *(Substantives),* co-operation, collaboration (709), union, agreement, consent (488), pulling together, alliance; complicity, connivance, collusion.

Voluntary concurrence (709).

(Verbs) To concur, co-operate, conspire, agree, conduce, contribute, unite, to pull together, hang together, join forces.

(Phrases) To have a hand in; to be in the same boat; to go hand in hand (709).

(Adjectives) Concurring, concurrent, conjoined, concomitant, associate, co-operating, conspiring, agreeing, correspondent, conformable,

179 Counteraction *(Substantives),* opposition, antagonism, polarity, clashing, etc., collision, contrariety (14), resistance, interference, friction.

Neutralization, nullification, compensation (30).

Reaction, retroaction (277), repercussion, rebound, recoil, ricochet, counterblast.

Check, obstacle, hindrance (706); antidote, counter-irritant, preventive, corrective, remedy (662).

Voluntary counteraction (708).

(Verbs) To counteract, oppose, cross, contravene, antagonize, interfere or conflict with, collide with,

pulling together, etc., of one mind, in alliance with, with one consent, of one mind, with one accord.

_____

clash, neutralize, undo, nullify, render null; to militate against, withstand, resist (719), hinder (706), repress, control, curb, check, rein in (174).

To react (277), countervail, counterpoise (30), overpoise.

(Adjectives) Counteracting, opposing, etc., counteractive, antagonistic, conflicting, reactionary, recalcitrant, opposite, retroactive, cohibitive, counter, contrary (14).

(Adverbs) Counter, notwithstanding, nevertheless, nathless, none the less, yet, still, although, though, albeit, howbeit, maugre, at all events.

But, even, however, in defiance of, in the teeth of, in the face of, in spite of, in despite of (708).

(Phrases) For all that; all the same; be that as it may; even so.

CLASS II

WORDS RELATING TO SPACE

SECTION I—SPACE IN GENERAL

1°. *Abstract Space*

180 Indefinite space.

Space *(Substantives)*, extension, extent, expanse, room, scope, range, purview, way, expansion, compass, sweep, play, amplitude, latitude, field, swing, spread, stretch; spare room, headway, elbow-room, freedom, house-room, stowage, roomage, margin.

Open space, void, space, vacuity (4), opening, waste, wilderness, moor, moorland, campagna, tundra.

Abyss (198); unlimited space, infinity (105).

(Adjectives) Spatial, two-dimensional, three-dimensional.

Spacious, roomy, commodious, extensive, expansive, capacious, ample.

Boundless, unlimited, unbounded, limitless, illimitable, infinite, uncircumscribed, shoreless, trackless, pathless.

(Adverbs) Extensively, etc., wherever, everywhere.

(Phrases) The length and the breadth of the land; far and near, far and wide; all over; all the world over; from China to Peru; from Land's End to John o' Groat's; in every quarter; in all quarters; in all lands; every hole and corner; here, there, and everywhere; from pole to pole; throughout the world; to the four winds; under the sun.

181 Definite space.

Region *(Substantives)*, sphere, ground, area, realm, quarter, district, orb, circuit, circle, compartment, domain, tract, department, territory, country, canton, county, shire, township, riding, hundred, parish, bailiwick, province, satrapy, *arrondissement*, commune, enclave, principality, duchy, kingdom, empire, dominion, colony, protectorate, mandate.

Arena, precincts, *enceinte*, walk, patch, plot, paddock, enclosure, field, compound.

Clime, climate, zone, meridian.

(Adjectives) Regional, territorial, provincial, parochial, local, etc.

Limited space, locality.

182 Place *(Substantives)*, spot, point, nook, corner, recess, hole, niche, compartment, premises, precinct, station, pitch, venue, abode (189).

Indefinite place.

(Adverbs) Somewhere, in some place, wherever it may be.

———

2°. *Relative Space*

183 Situation *(Substantives)*, position, locality, locale, status, latitude and longitude, footing, standing, post, stage, bearings, aspect, orientation, attitude, posture, lie, emplacement.

Place, site, station, pitch, seat, venue, whereabouts, direction, azimuth, etc. (278).

Topography, geography, chorography.

A map, chart, plan (554).

(Verbs) To be situated, to lie, to have its seat in.

(Adjectives) Local, topical; situate.

(Adverbs) In situ, here and there, *passim,* whereabouts.

184 Location *(Substantives),* localization, lodgment, deposition, reposition, stowage, establishment, settlement, fixation, grafting, insertion (300), lading, encampment, billet, installation.

A colony, settlement, cantonment.

A habitation, residence, dwelling (189).

(Phrases) Genius loci; the spirit of the place.

(Verbs) To place, situate, locate, localize, put, lay, set, seat, station, lodge, park, post, install, house, settle, stow, dump, establish, fix, root, plant, graft, stick in, tuck in, insert, wedge in, shelve, pitch, camp, posit, deposit, reposit, cradle, encamp, moor, pack, embed (or imbed), vest, stock, populate, people, colonize, domicile.

To billet on, quarter upon.

To pocket, pouch, put up, bag, load.

To inhabit, reside (186), domesticate, put up at, colonize.

(Phrase) To pitch one's tent.

(Adjectives) Placed, located, etc., situate, situated, ensconced, nestled, embosomed, housed, moored, rooted, unremoved.

185 Displacement *(Substantives),* dislodgment, eviction, ejectment (297), deportation, extradition, expatriation, banishment, exile.

Removal, remotion, transposition, relegation (270).

(Verbs) To displace, dislodge, unhouse, unkennel, break bulk, take off, eject, evict, chuck out, hoof out, expel, etc. (297), extradite, expatriate, banish, exile, relegate, oust, rusticate, ostracize, remove, transfer, transpose, transplant, transport (270), empty, clear, clear out, sweep off, sweep away, do away with, get rid of, root out, disestablish, unpeople, depopulate.

To vacate, leave (293), get out, heave out, bale out, lade out, pour out (297).

(Phrase) To make a clean sweep of.

(Adjectives) Displaced, etc., unhoused, houseless, homeless, stateless.

(Phrase) Like a fish out of water.

3°. Existence in Space

186 Presence *(Substantives),* occupancy, occupation, attendance, whereness.

Diffusion, permeation, pervasion, interpenetration, dissemination (73).

Ubiquity, ubiety, ubiquitousness, omnipresence.

(Verbs) To exist in space, to be present, attend, remain.

To occur in a place, lie, stand, occupy, colonize.

To inhabit, dwell, reside, live, abide, sojourn, lodge, nestle, perch, roost, put up at, hang out at, stay at,

187 Absence *(Substantives),* non-existence (2), non-residence, non-attendance, alibi, absenteeism.

Emptiness, void, vacuum, voidness, vacuity, vacancy, vacuousness.

An absentee, truant, nobody, nobody on earth.

(Verbs) To be absent, not present, etc., vacate, to keep away, to keep out of the way.

(Phrases) Make oneself scarce; absent oneself; take oneself off; stay away; play truant; be conspicuous by one's absence.

stop at, squat, hive, burrow, camp, encamp, bivouac, anchor, settle, take up one's quarters, pitch one's tent, get a footing, frequent, haunt, tenant, take root, strike root, revisit.

To fill, pervade, permeate, penetrate, interpenetrate, infiltrate, be diffused through, be disseminated through, overspread, run through.

(Adjectives) Present, occupying, inhabiting, etc., moored, at anchor, resident, residentiary, domiciled.

Ubiquitous, omnipresent.

(Adverbs) Here, there, where? everywhere, in residence, aboard, on board, at home, afield, etc., on the spot.

(Phrases) Here, there, and everywhere; at every turn.

(Adjectives) Absent, not present, away, gone, from home, missing, non-resident.

Empty, void, vacant, vacuous, blank, untenanted, tenantless, uninhabited, deserted, devoid, unoccupied, unpeopled.

(Phrases) Nowhere to be found; A.W.O.L. (absent without leave); *non est inventus*; not a soul; nobody present; the bird being flown.

(Adverbs) Without, minus, nowhere, elsewhere, sans.

(Phrases) One's back being turned; behind one's back.

---

188 Inhabitant *(Substantives)*, resident, residentiary, dweller, indweller, occupier, occupant, lodger, boarder, paying guest, inmate, tenant, sojourner, settler, squatter, backwoodsman, national, colonist, denizen, citizen, cit, cockney, townsman, burgess, countryman, villager, cottar, compatriot, garrison, crew, population, people.

Native, indigene, aborigines, autochthones, son of the soil.

A colony, settlement, household.

Newcomer (57).

(Adjectives) Indigenous, native, aboriginal, autochthonous, domestic, domiciled, domesticated, domiciliary.

---

189 Place of habitation.

Abode *(Substantives)*, dwelling, lodging, domicile, residence, address, habitation, berth, seat, lap, sojourn, housing, quarters, accommodation, headquarters, throne, ark, tabernacle.

Nest, nidus, lair, haunt, eyrie (or aerie), den, hole, earth, warren, rookery, hive, habitat, haunt, resort, retreat, nidification, perch, roost.

Bivouac, camp, encampment, cantonment, castrametation, tent, marquee, teepee, igloo.

Cave, cavern, cell, grove, grot, grotto, alcove, bower, arbour, cove, chamber (191).

Home, fatherland, motherland, native land, country, homestead, homestall, fireside, snuggery, hearth, Lares and Penates, household gods, roof, household, housing; 'dulce domum', Blighty.

Building, structure, edifice, fabric, erection, pile, tenement, messuage, farm, farmhouse, steading, grange.

Cot, cabin, hut, shack, chalet, croft, shed, hangar, penthouse, lean-to, booth, stall, hovel, outhouse, barn, kennel, sty, coop, hutch, cage, cote, stable, garage, offices.

House, mansion, villa, flat, flatlet, prefab, maisonette, cottage, box, lodge, *pied-à-terre*, bungalow, hermitage, summer-house, gazebo, folly, rotunda, tower, temple (1000), château, castle, pavilion, court, hall, palace, kiosk, house-boat.

Inn, hostel, hotel, roadhouse, motel, tavern, caravansery, hospice, rest-house, dak-bungalow, barrack, lodging-house, guest-house, doss-house, lodgings, apartments, diggings, digs.

Hamlet, village, clachan, thorp, dorp, kraal, borough, burgh, municipality, town, city, garden city, metropolis, suburb (227), conurbation, province, country.

Street, place, terrace, parade, road, avenue, row, lane, alley, court, wynd, close, yard, passage, rents, slum; square, polygon, quadrant, circus, crescent, mall, place, piazza, arcade, gardens.

Anchorage, roadstead, dock, basin, wharf, quay, port, harbour, haven.

(Adjectives) Urban, civic, metropolitan, municipal, provincial, rural, rustic, countrified; home-like, homy.

190 Things contained.

Contents *(Substantives)*, cargo, lading, filling, stuffing, freight, load, burden, ware (798).

191 Receptacle *(Substantives)*, recipient, receiver, reservatory, compartment (636).

Cell, cellule, loculus, follicle, hole, corner, niche, recess, nook, crypt, stall, pigeon-hole, lodging (189), bed, berth, bunk, doss, etc. (215), store-room, strong-room.

Capsule, vesicle, cyst, bladder, pod.

Stomach, belly, paunch, ventricle, crop, craw, maw, gizzard, bread-basket, kyte, ovary, womb (221).

Pocket, pouch, sporran, fob, sheath, scabbard, socket, bag, sac, sack, wallet, scrip, poke, kit, knapsack, rucksack, haversack, sabretache, satchel, cigar-case, cigarette-case, reticule, powder-box, flapjack, compact, vanity-case, vanity-bag, portfolio, budget.

Chest, box, hutch, coffer, case, casket, caddy, pyx (or pix), caisson, desk, davenport, escritoire, bureau, cabinet, reliquary; trunk, portmanteau, saratoga, grip-sack, grip, bandbox, valise, hold-all, attaché-case, dispatch-case, dispatch-box, writing-case, suit-case, dressing-case, kit-bag, brief-bag, brief-case, gladstone bag, boot, creel, crate, packing-case, snuff-box, mull.

Vessel, vase, bushel, barrel, canister, jar, can, pottle, basket, pannier, corbeille, punnet, hamper, tray, hod.

For liquids: cistern, reservoir, tank, vat, cauldron, barrel, cask, keg, runlet, firkin, kilderkin, demijohn, carboy, amphora, bottle, jar, decanter, carafe, tantalus, ewer, cruse, crock, kit, canteen, flagon, flask, flasket, thermos flask, vacuum flask, stoup, noggin, vial (or phial), cruet, caster, urn, samovar, billy.

Tub, bucket, pail, pot, tankard, beaker, jug, pitcher, mug, noggin, pipkin, gallipot, matrass, receiver, alembic, retort, test-tube, pipette, capsule, kettle, spittoon.

Bowl, basin, jorum, punch-bowl, cup, goblet, chalice, quaich, tumbler, glass, horn, can, pan, pannikin, plate, dish, trencher, tray, salver, patera, calabash, porringer, saucepan, skillet, casserole, tureen, saucer, platter, hod, scuttle, baikie, shovel, trowel, spoon, spatula, ladle.

Closet, cupboard, cellaret, chiffonier, wardrobe, bunker, bin, buffet, press, safe, sideboard, whatnot, drawer, chest of drawers, tallboy, lowboy, till.

Chamber, flat, storey, apartment, room, cabin, bower, office, court, hall, saloon, *salon*, parlour, state-room, presence-chamber, reception-room, drawing-room, sitting-room, living-room, gallery, cabinet, nursery, boudoir, library, study, snuggery, adytum, sanctum, den, phrontistery, lumber-room (636), dormitory, bedroom, dressing-room, refectory, dining-room, breakfast-room, billiard-room, smoking-room, pew, harem, seraglio, zenana.

Attic, loft, garret, cockloft, belfry, cellar, vault, hold, cockpit, ground-floor, *rez-de-chaussée*, basement, kitchen, kitchenette, pantry, scullery, bathroom, lavatory, water-closet, w.c., urinal, latrine, rear, toilet, convenience, comfort station, heads, thunder-box, offices.

Portico, porch, veranda, piazza, stoop, lobby, court, hall, vestibule, foyer, lounge, corridor, loggia, passage, anteroom, antechamber.

(Adjectives) Capsular, saccular, sacculate, recipient, ventricular, cystic, vascular, celled, cellular, cellulous, cellulose, camerated, chambered, locular, multilocular, roomed, two-roomed, etc., polygastric, pouched, marsupial.

SECTION II—DIMENSIONS

1°. *General Dimensions*

192 Size *(Substantives)*, magnitude, dimension, bulk, volume, largeness, bigness, greatness (31), expanse, amplitude, mass, massiveness.

Capacity, capaciousness, tonnage (or tunnage), calibre, scantling.

Average size, stock size.

Corpulence, adiposity, obesity, chubbiness, plumpness, *embonpoint*, stoutness, out-size; corporation, flesh and blood, brawn, brawniness.

Hugeness, vastness, enormousness, enormity, immensity, monstrousness, monstrosity; expansion (194) infinity (105).

A giant, Goliath, Brobdingnagian, Antaeus, Gargantua, monster, whale, leviathan, elephant, mammoth, colossus, tun, lump, chunk, bulk, block, boulder, mass, bushel, whacker, thumper, whopper, spanker, behemoth.

A mountain, mound, heap (72).

(Phrases) A Triton among the minnows; the lion's share.

(Verbs) To be large, etc., to become large (194).

(Adjectives) Large, big, great, considerable, bulky, voluminous, ample, massive, massy, capacious, comprehensive, mighty, king-sized.

Corpulent, obese, stout, fat, plump, rotund, buxom, sonsy, lusty, strapping, bouncing, portly, burly, brawny, fleshy, beefy, goodly, in good case, chopping, jolly, chubby, full-grown, chub-faced, lubberly, hulking, unwieldy, lumpish, husky, stalwart.

193 Littleness *(Substantives)*, smallness (32), minuteness, diminutiveness, exiguity, inextension, puniness, dwarfishness, epitome, duodecimo, rudiment, microcosm.

Leanness, emaciation, thinness, macilency, flaccidity, meagreness.

A dwarf, runt, pygmy, midget, Lilliputian, chit, bantam, urchin, elf, doll, puppet, skeleton, ghost, spindleshanks, shadow, Tom Thumb, manikin, *homunculus*.

Animalcule, mite, insect, emmet, fly, gnat, midge, shrimp, minnow, worm, grub, tit, tomtit, mouse, small fry, smout, mushroom, pollard, millet-seed, mustard-seed, grain of sand, molehill.

Atom, point, speck, dot, mote, ace, jot, iota, tittle, whit, particle, corpuscle, electron, molecule, monad, granule, grain, crumb, globule, nutshell, minim, drop, droplet, mouthful, thimbleful, sprinkling, dash, suspicion, *soupçon,* minimum, powder (330), driblet, patch, scrap, chip, inch, mathematical point; minutiae.

(Phrases) The shadow of a shade; a drop in the ocean; chicken feed; tip of the ice-berg.

(Verbs) To be small, etc., to become small, contract (195).

(Adjectives) Little, small, minute, diminutive, inconsiderable, exiguous, puny, tiny, wee, weeny, teeny-weeny, petty, mini, minikin, hop-o'-my-thumb, miniature, bijou, *petite,* pygmy, undersized, half-pint, dwarf,

Squab, dumpy (202), tubby, roly-poly, pursy, blowsy.

Huge, immense, enormous, mighty, unbounded, vast, vasty, amplitudinous, stupendous, inordinate, herculean, thumping, whacking, whopping, monster; gigantic, giant-like, colossal, titanic, mountainous, elephantine, mammoth, cyclopean, Antaean, Gargantuan, Falstaffian, Brobdingnagian; infinite, unbounded.

(Phrases) Large as life; plump as a partridge; fat as a pig; fat as butter; fat as bacon.

stunted, dwarfed, dwarfish, pollard, Lilliputian; pocket, thumb-nail, portative, portable, duodecimo.

Microscopic, infra-microscopic, evanescent, impalpable, imperceptible, invisible, inappreciable, infinitesimal, homoeopathic, atomic, corpuscular, molecular, rudimentary, rudimental.

Lean, thin, gaunt, meagre, emaciated, lank, macilent, ghostly, starved, starveling, fallen away, scrubby, reduced, shrunk, shrunken, attenuated, extenuated, shrivelled, tabid, flaccid, starved, skinny, wizen, wizened, scraggy, lanky, raw-boned, scrawny, spindle-shanked, lantern-jawed (203).

(Phrases) In a small compass; in a nutshell; on a small scale.

Worn to a shadow; skin and bone.

194 Expansion *(Substantives)*, enlargement, extension, augmentation, increase of size, amplification, ampliation, aggrandisement, spread, increment, growth, development, pullulation, swell, dilatation, rarefaction, turgescence, turgidity, thickening, tumefaction, intumescence, swelling, tumour, diastole, distension, puffing, inflation.

Overgrowth, hypertrophy, overdistension, tympany.

Bulb, knot, knob (249).

Superiority of size.

(Verbs) To become larger, to expand, widen, enlarge, extend, grow, increase, swell (202), gather, fill out, deploy, dilate, stretch, largen, spread, mantle, bud, burgeon, shoot, spring up, sprout, germinate, vegetate, pullulate, open, burst forth, put on flesh, outgrow.

To render larger, to expand, aggrandize, etc., distend, develop, open out, broaden, thicken, largen, amplify, tumefy, magnify, rarefy, inflate, puff, blow up, stuff, cram, pad, fill out.

To be larger than, to surpass, exceed, be beyond, cap, overtop (206, 33).

(Adjectives) Expanded, enlarged, increased, etc., swelled out, swollen, distended, bulbous; exaggerated,

195 Contraction *(Substantives)*, reduction, diminution, decrease of size, defalcation, lessening, decrement, shrinking, shrivelling, systole, collapse, emaciation, attenuation, tabefaction, tabes, consumption, marasmus, atrophy; hour-glass, neck (203).

Condensation, compression, squeezing.

Inferiority of size.

Corrugation, contractility, astringency.

(Verbs) To become smaller, to lessen, diminish, decrease, dwindle, shrink, contract, shrivel, collapse, wither, wilt, lose flesh, wizen, fall away, decay, purse up, waste, wane, ebb, to grow less.

To render smaller, to contract, lessen, etc., draw in, to condense, reduce, · clip, compress, constrict, cramp, squeeze, attenuate, chip, dwarf, bedwarf, stunt, cut short (201), corrugate, crumple, crush, purse up, pinch (203), deflate.

To be smaller than, to fall short of, not to come up to.

(Phrases) To grow 'small by degrees, and beautifully less' (659); to be on the wane; to hide its diminished head.

(Adjectives) Contracting, etc., astringent, styptic, tabid, contracted, lessened, etc., shrivelled, wasted,

bloated, tumid, turgid, puffy, full-blown, full-grown, full-formed, over-grown, hypertrophied, pot-bellied, swag-bellied, dropsical, oedematous.

(Phrase) 'A-swellin' wisibly.'

196 Distance, *(Substantives),* re-moteness, farness, longinquity, elon-gation, offing, removedness, parallax, reach, span.

Antipodes, outpost, outskirts, aphelion, apogee, horizon.

Separation (44), transference (270). Diffusion, dispersion (73).

(Phrases) Ultima Thule; ne plus ultra; the uttermost parts of the earth; the back of beyond.

(Verbs) To be distant, etc.; to extend to, stretch to, reach to, spread to, go to, get to, stretch away to; outgo, outstep (303); to go to great lengths.

To remain at a distance, keep away, stand off, keep off, keep clear, stand aloof, hold off.

(Adjectives) Distant, far, far off, remote, removed, distal, wide of, clear of, yon, yonder, at arm's length, apart, aloof, asunder, ulterior, transalpine, transatlantic, ultramundane, hyper-borean, antipodean, hull down.

Inaccessible, un-get-at-able, out of the way, unapproachable, unreach-able; incontiguous.

(Adverbs) Far, away, far away, afar, off, a long way off, afar off, wide away, aloof, wide of, clear of, out of the way, a great way off, out of reach, abroad.

Apart, asunder, few and far between.

Yonder, farther, beyond, *longo intervallo,* wide apart, poles apart.

(Phrases) Far and near; far and wide; over the hills and far away; a far cry to; from end to end; from pole to pole; from Indus to the Pole; from China to Peru; from Dan to Beer-sheba; to the ends of the earth; out of the sphere of; wide of the mark.

———

wizened, stunted, waning, ebbing, etc., neap, condensed.

Unexpanded, contractile, compres-sible.

(Phrase) Multum in parvo.

197 Nearness *(Substantives),* nigh-ness, proximity, propinquity, vicinity, vicinage, neighbourhood, adjacency, closeness; perihelion, perigee.

A short distance, a step, an ear-shot, close quarters, a stone's throw, a hair's breadth, a span, bowshot, gunshot, pistol-shot.

Purlieus, neighbourhood, environs (227), vicinity, *alentours,* suburbs, whereabouts, *banlieue,* borderland.

A bystander, neighbour.

Approach, approximation, appro-pinquation, appulse (286), junction (43), concentration, convergence (290).

Meeting, *rencontre* (292).

(Verbs) To be near, etc., to adjoin, hang about, trench on, border upon, stand by, approximate, tread on the heels of, cling to, clasp, hug, crowd, get near, etc., to approach (287), to meet (290).

To bring near, to crowd, pack, huddle together.

(Adjectives) Near, nigh, close, close at hand, neighbouring, proximate, approximate, adjacent, adjoining, intimate, bordering upon, close upon, hard upon, trenching on, treading on the heels of, verging on, at hand, handy, near the mark, home, at the point of, near run, in touch with, nearish.

(Adverbs) Near, nigh, hard by, fast by, close to, next door to, within reach, within call, within hearing, within an ace of, close upon, at hand, on the verge of, near the mark, in the environs, round the corner, at one's door, at one's feet, at one's elbow, at close quarters; within range, pistol-shot, a stone's throw, etc.; cheek by jowl, beside, alongside, at the heels of, at the threshold.

About, hereabouts, thereabouts, in the way, in presence of, in round numbers, approximately, roughly, as good as, *à peu près* (32).

198 Interval (*Substantives*), interspace (70), break, gap, opening (260), chasm, hiatus, caesura, interstice, lacuna, cleft, fosse, mesh, crevice, chink, creek, cranny, crack, slit, fissure, scissure, chap, rift, flaw, gash, cut, leak, dike (350), ha-ha, fracture, breach, rent, oscitation, gaping, yawning, pandiculation, insertion (300), pass, gorge, defile, ravine, canyon (or cañon), crevasse, chimney, couloir, *bergschrund*, gulf, gully, gulch, nullah, strait, sound, kyle, frith, furrow (*see* 259).

Thing interposed, go-between, interjacence (228).

(*Verbs*) To separate (44), gape, yawn.

---

199 Contiguity (*Substantives*), contact, proximity, apposition, juxtaposition, touching, tangency, tangent, osculation, meeting (292), syzygy, coincidence, register, co-existence, adhesion (46).

Confine, frontier, demarcation, border (233).

(*Verbs*) To be contiguous, etc., to touch, meet, adhere, (46), osculate, coincide, register, coexist, join, adjoin, abut on, graze, border, march with.

(*Adjectives*) Contiguous, touching, bordering on, meeting, in contact, conterminous, osculating, osculatory, tangential, proximate.

(*Phrases*) Hand to hand; end to end; tête-à-tête; next door to; with no interval; in juxtaposition, apposition, etc.; in register.

2°. *Linear Dimensions*

200 Length (*Substantives*), longitude, span, stretch.

A line, bar, rule, stripe, spoke, radius.

Lengthening, elongation, prolongation, production, producing, protraction, extension, tension, stretching.

(*Verbs*) To be long, etc., to extend to, reach, stretch to.

To render long, lengthen, extend, elongate, prolong, produce, stretch, draw out, protract, spin out, drawl.

(*Phrase*) To drag its slow length along.

(*Adjectives*) Long, longsome, lengthy, tedious, tiresome, wiredrawn, outstretched, lengthened, produced, etc., sesquipedalian, interminable, endless, unending, never-ending, there being no end of.

Linear, lineal, longitudinal, oblong.

(*Phrases*) As long as my arm; as long as to-day and to-morrow.

(*Adverbs*) Lengthwise, longitudially, in a line, along, from end to end, endways, from stem to stern, fore and aft, from head to foot, from top to toe, cap-à-pie.

201 Shortness (*Substantives*), brevity, briefness, a span, etc., *see* Smallness (193).

Shortening, abbreviation, abbreviature, abridgment, curtailment, reduction, contraction, compression (195), retrenchment, elision, ellipsis, compendium (596), conciseness (in style) (572).

(*Verbs*) To be short, brief, etc.

To render short, to shorten, curtail, abridge, abbreviate, epitomize, reduce, contract, compress, scrimp, skimp, boil down.

To retrench, cut short, cut down, pare down, whittle down, clip, dock, lop, poll, prune, pollard, crop, bob, shingle, bingle, snub, truncate, cut, hack, hew, foreshorten.

(*Adjectives*) Short, brief, curt, laconic, compendious, compact, stubby, squab, squabby, squat, chunky, stubby, stocky, dumpy, podgy, fubsy, skimpy, stumpy, pug, snub.

Oblate, elliptical.

Concise (572), summary.

---

202 Breadth *(Substantives)*, width, latitude, amplitude, diameter, bore, calibre, superficial, extent, expanse.

Thickness, crassitude (192), thickening, expansion, dilatation, etc. (194).

(Verbs) To be broad, thick, etc.

To broaden, to swell, dilate, expand, outspread, etc. (194); to thicken, incrassate.

(Adjectives) Broad, wide, ample, extended, fan-like, outstretched, etc.

Thick, corpulent, fat (192), squab, squabbly, squat, chunky, stubby, stocky, dumpy, podgy, fulsy, thick-set.

(Phrases) Wide as a church door; thick as a rope.

_____

203 Narrowness *(Substantives)*, slenderness, closeness, scantiness, exility, lankness, lankiness, fibrousness.

A line (205), a hair's breadth, a finger's breadth, strip, streak, vein.

Thinness, tenuity, leanness, meagreness.

A shaving, a slip (205), a mere skeleton, a shadow, an anatomy.

A middle constriction, stricture, neck, waist, isthmus, wasp, hourglass, bottle-neck, ridge, ravine, defile, gorge, pass (198).

Narrowing, coarctation, tapering, compression, squeezing, etc. (195).

(Phrases) A bag of bones; a living skeleton.

(Verbs) To be narrow, etc., to taper, contract, shrink.

To render narrow, etc., to narrow, contract, coarctate, attenuate, constrict, constringe, cramp, pinch, squeeze, compress, tweak, corrugate, warp.

To shave, pare, shear, etc.

(Adjectives) Narrow, strait, slender, thin, fine, tenuous, filiform, filamentary, filamentous, fibrous, funicular, capillary, stringy, wiredrawn, fine-spun, anguine, taper, dapper, slim, slight, gracile, scanty, scant, spare, delicate.

Meagre, lean, emaciated, lank, lanky, weedy, rangy, gangling, starveling, attenuated, pinched, skinny, scraggy, gaunt, cadaverous, skin and bone, raw-boned, scrawny, spindle-shanked (193), hatchet-faced, wasp-waisted, herring-gutted, spidery, spindly, reedy.

(Phrases) Thin as a lath; thin as a whipping-post; lean as a rake; thin as a thread-paper; thin as a wafer; thin as a shadow.

204 Layer *(Substantives)*, stratum, bed, zone, substratum, slab, escarpment, floor, flag, stage, course, storey, tier.

Plate, lamina, lamella, sheet, flake, scale, coat, pellicle, membrane, film, slice, shive, cut, shaving, rasher, board, plank, platter, trencher, spatula, leaf.

Stratification, scaliness, a nest of boxes, coats of an onion.

(Verbs) To slice, shave, etc.

(Adjectives) Lamellar, laminated, lamelliform, laminiferous, scaly, squamous, filmy, membranous, flaky, foliated, foliaceous, stratified, stratiform, tabular, nested.

205 Filament *(Substantives)*, line, fibre, fibril, tendril, hair, gossamer, wire, thread, cord, funicle, rope, yarn, string, twine (45), cilium, gimp.

Strip (51), shred, slip, spill, list, string, band, fillet, fascia, ribbon (or riband); roll, lath, slat, splinter, sliver, shiver, shaving, arborescence (256); strand.

A hair-stroke.

(Adjectives) Filamentary, fibrous, hairy, capillary, thread-like, wiry, funicular, stringy.

_____

206 Height *(Substantives)*, altitude, elevation, eminence, pitch, loftiness, sublimity.

Stature, tallness, procerity, culmination (210).

A giant, grenadier, guardsman, colossus, giraffe.

Alp, mountain, mount, hill, butte, ben, brae, hillock, kopje, monticule, fell, moorland, hummock, knap, knoll, cape, headland, foreland, promontory, ridge, *arête*, peak, pike, uplands, highlands, rising ground, downs, dune, mound, mole, steep, bluff, cliff, crag, vantage-ground, tor, eagle's nest, aerie.

Orography, Orology.

Tower, pillar, column, obelisk, monument, steeple, spire, *flèche*, campanile, belfry, minaret, turret, cupola, pilaster, skyscraper.

Pole, pikestaff, maypole, flagstaff, topmast, topgallant mast, crow's nest.

Ceiling, roof, awning, canopy (*see* 210), attic, loft, garret, housetop.

Growth, upgrowth (194).

(Verbs) To be high, etc., to tower, soar, ride, beetle, hover, cap, overtop, culminate, overhang, hang over, impend, overlie, bestride, mount, surmount, to cover (222), perch.

To render high, to heighten, exalt (307).

To become high, grow, upgrow, soar, tower, rise (305).

(Adjectives) High, elevated, eminent, exalted, lofty, supernal, tall, towering, beetling, soaring, colossal, gigantic (192), Patagonian, culminating, raised, elevated, etc., perched up, hanging (gardens), crowning, coronary.

Upland, moorland, hilly, mountainous, cloud-touching, heaven-kissing, cloud-topt, cloud-capt, Alpine, subalpine, aerial; orographical.

Upper, uppermost (210), topgallant.

Overhanging, impending, incumbent, overlying, superincumbent, supernatant, superimposed, hovering.

(Phrases) Tall as a maypole; tall as a steeple; tall as a poplar.

(Adverbs) On high, high up, aloft, above, upstairs, overhead, in the clouds, on tiptoe, on stilts, on the shoulders of, over head and ears.

Over, upwards, from top to bottom, from top to toe, from head to foot, cap-à-pie.

(Interjection) Excelsior!

207 Lowness *(Substantives)*, lowlands, depression, a molehill, recumbency, prostration.

Dwarf, pygmy bantam, Lilliputian.

Lowlands; molehill.

A ground-floor, basement, cellar, *rez de chaussée* (191), hold.

(Verbs) To be low, etc., lie low, grovel, wallow, crouch, slouch, lie flat.

To lower, depress (306), take down a peg, prostrate, subvert.

(Adjectives) Low, low-lying, neap, nether, prostrate, flat, level with the ground, grovelling, crouched, crouching, subjacent, underground, underlying, squat.

(Adverbs) Under, beneath, underneath, below, down, adown, downstairs, below stairs, over head and ears, downwards, underfoot, at the foot of, underground, at a low ebb.

———

208 Depth *(Substantives)*, deepness, profundity, profoundness, depression, bathos, anti-climax, depth of water, draught.

A hollow, pit, shaft, well, crater, gulf, abyss, abysm, bottomless pit, hell.

209 Shallowness *(Substantives)*, shoaliness, shoals.

(Adjectives) Shallow, skin-deep, superficial, shoaly.

———

Soundings, submersion, plunge, dive (310).

Plummit, lead, sounding-rod, probe; bathymetry.

Bathysphere, diving-bell, caisson, submarine; diver, frogman.

(Verbs) To be deep, etc.

To render deep, etc., to deepen, sink, submerge, plunge, dip, dive (310).

To dig, scoop out, hollow, sink, delve (252).

(Adjectives) Deep, deep-seated, profound, sunk, buried, submerged, etc., subaqueous, submarine, subterranean, underground, subterrene, abysmal; bathymetrical, bathymetric.

Bottomless, soundless, fathomless, unfathomed, unsounded, unplumbed, unfathomable.

(Phrases) Deep as a well; ankle-deep; knee-deep; breast-deep; chin-deep.

(Adverbs) Beyond one's depth, out of one's depth, underground.

(Phrases) Over head and ears; to Davy Jones's locker; in the bowels of the earth.

210 Summit *(Substantives)*, top, vertex, apex, zenith, pinnacle, acme, climax, culminating point, apogee, pitch, meridian, sky, pole, watershed.

Tip, tiptop, crest, crow's nest, mast-head, truck, peak, turning-point, pole.

Crown, brow, nib, head, nob, noddle, pate.

Capital, cornice, sconce, architrave, pediment, entablature, frieze.

Roof, ceiling, thatch, tiling, slating, awning, canopy (222).

(Adjectives) Top, topmost, uppermost, tiptop, culminating, meridian, capital, head, polar, supreme, crowning, coronary.

(Phrase) At the top of the tree.

211 Base *(Substantives)*, basement, plinth, foundation, substratum, ground, earth, pavement, floor, paving, flag, ground floor, deck, substructure, infrastructure, footing, groundwork.

The bottom, rock-bottom, nadir, foot, sole, toe, root, keel.

Dado, wainscot, skirting-board.

(Adjectives) Bottom, undermost, nethermost, fundamental, basic.

---

212 Verticality *(Substantives)*, erectness, uprightness, perpendicularity, aplomb, right angle, normal, plummet, plumb-line, azimuth, circle.

Wall, precipice, cliff.

Erection, raising, rearing.

(Verbs) To be vertical, etc., to stand up, to stand on end, to stand erect, to stand upright, to stick up.

To render vertical, to set up, stick up, erect, rear, raise up, cock up, prick up, raise on its legs.

(Adjectives) Vertical, upright, erect, perpendicular, sheer, normal, straight, standing up, etc., up on end, bolt upright, rampant.

213 Horizontality *(Substantives)*, a level, plane, dead level, flatness (251).

Recumbency, lying, lying down, reclination, decumbence, decumbency, supination, resupination, prostration; spirit-level.

A plain, floor, level, flat, platform, bowling-green, billiard-table, plateau, terrace, estrade, esplanade, parterre, table-land (204, 215).

(Verbs) To be horizontal, recumbent, etc., to lie, recline, lie down, couch, sit down, squat, lie flat, lie prostrate, sprawl, loll.

To render horizontal, etc., to lay, lay down, lay out, level, flatten, prostrate, knock down, fell, floor.

(Adverbs) Up, vertically, etc., on end, up on end, endways, endwise.

(Phrase) Straight up and down.

———

(Adjectives) Horizontal, level, plane, flat, even, discoid.

Recumbent, decumbent, lying, prone, supine, couchant, couching, jacent, prostrate, squat, squatting, sitting, reclining.

(Adverbs) Horizontally, etc., on one's back, on all fours, on one's hunkers.

(Phrases) Like a millpond.

214 Pendency *(Substantives)*, dependency, suspension, hanging.

A pendant, pedicel, peduncle, tail, train, flap, skirt, plait, pigtail, queue, tassel, earring, pendulum.

A peg, knob, button, stud, hook, nail, ring, fastener, zipper, clip, staple, knot (45), tenterhook.

(Verbs) To be pendant, etc., to hang, swing, dangle, swag, daggle, flap, trail.

To suspend, append, hang, sling, hook up, hitch, fasten to.

(Adjectives) Pendent, pendulous, pensile, hanging, dependent, swinging, etc., suspended, etc., loose, flowing, caudal.

Having a peduncle, etc., pedunculate, tailed, caudate.

(Adverbs) Dingle-dangle.

(Phrase) In the air.

———

215 Support *(Substantives)*, ground, foundation, base, basis, *terra firma*, fulcrum, foothold, toehold, *point d'appui, pou sto, locus standi,* landing, landing-place, resting-place, ground-work, substratum, floor, bed, stall, berth, lap, mount.

A supporter, prop, stand, strut, stray, shore, boom, yard, outrigger, truss, sleeper, staff, stick, walking-stick, crutch, stirrups, stilts, alpenstock, baton, anvil.

Post, pillar, shaft, column, buttress, pedicle, pedestal, plinth (211), baluster, banister.

A frame, framework, scaffold, scaffolding, skeleton, cadre, beam, rafter, lintel, joist, jamb, mullion, corner-stone, stanchion, summer, girder, cantilever, sponson, tie-beam, (45), columella, backbone, keystone, axle, axle-tree, axis, fuselage, chassis.

A board, form, ledge, platform, floor, stage, shelf, hob, bracket, arbor, rack, mantel, mantelpiece, mantel-shelf, counter, slab, console, dresser, flange, corbel, table, trestle, shoulder, perch, truss, horse, easel, desk.

A seat, throne, dais, divan, musnud, chair, arm-chair, easy-chair, *chaise longue*, hammock-chair, deck-chair, bench, sofa, davenport, lounge, settee, chesterfield, couch, *fauteuil*, stool, tripod, footstool, *tabouret*, trivet, woolsack, ottoman, settle, squab, bench, saddle, pillion, dicky, hassock, pouffe, cushion, howdah.

Bed, bedstead, chair-bedstead, bedding, pillow, bolster, mattress, shakedown, tester, pallet, hammock, bunk, stretcher, crib, cradle, cot, palliasse, donkey's breakfast, sleeping-bag, flea-bag.

Atlas, Persides, Atlantes, Caryatides, Hercules, Yggdrasil.

(Verbs) To be supported, etc., to lie, sit, recline, lean, loll, lounge, abut, bear, rest, stand, step, repose, etc., on, be based on, bestride, straddle, bestraddle.

To support, bear, carry, hold, sustain, shoulder, uphold, hold on, upbear, prop, underprop, shore up, underpin, bolster up, pillow.

To give, furnish, afford, supply, lend, etc., support or foundations; to bottom, found, ground, base, embed.

(Adjectives) Supported, etc., astride, astraddle; fundamental, basic.

216 Parallelism *(Substantives),* coextension.

(Verbs) To be parallel, etc.

(Adjectives) Parallel, coextensive.

(Adverbs) Alongside, abreast, beside.

(Phrases) Side by side; cheek by jowl.

---

217 Obliquity *(Substantives),* inclination, slope, leaning, slant, crookedness, bias, bend, bevel, tilt, list, dip, swag, cant, lurch, skew, skewness, bevelling, squint.

Acclivity, uphill, rise, ascent, gradient, rising ground, bank, ramp.

Declivity, downhill, fall, devexity.

A gentle or rapid slope, easy ascent or descent, chute, helter-skelter, switchback, *montagnes russes.*

Steepness, precipitousness, cliff, precipice, talus, scarp, escarp, escarpment; measure of inclination, clinometer.

Diagonal, zigzag, distortion, hypotenuse, angle (244).

(Phrase) The leaning tower of Pisa.

(Verbs) To be or render oblique, etc., to slope, slant, tilt, lean, incline, shelve, stoop, descend, bend, heel, careen, sag, swag, slouch, cant, sidle, skew, scarp, escarp, bevel, distort.

(Adjectives) Oblique, inclined, leaning, recumbent, sloping, shelving, skew, askew, skew-whiff, slant, aslant, slanting, slantendicular, plagioclastic, indirect, distorted, wry, awry, ajee, drawn, crooked, canted, tilted, biased, saggy, bevel, slouched, slouching, etc., out of the perpendicular, backhanded.

Uphill, rising, ascending, acclivitous.

Downhill, falling, descending, declining, declivitous, anticlinal.

Steep, abrupt, precipitous, break-neck.

Diagonal, transverse, athwart, transversal, antiparallel.

(Adverbs) Obliquely, etc., on one side, askew, edgewise, askant, askance, sideways, aslope, slopewise, all on one side, crinkum-crankum, asquint, at an angle.

(Phrase) Facilis descensus Averni.

---

218 Inversion *(Substantives),* contraposition, overturn, somersault (or somerset), *culbute,* subversion, retroversion, reversion, reversal, introversion, eversion, transposition, pronation and supination.

Anastrophe, metathesis, hysteron, proteron, spoonerism, palindrome.

(Verbs) To be inverted, etc., to turn turtle, loop the loop, bunt.

To render inverted, etc., to invert, reverse, upset, overset, overturn, turn over, upturn, subvert, retrovert, transpose, turn topsy-turvy, tilt over, *culbuter,* keel over, topple over, capsize.

(Adjectives) Inverted, inverse, upside down, topsy-turvy, top-heavy.

(Adverbs) Inversely, topsy-turvy, etc., inside out.

(Phrases) To turn the tables; to put the cart before the horse; to the

---

219 Crossing *(Substantives),* intersection, decussation, transversion, convolution.

Reticulation, network, inosculation, anastomosis, interweaving, twining, intertwining, matting, plaiting, interdigitation, mortise (or mortice).

Net, knot, plexus, web, mesh, twill, skein, hank, felt, lace, tulle, wattle, wicker, basket-work, basketry, mat, matting, plait, trellis, lattice, grille, *cancelli,* grid, griddle, grating, gridiron, tracery, fretwork, filigree, reticle, diaper.

Cross, chain, wreath, braid, cat's-cradle, dovetail, Greek cross, Latin cross, Maltese cross, cross of St. Anthony, St. Andrew's cross, cross of Lorraine, swastika, fylfot.

(Verbs) To cross, lace, intersect, decussate, interlace, intertwine, inter-

right about; bottom upwards; head over heels; the wrong side up; base over apex.

———

twist, pleach, plash, entwine, enlace, enmesh, weave, interweave, inweave, twine, twist, wreathe, interdigitate, interlock, anastomose, inosculate, dovetail, splice (43).

To mat, plait, plat, braid, felt, twill, tangle, entangle, ravel, net, knot (43), dishevel, raddle.

(Adjectives) Crossing, intersecting, etc., crossed, intersected, matted, etc., crucial, cruciform.

Retiform, reticulate, areolar, areolate, cancellated, grated, barred, streaked, traceried.

(Adverbs) Across, thwart, athwart, transversely, crosswise.

3°. Centrical Dimensions

1. GENERAL

220 Exteriority *(Substantives),* externality, outness, outside, exterior, surface, superficies, superstratum, eccentricity, extremity, frontage.

Disk, face, facet, front (234), skin (222).

(Verbs) To be exterior, etc.

To place exteriorly, or outwardly, to turn out.

(Adjectives) Exterior, external, outer, outward, outlying, outdoor, outside, extramural, superficial, skin-deep, frontal, discoid, eccentric, extrinsic.

(Adverbs) Externally, etc., out, without, outwards, outdoors, abroad.

(Phrases) Out of doors; *extra muros; ab extra*; in the open air; *sub Jove; à la belle étoile*; al fresco.

———

221 Interiority *(Substantives),* inside, interior, hinterland, back-blocks, interspace, substratum, sub-soil.

Vitals, viscera, pith, marrow, heart, bosom, breast, entrails, bowels, belly, intestines, guts, innards, womb, lap, backbone, *penetralia*, inmost recesses, cave, cavern (191).

(Verbs) To be interior, internal, within, etc.

To place or keep within, to enclose, circumscribe (*see* 231, 232).

(Adjectives) Interior, internal, inner, inside, intramural, inward, inlying, inmost, innermost, deep-seated, intestine, intestinal, splanchnic, intercostal, inland, interstitial, subcutaneous, intrinsic.

Home, domestic, indoor.

(Adverbs) Internally, inwards, inwardly, within, inly, therein, *ab intra*, withinside, indoors, within doors, ben, at home, *chez soi*, up country.

222 Covering *(Substantives),* cover, roof, ceiling, slates, tiles, thatch, cowling, canopy, baldachin, awning, tarpaulin, tilt, tent (189), lid, hatch, operculum (263), shed.

Integument, skin, tegument, pellicle, fleece, cuticle, scarf-skin, epidermis, hide, pelt, peel, crust, bark, rind, cortex, husk, scale, shell, carapace, capsule, coat, tunic, tunicle, sheath, case, casing, calyx, theca,

223 Centrality *(Substantives),* centre (68), middle, focus, epicentre, hub, core, kernel, marrow, pith, nucleus, nucleolus, heart, pole, axis, bull's-eye, nave, navel, umbilicus, omphalos; concentration, centralization.

(Verbs) To be central, etc.

To render central, centralize, concentrate.

To bring to a focus.

(Adjectives) Central, centrical,

sheathing, scabbard, wrapping, wrapper, envelope, tarpaulin, cloth, table-cloth, blanket, rug, quilt, eider-down, coverlet, (or coverlid), counter-pane, carpet, drugget, oilcloth, wax-cloth, linoleum.

Superposition, coating, facing, veneer, paint, enamel, varnish, anoint-ing, inunction, incrustation, plaster, stucco, wash, parget, patina.

(Verbs) To cover, superpose, super-impose, overspread, over-canopy, wrap, lap, overlap, face, case, encase, veneer, pave, upholster.

To coat, paint, enamel, varnish, pave, plaster, beplaster, daub, be-daub, encrust, stucco, dab, smear, besmear, anoint, spray, do over, gild, japan, lacquer (or lacker), plate, electroplate, parget.

(Phrase) To lay it on thick.

(Adjectives) Covering, etc., cutaneous, dermal, cortical, cuticular, tegu-mentary, skinny, scaly, squamous, imbricated, epidermal, loricated, armour-plated, iron-clad.

middle, middlemost, midmost, me-dian, azygous, axial, focal, umbilical, concentric.

(Adverbs) Midway, centrally, etc.

224 Lining *(Substantives)*, coating, facing, internal, incrustation, puddle, stalactite, stalagmite, wainscot, dado, wall.

Filling, stuffing, wadding, padding.

(Phrases) To line, encrust, stuff, pad, wad, face, puddle, bush.

(Adjectives) Lined, encrusted, etc.

---

225 Investment *(Substantives)*, dress, clothing, raiment, drapery, costume, attire, toilet, trim, rig, rigout, fig, habiliment, vesture, apparel, underwear, full dress, evening dress, soup-and-fish, glad rags, dinner-jacket, tuxedo, fancy dress, accoutrement, outfit, wardrobe, trousseau, uniform, regimentals, battle-dress, kit, equip-ment, livery, gear, harness, turn-out, caparison, suit, dress suit, lounge suit, bathing suit, swim-suit, tweeds, flannels, rigging, trappings, slops, traps, duds, togs, clobber, frippery, bloomers, haberdashery, housing.

Dishabille, morning dress, dressing-gown, undress, mufti, civvies, rags, *négligé*, tea-gown.

Clothes, garment, garb, garniture, vestment, pontificals, robe, tunic, caftan, paletot, habit, gown, coat, dress-coat, claw-hammer, frock, stole, blouse, shirt-waist, toga, haik, smock-frock, kimono, bikini.

Cloak, opera-cloak, cape, mantle, mantlet, dolman, shawl, wrap, wrapper, veil, fichu, yashmak, tippet, kirtle, plaid, mantilla, tabard, burn-ous, overcoat, great-coat, British

226 Divestment *(Substantives)*, nudity, bareness, nakedness, baldness, undress, dishabille, threadbareness.

Denuding, denudation, stripping, uncovering, decortication, peeling, flaying, excoriation, desquamation, moulting, exfoliation.

(Verbs) To divest, uncover, denude, bare, strip, unclothe, undress, unrobe, disrobe, disapparel, debag, disarray, take off, doff, cast off, peel, pare, decor-ticate, husk, uncoif, unbonnet, excoriate, skin, flay, expose, exfoliate, lay open, dismantle, unroof, uncase, unsheathe, moult, mew.

(Adjectives) Bare, naked, nude, stripped, denuded, undressed, un-clothed, unclad, undraped, uncovered, unshod, barefoot, bareheaded, un-bonneted, exposed, in dishabille, in buff, bald, threadbare, ragged, callow, roofless.

(Phrases) In a state of nature; stark-naked; *in puris naturalibus*; stripped to the buff; in one's birthday suit; bald as a coot; as bare as the back of one's hand; out at elbows.

---

warm, duffle coat, surtout, spencer, rain-coat, ulster, mackintosh, waterproof, oilskin, slicker, burberry, poncho, surplice, alb, cassock, pallium, etc., mask, domino, cardinal, pelerine.

Jacket, vest, under-vest, semmit, singlet, jerkin, lumberjacket, waistcoat, cardigan, sweater, jersey, pullover, slipover, jumper, windbreaker, windcheater, doublet, gaberdine, camisole, combinations, stays, corset, bodice, under-bodice, brassière, bra, corsage, cestus, petticoat, kilt, filibeg (or philibeg), stomacher, skirt, kirtle, crinoline, farthingale, underskirt, slip, apron, pinafore.

Trousers, trews, breeches, galligaskins, knickerbockers, plus-fours, knickers, drawers, scanties, pantaloons, pants, overalls, dungarees, boiler suit, rompers, unmentionables, inexpressibles, smalls, tights, bags, breeks, slacks, shorts, jeans, briefs.

Cap, hat, top-hat, silk hat, tile, bowler, panama, slouch-hat, trilby, Stetson, titfer, deerstalker, billycock, wide-awake, sou'wester, beaver, castor, bonnet, forage-cap, tam-o'-shanter, tammy, balmoral, glengarry, toque, sun-bonnet, hood, head-gear, head-dress, kerchief, scarf, muffler, comforter, boa, snood, coiffure, coif, skull-cap, calotte, biretta, cowl, chaplet, capote, calash, pelt, wig, peruke, periwig, toupee, transformation, chignon, turban, puggaree, fez, helmet, topi, shako, busby, képi, casque, beret.

Shirt, smock, shift, chemise, chemisette, nightshirt, nightgown, nightdress, pyjamas, bed-jacket, bed-gown, collar, cravat, neck-cloth, neck-tie, stock, handkerchief.

Shoe, pump, high-low, Oxford shoe, sabot, brogue, sand-shoe, plimsoll, rubbers, sneakers, boot, jack-boot, top-boot, Wellington, gumboot, slipper, mule, galosh, overshoe, legging, puttee, buskin, greaves, mocassin, gaiter, spatterdash, spat, stocking, sock, nylons, hose, sandal, clog, babouche.

Glove, gauntlet, mitten, sleeve, cuff, muff.

Outfitter, tailor, clothier, milliner, sempstress, costumier, hatter, hosier, shoemaker, cobbler.

(Verbs) To invest, cover, envelop, lap, involve, drape, enwrap, wrap up, lap up, sheathe, vest, clothe, array, enrobe, dress, dight, attire, apparel, accoutre, trick out, rig, fit out, fig out, caparison, adonize, dandify, titivate, don, put on, wear, have on, huddle on, slip on, roll up in, muffle, perk up, mantle, swathe, swaddle, equip, harness.

(Adjectives) Invested, clothed, arrayed, dight, etc., clad, shod, etc.; sartorial.

227 Circumjacence *(Substantives)*, circumambiency, encompassment, surroundings, environment, atmosphere, medium, setting, scene, outpost, skirt, outskirts, boulevards, suburbs, suburbia, rurbania, purlieus, precincts, faubourgs, environs, entourage, *banlieue*, green belt.

(Verbs) To lie around, surround, beset, set about, compass, encompass, environ, enclose, encircle, embrace, lap, gird, begird, engirdle, orb, enlace, skirt, twine round, hem in (231).

228 Interjacence *(Substantives)*, interlocation, intervention, insertion, interposition, interspersion, interpenetration, interdigitation, interpolation, interlineation, intercurrence, intrusion, obtrusion, insinuation, intercalation, insertion, intertwinement, interference, permeation, infiltration.

An intermedium, intermediary, a go-between, bodkin, intruder, interloper; interlude, episode; parenthesis, gag, flyleaf, *entresol* (68).

(Adjectives) Circumjacent, ambient, circumambient, surrounding, etc., circumfluent, circumferential, suburban, extramural, embosomed.

(Adverbs) Around, about, without, on every side, on all sides, right and left, all around, round about.

229 Outline *(Substantives)*, circumference, perimeter, periphery, ambit, circuit, lines, tournure, contour, profile, silhouette, sky-line.

Zone, belt, girth, band, baldric, zodiac, cordon, girdle, cingulum, clasp (247).

230 Edge *(Substantives)*, verge, brink, brow, brim, margin, marge, border, skirt, rim, side, mouth, jaws, lip, muzzle, door, porch, portal (260), kerb; shore, coast.

Frame, flounce, frill, ruffle, jabot, list, fringe, valance, edging, trimming, hem, selvedge, welt, furbelow.

(Verbs) to border, edge, skirt, coast, verge on.

(Adjectives) Border, marginal, coastal, skirting.

A partition, septum, panel, diaphragm, midriff, party-wall.

A half-way house, no-man's land.

(Verbs) To lie, come, or get between, intervene, intrude, butt in, slide in, permeate, put between, put in, interpose, interject, chip in, throw in, wedge in, thrust in, foist in, insert, intercalate, interpolate, parenthesize, interline, interleave, interlard, interdigitate, dovetail, sandwich, worm in, insinuate, obtrude (300), intersperse, infiltrate; to gag.

(Phrases) To put one's oar in; to stick one's nose into; to have a finger in the pie.

(Adjectives) Interjacent, intervening, etc., intermediary, intermediate, intercalary, interstitial, parenthetical, mediterranean.

(Adverbs) Between, betwixt, 'twixt, among, amongst, amid, amidst, midst, betwixt and between, sandwich-wise, parenthetically, between the lines, in the thick of.

———

231 Circumscription *(Substantives)*, limitation, enclosure, confinement, shutting up, circumvallation, entombment.

Imprisonment, incarceration (751).

(Verbs) To circumscribe, limit, delimit, localize, bound, confine, enclose, surround (227), compass about, impound, restrict, restrain (751), shut in, shut up, lock up, bottle up, dam, hem in, hedge in, wall in, rail in, fence, picket, pen, enfold, coop, corral, encage, cage, mew, entomb, bury, immure, encase, pack up, seal up, wrap up (225), etc.

(Adjectives) Circumscribed, etc., imprisoned, pent up (754), landlocked.

(Phrase) Not room to swing a cat.

232 Enclosure *(Substantives)*, envelope, case, box (191), pen, penfold, fold, sheep-fold, pound, paddock, enclave, *enceinte*, corral, ring fence, wall, hedge, hedgerow, espalier, exclosure, play-pen.

Barrier, bar, gate, gateway, door, barricade, cordon.

Dike (or dyke), ditch, fosse, moat.

Fence, pale, paling, balustrade, rail, railing, hurdle, palisade, battlement, rampart, embankment, breakwater, mole, groyne (717), circumvallation, contravallation.

233 Limit *(Substantives)*, boundary, bounds, confine, term, bourne, line of demarcation, termination, stint, frontier, border, precinct, marches, line of circumvallation, pillars of Hercules, Rubicon, turning-point, last word, *ne plus ultra*.

(Adjectives) Definite, conterminal, terminal, frontier.

(Phrases) To cross the Rubicon; thus far and no farther.

2. SPECIAL

234 Front *(Substantives)*, face, anteriority, fore-part, front rank, foreground, van, vanguard, advanced guard, outpost, proscenium, façade, frontage, foreword, preface, frontispiece (64).

Forehead, visage, physiognomy, phiz, countenance, mug, dial, puss, pan, beak, rostrum, bow, stem, prow.

Pioneer, avant-courier (64).

(In a medal) obverse; (in a coin) head.

(Verbs) To be in front, etc., to front, face, envisage, confront, bend forward, etc.

(Adjectives) Fore, anterior, front, frontal, facial.

(Adverbs) Before, in front, ahead, right ahead, in the van, foremost, vis-à-vis, in the foreground, face to face, before one's eyes.

---

236 Laterality *(Substantives)*, side, flank, quarter, hand, cheek, jowl, wing, profile, temple, loin, haunch, hip, broadside, lee-side, lee.

East, orient; West, occident.

(Verbs) To be on one side, etc., to flank, outflank, to sidle, skirt.

(Adjectives) Lateral, sidelong, collateral, sideling, bilateral, trilateral, quadrilateral, multilateral, many-sided, eastern, oriental, western, occidental, eastward, westward.

(Adverbs) Sideways, side by side (216), sidelong, abreast, abeam, alongside, aside, by the side of, to windward, to leeward.

(Phrases) Cheek by jowl; broadside on.

238 Dextrality *(Substantives)*, right, right hand, dexter, offside, starboard, recto.

(Adjectives) Dextral, right-handed; ambidextrous, ambidexter.

235 Rear *(Substantives)*, back, posteriority, the rear rank, rearguard, the background, heels, tail, scut, rump, croup, crupper, breech, backside, posterior, fanny, catastrophe, buttocks, haunches, hunkers, hurdies, hind quarters, *dorsum*, dorsal region, stern, poop, after-part, tailpiece, wake.

(In a medal) reverse; (in a coin) tail.

(Verbs) To be in the rear, behind, etc., to fall astern, to bend backwards, to back on.

(Phrases) Turn the back upon; bring up the rear.

(Adjectives) Back, rear, postern, hind, hinder, hindmost, sternmost, posterior, dorsal, after.

(Adverbs) Behind, in the rear, aft, abaft, astern, aback, rearward.

(Phrases) In the background; behind one's back; at the heels of; at the tail of; at the back of; back to back.

237 Antiposition *(Substantives)*, opposite side, contraposition, reverse, inverse, antipodes, opposition, inversion (218).

Polarity, opposite poles, North and South.

(Verbs) To be opposite, etc., subtend.

(Adjectives) Opposite, reverse, inverse, antipodal, subcontrary.

Fronting, facing, diametrically opposite, vis-à-vis.

Northern, boreal, septentrional, arctic; southern, austral, antarctic.

(Adverbs) Over, over the way, over against, facing, against, fronting (234), face to face, vis-à-vis.

239 Sinistrality *(Substantives)*, left, left hand, sinister, near side, port, larboard, verso.

(Adjectives) Sinistral, left-handed.

SECTION III—FORM

1°. General Form

240 Form *(Substantives)*, figure, shape, configuration, make, formation, frame, construction, conformation, cut, set, trim, build, make, stamp, cast, mould, fashion, structure.

Feature, lineament, phase (448), turn, attitude, posture, pose.

Morphology, isomorphism.

Formation, figuration, efformation, sculpture.

(Phrase) The cut of one's jib.

(Verbs) To form, shape, figure, fashion, carve, cut, chisel, chase, emboss, hew, rough-hew, cast, roughcast, hammer out, block out, trim, work, lick into shape, knock together, mould, sculpture, sculp, grave, stamp.

(Adjectives) Formed, graven, etc., receiving form, plastic, fictile.

Giving form, formative, plastic, plasmatic, plasmic.

241 Absence of form.

Amorphism *(Substantives)*, amorphousness, formlessness, shapelessness, disfigurement, defacement, mutilation (846).

Vandalism, vandal, Goth.

(Verbs) To destroy form, deform, deface, disfigure, disfeature (846), mutilate.

(Adjectives) Shapeless, amorphous, formless, unhewn, rough, rude, Gothic, unfashioned, unshapen, misshapen, inchoate.

---

242 Regularity of form.

Symmetry *(Substantives)*, shapeliness, eurhythmy, uniformity, finish, beauty (845), proportion, balance.

(Adjectives) Symmetrical, regular, shapely, eurhythmic, well-set, uniform, finished, well-proportioned, balanced, chaste, classic.

(Phrase) Teres atque rotundus.

---

243 Irregularity of form.

Distortion *(Substantives)*, twist, kink, wryness, asymmetry, gibbosity, contortion, malformation, ugliness, etc. (846), teratology.

(Verbs) To distort, twist, wrest, writhe, wring, contort, kink, buckle.

(Adjectives) Irregular, unsymmetrical, asymmetrical, distorted, twisted, wry, awry, askew, crooked, on one side, misshapen, deformed, ill-proportioned, ill-made, round-shouldered, pigeon-chested, humpbacked, hunchbacked, gibbous, gibbose; knock-kneed, bandy-legged, bow-legged, club-footed, splay-footed.

(Phrases) All manner of ways; all over the place.

2°. Special Form

244 Angularity *(Substantives)*, angulation, angle, cusp, bend, elbow, knee, knuckle, groin, crinkle-crankle, kink, crotch, crutch, crane, fluke, scythe, sickle, zigzag, anfractuosity, refraction; fold (258), corner (182).

Fork, bifurcation, dichotomy.

Right angle (212), salient angle, re-entrant angle, acute angle, obtuse angle.

A polygon, square, rectangle, pentagon, hexagon, heptagon, octagon, nonagon, decagon, lozenge, diamond, rhomb, rhombus, rhomboid, parallelogram, gore, gusset, wedge.

Cube, parallelepiped, pyramid, prism, rhombohedron, tetrahedron, pentahedron, hexahedron, octahedron, dodecahedron, icosahedron.

T-square, set-square, protractor, goniometer, theodolite, sextant, quadrant, clinometer.

(Verbs) To bend, refract, diffract, fork, bifurcate, angulate, crinkle, crankle, splay.

(Adjectives) Angular, triangular, quadrangular, rectangular, bent, crooked, hooked, aduncous, aquiline, jagged, serrated, falciform, falcated, furcated, forked, bifurcate, zigzag; dovetailed, knock-kneed, crinkled, akimbo, geniculated, polygonal, trigonal, pentagonal, etc., fusiform, sagittate, arrow-headed, wedge-shaped, cuneate, cuneiform, splayed, angulate, cubical, pyramidal, rhombohedral, tetrahedral, etc.

245 Curvature *(Substantives)*, curvation, incurvity, incurvation, bend, flexure, flexion, hook, crook, camber, bending, deflexion, inflexion, arcuation, diffraction, turn, deviation, detour, sweep, sinuosity, curl, curling, winding, recurvature, recurvation, refraction, flexibility (324).

A curve, arc, circle, ellipse (247), parabola, hyperbola, catenary, festoon, arch, arcade, vault, bow, crescent, half-moon, lunette, horseshoe, loop, bight, crane-neck, conchoid, ogee.

(Verbs) To be curved, etc., to bend, curve, etc., decline, turn, trend, deviate, re-enter, sweep.

To render curved; to bend, curve, incurvate, camber, deflect, inflect, crook, hook, turn, round, arch, arcurate, bow, curl, recurve, loop, frizzle.

(Adjectives) Curved, vent, etc., curvilinear, curviform, recurved, recurvous, circular, oval (247), parabolic, hyperbolic, bowed, crooked, bandy, arched, vaulted, arcuated, camerated, hooked, falcated, falciform, crescent-shaped, semilunar, semicircular, conchoidal, lunular, lunulate, cordiform, heart-shaped, reniform, pear-shaped; bow-legged, bandy-legged, knock-kneed, devious.

246 Straightness *(Substantives)*, rectilinearity, directness.

A straight line, a right line, a direct line; inflexibility (323).

(Verbs) To be straight, etc.

To render straight, to straighten, rectify, set or put straight, take the curl out of, unbend, unfold, uncurl, uncoil, unroll, unwind, unravel, untwist, unwreathe, unwrap.

(Adjectives) Straight, rectilinear (or rectilineal), direct, even, right, in a line; unbent; not inclining, not bending, not turning, not deviating to either side, undeviating, unturned, undistorted, unswerving.

(Phrases) Straight as an arrow; as the crow flies; in a bee line.

247 Simple circularity.

Circularity *(Substantives)*, roundness, rotundity (249).

A circle, circlet, ring, areola, hoop, roundlet, *annulus*, annulet, bracelet, bangle, armlet, anklet, ringlet, eye, loop, wheel, cycle, orb, orbit, rundle, zone, belt, cordon, band, sash, girdle, cestus, cincture, baldric, bandolier, fillet, cummerbund, fascia, wreath, garland, crown, corona, coronal, coronet, chaplet, necklace, rivière; noose, lasso.

An ellipse, oval, ovule, ellipsoid,

248 Complex circularity.

Convolution *(Substantives)*, winding, wave, undulation, circuit, tortuosity, anfractuosity, sinuosity, involution, sinuation, circumvolution, meander, circumbendibus, twist, twirl, squiggle, curl, curlicue, curlie-wurlie, tirlie-whirlie, crimp, frizz, frizzle, permanent wave, perm, windings and turnings, *ambages*, inosculation, peristalsis.

A coil, reel, roll, spiral, helix, corkscrew, worm, volute, scroll, cartouche, rundle, scallop (or scollop), escallop.

cycloid, epicycloid, epicycle, semi-circle, quadrant, sextant, sector, segment.

(Verbs) To make round, round, circle, encircle, environ (227).

(Adjectives) Round, rounded, circular, annular, orbicular.

Oval, elliptical, elliptic, ovate, egg-shaped; cycloidal, etc., moniliform.

———

Serpent, eel, maze, labyrinth.

(Verbs) To be convoluted, etc.

To wind, twine, twist, coil, roll, turn and twist, weave, twirl, wave, undulate, meander, scallop, curl, crimp, frizz, frizzle, perm, inosculate, entwine (219), enlace, twist together, goffer.

(Adjectives) Convoluted, winding, twisting, contorted, waving, waved, wavy, curly, undulating, undulant, undulatory, undated, serpentine, anguilline, mazy, labyrinthine, Daedalian, tortuous, sinuous, flexuous, snaky, involved, sigmate, sigmoid, sigmoidal, vermiform, vermicular, peristaltic, meandrine; scalloped (or scolloped), wreathed, wreathy, crisped, crimped, frizzed, frizzy, frizzled, frizzly, ravelled, twisted, dishevelled (61).

Spiral, coiled, helical, turbinate.

(Adverb) In and out.

249 Rotundity *(Substantives)*, roundness, cylindricity; cylinder, barrel, drum, cylindroid, roll, roller, rouleau, column, rolling-pin, rundle.

Cone, conoid; pear-shape, bell-shape.

Sphericity, spheroidity, globosity; a sphere, globe, ball, spheroid, ellipsoid, drop, spherule, globule, vesicle, bulb, bullet, pellet, pill, clue, marble, pea, knob, pommel.

(Verbs) To form into a sphere, render spherical, to sphere, ensphere, to roll into a ball, round off, give rotundity, etc.

(Adjectives) Rotund, round, cylindric, cylindrical, cylindroid, columnar, lumbriciform; conic, conical, conoidal.

Spherical, spheral, spheroidal, globular, globated, globous, globose, ovoid, egg-shaped, gibbous, bulbiform, bulbous, bell-shaped, campaniliform, campaniform, campanulate, fungiform, bead-like, moniliform, pyriform, cigar-shaped.

(Phrases) Round as an apple, as a ball; *teres atque rotundus*.

3°. *Superficial Form*

250 Convexity *(Substantives)*, prominence, projection, swelling, gibbosity, bulge, protuberance, intumescence, tumour, cancer, tuberosity, tubercle, tooth, knob, excrescence, elbow, process, condyle, bulb, nob, nubble, node, nodule, nodosity, tongue, *dorsum*, hump, hunch, hunk, bunch, boss, embossment, bump, lump, clump, sugarloaf, point (253), bow, bagginess.

Pimple, wen, papula, pustule, carbuncle, corn, wart, polyp, boil, furuncle, fungus, fungosity, bleb, blister, blain, chilblain, bunion.

Papilla, nipple, teat, pap, breast,

251 Flatness *(Substantives)*, plane; horizontality (213), layer (204), smoothness (255); plate, platter, slab, table, tablet; level.

(Verbs) To render flat, flatten, smooth, level.

(Adjectives) Flat, plane, even, level, etc. (213), flush, scutiform, scutellate.

(Phrases) Flat as a pancake; flat as a flounder; flat as a board; flat as my hand; a dead flat; a dead level.

252 Concavity *(Substantives)*, depression, hollow, hollowness, indentation, intaglio, cavity, dent, dint, dimple, follicle, pit, sinus, alveolus,

dug, udder, mamilla, proboscis, nose, neb, beak, snout, nozzle, belly, paunch, corporation, kyte, back, shoulder, elbow, lip, flange.

Peg, button, stud, ridge, rib, jetty, snag, eaves, mole, cupola, dome, balcony.

Cameo, high and low relief, bas-relief, *basso rilievo, alto rilievo*; repoussé work.

Mount, hill (206); cape, promontory, foreland, headland, ness, mull, salient, point of land, hummock, spur, hog's back, offset.

(Verbs) To be prominent, etc., to project, bulge, belly, jut out, bristle up, to hang over, overhang, beetle, bend over, protrude, stand out, stick out, poke out, stick up, start up, cock up, shoot up, swell.

To render prominent; to raise (307), to emboss, chase, stud, bestud, ridge.

(Adjectives) Convex, prominent, projecting, bulging, etc., bold, bossed, bossy, knobby, nubbly, lumpy, bumpy, nodose, embossed, chased, gibbous, salient, mamilliform, in relief, bowed, arched, bellied, baggy, cornute, odontoid, tuberous, tuberculous, ridged, ridgy.

lacuna, honeycomb, excavation, trough (259).

Cup, basin, crater, etc. (191); socket, thimble.

Valley, vale, dale, dell, dingle, coombe, strath, bottom, corrie, glade, glen, cave, cell, cavern, cove, grotto, grot, alcove, gully (198), cul-de-sac.

(Verbs) To be depressed, etc., to cave in, subside, retire.

To depress, hollow, scoop, gouge, dig, delve, excavate, dent, dint, stave in, mine, undermine, burrow, tunnel.

(Adjectives) Depressed, concave, hollow, stove in, retiring, retreating, cavernous, honeycombed, alveolar, cellular, funnel-shaped, infundibular, bell-shaped, campaniliform, porous (260).

---

253 Sharpness *(Substantives)*, keenness, pointedness, acuteness, acuity, acumination, spinosity, prickliness.

A point, spike, spine, spicule, needle, bodkin, (262), aiguille, pin, prickle, prick, prong, tine, caltrop, *chevaux de frise*, arrow, spear, bayonet, pike, sword, dagger (727), spur, rowel, barb, spit, cusp, horn, antler, snag, tag, jag, thorn, brier, bramble, thistle, nib, tooth, tusk, denticle, spoke, cog, ratchet, comb, bristle, beard, awn, *arête*, crest, cone, peak, spire, pyramid, steeple, porcupine, hedgehog.

Cutlery, blade, edge-tool, knife, jack-knife, penknife, clasp-knife, bowie, jocteleg, chisel, razor, scalpel, bistoury, lancet, axe, hatchet, pole-axe, pick-axe, pick, mattock, spade, adze, coulter, ploughshare, scythe, sickle, reaping-hook, bill, billhook, cleaver, scissors, shears, sécateurs.

Sharpener, knife-sharpener, strop, hone, grinder, grindstone, whetstone, steel, emery, carborundum.

(Verbs) To be sharp, etc., to taper to a point, to bristle with.

To render sharp, etc., to sharpen, point, aculeate, set, whet, strop, hone, grind, barb, bristle up.

(Adjectives) Sharp, keen, pointed, conical, acute, acicular, aculeated, arrowy, needle-shaped, spiked, spiky, spicular, spiculate, mucronate, mucronated, ensiform, peaked, acuminated, salient, cusped, cuspidate, cuspidated, cornute, prickly, spiny, spinous, thorny, jagged, bristling,

254 Bluntness *(Substantives)*, obtuseness, dullness.

(Verbs) To be blunt, etc., to render blunt, etc., to obtund, dull, take off the point or edge, turn.

(Adjectives) Blunt, obtuse, dull, bluff.

---

muricate, pectinated, studded, thistly, briery, snaggy, digitated, barbed, spurred, two-edged, tapering, fusiform, dentiform, denticular, denticulated, toothed, odontoid, cutting, trenchant, sharp-edged.

Starlike, stellated, stelliform.

(Phrases) Sharp as a needle, as a razor.

255 Smoothness *(Substantives)*, evenness, level (213), polish, gloss, glossiness, sleekness, slipperiness, lubricity, lubrication (332), down, velvet, velveteen velour, silk, satin, plush, glass, ice, enamel, macadam.

Burnisher, calender, mangle, iron, file, plane, sandpaper, emery-paper, roller.

(Verbs) To smooth, smoothen, plane, polish, burnish, calender, mangle, enamel, glaze, iron, file, roll, lubricate, macadamize.

(Adjectives) Smooth, even, level, plane, sleek, slick, polished, glazed, glossy, sleeky, silken, silky, satiny, velvety, glabrous, slippery, oily, soft, unwrinkled.

(Phrases) Smooth as glass, as velvet, as satin, as soil; slippery as an eel.

256 Roughness *(Substantives)*, unevenness, asperity, rugosity, ruggedness, scabrousness, salebrosity, cragginess, craggedness, corrugation, nodosity, crispness, plumosity, villosity; grain, texture, nap, pile.

Arborescence, branching, ramification.

Brush, bur, beard, shag, whisker, dundreary, mutton-chop, sideboards, side-burns, down, goatee, imperial, moustache, feather, plume, crest, tuft, *panache*, byssus, hair, chevelure, toupee, wool, fur, mane, cilia, fringe, *fimbriae*, tress, moss, plush, velvet, velveteen, velour, stubble.

(Verbs) To be rough, etc.

To render rough, to roughen, crisp, crumple, corrugate, rumple.

(Adjectives) Rough, uneven, scabrous, gnarled, rugged, rugose, rugous, salebrous, unpolished, matt, frosted, rough-hewn, craggy, cragged, prickly, scrubby.

Arborescent, dendriform, arboriform, branching, ramose, ramulose, dendroid.

Feathery, plumose, plumous, plumigerous, tufted, fimbriated, hairy, ciliated, hirsute, flocculent, bushy, hispid, tomentous, downy, woolly, velvety, villous (or villose), bearded, pilous, shaggy, shagged, stubbly, fringed, befringed, setaceous, filamentous.

(Phrases) rough as a nutmeg-grater; like quills upon the fretful porcupine; against the grain.

257 Notch *(Substantives)*, dent, dint, nick, cut, indent, indentation, dimple.

Embrasure, battlement, machicolation, machicoulis, saw, tooth, sprocket, crenelle, scallop (or scollop).

(Verbs) To notch, nick, cut, dent, indent, dint, jag, scotch, slash, scallop (or scollop), crenelate.

(Adjectives) Notched, etc., jagged, crenate, crenated, crenelated, dented, dentated, denticulated, toothed, palmated, indented, serrated.

258 Fold *(Substantives)*, plication, plait, ply, crease, pleat, tuck, hem, flexion, flexure, joint, elbow, doubling, duplicature, gather, wrinkle, crow's-foot, rimple, crinkle, crankle, crumple, rumple, rivel, ruck, ruffle, ruche, dog's-ear, corrugation, flounce, frounce, lapel, pucker, crimp.

(Verbs) To fold, double, plicate, plait, crease, wrinkle, crinkle, crankle, curl, cockle up, cocker, rimple, frizz, frizzle, rumple, flounce, frounce, rivel,

twill, corrugate, ruffle, crimp, crumple, pucker, to turn down, turn under, tuck, ruck.

(Adjectives) Folded, dog's eared (or dog-eared), etc.

259 Furrow *(Substantives)*, groove, rut, slit, scratch, streak, stria, crack, score, rib.

Channel, gutter, trench, ditch, dike, moat, fosse, trough, kennel, chamfer, ravine (198), fluting.

(Verbs) To furrow, etc., flute, plough.

(Adjectives) Furrowed, etc., ribbed, striated, striate, sulcated, fluted, canaliculate, bisulcate, trisulcate, etc., corduroy, corded, corrugated.

260 Opening *(Substantives)*, hole, foramen, perforation, eye, eyelet, key-hole, loophole, porthole, scuttle, mouse-hole, pigeon-hole, eye of a needle, pinhole, peep-hole, puncture.

Aperture, hiatus, yawning, oscitancy, dehiscence, patefaction, slot, chink, crevice (198).

Window, light, fanlight, skylight, casement, lattice, embrasure.

Orifice, inlet, intake, outlet, mouth, throat, muzzle, gullet, weasand, nozzle, portal, porch, gate, lych-gate, wicket, postern, gateway, door, embouchure, doorway, exit, vomitory, hatch, hatchway, gangway, arcade.

Channel (350), passage, pass, tube, pipe, vessel, tubule, canal, thoroughfare, gut, fistula, ajutage, tap, faucet, chimney, flue, vent, funnel, gully, tunnel, main, adit, pit, shaft, gallery, alley, aisle, glade, vista, bore, mine, calibre, pore, follicle, porosity, porousness, lacuna.

Sieve, cullender, colander, strainer, tamis, riddle, screen, honeycomb.

261 Closure *(Substantives)*, occlusion, blockade, shutting up, filling up, plugging, sealing, obstruction, impassableness, blocking up, obstipation, constipation, blind alley, blind corner, cul-de-sac, impasse, caecum.

Imperforation, imperviousness, impermeability, imporosity.

(Verbs) To close, occlude, steek, plug, block up, fill up, blockade, obstruct, bar, stop, bung up, seal, clinch, plumb, cork up, shut up, choke, throttle, ram down, dam up, cram, stuff up.

(Adjectives) Closed, shut, unopened, occluded, etc., impervious, imperforate, caecal, impassable, invious, pathless, untrodden, unpierced, unventilated, impermeable, imporous, operculated, tight, watertight, air-tight, hermetic.

(Phrase) Hermetically sealed.

Apertion, perforation, piercing, boring, mining, terebration, drilling, etc., impalement, pertusion, puncture, acupuncture, penetration (302).

Opener, tin-opener, key, master-key.

(Verbs) to open, ope, gape, yawn.

To perforate, lay open, pierce, empierce, tap, bore, mine, drill, scoop out, canalize, tunnel, transpierce, transfix, enfilade, rake, impale, spike, spear, gore, stab, pink, stick, prick, lance, puncture, riddle, honeycomb, punch, jab; uncover, unrip, stave in.

(Phrase) To cut a passage through.

(Adjectives) Open, pierced, perforated, etc., perforate, wide open, ajar, unclosed, unstopped, patulous, gaping, yawning, patent.

Tubular, tubulous, tubulate, tubuliform, cannular, fistulous, fistular, fistulate, pervious, permeable, foraminous, porous, follicular, cribriform, honeycombed, infundibular, windowed, fenestrated.

(Phrase) Open sesame!

262 Perforator *(Substantives)*, borer, auger, gimlet, stylet, drill, wimble, awl, bradawl, brog, scoop, corkscrew, dibble, trepan, probe, bodkin, needle, stiletto, lancet, punch, spike, bit, brace and bit, gouge, fleam.

(Verbs) To spike, gouge, scoop, punch, lance.

---

263 Stopper *(Substantives)*, stopple, plug, cork, bung, spigot, spike, spile, vent-peg, stopcock, tap, stopgap, rammer, ramrod, piston, wad, dossil, wadding, tompion, stuffing, tourniquet.

Cover, lid, operculum, covering, coverlid, door, etc. (222), valve.

A janitor, door-keeper, commissionaire, chucker-out, ostiary, concierge, porter, warder, beadle, Cerberus.

SECTION IV—MOTION

1°. *Motion in General*

264 Motion *(Substantives)*, movement, transit, transition, move, going, etc., passage, course, stir.

Step, gait, stride, tread, port, footfall, carriage, transference (270), locomotion, travel (266), voyage (267).

Mobility, restlessness, unrest, movability, movableness, inquietude, flux; kinematics.

(Verbs) To be moving, etc., to move, go, stir, hie, gang, budge, pass, flit, shift, glide, roll, roll on, flow (347, 348), sweep along, wander (279), change or shift one's place or quarters, dodge, keep going.

To put in motion, impel, etc. (276); to propel, project (284); to mobilize, motorize.

(Adjectives) Moving, in motion, on the move, going, transitional; kinematic.

Shifting, movable (270), mobile, restless, nomadic, wandering, vagrant, discursive, erratic (279), mercurial, unquiet.

(Adverbs) In transitu, under way, on the move.

---

265 Quiescence *(Substantives)*, rest, stillness, stagnation, stagnancy, fixedness, immobility, catalepsy, paralysis.

Quiet, quietness, quietude, tranquillity, calm, calmness, sedentariness, peace; steadiness, balance, equilibrium.

Pause, suspension, suspense, lull, stop, stoppage, interruption, stopping, stand, standstill, standing still, lying to, repose (687), respite.

Lock, deadlock, dead stop, embargo.

Resting-place, anchorage, moorings, bivouac, port (189, 666), bed, pillow, etc. (215).

(Verbs) To be quiescent, etc., to remain, stand, stand still, lie to, pull up, hold, halt, stop, anchor, stop short, stop dead, freeze, heave to, rest, pause, repose, keep quiet, take breath, stagnate, vegetate, settle; to mark time.

To stay, tarry, sojourn, dwell (186), pitch one's tent, cast anchor, settle, encamp, bivouac, moor, tether, picket, plant oneself, alight, land, etc. (292) ride at anchor.

(Phrases) Not to stir a peg (or step or inch); *'j'y suis, j'y reste'*; to come to a standstill; to come to a deadlock; to rest on one's oars or laurels.

To stop, suspend, arrest, lay to, hold one's hand, interrupt, intermit, discontinue (142), put a stop to, quell, becalm.

(Phrases) To bring to a standstill; to lay an embargo on.

(Adjectives) Quiescent, still, motionless, moveless, at rest, stationary, untravelled, stay-at-home, at a stand, at a standstill, stock-still, standing still, sedentary, undisturbed, unruffled, fast, stuck fast, fixed, transfixed, rooted, moored, aground, at anchor, tethered, becalmed, stagnant, quiet, calm, breathless, peaceful, unmoved, unstirred, immovable, immobile, restful, cataleptic, paralysed, frozen, irremovable, stable, steady, steadfast.

(Phrases) Still as a statue; still as a post; quiet or still as a mouse.

(Interjections) Soho! stop! stay! avast! belay! halt! as you were! hold hard! hold your horses! hold on! whoa!

---

266 Locomotion by land.

Journey *(Substantives)*, travel, travelling, excursion, expedition, tour, trip, trek, circuit, peregrination, discursion, ramble, outing, pilgrimage, Odyssey, course, ambulation, march, route march, marching, walk, walking, promenade, stroll, saunter, dander, turn, trot, tramp, hike, stalk, noctambulation, perambulation, ride, equitation, drive, jogtrot, airing, constitutional, spin, jaunt, joy-ride, change of scene.

Roving, vagrancy, flit, flitting, migration, emigration, immigration, intermigration; *Wanderlust*.

Map, plan, itinerary, road-book, Guide, Baedeker, Bradshaw, A B C.

Procession, caravan, cavalcade, column, cortège.

Organs and instruments of locomotion, legs, feet, pins, stilt, skate, ski, snow-shoe, locomotive, vehicle (272, 273), velocipede, penny-farthing, bone-shaker, bicycle, cycle, bike, push cycle, tandem, tricycle, fairy-cycle, scooter.

(Phrase) Shanks's mare.

(Verbs) To travel, journey, trek, walk, ramble, roam, rove, course, wander, itinerate, perambulate, stroll, straggle, expatiate, range, gad about, gallivant, knock about, to go or take a walk, journey, tour, turn, trip, etc.; to prowl, stray, saunter, tour, make a tour, knock about, emigrate, flit, migrate.

To walk, march, counter-march, step, tread, pace, wend, wend one's way, promenade, perambulate, circumambulate, take a walk, go for a walk, take the air, trudge, trapes, stalk, stride, straddle, strut, foot it, hoof it, stump, clump, plod, peg along, bundle, toddle, patter, shuffle on,

267 Locomotion by water, or air, or through space.

Navigation *(Substantives)*, voyage, sail, cruise, Odyssey, circumnavigation, periplus, seafaring, yachting, boating; drifting, headway, sternway, leeway.

Natation, swimming, surf-riding.

Flight, flying, flip, volitation, aerostation, aeronautics, aerostatics, ballooning, aviation, gliding.

Space travel, astronautics.

Wing, pinion, fin, flipper; oar, scull, canvas, sail, rotor, paddle, punt-pole, paddle-wheel, screw, turbine, jet.

(Verbs) To sail, make sail, warp, put to sea, navigate, take ship, get under way, spread sail, spread canvas, carry sail, plough the waves, plough the deep, scud, boom, drift, course, cruise, coast, circumnavigate, aviate.

To row, pull, paddle, scull, punt, steam.

To swim, float, buffet the waves, skim, *effleurer,* dive, wade.

To fly, aviate, hedge-hop, be wafted, hover, soar, glide, wing; to flush.

(Phrases) To take wing; to take flight.

(Adjectives) Sailing, etc., seafaring, under way, under sail, on the wing, volant, nautical; airborne, aeronautic, aeronautical, aerostatic; astronautical.

(Phrases) In sail; under canvas.

---

tramp, hike, footslog, traverse, bend one's steps, thread one's way, make one's way, find one's way, tread a path, take a course, take wing, take flight, defile, file off.

Ride, jog on, trot, amble, canter, gallop, take horse, prance, frisk, tittup, caracole, have a run, ride and tie, hitch-hike, lorry-hop.

To drive, slide, glide, skim, skate, toboggan, ski.

To go to, repair to, resort to, hie to.

(Phrase) To pad the hoof; to hump bluey.

(Adjectives) Travelling, etc., ambulatory, itinerant, wayfaring, peripatetic, discursive, vagrant, migratory, nomadic, on the wing, etc., circumforanean, overland.

(Adverbs) By the way, *chemin faisant,* on the road, *en passant, en route,* on foot, afoot.

268 Traveller *(Substantives),* wayfarer, voyager, itinerant, passenger, commuter, tourist, tripper, excursionist, wanderer, rover, straggler, rambler, hiker, bird of passage, gad-about, globe-trotter, vagrant, tramp, hobo, bum, swagman, sundowner, vagabond, rolling-stone, nomad, pilgrim, hadji, palmer, runner, courier, pedestrian, peripatetic, emigrant, fugitive.

Rider, horseman, equestrian, cavalier, jockey, postilion, rough-rider, scout, motorist.

Mercury, Iris, Ariel.

269 Mariner *(Substantives),* navigator, seaman, sailor, seafarer, shipman, tar, old salt, bluejacket, marine, jolly, boatman, *voyageur,* ferryman, waterman, lighterman, bargee, gondolier, longshoreman, crew, oarsman.

An aerial navigator, aeronaut, balloonist, aviator, airman, flying man, pilot.

Astronaut, cosmonaut, spaceman.

---

270 Tranference *(Substantives),* transfer, displacement, metathesis, transposition (148), remotion, removal (185), relegation, deportation, extradition, conveyance, draft, carriage, carrying, convection, conduction, export, import.

Transmission, passage, transit, transition, ferry, transport, gestation, portage, porterage, cartage, carting, shovelling, shipment, transhipment, air lift, air drop, freight, wafture, transportation, transumption, transplantation, transfusion, translation, shifting, dodging, dispersion (73), traction (285).

(Verbs) To transfer, convey, transmit, transport, transplant, transfuse, carry, bear, carry over, hand over, pass forward, remove (185), transpose (148), shift, export, import, convey, conduct, convoy, send, relegate, extradite, turn over to, deliver, waft, ship, tranship, ferry over.

To bring, fetch, reach, draft.

To load, lade, charge, unload, shovel, ladle, decant, empty, break bulk.

(Adjectives) Transferred, etc., movable, portable, portative.

(Adverbs) From hand to hand, on the way, *en route, en passant, in transitu,* from pillar to post.

271 Carrier *(Substantives),* porter, bearer, coolie, *hammal,* conveyor, transport-worker, stevedore (690), conductor, locomotive (285).

Beast of burden, cattle, horse, blood-horse, arab, steed, nag, palfrey, galloway, charger, destrier, war-horse, courser, racer, racehorse, hunter, pony, filly, colt, foal, barb, jade, hack, *bidet,* pad, cob, tit, punch, roadster, goer, pack-horse, draught horse, cart-horse, post-horse, shelty, jennet, bayard, mare, stallion, gelding, gee-gee, gee, stud.

Ass, donkey, moke, cuddy, jackass, mule, hinny, sumpter-mule.

Camel, dromedary, llama, zebra, reindeer, yak, elephant, carrier-pigeon.

272 Vehicle (*Substantives*), conveyance.

Carriage, caravan, van, furniture van, pantechnicon, wagon, stage-wagon, wain, dray, cart, float, trolley, sledge, sleigh, bob-sleigh, *luge*, toboggan, truck, tumbril, pontoon, barrow, wheelbarrow, hand-barrow, lorry.

Train, railway train, goods train, freight train, rolling stock, Pullman car, parlour car, restaurant-car, dining-car, diner, buffet-car, sleeping-car, sleeper, horse-box, cattle-truck, rail-car, tender.

Equipage, turn-out, carriage, coach, chariot, chaise, post-chaise, phaeton, curricle, tilbury, whisky, victoria, landau, brougham, clarence, gig, calash, dog-cart, governess-cart, trap, buggy, carriole, jingle, wagonette, jaunting-car, shandrydan, droshky, kibitka, berlin, stage, stage-coach, diligence, car, omnibus, bus, charabanc, brake, cabriolet, cab, hackney cab, four-wheeler, growler, fly, hansom.

Motor-car, motor, automobile, autocar, touring-car, tourer, sports car, torpedo, landaulette, limousine, saloon, sedan, two-seater, runabout, coupé, jalopy, tricar, motor-cycle, side-car, autocycle, moped, corgi, motor-bus, motor-coach, autobus, taxi-cab, taxi, motor-van, jeep; trolley-bus, tram-car, tram, street-car.

Tank, armoured car, half-track, amtrac, duck.

Bath-chair, wheel-chair, sedan chair, palanquin (or palankeen), litter, jinricksha (or rickshaw), brancard, stretcher, perambulator, pram, mail-cart, bassinette, baby-carriage.

Shovel, spoon, spatula, ladle, hod.

273 Ship (*Substantives*), vessel, bottom, craft, shipping, marine, fleet, flotilla, squadron, three-master, barque (or bark), barquentine, brig, brigantine, schooner, sloop, cutter, skiff, yawl, ketch, smack, dogger,

hoy, lugger, barge, wherry, lighter, hulk, buss, packet, clipper, rotor ship.

Navy, armada, warship, man-of-war, ironclad, capital ship, super-dreadnought, dreadnought, battle-ship, battle-cruiser, cruiser, frigate, corvette, gunboat, aircraft-carrier, monitor, torpedo boat destroyer, destroyer, torpedo boat, mine-sweeper, mine-layer, submarine, Q-boat, troop-ship, trooper, transport, hospital ship, flagship; ship of the line, first-rate, seventy-four, fireship.

Liner, merchantman, tramp, slaver, steamer, steamboat, steam-packet, paddle-steamer, stern-wheeler, screw-steamer, turbine, tender, tug, collier, whaler, coaster, tanker.

Argosy, bireme, trireme, quadrireme, quinquereme, galley, galleon, carrack, caravel, galliot, polacca, tartan, junk, praam, saic, dhow, proa, sampan, xebec.

Boat, motor-boat, long-boat, pinnace, launch, cabin cruiser, yacht, shallop, jolly-boat, gig, funny, dinghy, bumboat, fly-boat, wherry, coble, cock-boat, punt, cog, kedge, outrigger, catamaran, fishing-boat, coracle, hooker, life-boat, gondola, felucca, dahebeeyah, caique, canoe, dug-out, raft, float.

(*Adverbs*) Afloat, aboard.

273A Aircraft (*Substantives*), flying machine, aeroplane, monoplane, biplane, seaplane, hydroplane, plane, flying boat, amphibian, air-liner, flying wing, stratocruiser, stratoliner, sky-master, jet aircraft, jet, turbo-jet, autogiro, helicopter, hoverplane, whirlybird, planicopter, glider; fighter, bomber, fighter-bomber, flying fortress, super-fortress.

Balloon, air-balloon, aerostat, Montgolfier, pilot balloon, blimp, kite, airship, dirigible, Zeppelin.

Space ship, rocket, sputnik, lunik, satellite.

(*Adjective*) Airborne; orbital.

2°. *Degrees of Motion*

274 Velocity *(Substantives)*, speed, celerity, swiftness, rapidity, fleetness, expedition, speediness, quickness, nimbleness, briskness, agility, promptness, promptitude (682), dispatch, acceleration (684).

Gallop, full gallop, canter, trot, run, rush, scamper, scoot, scorch, hand-gallop, lope; flight, dart, bolt, dash, spurt, sprint.

Haste, hurry, scurry, bounce, bolt, precipitation, precipitancy (684), forced march, race, steeplechase, Marathon race.

Rate, pace, step, gait, course, progress.

Lightning, light, cannon-ball, bullet, wind, rocket, arrow, dart, quicksilver, telegraph, express train, clipper.

An eagle, antelope, doe, courser, racehorse, racer, gazelle, greyhound, hare, squirrel, bandersnatch.

Mercury, Ariel, Camilla.

Speed indicator, speedometer, tachometer, log, log-line.

(Verbs) To move quickly; to trip, speed, haste, hie, hasten, hurry, fly, press, press on, press forward, post, push on, whip, scamper, run, sprint, race, scud, scour, scurry, scuttle, spin, scoot, scorch, rip, clip, shoot, tear, whisk, sweep, skim, brush, glance, cut along, dash on, dash forward, trot, gallop, lope, rush, bound, bounce, flounce, frisk, tittup, bolt, flit, spring, boom, dart.

To hasten, accelerate, expedite, dispatch, urge, whip, forward, buck up, express, speed-up, hurry, precipitate, quicken pace, gather way, ride hard.

To keep up with, keep pace with, race, race with, outpace, outmarch, distance, outdistance, lap, leave behind, outrun, outstrip, gain ground.

(Phrases) To cover the ground; to clap on sail; take to one's heels; clap spurs to one's horse; to run like mad; ride hard; outstrip the wind; to make rapid strides; wing one's way; be off like a shot; run a race; stir one's stumps; do a scoot; get a move on; get cracking; step on it; give her the gun; let it rip.

275 Slowness *(Substantives)*, tardiness, dilatoriness, slackness, lentor, languor (683), drawl.

Hobbling, creeping, lounging, etc., shambling, claudication, halting, walk, amble, jog-trot, dog-trot, mincing steps, foot-pace, crawl.

A slow-goer, dawdle, dawdler, lingerer, slow-coach, lame duck, drone, tortoise, snail, slug, sluggard, slacker.

Retardation, slackening, slowing down, delay (133).

(Verbs) To move slowly, to creep, crawl, lag, slug, drawl, dawdle, linger, loiter (683), plod, trudge, flag, saunter, lounge, lumber, trail, drag, grovel, glide, laze, amble, steal along, inch along, jog on, rub on, bundle on, toddle, waddle, shuffle, halt, hobble, limp, claudicate, shamble, mince, falter, totter, stagger.

To retard, slacken, relax, check, rein in, curb, strike sail, reef, slow up, slow down.

(Phrases) To 'drag its slow length along'; to hang fire; to march in slow time, in funeral procession; to lose ground.

To put on the drag; apply the brake; clip the wings; take in sail; take one's time; ca' canny; *festina lente*.

(Adjectives) Slow, slack, tardy, dilatory, easy, gentle, leisurely, deliberate, lazy, languid, drowsy, sleepy, heavy, drawling, leaden, sluggish, snail-like, creeping, crawling, etc., dawdling, lumbering, hobbling, tardigrade.

(Adverbs) Slowly, etc., gingerly, softly, leisurely, deliberately, gradually, etc. (144), *piano, adagio, largo*.

(Phrases) In slow motion; just ticking over; under easy sail; at a snail's pace; with mincing steps; with clipped wings; by degrees; little by little; inch by inch.

(Adjectives) Fast, speedy, swift, rapid, full-drive, quick, double-quick, fleet, nimble, agile, expeditious, prompt, brisk, frisky, hasty, hurried, flying, etc., precipitate, furious, light-footed, winged, eagle-winged, mercurial, electric, telegraphic, light-legged; accelerative.

(Phrases) Swift as an arrow; as a doe, as a lamplighter; off like a shot; quick as lightning; quick as thought.

(Adverbs) Swiftly, with speed, speedily, trippingly, etc., full-tilt, full speed, apace, post-haste, *presto*, tantivy, by express, by telegraph, slap, slap-dash, headlong, hurry-scurry, hand over hand, at a round trot.

(Phrases) Under press of sail, or canvas; *velis et remis*; on eagle's wings; at the double, in double-quick time; with giant, or gigantic steps; *à pas de géant*; in seven-league boots; whip and spur; *ventre à terre*; as fast as one's legs or heels will carry one; *sauve qui peut*; the devil take the hindmost; *vires acquirit eundo;* with rapid strides; at top speed; in top gear; flat out; all out; like greased lightning; like the wind.

3°. *Motion conjoined with Force*

276 Impulse *(Substantives)*, momentum, impetus, push, impulsion, thrust, shove, fling, jog, jolt, brunt, throw, volley, explosion (173), propulsion (284).

Percussion, collision, concussion, impact, clash, encounter, cannon, carom, carambole, appulse, shock, crash, bump, charge, tackle (716), foul.

Blow, stroke, knock, tap, fillip, pat, rap, dab, dig, jab, smack, slap, hit, putt, cuff, bang, crack, whack, thwack, slog, belt, wipe, clout, swipe, clip, squash, dowse, punch, thump, pelt, kick, lunge, buffet, beating (972).

277 Recoil *(Substantives)*, retroaction, revulsion, reaction, rebound, bounce, stot, repercussion, ricochet, rebuff, reverberation, reflux, reflex, kick, springing back, ducks and drakes.

A boomerang, spring (325).

(Verbs) To recoil, react, spring back, fly back, bound back, rebound, stot, reverberate, repercuss.

(Adjectives) Recoiling, etc., on the recoil, etc., refluent, repercussive, reactionary, retroactive.

(Phrase) On the rebound.

Hammer, mallet, mall, maul, beetle, flail, cudgel, bludgeon, life-preserver, cosh, baton, truncheon, knobkerrie, shillelagh, staff, lathi, cane, stick, club, racket, bat, driver, brassy, baffy, spoon, putter, cleek, iron, mashie, niblick, ram, battering-ram, monkey-engine, catapult, pile-driver, rammer, sledgehammer, steam hammer.

Dynamics; seismometer.

(Verbs) To impel, push, give impetus, etc., drive, urge, hurtle, boom, thrust, elbow, shoulder, charge, tackle, jostle, justle, hustle, shove, jog, jolt, encounter, collide, clash, cannon, foul.

To strike, knock, tap, slap, dab, pat, slam, hit, bat, putt, rap, prod, jerk, dig, cuff, smite, butt, impinge, thump, bethump, beat, bang, whang, biff, punch, thwack, whack, spank, skelp, swat, lay into, shin, slog, clout, wipe, swipe, batter, dowse, baste, pummel, pelt, patter, drub, buffet, belabour, cane, whip (972), poke at, hoof, jab, pink, lunge, kick, recalcitrate.

To throw, etc. (284), to set going, mobilize.

(Adjectives) Impelling, etc., impulsive, impellent, impelled, etc., dynamic, dynamical.

(Interjections) Bang! boom! wham!

4°. *Motion with reference to Direction*

278 Direction *(Substantives)*, bearing, course, route, bent, inclination, drift, tenor, tendency, incidence, set, leaning, bending, trend, dip, steerage, tack, steering, aim, alignment (or alinement), orientation, collimation.

A line, bee-line, path, road, aim, range, quarter, point of the compass, rhumb, great circle, azimuth, line of collimation.

(Verbs) To tend towards, go to, point to, or at; trend, verge, align (or aline), incline, conduct to, determine.

To make for, or towards, aim at, take aim, level at, steer for, keep or hold a course, be bound for, bend one's steps towards, direct or shape one's course.

To ascertain one's direction, orient (or orientate) oneself, to see which way the wind blows.

(Adjectives) Directed, etc., direct, straight, undeviating, unswerving, aligned (or alined) with, determinate, point-to-point.

(Adverbs) Towards, to, *versus*, thither, directly, point-blank, full tilt at, whither, in a line with, as the crow flies.

By way of, via, in all directions, *quaquaversum*, in all manner of ways, to the four winds.

---

280 Going before.

Precession *(Substantives)*, leading, heading.

Precedence in order (62), priority (116), precursor (64), front (234).

(Verbs) To precede, forerun, lead, head, herald, introduce, usher in (62), go ahead.

(Phrases) Go in the van; take the lead; lead the way; open the ball; have the start; to get before; steal a march.

(Adjectives) Preceding, leading, etc.

(Adverbs) In advance, before (62), in the van, ahead.

279 Deviation *(Substantives)*, swerving, aberration, obliquation, *ambages*, warp, bending, flexion, deflection, refraction, sidling, side-slip, skid, half-roll, barrel-roll, loop, straying, straggling, warping, etc., digression, circuit, detour, departure from, divergence (291), desultory motion; slice, pull, hook, leg-break, off-break, googly.

Motion sideways, side-step.

(Verbs) To alter one's course, divert, deviate, depart from, turn, bend, swerve, break, switch, skid, side-slip, zoom, bank, loop, bunt, jib, shift, warp, stray, straggle, sidle, diverge (291), digress, wander, meander, veer, wear, tack, yaw, turn aside, turn a corner, turn away from, face about, wheel, wheel about, steer clear of, ramble, rove, go astray, step aside, shunt, side-track, jay walk.

(Phrases) To fly off at a tangent; to face to the right-about; to go out of one's way; to lose one's way.

(Adjectives) Deviating, etc., aberrant, discursive, devious, desultory, erratic, vagrant, stray, undirected, circuitous, roundabout, crab-like, zigzag.

(Adverbs) Astray from, round about.

(Phrases) To the right-about; all manner of ways; like the knight's move in chess.

---

281 Going after.

Sequence *(Substantives)*, following, pursuit, chase, hunt (622).

A follower, pursuer, attendant, shadow, satellite, hanger-on, train.

Sequence in order (63), in time (117).

(Verbs) To follow, pursue, chase, hunt, hound, shadow, dog, tail, trail, lag.

(Phrases) Go in the rear, or in the wake of; tread in the steps of; tread on the heels of; go after; fly after; to follow as a shadow; to lag behind; to bring up the rear; to fall behind; to tail off.

(Adjectives) Following, etc.

(Adverbs) Behind, in the rear, etc.

282 Motion forwards.

Progression *(Substantives)*, advance, advancement, progress (658), on-going, progressiveness, progressive motion, flood-tide, headway, advancing, etc., pursuit, steeplechase (622), journey, march (266).

(Verbs) To advance, proceed, progress, go, move, bend or pass forward, go on, move on, pass on, get on, get along, jog on, push on, go one's way, go ahead, forge ahead, make head, make way, make headway, work one's way, press forward, edge forward, get over the ground, gain ground, make progress, keep or hold on one's course, keep up with, get forward, distance.

(Phrases) To make up leeway; to go with the stream; to make rapid strides; to push or elbow or cleave one's way; to go full tilt at.

(Adjectives) Advancing, etc., progressive, go-ahead, avant-garde, profluent, undeviating.

(Adverbs) Forward, onward, forth, on, in advance, ahead, under way, straightforward.

(Phrases) Vestigia nulla retrorsum; en avant.

283 Motion backwards.

Regression *(Substantives)*, regress, recess, retrogression, retrogradation, retreat, withdrawal, retirement, recession (287), refluence, reflux, retroaction, return, reflexion, reflex (277), ebb, countermovement, counter-march, veering, regurgitation, back-wash.

(Verbs) To recede, retrograde, return, rebound, back, fall back, fall or drop astern, lose ground, put about, go back, turn back, hark back, double back, countermarch, turn tail, draw back, get back, retrace one's steps, wheel about, back water, regurgitate, yield, give.

(Phrases) Dance the back step; beat a retreat.

(Adjectives) Receding, etc., retrograde, retrogressive, regressive, refluent, reflex, recidivous, resilient.

(Adverbs) Backwards, reflexively, to the right-about, about turn, *à reculons, à rebours.*

(Phrase) Revenons à nos moutons.

---

284 Motion given to an object in front.

Propulsion *(Substantives)*, push, pushing (276), projection, jaculation, ejaculation, throw, fling, fillip, toss, shot, discharge, shy.

Ballistics, gunnery; *vis a tergo.*

Missile, projectile, shot, shell, ball, bolt, dart, arrow, bullet, stone, shaft, brickbat, discus, quoit, caber.

Bow, sling, pea-shooter, catapult etc. (727).

(Verbs) To propel, project, throw, fling, cast, pitch, chuck, bung, toss, lob, loft, jerk, jaculate, ejaculate, hurl, boost, bolt, drive, sling, flirt, flip, flick, shy, dart, send, roll, send

285 Motion given to an object behind.

Traction *(Substantives)*, drawing, draught, pull, pulling, towage, haulage.

Traction engine, locomotive; hauler, haulier, tractor, tug; trailer.

(Phrase) A long pull, a strong pull, and a pull all together.

(Verbs) To draw, pull, haul, lug, drag, tug, tow, trail, train, wrench, jerk, twitch, yank.

(Phrase) To take in tow.

(Adjectives) Drawing, etc., tractile.

---

off, let off, discharge, fire off, shoot, launch, let fly, dash, punt, volley, heave, pitchfork.

To bowl, trundle, roll along (312).

To put in motion, start, give an impulse, impel (276), expel (297).

(Phrases) To carry off one's feet; to put to flight.

(Adjectives) Propelling, etc., propulsive, projectile, etc.

286 Motion towards.

Approach *(Substantives)*, approximation, appropinquation, access, appulse, afflux, affluxion, pursuit (622), collision (276), arrival (292).

(Verbs) To approach, draw near, approximate, to near; to come, get, go, etc., near; to set in towards, make up to, snuggle up to, gain upon, gain ground upon.

(Phrases) To tread on the heels of; to hug the shore.

(Adjectives) Approaching, etc., approximative.

287 Motion from.

Recession *(Substantives)*, retirement, withdrawal, retreat, retrocession (283), departure (293), recoil (277), decampment, flight, stampede, skedaddle.

A runaway, a fugitive.

(Verbs) To recede, go, move or fly from, retire, retreat, withdraw, come away, go or get away, draw back, shrink, move away.

To move off, stand off, draw off, buzz off, fall back, turn tail, march off, decamp, absquatulate, skedaddle, vamoose, sheer off, bolt, scram, hop it, beat it, slip away, run away, pack off, fly, remove, abscond, sneak off, slink away.

(Phrases) To take French leave; to cut and run; take to one's heels; to give leg-bail; take one's hook; *sauve qui peut*; the devil take the hindmost; beat a retreat; make oneself scarce; do a bolt; do a guy; make tracks; cut one's lucky.

(Adjectives) Receding, etc., fugitive, runaway (671).

288 Motion towards, actively.

Attraction *(Substantives)*, drawing to, pulling towards, adduction, attractiveness, magnetism, gravity, gravitation.

A loadstone, magnet.

(Verbs) To attract, draw, pull, drag, etc., towards, adduce.

(Adjectives) Attracting, etc., adducent, attrahent, adductive, attractive, magnetic, gravitational.

(Interjections) Come! come here! approach! come near!

289 Motion from, actively.

Repulsion *(Substantives)*, push (276), driving from, repulse, expulsion (297).

(Verbs) To repel, repulse; push, drive, etc., from, drive away, cold-shoulder, send packing.

(Phrases) To give the frozen mitt to; send away with a flea in one's ear; send to the right-about (678).

(Adjectives) Repelling, etc., repellent, repulsive, forbidding.

(Interjections) Get out! be off! scram! avaunt! (293, 297).

290 Motion nearer to.

Convergence *(Substantives)*, appulse, meeting, confluence, concourse, conflux, congress, concurrence, concentration.

Resort, assemblage, synod (72), focus (74), asymptote.

(Verbs) To converge, come together, unite, meet, fall in with, close in upon, centre in, enter in, meet, come across, come up against.

To gather together, unite, concentrate, etc.

291 Motion farther off.

Divergence *(Substantives)*, aberration, peregrination, wandering, divarication, radiation, ramification, separation (44), dispersion, diffusion, dissemination (73); deviation (279).

(Verbs) To diverge, divaricate, deviate, wander, stray (279), radiate, branch off, ramify, file off, draw aside.

To spread, disperse, scatter, distribute, decentralize, diffuse, disseminate, shed, sow broadcast, broadcast, sprinkle.

(Adjectives) Converging, etc., convergent, confluent, concurring, concurrent, centripetal, asymptotical.

---

292 Terminal motion at.

Arrival (Substantives), advent, reception, welcome, return, disembarkation, debarkation, remigration.

Home, goal, resting-place, destination, journey's end, harbour, haven, port, dock, pier, landing-place, landing-stage, landing-ground, airfield, airstrip, airstop, airport, aerodrome, helidrome, terminus, station.

Meeting, rencontre, rencounter, encounter.

Caller, visitor, visitant, guest.

(Verbs) To arrive, get to, come, come to, reach, attain, come up with, come up to, catch up, make, fetch, overtake, overhaul.

To light, alight, land, dismount, disembark, debark, detrain, outspan, debus, put in, put into, visit, cast, anchor.

To come upon, light upon, pitch upon, hit upon, drop in, pop upon, bounce upon, plump upon, bump against, run against, run across, close with.

To come back, return, get back, get home, sit down.

To meet, encounter, rencounter, contact, come in contact (199).

(Phrase) To be in at the death.

(Adjectives) Arriving, etc., homeward bound.

(Adverbs) Here, hither.

(Interjections) Welcome! hallo! hail! all hail! good day ! good morrow! ave!

To part, part company, turn away from, wander from, separate (44).

(Phrase) To go or fly off at a tangent.

(Adjectives) Diverging, etc., divergent, radiant, wandering, aberring, aberrant, centrifugal.

(Adverb) Broadcast.

293 Initial motion from.

Departure (Substantives), outset, removal, exit, exodus, decampment, embarkation, flight, hegira.

Valediction, adieu, farewell, goodbye, leave-taking, send-off; stirrup-cup, doch-an-doris, one for the road.

A starting point or post, place of departure or embarkation, airfield, terminus, etc. (292).

(Phrase) The foot being in the stirrup.

(Verbs) To depart, go, set out, set off, start, start off, issue, go forth, sally, debouch, sally forth, set forward, be off, move off, pack off, buzz off, scram, begone, get off, sheer off, clear out, vamoose, skedaddle, absquatulate.

To leave a place, quit, retire, withdraw, go one's way, take wing, flit, embus, inspan, entrain, embark, go on board, set sail, put to sea, weigh anchor, slip cable, decamp (671).

(Phrases) To take leave; bid or take adieu; bid farewell; to say goodbye; make one's exit; take a run-out powder.

(Adjectives) Departing, etc., valedictory, outward bound.

(Adverbs) Whence, hence, thence.

(Interjections) Be off! get out! clear out! scram! buzz off! hop it! beat it! begone! get you gone! go along! off with you! avaunt! away with you! go about your business!

Good-bye! bye-bye! 'bye! ta ta! farewell! fare you well! adieu! au revoir! auf wiedersehen! a rivederci! bon voyage! vale! hasta la vista! sayonara! so long! cheerio! chin-chin! tinkety-tonk! pip-pip! tootle-oo! bung-ho!

---

294 Motion into.

Ingress (Substantives), ingoing, entrance, entry, introgression, admission, admittance, intromission,

295 Motion out of.

Egress (Substantives), exit, issue, emersion, emergence.

Exudation, extravasation,

introduction, insinuation, insertion (300), intrusion, inroad, incursion, influx, irruption, invasion, penetration, interpenetration, infiltration, import, importation, illapse, immigration.

A mouth, door (260); an entrant.

(*Verbs*) To enter, go into, come into, set foot in, intrude, invade, flow into, pop into, insinuate itself, penetrate, interpenetrate, infiltrate, soak into; to put into, etc., bring in, insert, drive in, run in, wedge in, ram in (300), intromit, introduce, import, smuggle.

(*Phrases*) To find one's way into; creep into; worm oneself into; to darken one's door; have the *entrée*; to open the door to.

(*Adjectives*) Ingoing, incoming, penetrative, penetrant.

(*Adverb*) Inwards.

———

296 Motion into, actively.

Reception (*Substantives*), admission, admittance, importation, immission, introduction, ingestion, imbibition, absorption, resorption, ingurgitation, inhalation (300).

Eating, swallowing, deglutition, devouring, gulp, gulping, gorge, gorging, carousal.

Drinking, potation, sipping, supping, suction, sucking, draught, libation; smoking, snuffing.

Mastication, manducation, rumination, chewing; hippophagy, ichthyophagy, anthropophagy.

(*Verbs*) To admit, receive, intromit, import, ingest, absorb, resorb, imbibe, inhale, let in, take in, readmit, resorb, reabsorb, snuff up, sop up, suck, suck in, swallow, take down, ingurgitate, engulf.

To eat, fare, feed, devour, tuck in, gulp, bolt, snap, get down, pick, peck, gorge, engorge, fall to, stuff, cram, gobble, guttle, guzzle, wolf, raven, eat heartily, do justice to, overeat, gormandize (957), dispatch, discuss.

To feed upon, live on, feast upon,

transudation (348), leakage, seepage, percolation, distillation, oozing, effluence, efflux, effusion, drain, dropping, dripping, dribbling, drip, dribble, drainage, filtering, defluxion, trickling, eruption, outbreak, outburst, outpouring, gush (348), emanation, aura.

Export, expatriation, emigration, remigration, repatriation, exodus (293).

An outlet, vent, spout, tap, faucet, sluice, flue, chimney, pore, drain, sewer (350).

(*Verbs*) To emerge, emanate, issue, go, come, move, pass, pour, flow, etc., out of, find vent, pass off, evacuate.

To transude, exude, leak, seep, well out, percolate, transcolate, strain, distil, drain, ooze, filter, filtrate, dribble, trickle, drizzle, drip, gush, spout, run, flow out, effuse, extravasate, disembogue, debouch (348).

(*Adjectives*) Dripping, outgoing, etc., oozy, leaky, trickly, dribbly.

297 Motion out of, actively.

Ejection (*Substantives*), emission, effusion, rejection, expulsion, detrusion, extrusion, eviction.

Discharge, egestion, evacuation, vomition, eructation, belch; bloodletting, venesection, phlebotomy, tapping.

Deportation, exile, rustication, banishment, relegation, extradition.

(*Phrases*) The rogue's march; the bum's rush.

(*Verbs*) To emit, eject, expel, export, reject, discharge, give out, let out, cast out, clear out, sweep out, clean out, gut, fillet, wipe off, turn out, chuck out, elbow out, kick out, hoof out, sack, dismiss, bounce, drive out, root out, pour out, ooze, shed, void, evacuate, disgorge, extrude, empty, detrude, throw off, spit, spit out, expectorate, spirt, spill, slop, drain.

To vomit, spue, cat, puke, cast up, keck, retch, spatter, splutter, slobber, slaver, slabber, squirt, eructate, belch, burp, give vent to, tap, broach, open the sluices, heave out, bale out, shake off.

regale, carouse, batten upon, fatten upon, dine, etc., browse, graze, crop, chew, champ, munch, gnaw, nibble, crunch, ruminate, masticate, manducate, mumble.

To drink, quaff, swig, booze, drench, sip, sup, lap, drink up, drain up, toss off, drain the cup, tipple (959).

(Phrases) To give entrance or admittance to; open the door to; usher in.

To refresh the inner man; restore one's tissues; play a good knife and fork; get outside of; wrap oneself round.

To drink one's fill; wet one's whistle; empty one's glass; crook or lift one's elbow; crack a bottle.

(Adjectives) Admitting, etc., admitted, etc., admissible; absorbent, absorptive.

Hippophagous, ichthyophagous, anthropophagous, herbivorous, graminivorous, granivorous, omnivorous.

To throw, project (284); to push, thrust (276).

To unpack, unlade, unload (270).

To banish, exile, extradite, deport; ostracize, boycott, send to Coventry.

(Phrases) To send packing; to send to the right about; to send about one's business; to give the sack to; to show the door to; to turn out neck and crop; to make a clean sweep of; to send away with a flea in one's ear.

(Adjectives) Emitting, etc., emitted, etc.

(Interjections) Be off! get out! scram! (293), scat! fade! chase yourself! *allez-vous-en!*

———

298 Food *(Substantives)*, pabulum, aliment, nourishment, nutriment, sustenance, sustentation, nurture, subsistence, provender, fodder, provision, prey, forage, pasture, pasturage, keep, fare, cheer, rations, diet, regimen.

Comestibles, eatables, victuals, prog, grub, chow, chuck, toke, eats, meat, bread, breadstuffs, cake, pastry, viands, cates, delicacy, delicatessen, dainty, creature comforts, bellytimber, staff of life, dish, flesh-pots, pottage, pudding, ragout, omelet, sundae, kickshaws.

299 Excretion *(Substantives)*, discharge, emanation, exhalation, exudation, secretion, extrusion, effusion, extravasation, evacuation, faeces, excrement (653), perspiration, sweat, saliva, salivation, spittle, diaphoresis; bleeding, haemorrhage, flux.

(Verbs) To emanate, exhale, excern, excrete, exude, effuse, secrete, secern, extravasate, evacuate, urinate, discharge, etc. (297).

———

Table, board, commons, good cheer, bill of fare, menu, commissariat, table d'hôte, ordinary, cuisine.

Canteen, Naffy, restaurant, chop-house, café, cafeteria, eating-house, tea-room, tea-shop, coffee-house, coffee-stall, bar, milk bar, snack bar, public house, pot-house, ale-house, wineshop, brasserie, bodega, tavern (189).

Meal, repast, feed, mess, spread, course, regale, regalement, entertainment, feast, banquet, junket, refreshment, refection; breakfast, *chota hazri*, elevenses, *déjeuner*, lunch, bever, luncheon, tiffin, tea, afternoon tea, five-o'clock tea, high tea, dinner, supper, whet, appetizer, aperitif, bait, dessert, *entremet, hors d'oeuvre*, picnic, bottle-party, wayz-goose, beanfeast, blow-out, tuck-in, snack, pot-luck table d'hôte, *déjeuner à la fourchette*.

Mouthful, bolus, gobbet, sip, sup, sop, tot, snort, hoot, dram, peg, cocktail (615), nip, *chasse*, liqueur.

Drink, hard drink, soft drink, tipple, beverage, liquor, broth, soup, etc., symposium.

(Phrases) A good tuck-in; a modest quencher.

(Adjectives) Eatable, edible, esculent, comestible, alimentary, cereal, culinary, nutritious, nutritive, nutrient, nutrimental, succulent, potable, drinkable.

298ᴀ Tobacco, the weed, bacca, baccy, honeydew, cavendish, bird's-eye, shag, virginia, latakia, perique, plug, twist.

Cigar, segar, cheroot, havana, manila, weed, whiff, cigarette, fag, gasper, stinker, coffin-nail.

Snuff, rappee.

A smoke, draw, puff, pinch, quid, chew, chaw.

Tobacco-pipe, pipe, briar, meerschaum, calabash, corncob, clay pipe, clay, churchwarden, dudeen (or dudheen), cutty, hookah, hubble-bubble, chibouque, narghile, calumet.

(Verbs) To smoke, chew, take snuff.

(Adjective) Nicotian.

300 Forcible ingress.

Insertion *(Substantives)*, putting in, implantation, introduction, interjection, insinuation, planting, intercalation, embolism, injection, inoculation, vaccination, importation, intervention (228), dovetailing, tenon, wedge.

Immersion, dip, plunge, bath (337), submergence, submersion, souse, duck, soak.

Interment, burying, etc. (363).

(Verbs) To insert, introduce, intromit, put into, import, throw in, interlard, inject, interject, intercalate, infuse, instil, inoculate, vaccinate, pasteurize, impregnate, imbue, imbrue, graft, engraft, bud, plant, implant, embed, obtrude, foist in, worm in, thrust in, stick in, ram in, stuff in, tuck in, plough in, let in, dovetail, mortise (or mortice), insinuate, wedge in, press in, impact, drive in, run in, empierce (260).

To immerse, dip, steep, immerge, merge, submerge, bathe, plunge, drop in, souse, douse, soak, duck, drown.

To inter, bury, etc. (363).

(Adjectives) Inserting, inserted, implanted, embedded, etc., ingrowing.

301 Forcible egress.

Extraction *(Substantives)*, taking out, removal, elimination, extrication, evulsion, avulsion, eradication, extirpation, wrench.

Expression, squeezing; ejection (297).

Extractor, corkscrew, pincers, pliers, forceps.

(Verbs) To extract, take out, draw, draw out, pull out, tear out, pluck out, extort, wring from, prise, wrench, rake out, rake up, grub up, root up, uproot, eradicate, extirpate, dredge, remove, get out (185), elicit, extricate, eliminate.

To express, squeeze out, wring out, pick out, disembowel, eviscerate, exenterate.

(Adjectives) Extracted, etc.

———

302 Motion through.

Passage *(Substantives)*, transmission, permeation, penetration, interpenetration (294), filtration, infiltration, percolation, transudation, osmosis (or osmose), capillary action, endosmosis (or endosmose), exosmosis (or exosmose), intercurrence; way, path (627); channel, pipe (350).

Terebration, impalement, etc. (260).

(Verbs) To pass, pass through, traverse, terebrate, stick, pierce, impale, spear, spike, spit (260), penetrate, percolate, permeate, thread, thrid, enfilade,

go through, cross, go across, go over, pass over, get over, clear, negotiate, cut across, pass and repass; work, thread or worm one's way, force a passage; to transmit.

(Adjectives) Passing, intercurrent, penetrative, transudatory, etc.

303 Motion beyond.
Transcursion *(Substantives)*, transilience, transgression, trespass, encroachment, infringement, extravagation, transcendence, enjambement, overrunning.

(Verbs) To transgress, overstep, surpass, overpass, overrun, overgo, beat, outstrip, outgo, outstep, outrun, outdo, overreach, overleap, outleap, pass, go by, strain, overshoot the mark, overjump, overskip, overlap, go beyond, outpace, outmarch, transcend, distance, outdistance, lap, encroach, exceed, trespass, infringe, trench upon.

(Phrases) To stretch a point; to steal a march on; to pass the Rubicon; to shoot ahead of; to throw into the shade.

(Adverbs) Beyond the mark, out of bounds.

304 Motion short of.
Shortcoming *(Substantives)*, failure, falling short (732), defalcation, default, backlog, leeway, incompleteness (53); imperfection (651); insufficiency (640).

(Verbs) To come or fall short of, not to reach, keep within bounds, keep within compass, to stop short, be wanting, lose ground, miss the mark.

(Adjectives) Unreached, deficient (53), short, minus.

(Adverbs) Within the mark, within compass, within bounds, etc., behindhand.

---

305 Motion upwards.
Ascent *(Substantives)*, rise, climb, ascension, upgrowth, leap (309).

A rocket, sky-rocket, lark, skylark; a climber, mountaineer, Alpinist, stegophilist.

(Verbs) To ascend, rise, mount, arise, uprise, go up, get up, climb, clamber, swarm, shin, scale, scramble, escalade, surmount, aspire.

To tower, soar, zoom, hover, spire, plane, swim, float, surge.

(Phrase) To make one's way up.

(Adjectives) Rising, etc., scandent, buoyant, floating, supernatant, superfluitant.

(Adverbs) Uphill, on the up grade.
(Interjection) Excelsior!

306 Motion downwards.
Descent *(Substantives)*, fall, descension, declension, declination, drop, cadence, subsidence, lapse, downfall, tumble, tilt, toppling, trip, lurch, *culbute*, spill, cropper, purler, crash.

Titubation, shamble, shambling, stumble.

An avalanche, landslip, landslide, debacle, slump.

(Phrase) The fate of Icarus.

(Verbs) To descend, come or go down, fall, sink, gravitate, drop, drop down, droop, decline, come down, dismount, alight, light, settle, subside, slide, slip, slither, glissade, toboggan, coast, volplane, dive (310).

To tumble, slip, trip, stumble, pitch, lurch, swag, topple, topple over, swoop, tilt, sprawl, plump down, measure one's length, bite the dust, heel over, careen (217), slump, crash.

To alight, dismount, get down.

(Adjectives) Descending, etc., descendent, decurrent, decursive, deciduous.

(Phrase) Nodding to its fall.

(Adverbs) Downhill, on the down grade.

307 Elevation (*Substantives*), raising, lifting, erection, lift, uplift, upheaval, upcast.

Lift, elevator, hoist, escalator, crane, derrick, winch, windlass, jack, lever.

(*Verbs*) To elevate, raise, lift, uplift, upraise, set up, erect, stick up, rear, uprear, upbear, upcast, hoist, uphoist, heave, upheave, weigh, exalt, promote, give a lift, help up, prick up, perk up.

To drag up, fish up, dredge.

To stand up, rise up, ramp.

(*Phrases*) To set on a pedestal; to get up on one's hind legs.

(*Adjectives*) Elevated, etc., rampant.

(*Adverbs*) On stilts, on the shoulders of.

———

308 Depression (*Substantives*), lowering, abasement, abasing, detrusion, reduction.

Overthrow, upset, prostration, subversion, overset, overturn, precipitation.

Bow, curtsy (or curtsey), genuflexion, obeisance, kowtow, salaam.

(*Verbs*) To depress, lower, let down, take down, sink, debase, abase, reduce, demote, detrude, let fall, cast down, to grass, send to grass.

To overthrow, overturn, upset, overset, subvert, prostrate, level, raze, fell; cast, take, throw, fling, dash, pull, cut, knock, hew, etc., down.

To stoop, bend, bow, curtsy (or curtsey), bob, duck, kneel, crouch, cower, lout, kowtow, salaam, bend the head or knee; to recline, sit, sit down, couch, squat.

(*Phrases*) To take down a peg; to pull about one's ears; to trample in the dust.

(*Adjectives*) Depressed, sunk, prostrate.

309 Leap (*Substantives*), jump, hop, spring, bound, vault, saltation.

Dance, caper, curvet, caracole, *entrechat*, gambade, gambado, capriole, dido, demivolt.

Kangaroo, jerboa, chamois, goat, frog, grasshopper, flea, buck-jumper.

(*Phrases*) Hop, skip, and jump; on the light fantastic toe.

(*Verbs*) To leap, jump, bound, spring, take off, buck, buck-jump, hop, skip, vault, dance, bob, curvet, romp, caracole, caper, cut capers.

310 Plunge (*Substantives*), dip, dive, ducking, header.

Diver, frogman.

(*Verbs*) To plunge, dip, souse, duck, dive, plump, plop, submerge, submerse, bathe, douse, sink, engulf, founder.

———

(*Adjectives*) Leaping, etc., saltatory, Terpsichorean, frisky.

311 Curvilinear motion.

Circuition (*Substantives*), turn, wind, circuit, curvet, detour, excursion, circumbendibus, circumvention, circumnavigation, north-west passage, circulation.

Turning, winding, twist, twisting, wrench, evolution, twining, coil, circumambulation, meandering.

(*Verbs*) To turn, bend, wheel, put about, switch, circle, go round, or round about, circumnavigate, circumambulate, turn a corner, double a point, wind, meander, whisk, twirl, twist (248), twill; to turn on one's heel.

(*Phrases*) To lead a pretty dance; to go the round; to turn on one's heel.

(*Adjectives*) Turning, etc., circuitous, circumforaneous, circumfluent.

(*Adverb*) Round about.

312 Motion in a continued circle.

Rotation *(Substantives)*, revolution, gyration, roll, circumrotation, circumgyration, gurgitation, pirouette, circumvolution, convolution, turbination, whir, whirl, eddy, vortex, whirlpool, cyclone, anticyclone, tornado, typhoon, whirlwind, willy-willy, waterspout, surge, dizzy round, maelstrom, Charybdis.

A wheel, flywheel, screw, reel, whirligig, rolling stone, windmill, top, teetotum, merry-go-round, roundabout, gyroscope, gyrostat.

313 Motion in a reverse circle.

Evolution *(Substantives)*, unfolding, etc., development, introversion, reversion, eversion.

(Verbs) To evolve, unfold, unroll, unwind, uncoil, untwist, unfurl, untwine, unravel disentangle (44), develop, introvert, reverse.

(Adjectives) Evolving, evolved, etc.
(Adverb) Against.

———

Axis, axle, spindle, pivot, pin, hinge, pole, swivel, gimbals, mandrel.

(Verbs) To rotate, roll, revolve, spin, turn, turn round, circumvolve, circulate, gyre, gyrate, gimble, wheel, reel, whirl, twirl, birl, thrum, trundle, troll, twiddle, bowl, roll up, furl, wallow, welter.

(Phrases) To box the compass; to spin like a top.

(Adjectives) Rotating, etc., rotatory, rotary, circumrotatory, turbinate, trochoid, vortiginous, vortical, gyratory.

(Phrase) Like a squirrel in a cage.

(Adverbs) Clockwise, with the sun, deiseal (or deisil); counter-clockwise, against the sun, withershins (or widdershins).

314 Reciprocating motion, motion to and fro.

Oscillation *(Substantives)*, vibration, undulation, pulsation, pulse, systole, diastole, libration, nutation, swing, beat, shake, seesaw, alternation, wag, evolution, vibratiuncle, coming and going, ebb and flow, flux and reflux; vibratility.

Fluctuation, vacillation, dance, lurch, dodge, rolling, tossing, etc.

A pendulum, seesaw, rocker, rocking-chair, rocking-horse, etc.

(Verbs) To oscillate, vibrate, undulate, librate, wave, rock, swing, sway, pulsate, beat, wag, waggle, wiggle, wobble, shoogle, nod, bob, tick, play, wamble, wabble, waddle, dangle, swag, curtsy.

To fluctuate, vacillate, alternate, dance, curvet, reel, quake, quiver, quaver, roll, top, pitch, flounder, stagger, totter, brandish, shake, flicker, flourish, seesaw, teeter, move up and down, to and fro, backwards and forwards, to pass and repass, to beat up and down.

(Adjectives) Oscillating, etc., oscillatory, vibratory, vibratile, vibrant, vibrational, undulatory, pulsatory, pendulous, libratory, systaltic.

(Adverbs) To and fro, up and down, backwards and forwards, seesaw, zigzag, wibble-wabble.

315 Irregular motion.

Agitation *(Substantives)*, stir, tremor, shake, ripple, jog, jolt, jar, succussion, trepidation, quiver, quaver, dance, jactitation, jactitancy, restlessness, shuffling, twitter, flicker, flutter, bobbing.

Disturbance, perturbation, commotion, turmoil, welter, bobbery; turbulence, tumult, tumultuation, bustle, fuss, flap, tirrivee, jerk, throw, convulsion, spasm (173), twitch, tic, staggers, St. Vitus's dance, epilepsy, writhing, ferment, fermentation, efferverscence, ebullition, hurly-burly, hubbub, stramash, *tohu-bohu*; tempest, storm, whirlwind, cyclone (312), ground swell.

(Verbs) To be agitated, to shake, tremble, quiver, quaver, shiver, dither,

twitter, twire, writhe, toss about, tumble, stagger, bob, reel, sway, wag, waggle, wiggle, wobble, shoogle, dance, wriggle, squirm, stumble, flounder, shuffle, totter, dodder, shamble, flounce, flop, curvet, prance, cavort, throb, pulsate, beat, palpitate, go pit-a-pat, fidget, flutter, flitter, flicker, bicker, twitch, jounce, ferment, effervesce, boil.

To agitate, shake, convulse, toss, tumble, bandy, wield, brandish, flap, flourish, whisk, switch, jerk, hitch, jolt, jog, hoggle, jostle, hustle, disturb, shake up, churn.

(Phrases) To jump like a parched pea; to be in a spin; to shake like an aspen leaf; to drive from pillar to post.

(Adjectives) Shaking, etc., agitated, tremulous, shivery, tottery, jerky, shaky, shoogly, quivery, quavery, trembly, choppy, rocky, wriggly, desultory, subsultory, shambling, giddy-paced, saltatory.

(Phrases) All of a tremble or twitter; like a pea on a drum; like a cat on hot bricks; like a hen on a hot griddle.

(Adverbs) By fits and starts; subsultorily, *per saltum* (139).

CLASS III
WORDS RELATING TO MATTER

SECTION I — MATTER IN GENERAL

316 Materiality *(Substantives)* corporeity, corporality, materialness, substantiality, physical condition.

Matter, body, substance, brute matter, stuff, element, principle, parenchyma, material, substratum, frame, *corpus pabulum*, flesh and blood.

Thing, object, article, still life, stocks and stones.

Physics, somatology, somatics, natural philosophy, physiography, physical science, experimental philosophy, positivism, materialism.

(Verbs) To materialize, embody, incarnate, objectify, externalize.

(Adjectives) Material, bodily, corporeal, corporal, carnal, temporal, physical, somatic, somatological, materialistic, sensible, palpable, tangible, ponderable, concrete, impersonal, objective, bodied.

317 Immateriality *(Substantives)*, incorporeity, spirituality, spirit, etc. (450), inextension.

Personality, I, me, myself, ego.

Spiritualism, spiritism, idealism, immaterialism.

(Verbs) To disembody, spiritualize, immaterialize.

(Adjectives) Immaterial, incorporeal, ideal, unextended, intangible, impalpable, imponderable, bodiless, unbodied, disembodied, extra-sensory, astral, psychical, psychic, extramundane, unearthly, supernatural, supranatural, transcendent, transcendental, pneumatoscopic, spiritualistic, spiritual (450).

Personal, subjective.

———

318 World *(Substantives)*, nature, creation, universe; earth, globe, wide world, cosmos, sphere, macrocosm.

The heavens, sky, welkin, empyrean, starry heaven, firmament, ether; vault or canopy of heaven; celestial spaces, starry host, heavenly bodies, star, constellation, galaxy, Milky Way, *via lactea*, nebula, etc., sun, moon, planet, asteroid, planetoid, satellite, comet, meteor, meteorite, shooting star.

Zodiac, ecliptic, colure, orbit.

Astronomy, astrophysics, uranography, uranology, cosmology, cosmography, cosmogony; planetarium, orrery.

An astronomer, star-gazer, cosmographer; observatory.

(Adjectives) Cosmic, cosmical, mundane, terrestrial, terraqueous, terrene, telluric, sublunary, under the sun, subastral, worldwide, global.

Celestial, heavenly, spheral, starry, stellar, nebular, etc., sidereal, sideral, astral, solar, lunar.

319 Heaviness *(Substantives)*, weight, gravity, gravitation, ponderosity, ponderousness, avoirdupois, pressure, load, burden, ballast; a

320 Lightness *(Substantives)*, levity, imponderability, subtlety, buoyancy, airiness, portability, volatility.

lump, mass, weight, counterweight, counterpoise; ponderability.

Lead, millstone, mountain.

Balance, spring balance, scales, steelyard, weighbridge.

Statics.

(Phrase) Pelion on Ossa.

(Verbs) To be heavy, to gravitate, weigh, press, cumber, load.

(Adjectives) Weighty, heavy, ponderous, gravitating, weighing, etc., ponderable, lumpish, cumbersome, hefty, massive, unwieldy, cumbrous, incumbent, superincumbent; gravitational.

(Phrase) Heavy as lead.

A feather, dust, mote, down, thistledown, flue, ooss, fluff, cobweb, gossamer, straw, cork, bubble; float, buoy; featherweight.

(Verbs) To be light, float, swim, be buoyed up.

(Adjectives) Light, subtle, airy, vaporous, imponderous, astatic, weightless, imponderable, ethereal, sublimated, floating, swimming, buoyant, air-borne, portable, uncompressed, volatile.

(Phrases) Light as a feather; light as thistledown; 'trifles light as air.'

SECTION II—INORGANIC MATTER

1°. *Solid Matter*

321 Density *(Substantives)*, denseness, solidness, solidity, impenetrability, incompressibility, cohesion, coherence, cohesiveness (46), imporosity, impermeability, closeness, compactness, constipation, consistence, spissitude, thickness.

Specific gravity; hydrometer, araeometer.

Condensation, consolidation, solidification, concretion, coagulation, conglomeration, petrification, lapidification, vitrification, crystallization, precipitation, inspissation, thickening, grittiness, knottiness, induration (323).

Indivisibility, indiscerptibility, indissolubility.

322 Rarity *(Substantives)*, tenuity, absence of solidity, subtility, sponginess, compressibility; hollowness (252).

Rarefaction, expansion, dilatation, inflation, dilution, attenuation, subtilization.

Ether, vapour, air, gas (334).

(Verbs) To rarefy, expand, dilate, dilute, attenuate, subtilize, thin out.

(Adjectives) Rare, subtle, sparse, slight, thin, fine, tenuous, compressible.

Porous, cavernous, spongy, bibulous, spongious, spongeous.

Rarefied, expanded, dilated, subtilized, unsubstantial, hollow (252).

A solid body, mass, block, knot, lump, concretion, concrete, cake, clot, stone, curd, coagulum, clinker, nugget; deposit, precipitate.

(Verbs) To be dense, etc.

To become or render solid; solidify, solidate, concrete, set, consolidate, congeal, jelly, jell, coagulate, curdle, curd, fix, clot, cake, cohere, crystallize, petrify, vitrify, condense, incrassate, thicken, inspissate, compact, concentrate, compress, squeeze, ram down, constipate.

(Adjectives) Dense, solid, solidified, consolidated, etc., coherent, cohesive, compact, close, thick-set, serried, substantial, massive, lumpish, impenetrable, incompressible, impermeable, imporous, constipated, concrete, knotted, gnarled, crystalline, crystallizable, vitreous, coagulated, thick, incrassated, inspissated, curdled, clotted, grumous.

Undissolved, unmelted, unliquefied, unthawed,

Indivisible, indiscerptible, infrangible, indissolvable, indissoluble, insoluble, infusible.

323 Hardness (*Substantives*), rigidity, rigescence, firmness, renitence, inflexibility, stiffness, starchiness, starchedness, temper, callosity, durity, induration, grittiness, petrifaction, etc. (321), ossification, sclerosis.

A stone, pebble, flint, marble, rock, granite, brick, iron, steel, corundum, diamond, adamant, bone, callus.

(*Verbs*) To render hard, harden, stiffen, indurate, petrify, vitrify, temper, ossify.

(*Adjectives*) Hard, horny, corneous, bony, osseous, rigid, rigescent, stiff, firm, starch, stark, unbending, unyielding, inflexible, tense, indurate, indurated, gritty, stony, proof, adamantean, adamantine.

(*Phrases*) Hard as iron, etc.; hard as a brick; hard as a nail; hard as a deal board; 'as hard as a piece of the nether millstone'; stiff as buckram; stiff as a poker.

---

325 Elasticity (*Substantives*), springiness, spring, resilience, buoyancy, renitency, contractility (195), compressibility.

Indiarubber, rubber, caoutchouc, whalebone, elastic.

(*Verbs*) To be elastic, etc., to spring back, fly back, rebound, recoil (277).

(*Adjectives*) Elastic, tensile, springy, resilient, buoyant.

327 Toughness (*Substantives*), tenacity, strength, cohesion (46), stubbornness (606).

Leather, gristle, cartilage.

(*Verbs*) To be tenacious, etc., to resist fracture.

(*Adjectives*) Tenacious, tough, wiry, sinewy, stringy, stubborn, cohesive, strong, resisting, resistant, leathery, coriaceous.

(*Phrase*) Tough as leather.

---

324 Softness (*Substantives*), tenderness, flexibility, pliancy, pliableness, pliantness, litheness, pliability, suppleness, sequacity, ductility, malleability, tractility, extensibility, plasticity, inelasticity, laxity, flaccidity, flabbiness, limpness.

Clay, wax, butter, dough; a cushion, pillow, featherbed, down, padding, wadding, cotton-wool.

Mollification, softening, etc.

(*Verbs*) To render soft, soften, mollify, relax, temper, mash, pulp, knead, squash.

To bend, yield, give, relent, relax.

(*Adjectives*) Soft, tender, supple, pliable, limp, limber, flexible, flexile, lithe, lissom, *svelte*, willowy, pliant, plastic, waxen, ductile, tractile, tractable, malleable, extensile, sequacious.

Yielding, bending, flabby, flaccid, lymphatic, flocculent, downy, flimsy, spongy, oedematous, doughy, argillaceous, mellow; emollient, softening, etc.

(*Phrases*) Soft as butter; soft as down; soft as silk; yielding as wax; tender as a chicken.

326 Inelasticity (*Substantives*), want or absence of elasticity, softness, etc. (324).

(*Adjectives*) Inelastic, ductile, limber, etc. (324).

---

328 Brittleness (*Substantives*), fragility, crispness, friability, frangibility, fissility.

(*Verbs*) To be brittle, break, crack, snap, split, shiver, splinter, fracture, crumble, break short, burst, fly.

(*Adjectives*) Brittle, frangible, fragile, frail, jerry-built, gimcrack, shivery, fissile, splitting, splintery, lacerable, crisp, friable, short, crumbling.

(*Phrases*) Brittle as glass; a house of cards.

329 Texture *(Substantives)* structure, construction, organization, set-up, organism, anatomy, frame, mould, fabric, framework, carcass, architecture, *compages*; substance, stuff, parenchyma, constitution, intertexture, contexture, tissue, grain, web, warp, woof, nap (256).

Fineness or coarseness of grain.

Histology.

(Adjectives) Textural, structural, organic, anatomic, anatomical; fine, delicate, subtle, fine-grained; coarse, homespun, rough-grained, coarse-grained; flimsy, unsubstantial, gossamery, filmy, gauzy.

330 Pulverulence *(Substantives)*, state of powder, powderiness, efflorescence, sandiness, friability.

Dust, stour (or stoor), powder, sand, shingle, sawdust, grit, meal, bran, flour, limature, filings, debris, detritus, moraine, scobs, crumb, seed, grain, spore, atom, particle (32), flocculence.

Reduction to powder, pulverization, comminution, granulation, disintegration, weathering, subaction, contusion, trituration, levigation, abrasion, detrition, filing, etc. (331).

Mill, quern, grater, nutmeg grater, rasp, file, pestle and mortar.

(Verbs) To reduce to powder, to pulverize, comminute, granulate, triturate, levigate, scrape, file, abrade, rub down, grind, grate, rasp, mill, pound, bray, bruise, contuse, contund, beat, crush, crunch, scrunch, crumble, disintegrate, weather.

(Adjectives) Powdery, granular, mealy, floury, branny, farinaceous, furfuraceous, flocculent, dusty, sandy, sabulous, arenaceous, gritty, efflorescent, impalpable; pulverizable, pulverulent, friable, crumbly, shivery, pulverized, etc., attrite.

331 Friction *(Substantives)*, attrition, rubbing, massage, abrasion, rub, scouring, limature, filing, rasping, frication, elbow-grease.

Grindstone, whetstone, buff, hone, strop (253).

(Verbs) To rub, abrade, scratch, scrape, scrub, grate, fray, rasp, pare, scour, polish, massage, curry, shampoo, rub out.

332 Absence of friction.

Lubrication *(Substantives)*, prevention of friction, oiling, etc., anointment.

Lubricant, oil, lard, grease, etc. (356); synovia, saliva.

(Verbs) To lubricate, oil, grease, anoint, wax; smooth (255).

(Adjectives) Lubricated, etc.

2°. *Fluid Matter*

1. FLUIDS IN GENERAL

333 Fluidity *(Substantives)*, fluid (including both inelastic and elastic fluids).

Inelastic fluid.

Liquidity, liquidness, aquosity, a liquid, liquor, lymph, humour, juice, sap, blood, serum, serosity, gravy, chyle, rheum, ichor, sanies; solubility.

Hydrology, hydrostatics, hydrodynamics.

334 Elastic fluid.

Gaseity, vaporousness, flatulence, flatulency; gas, air, vapour, ether, steam, fume, reek, effluvium.

Smoke, cloud (353).

Pneumatics, aerostatics, aerodynamics; gas-meter, gasometer.

(Verbs) To be fluid or liquid, to flow, run (348).

(Adjectives) Liquid, fluid, fluent, running, flowing, serous, juicy, succulent, sappy, lush.

Liquefied, uncongealed, melted, etc. (335).

(Verbs) To emit vapour, evaporate, to steam, fume, reek, smoke, puff, smoulder.

(Adjectives) Gaseous, aeriform, ethereal, aerial, airy, vaporous, vapoury, flatulent, volatile, evaporable.

335 Liquefaction *(Substantives)*, liquescence, fusion, melting, thaw, deliquation, deliquescence, lixiviation.

Solution, dissolution, decoction, infusion, apozem, flux.

Solvent, menstruum, alkahest.

(Verbs) To render liquid, to liquefy, deliquesce, run, melt, thaw, fuse, solve, dissolve, resolve, to hold in solution.

(Adjectives) Liquefied, melted, unfrozen, molten, liquescent, liquefiable, deliquescent, diffluent, soluble, dissoluble.

336 Vaporization *(Substantives)*, gasification, volatilization, evaporation, distillation, sublimation, exhalation, volatility.

Vaporizer, retort, still.

(Verbs) To render gaseous, vaporize, volatilize, evaporate, exhale, distil, sublime, sublimate.

(Adjectives) Volatilized, etc., volatile, evaporable, vaporizable.

------

2. SPECIFIC FLUIDS

337 Water *(Substantives)*, heavy water, serum, lymph, rheum, whey.

Dilution, immersion, maceration, humectation, infiltration, sprinkling, washing, spraying, aspersion, affusion, irrigation, douche, balneation, bath, shower-bath, inundation, deluge (348), a diluent.

(Verbs) To be watery, etc., to reek.

To add water, to water, wet, moisten (339), dilute, dip, immerse, plunge, merge, immerge, steep, souse, duck, submerge, drown, soak, saturate, sop, macerate, pickle, blunge, wash, lave, springle, asperge, asperse, dabble, bedabble, affuse, splash, splatter, spray, swash, douse, drench, slop, slobber, irrigate, inundate, deluge, flood.

To take a bath, to tub, bathe, bath, paddle.

To syringe, inject, gargle.

(Adjectives) Watery (339), aqueous, aquatic, lymphatic, diluted, etc., reeking, dripping, sodden, drenched, soaking, sopping.

338 Air *(Substantives)*, common air, atmospheric air.

The atmosphere, troposphere, tropopause, stratosphere, ionosphere, Heaviside layer, Appleton layer; the sky, the ether, the open air, ozone, weather, climate.

Meteorology, climatology, isobar, barometer, aneroid barometer, weather-glass, weather-chart, weather station, weather ship.

Exposure to the air or weather, airing, weathering (330).

(Verbs) To aerate, oxygenate, arterialize, ventilate, air-condition.

(Adjectives) Containing air, windy, flatulent, aerated, effervescent.

Atmospheric, airy, open-air, *plein-air*, alfresco, aerial, aeriform; meteorological, barometric, weather-wise.

(Adverbs) In the open air, *à la belle étoile*, sub Jove.

Wet, washy, sloppy, squashy, splashy, soppy, soggy, slobbery, diluent, balneal.

(Phrases) Wet as a drowned rat; soaked to the skin; wet as a rag; wet through.

339 Moisture (*Substantives*), moistness, humidity, dampness, damp, wetness, wet, humectation, madefaction, dew, muddiness, marsh (345).

Hygrometer, hygrometry, hygrology.

(*Verbs*) To be moist, etc.

To moisten, wet, humectate, sponge, damp, dampen, bedew, imbue, infiltrate, imbrue; soak, saturate (337).

(*Adjectives*) Moist, damp, watery, humid, wet, dank, muggy, dewy, roral, rorid, roscid, juicy, swampy (345), humectant, sopping, dripping, sodden.

(*Phrase*) Wringing wet.

340 Dryness (*Substantives*), siccity, aridity, drought.

Exsiccation, desiccation, arefaction, drainage.

(*Verbs*) To be dry, etc.

To render dry, to dry, dry up, sop up, swab, wipe, blot, exsiccate, desiccate, dehydrate, drain, parch.

(*Adjectives*) Dry, anhydrous, dehydrated, arid, dried, etc., unwatered, undamped, waterproof, husky, juiceless, sapless; siccative, desiccative.

(*Phrases*) Dry as a bone; dry as dust; dry as a stick; dry as a mummy; dry as a biscuit; dry as a limekiln.

---

341 Ocean (*Substantives*), sea, main, the deep, brine, salt water, blue water, high seas, offing, tide, wave, surge, ooze, etc. (348).

Hydrography, oceanography.

Neptune, Thetis, Triton, Oceanid, Nereid, sea-nymph, siren, mermaid, merman, dolphin; trident.

(*Phrases*) The vasty deep; the briny; the ditch; the drink.

(*Adjectives*) Oceanic, marine, maritime, thalassic, pelagic, pelagian, seagoing, hydrographic.

(*Adverbs*) At sea, on sea, afloat.

342 Land (*Substantives*), earth, ground, terra firma, continent, mainland, peninsula, delta, alluvium, polder, tongue of land, neck of land, isthmus, oasis.

Coast, shore, seaboard, seaside, seabank, strand, beach, bank, lea.

Cape, promontory, etc. (250), headland, point of land, highland (206).

Soil, glebe, clay, humus, loam, marl, clod, clot, rock, crag, chalk, gravel, mould, subsoil.

(*Adjectives*) Terrene, continental, earthy, terraqueous, terrestrial.

Littoral, riparian, alluvial, midland.

(*Adverbs*) Ashore, on shore, on land.

---

343 Gulf (*Substantives*), bay, inlet, bight, estuary, roadstead, roads, arm of the sea, armlet, sound, frith, firth, fiord, lagoon, cove, creek, strait, belt, kyle, Euripus.

(*Adjectives*) Estuarine.

Lake (*Substantives*), loch, lough, mere, tarn, linn, plash, broad, pond, dew-pond, pool, puddle, well, reservoir, standing water, dead water, a sheet of water, fish-pond, ditch, dike, backwater.

(*Adjectives*) Lacustrine (or lacustrian), lacuscular.

344 Plain (*Substantives*), tableland, open country, the face of the country, champaign country, basin, downs, waste, wild, weald, steppe, pampas, savanna, llano, prairie, tundra, heath, common, wold, moor, moorland, the bush; plateau, flat (213).

Meadow, mead, haugh, pasturage, park, field, lawn, green, plot, plat, terrace, esplanade, sward, turf, sod, heather, lea, grounds, pleasuregrounds, playing-fields, campus.

(*Phrase*) A weary waste.

(*Adjectives*) Campestrian, champaign, lawny.

345 Marsh *(Substantives)*, marish, swamp, morass, moss, fen, bog, quag, quagmire, slough, sump, wash.

(Adjectives) Marshy, marish, swampy, boggy, quaggy, fenny, soft, plashy, poachy, paludal.

346 Island *(Substantives)*, isle, islet, ait, eyot, inch, holm, reef, atoll; archipelago.

(Adjectives) Insular, sea-girt.

3. FLUIDS IN MOTION

347 Fluid in motion.

Stream *(Substantives)*, flow, current, jet, undercurrent, course (348).

(Verb) To flow, stream, issue, run.

348 Water in motion.

River *(Substantives)*, running water, jet, spurt, squirt, spout, splash, rush, gush, water-spout, sluice, linn, waterfall, cascade, force, catadupe, cataract, debacle, cataclysm, inundation, deluge, avalanche, spate.

Rain, shower, scud, driving rain, downpour, drencher, soaker, cloudburst, mizzle, drizzle, Scotch mist, smirr, dripping, stillicidium; flux, flow, profluence, effluence, efflux, effluxion, defluxion.

Irrigation (337).

Spring, fountain, fount, rill, rivulet, gill, gullet, rillet, streamlet, runnel, sike, burn, beck, brooklet, brook, stream, reach, torrent, rapids, race, flush, flood, swash.

Tide, spring tide, high tide, tidal wave, bore, eagre, freshet, current, indraught, reflux, eddy, whirlpool, vortex, maelstrom, regurgitation.

Tributary, confluent, effluent, billabong; corrivation, confluence, effluence.

Wave, billow, surge, swell, chop, ripple, ground swell, surf, breaker, roller, comber, white caps, white horses.

Irrigation (337); sprinkler, sprayer, spray, atomizer, aspergillum, aspersorium, water-cart, watering-pot, watering-can, pump, syringe, hydrant.

Hydraulics, hydrodynamics, hydrography; rain-gauge.

(Verbs) To flow, run, meander, gush, spout, roll, billow, surge, jet, well, drop, drip, trickle, dribble, ooze (295), percolate, distil, transude,

349 Air in motion.

Wind *(Substantives)*, draught, current, breath, air, breath of air, puff, whiff, zephyr, blow, drift, aura.

Gust, blast, breeze, squall, gale, storm, tempest, hurricane, whirlwind, tornado, cyclone, typhoon, blizzard, simoom, samiel, harmattan, monsoon, trade wind, sirocco, mistral, *bise, tramontana, föhn,* pampero; windiness, ventosity.

Aeolus, Boreas, Auster, Euroclydon, the cave of Aeolus.

Bellows, blowpipe, fan, ventilator, punkah.

Anemometer, anemograph, windgauge, weathercock, vane.

Insufflation, sufflation, perflation, blowing, fanning, ventilation, blowing up, inflation, afflation; respiration, inspiration, expiration, sneezing, sternutation, cough, hiccup.

(Phrase) A capful of wind.

(Verbs) To blow, waft, blow hard, blow a hurricane, breathe, respire, inspire, expire, insufflate, puff, whiff, sough, whiffle, wheeze, gasp, snuffle, sniffle, sneeze, cough.

To fan, ventilate, inflate, perflate, blow up.

(Phrase) To blow great guns.

(Adjectives) Blowing, etc., rough, blowy, windy, breezy, gusty, squally, puffy, stormy, tempestuous, blustering.

stream, sweat, perspire (299), overflow, flow over, splash, swash, guggle, murmur, babble, bubble, purl, gurgle, sputter, spurt, regurgitate, surge.

To rain, rain hard, pour with rain, drizzle, spit, mizzle, set in.

To flow into, fall into, open into, drain into, discharge itself, disembogue, disgorge, debouch.

(Phrases) To rain cats and dogs; to rain in torrents.

To cause a flow, to pour, drop, distil, splash, squirt, spill, drain, empty, discharge, pour out, open the sluices or flood-gates; shower down, irrigate (337).

To stop a flow, to stanch, dam, dam up (261), intercept.

(Adjectives) Fluent, profluent, affluent, confluent, diffluent, tidal, flowing, etc., babbling, bubbling, gurgling, meandering, meandrous.

Fluviatile, fluvial, riverine, streamy, showery, drizzly, rainy, pluvial, pouring.

350 Channel for the passage of water.

Conduit *(Substantives)*, channel, duct, watercourse, watershed, race, adit, aqueduct, canal, sluice, dike, main, gully, moat, ditch, lode, leat, rhine, trough, gutter, drain, sewer, culvert, cloaca, sough, kennel, siphon, pipe (260), emunctory, gully-hole, artery, aorta, pore, spout, funnel, tap, faucet, scupper, adjutage (or ajutage), waste-pipe, hose, rose, gargoyle, artesian well.

Floodgate, dam, weir, levee, water-gate, lock, valve.

351 Channel for the passage of air.

Air-pipe *(Substantives)*, air-tube, shaft, flue, chimney, lum, funnel, smoke-stack, exhaust-pipe, exhaust, vent, blow-hole, nostril, nozzle, throat, weasand, trachea, larynx, windpipe, thrapple, spiracle, ventiduct.

Ventilator, louvre, register.

Tobacco-pipe, pipe, etc. (298A).

———

3°. *Imperfect Fluids*

352 Semiliquidity *(Substantives)*, pulpiness, viscidity, viscosity, ropiness, sliminess, gumminess, glutinosity, gummosity, siziness, clamminess, mucosity, spissitude, lentor, thickness, crassitude.

Inspissation, thickening, incrassation.

Jelly, mucilage, gelatine, mucus, chyme, phlegm, gum, glue, gluten, goo, colloid, albumen, size, milk, cream, emulsion, soup, broth, starch, treacle, squash, mud, clart, glaur, slush, slime, ooze, dope, glycerine; lava.

Pitch, tar, bitumen, asphalt, resin, rosin, varnish, copal, mastic, wax, amber.

(Verbs) To inspissate, thicken, incrassate, jelly, jellify, mash, squash, churn, beat up, pulp.

(Adjectives) Semi-fluid, semi-

353 Mixture of air and water.

Bubble *(Substantives)*, soda-water, aerated water, foam, froth, head, spume, lather, bleb, spray, spindrift, surf, yeast, barm, suds.

Cloud, vapour, fog, mist, smog, haze, steam, nebulosity (422); scud, rack, cumulus, cirrus, stratus, nimbus, mare's tail, mackerel sky.

Nephelology; Fido.

Effervescence, foaming, mantling, fermentation, frothing, etc.

(Verbs) To bubble, boil, foam, froth, mantle, sparkle, guggle, gurgle, effervesce, fizz, ferment.

(Adjectives) Bubbling, etc., frothy, yeasty, barmy, nappy, effervescent, fizzy, up, boiling, fermenting, sparkling, mantling, *mousseux*.

Cloudy, foggy, misty, vaporous, nebulous.

———

liquid, milky, emulsive, creamy, lacteal, lacteous, curdy, curdled, soupy, muddy, slushy, clarty, thick, succulent, squashy.

Gelatinous, albuminous, gummy, colloid, amylaceous, mucilaginous, glairy, slimy, ropy, stringy, clammy, glutinous (46), viscid, viscous, sticky, gooey, slab, slabby, sizy, lentous, tacky.

Tarry, pitchy, resinous, bituminous.

354 Pulpiness (*Substantives*), pulp, paste, dough, curd, pap, pudding, poultice, soup, squash, mud, slush, grume, jam, preserve.

(*Adjectives*) Pulpy, pulpous, pultaceous, doughy, grumous.

355 Unctuousness (*Substantives*), unctuosity, oiliness, greasiness, slipperiness, lubricity.

Lubrication (332), anointment, unction; ointment (356).

(*Verbs*) To oil, grease, anoint, wax, lubricate (332).

(*Adjectives*) Unctuous, oily, oleaginous, adipose, sebaceous, fat, fatty, greasy, waxy, butyraceous, soapy, saponaceous, pinguid, stearic, lardaceous.

356 Oil (*Substantives*), fat, butter, margarine, cream, grease, tallow, suet, lard, dripping, blubber, pomatum, pomade, stearin, lanoline, soap, soft soap, wax, beeswax, sealing-wax, ambergris, spermaceti, adipocere, ointment, unguent, liniment, paraffin, kerosene, gasolene, petroleum, petrol, mineral oil, vegetable oil, olive oil, castor oil, linseed oil, train oil.

SECTION III—ORGANIC MATTER

1°. *Vitality*

1. VITALITY IN GENERAL

357 Organization (*Substantives*), the organized world, organized nature, living nature, animated nature, living beings; protoplasm, protein.

Biology, ecology (or oecology), natural, history, organic chemistry, zoology (368), botany (369).

(*Adjectives*) Organic, animate.

358 Inorganization (*Substantives*), the mineral world or kingdom; unorganized, inorganic, brute, or inanimate matter.

Mineralogy, geognosy, petrology, lithology, geology, metallurgy, inorganic chemistry.

(*Adjectives*) Inorganic, azoic, mineral, inanimate.

359 Life (*Substantives*), vitality, animation, viability, the vital spark or flame or principle, the breath of life, life-blood; existence (1).

Vivification, revivification.

Physiology, biology; metabolism.

(*Phrase*) The breath of one's nostrils.

(*Verbs*) To be living, alive, etc., to live, subsist (1), breathe, fetch breath, respire, draw breath, to be born, be spared.

360 Death (*Substantives*), decease, dissolution, demise, departure, obit, expiration; termination, close or extinction of life, existence, etc.; mortality, fall, doom, fate, release, rest, end, quietus, loss, bereavement, euthanasia, katabolism.

Last breath, last gasp, last agonies, the death-rattle, dying breath, agonies of death, dying agonies.

Necrology, death-roll, obituary.

(*Phrases*) The ebb of life; the king

To come to life, to revive, come to.

To give birth to (161); to bring, restore, or recall to life, to vivify, revive, revivify, quicken, reanimate, vitalize.

(Phrases) To see the light; to come into the world; to walk the earth; to draw breath.

To keep body and soul together; to support life.

(Adjectives) Living, alive, in life, above ground, breathing, animated, quick, viable.

Vital, vivifying, vivified, Promethean, metabolic.

(Phrases) Alive and kicking; in the land of the living; on this side of the grave.

———

of terrors; the jaws of death; the swan-song; the Stygian shore; the sleep that knows no waking; a watery grave.

(Verbs) To die, perish, expire.

(Phrases) Breathe one's last; cease to live; depart this life; end one's days; be no more; go off; drop off; pop off; peg out; lose one's life; drop down dead; resign, relinquish, lay down, or surrender one's life; drop or sink into the grave; close one's eyes; break one's neck.

To give up the ghost; to be all over with one; to pay the debt to nature; to make the great change; to take one's last sleep; to shuffle off this mortal coil; to go to one's last home; to go the way of all flesh; to kick the bucket; to hop the twig; to turn up one's toes; to slip one's cable; to cross the Stygian ferry.

To snuff out; to go off the hooks; to go to one's account; to go aloft; to join the majority; to go west; to have had it; to be numbered with the dead; to die a natural death; to hand in one's checks; to pass away or over.

(Adjectives) Dead, lifeless, deceased, demised, gone, departed, defunct, exanimate, inanimate, *kaput*, out of the world, mortuary; still-born.

Dying, expiring, moribund, *in articulo mortis, in extremis,* in the agony of death, etc., going, life ebbing, going off, life failing, *aux abois,* booked, having received one's death warrant.

(Phrases) Dead and gone; dead as a door-nail, as mutton, as a doorpost, as a herring; stone-dead; launched into eternity; gone to one's last home; gathered to one's fathers; gone to Davy Jones's locker; gone west; gone for a Burton; pushing up the daisies.

At death's door; on one's death-bed; in the jaws of death; death staring one in the face; one's hour being come; one's days being numbered; one's race being run; one foot in the grave; on one's last legs; life hanging by a thread; at one's last gasp.

(Adverbs) Post-mortem, post-obit.

361 Destruction of life, violent death.

Killing *(Substantives)*, homicide, parricide, matricide, fratricide, sororicide, infanticide, regicide, tyrannicide, vaticide, genocide, manslaughter, murder, assassination, blood, gore, bloodshed, slaughter, carnage, butchery, massacre, immolation, holocaust, fusillade, *noyade*, thuggee, thuggery, thuggism; casualty, fatality.

Death-blow, kiss of death, *coup de grâce*, grace-stroke, mercy killing, euthanasia.

Suicide, felo-de-se, hara-kiri, happy dispatch, suttee, martyrdom, execution.

Destruction of animals, slaughtering, battue, hecatomb.

Slaughter-house, shambles, abattoir.

A butcher, slayer, murderer, homicide, parricide, matricide, etc., assassin, cut-throat, bravo, thug, executioner (975).

(Verbs) To kill, put to death, do to death, slay, murder, assassinate, slaughter, butcher, immolate, massacre, decimate, take away or deprive of life, make away with, dispatch, burke, lynch, settle, do for, do in, bump off, brain, spifflicate.

To strangle, throttle, bowstring, choke, garrotte, stifle, suffocate, smother, asphyxiate, drown, hang, turn off, string up.

To cut down, sabre, cut to pieces, cut off, cut the throat, stab, knife, bayonet, shoot, behead, decapitate, stone, lapidate, execute (972).

To commit suicide, to make away with oneself.

(Phrases) To put to the sword; put to the edge of the sword; give no quarter to; run through the body; knock on the head; give one the works; put one on the spot; blow the brains out; give the death blow; the *coup de grâce*; put out of one's misery; launch into eternity; give a quietus to.

(Adjectives) Killing, etc., murderous, slaughterous, sanguinary, ensanguined, gory, bloody, blood-stained, blood-guilty, red-handed.

Mortal, fatal, deadly, lethal, internecine, suicidal, homicidal, fratricidal, etc.

362 Corpse *(Substantives)*, corse, carcass, bones, skeleton, carrion, defunct, relic, remains, ashes, earth, dust, clay, mummy.

Shade, ghost, *manes*; the dead, the majority, the great majority.

(Phrases) All that was mortal; this tenement of clay; food for worms or fishes.

(Adjectives) Cadaverous, corpse-like.

363 Interment *(Substantives)*, burial, sepulture, inhumation, obsequies, exequies, funeral, wake, lyke-wake, pyre, funeral pile, cremation.

Funeral rite or solemnity, knell, passing-bell, tolling, dirge, lament, coronach, keening (839), requiem, epicedium, obit, elegy, funeral oration, epitaph, death march, dead march, lying in state.

Grave-clothes, shroud, winding-sheet, cerecloth, cerement.

Coffin, casket, shell, sarcophagus, urn, pall, bier, hearse, catafalque.

Grave, pit, sepulchre, tomb, vault, catacomb, mausoleum, house of death, burial-place, cemetery, necropolis, churchyard, graveyard, God's acre, burial-ground, cromlech, dolmen, barrow, tumulus, cairn, ossuary, charnel-house, morgue, mortuary, crematorium, cinerator; Valhalla.

Monument, tombstone, gravestone, shrine, cenotaph.

Exhumation, disinterment; autopsy, necropsy, post-mortem.

Undertaker, mortician, mute, sexton, grave-digger.

(Verbs) To inter, bury, lay in the grave, consign to the grave or tomb, entomb, inhume, cremate, lay out, embalm, mummify.

To exhume, disinter.

(Adjectives) Buried, etc., burial, funereal, funebrial, funerary, mortuary, sepulchral, cinerary; elegiac.

(Phrases) Hic jacet; R.I.P.

2. SPECIAL VITALITY

364 Animality *(Substantives)*, animal life, animality, animation, breath, animalization.

Flesh, flesh and blood, physique.

(Verb) To animalize.

(Adjectives) Fleshly, corporal, carnal.

365 Vegetability *(Substantives)*, vegetable life, vegetation.

(Adjectives) Lush, rank, luxuriant.

366 Animal (*Substantives*), the animal kingdom, brute creation, fauna, avifauna.

A beast, brute, creature, created being; creeping or living thing, dumb creature, flocks and herds, live-stock.

Cattle, kine, etc.

Game, *fera natura*, wild life.

Mammal, quadruped, bird, reptile, fish, mollusc, worm, insect, zoophyte, animalcule, etc.

(*Phrases*) The beasts of the field; fowls of the air; denizens of the deep.

(*Adjectives*) Animal, zoological, piscatory, fishy, molluscous, vermicular, etc., feral.

368 The science of animals.

Zoology (*Substantives*), zoography, anatomy, zootomy, comparative anatomy, physiology, morphology.

Ornithology, ichthyology, herpetology, ophiology, malacology, helminthology, entomology, palaeontology.

370 The economy or management of animals.

Taming (*Substantives*), domestication, domesticity; training, breaking-in, manège, breeding, pisciculture; veterinary art.

Menagerie, zoological garden, game reserve, aviary, apiary, vivarium, aquarium, fishery, fish-pond, duck-pond.

(*Verbs*) To tame, domesticate, train, tend, break in.

(*Adjectives*) Pastoral, bucolic.

367 Plant (*Substantives*), vegetable, the vegetable kingdom, flora.

Tree, fruit-tree, shrub, bush, creeper, herb, herbage, grass, fern, fungus, lichen, moss, weed, seaweed, alga; annual, biennial, perennial; exotic.

Forest, wood, hurst, holt, greenwood, woodland, brake, grove, copse, coppice, hedgerow, boscage, plantation, thicket, spinney, underwood, undergrowth, brushwood, clump of trees, park, chase, weald, scrub, jungle, prairie.

Foliage, florescence, flower, blossom, branch, bough, spray, twig, leaf.

(*Adjectives*) Vegetable, vegetal, arboreal, herbaceous, herbal, botanic, sylvan, woodland, woody, wooded, well-wooded, shrubby, grassy, verdurous, verdant, floral, mossy.

369 The science of plants.

Botany (*Substantives*), phytography, phytology, vegetable physiology, herborization, dendrology, mycology, Pomona, Flora, Ceres.

Herbarium, herbal, *hortus siccus*, vasculum.

(*Verbs*) To botanize, herborize.

371 The economy or management of plants.

Agriculture (*Substantives*), cultivation, culture, intensive cultivation, husbandry, agronomy, geoponics, hydroponics, georgics, tillage, gardening, arboriculture, floriculture, the topiary art.

Vineyard, vinery, garden, kitchen garden, market garden, nursery, bed, plot, herbaceous border, parterre, hothouse, greenhouse, conservatory, espalier, shrubbery, orchard, rock garden, rockery, winter garden, pinery, arboretum, allotment.

A husbandman, horticulturist, gardener, florist, agriculturist, agriculturalist, woodcutter, backwoodsman, forester, land girl, farmer, yeoman, cultivator.

(*Verbs*) To cultivate, till, garden, farm; delve, dibble, dig, sow, plant, graft; plough, harrow, rake, reap, mow, cut, weed.

(*Adjectives*) Agricultural, agrarian, arable, rural, country, rustic, agrestic.

372 Mankind *(Substantives)*, the human race or species; man, human nature, humanity, mortality, flesh, generation; Everyman.

Anthropology, anthropography, ethnology, ethnography, demography, sociology, social economics; civics.

Anthropomorphism.

Human being, person, individual, type, creature, fellow creature, mortal, body, somebody, one, someone, a soul, living soul, earthling, party, personage, inhabitant; *dramatis personae*.

People, persons, folk, population, public, world, race, society, community, the million, commonalty (876), nation, state, realm, community, commonwealth, republic, commonweal, polity, nationality; civilized society, civilization.

Anthropologist, ethnologist, sociologist, etc.

(Phrases) The lords of creation; the body politic.

(Adjectives) National, civic, public, human, mortal, personal, individual, social, cosmopolitan, ethnic, racial; sociological, anthropological, ethnological, anthropomorphic, anthropomorphous, anthropoid, manlike.

373 Man *(Substantives)*, manhood, manliness, virility, he, menfolk.

A human being, man, male, mortal, person, body, soul, individual, fellow creature, one, someone, somebody, so-and-so.

Personage, a gentleman, sir, master, yeoman, citizen, denizen, burgess, burgher, cosmopolite, wight, swain, fellow, blade, bloke, beau, chap, guy, bod, type, cove, gossoon, buffer, gaffer, goodman; husband (903).

(Adjectives) Human, manly, male, masculine, manlike, mannish, virile, mannish, unwomanly, unfeminine.

(Phrase) The spear side.

374 Woman *(Substantives)*, female, feminality, femininity, womanhood, muliebrity, girlhood, she, womenfolk.

Womankind, the sex, the fair, the fair sex, the softer sex, the weaker vessel, a petticoat, skirt.

Dame, madam, madame, ma'am, mistress, lady, gentlewoman, donna, belle, matron, dowager, goody, gammer, good woman, goodwife; wife (903).

Damsel, girl, lass, lassie, maid (209), maiden, *demoiselle*, flapper, miss, missie, nymph, wench, bint, floosy, popsy, pusher, jade, dona, grisette, colleen.

(Adjectives) Female, feminine, womanly, ladylike, matronly, maidenly, girlish; womanish, effeminate, unmanly, pansy.

(Phrase) The distaff side.

2°. Sensation

1. SENSATION IN GENERAL

375 Physical Sensibility *(Substantives)*, sensitiveness, sensitivity, feeling, perceptivity, acuteness; allergy, idiosyncrasy; moral sensibility (822).

Sensation, impression consciousness (490).

The external senses.

(Verbs) To be sensible of, to feel, perceive, be conscious of, respond to, react to.

376 Physical Insensibility *(Substantives)*, obtuseness, dullness, paralysis, anaesthesia, analgesia, sleep, trance, stupor, coma, catalepsy; moral insensibility (823).

Anaesthetic, opium, ether, chloroform, chloral, cocaine, morphia, laudanum, nitrous oxide, laughing gas.

Anaesthetics.

(Verbs) To be insensible, etc. To

To render sensible, to sharpen, cultivate, train, tutor, condition.

To cause sensation; to impress, excite, or produce an impression.

(Adjectives) Sensible, conscious, sensitive, sensuous, aesthetic, perceptive.

Hypersensitive, thin-skinned, neurotic, hyperaesthetic, allergic.

Acute, sharp, keen, vivid, lively, impressive.

(Adverb) To the quick.

render insensible, to blunt, dull, obtund, benumb, deaden, stupefy, stun, paralyse, anaesthetize, dope, hocus, gas.

(Adjectives) Insensible, unfeeling, senseless, impercipient, impassable, thick-skinned, pachydermatous, hardened, proof, apathetic, obtuse, dull, anaesthetic, paralytic, palsied, numb, dead, unaffected, untouched.

(Phrase) Having a rhinoceros hide.

377 Physical Pleasure (*Substantives*), bodily enjoyment, gratification, titillation, comfort, luxury, voluptuousness, sensuousness, sensuality; mental pleasure (827).

(Phrases) The flesh-pots of Egypt; creature comforts; a bed of roses; a bed of down; on velvet; in clover.

(Verbs) To feel, experience, receive, etc., pleasure, to enjoy, relish, luxuriate, revel, riot, bask, wallow in, feast on, gloat over, have oneself a ball.

To cause or give physical pleasure, to gratify, tickle, regale, etc. (829).

(Adjectives) Enjoying, etc., luxurious, sensual, voluptuous, comfortable, cosy, snug.

Pleasant, pleasing, agreeable, grateful, refreshing, comforting.

378 Physical Pain (*Substantives*), bodily pain, suffering, sufferance, dolour, ache, aching, smart, smarting, shoot, shooting, twinge, twitch, gripe, headache, toothache, earache, sore, hurt, discomfort, malaise; mental pain (828).

Spasm, cramp, nightmare, crick, stitch, convulsion, throe.

Pang, anguish, agony, torment, torture, rack, cruciation, crucifixion, martyrdom.

(Verbs) To feel, experience, suffer, etc., pain; to suffer, ache, smart, bleed, tingle, shoot, twinge, lancinate, wince, writhe, twitch.

(Phrases) To sit on thorns; to sit on pins and needles.

To give or inflict pain; to pain, hurt, chafe, sting, bite, gnaw, pinch, tweak, grate, gall, fret, prick, pierce, gripe, etc., wring, torment, torture, rack, agonize, break on the wheel, put on the rack, convulse.

(Adjectives) In pain, in a state of pain; uncomfortable, pained, etc.
Painful, aching, etc., sore, raw, agonizing, excruciating.

---

2. SPECIAL SENSATION

(1) *Touch*

379 Sensation of pressure.

Touch (*Substantives*), taction, tactility, feeling, palpation, manipulation, tangibility, palpability.

Organ of touch; hand, finger, forefinger, thumb, paw, feeler, antenna.

(Verbs) To touch, feel, handle, finger, thumb, paw, fumble, grope, grabble, scrabble; pass, or run the fingers over, manipulate.

(Phrase) To throw out a feeler.

(Adjectives) Tactual, tangible, palpable, tactile.

380 Sensations of Touch *(Substantives)*, itching, titillation, formication, etc., creeping, aura, tingling, thrilling.

(Verbs) To itch, tingle, creep, thrill; sting, prick, prickle, tickle, kittle, titillate.

(Adjectives) Itching, etc., ticklish, kittly.

381 Insensibility to touch.

Numbness *(Substantives)*, deadness, anaesthesia (376); pins and needles.

(Verbs) To benumb, paralyse, anaesthetize; to chloroform, inject with cocaine, etc. (376).

(Adjectives) Numb, benumbed; intangible, impalpable.

(2) *Heat*

382 Heat *(Substantives)*, caloric, temperature, warmth, fervour, calidity, incalescence, candescence, incandescence, glow, flush, hectic, fever, pyrexia, hyperpyrexia.

Fire, spark, scintillation, flash, flame, blaze, bonfire, firework, wildfire, pyrotechny, ignition (384).

Insolation, summer, dog-days, tropical heat, heat-wave, summer heat, blood heat, sirocco, simoom; isotherm.

Hot spring, thermal spring, geyser.

Pyrology, thermology, thermotics, calorimetry, thermodynamics; thermometer (389).

(Phrase) The devouring element.

(Verbs) To be hot, to glow, flush, sweat, swelter, bask, smoke, reek, stew, simmer, seethe, boil, burn, broil, bake, parch, fume, blaze, smoulder.

(Phrases) To be in a heat, in a glow, in a fever, in a blaze, etc.

(Adjectives) Hot, warm, mild, unfrozen, genial, tepid, lukewarm, blood-hot, thermal, thermotic, calorific, sunny, close, sweltering, stuffy, sultry, baking, boiling, broiling, torrid, tropical, aestival, canicular, glowing, piping, scalding, reeking, etc., on fire, afire, ablaze, alight, aglow, fervid, fervent, ardent, unquenched; isothermal, sotheral; feverish, pyretic, pyrexial, pyrexical.

Igneous, plutonic, fiery, candescent, incandescent, red-hot, white-hot, incalescent, smoking, blazing, unextinguished, smouldering.

(Phrases) Hot as fire; warm as toast; warm as wool; piping hot; like an oven; hot enough to roast an ox.

383 Cold *(Substantives)*, coldness, frigidity, coolness, coolth, gelidity, chill, chilliness, freshness, inclemency; cold storage.

Frost, ice, snow, snowflake, sleet, hail, hailstone, rime, hoar-frost, icicle, iceberg, ice-floe, glacier, winter.

Sensation of cold; chilliness, shivering, shuddering, goose-skin, goose-pimples, goose-flesh, rigor, horripilation, chattering of teeth.

(Verbs) To be cold, etc., to shiver, quake, shake, tremble, shudder, dither, quiver, starve.

(Adjectives) Cold, cool, chill, chilly, gelid, frigid, algid, bleak, raw, inclement, bitter, biting, cutting, nipping, piercing, pinching, clay-cold, fresh, keen; pinched, starved, perished, shivering, etc., aguish, frozen, frost-bitten, frost-nipped, frost-bound, unthawed, unwarmed; isocheimal, isochimenal.

Icy, glacial, frosty, freezing, wintry, brumal, hibernal, boreal, arctic, hiemal, hyperborean, icebound.

(Phrases) Cold as a stone; cold as marble; cold as a frog; cold as charity; cold as Christmas; cool as a cucumber; cool as a custard.

---

384 Calefaction *(Substantives)*, increase of temperature, heating, tepefaction.

Melting, fusion, liquefaction, thaw,

385 Refrigeration *(Substantives)*, infrigidation, reduction of temperature, cooling, freezing, congealing, congelation, glaciation.

liquescence (335), liquation, incandescence.

Burning, combustion, incension, accension, cremation, cautery, cauterization, roasting, broiling, frying, ustulation, torrefaction, scorification, branding, calcination, carbonization, incineration, cineration.

Boiling, coction, ebullition, simmering, scalding, decoction, smelting.

Ignition, inflammation, setting fire to, flagration, deflagration, conflagration, arson, incendiarism, fire-raising; *auto da fé*, suttee.

Inflammability, combustibility; incendiary, fire-bug, fire-ship, *pétroleur*.

Transmission of heat, diathermancy.

(Verbs) To heat, warm, mull, chafe, fire, set fire to, set on fire, kindle enkindle, light, ignite, relume, rekindle.

To melt, thaw, fuse, liquefy (335); defrost, de-ice.

To burn, inflame, roast, broil, fry, grill, brander, singe, parch, sweal, scorch, brand, scorify, torrify, bake, cauterize, sear, char, carbonize, calcine, incinerate, smelt.

To boil, stew, cook, seethe, scald, parboil, simmer.

To take fire, catch fire, kindle, light, ignite.

(Phrases) To stir the fire; blow the fire; fan the flame; apply a match to; make a bonfire of; to take the chill off.

To consign to the flames; to reduce to ashes; to burn to a cinder.

(Adjectives) Combustible, inflammable, heating, etc., heated, warmed, melted, molten, unfrozen, boiled, stewed, sodden, adust.

Fire-brigade, fire-extinguisher, fire-engine, fireman; incombustability.

(Verbs) To cool, refrigerate, congeal, freeze, glaciate, ice, benumb, refresh, damp, slack, quench, put out, blow out, extinguish, starve, pinch, pierce, cut.

To go out.

(Adjectives) Cooled, frozen, benumbed, etc., shivery, frigorific, refrigerant.

Incombustible, non-inflammable, fire-proof.

_____

386 Furnace *(Substantives)*, fire, gas fire, electric fire, stove, kiln, oven, bakehouse, hothouse, conservatory, fire-place, grate, hearth, radiator, register, reverberatory, range, hob, hypocaust, crematorium, incinerator, forge, blast-furnace, brasier, salamander, geyser, heater, hot-plate, hot-water bottle, electric blanket, warming-pan, stew-pan, boiler, cauldron, kettle, pot, urn, chafing-dish, gridiron, saucepan, frying-pan; sudatorium, sudatory, Turkish bath, *hammam*, vapour bath.

387 Refrigeratory *(Substantives)*, refrigerator, frig, ice-pail, ice-bag, ice-house, freezing-mixture, cooler, freezer.

_____

388 Fuel *(Substantives)*, firing, coal, anthracite, coke, charcoal, briquette, peat, combustible, log, tinder, touchwood.

Lucifer, ingle, brand, match, vesuvian, vesta, safety-match, fusee, lighter, spill, embers, faggot, firebrand, incendiary, port-fire, fire-ball, fire-barrel.

389 Thermometer *(Substantives)*, clinical thermometer, pyrometer, calorimeter, thermoscope, thermograph, thermostat, thermopile.

Fahrenheit, Centigrade, Celsius, Réaumur.

Thermometry, therm.

(3) *Taste*

390 Taste (*Substantives*), flavour, gust, gusto, zest, savour, sapor, tang, twang, smack, relish, aftertaste, smatch, sapidity.

Tasting, gustation, degustation.

Palate, tongue, tooth, sweet tooth, stomach.

(*Verbs*) To taste, savour, smack, smatch, flavour, twang.

(*Phrases*) To tickle the palate; to smack the lips.

(*Adjectives*) Sapid, gustable, gustatory, saporific, strong, appetizing, palatable (394).

391 Insipidity (*Substantives*), tastelessness, insipidness, vapidness, vapidity, mawkishness, wershness, mildness; wish-wash, milk and water, slops.

(*Verbs*) To be void of taste, tasteless, etc.

(*Adjectives*) Insipid, tasteless, savourless, mawkish, wersh, flat, vapid, *fade*, wishy-washy, watery, weak, mild; untasted.

---

392 Pungency (*Substantives*), *haut-goût*, strong taste, twang, raciness, race, saltness, sharpness, roughness.

Ginger, caviare, cordial, condiment (393).

(*Verbs*) To be pungent, etc.

To render pungent, to season, spice, salt, pepper, pickle, brine, devil.

(*Adjectives*) Pungent, high-flavoured, high-tasted, high, sharp, strong, rough, stinging, piquant, racy, biting, mordant, spicy, seasoned, hot, peppery, gingery, high-seasoned, gamy, salt, saline, brackish.

(*Phrases*) Salt as brine; salt as a herring; salt as Lot's wife; hot as pepper.

393 Condiment (*Substantives*), salt, mustard, pepper, cayenne, vinegar, curry, chutney, seasoning, spice, ginger, sauce, dressing, *sauce piquante*, caviare, potherbs, pickles, onion, garlic, sybo.

394 Savouriness (*Substantives*), palatableness, toothsomeness, daintiness, delicacy, relish, zest.

A titbit, dainty, delicacy, ambrosia, nectar, *bonne-bouche*.

(*Verbs*) To be savoury, etc.

To render palatable, etc.

To relish, like, fancy, be partial to.

(*Adjectives*) Savoury, well-tasted, palatable, nice, good, dainty, delectable, toothsome, tasty, appetizing, delicate, delicious, exquisite, rich, luscious, ambrosial, meaty, fruity.

395 Unsavouriness (*Substantives*), unpalatableness, bitterness, acridness, acridity, acrimony, roughness, acerbity, austerity; gall and wormwood, rue; sickener, scunner.

(*Verbs*) To be unpalatable, etc.

To sicken, disgust, nauseate, pall, turn the stomach.

(*Adjectives*) Unsavoury, unpalatable, ill-flavoured, bitter, acrid, acrimonious, unsweetened, rough, austere, uneatable, inedible.

Offensive, repulsive, nasty, fulsome, sickening, nauseous, nauseating, disgusting, loathsome, palling.

(*Phrases*) Bitter as gall; bitter as aloes.

---

396 Sweetness (*Substantives*), dulcitude, dulcification, sweetening.

Sugar, saccharine, glucose, syrup, treacle, molasses, honey, manna, confection, confectionery, candy,

397 Sourness (*Substantives*), acid, acidity, tartness, crabbedness, hardness, roughness, acetous fermentation.

Vinegar, verjuice, crab, alum.

(*Verbs*) To be sour, etc.

conserve, jam, jelly, marmalade, preserve, liquorice, julep, sugar-candy, toffee, caramel, butterscotch, plum, sugar-plum, lollipop, bonbon, jujube, lozenge, pastille, comfit, fudge, chocolate, sweet, sweetmeat, marzipan, marchpane, fondant, nougat; mead, nectar, hydromel, honeysuckle.

(Verbs) To be sweet, etc.

To render sweet, to sweeten, sugar, mull, edulcorate, candy, dulcify, saccharify.

(Adjectives) Sweet, saccharine, sacchariferous, sugary, dulcet, candied, honeyed, luscious, edulcorated, nectarous, nectareous, sweetish, sugary.

(Phrases) Sweet as a nut; sweet as honey.

To render or turn sour, to sour, acidify, acidulate.

(Phrase) To set the teeth on edge.

(Adjectives) Sour, acid, acidulous, acidulated, sourish, subacid, vinegary, tart, crabbed, acerb, acetic, acetous, acescent, acetose, styptic, hard, rough.

(Phrases) Sour as vinegar; sour as a crab.

———

(4) *Odour*

398 Odour *(Substantives)*, smell, scent, effluvium, emanation, fume, exhalation, essence; trail, nidor, redolence.

The sense of smell, act of smelling.

(Verbs) To have an odour, to smell of, to exhale, to give out a smell, etc.

To smell, scent, snuff, sniff, inhale, nose, snowk.

(Adjectives) Odorous, odorant, odoriferous, smelling, strong-scented, graveolent, redolent, nidorous, pungent.

Relating to the sense of smell; olfactory, keen-scented.

399 Inodorousness *(Substantives)*, absence, or want of smell; deodorization.

(Verbs) To be inodorous, etc., deodorize (652).

(Adjectives) Inodorous, odourless, scentless, smell-less, wanting smell.

———

400 Fragrance *(Substantives)*, aroma, redolence, perfume, savour, bouquet.

Incense, musk, myrrh, frankincense, ambrosia, attar (or otto), eau de-Cologne, civet, castor, ambergris, bergamot, lavender, sandalwood, orris root, balm, pot-pourri, pulvil; scent-bag, scent-bottle, sachet, nosegay.

(Phrase) 'All the perfumes of Arabia.'

(Verbs) To perfume, scent, embalm.

(Adjectives) Fragrant, aromatic, redolent, balmy, scented, sweet-smelling, sweet-scented, ambrosial, perfumed, musky.

———

401 Fetor *(Substantives)*, bad smell, empyreuma, stench, stink, mustiness, fustiness, frowziness, frowst, fug, rancidity, foulness, putrescence, putridity, mephitis.

A pole-cat, skunk, badger, teledu, asafoetida, cacodyl, stinkard, stink-bomb, stinkpot.

(Verbs) To smell, stink, hum, niff, pong.

(Phrase) To stink in the nostrils.

(Adjectives) Fetid, strong-smelling, smelly, whiffy, malodorous, noisome, offensive, rank, rancid, reasty, mouldy, fusty, musty, stuffy, frowsty, fuggy, foul, frowzy, olid, nidorous, stinking, rotten, putrescent, putrid, putrefying, tainted, high (653), mephitic, empyreumatic.

(5) *Sound*

(I) SOUND IN GENERAL

402 Sound (*Substantives*), sonance, noise, strain, voice (580), accent, twang, intonation, tone, resonance (408); sonority, sonorousness, audibleness, audibility.

Acoustics, phonics, phonetics, phonology, diacoustics.

(*Verbs*) To produce sound; to sound, make a noise, give out or emit sound, to resound.

(*Adjectives*) Sonorous, sounding, soniferous, sonorific, sonoriferous, resonant, canorous, audible, distinct, phonic, phonetic.

---

403 Silence (*Substantives*), stillness, quiet, peace, calm, hush, lull; muteness (581).

A silencer, mute, damper, sordine.

(*Verbs*) To be silent, etc.

To render silent, to silence, still, hush, stifle, muffle, stop, muzzle, mute, damp, gag.

(*Phrases*) To keep silence; to hold one's tongue; to hold one's peace.

(*Adjectives*) Silent, still, stilly, noiseless, soundless, inaudible, hushed, etc., mute, mum, mumchance (581), solemn, awful, deathlike.

(*Phrases*) Still as a mouse; deathlike silence; silent as the grave; one might hear a pin drop.

(*Adverbs*) Silently, softly, etc., *sub silentio.*

(*Interjections*) Hush! silence! soft! mum! whist! chut! *tace!*

---

404 Loudness (*Substantives*), clatter, din, clangour, clang, roar, uproar, racket, hubbub, flourish of trumpets, tucket, tantara, taratantara, fanfare, blare, alarum, peal, swell, blast, boom, echo, fracas, shindy, row, rumpus, bobbery, clamour, hullaballoo, chorus, hue and cry, shout, yell, whoop, charivari, shivaree, vociferation; Stentor, Boanerges.

Speaking-trumpet, megaphone, loud-speaker, microphone, mike, amplifier, resonator.

Artillery, cannon, thunder.

(*Verbs*) To be loud, etc., to resound, echo, re-echo, peal, swell, clang, boom, blare, thunder, fulminate, roar, whoop, shout (411).

(*Phrases*) To din in the ear; to pierce, split, or rend the ears, or head; to shout, or thunder at the pitch of one's breath, or at the top of one's voice; to make the welkin ring; to rend the air; *faire le diable à quatre.*

(*Adjectives*) Loud, sonorous, resounding, etc., high-sounding, big-sounding, deep, full, swelling, clamorous, clangorous, multisonous, noisy, blatant, plangent, vocal, vociferous, stunning, piercing, splitting, rending, thundering, deafening, ear-deafening, ear-piercing, obstreperous,

---

405 Faintness (*Substantives*), lowness, faint sounds, whisper, undertone, breath, underbreath, murmur, mutter, hum, susurration, tinkle, rustle.

Hoarseness, huskiness, raucity.

(*Verbs*) To whisper, breathe, murmur, mutter, mumble, purl, hum, croon, gurgle, ripple, babble, tinkle.

(*Phrases*) Steal on the ear; melt, float on the air.

(*Adjectives*) Inaudible, scarcely audible, low, dull, stifled, muffled, hoarse, husky, gentle, faint, breathed, etc., soft, floating, purling, etc., liquid, mellifluous, dulcet, flowing, soothing.

(*Adverbs*) In a whisper, with bated breath, under one's breath, *sotto voce,* between the teeth, from the side of one's mouth, aside, *piano, pianissimo, à la sourdine.*

blaring, deep-mouthed, open-mouthed, trumpet-tongued, uproarious, rackety, stentorian.

(Phrases) Enough to split the head or ears; enough to wake the dead; enough to wake the Seven Sleepers.

(Adverbs) Loudly, aloud, etc., *forte, fortissimo.*

(Phrases) At the top of one's voice; in full cry.

(2) SPECIFIC SOUNDS

406 Sudden and violent sounds.

Snap *(Substantives)*, knock, rap, tap, click, clash, slam, clack, crack, crackle, crackling, crepitation, decrepitation, report, pop, plop, bang, thud, thump, ping, zip, clap, burst, explosion, discharge, crash, detonation, firing, salvo, atmospherics.

Squib, cracker, gun, pop-gun.

(Verbs) To snap, knock, etc.

(Adjectives) Snapping, etc.

407 Repeated and protracted sounds.

Roll *(Substantives)*, rumble, rumbling, hum, humming, shake, trill, whirr, chime, tick, beat, toll, ticking, tick-tack, patter, tattoo, ding-dong, drumming, quaver, tremolo, ratatat, tantara, rataplan, rat-tat, clatter, clutter, rattle, racket, rub-a-dub; reverberation (408).

(Phrases) The devil's tattoo; tuck of drum.

(Verbs) To roll, beat, tick, toll, drum, etc., rattle, clatter, patter, shake, trill, whirr, chime, beat; to drum or din in the ear.

(Adjectives) Rolling, rumbling, etc.

408 Resonance *(Substantives)*, ring, ringing, jingle, chink, tinkle, ting, tink, tintinnabulation, gurgle, chime, toot, tootle, clang, etc. (404).

Reflection, reverberation, echo.

(Verbs) To resound, reverberate, re-echo, ring, jingle, clink, chime, tinkle, etc.

(Adjectives) Resounding, resonant, tintinnabular, ringing, etc.

(Phrase) Clear as a bell.

Bass *(Substantives)*, low, flat or grave note, chest-note, baritone, contralto.

(Adjectives) Deep-toned, deep-sounding, deep-mouthed, hollow, sepulchral, *basso profondo.*

409 Hissing sounds.

Sibilation *(Substantives)*, hiss, swish, buzz, whiz, rustle, fizz, fizzle, wheeze, whistle, snuffle, sneeze, sternutation.

(Verbs) To hiss, buzz, etc.

(Adjectives) Sibilant, hissing, buzzing, etc., wheezy.

Soprano *(Substantives)*, high note (410).

410 Harsh sounds.

Stridor *(Substantives)*, jar, grating, creak, clank, twang, jangle, jarring, creaking, rustling, roughness, gruffness, sharpness, cacophony.

High note, shrillness, acuteness, soprano, falsetto, treble, alto, counter-tenor, penny trumpet, head-note.

(Verbs) To creak, grate, jar, burr, pipe, twang, jangle, rustle, clank; to shrill, shriek, screech, squeal, skirl (411), stridulate.

(Phrases) To set the teeth on edge; to grate upon the ear.

(Adjectives) Strident, stridulous, jarring, etc., harsh, hoarse, horrisonous, discordant, scrannel (414), cacophonous, rough, gruff, sepulchral, grating.

Sharp, high, acute, shrill, piping, screaming.

411 Human sounds.

Cry *(Substantives)*, voice (580), vociferation, outcry, roar, shout, bawl, bellow, brawl, halloo, hullaballoo, hoop, whoop, yell, cheer, hoot, howl, chorus, scream, screech, screak, shriek, squeak, squawk, squeal, skirl, yawp, squall, whine, pule, pipe, grumble, plaint, groan, moan, snore, snort.

(Verbs) To vociferate, roar, shout, bawl, etc., sing out, thunder, raise or lift up the voice.

(Adjectives) Vociferating, etc., clamant, clamorous, vociferous, stertorous.

412 Animal sounds.

Ululation *(Substantives)*, latration, cry, roar, bellow, reboation, bark, yelp, howl, bay, baying, yap, growl, grunt, gruntle, snort, neigh, nicker, whinny, bray, croak, snarl, howl, caterwauling, mew, mewl, miaow, miaul, purr, pule, bleat, baa, low, moo, boo, caw, coo, croodle, cackle, gobble, quack, gaggle, squeak, squawk, squeal, chuckle, chuck, cluck, clack, chirp, chirrup, crow, woodnote, twitter, peep.

Insect cry, drone, buzz, hum.

Cuckoo, screech-owl.

(Verbs) To cry, bellow, rebellow, etc., bell, boom, trumpet, give tongue.

(Phrases) To bay the moon; to roar like a bull or lion.

(Adjectives) Crying, etc., blatant, latrant, remugient.

(3) MUSICAL SOUND

413 Melody *(Substantives)*, melodiousness, *melos.*

Pitch, note, interval, tone, intonation, timbre; high or low, acute or grave notes, treble, alto, tenor, bass, soprano, mezzo-soprano, contralto, countertenor, baritone, *basso profondo.*

Scale, gamut, diapason; diatonic, chromatic, enharmonic, whole-tone, etc., scales; key, clef; major, minor, Dorian, Phrygian, Lydian, etc., modes; tetrachord, hexachord, pentatonic scale; tuning, modulation, temperament; solmization, solfeggio, solfa.

Staff (or stave), lines, spaces, brace; bar, double bar, rest.

414 Discord *(Substantives)*, discordance, dissonance, jar, jarring, caterwauling, cocophony.

Hoarseness, croaking, etc. (410).

Confused sounds, babel, Dutch concert, cat's concert, marrow-bones and cleavers, charivari (404).

(Verbs) To be discordant, etc., to croak, jar (410).

(Adjectives) Discordant, dissonant, out of tune, sharp, flat, tuneless, absonant, unmusical, inharmonous, unmelodious, untuneful, untunable, singsong.

Cacophonous, harsh, hoarse, croaking, jarring, stridulous, etc. (410).

Notes of the scale: sharps, flats, naturals, accidentals; breve, semibreve, minim, crotchet, quaver, semiquaver, demisemiquaver, etc.

Tonic, keynote, supertonic, mediant, subdominant, dominant, submediant, leading note, octave; primes, seconds, triads, etc.

Harmonic, overtone, partial, fundamental, note, hum-note.

Harmony, harmoniousness, concord, concordance, unison, homophony, chord, chime, consonance, concert, euphony; counterpoint, polyphony; tonality, atonality; thorough-bass, figured bass.

Rhythm, time, tempo; common, duple, triple, six-eight, etc., time; *tempo rubato,* syncopation, ragtime, jazz, swing, jive, boogie-woogie, bebop, skiffle, rock-and-roll.

(Verbs) To harmonize, chime, be in unison; put in tune, tune, accord.

(Adjectives) Harmonious, harmonic, harmonical, in harmony, in

tune, etc., unisonant, unisonal, univocal, symphonic, homophonous; contrapuntal, chordal; diatonic, chromatic, enharmonic, tonal, atonal.

Measured, rhythmical, in time, on the beat, hot.

Melodious, musical, tuneful, tunable, sweet, dulcet, canorous, mellow, mellifluous, silver, toned, silvery, euphonious, euphonic, euphonical; enchanting, ravishing, etc., Orphean.

415 Music (*Substantives*), tune, air, lilt, melody, refrain, burden, cadence, theme, motive, motif, *leit-motiv*, subject, counter-subject, episode, modulation, introduction, finale, etc.

Composition, work, opus, score, full score, vocal score, etc.

Solo, duet, trio, quartet, etc., concerted music, chorus, chamber music.

Instrumental music: Symphony, *sinfonietta*, symphonic poem, tone-poem, concerto, sonata, sonatina; *allegro, andante, largo,* scherzo, rondo, etc.; overture, prelude, intermezzo, postlude, voluntary; ballade, nocturne, serenade, aubade, barcarolle, *berceuse,* etc.; fugue, fugato, canon; variations, humoresque, rhapsody, caprice, *capriccio,* fantasia, impromptu; arrangement, pot-pourri; march, pibroch, minuet, gavotte, waltz, mazurka, etc. (840); accompaniment, *obbligato;* programme music.

Vocal music: Chant, plain-song, Gregorian music, neume, psalmody, psalm, hymn, anthem, motet, antiphon, canticle, introit, etc., service, song, ballad, *lied, chanson,* cavatina, canzonet, serenade, lullaby, ditty, chanty, folk-song, dithyramb; part-song, glee, catch, round, canon, madrigal, chorus, cantata, oratorio, etc.; opera (599).

Dirge, requiem, *nenia,* knell, lament, coronach, dead march.

Musical ornament; grace-note, appoggiatura, trill, shake, turn, beat, mordent, etc.; cadenza, roulade, bravura, colorature, *coloratura.*

Scale, run, arpeggio, chord; five-finger exercise, study, *étude,* toccata.

Performance, execution, technique, touch, expression, tone-colour, rendering, interpretation; voice-production, *bel canto; embouchure*, lipping, bowing.

Concert, recital, performance, ballad concert, etc., musicale, sing-song.

Minstrelsy, musicianship, musicality, musicalness, an ear for music; composition, composing, orchestration, scoring, filling in the parts.

Composer, harmonist, contrapuntist.

Apollo, the Muses, Erato, Euterpe, Terpsichore.

(*Verbs*) To play, fiddle, bow, strike, strike up, thrum, strum, grind, touch, tweedle, scrape, blow, pipe, tootle, blare, etc.; to execute, perform, render, interpret, conduct, accompany, vamp, arrange, prelude, improvise (612).

To sing, chant, vocalize, warble, carol, troll, lilt, hum, croon, chirp, chirrup, twitter, quaver, trill, shake, whistle, yodel.

To compose, set to music, score, harmonize, orchestrate.

To put in tune, tune, attune, accord, string, pitch.

(*Adjectives*) Musical, harmonious, etc. (413), instrumental, orchestral, pianistic, vocal, choral, operatic, etc.; musicianly, having a good ear.

(*Phrase*) *Fanatico per la musica.*

(*Adverbs*) *Adagio, largo, larghetto, andante, andantino, maestoso, moderato, allegretto, con moto, vivace, veloce, allegro, presto, prestissimo, strepitoso,* etc.; *scherzando, legato, staccato, crescendo, diminuendo, morendo, sostenuto, sforzando, accelerando, stringendo, più mosso, meno mosso, allargando, rallentando, ritenuto, a piacere,* etc.; *arpeggiando, pizzicato, glissando, martellato, da capo.*

416 Musician (*Substantives*), minstrel, performer, player, soloist, virtuoso, maestro.

Organist, pianist, violinist, fiddler, cellist, harper, harpist, flautist, fifer, clarinettist, trombonist, etc., trumpeter, bugler, piper, bagpiper, drummer, timpanist; campanologist; band, orchestra, brass band, military band, string band, pipe band, waits; conductor, bandmaster, drum-major, leader, *chef d'orchestre*, etc., accompanist.

Vocalist, singer, songster, songstress, chanter, chantress, *cantatrice, lieder-*singer, ballad-singer, etc.; troubadour, minnesinger, gleeman; nightingale, Philomel, thrush, throstle, Orpheus.

Chorus, choir, chorister.

(Phrase) The tuneful Nine.

417 Musical Instruments.

1. Stringed instruments: Monochord, polycord, harp lyre, lute, theorbo, mandolin, guitar, gittern, cithern, banjo, ukelele, balalaika.

Violin, fiddle, Cremona, Stradivarius (or Strad), kit, viola (or tenor), violoncello (or cello), double-bass (or bass-viol), viol, viola d'amore, viola da gamba, violone, rebeck, psaltery.

Pianoforte (or piano), harpsichord, clavier, clavichord, clavicembalo, spinet, cembalo, virginal, zither, dulcimer.

2. Wind instruments: Organ, siren, pipe, pitch-pipe, Pan-pipes; piccolo, flute, bass-flute, oboe (or hautboy), oboe d'amore, cor anglais, clarinet, basset-horn, bass-clarinet, bassoon, double-bassoon, saxophone, horn, French horn, tuba, trumpet, cornet, cornet-à-piston, trombone, euphonium; fife, flageolot, whistle, penny-whistle, ocarina, bugle, serpent, ophicleide, clarion, bagpipe, musette; harmonium, American organ, seraphina, concertina, accordion, melodeon, mouth-organ, etc.; great, swell, choir, solo and echo organs.

3. Vibrating surfaces: Cymbal, bell, carillon, gong, tabor, tambourine, timbrel, drum, side-drum, bass-drum, kettle-drum, timpano, military drum, tom-tom, castanet; musical glasses, harmonica, glockenspiel; sounding-board.

4. Vibrating bars: Tuning-fork, triangle, xylophone, Jew's harp.

5. Mechanical instruments: Musical box, hurdy-gurdy, barrel-organ, piano-organ, orchestrion, piano-player, pianola, etc.; gramophone, phonograph, tape recorder, juke box, nickelodeon.

Key, string, bow, drumstick, bellows, sound-box, pedal, stop; loud or sustaining pedal, soft pedal, mute, sordine, sourdine, damper, swell-box; keyboard, finger-board, console; organ-loft, concert platform, orchestra, choir, singing-gallery, belfry, campanile.

(4) PERCEPTION OF SOUND

418 Sense of sound.

Hearing *(Substantives)*, audition, auscultation, listening, eavesdropping, audibility.

Acuteness, nicety, delicacy, of ear.

Ear, auricle, acoustic organs, auditory apparatus, lug, ear-drum, tympanum.

Telephone, speaking-tube, ear-trumpet, audiphone, audiometer, earphone, phone, gramophone, phonograph, dictaphone, intercom, receiver.

Wireless telephony, broadcasting, wireless, radio, transmitter, walkie-talkie, radiogram, microphone, mike.

419 Deafness *(Substantives)*, hardness of hearing, surdity; inaudibility.

(Verbs) To be deaf, to shut, stop, or close one's ears.

To render deaf, to stun, deafen.

(Phrase) To turn a deaf ear to.

(Adjectives) Deaf, stone deaf, tone deaf, hard of hearing, earless, surd, dull of hearing, deaf-mute, stunned, deafened, having no ear.

Inaudible, out of earshot.

(Phrases) Deaf as a post; deaf as a beetle; deaf as an adder.

A hearer, auditor, listener, eavesdropper, auditory, audience.

(Verbs) To hear, overhear, hark, listen, list, hearken, give or lend an ear, prick up one's ears, give a hearing or audience to, listen in.

To become audible, to catch the ear, to be heard.

(Phrases) To hang upon the lips of; to be all ears.

(Adjectives) Hearing, etc., auditory, auricular, acoustic.

(Interjections) Hark! list! hear! listen! oyez! (or oyes!)

(Adverbs) *Arrectis auribus;* with ears flapping.

(6) *Light*

(I) LIGHT IN GENERAL

420 Light *(Substantives)*, ray, beam, stream, gleam, streak, pencil, sunbeam, moonbeam, starbeam.

Day, daylight, sunshine, sunlight, moonlight, starlight, the light of day, the light of heaven, noontide, noonday, noontide light, broad daylight.

Glimmer, glimmering, glow, afterglow, phosphorescence, lambent flame, play of light.

Flush, halo, aureole, nimbus, glory, corona.

Spark, sparkle, scintilla, sparkling, scintillation, flame, flash, blaze, coruscation, fulguration, lightning, flood of light, glint.

Lustre, shine, sheen, gloss, tinsel, spangle, brightness, brilliancy, refulgence, dazzlement, splendour, resplendence, luminousness, luminosity, luminescence, lucidity, lucidness, incandescence, radiance, illumination, irradiation, glare, flare, flush, effulgence, fulgency, fluorescence, lucency, lambency.

Optics, photology, photometry, dioptrics, catoptrics.

Radioactivity, radiography, radiograph, radiometer, radioscopy, radiotherapy.

(Verbs) To shine, glow, glitter, glisten, glister, glint, twinkle, gleam, flicker, flare, glare, beam, radiate, shoot beams, shimmer, sparkle, scintillate, coruscate, flash, blaze, fizzle, daze, dazzle, bedazzle, to clear up, to brighten.

To illuminate, illume, illumine, lighten, enlighten, light, light up, irradiate, flush, shine upon, cast lustre upon; cast, throw, or shed a light upon, brighten, clear, relume.

421 Darkness *(Substantives)*, night, midnight, obscurity, dusk (422), duskiness, gloom, gloominess, murk, mirk, murkiness, shadow, shade, umbrage, shadiness, umbra, penumbra, Erebus.

Obscuration, adumbration, obumbration, obtenebration, obfuscation, black-out, extinction, eclipse, gathering of the clouds, dimness (422).

(Phrases) Dead of night; darkness visible; darkness that can be felt; blind man's holiday.

(Verbs) To be dark, etc.; to lour (or lower).

To darken, obscure, shade, shadow, dim, bedarken, overcast, overshadow, obfuscate, obumbrate, adumbrate, cast in the shade, becloud, overcloud, bedim, put out, snuff out, blow out, extinguish, dout, douse.

To cast, throw, spread a shade or gloom.

(Phrase) To douse the glim.

(Adjectives) Dark, obscure, darksome, darkling, tenebrous, tenebrific, rayless, beamless, sunless, moonless, starless, pitch-dark, pitchy; Stygian, Cimmerian.

Sombre, dusky, unilluminated, unillumined, unlit, unsunned, nocturnal, dingy, lurid, overcast, louring (or lowering), cloudy, murky, murksome, shady, shadowy, umbrageous.

Benighted, noctivagant, noctivagous.

(Phrases) Dark as pitch; dark as a pit; dark as Erebus; dark as a wolf's mouth; the palpable obscure.

422 Dimness *(Substantives)*, dim-

(Phrase) To strike a light.

(Adjectives) Luminous, luminiferous, shining, glowing, etc., lambent, glossy, lucid, lucent, luculent, lustrous, lucific, glassy, clear, bright, scintillant, light, lightsome, unclouded, sunny, orient, noonday, noontide, beaming, beamy, vivid, alight, splendent, radiant, radiating, cloudless, unobscured; radioactive, fluorescent, phosphorescent.

Garish, resplendent, refulgent, fulgent, effulgent, in a blaze, ablaze, relucent, splendid, blazing, rutilant, meteoric, burnished.

(Phrases) Bright as silver, as day, as noonday.

-out, brown-out, paleness, glimmer, glimmering, owl-light, nebulousness, nebulosity, nebula, cloud, film, mist, haze, fog, brume, smog, smoke, haziness, eclipse, dusk, cloudiness, dawn, aurora, twilight, crepuscule, cockshut time, gloaming, daybreak, dawn, half-light, moonlight; moonshine, moonbeam, starlight, starshine, starbeam, candle-light.

(Verbs) To be dim, etc., to glimmer, loom, lour, twinkle.

To grow dim, to fade, to render dim, to dim, obscure, pale.

(Adjectives) Dim, dull, lack-lustre, dingy, darkish, glassy, faint, confused.

Cloudy, misty, hazy, foggy, brumous, muggy, fuliginous, nebulous, lowering, overcast, crepuscular, muddy, lurid, looming.

(Phrase) Shorn of its beams.

---

423 Source of light, self-luminous body.

Luminary *(Substantives)*, sun, Phoebus, star, orb, meteor, galaxy, constellation, blazing star, glowworm, firefly.

Meteor, northern lights, aurora borealis, aurora australis, fire-drake, ignis fatuus, jack-o'-lantern, will-o'-the-wisp, friar's lantern.

Artificial light, flame, gas-light, incandescent gas-light, electric light, limelight, acetylene, torch, candle, flash-lamp, flashlight, flambeau, link, light, taper, lamp, arc-lamp, mercury vapour lamp, neon lighting, lantern (or lanthorn), rushlight, farthing rushlight, night-light, firework, rocket, Very light, blue lights, fizgig, flare.

Chandelier, gaselier, electrolier, candelabra, girandole, lustre, sconce, gas-bracket, gas-jet, gas-burner, batswing; gas-mantle, electric bulb, filament.

Lighthouse, lightship, pharos, beacon, watch-fire, cresset, brand.

(Adjectives) Self-luminous, phosphoric, phosphorescent, radiant (420).

424 Shade *(Substantives)*, awning, parasol, sunshade, screen, curtain, veil, mantle, mask, gauze, blind, shutter, cloud, mist.

A shadow, chiaroscuro, umbrage, penumbra (421).

(Adjectives) Shady, umbrageous.

---

425 Transparency *(Substantives)*, transparence, diaphaneity, translucence, translucency, lucidity, pellucidity, limpidity, clarity.

Glass, crystal, mica, lymph, water.

(Verbs) To be transparent, etc., to transmit light.

(Adjectives) Transparent, pellucid,

426 Opacity *(Substantives)*, thickness, opaqueness, turbidity, turbidness, muddiness.

Cloud, film, haze.

(Verbs) To be opaque, etc., to obfuscate, not to transmit, to obstruct the passage of light.

(Adjectives) Opaque, turbid, roily,

lucid, diaphanous, translucent, relucent, limpid, clear, crystalline, vitreous, transpicuous, glassy, hyaline.

(Phrase) Clear as crystal.

(Adjectives) Semitransparent, escent, gauzy, pearly, milky.

thick, muddy, opacous, obfuscated, fuliginous, cloudy, hazy, misty, foggy, impervious to light.

427 Semitransparency, opalescence, pearliness, milkiness.

Film, gauze, muslin.

semi-diaphanous, semi-opaque, opal-

(2) SPECIFIC LIGHT

428 Colour *(Substantives)*, hue, tint, tinge, dye, complexion, shade, spectrum, tincture, blazonry, cast, livery, coloration, glow, flush, tone, key.

Pure or positive colour, primary colour.

Broken colour, secondary or tertiary colour.

Chromatics: prism, spectroscope.

A pigment, colouring matter, medium, paint, dye, wash, stain, distemper, mordant.

(Verbs) To colour, dye, tinge, stain, tinct, tincture, paint, wash, illuminate, blazon, emblazon, bedizen, imbue, distemper.

(Adjectives) Coloured, colorific, chromatic, prismatic, full-coloured, lush, dyed; tinctorial.

Bright, deep, vivid, florid, fresh, high-coloured, unfaded, gay, showy, gaudy, garish, flaunting, vivid, gorgeous, glaring, flaring, flashy, tawdry, meretricious, raw, intense, double-dyed, loud, noisy.

Mellow, harmonious, pearly, light, quiet, delicate, pastel.

429 Absence of colour.

Achromatism *(Substantives)*, decoloration, discoloration, paleness, pallidity, pallidness, pallor, etiolation, anaemia, chlorosis, albinism, neutral tint, colourlessness; monochrome, black and white.

(Verbs) To lose colour, to fade, pale, blanch, become colourless.

To deprive of colour, discolour, bleach, tarnish, decolour, decolorate, decolorize, achromatize, tone down.

(Adjectives) Colourless, uncoloured, untinged, untinctured, achromatic, aplanatic, hueless, undyed, pale, pallid, pale-faced, pasty, etiolated, anaemic, chlorotic, faint, faded, dull, cold, muddy, wan, sallow, dead, dingy, ashy, ashen, cadaverous, glassy, lack-lustre, tarnished, bleached, discoloured.

(Phrases) Pale as death, as ashes, as a witch, as a ghost, as a corpse.

430 Whiteness *(Substantives)*, miliness, hoariness.

Albification, etiolation.

Snow, paper, chalk, milk, lily, sheet, ivory, silver, alabaster.

(Verbs) To be white, etc.

To render white, whiten, bleach, whitewash, blanch, etiolate.

(Adjectives) White, milk-white, snow-white, snowy, niveous, chalky, hoary, hoar, silvery, argent.

431 Blackness *(Substantives)*, darkness (421), swarthiness, dinginess, lividity, inkiness, pitchiness, nigritude.

Nigrification.

Jet, ink, ebony, coal, pitch, charcoal, soot, sloe, smut, raven, crow; negro, nigger, darkie, coon, blackamoor.

(Verbs) To be black, etc.

To render black, to blacken, nigrify,

Whitish, off-white, cream-coloured, creamy, pearly, fair, blonde, etiolated, albescent.

(Phrases) White as the driven snow; white as a sheet.

denigrate, blot, blotch, smirch, smutch.

(Adjectives) Black, sable, swarthy, swart, sombre, inky, ebon, livid, coal-black, jet-black, pitch-black, fuliginous, dingy, dusky, Ethiopic, nigrescent.

(Phrases) Black as my hat; black as ink; black as coal; black as a crow; black as thunder.

432 Grey *(Substantives)*, neutral tint, dun.

(Adjectives) Grey, etc., drab, dingy, sombre, leaden, livid, ashen, mouse-coloured, slate-coloured, stone-coloured, cinereous, cineritious, grizzly, grizzled.

433 Brown *(Substantives)*, bistre, ochre, sepia.

(Adjectives) Brown, etc., bay, dapple, auburn, chestnut, nut-brown, umber, cinnamon, fawn, russet, olive, hazel, tawny, fuscous, chocolate, liver-coloured, tan, brunette, maroon, khaki, foxy, bronzed, sunburnt, tanned.

(Phrases) Brown as a berry, as mahogany, as a gipsy.

(Verbs) To render brown, embrown, to tan, bronze, etc.

Primitive Colours

434 Redness *(Substantives)*, red, scarlet, vermilion, crimson, carmine, pink, lake, maroon, carnation, damask, ruby, rose, blush colour, peach colour, flesh colour, gules, solferino.

Rust, cinnabar, cochineal, madder, red lead, ruddle; blood, lobster, cherry, pillar-box.

Erubescence, rubescence, rubefaction, rosiness, rufescence, ruddiness, rubicundity.

(Verbs) To become red, to blush, flush, mantle, redden, colour.

435 Greenness *(Substantives)*, verdure, viridescence, viridity.

Emerald, jasper, verd-antique, verdigris, beryl, aquamarine, malachite, grass.

(Adjectives) Green, verdant, pea-green, grass-green, apple-green, sea-green, turquoise-green, olive-green, bottle-green, glaucous, virescent, aeruginous, vert.

(Phrase) Green as grass.

To render red, redden, rouge, rubefy, rubricate, incarnadine.

(Adjectives) Red, scarlet, vermilion, carmine, rose, ruby, crimson, pink, etc., ruddy, rufous, florid, rosy, roseate, auroral, rose-coloured, blushing, mantling, etc., erubescent, blowzy, rubicund, stammel, blood-red, ensanguined, rubiform, cardinal, cerise, *sang-de-boeuf*, murrey, carroty, sorrel, brick-coloured, brick-red, lateritic, cherry-coloured, salmon-coloured.

(Phrases) Red as fire, as blood, as scarlet, as a turkey-cock, as a cherry.

436 Yellowness *(Substantives)*, buff colour, orpiment, yellow ochre, gamboge, crocus, saffron, xanthin, topaz.

437 Purple *(Substantives)*, violet, plum, prune, lavender, lilac, peach colour, puce, gridelin, lividness, lividity, bishop's purple, magenta, mauve.

Lemon, mustard, jaundice, gold.

(*Adjectives*) Yellow, citron, gold, golden, aureate, citrine, fallow, tawny, flavous, fulvous, saffron, croceate, lemon, xanthic, xanthous, sulphur, amber, straw-coloured, sandy, lurid, Claude-tint, luteous, primrose-coloured, cream-coloured, buff, chrome.

(*Phrases*) Yellow as a quince, as a guinea, as a crow's foot.

438 Blueness (*Substantives*), bluishness, azure, indigo, ultramarine, Prussian blue, mazarine, bloom, bice.

Sky, sea, lapis lazuli, cobalt, sapphire, turquoise.

(*Adjectives*) Blue, cerulean, sky-blue, sky-coloured, sky-dyed, watchet, azure, bluish, sapphire, Garter-blue.

Amethyst, murex.

(*Verb*) To empurple.

(*Adjectives*) Purple, violet, plum-coloured, lilac, mauve, livid, etc.

---

439 Orange (*Substantives*), gold, flame, copper, brass, apricot colour; aureolin, nacarat.

Ochre, cadmium.

(*Adjectives*) Orange, golden, ochreous, etc., buff, flame-coloured.

---

440 Variegation (*Substantives*), dichroism, trichroism, iridescence, play of colours, *reflet*, variegatedness, patchwork, check, plaid, chess-board, tartan, maculation, spottiness, pointillism, parquetry, marquetry, mosaic, inlay, buhl, striae, spectrum.

A rainbow, iris, tulip, peacock, chameleon, butterfly, tortoise-shell, leopard, zebra, harlequin, motley, mother-of-pearl, nacre, opal, marble.

(*Verbs*) To be variegated, etc.

To variegate, speckle, stripe, streak, chequer, bespeckle, fleck, freckle, inlay, stipple, spot, dot, damascene, embroider, tattoo.

(*Adjectives*) Variegated, varicoloured, many-coloured, versicolour, many-hued, divers-coloured, particoloured, polychromatic, bicolour, tricolour, dichromatic.

Iridescent, prismatic, opaline, nacreous, pearly, opalescent, shot, watered, *chatoyant, gorge de pigeon,* all manner of colours, pied, piebald, skewbald, daedal, motley, mottled, veined, marbled, paned, dappled, clouded, cymophanous.

Mosaic, inlaid, tessellated, chequered, tartan, tortoiseshell.

Dotted, spotted, bespotted, spotty, speckled, bespeckled, punctate, maculated, freckled, fleckered, flecked, flea-bitten, studded, tattooed.

Striped, striated, streaked, barred, veined, brinded, brindled, tabby, roan, grizzled, listed, stippled.

(*Phrase*) All the colours of the rainbow.

(3) PERCEPTIONS OF LIGHT

441 Vision (*Substantives*), sight, optics, eyesight.

View, espial, glance, glimpse, peep, peek, look, squint, dekko, gander, the once-over, gaze, stare, leer, perlustration, contemplation, sight-seeing, regard, survey, reconnaissance, introspection, inspection, speculation,

442 Blindness (*Substantives*), night-blindness, snow-blindness, cecity, amaurosis, cataract, ablepsy, nictitation, wink, blink.

A blinkard.

(*Verbs*) To be blind, etc., not to see, to lose sight of.

Not to look, to close or shut the

watch, *coup d'oeil,* oeillade, glad eye, bo-peep, ocular demonstration, autopsy, visualization, envisagement.

A point of view, gazebo, vista, loop-hole, peep-hole, look-out, belvedere, field of view, watch-tower, observation post, crow's nest, theatre, amphitheatre, horizon, arena, commanding view, bird's-eye view, coign of vantage, observatory, periscope.

The organ of vision, eye, the naked or unassisted eye, retina, pupil, iris, cornea, white, optics, peepers.

Perspicacity, penetration, discernment.

Cat, hawk, lynx, eagle, Argus.

Evil eye; cockatrice, basilisk.

(Verbs) To see, behold, discern, have in sight, descry, sight, catch a sight, glance, or glimpse of, spy, espy, to get a sight of.

eyes, to look another way, to turn away or avert the eyes, to wink, blink, nictitate.

To render blind, etc., to put out the eyes, to blind, blindfold, hoodwink, daze, dazzle.

(Phrase) To throw, dust in the eyes.

(Adjectives) Blind, eyeless, sightless, visionless, dark, stone-blind, sand-blind, stark-blind, mope-eyed, dazzled, hoodwinked, blindfolded, undiscerning.

(Phrases) Blind as a bat, as a buzzard, as a beetle, as a mole, as an owl.

(Adverbs) Blindly, etc., blindfold, darkly.

———

To look, view, eye, open one's eyes, glance on, cast or set one's eyes on, clap eyes on, look on or upon, turn or bend one's looks upon, turn the eyes to, envisage, visualize, peep, peer, peek, pry, scan, survey, reconnoitre, contemplate, regard, inspect, recognize, mark, discover, distinguish, see through, speculate; to see sights, lionize.

To look intently, strain one's eyes, be all eyes, look full in the face, look hard at, stare, gaze, pore over, gloat on, leer, to see with half an eye, to blink, goggle, ogle, make eyes at; to play at bo-peep.

(Phrases) To have an eye upon; keep in sight; look about one; glance round; run the eye over; lift up one's eyes; see at a glance, or with half an eye; keep a look-out for; to keep one's eyes skinned; to be a spectator of; to see with one's own eyes.

(Adjectives) Visual, ocular, optic, optical, ophthalmic.

Seeing, etc., the eyes being directed to, fixed, riveted upon.

Clear-sighted, sharp-sighted, quick-sighted, eagle-eyed, hawk-eyed, lynx-eyed, keen-eyed, Argus-eyed, piercing, penetrating.

(Phrase) The scales falling from one's eyes.

(Adverbs) Visibly, etc., at sight, in sight of, to one's face, before one's face, with one's eyes open, at a glance, at first sight, at sight.

(Interjections) Look! behold! see! lo! mark! observe! lo and behold!

443 Imperfect vision.

Dim-sightedness *(Substantives),* purblindness, lippitude, confusion of vision, scotomy, failing sight, short-sightedness, near-sightedness, myopia, nictitation, long-sightedness, amblyopia, presbyopia, hypermetropia, nyctalopia (or nyctalopy), nystagmus, astigmatism, squint, strabismus, wall-eye, swivel-eye, cast of the eye, double sight; an albino, blinkard.

Fallacies of vision; *deceptio visus,* refraction, false light, phantasm, anamorphosis, distortion, looming, mirage, *fata morgana,* the spectre of the Brocken, ignis fatuus, phantasmagoria, dissolving views.

Colour-blindness, Daltonism.

Limitation of vision, blinker, screen.

(Verbs) To be dim-sighted, etc., to see double, to have a mote in the eye,

to squint, goggle, look askance (or askant), to see through a prism, wink, nictitate.

To glare, dazzle, loom.

(Adjectives) Dim-sighted, half-sighted, short-sighted, near-sighted, purblind, myopic, long-sighted, hypermetropic, presbyopic, moon-eyed, mope-eyed, bleareyed, goggle-eyed, wall-eyed, one-eyed, nictitating, winking, monoculous, amblyopic, astigmatic.

444 Spectator *(Substantives)*, looker-on, onlooker, watcher, sightseer, bystander, *voyeur,* inspector, snooper, rubberneck (455), spy, beholder, witness, eyewitness, observer, star-gazer, etc., scout.

(Verbs) To witness, behold, look on at, spectate.

445 Optical Instruments *(Substantives)*, lens, meniscus, magnifier, readingglass, microscope, megascope, spectacles, specs, glasses, barnacles, goggles, pince-nez, lorgnette, folders, eye-glass, monocle, contact lens, periscope, telescope, spy-glass, monocular, binoculars, field-glass, night-glass, opera-glass, glass, view-finder, range-finder.

Mirror, reflector, speculum, looking-glass, pier-glass, cheval-glass, kaleidoscope.

Prism, camera, cine-camera, cinematograph (448), camera lucida, camera obscura, magic lantern, phantasmagoria, thaumatrope, chromatrope, stereoscope, pseudoscope, bioscope.

Photometer, polariscope, spectroscope, collimator, polemoscope, eriometer, actinometer, exposure meter, lucimeter.

446 Visibility *(Substantives)*, perceptibility, conspicuousness, distinctness, conspicuity, appearance, exposure.

(Verbs) To be visible, etc., to appear, come in sight, come into view, heave in sight, open to the view, catch the eye, show its face, present itself, show itself, manifest itself, produce itself, discover itself, expose itself, come out, come to light, come forth, come forward, stand forth, stand out, arise, peep out, peer out, show up, turn up, crop up, start up, loom, burst forth, break through the clouds, glare, reveal itself, betray itself.

(Phrases) to show its colours; to see the light of day; to show one's face; to tell its own tale; to leap to the eye; *cela saute aux yeux;* to stare one in the face.

(Adjectives) Visible, perceptible, perceivable, discernible, in sight, apparent, plain, manifest, patent, obvious (525), clear, distinct, definite, well-defined, well-marked, recognizable, evident, unmistakable, palpable, naked, bare, barefaced, ostensible,

447 Invisibility *(Substantives)*, indistinctness, inconspicuousness, imperceptibility, nonappearance, delitescence, latency (526), concealment (528).

(Verbs) To be invisible, escape notice, etc., to lie hidden, concealed, etc. (528), to be in or under a cloud, in a mist, in a haze, etc.; to lurk, lie in ambush, skulk.

Not to see, etc., to be blind to.

To render invisible, to hide, conceal (528).

(Adjectives) Invisible, imperceptible, unseen, unbeheld, undiscerned, viewless, undiscernible, indiscernible, sightless, undescried, unespied, unapparent, non-apparent, inconspicuous, unconspicuous, hidden, concealed, etc. (528), covert, eclipsed.

Confused, dim, obscure, dark, misty, hazy, foggy, indistinct, illdefined, indefinite, ill-marked, blurred, shadowy, nebulous, shaded, screened, veiled, masked.

(Phrases) Out of sight; not in sight; out of focus.

conspicuous, prominent, staring, glaring, notable, notorious, overt; periscopic, panoramic, stereoscopic.

(Phrases) Open as day; clear as day; plain as a pikestaff; there is no mistaking; plain as the nose on one's face; before one's eyes; above-board;. exposed to view; under one's nose; in bold relief; in the limelight.

448 Appearance *(Substantives),* phenomenon, sight, spectacle, show, premonstration, scene, species, view, *coup d'œil,* look-out, prospect, outlook, vista, perspective, bird's-eye view, scenery, landscape, seascape, streetscape, picture, tableau, *mise en scène,* display, exposure, exhibition, manifestation.

Pageant, pageantry, peep-show, raree-show, panorama, diorama, cosmorama, georama, *coup de théâtre, jeu de théâtre.*

Bioscope, biograph, magic lantern, epidiascope, cinematograph (or kinematograph).

Phantasm, phasma, phantom, spectrum, apparition, spectre, mirage, etc. (4, 443).

Aspect, phase, *phasis,* seeming, guise, look, complexion, shape, mien, air, cast, carriage, manner, bearing, deportment, port, demeanour, presence, expression.

Lineament, feature, trait, lines, outline, contour, face, countenance, physiognomy, visage, phiz, mug, dial, puss, pan, profile, *tournure.*

(Verbs) To seem, look, appear; to present, wear, carry, have, bear, exhibit, take, take on, or assume the appearance of; to play, to look like, to be visible, to reappear; to materialize.

To show, to manifest.

(Adjectives) Apparent, seeming, etc., ostensible.

(Adverbs) Apparently, to all appearance, etc., ostensibly, seemingly, on the face of it, *prima facie,* at the first blush, at first sight.

449 Disappearance *(Substantives),* evanescence, eclipse, occultation.

Dissolving views, fade-out.

(Verbs) To disappear, vanish, dissolve, fade, melt away, pass, be gone, be lost, etc.

To efface, blot, blot out, erase, rub out, expunge (552).

(Phrase) To go off the stage.

(Adjectives) Disappearing, etc., lost, vanishing, evanescent, gone, missing.

Inconspicuous, unconspicuous (447).

(Phrases) Lost in the clouds; leaving no trace; out of sight.

(Interjections) Avaunt! vanish! disappear! (297).

CLASS IV

WORDS RELATING TO THE INTELLECTUAL FACULTIES

DIVISION I—FORMATION OF IDEAS

SECTION I—OPERATIONS OF INTELLECT IN GENERAL

450 Intellect *(Substantives)*, mind, understanding, reason, thinking principle, nous, noesis, faculties, sense, common sense, consciousness, capacity, intelligence, percipience, intellection, intuition, instinct, conception, judgment, talent, genius, parts, wit, wits, shrewdness, intellectuality; the five senses; rationalism; ability, skill (698); wisdom (498).

Subconsciousness, subconscious mind, unconscious, id.

Soul, spirit, psyche, ghost, inner man, heart, breast, bosom.

Organ or seat of thought: *sensorium,* sensory, brain, head, headpiece, pate, noddle, nut, loaf, skull, brain-pan, grey matter, pericranium, cerebrum, cerebellum, cranium, upper storey, belfry.

Science of mind, phrenology, mental philosophy, metaphysics, psychology, psychics, psycho-analysis; ideology, idealism, ideality, pneumatology, immaterialism, intuitionism, realism; transcendentalism, spiritualism.

Metaphysician, psychologist, psychiatrist, psycho-analyst, psychotherapist.

(Verbs) Appreciate, realize, be aware of, be conscious of, take in, mark, note, notice.

(Adjectives) Intellectual, noetic, rational, reasoning, gnostic, mental, spiritual, subjective, metaphysical, psychical, psychological, noumenal, ghostly, immaterial (317), cerebral; subconscious, subliminal, Freudian.

450A Absence or want of intellect, imbecility (499), materialism.

(Adjectives) Material, objective, unreasoning.

———

451 Thought *(Substantives)*, reflection, cogitation, cerebration, consideration, meditation, study, lucubration, speculation, deliberation, pondering, head-work, brain-work, application, attention (457).

Abstraction, contemplation, musing, brown study, reverie (458); depth of thought, workings of the mind, inmost thoughts, self-counsel, self-communing, self-examination, introspection; succession, flow, train,

452 Absence or want of thought.

Incogitancy *(Substantives)*, vacancy, inanity, fatuity (499), thoughtlessness (458).

(Verbs) Not to think, to take no thought of, not to trouble oneself about, to put away thought; to inhibit, dismiss, discard, or discharge from one's thoughts, or from the mind; to drop the subject, set aside, turn aside, turn away from, turn

130

current, etc., of thought or of ideas, brain-wave.

Afterthought, second thoughts, hindsight, reconsideration, retrospection, retrospect (505), examination (461), imagination (515).

Thoughtfulness, pensiveness, intentness.

Telepathy, thought-transference, mind-reading, extra-sensory perception, retrocognition, telekinesis.

(Verbs) To think, reflect, cogitate, excogitate, consider, deliberate, speculate, contemplate, mediate, introspect, ponder, muse, ruminate, think over, brood over, reconsider, animadvert, con, con over, mull over, study, bend or apply the mind, digest, discuss, hammer at, puzzle out, weigh, perpend, fancy, trow, dream of.

To occur, present itself, pass in the mind, suggest itself, strike one.

To harbour, entertain, cherish, nurture, etc., an idea, a thought, a notion, a view, etc.

(Phrases) Take into account; take into consideration; to take counsel; to commune with oneself; to collect one's thoughts; to advise with one's pillow; to sleep on or over it; to chew the cud upon; revolve in the mind; turn over in the mind; to rack or cudgel one's brains; to put on one's thinking-cap.

To flash on the mind; to flit across the view; to enter the mind; come into the head; come uppermost; run in one's head.

To make an impression; to sink or penetrate into the mind; fasten itself on the mind; to engross one's thoughts.

(Adjectives) Thinking, etc., thoughtful, pensive, meditative, reflective, ruminant, introspective, wistful, contemplative, speculative, deliberative, studious, abstracted, introspective, sedate, philosophical, conceptual.

Close, active, diligent, mature, deliberate, laboured, steadfast, deep, profound, intense, etc., thought, study, reflection, etc.

Intent, engrossed, absorbed, deep-musing, rapt (or wrapt), abstracted; sedate.

(Phrases) Having the mind on the stretch; lost in thought; the mind or head running upon.

one's attention from, abstract oneself, dream.

To unbend, relax, divert the mind.

(Adjectives) Vacant, unintellectual (499), unoccupied, unthinking, inconsiderate, thoughtless, idealess, unidea'd, absent, *distrait*, abstracted, inattentive (458), diverted, distracted, distraught, unbent, relaxed.

Unthought-of, unconsidered, incogitable, undreamed-of, off one's mind.

(Phrase) In nubibus.

---

453 Object of thought.

Idea *(Substantives)*, notion, conception, apprehension, concept, thought, fancy, conceit, impression, perception, apperception, percept, ideation, image, eidolon, sentiment (484), fantasy, flight of fancy.

Point of view, light, aspect (448), field of view, standpoint; theory (514); fixed idea (481).

---

454 Subject of thought.

Topic *(Substantives)*, subject, matter, theme, motif, thesis, text, subject-matter, point, proposition, theorem, business, affair, case, matter in hand, question, argument, motion, resolution, moot point (461), head, chapter; nice or subtle point, quodlibet.

(Phrases) Food for thought; mental pabulum.

(Adverbs) In question, under consideration, on the carpet, *sur le tapis*, relative to, *re, in re* (9), concerning, touching.

SECTION II—PRECURSORY CONDITIONS AND OPERATIONS

455 The desire for knowlege.

Curiosity *(Substantives)*, curiousness, inquisitiveness, an inquiring mind.

A quidnunc, busybody, eavesdropper, snooper, rubberneck, Peeping Tom, Nosy Parker, Paul Pry, newsmonger, gossip.

(Verbs) To be curious, etc., to take an interest in, to stare, gape, pry, snoop, rubber, lionize.

(Adjectives) Curious, inquisitive, inquiring, inquisitorial, all agog, staring, prying, snoopy, gaping, agape, over-curious, nosy.

(Adverbs) With open mouth, on tiptoe, with ears flapping, *arrectis auribus*.

457 Attention *(Substantives)*, advertence, advertency, observance, observation, interest, notice, heed, look, regard, view, remark, inspection, introspection, heedfulness, mindfulness, look-out, watch, vigilance, circumspection, surveillance, consideration, scrutiny, revision, revisal, recension, review, revise, particularity (459).

Close, intense, deep, profound, etc., attention, application, or study.

(Verbs) To be attentive, etc.; to attend, advert to, mind, observe, look, look at, see, view, look to, see to, remark, heed, notice, spot, twig, pipe, take heed, take notice, mark; give or pay attention to; give heed to, have an eye to; turn, apply, or direct the mind, the eye, or the attention to; look after, give a thought to, animadvert on, occupy oneself with, be interested in, devote oneself to, give oneself up to, see about.

To examine cursorily; to glance at, upon, or over; cast or pass the eyes over, run over, turn over the leaves, dip into, skim, perstringe.

To examine closely or intently, scrutinize, consider, give one's mind to, overhaul, pore over, perpend, note, mark, inspect, review, size up, take stock of, fix the eye, mind,

456 Absence of curiosity.

Incuriosity *(Substantives)*, incuriousness, insouciance, nonchalance, want of interest, indifference (866).

(Verbs) To be incurious, etc., to have no curiosity, take no interest in, not to care, not to mind; to mind one's own business.

(Phrases) Not to trouble oneself about; one couldn't care less; the devil may care; san fairy ann.

(Adjectives) Incurious, uninquisitive, indifferent, *sans souci*, insouciant, nonchalant, aloof, detached, apathetic, uninterested.

458 Inattention *(Substantives)* inconsideration, inconsiderateness, inadvertence, inadvertency, non-observance, inobservance, disregard, oversight, unmindfulness, giddiness, respectlessness, thoughtlessness (460), insouciance; wandering, distracted, etc., attention.

Absence of mind, abstraction, preoccupation, distraction, reverie, brown study, day-dream, day-dreaming, wool-gathering.

(Phrases) The wits going wool-gathering; the attention wandering; building castles in the air, or castles in Spain.

(Verbs) To be inattentive, etc., to overlook, disregard, pass by, slur over, pass over, gloss over, blink, miss, skim, skim the surface, *effleur* (460).

To call off, draw off, call away, divert, etc., the attention; to distract; to disconcert, put out, rattle, discompose, confuse, perplex, bewilder, bemuse, moider, bemuddle, muddle, dazzle, obfuscate, faze, fluster, flurry, flummox, befog.

(Phrases) To take no account of; to drop the subject; to turn a deaf ear to; to come in at one ear and go out of the other; to reckon without one's host.

thoughts, or attention on, keep in view, contemplate, revert to, etc. (451).

To fall under one's notice, observation, etc., to catch the eye; to catch, awaken, wake, invite, solicit, attract, claim, excite, engage, occupy, strike, arrest, fix, engross, monopolize, preoccupy, obsess, absorb, rivet, etc., the attention, mind, or thoughts; to interest.

To call attention to, point out, indicate (550).

(Phrases) To trouble one's head about; lend or incline an ear to; to take cognizance of; to prick up one's ears; to have one's eyes open; to keep one's eyes skinned.

To have one's wits about one; to bear in mind; to come to the point; to take into account; to read, mark, learn.

(Adjectives) Attentive, mindful, heedful, regardful, alive to, awake to, bearing in mind, occupied with, engaged, taken up with, interested, engrossed, wrapped in, absorbed, rapt.

Awake, watchful, on the watch (459), broad awake, wide awake, agape, intent on, with eyes fixed on, open-eyed, unwinking, undistracted, with bated breath, breathless, upon the stretch.

(Interjections) See! look! say! attention! hey! oy! mark! lo! behold! achtung! nota bene! N.B.

(Adjectives) Inattentive, mindless, unobservant, unmindful, uninterested, inadvertent, heedless, regardless, respectless, careless (460), insouciant, unwatchful, listless, cursory, blind, deaf, etc.

Absent, abstracted, *distrait,* absent-minded, lost, preoccupied, bemused, dreamy, moony, napping.

Disconcerted, put out, etc., dizzy, muzzy (460).

(Phrase) Caught napping.

(Adverbs) Inattentively, etc., cavalierly.

———

459 Care *(Substantives)*, caution, heed, heedfulness, attention (457), wariness, prudence, discretion, watch, watchfulness, alertness, vigil, vigilance, circumspection, watch and ward, deliberation, forethought (510), predeliberation, solicitude, precaution (673), scruple, scrupulousness, scrupulosity, particularity, surveillance.

(Phrases) The eyes of Argus; *l'œil du maître.*

(Verbs) To be careful, etc., to take care, have a care, beware, look to it, reck, heed, take heed, provide for, see to, see after, keep watch, keep watch and ward, look sharp, look about one, set watch, take precautions, take tent, see about.

(Phrases) To have all one's wits about one; to mind one's P's and Q's; to speak by the card; to pick one's steps; keep a sharp look out; keep one's weather eye open; to keep an eye on.

(Adjectives) Careful, cautious,

460 Neglect *(Substantives)*, negligence, omission, trifling, laches, heedlessness, carelessness, perfunctoriness, remissness, imprudence, secureness, indiscretion, *étourderie*, incautiousness, indiscrimination, rashness (863), recklessness, nonchalance, inattention (458); slovenliness, sluttishness.

Trifler, flibbertigibbet, Micawber; slattern, slut, sloven.

(Verbs) To be negligent, etc., to neglect, scamp, pass over, cut, omit, pretermit, set aside, cast or put aside.

To overlook, disregard, ignore, slight, pay no regard to, make light of, trifle with, blink, wink at, connive at; take or make no account of; gloss over, slur over, slip over, skip, skim, miss, shelve, sink, jump over, shirk (623), discount.

To waste time, trifle, frivol, fribble (683).

heedful, wary, canny, guarded, on one's guard, alert, on the alert, on the watch, watchful, on the look out, *aux aguets*, awake, vigilant, circumspect, broad awake, having the eyes open, Argus-eyed.

Discreet, prudent, sure-footed, provident, scrupulous, particular, meticulous.

(Phrase) On the *qui vive.*

(Adverbs) Carefully, etc., with care, etc., gingerly, considerately.

(Phrases) Let sleeping dogs lie; catching a weasel asleep.

(Interjections) Look out! mind your eye! watch! beware! cave! fore! heads!

To render neglectful, etc., to put or throw off one's guard.

(Phrases) To give to the winds; take no account of; turn a deaf ear to; shut one's eyes to; not to mind; think no more of; set at naught; give the go-by to.

(Adjectives) Neglecting, etc., unmindful, heedless, careless, *sans souci*, negligent, neglectful, slovenly, sluttish, remiss, perfunctory, thoughtless, unthoughtful, unheedful, off one's guard, unwary, incautious, unguarded, indiscreet, inconsiderate, imprudent, improvident, rash, headlong, reckless, heels over head, witless, hare-brained, giddy-brained, offhand, slapdash, happy-go-lucky, cursory, brain-sick, scatterbrained.

Neglected, missed, abandoned, shunted, shelved, unheeded, unperceived, unseen, unobserved, unnoticed, unnoted, unmarked, unattended to, untended, unwatched, unthought-of, overlooked, unmissed, unexamined, unsearched, unscanned, unweighed, unsifted, untested, unweeded, undetermined.

(Phrases) In an unguarded moment; buried in a napkin.

(Adverbs) Negligently, etc., anyhow, any old way.

(Interjections) Let it pass! never mind! no matter! I should worry! san fairy ann! *nichevo!*

---

461 Inquiry *(Substantives)*, search, research, quest, pursuit (622), examination, review, scrutiny, investigation, perquisition, perscrutation, referendum, straw vote, Gallup poll; discussion, symposium, inquest, inquisition, exploration, exploitation, sifting, screening, calculation, analysis, dissection, resolution, induction; the Baconian method.

Questioning, asking, interrogation, interpellation, interrogatory, the Socratic method, examination, crossexamination, cross-questioning, third degree, quiz, catechism.

Reconnoitring, reconnaissance, feeler, *ballon d'essai*, prying, spying, espionage, the lantern of Diogenes, searchlight.

Question, query, difficulty, problem, proposition, desideratum, point to be solved; point or matter in dispute; moot point, question at issue,

462 Answer *(Substantives).* response, reply, replication, riposte, rejoinder, rebutter, surrejoinder, surrebutter, retort, come-back, repartee, rescript, antiphony, rescription, acknowledgment.

Explanation, solution, deduction, resolution, exposition, rationale, interpretation (522).

A key, master-key, open sesame, *passepartout*, clue.

Oedipus, oracle (513), solutionist.

(Verbs) To answer, respond, reply, rebut, retort, rejoin, return for answer, acknowledge, echo.

To explain, solve, resolve, expound, decipher, spell, interpret (522), to unriddle, unlock, cut the knot, unravel, fathom, pick or open the lock, discover, fish up, to find a clue to, get to the bottom of.

(Phrases) To turn the tables upon; Q.E.D.

bone of contention, plain question, fair question, open question, knotty point, vexed question, crux.

Enigma, riddle, conundrum, crossword, bone to pick, quodlibet, Gordian knot.

(Adjectives) Answering, responding, etc., responsive, respondent.

(Adverb) On the right scent.

(Interjections) Eureka!

———

An inquirer, querist, questioner, heckler, inquisitor, scrutator, scrutineer, examiner, inspector, analyst, quidnunc, newsmonger, gossip (527, 532); investigator, detective, bloodhound, sleuth-hound, sleuth, inquiry agent, private eye, Sherlock Holmes, busy, dick, rozzer, flattie, G-men; secret police, Cheka, Ogpu, Gestapo.

(Verbs) To inquire, seek, search, look for, look about for, look out for, cast about for, beat up for, grope for, feel for, reconnoitre, explore, sound, rummage, fossick, ransack, pry, snoop, look round, look over, look through, scan, peruse.

To pursue, hunt, track, trail, mouse-dodge, trace, shadow, tail, dog (622), nose out, ferret out, unearth, hunt up.

To investigate; to take up, follow up, institute, pursue, conduct, carry on, prosecute, etc., an inquiry, etc.; to overhaul, examine, study, consider, fathom, take into consideration, dip into, look into, calculate, pre-examine, dive into, to delve into, rake, rake over, discuss, canvass, thrash out, probe, fathom, sound, scrutinize, analyse, anatomize, dissect, sift, screen, winnow, resolve, traverse, see into.

To ask, speer, question, query, demand; to put, propose, propound, moot, raise, stir, suggest, put forth, start, pop, etc., a question; to interrogate, catechize, pump, cross-question, cross-examine, grill, badger, heckle, dodge, require an answer.

(Phrases) To look, peer, or pry into every hole and corner, to beat the bushes; to leave no stone unturned; to seek a needle in a bundle of hay; to scratch the head.

To subject to examination; to grapple with a question; to put to the proof; pass in review; take into consideration; to ventilate a question; seek a clue; throw out a feeler.

To undergo examination; to be in course of inquiry; to be under consideration.

(Adjectives) Inquiring, etc., inquisitive, requisitive, requisitory, catechetical, inquisitorial, heuristic, analytic, in search of, in quest of, on the look out for, interrogative, zetetic.

Undetermined, untried, undecided, to be resolved, etc., in question, in dispute, under discussion, under consideration, *sub judice*, moot, proposed, doubtful.

(Adverbs) Why? wherefore? whence? *quaere?* how comes it? how happens it? how is it? what is the reason? what's in the wind? what's cooking?

463 Experiment *(Substantives)*, essay, trial, tryout, tentative method, *tâtonnement*, verification, probation, proof, criterion, test, acid test, reagent, check, control, touchstone, pyx, assay, ordeal; empiricism, rule of thumb method of trial and error.

A feeler, *ballon d'essai*, pilot-balloon, messenger-balloon; pilot-engine; straw to show the wind.

(Verbs) To experiment, essay, try, explore, grope, angle, cast about, beat the bushes; feel or grope one's way; to thread one's way; to make an experiment, make trial of.

To subject to trial, etc., to experiment upon, try over, rehearse, give a trial to, put, bring, or submit to the test or proof; to prove, verify, test, assay, touch, practise upon.

(Phrases) To see how the land lies; to see how the wind blows; to feel the pulse; to throw out a feeler; to have a try; to have a go.

(Adjectives) Experimental, crucial, tentative, probationary, empirical, *sub judice*, under probation, on trial, on approval.

(Adverb) A tâtons.

464 Comparison *(Substantives)*, collation, contrast, antithesis, identification.

A comparison, simile, similitude, analogy, parallel, parable, metaphor, allegory (521).

(Verbs) To compare to or with; to collate, confront, place side by side or in juxtaposition, to draw a parallel, institute a comparison, contrast, balance, identify.

(Adjectives) Comparative, metaphorical, figurative, allegorical, comparable, compared with, pitted against, placed by the side of.

465 Discrimination *(Substantives)*, distinction, differentiation, perception or appreciation of difference, nicety, refinement, taste (850), judgment, discernment, nice perception, tact, critique.

(Verbs) To discriminate, distinguish, differentiate, draw the line, sift, screen.

(Phrases) To split hairs; to cut blocks with a razor; to separate the chaff from the wheat or the sheep from the goats.

465A Indiscrimination *(Substantives)*, indistinctness, indistinction (460).

(Verbs) Not to distinguish or discriminate, to confound, confuse; to neglect, overlook, lose sight of a distinction.

(Adjectives) Indiscriminate, undistinguished, undistinguishable, unmeasured, sweeping, wholesale.

(Adjectives) Discriminating, etc., discriminative, distinctive, diagnostic, nice, judicial.

466 Measurement *(Substantives)*, admeasurement, mensuration, triangulation, survey, valuation, appraisement, assessment, assize, estimation, reckoning, evaluation, gauging; mileage, voltage, horse power.

Geometry, geodetics, geodesy, orthometry, altimetry, sounding, surveying, weighing, ponderation, trutination, dead reckoning, metrology.

A measure, standard, rule, yardstick, compass, callipers, dividers, gauge, meter, line, rod, plumb-line, plummet, log, log-line, sound, sounding-rod, sounding-line, lead-line, index, flood-mark, Plimsoll line (or mark), check.

Scale, graduation, graduated scale, vernier, quadrant, theodolite, slide-rule, balance, spring balance, scales, steelyard, beam, weather-glass, barometer, aneroid, barograph, araeometer, altimeter, clinometer, graphometer, goniometer, thermometer, speedometer, tachometer, pedometer, ammeter, voltmeter, micrometer, etc.

A surveyor, geometer, leadsman, etc.

(Verbs) To measure, mete, value, assess, rate, appraise, estimate, form an estimate, set a value on, appreciate, span, pace, step; apply the compass, rule, scale, etc., gauge, plump, probe, sound, fathom, heave the log, survey, weigh, poise, balance, hold the scales, take an average, graduate, evaluate, size up, to place in the beam, to take into account, price.

(Adjectives) Measuring, etc., metrical, ponderable, measurable, mensurable.

SECTION III—MATERIALS FOR REASONING

467 Evidence, on one side *(Substantives)*, premises, data, grounds, *praecognita*, indication (550).

Oral, hearsay, internal, external, documentary, presumptive evidence.

Testimony, testimonial, deposition, declaration, attestation, testification, authority, warrant, warranty, guarantee, surety, handwriting, autograph, signature, endorsement, seal, sigil, signet (550), superscription, entry, finger-print.

Voucher, credential, certificate, deed, indenture, docket, dossier, probate, affidavit, diploma; admission, concession, allegation, deposition, citation, quotation, reference; admissibility.

Criterion, test, reagent, touchstone, check, control, prerogative, fact, argument, shibboleth.

A witness, eye-witness, indicator, ear-witness, deponent, telltale, informer, sponsor, special pleader.

Assumption, presumption, show of reason, postulation, postulate, lemma.

Reason, proof (478), circumstantial evidence.

Ex-parte evidence, one-sided view.

Secondary evidence, confirmation, corroboration, ratification, authentication, support, approval, compurgation.

(Phrases) A case in point; *ecce signum; ex pede Herculem.*

(Verbs) To be evidence, etc., to evidence, evince, show, indicate (550), imply, involve, entail, necessitate, argue, bespeak, admit, allow, concede, homologate, certify, testify, attest, bear testimony, depose, depone, witness, vouch for, sign, seal, set one's hand and seal to, endorse, confirm, ratify, corroborate, support, establish, uphold, bear upon, bear out, warrant, guarantee.

To adduce, cite, quote, refer to, appeal to, call, bring forward, produce, bring into court, confront witnesses, collect, bring together, rake up evidence, to make a case, make good, authenticate, substantiate, go bail for.

To allege, plead, assume, postulate, posit, presume; to beg the question.

468 Evidence on the other side, on the other hand.

Counter-evidence *(Substantives)*, disproof, contradiction, rejoinder, rebutter, answer (462), weak point, conflicting evidence, refutation (479), negation (536).

(Phrases) A *tu quoque* argument; the other side of the shield.

(Verbs) To countervail, oppose, rebut, check, weaken, invalidate, contradict, contravene.

(Phrases) To tell another story; to cut both ways.

(Adjectives) Countervailing, etc., contradictory; unauthenticated, unattested, unvouched-for.

(Adverbs) Although, though, albeit, but, *per contra.*

(Phrase) Audi alteram partem.

469 Qualification *(Substantives)*, limitation, modification, allowance, grains of allowance, consideration, extenuating circumstance, condition, proviso, saving clause, penalty clause, exception (83), assumption (514).

(Verbs) To qualify, limit, modify, tone down, colour, discount, allow for, make allowance for, take into account, introduce new conditions, admit exceptions, take exception.

(Adjectives) Qualifying, etc., conditional, exceptional (83), contingent, postulatory, hypothetical, supposititious (514).

(Adverbs) Provided, if, unless, but, yet, according as, conditionally, admitting, supposing, granted that; on the supposition, assumption, presumption, allegation, hypothesis, etc., of; with the understanding, even, although, for all that, at all events, after all.

(Phrases) With a grain of salt; *cum grano salis.*

(Phrases) To hold good, hold water; to speak volumes; to bring home to; to bring to book; to quote chapter and verse; to speak for itself; tell its own tale.

(Adjectives) Showing, etc., indicating, indicative, indicatory, evidential, evidentiary, following, deducible, consequential, collateral, corroborative, confirmatory, postulatory, presumptive.

Sound, logical, strong, valid, cogent, decisive, persuasive, persuasory, demonstrative, irrefragable, irresistible, etc. (578).

(Adverbs) According to, witness, admittedly, confessedly, *a fortiori,* still more, still less, all the more reason for.

Degrees of Evidence

470 Possibility *(Substantives),* potentiality, contingency (156), what may be, what is possible, etc.

Practicability, feasibility (705), compatibility (23).

(Verbs) To be possible, etc., to admit of, to bear.

To render possible, etc., to put into the way of.

(Adjectives) Possible, contingent (475), conceivable, credible.

Practicable, feasible, achievable, performable, viable, accessible, surmountable, attainable, obtainable, compatible.

(Adverbs) Possibly, by possibility, maybe, perhaps, mayhap, haply, perchance, peradventure, *in posse* (156).

(Phrases) Wind and weather permitting; within the bounds of possibility; on the cards; D.V.

471 Impossibility *(Substantives),* what cannot be, what can never be, imposs, no go, hopelessness (859).

Impracticability, incompatibility (704), incredibility.

(Verbs) To be impossible, etc., to have no chance whatever.

(Phrases) To make a silk purse out of a sow's ear; to wash a blackamoor white; to make bricks without straw; to get blood from a stone; to take the breeks off a highlandman; to square the circle; to eat one's cake and have it too.

(Adjectives) Impossible, contrary to reason, inconceivable, unreasonable, absurd, incredible, visionary, chimerical, prodigious (870), desperate, hopeless, unheard-of, unthinkable.

Impracticable, unattainable, unachievable, unfeasible, infeasible, beyond control, unobtainable, unprocurable, insuperable, unsurmountable, inaccessible, inextricable.

(Phrases) Out of the question; sour grapes; *non possumus.*

472 Probability *(Substantives),* likelihood, *vraisemblance,* verisimilitude, plausibility, show of, colour of, credibility, reasonable chance, favourable chance, fair chance, hope, prospect, presumption, presumptive evidence, circumstantial evidence, the main chance, a *prima facie* case.

Probabilism, probabiliorism.

(Verbs) To be probable, likely, etc.; to think likely, dare say, expect (507).

(Phrases) To bid fair; to stand fair for; to stand a good chance; to stand to reason.

473 Improbability *(Substantives),* unlikelihood, unfavourable chances, small chance, off-chance, bare possibility, long odds, incredibility.

(Verbs) To be improbable, etc., to have or stand a small, little, poor, remote, etc., chance; to whistle for.

(Adjectives) Improbable, unheard-of, incredible, unbelievable, unlikely.

(Phrases) Contrary to all reasonable expectation; having scarcely a chance; a chance in a thousand.

(Adjectives) Probable, likely, hopeful, well-founded.

Plausible, specious, ostensible, colourable, standing to reason, reasonable, credible, tenable, easy of belief, presumable, presumptive, *ben trovato*.

(Phrases) Likely to happen; in a fair way; appearances favouring; according to every reasonable expectation; the odds being in favour.

(Adverbs) Probably, etc., belike, in all probability, or likelihood, apparently, to all appearance, on the face of it, in the long run, *prima facie*, very likely, like enough, arguably, ten to one.

(Phrase) All Lombard Street to a china orange.

474 Certainty *(Substantives)*, certitude, positiveness, a dead certainty, dead cert, infallibleness, infallibility, gospel, scripture, surety, assurance, indisputableness, moral certainty.

Fact, matter of fact, *fait accompli*.

Bigotry, dogmatism, *ipse dixit*.

Bigot, dogmatist, Sir Oracle.

(Verbs) To be certain, etc., to believe (484).

To render certain, etc., to ensure, to assure, clinch, determine, decide.

To dogmatize, lay down the law.

(Phrases) To stand to reason; to make assurance doubly sure.

(Adjectives) Certain, sure, assured, solid, absolute, positive, flat, determinate, categorical, unequivocal, inevitable, unavoidable, avoidless, unerring, infallible, indubitable, indubious, indisputable, undisputed, uncontested, undeniable, incontestable, irrefutable, unimpeachable, incontrovertible, undoubted, doubtless, without doubt, beyond a doubt, past dispute, unanswerable, decided, unquestionable, beyond all question, unquestioned, questionless, irrefragable, evident, self-evident, axiomatic, demonstrable (478), authoritative, authentic, official, unerring, infallible, trustworthy (939).

(Phrases) Sure as fate; and no mistake; sure as a gun; clear as the sun at noonday; sure as death (and taxes); bet your life; you bet; *cela va sans dire*; it's in the bag; that's flat.

(Adverbs) Certainly, assuredly, etc., for certain, *in esse*, sure, surely, sure enough, to be sure, of course, as a matter of course, yes (488), depend upon it, that's so, by all manner of means, beyond a peradventure.

475 Uncertainty *(Substantives)*, incertitude, doubt (485), doubtfulness, dubiety, dubiousness, suspense, precariousness, indefiniteness, indetermination, slipperiness, fallibility, perplexity, embarrassment, dilemma, ambiguity (520), hesitation, vacillation (605), equivoque, vagueness, peradventure, touch-and-go.

(Phrases) A blind bargain; a pig in a poke; a leap in the dark; a moot point; an open question.

(Verbs) To be uncertain, etc.,; to vacillate, hesitate, waver.

To render uncertain, etc., to perplex, embarrass, confuse, moider, confound, bewilder, disorientate.

(Phrases) To be in a state of uncertainty; not to know which way to turn; to be at a loss; to be at fault; to lose the scent.

To tremble in the balance; to hang by a thread.

(Adjectives) Uncertain, doubtful, dubious, precarious (665), chancy, casual, random, contingent, indecisive, dependent on circumstances, undecided, unsettled, undetermined, pending, pendent, vague, indeterminate, indefinite, ambiguous, undefined, equivocal, undefinable, puzzling, enigmatic, debatable, disputable, questionable, apocryphal, problematical, hypothetical, controvertible, fallible, fallacious, suspicious, fishy, slippery, ticklish.

Unauthentic, unconfirmed, undemonstrated, undemonstrable, unreliable, untrustworthy.

SECTION IV—REASONING PROCESSES

476 Reasoning (*Substantives*), ratiocination, dialectics, induction, deduction, generalization; inquiry (461).

Argumentation, discussion, *pourparler*, controversy, polemics, debate, wrangling, logomachy, apology, apologetics, ergotism, disputation, disceptation.

The art of reasoning, logic, process, train or chain of reasoning, analysis, synthesis, argument, lemma, proposition, terms, premises, postulate, data, starting-point, principle, inference, result, conclusion.

Syllogism, prosyllogism, enthymeme, sorites, dilemma, *perilepsis*, pros and cons, a comprehensive argument.

Correctness, soundness, force, validity, cogency, conclusiveness.

A thinker, reasoner, disputant, controversialist, logician, dialectician, polemic, wrangler, arguer, debater.

(*Phrases*) A paper war; a war of words; a battle of the books; a full-dress debate.

The horns of a dilemma; *reductio ad absurdum*; *argumentum ad hominem*; *onus probandi*.

(*Verbs*) To reason, argue, discuss, debate, dispute, wrangle; bandy words or arguments; hold or carry on an argument, controvert, contravene (536), consider (461), comment upon, moralize upon, spiritualize.

(*Phrases*) To open a discussion or case; to moot; to join issue; to ventilate a question; to talk it over; to have it out; to take up a side or case.

To chop logic; to try conclusions; to impale on the horns of a dilemma; to cut the matter short; to hit the nail on the head; to take one's stand upon; to have the last word.

(*Adjectives*) Reasoning, etc., rational, rationalistic, ratiocinative, argumentative, controversial, dialectic, polemical, discursory, discursive, debatable, controvertible, disputatious; correct, just, fair, sound, valid,

477 The absence of reasoning.

Intuition (*Substantives*), instinct, association, presentiment, insight, second sight, sixth sense.

False or vicious reasoning, show of reason.

Misjudgment, miscalculation (481).

Sophistry (*Substantives*), paralogy, fallacy, perversion, casuistry, jesuitry, quibble, equivocation, evasion, chicanery, special pleading, quiddity, mystification; nonsense (497).

Sophism, solecism, paralogism, elenchus, fallacy, quodlibet, subterfuge, subtlety, quillet, inconsistency, antilogy.

Speciousness, plausibility, illusiveness, irrelevancy, invalidity; clap-trap, hot air.

Quibbler, casuist, *advocatus diaboli*.

(*Phrases*) Begging the question; *petitio principii*; *ignoratio elenchi*; reasoning in a circle; *post hoc, ergo propter hoc; ignotum per ignotius*.

The meshes or cobwebs of sophistry; a flaw in an argument; an argument falling to the ground.

(*Verbs*) To envisage, to judge intuitively, etc.

To reason ill, falsely, etc.; to pervert, quibble, equivocate, mystify, evade, elude, gloss over, varnish, misjudge, miscalculate (481).

To refine, subtilize, cavil, sophisticate, mislead.

(*Phrases*) To split hairs; to cut blocks with a razor; throw off the scent; to beg the question; reason in a circle; beat about the bush; prove that black is white; not have a leg to stand on; lose one's reckoning.

(*Adjectives*) Intuitive, instinctive, impulsive, unreasoning, independent of or anterior to reason.

Sophistical, unreasonable, irrational, illogical, false, unsound, not following, not pertinent, inconsequent, inconsequential, unwarranted, untenable, inconclusive, incorrect, fallacious, inconsistent, groundless, fallible, unproved, indecisive,

cogent, logical, demonstrative (478), relevant, pertinent (9, 23).

(Phrases) To the point; in point; to the purpose; *ad rem.*

(Adverbs) For, because, for that reason, forasmuch as, inasmuch as, since, hence, whence, whereas, considering, therefore, consequently, *ergo,* then, thus, accordingly, wherefore, *a fortiori, a priori, ex concesso.*

(Phrases) In consideration of; in conclusion; in fine; after all; *au bout du compte;* on the whole; taking one thing with another.

---

478 Demonstration *(Substantives),* proof, conclusiveness, probation, comprobation, clincher, *experimentum crucis,* test, etc. (463), argument (476).

(Verbs) To demonstrate, prove, establish, show, evince, verify, substantiate; to follow.

(Phrases) Make good; set at rest; settle the question; reduce to demonstration; to make out a case; to prove one's point; to clinch an argument; bring home to; bear out.

(Adjectives) Demonstrating, etc., demonstrative, probative, demonstrable, unanswerable, conclusive, final, apodictic (or apodeictic), irrefutable, irrefragable, unimpeachable, categorical, decisive, crucial.

Demonstrated, proved, proven, etc., unconfuted, unrefuted; evident, self-evident, axiomatic (474); deducible, consequential, inferential.

(Phrases) Probatum est; it stands to reason; it holds good; there being nothing more to be said; Q.E.D.

(Adverbs) Of course, in consequence, consequently, as a matter of course, no wonder.

deceptive, illusive, illusory, specious, hollow, jesuitical, plausible, irrelevant.

Weak, feeble, poor, flimsy, trivial, trumpery, trashy, puerile, childish, irrational, silly, foolish, imbecile, absurd (499), extravagant, far-fetched, pettifogging, quibbling, fine-spun, hair-splitting.

(Phrases) Non constat; non sequitur; not holding water; away from the point; foreign to the purpose or subject; having nothing to do with the matter; not of the essence; *nihil ad rem;* not bearing upon the point in question; not the point; beside the mark.

479 Confutation *(Substantives),* refutation, disproof, conviction, redargution, invalidation, exposure, exposition; demolition of an argument; answer, come-back, counter, retort.

(Phrases) Reductio ad absurdum; a knock-down argument; a *tu quoque* argument.

(Verbs) To confute, refute, disprove, redargue, expose, show the fallacy of, knock the bottom out of, rebut, parry, negative, defeat, overthrow, demolish, explode, riddle, overturn, invalidate, silence, reduce to silence, shut up, put down.

(Phrases) To cut the ground from one's feet; to give one a set-down.

(Adjectives) Confuting, etc., confuted, etc., capable of refutation, refutable, confutable, etc.; unproved, etc.

(Phrases) The argument falls to the ground; it won't hold water; that cock won't fight.

SECTION V—RESULTS OF REASONING

480 Judgment *(Substantives)*, conclusion, determination, deduction, inference, result, illation, corollary, rider, porism, consectary.

Estimation, valuation, appreciation, judication, adjudication, arbitrament, arbitration, assessment, award, ponderation.

Decision, sentence, verdict, moral, ruling, finding; detection, discovery, estimate; *chose jugée.*

Criticism, critique, review, report, notice; plebiscite, casting vote.

A judge, umpire, arbiter, arbitrator, assessor, censor, referee, critic, connoisseur, reviewer.

(Verbs) To judge, deduce, conclude, draw a conclusion, infer, make a deduction, draw an inference, put two and two together; come to, arrive or jump at a conclusion; to derive, gather, collect.

To estimate, appreciate, value, count, assess, rate, account, rank, regard, review, settle, decide, pronounce, arbitrate, perpend, size up.

(Phrases) To sit in judgment; to hold the scales; to pass an opinion; to pass judgment.

(Adjectives) Judging, etc., deducible (467); impartial, unbiased, unprejudiced, unwarped, unbigoted, equitable, fair, sound, rational, judicious, shrewd.

480ᴀ Detection *(Substantive)*, discovery.

(Verbs) To ascertain, determine, find, find out, make out, detect, discover, elicit, recognize, trace, get at; get or arrive at the truth; meet with, fall upon, light upon, hit upon, fall in with, stumble upon, lay the finger on, spot, solve, resolve, unravel, fish out, worm out, ferret out, root out, nose out, disinter, unearth, grub up, fish up, investigate (461).

To be near the truth, to get warm, to burn.

(Phrase) To smell a rat.

(Interjection) Eureka!

481 Misjudgment *(Substantives)*, obliquity of judgment, misconception, error (495), miscalculation, miscomputation, presumption.

Prejudgment, prejudication, prejudice, prenotion, *parti pris*, prevention, preconception, predilection, prepossession, preapprehension, presentiment, *esprit de corps,* clannishness, party spirit, partisanship, partiality.

Bias, warp, twist, fad, whim, crotchet, fike; narrow-mindedness, bigotry, dogmatism, intolerance, tenacity, obstinacy (606); blind side; one-sided, partial, narrow or confined views, ideas, conceptions, or notions; *idée fixe,* fixed idea, obsession, monomania, infatuation.

(Phrases) A bee in one's bonnet; a mote in the eye; a fool's paradise.

(Verbs) To misjudge, misestimate, misconceive, misreckon, etc. (495).

To prejudge, forejudge, prejudicate, dogmatize, have a bias, etc., presuppose, presume.

To produce a bias, twist, etc.; to bias, warp, twist, prejudice, obsess, infatuate, prepossess.

(Phrases) To have on the brain; to look only at one side of the shield; to view with jaundiced eye; to run away with the notion; to jump to a conclusion.

(Adjectives) Prejudging, misjudging, etc., prejudiced, jaundiced, narrow-minded, dogmatic, intolerant, illiberal, blimpish, besotted, infatuated, fanatical, *entêté*, positive, obstinate (606), tenacious, pig-headed, having a bias, twist, etc., warped, partial, one-sided, biased, bigoted, hide-bound, tendentious, opinionated, opinionative, opinioned, selfopinioned, self-opinionated, crotchety, pernickety, faddy, fussy, fiky.

(Phrases) Wedded to an opinion; the wish being father to the thought.

482 Overestimation *(Substantive),* exaggeration.

(Phrases) Much ado about nothing; much cry and little wool; a storm in a tea-cup.

(Verbs) To overestimate, estimate too highly, overrate, overvalue, overprize, overpraise, overweigh, outreckon; exaggerate, extol, puff, boost, make too much of, overstrain.

(Phrases) To set too high a value upon; to make a mountain out of a molehill; *parturiunt montes, nascetur ridiculus mus*; to make two bites of a cherry; all his geese are swans.

(Adjectives) Overestimated, etc.

---

483 Underestimation *(Substantives),* depreciation, disparagement, detraction (934), underrating, undervaluing, etc.

(Verbs) To depreciate, disparage, detract, underrate, underestimate, undervalue, underreckon, underprize, misprize, disprize, not to do justice to, make light of, slight, belittle, knock, slam, make little of, think nothing of, hold cheap, cheapen, disregard, to care nothing for, despise, set at naught, minimize, discount, deride, derogate, decry, cry down, crab, denigrate, smear, vilipend, run down (934).

To scout, deride, pooh-pooh, mock, scoff at, laugh at, whistle at, play with, trifle with, fribble, niggle, ridicule (856).

(Phrases) To snap one's fingers at; throw into the shade; not to care a pin, rush, hoot, tinker's cuss, etc., for; to damn with faint praise.

(Adjectives) Depreciating, etc., derogatory, cynical.

Depreciated, etc., unvalued, unprized.

---

484 Belief *(Substantives),* credence, faith, trust, troth, confidence, credit, dependence on, reliance, assurance.

Opinion, notion, idea (453), conception, apprehension, impression, conceit, mind, view, persuasion, conviction, convincement, sentiment, voice, conclusion, judgment (480), estimation, self-conviction.

System of opinions, creed, credo, religion (983, 987), doctrine, tenet, dogma, principle, school, ideology, articles of belief, way of thinking, popular belief, *vox populi,* public opinion, *esprit de corps,* partisanship; ism, doxy.

Change of opinion (607), proselytism, propagandism (537).

A convert, pervert, vert, proselyte.

(Verbs) To believe, credit, receive, give faith to, give credit to, rely upon, make no doubt, reckon, doubt not, confide in, count upon, depend upon, build upon, calculate upon, take upon trust, swallow, gulp down, take one's word for, take upon credit, swear by.

To be of opinion, to opine, presume;

---

485 Unbelief *(Substantives),* disbelief, misbelief, discredit, agnosticism, atheism (988), heresy (984), dissent (489).

Doubt, dubitation, scepticism, *diaporesis,* misgiving, demur, cliff-hanging, suspense; shade or shadow of doubt, distrust, mistrust, misdoubt, suspicion, shyness, embarrassment, hesitation, uncertainty (475), scruple, qualm, dilemma; casuistry, paradox; schism (489), incredulity (487).

Unbeliever, sceptic (487); Doubting Thomas.

(Verbs) To disbelieve, discredit, not to believe; refuse to admit or believe; misbelieve, controvert; put or set aside; join issue, dispute, etc.

To doubt, be doubtful, etc., diffide, distrust, mistrust, suspect, scent, jalouse; have, harbour, entertain, etc., doubts; demur, stick at, pause, hesitate, scruple, question, query, call in question, look askance (or askant).

To cause, raise, suggest, or start a doubt; to pose, stagger, floor, startle, embarrass, puzzle (704); shake or stagger one's faith or belief.

(Phrases) Not to know what to

to have, hold, possess, entertain, adopt, imbibe, embrace, foster, nurture, cherish, etc.; to think, look upon, view, consider, take, take it, hold, trow, ween, conceive, fancy, apprehend, regard, esteem, deem, account; meseems, methinks.

To cause to be believed, thought, or esteemed; to satisfy, persuade, assure, convince, convert, bring over, win over, indoctrinate, proselytize (537), evangelize; to vert.

(Phrases) To pin one's faith to; to take at one's word.

To take it into one's head; to run away with the notion; to come round to an opinion.

To cram down the throat; to bring home to; to find credence; to carry conviction; pass current; pass muster; to hold water; to go down.

make of; to smell a rat; to hang in doubt; to have one's doubts; to float in a sea of doubts.

(Adjectives) Unbelieving, doubting, etc., incredulous, scrupulous, suspicious, sceptical, shy of belief, at sea, at a loss (487).

Unworthy or undeserving of belief, hard to believe, doubtful (475), dubious, unreliable, fishy, questionable, suspect, staggering, puzzling, etc., **paradoxical, incredible, inconceivable.**

(Phrases) With a grain of salt; *cum grano salis; timeo Danaos et dona ferentes*; all is not gold that glitters; the cowl does not make the monk.

(Adjectives) Believing, etc., impressed with, imbued with, wedded to, unsuspecting, unsuspicious, void of suspicion, etc., credulous (486), convinced, positive, sure, assured, cocksure, certain, confident.

Believed, etc., credited, accredited, unsuspected, received, current, popular.

Worthy or deserving of belief, commanding belief, believable, persuasive, impressive, reliable, dependable, trustworthy (939), credible, probable (572), fiducial, fiduciary; relating to belief, doctrinal.

(Adverbs) In the opinion of, in the eyes of, on the strength of, to the best of one's belief, *me judice*.

486 Credulity *(Substantives)*, credulousness, gullibility, infatuation, self-delusion, self-deception, superstition, gross credulity, bigotry, dogmatism.

A credulous person, gull, gobemouche; dupe (547).

(Verbs) To be credulous, etc., to follow implicitly, swallow, take on trust, take for gospel.

To impose upon, practise upon, palm off upon, cajole, etc., deceive (545).

(Phrases) Credo quia absurdum; the wish being father to the thought.

(Adjectives) Credulous, gullible, confiding, trusting; easily deceived, cajoled, etc.; green, verdant, superstitious, simple, unsuspicious, etc. (484), soft, childish, silly, stupid, over-credulous, over-confident.

487 Incredulity *(Substantives)*, incredulousness, scepticism, pyrrhonism, nihilism, suspicion (485), suspiciousness, scrupulousness, scrupulosity.

An unbeliever, sceptic, misbeliever, pyrrhonist; nihilist.

(Verbs) To be incredulous, etc., to distrust (485).

(Adjectives) Incredulous, hard of belief, sceptical, unbelieving, inconvincible, shy of belief, doubting, distrustful, suspicious (485).

(Phrases) Oh yeah? says you! a likely story! rats! that be hanged for a tale; tell that to the marines; it won't wash; that cock won't fight; *credat Judaeus Apella*.

488 Assent *(Substantives)*, acquiescence, admission, assentation, nod, consent, concession, accord, accordance, agreement (23), concord (714), concordance, concurrence, ratification, confirmation, corroboration, approval, recognition, acknowledgment, acceptance, granting, avowal, confession.

Unanimity, chorus; affirmation (535), common consent, acclamation, consensus.

Yes-man, sycophant, echo.

(Verbs) To assent, acquiesce, agree, yield assent, accord, concur, consent, nod assent, accept, coincide, go with, go along with, be at one with, chime in with, strike in with, close with, vote for, conform with, defer to; say yes, ay, ditto, amen, etc.

To acknowledge, own, avow, confess, concede, subscribe to, abide by, admit, allow, recognize, grant, endorse, ratify, countersign, O.K., okay, approve, carry.

(Phrases) To go or be solid for; to come to an understanding; to come to terms; one could not agree more.

(Adjectives) Assenting, etc., acquiescent, content, consentient, willing; approved, agreed, carried; uncontradicted, unchallenged, unquestioned, uncontroverted; unanimous.

(Phrase) Of one mind.

(Adverbs) Affirmatively, in the affirmative (535).

Yes, yea, yeah, yep, ay, aye, uh-huh, sure, very well, even so, just so, quite so, to be sure, all right, right oh! right you are, you said it, definitely, absolutely, exactly, precisely, truly, certainly, assuredly, no doubt, doubtless, verily, very true (494), *ex concesso.*

Be it so, so be it, by all means, granted, O.K., okay, oke, okeydoke, by all manner of means, *à la bonne heure,* amen, willingly, etc. (602).

With one voice, with one accord, *una voce,* unanimously, in chorus, as one man, to a man, *nem. con.* or *nemine contradicente, nemine dissentiente, en bloc,* without a dissentient voice, one and all, on all hands.

489 Dissent *(Substantives)*, dissidence, discordance, denial (536), dissonance, disagreement; difference or diversity of opinion, recusancy, contradiction, nonconformity, schism (984), secession; protest.

A dissentient, dissenter, protestant, nonconformist, recusant, heretic; deviationist, nonjuror, schismatic, seceder.

(Verbs) To dissent, demur, deny, disagree, refuse assent, say no, differ, cavil, ignore, protest, contradict, secede, repudiate, refuse to admit.

(Phrases) To shake the head; to shrug the shoulders; to join issue; to give the lie; to differ *toto caelo.*

(Adjectives) Dissenting, etc., dissentient, dissident, discordant, protestant, nonconforming, recusant, nonjuring, non-content, schismatic, deviationist; unconvinced, unconverted, unavowed, unacknowledged.

Unwilling, reluctant, extorted, etc.

(Adverbs) Negatively, in the negative (536), at variance with.

No, nay, nope, nit, na, not, not so, not at all, nohow, nowise, not in the least, not a bit, not a whit, not a jot, by no means, by no manner of means, not for the world, on no account, in no respect.

(Phrases) Many men, many minds; *quot homines, tot sententiae; tant s'en faut;* the answer is in the negative; *il s'en faut bien.*

(Interjections) No sir! God forbid! I'll be hanged first! I'll see you far enough! not bloody likely! not on your nelly! not if I know it! over my dead body! pardon me! I beg your pardon!

---

490 Knowledge *(Substantives)*, cognizance, cognition, cognoscence, awareness, gnosis, acquaintance, experience, ken, privity, insight,

491 Ignorance *(Substantives)*, nescience, nescientness, unacquaintance, unconsciousness, darkness, blindness, incomprehension,

familiarity, apprehension, comprehension, understanding, recognition; discovery (480), appreciation; knowability.

Intuition, clairvoyance, consciousness, conscience, perception, precognition, light, enlightenment, glimpse, inkling, glimmer, dawn, scent, suspicion; conception, notion, idea (453).

Self-consciousness, self-knowledge, apperception.

System or body of knowledge, science, philosophy, pansophy, pandect, doctrine, ideology, theory, aetiology, literature, *belles-lettres*, *literae humaniores*, the humanities, humanism; ology.

Erudition, learning, lore, scholarship, letters, book-learning, bookishness, bibliomania, bibliolatry, education, instruction, information, acquisitions, acquirements, accomplishments, attainments, proficiency, cultivation, culture; a liberal education, encyclopaedic knowledge, omniscience.

Elements, rudiments, abecedary (542), cyclopaedia, encyclopaedia, school, academy, etc.

Depth, extent, profoundness, profundity, stores, etc., solidity, accuracy, etc., of knowledge.

(Phrases) The march of intellect; the progress, advance, etc., of science; the schoolmaster being abroad.

(Verbs) To know, be aware of, savvy, ken, wot, ween, trow, have, possess, perceive, conceive, apprehend, ideate, understand, comprehend, make out, recognize, be master of, know full well, possess the knowledge of, experience, discern, perceive, see, see through, have in one's head.

(Phrases) To know what's what; to know how the wind blows; to know the ropes; to have at one's finger-tips or finger-ends.

(Adjectives) Knowing, aware of, etc., cognizant of, acquainted with, privy to, conscious of, no stranger to, *au fait, au courant*, versed in, hep,

incognizance, inexperience, emptiness.

Imperfect knowledge, smattering, sciolism, glimmering; bewilderment, perplexity (475); incapacity.

Affectation of knowledge, pedantry, charlatanry, quackery, dilettantism.

(Phrases) Crass ignorance; monumental ignorance.

A sealed book; unexplored ground; an unknown quantity; *terra incognita*.

(Verbs) To be ignorant, etc., not to know, to know nothing of, not to be aware of, to be at a loss, to be out of it, to be at fault, to ignore, to be blind to, etc., not to understand, etc.

(Phrases) To be caught tripping; not to know what to make of; to have no idea or notion; not to be able to make head or tail of; not to know a hawk from a handsaw; to lose one's bearings.

(Adjectives) Ignorant, unknowing, unconscious, unaware, unwitting, witless, a stranger to, unacquainted, unconversant, unenlightened, unilluminated, incognizant, unversed, uncultivated, clueless.

Uninformed, uninstructed, untaught, unapprised, untutored, unschooled, unguided.

Shallow, superficial, green, verdant, rude, half-learned, illiterate, unread, uneducated, unlearned, uncultured, Philistine, unlettered, empty-headed, having a smattering, etc., pedantic.

Confused, puzzled, bewildered, bemused, muddled, bemuddled, lost, benighted, belated, at sea, at fault, posed, blinded, abroad, distracted, in a maze, misinformed, hoodwinked, in the dark, at a loss, *désorienté*.

Unknown, novel, unapprehended, unexplained, unascertained, uninvestigated, unexplored, untravelled, uncharted, chartless, unheard-of, unperceived, unknowable.

(Phrases) Having a film over the eyes; wide of the mark; at cross purposes.

(Adverbs) Ignorantly, unwittingly,

up in, up to, alive to, wise to, conversant with, proficient in, read in, familiar with.

Apprised of, made acquainted with, informed of; undeceived.

Erudite, instructed, learned, well-read, lettered, literate, educated, cultivated, cultured, knowledgeable, enlightened, well-informed, shrewd, bookish, scholarly, scholastic, deep-read; self-taught, well-grounded, well-conned.

Known, etc., well-known, recognized, received, notorious, noted, proverbial, familiar; hackneyed, trite, commonplace; cognoscible, knowable; experiential.

(Phrases) Behind the scenes; in the know; at home in; the scales fallen from one's eyes.

(Adverbs) To one's knowledge, to the best of one's knowledge.

(Phrase) Experto crede.

unawares; for anything one knows; for aught one knows.

(Phrase) 'A little learning is a dangerous thing.'

---

492 Scholar *(Substantives)*, student (541); savant, scientist, humanist, grammarian, intellectual, pundit, schoolman, don, professor, lecturer, reader, demonstrator, graduate, doctor, master of arts, licentiate, wrangler, gownsman, philosopher, philomath, clerk, encyclopaedist.

Linguist; *littérateur, literati, illuminati,* intelligentsia.

Pedant, pedagogue, bookworm, *helluo librorum,* bibliomaniac, bibliophile, blue-stocking, *bas-bleu,* highbrow, bigwig, bookman; swot, grind.

(Phrases) Man of letters; man of learning; at the feet of Gamaliel; a walking dictionary.

(Adjectives) Erudite, learned, scholarly (490).

493 Ignoramus *(Substantives)*, sciolist, smatterer, novice, greenhorn, half-scholar, schoolboy, booby, dunce (501); bigot (481); quack, mountebank, charlatan, dilettante, low-brow, amateur, Philistine, obscurant, obscurantist.

(Phrase) The wooden spoon.

(Adjectives) Bookless, shallow (499), ignorant, etc. (491), prejudiced (481), obscurantist.

---

494 Object of knowledge.
Truth *(Substantives)*, verity, actual existence (1), reality, fact, matter of fact, actuality, nature, principle, orthodoxy, gospel, holy writ, substantiality, genuineness, authenticity, realism.

Accuracy, exactness, exactitude, precision, preciseness, nicety, delicacy, fineness, strictness, rigour, punctuality.

(Phrases) The plain truth; the honest truth; the naked truth; the sober truth; the very thing; a stubborn fact; not a dream, fancy, illusion, etc.; the exact truth; 'the truth, the whole truth, and nothing but the

495 Untruth (546).
Error *(Substantives)*, mistake, miss, fallacy, misconception, misapprehension, misunderstanding, inaccuracy, incorrectness, inexactness, misconstruction (523), miscomputation, miscalculation (481).

Fault, blunder, *faux pas,* bull, Irish bull, Irishism, bloomer, howler, floater, clanger, boner, lapse, slip of the tongue, *lapsus linguae,* Spoonerism, slip of the pen, malapropism, equivoque, cross purposes, oversight, flaw, misprint, erratum; heresy, misstatement, misreport, bad shot.

Illusion, delusion, self-deceit, self-deception, hallucination, monomania,

truth'; 'a round unvarnished tale'; *ipsissima verba*; the real Simon Pure.

(Verbs) To be true, real, etc., to hold good, to be the case.

To render true, legitimatize, legitimize, substantiate, realize, actualize, to make good, establish.

To get at the truth (480).

(Phrases) Vitam impendere vero; magna est veritas et praevalebit.

(Adjectives) True, real, veritable, veracious, actual, certain, positive, absolute, existing (1), substantial, categorical, realistic, factual; unrefuted, unconfuted, unideal, unimagined.

Exact, accurate, definite, precise, well-defined, just, correct, right, strict, hard-and-fast, literal, rigid, rigorous, scrupulous, conscientious, religious, punctilious, nice, mathematical, axiomatic, demonstrable, scientific, unerring, constant, faithful, bona fide, curious, delicate, meticulous.

Genuine, authentic, legitimate, pukka, orthodox, official, *ex officio*, pure, sound, sterling, hall-marked unsophisticated, unadulterated, unvarnished; solid, substantial, undistorted, undisguised, unaffected, unflattering, unexaggerated, unromantic.

(Phrases) Just the thing; neither more nor less; to a hair.

(Adverbs) Truly, verily, veritable, troth, certainly, certes, assuredly, in truth, in good truth, of a truth, really, indubitably, in sooth, for sooth, in reality, in fact, in point of fact, as a matter of fact, strictly speaking, *de facto*, indeed, in effect, actually, *ipso facto*, definitely, literally, positively, virtually, at bottom, *au fond*.

Precisely, accurately, *ad amussim*, etc., mathematically, to a nicety, to a hair, to a T, to an inch; to the letter, *au pied de la lettre*.

aberration; fable, dream, shadow, fancy, bubble, false light (443), the mists of error, will-o'-the wisp, jack-o'-lantern, ignis fatuus, chimera (515), *maya*.

(Verbs) To be erroneous, false, etc., to cause error, to mislead, lead astray, lead into error, delude, give a false impression or idea, to falsify, misstate, misrelate, misinform, misrepresent (544), deceive (545), beguile.

To err, be in error, to mistake, to receive a false impression; to lie or labour under an error, mistake, etc., to blunder, be in the wrong, be at fault, to misapprehend, misconceive, misunderstand, misremember, misreckon, miscalculate, miscount, misestimate, misjudge, misthink, flounder, trip.

(Phrases) To take the shadow for the substance; to go on a fool's errand; to have the wrong sow by the ear; to put one's foot in it; to pull a boner; to drop a brick.

(Adjectives) Erroneous, untrue, false, fallacious, duff, unreal, unsubstantial, baseless, groundless, less, ungrounded, unauthenticated, untrustworthy, heretical.

Inexact, incorrect, wrong, illogical, partial, one-sided, unreasonable, absonous, absonant, indefinite, unscientific, inaccurate, aberrant.

In error, mistaken, etc., tripping, floundering, etc.

Illusive, illusory, ideal, imaginary, fanciful, chimerical, visionary, shadowy, mock, futile.

Spurious, apocryphal, bogus, illegitimate, phoney, pseudo, bastard, meretricious, deceitful, sophisticated, adulterated.

(Phrases) Wide of the mark; on the wrong scent; barking up the wrong tree; out of it; without a leg to stand upon.

In every respect, in all respects, *sous tous les rapports,* at any rate, at all events, by all means.

(Phrases) Joking apart; in good earnest; in sober earnest; sooth to say.

496 Maxim *(Substantives)*, aphorism, apophthegm, dictum, saying, *mot*, adage, gnome, saw, proverb, wisecrack, sentence, precept, rule, formula, tag, code, motto, slogan, catchword, word, byword, moral, sentiment, phylactery, conclusion, reflection, thought, golden rule, axiom, theorem, scholium, lemma, truism.

Catechism, creed (484), profession of faith.

(Adjectives) Aphoristic, gnomic, proverbial, phylacteric, axiomatic; hackneyed, trite.

(Phrases) 'Wise saws and modern instances'; as the saying is or goes.

---

497 Absurdity *(Substantives)*, absurdness, nonsense, folly, paradox, inconsistency, quibble, sophism (477), stultiloquy, stultiloquence, Irish bull, Irishism, Hibernicism, sciamachy, imbecility (499).

Jargon, gibberish, rigmarole, double-Dutch, fustian, rant, bombast, bathos, amphigouri, rhapsody, extravagance, rodomontade, romance; nonsense verse, limerick, clerihew.

Twaddle, claptrap, flapdoodle, bunkum, blah, fudge, rubbish, piffle, verbiage, trash, truism, stuff, balderdash, slipslop, *bavardage,* palaver, *baragouin,* moonshine, fiddlestick, wish-wash, platitude, cliché, flummery, inanity, fiddle-faddle, rot, tommy-rot, bosh, tosh, hot air, havers, blethers, tripe, bilge, bull, hooey, hokum, boloney.

Vagary, foolery, tomfoolery, mummery, monkey-trick, monkey-shine, dido, *boutade,* lark, escapade, ploy, rag.

(Phrases) A cock-and-bull story; a mare's-nest; a wild-goose chase; talking through one's hat; 'a tale told by an idiot, full of sound and fury, signifying nothing'; clotted nonsense; arrant rot.

(Adjectives) Absurd, nonsensical, foolish, senseless, preposterous (499), sophistical, inconsistent, extravagant, ridiculous, cock-and-bull, quibbling, trashy, washy, wishy-washy, twaddling, etc.; topsy-turvy, Gilbertian.

498 Intelligence *(Substantives)*, capacity, nous, parts, talent, sagacity, sagaciousness, wit, mother-wit, *esprit*, gumption, comprehension, understanding, quick parts, grasp of intellect.

Acuteness, acumen, shrewdness, astuteness, arguteness, sharpness, aptness, aptitude, quickness, receptiveness, subtlety, archness, penetration, perspicacity, perspicaciousness, clear-sightedness, discrimination, discernment, flair, refinement (850).

Head, brains, headpiece, a long head.

Wisdom, sapience, sense, good sense, common sense, plain sense, horse-sense, reason, reasonableness, rationality, judgment, judiciousness, solidity, depth, profoundness, catholicity, breadth of view, enlarged views, reach or compass of thoughts.

Genius, inspiration, the fire of genius.

499 Imbecility *(Substantives)*, incapacity, vacancy of mind, poverty of intellect, shallowness, dullness, stupidity, asininity, obtuseness, stolidity, hebetude, doltishness, muddle-headedness, vacuity, short-sightedness, incompetence.

Silliness, simplicity, childishness, puerility, babyhood; dotage, second childhood, anility, fatuity, idiocy, idiotism (503).

Folly, unwisdom, absurdity, infatuation, irrationality, senselessness, foolishness, frivolity, inconsistency, lip-wisdom, conceit, vanity, irresponsibility, giddiness, extravagance, oddity, eccentricity (503), ridiculousness, desipience.

Act of folly (497), imprudence (699), rashness, fanaticism.

(Phrases) A fool's paradise; apartments to let; one's wits going wool-gathering; the meanest capacity.

Wisdom in action, prudence, discretion, self-possession, aplomb (698), sobriety, tact, ballast.

(Phrase) Discretion being the better part of valour.

(Verbs) To be intelligent, wise, etc., to reason (476), to discern (441), discriminate (465), to penetrate, to see far into.

(Phrases) To have all one's wits about one; to see as far through a brick wall as anybody.

(Adjectives) Applied to persons: Intelligent, sagacious, receptive, quick, sharp, acute, fly, smart, shrewd, gumptious, canny, astute, sharp-sighted, quick-sighted, quick-eyed, keen, keen-eyed, keen-sighted, keen-witted, sharp-witted, quick-witted, needle-witted, penetrating, piercing, clear-sighted, perspicacious, discerning, discriminating, discriminative, clever (698), knowledgeable.

Wise, sage, sapient, sagacious, reasonable, rational, sound, common-sense, sane, sensible, judicious, judgmatic, enlightened, impartial, catholic, broad-minded, open-minded, unprejudiced, unbiased, unprepossessed, undazzled, unperplexed, judicial, impartial, fair, progressive.

Cool, cool-headed, long-headed, hard-headed, long-sighted, calculating, thoughtful, reflective, oracular, heaven-directed.

Prudent, discreet, sober, staid, deep, solid, considerate, provident, politic, diplomatic, tactful.

Applied to actions: Wise, sensible, reasonable, judicious, well-judged, well-advised, prudent, prudential, politic (646), expedient.

(Phrases) Wise as a serpent; wise in one's generation; not born yesterday; up to snuff; no flies on him; wise as Solomon.

———

(Verbs) To be imbecile, foolish, etc., to trifle, drivel, ramble, dote, *radoter*, blether, haver; to fool, to monkey, to footle.

(Phrases) To play the fool; to play the giddy goat; to make an ass of oneself; to go on a fool's errand; to pursue a wild-goose chase; *battre la campagne*; Homer nods.

(Adjectives) Applied to persons: Unintelligent, unintellectual, witless, reasonless, not bright, imbecile, shallow, *borné*, weak, soft, simple, sappy, spoony, weak-headed, weak-minded, feeble-minded, half-witted, short-witted, half-baked, not all there, deficient, wanting, shallow-pated, shallow-brained, dull, dumb, dense, crass, stupid, heavy, obtuse, stolid, doltish, asinine, addle-headed, dull-witted, blunt, dull-brained, dim-sighted, vacuous.

Childish, infantine, infantile, babyish, childlike, puerile, callow; anile.

Fatuous, idiotic, lack-brained, drivelling, blatant, brainless, blunt-witted, beef-witted, fat-witted, fat-headed, boneheaded, insulse, having no head or brains, thick-skulled, ivory-skulled, blockish, Boeotian.

Foolish, silly, senseless, irrational, insensate, nonsensical, blunder-headed, chuckle-headed, puzzle-headed, muddle-headed, muddy-headed, undiscerning, unenlightened, unphilosophical; prejudiced, bigoted, purblind, narrow-minded, wrong-headed, tactless, crotchety, conceited, self-opinionated, pig-headed, mulish, unprogressive, one-ideaed, stick-in-the-mud, reactionary, blimpish, besotted, infatuated, unreasoning.

Wild, giddy, dizzy, thoughtless, eccentric, odd, extravagant, quixotic, light-headed, rantipole, high-flying, crack-brained, cracked, cranky, hare-brained, scatter-brained, scatter-pated, unballasted, ridiculous, frivolous, balmy (or barmy), daft (503).

Applied to actions: Foolish, unwise, injudicious, improper, imprudent, unreasonable, nonsensical, absurd, ridiculous, silly, stupid, asinine, ill-imagined, ill-advised, ill-judged, ill-devised, tactless, inconsistent, irrational, unphilosophical, extravagant, preposterous, egregious, footling, imprudent, indiscreet, improvident, impolitic, improper (645, 647).

(Phrases) Dead from the neck up; concrete above the ears.
Without rhyme or reason; penny-wise and pound-foolish.

500 Sage *(Substantives)*, wise man, master-mind, thinker, *savant*, expert, luminary, adept, authority, egghead.

Oracle, a shining light, *esprit fort*, intellectual, high-brow, pundit, academist, academician, philomath, schoolman, magi, a Solomon, Nestor, Solon, Socrates, a second Daniel.

(Adjectives) Venerable, reverend, authoritative.

(Phrases) 'A Daniel come to judgment'; the wise men of the East.

(Ironically) Wiseacre, know-all, bigwig.

———

501 Fool *(Substantives)*, block-head, bonehead, idiot, tom-fool, lowbrow, simpleton, simp, sap, softy, sawney, witling, ass, donkey, goat, goose, ninny, dolt, booby, boob, noodle, muff, mug, muggins, juggins, owl, cuckoo, gowk, numskull, noddy, dumb-bell, gomeril, half-wit, imbecile, ninnyhammer, mutt, driveller, cretin, moron, natural, lackbrain, child, infant, baby, innocent, greenhorn, zany, zombie, gaby.

Dunce, lout, loon, oaf, dullard, duffer, calf, colt, buzzard, block, stick, stock, clod-poll, clot-poll, clodhopper, clod, lubber, bull-calf, bullhead, fat-head, thick-skull, dunderhead, addle-head, dizzard, hoddy-doddy, looby, Joe Soap, nincompoop, poop, put, *un sot à triple étage*, loggerhead, sot, shallow-brain, jobbernowl, changeling, dotard, driveller, moon-calf, giddy-head, gobemouche, rantipole, muddler, stick-in-the-mud, old woman, April fool.

(Phrases) One who is not likely to set the Thames on fire; one who did not invent gunpowder; one who is no conjurer; *qui n'a pas inventé la poudre*; who could not say 'Bo' to a goose; one with his upper storey to let; no fool like an old fool.

Men of Gotham; men of Boeotia.

502 Sanity *(Substantives)*, rationality; being in one's senses, in one's right mind, in one's sober senses; sobriety, lucidity, lucid interval, sound mind, *mens sana.*

(Verbs) To be sane, etc., to retain one's senses, reason, etc.

To become sane, come to one's senses, sober down.

To render sane, bring to one's senses, to sober.

(Adjectives) Sane, rational, reasonable, *compos*, in one's sober senses, in one's right mind, sober-minded.

(Phrase) In full possession of one's faculties.

(Adverbs) Sanely, soberly, etc.

———

503 Insanity *(Substantives)*, lunacy, madness, unsoundness, derangement, psychosis, neurosis, alienation, aberration, schizophrenia, split personality, dementia, paranoia, mania, melancholia, hypochondria, calenture, frenzy, phrenitis, raving, monomania, megalomania, kleptomania, dipsomania, etc., disordered intellect, incoherence, wandering, delirium, hallucination, lycanthropy, eccentricity (499), dementation; Bedlam.

(Phrases) The horrors; the jim-jams; pink spiders; snakes in the boots.

(Verbs) To be or become insane, etc., to lose one's senses, wits, reason, faculties, etc., to run mad, run amuck, go off one's head, rave, dote, ramble, wander, drivel.

To render or drive mad; to madden, dementate, turn the brain, addle the wits, turn one's head, befool, infatuate, craze.

(Phrases) Battre la campagne; avoir le diable au corps.

(Adjectives) Insane, mad, lunatic, crazy, crazed, *non compos*, cracked, cranky, loco, touched, deficient, wanting, out of one's mind, off one's head or nut or onion, bereft of reason, unsettled in one's mind, unhinged, insensate, reasonless, beside oneself.

Demented, daft, dotty, potty, dippy, scatty, loopy, batty, bats, wacky, crackers, cuckoo, haywire, bughouse, bugs, nuts, possessed, maddened, moon-struck, mad-brained, maniac, maniacal, delirious, incoherent, rambling, doting, doited, gaga.

Wandering, frantic, phrenetic, paranoiac, schizophrenic, megalomaniacal, kleptomaniacal, etc., raving, corybantic, dithyrambic, rabid, pixillated, light-headed, giddy, vertiginous, wild, haggard, flighty, neurotic, distracted, distraught, hag-ridden, *écervelé, tête montée*.

(Phrases) The head being turned; having a screw (or a tile) loose; far gone; stark staring mad; mad as a March hare; mad as a hatter; of unsound mind; up the pole; bats in the belfry; the devil being in one; dizzy as a goose; candidate for Bedlam; like one possessed.

The wits going wool-gathering or bird's-nesting.

504 Madman *(Substantives)*, lunatic, maniac, bedlamite, energumen, raver, monomaniac, paranoiac, schizophrenic, nut, screwball, crackpot, madcap, megalomaniac, dipsomaniac, kleptomaniac, psychopath, hypochondriac, *malade imaginaire*, crank, maenad.

SECTION VI—EXTENSION OF THOUGHT

1°. *To the Past*

505 Memory *(Substantives)*, remembrance, reminiscence, recognition, anamnesis, retention, retentiveness, readiness, tenacity.

Recurrence, recollection, retrospection, retrospect, flash-back, afterthought, hindsight.

Token of remembrance, reminder, memorial, memento, souvenir, keepsake, relic, reliquary, memorandum, aide-mémoire, remembrancer, prompter.

Things to be remembered, *memorabilia*.

Art of memory, artificial memory, *memoria technica*, mnemonics; Mnemosyne.

(Phrases) The tablets of the memory; *l'esprit de l'escalier*.

(Verbs) To remember, retain, mind, bear or keep in mind, have or carry in the memory, know by heart or by rote; recognize.

506 Oblivion *(Substantives)*, forgetfulness, amnesia, obliteration (552), a short memory; a lapse of memory; the memory failing, being in fault, or deserting one; the waters of Lethe, Nepenthe, *tabula rasa*.

(Verbs) To forget, lose, unlearn, efface, expunge, blot out, etc. (552); discharge from the memory.

To slip, escape, fade, die away from the memory, to sink into oblivion.

(Phrases) To cast behind one's back; to have a short memory; to put out of one's head; to apply the sponge; to think no more of; to consign to oblivion; to let bygones be bygones.

(Adjectives) Forgotten, etc., lost, effaced, blotted out, obliterated, discharged, sponged out, buried or sunk in oblivion, out of mind, clean out

To be deeply impressed, live, remain, or dwell in the memory; to be stored up, bottled up, to sink in the mind, to rankle, etc.

To recollect, call to mind, bethink oneself, recall, call up, retrace, carry one's thoughts back, review, look back, rake up, brush up, think upon, call to remembrance, tax the memory.

To suggest, prompt, hint, recall to mind, put in mind, remind, whisper, call up, summon up, renew, commend to.

To say by heart, by rote, say one's lesson, repeat as a parrot.

To commit to memory, get or learn by heart or rote, memorize, con, con over, repeat; to fix, imprint, impress, stamp, grave, engrave, store, treasure up, bottle up, embalm, enshrine, etc., in the memory; to load, store, stuff, or burden the memory with; to commemorate (883).

(Phrase) To have at one's fingers' ends.

To jog or refresh the memory; to pull by the sleeve; to bring back to the memory; to keep the memory alive; to keep the wound green; to reopen old sores; to put in remembrance.

(Adjectives) Remembering, etc., mindful, remembered, etc., fresh, green, unforgotten, present to the mind; living in, being in, or within one's memory; indelible, ineffaceable, green in remembrance, reminiscential, commemorative.

(Adverbs) By heart, by vote, *memoriter*, without book; in memory of, in memoriam.

of one's head or recollection, past recollection, unremembered.

Forgetful, oblivious, unmindful, mindless; Lethean.

2°. To the Future

507 Expectation *(Substantives)*, expectance, expectancy, anticipation, forestalling, foreseeing (510); reckoning, calculation.

Contemplation, prospect, look-out, outlook (121), perspective, horizon, vista, hope, trust (858), abeyance, waiting, suspense.

(Phrase) The torments of Tantalus.

(Verbs) To expect, look for, look out for, look forward to, anticipate, contemplate, flatter oneself, to dare to say, foresee (510), forestall, reckon upon, count upon, lay one's account to, to calculate upon, rely upon, build upon, make sure of, prepare oneself for, keep in view, not to wonder at.

To wait, tarry, lie in wait, watch for, abide, to bide one's time.

To hold out, raise, or excite expectation, to bid fair, to promise, to augur, etc. (511).

(Phrases) To count one's chickens before they are hatched.

508 Inexpectation *(Substantives)*, non-expectation; blow, shock, surprise (870).

False or vain expectation, miscalculation.

(Phrase) A bolt from the blue.

(Verbs) Not to expect, not to look for, etc., to be taken by surprise, to start, come upon, to fall upon, not to bargain for, to miscalculate.

To be unexpected, etc., to crop up, pop up, to come unawares, suddenly, abruptly, like a thunderbolt, creep upon, burst upon, bounce upon; surprise, take aback, stun, stagger, startle.

(Phrases) To reckon without one's host; to trust to a broken reed.

To drop from the clouds; you could have knocked me down with a feather.

(Adjectives) Non-expectant, surprised, taken by surprise, unwarned, unaware, startled, etc., taken aback.

Unexpected, unanticipated, unlooked-for, unhoped-for, unforeseen,

To have in store for; to have a rod in pickle.

(Adjectives) Expectant, expecting, etc., prepared for, gaping for, ready for, agog, anxious, ardent, eager, breathless, sanguine.

Expected, anticipated, foreseen, etc., long expected, impending, prospective, in prospect.

(Adverbs) With breathless expectation, on tenterhooks.

(Phrases) On the tiptoe of expectation; on edge; looming in the distance; the wish father to the thought; we shall see; *nous verrons*.

————

beyond expectation, abrupt, sudden, contrary to or against expectation, unannounced, unheralded back-handed.

(Adverbs) Suddenly, abruptly, unexpectedly, plump, pop, *à l'improviste*, unawares, without notice or warning (113).

(Phrases) Like a thief in the night; who would have thought it?

509 Failure of expectation.

Disappointment *(Substantives)*, vain expectation, blighted hope, surprise, astonishment (870); balk, afterclap, miscalculation.

(Phrase) 'There's many a slip 'twixt cup and lip.'

(Verbs) To be disappointed, etc., to miscalculate; to look blank, to look blue, to look or stand aghast.

To disappoint, balk, bilk, tantalize, let down, play false, stand up, dumbfound, dash one's hope (859), sell.

(Adjectives) Disappointed, disconcerted, aghast, blue, out of one's reckoning.

Happening, contrary to or against expectation.

(Phrase) Parturiunt montes, nascetur, ridiculus mus.

510 Foresight *(Substantives)*, prospiscience, prescience, foreknowledge, forethought, forecast, prevision, prognosis, precognition, second sight, clairvoyance.

Anticipation, foretaste, prenotion, presentiment, foregone conclusion, providence, discretion, prudence, sagacity.

Announcement, prospectus, programme, policy (626).

(Verbs) To foresee, foreknow, forejudge, forecast, predict (511), anticipate, look forwards or beyond; look, peep, or pry into the future.

(Phrases) To keep a sharp look out for; to have an eye to the future; *respice finem*.

(Adjectives) Foreseeing, etc., prescient, weather-wise, far-sighted, far-seeing; provident, prudent, rational, sagacious, perspicacious.

511 Prediction *(Substantives)*, announcement, prognosis, forecast, weird, prophecy, vaticination, mantology, prognostication, astrology, horoscopy, haruspicy, auguration, auspices, bodement, omination, augury, foreboding, abodement, aboding, horoscope, nativity, genethliacs, fortune-telling, crystal-gazing, palmistry, chiromancy, oneiromancy, sortilege, *sortes Virgilianae*, soothsaying, ominousness, divination (992).

Place of prediction, adytum, tripod.

(Verbs) To predict, prognosticate, prophesy, vaticinate, presage, augur, bode, forebode, divine, foretell, croak, soothsay, auspicate, to cast a horoscope or nativity, tell one's fortune, read one's hand.

To foretoken, betoken, prefigure, portend, foreshadow, foreshow, usher in, herald, signify, premise, announce, point to, admonish, warn, forewarn, advise.

(Adjectives) Predicting, etc., predictive, prophetic, fatidical, vaticinal, oracular, Sibylline.

Ominous, portentous, augural, auspicious, monitory, premonitory, significant of, pregnant with, weatherwise, bodeful, big with fate.

(Phrase) 'Coming events cast their shadows before.'

512 Omen *(Substantives)*, portent, presage, prognostic, augury, auspice, sign, forerunner, precursor (64), harbinger, herald, monition, warning, avant-courier, pilot-balloon, handwriting on the wall, rise and fall of the barometer, a bird of ill omen, a sign of the times, gathering clouds.

(Phrases) Touch wood! *absit omen.*

513 Oracle *(Substantives)*, prophet, seer, soothsayer, haruspex, fortune-teller, spaewife, palmist, gipsy, wizard, witch, geomancer, Sibyl, Python, Pythoness, *Pythia,* Pythian oracle, Delphic oracle, Old Moore, Zadkiel, Mother Shipton, Witch of Endor, Sphinx, Tiresias, Cassandra, Oedipus, Sibylline leaves.

SECTION VII—CREATIVE THOUGHT

514 Supposition *(Substantives)*, conjecture, surmise, presurmise, speculation, inkling, guess, guess-work, shot, divination, conceit; assumption, postulation, hypothesis, presupposition, postulate, *postulatum*, presumption, theory, thesis; suggestion, proposition, motion, proposal, allusion, insinuation, innuendo.

(Phrases) A rough guess; a lucky shot.

(Verbs) To suppose, conjecture, surmise, guess, divine, theorize, give a guess, make a shot, hazard a conjecture, throw out a conjecture, etc., presuppose, fancy, wis, take it, dare to say, take it into one's head, assume, believe, postulate, posit, presume, presurmise.

To suggest, hint, insinuate, put forth, propound, propose, start, allude to, prompt, put a case, move, make a motion.

To suggest itself, occur to one, come into one's head; to run in the head; to haunt (505).

(Phrases) To put it into one's head; 'thereby hangs a tale.'

(Adjectives) Supposing, etc., supposed, supposititious, suppositious, suppositive, reputed, putative, suggestive, allusive, conjectural, presumptive, hypothetical, theoretical, warranted, authorized, mooted, conjecturable, supposable.

(Adverbs) If, if so be, an, gin, maybe, perhaps, on the supposition, in the event of, as if, *ex hypothesi, quasi.*

515 Imagination *(Substantives)*, fancy, conception, ideality, idealism, inspiration, afflatus, verve, dreaming, somnambulism, frenzy, ecstasy, excogitation, reverie, *Schwärmerei,* trance, imagery, vision; Pegasus.

Invention, inventiveness, originality, fertility, romanticism, utopianism, castle-building.

Conceit, maggot, figment, coinage, fiction, romance, novel (594), myth, Arabian Nights, fairyland, faerie, the man in the moon, dream, day-dream, pipe-dream, nightmare, vapour, chimera, phantom, phantasy, fantasia, whim, whimsy, vagary, rhapsody, extravaganza, air-drawn dagger, bugbear, men in buckram, castle in the air, air-built castle, castle in Spain, will-o'-the-wisp, ignis fatuus, jack-o'-lantern, Utopia, Atlantis, Shangri-la, land of Prester John, millennium, golden age, *fata morgana* (443).

A visionary, romancer, rhapsodist, high-flyer, enthusiast, idealist, energumen, dreamer, seer, fanatic, knight-errant, Don Quixote.

(*Phrases*) Flight of fancy; fumes of fancy; fine frenzy; thick-coming fancies; coinage of the brain; the mind's eye; a stretch of imagination; 'such stuff as dreams are made on.'

(*Verbs*) To imagine, fancy, conceive, ideate, idealize, realize, objectify; fancy or picture to oneself; create, originate, devise, invent, coin, fabricate, make up, mint, improvise, excogitate, conjure up.

(*Phrases*) To take into one's head; to figure to oneself; to strain or crack one's invention; to strike out something new; to give a loose to the fancy; to give the reins to the imagination; to set one's wits to work; to rack or cudgel one's brains.

(*Adjectives*) Imagining, imagined, etc.; ideal, unreal, unsubstantial, imaginary, *in nubibus*, fabulous, fictitious, legendary, mythological, chimerical, *ben trovato*, fanciful, faerie, fairylike, air-drawn, air-built, original, fantastic, fantastical, whimsical, high-flown.

Imaginative, inventive, creative, fertile, romantic, flighty, extravagant, high-flown, fanatic, enthusiastic, Utopian, Quixotic.

DIVISION II—COMMUNICATION OF IDEAS

SECTION I—NATURE OF IDEAS COMMUNICATED

516 Idea to be conveyed.

Meaning (*Substantives*), signification, sense, import, purport, significance, drift, gist, acceptation, acceptance, bearing, interpretation (522), reading, tenor, allusion, spirit, colouring, expression.

Literal meaning, literality, obvious meaning, grammatical sense, first blush, *prima facie* meaning; after-acceptation.

Equivalent meaning, synonym, synonymity.

Thing signified: Matter, subject, substance, pith, marrow, argument, text; sum and substance.

(*Verbs*) To mean, signify, express, import, purport, convey, breathe, imply, bespeak, speak of, tell of, touch on, bear a sense, involve, declare (527), insinuate, allude to, point to, indicate, drive at; to come to the point, give vent to; to stand for.

To take, understand, receive, or accept in a particular sense.

(*Adjectives*) Meaning, etc., significant, significative, significatory, literal, expressive, explicit, suggestive, allusive; pithy, pointed, epigrammatic, pregnant with meaning.

517 Absence of meaning.

Unmeaningness (*Substantives*), empty sound, a dead letter, scrabble, scribble; inexpressiveness, vagueness (519).

Nonsense, stuff, balderdash (497), jabber, gibberish, palaver, rigmarole, twaddle, tosh, bosh, bull, rubbish, rot, empty babble, empty sound, verbiage, *nugae*, truism, moonshine, inanity.

(*Verbs*) To mean nothing, to be unmeaning, etc.; to scribble, jabber, gibber, babble.

(*Adjectives*) Unmeaning, meaningless, nonsensical, void of meaning, of sense, etc., senseless, not significant, undefined, tacit, not expressed.

Inexpressible, indefinable, undefinable, unmeant, unconceived.

Trashy, trumpery, twaddling, etc.

(*Phrases*) Vox et praeterea nihil; 'a tale told by an idiot, full of sound and fury, signifying nothing'; 'sounding brass and tinkling cymbal.'

(*Adverb*) Tacitly.

telling, striking, full of meaning,

Synonymous, equivalent, tantamount; the same thing as.

Implied, tacit, understood, implicit, inferred, latent.

(Adverbs) Meaningly, literally, etc., *videlicet* (522), viz., i.e.

(Phrases) Au pied de la lettre; so to speak; to that effect; so to express oneself; as it were; that is to say; *façon de parler*.

---

518   Intelligibility *(Substantives)*, clearness, lucidity, perspicuity, explicitness, distinctness, plain speaking, expressiveness, legibility, visibility (446); precision (494).

Intelligence, comprehension, understanding, learning (539).

(Phrases) A word to the wise; *verbum sapienti.*

(Verbs) To be intelligible, etc.

To render intelligible, etc., to simplify, clear up, throw light upon.

To understand, comprehend, follow, take, take in, catch, catch on to, twig, dig, get the hang of, get wise to, grasp, sense, make out, get, collect; master, tumble to, rumble.

(Phrases) It tells its own tale; he who runs may read; to stand to reason; to speak for itself.

To come to an understanding; to see with half an eye.

(Adjectives) Intelligible, clear, lucid, understandable, explicit, expressive, significant, express, distinct, precise, definite, well-defined, perspicuous, transpicuous, striking, plain, obvious, manifest, palpable, glaring, transparent, above-board, unambiguous, unmistakable, legible, open, positive, expressive (516), unconfused, unequivocal, pronounced, graphic, readable.

(Phrases) Clear as day; clear as crystal; clear as noonday; not to be mistaken; plain to the meanest capacity; plain as a pikestaff; in plain English.

519   Unintelligibility *(Substantives)*, incomprehensibility, inconceivability, darkness (421), imperspicuity, obscurity, confusion, perplexity, imbroglio, indistinctness, mistiness, indefiniteness, vagueness, ambiguity, looseness, uncertainty, mysteriousness (526), paradox, inexplicability, incommunicability, spinosity.

Jargon, gibberish, rigmarole, rodomontade, etc. (497); paradox, riddle, enigma, puzzle (533).

Double or High Dutch, Greek, Hebrew, etc.

(Verbs) To be unintelligible, etc., to pass comprehension.

To render unintelligible, etc., to perplex, confuse, confound, bewilder, darken, moither (475).

Not to understand, etc., to lose, miss, etc., to lose the clue.

(Phrases) Not to know what to make of; not to be able to make either head or tail of; to be all at sea; to play at cross purposes; to beat about the bush.

(Adjectives) Unintelligible, incognizable, inapprehensible, incomprehensible, inconceivable, unimaginable, unknowable, inexpressible, undefinable, incommunicable, above or past or beyond comprehension, inexplicable, illegible, undecipherable, inscrutable, unfathomable, beyond one's depth, paradoxical, insoluble, impenetrable.

Obscure, dark, confused, indistinct, indefinite, misty, nebulous, intricate, undefined, ill-defined, indeterminate, perplexed, loose, vague, ambiguous, disconnected, incoherent, unaccount-

able, puzzling, enigmatical, hieroglyphic, mysterious, mystic, mystical, at cross purposes.

Hidden, recondite, abstruse, crabbed, transcendental, far-fetched, *in nubibus,* searchless, unconceived, unimagined.

(Phrases) Greek to one; without rhyme or reason; *obscurum per obscurius; lucus a non lucendo.*

520 Having a double sense.

Equivocalness *(Substantives)*, double meaning, quibble, equivoque, equivocation, *double-entendre*, paragram, anagram, amphibology, amphiboly, ambiloquy, prevarication, white lie, mental reservation, tergiversation, slip of the tongue, *lapsus linguae*, a pun, play on words, homonym.

Having a doubtful meaning, ambiguity (475), homonymy.

Having a false meaning (544), *suggestio falsi.*

(Verbs) To be equivocal, etc., to have two senses, etc., to equivocate, prevaricate, tergiversate, palter to the understanding, to pun.

(Adjectives) Equivocal, ambiguous, amphibolous, amphibological, homonymous, double-tongued, double-edged, left-handed, equivocatory, paltering.

(Adverb) Over the left.

521 Metaphor *(Substantives)*, figure, metonymy, trope, catachresis, synecdoche, figure of speech, figurativeness, image, imagery, metalepsis, type (22), symbol, symbolism (550), tropology.

Personification, prosopopaeia, allegory, apologue, parable.

Implication, inference, allusion, application, adumbration, hidden meaning.

Allegorist, tropist, symbolist.

(Verbs) To employ metaphor, etc., to personify, allegorize, adumbrate, shadow forth, imply, understand, apply, allude to.

(Adjectives) Metaphorical, figurative, catachrestical, typical, tropical, parabolic, allegorical, allusive, symbolic (550), symbolistic, implied, inferential, implicit, understood.

(Adverbs) So to speak, as it were.

(Phrases) Where more is meant than meets the ear; in a manner of speaking; *façon de parler*; in a Pickwickian sense.

522 Interpretation *(Substantives)*, exegesis, explanation, meaning (516), explication, expounding, exposition, rendition, reddition.

Translation, version, rendering, construction, reading, spelling, restoration, metaphrase, literal translation, free translation, paraphrase.

Comment, commentary, inference, illustration, exemplification, definition, *éclaircissement*, elucidation, crib, cab, gloss, glossary, annotation, *scholium*, marginalia, note, clue, key, sidelight, master-key (631), rationale, denouement, solution, answer (462), object lesson.

Palaeography, dictionary, glossology, etc. (562), semantics, semasiology, oneirocritics, oneirocriticism, hermeneutics.

(Verbs) To interpret, expound, explain, clear up, construe, translate, render, English, do into, turn into, transfuse the sense of.

To read, spell, make out, decipher, decode, unfold, disentangle, elicit the

523 Misinterpretation *(Substantives)*, misapprehension, misunderstanding, misacceptation, misconstruction, misspelling, misapplication, catachresis, mistake (495), cross-reading, cross-purpose.

Misrepresentation, perversion, falsification, misquotation, garbling, exaggeration (549), false colouring, abuse of terms, parody, travesty, misstatement, etc. (544).

(Verbs) To misinterpret, misapprehend, misunderstand, misconceive, misdeem, misspell, mistranslate, misconstrue, misapply, mistake (495).

To misstate, etc. (544); to pervert, falsify, distort, misrepresent, torture, travesty; to stretch, strain, wring, or wrest the sense or meaning; to put a bad or false construction on; to misquote, garble, belie, explain away.

(Phrases) To give a false colouring to; to be or play at cross-purposes; to put a false construction on.

meaning of, make sense of, find the key of, unriddle, unravel, solve, resolve (480), restore.

To elucidate, throw light upon, illustrate, exemplify, expound, annotate, comment upon, define, unfold.

(Adjectives) Explanatory, expository, explicatory, explicative, exegetical, hermeneutic, constructive, inferential.

Paraphrastic, metaphrastic; literal, plain, simple, strict, synonymous; polyglot.

(Adverbs) That is to say, *id est* (or i.e.), *videlicet* (or viz.), in other words, in plain words, simply, in plain English.

Literally, word for word, verbatim, *au pied de la lettre,* strictly speaking (494).

(Adjectives) Misinterpreted, etc., untranslated, untranslatable.

(Phrase) Traduttori traditori.

---

524 Interpreter *(Substantives)*, expositor, expounder, exponent, demonstrator, scholiast, commentator, annotator, metaphrast, paraphrast, palaeographer, spokesman, speaker, mouthpiece, guide, dragoman, cicerone, conductor, courier, showman, barker, oneirocritic; Oedipus (513).

SECTION II—MODES OF COMMUNICATION

525 Manifestation *(Substantives)*, expression, showing, etc., disclosure (529), presentation, indication, exposition, demonstration, exhibition, production, display, showing off.

An exhibit, an exhibitor.

Openness, frankness, plain speaking (543), publication, publicity (531).

(Verbs) To manifest, make manifest, etc., show, express, indicate, point out, bring forth, bring forward, trot out, set forth, exhibit, expose, produce, present, bring into view, set before one, hold up to view, lay open, lay bare, expose to view, set before one's eyes, show up, shadow forth, bring to light, display, demonstrate, unroll, unveil, unmask, disclose (529).

To elicit, educe, draw out, bring out, unearth, disinter.

To be manifested, etc., to appear, transpire, come to light (446), to come out, to crop up, get wind.

(Phrases) Hold up the mirror; draw, lift up, raise, or remove the curtain; show one's true colours; throw off the mask.

To speak for itself; to stand to reason; to stare one in the face; to tell its own tale; to give vent to.

526 Latency *(Substantives)*, secrecy, secretness, privacy, invisibility (447), mystery, occultness, darkness, reticence, silence (585), closeness, reserve, inexpression; a sealed book, a dark horse, an undercurrent.

Retirement, delitescence, seclusion (893).

(Phrases) More is meant than meets the ear (or eye).

(Verbs) To be latent, etc., to lurk, underlie, escape observation, smoulder; to keep back, reserve, suppress, keep close, etc. (528).

To render latent (528).

(Phrases) Hold one's tongue; hold one's peace; leave in the dark; to keep one's own counsel; to keep mum; to seal the lips; not to breathe a syllable about.

(Adjectives) Latent, lurking, secret, close, unapparent, unknown (491), dark, delitescent, in the background, occult, cryptic, snug, private, privy, *in petto*, anagogic, sequestered, dormant, smouldering.

Inconspicuous, unperceived, invisible (447), unseen, unwitnessed, impenetrable, unespied, unsuspected.

(Adjectives) Manifest, clear, apparent, evident, visible (446), prominent, in the foreground, salient, signal, striking, notable, conspicuous, palpable, patent, overt, flagrant, stark, glaring, open.

Manifested, shown, expressed, etc., disclosed (529), frank, capable of being shown, producible.

(Phrases) As plain as a pikestaff; as plain as the nose on one's face.

(Adverbs) Openly, before one's eyes, face to face, above-board, in open court, in open daylight, in the light of day, in the open streets, on the stage, on show.

Untold, unsaid, unwritten, unpublished, unmentioned, unbreathed, untalked of, unsung, unpronounced, unpromulgated, unreported, unexposed, unproclaimed, unexpressed, not expressed, tacit, implicit, implied, undeveloped, embryonic, unsolved, unexplained, undiscovered, untraced, untracked, unexplored.

(Phrase) No news being good news.

(Adverbs) Secretly, etc., *sub silentio*.

(Phrases) In the background; behind one's back; under the table; behind the scenes; between the lines.

---

527 Information *(Substantives)*, gen, pukka gen, low-down, enlightenment, communication, intimation, notice, notification, enunciation, announcement, annunciation, statement, specification, report, advice, monition, mention, acquaintance (490), acquainting, etc., outpouring, intercommunication, communicativeness.

An informant, teller, tipster, spy, nose, nark, stool-pigeon, intelligencer, correspondent, reporter, messenger, newsmonger, gossip (532).

Hint, suggestion (514), wrinkle, tip, pointer, insinuation, innuendo, wink, glance, leer, nod, shrug, gesture, whisper, implication, cue, office, by-play, eye-opener.

(Phrases) A word to the wise; *verbum sapienti*; a broad hint; a straight tip; a stage whisper.

(Verbs) To inform, acquaint, tell, mention, express, intimate, impart, communicate, apprise, post, make known, notify, signify to, let one know, advise, state, specify, give notice, announce, annunciate, publish, report, set forth, bring word, send word, leave word, write word, declare, certify, depose, pronounce, explain, undeceive, enlighten, put wise, set right, open the eyes of, convey the knowledge of, give an account of; instruct (537).

To hint, give an inkling of; give, throw out, or drop a hint, insinuate, allude to, glance at, touch on, make

528 Concealment *(Substantives)*, hiding, occultation, etc., secrecy, stealth, stealthiness, slyness (702), disguise, incognito, privacy, masquerade, camouflage, smoke screen, mystery, mystification, freemasonry, reservation, suppression, secretiveness, reticence, reserve, uncommunicativeness; secret path.

A mask, visor, ambush, etc. (530), enigma, etc. (533).

(Phrases) A needle in a bundle of hay; a nigger in the woodpile; a skeleton in the cupboard; a family skeleton.

(Verbs) To conceal, hide, put out of sight, secrete, cover, envelop, screen, cloak, veil, shroud, enshroud, shade, muffle, mask, disguise, camouflage, ensconce, eclipse.

To keep from, lock up, bury, cache, sink, suppress, stifle, withhold, reserve, burke, hush up, keep snug or close or dark.

To keep in ignorance, blind, hoodwink, mystify, pose, puzzle, perplex, embarrass, flummox, bewilder, bamboozle, etc. (545).

To be concealed, etc., to lurk, skulk, smoulder, lie hid, lie in ambush, lie perdu, lie low, lie doggo, sneak, slink, prowl, gumshoe, retire, steal into, steal along.

To conceal oneself, put on a veil, etc. (530), masquerade.

(Phrases) To draw or close the curtain; not breathe a word about;

allusion to, to wink, to tip the wink, glance, leer, nod, shrug, give the cue, give the office, give the tip, wave, whisper, suggest, prompt, whisper in the ear, give one to understand.

To be informed, etc., of, made acquainted with; to hear of, get a line on, understand.

To come to one's ears, to come to one's knowledge, to reach one's ears.

(*Adjectives*) Informed, etc., of, made acquainted with, in the know, hep; undeceived.

Reported, made known (531), bruited.

Expressive, significant, pregnant with meaning, etc. (516), declaratory, enunciative, nuncupatory, expository, communicatory, communicative, insinuative.

(*Adverbs*) Expressively, significantly, etc.

(*Phrases*) A little bird told me; *on dit*; from information received.

———

let it go no farther; keep it under your hat.

To play at bo-peep; to play at hide-and-seek; to hide under a bushel; to throw dust in the eyes.

(*Adjectives*) Concealed, hid, hidden, etc., secret, clandestine, perdu, close, private, privy, furtive, surreptitious, stealthy, feline, underhand, sly, sneaking, skulking, hole-and-corner, undivulged, unrevealed, undisclosed, incognito, incommunicado.

Mysterious, mystic, mystical, dark, enigmatical, problematical, anagogical, paradoxical, occult, cryptic, gnostic, cabbalistic, esoteric, recondite, abstruse, unexplained, impenetrable, undiscoverable, inexplicable, unknowable, bewildering, baffling.

Covered, closed, shrouded, veiled, masked, screened, shaded, disguised, under cover, under a cloud, veil, etc., in a fog, haze, mist, etc., under an eclipse; inviolate, inviolable, confidential, under wraps.

Reserved, uncommunicative, secretive, buttoned up, taciturn (585).

(*Phrase*) Close as wax.

(*Adverbs*) Secretly, clandestinely, incognito, privily, in secret, *in camera*, with closed doors, *à huis clos*, *à la dérobée*, under the rose, *sub rosa*, privately, in private, aside, on the sly, *sub silentio*, behind one's back, under the counter, behind the curtain, behind the scenes.

Confidentially, between ourselves, between you and me, *entre nous, inter nos*, in strict confidence, on the strict q.t., off the record, it must go no farther.

(*Phrases*) Like a thief in the night; under the seal of secrecy, of confession; between you and me and the gate-post; 'tell it not in Gath'; nobody any the wiser.

529 Disclosure (*Substantives*), revealment, revelation, disinterment, exposition, show-down, exposure, effusion, outpouring.

Acknowledgment, avowal, confession; an *exposé*, denouement.

A telltale, talebearer, informer, stool-pigeon, nark, nose.

(*Verbs*) To disclose, open, lay open, divulge, reveal, bewray, discover, unfold, let drop, let fall, let out, let on, spill, lay open, acknowledge, allow, concede, grant, admit, own, own up, confess, avow, unseal, unveil, unmask, uncover, unkennel, unearth (525).

530 Ambush (*Substantives*), hiding-place, hide, retreat, cover, lurking-hole, secret place, cubby-hole, recess, closet, priest's hole, crypt, cache, ambuscade, *guet-apens, adytum,* dungeon, oubliette.

A mask, veil, visor (or vizor), eye-shade, blinkers, cloak, screen, hoarding, curtain, shade, cover, disguise, masquerade dress, domino.

(*Verbs*) To lie in ambush, lurk, couch, lie in wait for, lay or set a trap for (545).

———

To blab, peach, squeal, let out, let fall, let on, betray, give away, tell tales, speak out, blurt out, vent, give vent to, come out with, round on, split; publish (531).

To make no secret of, to disabuse, unbeguile, undeceive, set right, correct.

To be disclosed, revealed, etc., to come out, to transpire, to ooze out, to leak out, to creep out, to get wind, to come to light.

(Phrases) To let into the secret; to let the cat out of the bag; to spill the beans; to unburden or disburden one's mind or conscience; to open one's mind; to unbosom oneself; to make a clean breast of it; to come clean; to give the show away; to own the soft impeachment; to tell tales out of school; to show one's hand; to turn Queen's (or King's or State's) evidence.

Murder will out.

(Adjectives) Disclosed, revealed, divulged, laid open, etc., unriddled, etc.; outspoken, etc. (543).

Open, public, exoteric.

(Interjection) Out with it!

531 Publication *(Substantives)*, announcement, notification, enunciation, annunciation, advertisement, promulgation, circulation, propagation, edition, redaction, proclamation, hue and cry, the Press, journalism, wireless, radio, broadcasting, television.

Publicity, notoriety, currency, cry, bruit, rumour, fame, report (532), on dit, flagrancy, limelight, town-talk, small talk, table-talk, puffery, bally-hoo, *réclame*, the light of day, daylight.

Notice, notification, manifesto, propaganda, advertisement, blurb, circular, placard, bill, *affiche*, poster, newspaper, journal, daily, periodical, weekly, gazette; personal column, agony column.

Publisher (593), publicity agent, advertising agent; tout, barker, town crier.

(Phrases) An open secret; *un secret de Polichinelle*.

(Verbs) To publish, make known, announce, notify, annunciate, gazette, set forth, give forth, give out, broach, voice, utter, advertise, circularize, placard, *afficher*, circulate, propagate, spread, spread abroad, broadcast, edit, redact, rumour, diffuse, disseminate, celebrate, blaze about; blaze or noise abroad; bruit, buzz, bandy, hawk about, trumpet, proclaim, herald, puff, boost, splash, plug, boom, give tongue, raise a cry, raise a hue and cry, tell the world, popularize; bring, lay or drag before the public, give currency to, ventilate, bring out.

(Phrases) To proclaim from the house-tops; to publish in the gazette; to send round the crier; with beat of drum.

To be published, etc., to become public, to go forth, get abroad, get about, get wind, take air, get afloat, acquire currency, get in the papers, spread, go the rounds, buzz about, blow about.

To pass from mouth to mouth; to spread like wildfire.

(Adjectives) Published, etc., made public, in circulation, exoteric, rumoured, rife, current, afloat, notorious, flagrant, whispered, buzzed about, in every one's mouth, reported, trumpet-tongued; encyclical.

(Phrases) As the story runs; to all whom it may concern.

(Interjections) Oyez! O yes! notice is hereby given!

532 News *(Substantives)*, piece of information, intelligence, tidings, budget of news, word, advice, message, communication, errand, embassy, dispatch, bulletin.

533 Secret *(Substantives)*, arcanum, penetralia, profound secret, mystery, crux, problem, enigma, teaser, poser, riddle, puzzle, conundrum, charade, rebus, logogriph,

Report, story, scoop, beat, rumour, canard, hearsay, *on dit*, fame, talk, gossip, tittle-tattle, *oui-dire*, scandal, buzz, bruit, *chronique scandaleuse*, town talk.

Letter, postcard, airgraph, telegram, wire, cable, wireless message, radiogram.

Newsmonger, scandalmonger, scaremonger, alarmist, talebearer, tattler, gossip (527), local correspondent, special correspondent, reporter (590).

anagram, acrostic, cross-word, cipher, code, cryptogram, monogram, paradox, maze, labyrinth, perplexity, chaos (528), the Hercynian wood; *terra incognita*.

Iron curtain, bamboo curtain, censorship, counter-intelligence.

(Phrases) The secrets of the prison-house; a sealed book.

(Adjectives) Secret, top secret, hush-hush, undercover, clandestine (528).

---

534 Messenger *(Substantives)*, envoy, nuncio, internuncio, intermediary, go-between, herald, ambassador, legate, emissary, *corps diplomatique*.

Marshal, crier, trumpeter, pursuivant, *parlementaire,* courier, runner, postman, telegraph-boy, errand-boy, bell-boy, bell-hop, Mercury, Hermes, Iris, Ariel, carrier pigeon.

Narrator, etc., talebearer, spy, secret-service agent, scout.

Mail, post (592), post office, telegraph, telephone, wireless, radio; grapevine, bush telegraph.

---

535 Affirmation *(Substantives)*, statement, predication, assertion, declaration, word, averment, asseveration, protestation, swearing, adjuration, protest, profession, deposition, avouchment, affirmance, assurance, allegation, acknowledgment, avowal, confession, confession of faith, oath, affidavit; vote, voice.

Remark, observation, position, thesis, proposition, saying, dictum, theorem, sentence.

Positiveness (474), dogmatism, *ipse dixit.*

A dogmatist, doctrinaire.

(Phrase) The big bow-wow style.

(Verbs) To assert, make an assertion, etc., say, affirm, predicate, enunciate, state, declare, profess, aver, avouch, put forth, advance, express, allege, pose, propose, propound, broach, set forth, maintain, contend, pronounce, pretend, pass an opinion, etc.; to reassert, reaffirm, reiterate; quoth, *dixit, dixi.*

To vouch, assure, vow, swear, take oath, depose, depone, recognize, avow, acknowledge, own, confess, announce, hazard or venture an opinion.

536 Negation *(Substantives)*, abnegation, denial, denegation, disavowal, disclaimer, abjuration, contradiction, *démenti*, contravention, recusation, retraction, retractation, recantation, renunciation, palinode, recusancy, protest.

Qualification, modification (469); rejection (610); refusal (764).

(Verbs) To deny, disown, contradict, negative, gainsay, contravene, disclaim, withdraw, recant, disavow, retract, revoke, abjure, negate.

(Phrases) To deny flatly; eat one's words; go back from, or upon one's word.

To dispute, impugn, controvert, confute (479), question, call in question, give the lie to, rebut, belie.

(Adjectives) Denying, etc., denied, etc., negative, contradictory, recusant.

(Adverbs) No, nay, not, nohow, not at all, by no means (489), far from it, anything but, on the contrary, quite the reverse.

To dogmatize, lay down, lay down the law; to call heaven to witness, protest, certify, warrant, posit, go bail for.

(Phrases) I doubt not; I warrant you; I'll engage; take my word for it; depend upon it; I'll be bound; I am sure; I have no doubt; sure enough; to be sure; what I have said, I have said; faith! that's flat.

To swear till one is black in the face; to swear by all the saints in the calendar; to call heaven to witness.

(Adjectives) Asserting, etc., dogmatic, positive, emphatic, declaratory, affirmative, predicable, pronounced, unretracted.

Positive, broad, round, express, explicit, marked, definitive, distinct, decided, formal, solemn, categorical, peremptory, absolute, fiat, pronounced.

(Adverbs) Ex cathedra, positively, avowedly, confessedly, broadly, roundly, etc.; ay, yes, indeed; by Jove, by George, by James, by jingo.

537 Teaching *(Substantives),* instruction, direction, guidance, tuition, culture, inculcation, inoculation, indoctrination.

Education, co-education, initiation, preparation, practice, training, upbringing, schooling, discipline, exercise, drill, exercitation, breaking in, taming, drilling, etc., preachment, persuasion, edification, proselytism, propagandism.

A lesson, lecture, prolusion, prelection, exercise, task; curriculum, course.

Rudiments, ABC, elements, three Rs, grammar, text-book, vademecum, school-book (593).

Physical training, P.T., gymnastics, callisthenics.

(Verbs) To teach, instruct, enlighten, edify, inculcate, indoctrinate, instil, imbue, inoculate, infuse, impregnate, graft, infix, engraft, implant, sow the seeds of, infiltrate, give an idea of, cram, coach, put up to.

To explain, expound, lecture, hold forth, read a lecture or sermon, give a lesson, preach; sermonize, moralize, point a moral.

To educate, train, discipline, school, form, ground, tutor, prepare, qualify, prime, drill, exercise, practise, bring up, rear, nurture, dry-nurse, breed, break in, tame, domesticate, condition.

To direct, guide, initiate, put in the way of, proselytize, bring round to an opinion, bring over, win over, brainwash, re-educate, persuade, convince, convict, set right, enlighten, give one new ideas, put one up to, bring home to.

538 Misteaching *(Substantives),* misdirection, misleading, misinformation, misguidance, perversion, false teaching, sophistry.

Indocility, incapacity, misintelligence, dullness, backwardness.

(Verbs) To misinform, misteach, mislead, misdirect, misguide, miscorrect, pervert, lead into error, bewilder, mystify (528), throw off the scent; to unteach.

(Phrases) To teach one's grandmother; *obscurum per obscurius;* the blind leading the blind.

(Adjectives) Misteaching, etc., unedifying.

539 Learning *(Substantives),* acquisition of knowledge, acquirement, attainment, scholarship, erudition, instruction, study, etc. (490).

Docility (602), aptitude (698), aptness to be taught, teachableness, persuasibility, capacity.

(Verbs) to learn; to acquire, gain, catch, receive, imbibe, pick up, gather, collect, glean, etc., knowledge or information.

To hear, overhear, catch hold of, take in, fish up, drink in, run away with an idea, to make oneself acquainted with, master, read, spell, turn over the leaves, pore over, run through, peruse, study, grind, cram, mug, swot, go to school; to get up a subject; to serve one's time or apprenticeship.

To be taught, etc.

(Phrases) To teach the young idea how to shoot; to sharpen the wits; to enlarge the mind.

(Adjectives) Teaching, etc., taught, etc., educational.

Didactic, academic, doctrinal, disciplinal, disciplinary, instructive, scholastic, persuasive.

(Adjectives) Docile, apt, teachable, persuasible, studious, industrious, scholastic, scholarly.

(Phrase) To burn the midnight oil.

———

540 Teacher *(Substantives)*, instructor, apostle, master, director, tutor, preceptor, institutor, mentor, adviser, monitor, counsellor, expositor, dry-nurse, trainer, coach, crammer, grinder, governor, bear-leader, disciplinarian, martinet, guide, cicerone, pioneer, governess, duenna.

Orator, speaker, mouthpiece (582).

Professor, lecturer, reader, demonstrator, praelector, prolocutor, schoolmaster, schoolmistress, schoolmarm, usher, pedagogue, monitor, pupil-teacher, dominie, dame, moonshee; missionary, propagandist.

(Adjectives) Tutorial, professorial.

541 Learner *(Substantives)*, scholar, student, alumnus, disciple, pupil, *élève*, schoolboy, schoolgirl, beginner, tyro (or tiro), abecedarian, novice, neophyte, chela, inceptor, probationer, apprentice, tenderfoot, freshman, bejan (or bejant), undergraduate, undergraduette, sophomore.

Proselyte, convert, catechumen, sectator; class, form.

Pupilage, pupilarity, pupilship, tutelage, apprenticeship, novitiate, leading-strings, matriculation.

(Phrases) Freshwater sailor; *in statu pupillari.*

542 School *(Substantives)*, day school, boarding school, public school, council school, national school, board school, private school, preparatory school, elementary school, primary school, secondary school, senior school, grammar school, high school, academy, university, Alma Mater, university extension, correspondence school, college, seminary, lyceum, polytechnic, nursery, institute, institution, palaestra, gymnasium, class, form, standard; nursery school, infant school, kindergarten, crèche; reformatory, Borstal, approved school.

Horn-book, rudiments, vade-mecum, abecedary, manual, primer, school-book, text-book.

Professorship, lectureship, readership, chair; pulpit, ambo, theatre, amphitheatre, forum, stage, rostrum, platform.

(Adjectives) Scholastic, academic, collegiate.

543 Veracity *(Substantives)*, truthfulness, truth, sincerity, frankness, straightforwardness, ingenuousness, candour, honesty, fidelity, bona fides, openness, unreservedness, bluntness, plainness, plain speaking, plain dealing; simplicity, bonhomie, naïveté, artlessness (703), love of truth.

A plain-dealer, truth-teller, man of his word.

(Verbs) To speak the truth, speak one's mind, open out, think aloud.

(Phrases) Tell the truth and shame the devil; to deal faithfully with; to show oneself in one's true colours.

544 Falseness *(Substantives)*, falsehood, untruthfulness, untruth (546), falsity, mendacity, falsification, perversion of truth, perjury, fabrication, romance, forgery, prevarication, equivocation, shuffling, evasion, fencing, duplicity, double-dealing, unfairness, dishonesty, fraud, misrepresentation, *suggestio falsi, suppressio veri,* Punic faith, giving the go-by, disguise, disguisement, irony, understatement.

Insincerity, dissimulation, dissembling, deceit (545), shiftiness, hypocrisy, cant, humbug, gammon,

(Adjectives) Truthful, true, veracious, uncompromising, veridical, veridicious, sincere, candid, frank, open, outspoken, unreserved, free-spoken, open-hearted, honest, simple, simple-hearted, ingenuous, blunt, plain-spoken, true-blue, straightforward, straight, fair, fair-minded, single-minded, artless, guileless, natural, unaffected, simple-minded, undisguised, unfeigned, unflattering, warts and all.

(Adverbs) Truly, etc. (494), above-board, broadly.

(Phrases) In plain English; without mincing the matter; honour bright; honest Injun; bona fide; *sans phrase*.

jesuitry, pharisaism, mental reservation, lip-service, simulation, acting, sham, malingering, pretending, pretence, crocodile tears, false colouring, art, artfulness (702).

Deceiver (548).

(Verbs) To be false, etc., to play false, speak falsely, lie, fib, tell a lie or untruth, etc. (546), to mistake, misreport, misrepresent, misquote, belie, falsify, prevaricate, equivocate, quibble, palter, shuffle, fence, hedge, understate, mince the truth.

To forswear, swear false, perjure oneself, bear false witness.

To garble, gloss over, disguise, pervert, distort, twist, colour, varnish, cook, doctor, embroider, fiddle, wangle, gerrymander, put a false colouring or construction upon (523).

To invent, make up, fabricate, concoct, trump up, forge, fake, romance.

To dissemble, dissimulate, feign, pretend, assume, act or play a part, simulate, pass off for, counterfeit, sham, malinger, make believe, cant, put on.

(Phrases) To play the hypocrite; to give the go-by; to play fast and loose; to play a double game; to blow hot and cold; to lie like a conjurer; sham Abraham; to look as if butter would not melt in one's mouth; to sail under false colours; to ring false.

(Adjectives) False, dishonest, faithless, deceitful, mendacious, unveracious, truthless, trothless, unfair, uncandid, disingenuous, shady, shifty, underhand, underhanded, hollow, insincere, canting, hypocritical, jesuitical, sanctimonious, pharisaical, tartuffian, double, double-tongued, double-faced, smooth-spoken, smooth-tongued, plausible, mealy-mouthed, snide.

Artful, insidious, sly, designing, diplomatic, Machiavellian.

Untrue, unfounded, fictitious, invented, made up, *ben trovato*, forged, falsified, counterfeit, spurious, factitious, self-styled, bastard, sham, bogus, phoney, mock, pseudo, disguised, simulated, artificial, colourable, catchpenny, meretricious, tinsel, Brummagem, postiche, pinchbeck, illusory, elusory, supposititious, surreptitious, ironical, apocryphal.

(Phrase) All is not gold that glitters.

(Adverbs) Falsely, etc., slyly, stealthily, underhand.

545 Deception *(Substantives)*, falseness (544), fraud, deceit, imposition, artifice, juggle, juggling, sleight of hand, legerdemain, conjuration, hocus-pocus, jockeyship, trickery, coggery, fraudulence, imposture, *supercherie*, chicane, chicanery, covin, cozenage, circumvention, ingannation, prestidigitation, subreption, collusion, complicity, guile, gullery, hanky-panky, jiggery-pokery, rannygazoo.

Quackery, charlatanism, charlatanry, empiricism, humbug, hokum, eye-wash, hypocrisy, gammon, flapdoodle, bunkum, *blague*, bluff, mummery, borrowed plumes.

Stratagem, trick, cheat, wile, artifice, cross, deception, take-in, camouflage, make-believe, ruse, manoeuvre, finesse, hoax, canard, hum, kid, chouse, bubble, fetch, catch, spoof, swindle, plant, sell, hocus, dodge, bite, forgery, counterfeit, sham, fake, fakement, rig, delusion, stalking-horse.

Snare, trap, pitfall, decoy, gin, spring, noose, hook, bait, net, meshes, mousetrap, trap-door, false bottom, ambush, ambuscade (530), masked battery, mine, mystery-ship, Q-boat.

(Phrases) A wolf in sheep's clothing; a whited (or painted) sepulchre; a pious fraud; a man of straw.

(Verbs) To deceive, mislead, cheat, impose upon, practise upon, circumvent, play upon, put upon, bluff, dupe, mystify, blind, hoodwink, best, outreach, trick, hoax, kid, gammon, spoof, hocus, bamboozle, hornswoggle, juggle, trepan, nick, entrap, beguile, lure, inveigle, decoy, lime, ensnare, entangle, lay a snare for, trip up, stuff the go-by.

To defraud, fiddle, take in, jockey, do, do brown, cozen, diddle, have, have on, chouse, welsh, bilk, bite, pluck, swindle, victimize, outwit, over-reach, nobble, palm upon, work off upon, foist upon, fob off, balk, trump up.

(Phrases) To throw dust in the eyes; to play a trick upon; to pull one's leg; to try it on; to cog the dice; to mark the cards; to live by one's wits; to play a part; to throw a tub to the whale.

(Adjectives) Deceiving, cheating, etc.; hypocritical, Pecksniffian; deceived, duped, done, had, etc., led astray.

Deceptive, deceitful, deceptious, illusive, illusory, delusory, prestigious, elusive, bogus, counterfeit, insidious, *ad captandum, ben trovato.*

(Phrase) Fronti nulla fides; timeo Danaos et dona ferentes.

546 Untruth *(Substantives)*, falsehood, lie, falsity, fiction, fabrication, fib, whopper, bouncer, cracker, crammer, tarradiddle, story, fable, novel, romance, flam, bull, gammon, flim-flam, *guet-apens*, white lie, pious, fraud, canard, nursery tale, fairy-tale, tall story.

Falsification, perjury, forgery, false swearing, misstatement, misrepresentation, inexactitude.

Pretence, pretext, subterfuge, irony, evasion, blind, disguise, plea, claptrap, shuffle, make-believe, shift, mask, cloak, visor, veil, masquerade, gloss, cobweb.

(Phrases) A pack of lies; a tissue of falsehoods; a cock-and-bull story; a trumped-up story; all my eye and Betty Martin; a mare's-nest.

547 Dupe *(Substantives)*, gull (486), gudgeon, gobemouche, cully, victim, sucker, flat, greenhorn, puppet, cat's paw, April fool, simple Simon, Joe Soap, pushover, soft mark.

(Phrases) To be the goat; to hold the baby; to carry the can; *qui vult decipi, decipiatur.*

548 Deceiver *(Substantives)*, liar, hypocrite, tale-teller, shuffler, shammer, dissembler, serpent, cockatrice; Janus, Tartuffe, Pecksniff, Joseph Surface, Cagliostro.

Pretender, impostor, knave, cheat, rogue, trickster, swindler, spiv, adventurer, humbug, sharper, jockey, welsher, leg, blackleg, rook, shark, confidence man, con man, confidence trickster, decoy, decoy-duck, stool-pigeon, gipsy.

Quack, charlatan, mountebank, empiric, quacksalver, *saltimbanco*, medicaster, *soi-disant*.

Actor, player, mummer, tumbler, posture-master, jack-pudding; illusionist, conjurer (994).

(Phrases) A wolf in sheep's clothing; a snake in the grass; one who lives by his wits.

549 Exaggeration *(Substantives),* hyperbole, overstatement, stretch, strain, colouring, bounce, flourish, vagary, bombast (884), yarn, figure of speech, flight of fancy, *façon de parler,* extravagance, rhodomontade, heroics, sensationalism, highfalutin; tale of Baron Munchausen, traveller's tale.

(Phrases) A storm in a teacup; much ado about nothing.

(Verbs) To exaggerate, amplify, magnify, heighten, overcharge, overstate, overcolour, overlay, overdo, strain, stretch, bounce, flourish, embroider; to hyperbolize, aggravate, to make the most of.

(Phrases) To make a song about; spin a long yarn; draw the long bow; deal in the marvellous; out-herod Herod; lay it on thick; pile it on; make a mountain of a molehill.

(Adjectives) Exaggerated, etc., hyperbolical, turgid, tumid, fabulous, extravagant, magniloquent, bombastic, *outré,* highly coloured, high-flying, high-flown, high-falutin, sensational, blood-and-thunder, lurid.

(Phrases) All his geese are swans; much cry and little wool.

SECTION III—MEANS OF COMMUNICATING IDEAS

1°. *Natural Means*

550 Indication *(Substantives),* symbolization, symbolism, typification, notation, connotation, prefigurement, representation (554), exposition, notice (527), trace (551), name (564).

A sign, symbol, index, placard, exponent, indicator, pointer, mark, token, symptom, type, emblem, figure, cipher, code, device, epigraph, motto, posy.

Science of signs, sematology, semeiology, semeiotics.

Lineament, feature, line, stroke, dash, trait, characteristic, idiosyncrasy, score, stripe, streak, scratch, tick, dot, point, notch, nick, asterisk, red letter, rubric, italics, print, stamp, impress, imprint, sublineation, underlining, display, jotting.

For identification: Badge, criterion, check, countercheck, countersign, stub, counterfoil, duplicate, tally, label, book-plate, *ex-libris,* ticket, billet, card, visiting-card, *carte de visite,* identity-card, passport, bill, bill-head, facia, signboard, witness, voucher, coupon, trade mark, hall-mark, signature, handwriting, sign manual, monogram, seal, sigil, signet, chop, autograph, autography, superscription, endorsement, *visé,* title, heading, caption, docket, watchword, password, shibboleth, *mot du guet,* catchword; fingerprint.

Insignia: Banner, banneret, flag, colours, bunting, streamer, standard, eagle, ensign, pennon, pennant, pendant, burgee, jack, ancient, labarum, oriflamme; gonfalon, banderole, Union Jack, Royal Standard, Stars and Stripes, Tricolour, etc.; crest, arms, coat of arms, armorial bearings, shield, scutcheon, escutcheon, uniform, livery, cockade, epaulet, chevron, cordon, totem.

Indication of locality: Beacon, cairn, post, staff, flagstaff, hand, pointer, vane, guide-post, finger-post, signpost, landmark, sea-mark, lighthouse, lightship, pole-star, lodestar, cynosure, guide, address, direction, rocket, blue-light, watch-fire, blaze.

Indication of an event: Signal, nod, wink, glance, leer, shrug, beck, cue, gesture, gesticulation, deaf-and-dumb alphabet, by-play, dumb-show, pantomime, touch, nudge, freemasonry, telegraph, heliograph, semaphore.

Indication of time: Time-signal, clock (114), alarm-clock, hooter, blower, buzzer, siren; tattoo, reveille, last post, taps.

Indication of danger: Alarm, alarum, alarm-bell, alert, fog-signal, detonator, red light, tocsin, fire-hooter, maroon, S O S, beat of drum, fiery cross, sound of trumpet, war-cry, war-whoop, slogan.

Indication of safety; all-clear, green light.

(Verbs) To indicate, point out, be the sign, etc., of, denote, betoken, connote, connotate, represent, stand for, typify, symbolize, shadow forth, argue, bear the impress of, witness, attest, testify.

To put an indication, mark, etc.; to note, mark, stamp, impress, earmark, brand, label, ticket, docket, endorse, sign, countersign; put, append, or affix a seal or signature; dot, jot down, book, score, dash, trace, chalk, underline, italicize, print, imprint, engrave, stereotype, rubricate, star, obelize, initial.

To make a sign, signal, etc., signalize; give or hang out a signal; give notice, gesticulate, beckon, beck, nod, wink, nudge, tip the wink; give the cue, tip, or office; wave, unfurl, hoist, or hang out a banner, flag, etc., show one's colours, give or sound an alarm, beat the drum, sound the trumpets, raise a cry, etc.

(Adjectives) Indicating, etc., indicatory, indicative, sematic, semeiological, denotative, representative, typical, typic, symbolic, symbolical, diacritical, connotative, pathognomic, symptomatic, exponential, emblematic, pantomimic, attesting; armorial, totemistic.

Indicated, etc., typified, impressed, etc.

Capable of being denoted, denotable, indelible.

(Phrases) Ecce signum; in token of.

---

551 Record *(Substantives)*, trace, mark, tradition, vestige, footstep, footmark, footprint, footfall, wake, track, trail, slot, spoor, pug, scent.

Monument, relic, remains, trophy, hatchment, achievement, obelisk, monolith, pillar, stele, column, slab, tablet, medal, testimonial, memorial.

Note, minute, register, registry, index, inventory, catalogue, list (86), memorandum, jotting, document, account, score, tally, invoice, docket, voucher, protocol, inscription.

Paper, parchment, scroll, instrument, deed, indenture, debenture, roll, archive, schedule, file, dossier, cartulary, table, *procès verbal*, affidavit, certificate, attestation, entry, diploma, protest, round-robin, roster, rota, muster-roll, muster-book, notebook, commonplace-book, *adversaria*, portfolio.

552 Suppression of sign.

Obliteration *(Substantives)*, erasure, rasure, cancel, cancellation, circumduction, deletion.

(Verbs) To efface, obliterate, erase, raze, expunge, cancel, delete, blot out, take out, rub out, scratch out, strike out, elide, wipe out, wash out, black out, write off, render illegible.

To be effaced, etc., to leave no trace.

(Phrases) To draw the pen through; to apply the sponge.

(Adjectives) Obliterated, effaced, etc., printless, leaving no trace.

Unrecorded, unattested, unregistered, intestate.

(Interjections) Dele; out with it!

Chronicle, annals, gazette, Hansard, history (594), newspaper, magazine, gazetteer, blue-book, almanac, calendar, ephemeris, diary, log, journal, daybook, ledger.

Registration, tabulation, enrolment, booking.

(Verbs) To record, note, register, chronicle, calendar, make an entry of, enter, book, take a note of, post, enrol, jot down, take down, mark, sign, etc. (550), tabulate, catalogue, file, index, commemorate (883).

(Adjectives) Registered, etc.

(Adverbs) Under one's hand and seal, on record.

553 Recorder *(Substantives)*, notary, clerk, registrar, registry, register, prothonotary, secretary, stenographer, amanuensis, scribe, remembrancer, journalist, historian, historiographer, annalist, chronicler, biographer, bookkeeper.

Recordership, secretaryship, secretariat, clerkship.

554 Representation *(Substantives)*, delineation, representment, reproduction, depictment, personification.

Art, the fine arts, the graphic arts, design, designing, illustration, imitation (19), copy (21), portraiture, iconography, photography.

A picture, drawing, tracing, photograph.

An image, likeness, icon, portrait, effigy, facsimile, autotype, imagery, figure, puppet, dummy, lay figure, figurehead, doll, manikin, *mannequin,* mammet, marionette, *fantoccini* (599) statue (557), waxwork.

Hieroglyphic, hieroglyph, inscription, diagram, monogram, draught (or draft), outline, scheme, *schema,* schedule.

Map, plan, chart, ground-plan, projection, elevation, ichnography, atlas; cartography, chorography.

(Verbs) To represent, present, depict, portray, photograph, delineate, design, figure, adumbrate, shadow forth, copy, draft, mould, diagrammatize, schematize, map.

To imitate, impersonate, personate, personify, act, take off, hit off, figure as; to paint (556); carve (557); engrave (558).

(Adjectives) Representing, etc.; artistic; imitative, representative, illustrative, figurative, hieroglyphic, hieroglyphical, diagrammatic, schematic.

555 Misrepresentation *(Substantives)*, distortion (243), caricature, burlesque (856), a bad likeness, daub, scratch, sign-painting, anamorphosis; misprint, *erratum.*

(Verbs) To misrepresent, distort, falsify, caricature, wrest the sense (or meaning).

———

556 Painting *(Substantives)*, depicting, drawing; perspective, composition, treatment.

Drawing in pencil, crayon, pastel, chalk, water-colour, etc.

Painting in oils, in distemper, in gouache, in fresco; encaustic painting, enamel painting, scene-painting; wash (428), body-colour, impasto.

A picture, drawing, painting, sketch, illustration, scratch, *graffito,* outline, tableau, cartoon, fresco, illumination; pencil, pen-and-ink, etc., drawing; oil, etc., painting; photograph; silver print; P.O.P., bromide, gaslight, bromoil, platinotype, carbon print; autochrome, Kodachrome; daguerreotype, calotype; mosaic, tapestry, etc., picture-gallery.

Portrait, portraiture, likeness, full-length, etc., miniature, kitcat, shade, profile, silhouette, still, snapshot.

Landscape, seascape, nocturne, view, still-life, *genre,* panorama, diorama.

Pre-Raphaelitism, impressionism, etc. (559).

(Verbs) To paint, depict, portray, limn, draw, sketch, pencil, scratch, scrawl, block in, rough in, dash off, chalk out, shadow forth, adumbrate, outline, illustrate, illuminate; to take a portrait, take a likeness, to photograph, snap, pan.

(Phrases) Fecit, *pinxit, delineavit.*

(Adjectives) Painted, etc.; pictorial, graphic, picturesque, Giottesque, Raphaelesque, Turneresque, etc.; like, similar (17).

557 Sculpture *(Substantives)*, insculpture, carving, modelling.

A statue, statuary, statuette, figure, figurine, model, bust, image, high relief, low relief, alto-rilievo, mezzo-rilievo, basso-rilievo, bas-relief, cast, marble, bronze, intaglio, anaglyph; medallion, cameo.

(Verbs) To sculpture, sculp, carve, cut, chisel, model, mould, cast.

(Adjectives) Sculptured, etc., sculptural, sculpturesque, anaglyphic, cero-plastic, ceramic.

558 Engraving *(Substantives)*, etching, wood-engraving, process-engraving, xylography, chalcography, cerography, glyptography; poker-work.

A print, engraving, impression, plate, cut, wood-cut, steel-cut, linocut, vignette.

An etching, dry-point, stipple, roulette; copper-plate, mezzotint, aquatint, lithograph, chromolithograph, chromo, photo-lithograph, photogravure, anastatic-printing, collotype, electrotype, stereotype.

Matrix, flong.

(Verbs) To engrave, etc., lithograph, print, etc.

559 Artist *(Substantives)*, painter, limner, draughtsman, black-and-white artist, cartoonist, caricaturist, drawer, sketcher, pavement artist, screever, designer, engraver, copyist, photographer.

Academician; historical, landscape, portrait, miniature, scene, sign, etc., painter; an Apelles.

Primitive, Pre-Raphaelite, old master, quattrocentist, cinquecentist, impressionist, post-impressionist, futurist, vorticist, cubist, surrealist, Dadaist, pointillist.

A sculptor, carver, modeller, goldsmith, silversmith, *figuriste*; a Phidias, Praxiteles, Royal Academician, R.A.

Implements of art: pen, pencil, brush, charcoal, chalk, pastel, crayon; paint (428); stump, graver, style, burin; canvas, easel, palette, maul-stick, palette-knife; studio, *atelier*.

2°. *Conventional Means*

1. LANGUAGE GENERALLY

560 Language *(Substantives)*, tongue, speech, lingo, vernacular, mother-tongue, native tongue, standard English, King's (or Queen's) English, the genius of a language.

Dialect, local dialect, class dialect, provincialism, vulgarism, colloquialism, Americanism, Scotticism, Cockney speech, brogue, patois, patter, slang, cant, argot, Anglic, Basic English, broken English, pidgin English, lingua franca.

Universal languages: Esperanto, Volapük, Ido, Interglossa.

Philology, etymology (562), linguistics, glossology, dialectology, phonetics.

Literature, letters, polite literature, belles lettres, the muses, humanities, the republic of letters, dead languages, classics, *literae humaniores*.

Scholarship (490), linguist, scholar (492), writer (593), glossographer.

(Verbs) To express by words, to couch in terms, to clothe in language.

(Adjectives) Literary, belletristic, linguistic, dialectal, vernacular, colloquial, slang, current, polyglot, pantomimic.

(Adverbs) In plain terms, in common parlance, in household words.

561 Letter *(Substantives)*, alphabet, A B C, abecedary, spelling-book, horn-book, criss-cross-row; character (591), writing (590), hieroglyph, hieroglyphic; consonant, vowel, diphthong, triphthong; mute, liquid, labial, palatal, dental, guttural; spelling, orthography, phonetic spelling, misspelling; spelling-bee.

Syllable, monosyllable, dissyllable, trisyllable, polysyllable; anagram.

(Verbs) To spell, spell out.

(Adjectives) Literal, alphabetical, abecedarian, orthographic; syllabic, disyllabic, etc.

562 Word *(Substantives)*, term, vocable, terminology, part of speech (567), root, etymon.

Word similarly pronounced, homonym, homophone, paronym.

A dictionary, vocabulary, lexicon, index, polyglot, glossary, thesaurus, concordance, onomasticon, gradus; lexicography, lexicographer.

Derivation, etymology, glossology.

(Adjectives) Verbal, literal, titular, nominal, etymological, terminological.

Similarly derived, conjugate, paronymous.

(Adverbs) Nominally, etc., *verbatim*, word for word, in so many words, literally, *sic, totidem verbis, ipsissimis verbis, literatim*.

563 Neology *(Substantives)*, neologism, slang, cant, byword, hard word, jaw-breaker, dog Latin, monkish Latin, loan word, vogue word, nonce word, Gallicism.

A pun, play upon words, paronomasia, *jeu de mots, calembour,* palindrome, conundrum, acrostic, anagram (533).

Dialect (560).

Neologian, neologist.

(Verbs) To neologize, archaize, pun.

(Phrase) To coin or mint words.

(Adjectives) Neological, neologistic, paronomastic.

564 Nomenclature *(Substantives)*, nomination, naming, nuncupation.

A name, appellation, designation, appellative, denomination, term, expression, noun, byword, moniker, epithet, style, title, prenomen, forename, Christian name, baptismal name, given name, cognomen, agnomen, patronymic, surname, family name.

Synonym, namesake; euphemism, antonomasia, onomatopoeia.

Quotation, citation, chapter and verse.

(Verbs) To name, call, term, denominate, designate, style, clepe, entitle, dub, christen, baptize, characterize, specify, label (550).

To be called, etc., to take the name of, pass under the name of; to quote, cite.

(Phrases) To call a spade a spade; to rejoice in the name of.

(Adjectives) Named, called, etc., hight, yclept, known as; nuncupatory, nuncupative, cognominal, titular, nominal.

Literal, verbal, discriminative.

565 Misnomer *(Substantives)*, missaying, malaprop, malapropism, antiphrasis, nickname, sobriquet, byname, assumed name or title, alias, *nom de guerre, nom de plume*, pen-name, pseudonym, pet name, euphemism.

So-and-so, what's-his-name, thingummy, thingumbob, thingumajig, dingus, *Je ne sais quoi.*

A Mrs. Malaprop.

(Phrase) Lucus a non lucendo.

(Verbs) To misname, missay, miscall, misterm, nickname.

To assume a name.

(Adjectives) Misnamed, etc., malapropian, pseudonymous, *soi-disant,* self-called, self-styled, so-called.

Nameless, anonymous, without a name, having no name, innominate, unnamed.

566 Phrase (*Substantives*), expression, phraseology, paraphrase, periphrasis, circumlocution (573), set phrase, round terms; mode or turn of expression; idiom, wording, *façon de parler*, mannerism, plain terms, plain English.

Sentence, paragraph, motto.

Figure, trope, metaphor (521), wisecrack, proverb (496).

(*Verbs*) To express, phrase, put; couch, clothe in words, give words to; to word.

(*Adjectives*) Expressed, etc., couched in, phraseological, idiomatic, paraphrastic, periphrastic, circumlocutory (573), proverbial.

(*Phrase*) As the saying is; in good set terms; *sans phrase*.

567 Grammar (*Substantives*), accidence, syntax, parsing, analysis, praxis, punctuation, conjugation, declension, inflexion, case, voice, person, number; philology (560), parts of speech.

(*Phrase*) *Jus et norma loquendi.*

(*Verbs*) To parse, analyse, conjugate, decline, inflect, punctuate.

(*Adjectives*) Grammatical, syntatic, inflexional.

568 Solecism (*Substantives*), bad or false grammar, slip of the pen or tongue, bull, howler, floater, clanger, *lapsus linguae*, barbarism, vulgarism; dog Latin.

(*Verbs*) To use bad or faulty grammar, to solecize, commit a solecism.

(*Phrases*) To murder the king's English; to break Priscian's head.

(*Adjectives*) Ungrammatical, barbarous, slipshod, incorrect, faulty, inaccurate.

569 Style (*Substantives*), diction, phraseology, wording, turn of expression, idiom, manner, strain, composition, authorship; stylist.

(*Adjectives*) Stylistic, idiomatic, mannered.

(*Phrases*) Command of language; a ready pen; *le style, c'est l'homme même*.

Various Qualities of Style

570 Perspicuity (*Substantives*), lucidity, lucidness, clearness, clarity, perspicacity, plain speaking, intelligibility (518).

(*Adjectives*), Perspicuous, clear (525), lucid, intelligible, plain, transparent, explicit.

571 Obscurity (*Substantives*), ambiguity (520), unintelligibility (519), involution, involvedness, vagueness.

(*Adjectives*) Obscure, confused, crabbed, ambiguous, vague, unintelligible, etc., involved, wiredrawn, tortuous.

572 Conciseness (*Substantives*), brevity, terseness, compression (195), condensation, concision, closeness, laconism, portmanteau word, telegraphese, pithiness, succinctness, quaintness, stiffness, ellipsis, ellipse, syncope.

Abridgment, epitome (596).

(*Verbs*) To be concise, etc., to condense, compress, abridge, abbreviate, cut short, curtail, abstract.

(*Phrase*) To cut the cackle and come to the horses.

573 Diffuseness (*Substantives*), prolixity, verbosity, macrology, pleonasm, tautology, copiousness, exuberance, laxity, looseness, verbiage, flow, flow of words, fluency, *copia verborum,* loquacity (584), redundancy, redundance, digression, amplification, *longueur*, padding, circumlocution, ambages, periphrasis, officialese, commercialese, gobbledygook, episode, expletive.

(*Verbs*) To be diffuse, etc., to expatiate, enlarge, launch out, dilate, expand, pad out, spin out, run on,

(Adjectives) Concise, brief, crisp, curt, short, terse, laconic, sententious, gnomic, snappy, pithy, nervous, pregnant, succinct, *guindé*, stiff, compact, summary, compendious (596), close, cramped, elliptical, telegraphic, epigrammatic, lapidary.

(Adverbs) Concisely, briefly, etc., in a word, to the point, in short.

(Phrases) The long and short of it; *multum in parvo*; it comes to this; for shortness' sake; to make a long story short; to put it in a nutshell.

amplify, swell out, inflate, dwell on, harp on, descant, digress, ramble, maunder, rant.

(Phrases) To beat about the bush; to spin a long yarn; to make a long story of.

(Adjectives) Diffuse, wordy, verbose, prolix, copious, exuberant, flowing, fluent, bombastic, lengthy, long-winded, talkative (584), prosy, spun out, long-spun, loose, lax, slovenly, washy, slipslop, sloppy, frothy, flatulent, windy, digressive, discursive, excursive, tripping, rambling, ambagious, pleonastic, redundant, periphrastic, episodic, circumlocutory, roundabout.

Minute, detailed, particular, circumstantial.
(Adverbs) In detail, at great length, *in extenso*, about it and about, *currente calamo, usque ad nauseam*.

574 Vigour *(Substantives)*, energy, power, force, spirit, point, vim, snap, punch, ginger, *élan*, pep, go, raciness, liveliness, fire, glow, verve, piquancy, pungency, spice, boldness, gravity, warmth, sententiousness, elevation, loftiness, sublimity, eloquence, individuality, distinction, emphasis, virility.

(Phrase) 'Thoughts that glow and words that burn.'

(Adjectives) Vigorous, energetic, powerful, strong, forcible, nervous, spirited, vivid, virile, expressive, lively, glowing, sparkling, racy, bold, slashing, incisive, trenchant, snappy, mordant, poignant, piquant, pungent, spicy, meaty, pithy, juicy, pointed, antithetical, sententious, emphatic, individual, lofty, elevated, sublime, Miltonic, eloquent.

575 Feebleness *(Substantives)*, baldness, tameness, meagreness, coldness, frigidity, poverty, puerility, childishness, dullness, dryness, jejuneness, monotony.

(Adjectives) Feeble, bald, dry, flat, insipid, tame, meagre, invertebrate, weak, mealy-mouthed, wishy-washy, wersh, banal, uninteresting, jejune, vapid, cold, frigid, poor, dull (843), languid, anaemic, prosy, prosaic, pedestrian, platitudinous, conventional, mechanical, decadent, trashy, namby-pamby (866), puerile, childish, emasculate.

athletic, distinguished, original,

576 Plainness *(Substantives)*, simplicity, homeliness, chasteness, chastity, neatness, monotony, severity.

(Adjectives) Simple, unornamented, unvarnished, straightforward, artless, unaffected, downright, plain, unadorned, unvaried, monotonous, severe, chaste, blunt, homespun.

577 Ornament *(Substantives)*, floridness, floridity, flamboyance, richness, opulence, turgidity, tumidity, pomposity, inflation, altiloquence, spreadeagleism, pretension, fustian, affectation, euphuism, gongorism, mannerism, metaphor, preciosity, inversion, figurativeness, sesquipedalianism, *sesquipedalia verba*, rant, bombast, frothiness; flowers of speech, high-sounding words, well-rounded periods, purple patches.

A phrase-monger, euphuist.

(Verbs) To ornament, overcharge, overlay with ornament, lard or garnish with metaphors, lay the colours on thick, round a period, mouth.

(Adjectives) Ornamented, etc., ornate, florid, flamboyant, rich, opulent, golden-mouthed, figurative, metaphorical, pedantic, affected, pretentious, falsetto, euphuistic, Della Cruscan, pompous, fustian, high-sounding, mouthy, inflated, high-falutin (or high-faluting), bombastic, stilted, mannered, high-flowing, frothy, flowery, luscious, turgid, tumid, swelling, declamatory, rhapsodic, rhetorical, orotund, sententious, grandiose, grandiloquent, magniloquent, altiloquent, sesquipedalian, Johnsonian, ponderous.

(Adverb) Ore rotundo.

578 Elegance *(Substantives)*, grace, ease, naturalness, purity, concinnity, readiness, euphony; a purist.

(Phrases) A ready pen; flowing periods; *curiosa felicitas.*

(Adjectives) Elegant, graceful, Attic, Ciceronian, classical, natural, easy, felicitous, unaffected, unlaboured, chaste, pure, correct, flowing, mellifluous, euphonious, rhythmical, puristic, well-expressed, neatly put.

(Phrases) To round a period; 'to point a moral and adorn a tale.'

579 Inelegance *(Substantives)*, stiffness, uncouthness, barbarism, archaism, rudeness, crudeness, bluntness, brusquerie, ruggedness, abruptness, artificiality, cacophony.

(Phrases) Words that dislocate the jaw, that break the teeth.

(Verbs) To be inelegant, etc.

(Phrase) To smell of the lamp.

(Adjectives) Inelegant, ungraceful, stiff, forced, laboured, clumsy, contorted, tortuous, harsh, cramped, rude, rugged, dislocated, crude, crabbed, uncouth, barbarous, archaic, archaistic, affected (577), artificial, abrupt, blunt, brusque, incondite.

2. SPOKEN LANGUAGE

580 Voice *(Substantives)*, vocality, vocalization, utterance, cry, strain, articulate sound, prolation, articulation, enunciation, delivery, vocalism, pronunciation, orthoepy, euphony.

Cadence, accent, accentuation, emphasis, stress, tone, intonation, exclamation, ejaculation, vociferation, ventriloquism, polyphonism.

A ventriloquist, polyphonist.

Phonetics, phonology; voice-production.

(Verbs) To utter, breathe, cry, exclaim, shout, ejaculate, vociferate; raise, lift, strain the voice or lungs; to vocalize, prolate, articulate, enunciate, pronounce, accentuate, aspirate, deliver, mouth, rap out, speak out, speak up.

(Phrase) To whisper in the ear.

(Adjectives) Vocal, oral, phonetic, articulate.

Silvery, mellow, soft (413).

581 Aphony *(Substantives)*, obmutescence, absence or want of voice, dumbness, muteness, mutism, speechlessness, aphasia, hoarseness, raucity; silence (585).

A dummy, a mute, deaf-mute.

(Verbs) To render mute, to muzzle, muffle, suppress, smother, gag (585); to whisper (405).

(Phrases) To stick in the throat; to close one's lips; to shut up.

(Adjectives) Aphonous, dumb, speechless, mute, tongueless, muzzled, tongue-tied, inarticulate, inaudible, unspoken, unsaid, mum, mumchance, lips close or sealed, wordless; raucous, hoarse, husky, sepulchral.

(Phrases) Mute as a fish; hoarse as a raven; with bated breath; *sotto voce*; with the finger on the lips; mum's the word.

582 Speech *(Substantives)*, locution, talk, parlance, verbal intercourse, oral communication word of mouth, palaver, prattle, effusion, narrative (594), tale, story, yarn, oration, recitation, delivery, say, harangue, formal speech, speechifying, sermon, homily, discourse (998), lecture, curtain lecture, pi-jaw, address, tirade, pep-talk, screed; preamble, peroration; soliloquy (589).

Oratory, elocution, rhetoric, declamation, eloquence, gift of the gab, *copia verborum*, grandiloquence, magniloquence.

A speaker, spokesman, prolocutor, mouthpiece, lecturer, orator, stumporator, speechifier; a Cicero, a Demosthenes.

(Verbs) To speak, break silence, say, tell, utter, pronounce (580), open one's lips, give tongue, hold forth, make or deliver a speech, speechify, harangue, talk, discourse, declaim, stump, flourish, spout, rant, recite, rattle off, intone, breathe, let fall, whisper in the ear, expatiate, run on; to lecture, preach, address, sermonize, preachify; to soliloquize (589); quoth he.

(Phrases) To have a tongue in one's head; to have on the tip of one's tongue; to have on one's lips; to pass one's lips; to find one's tongue.

(Adjectives) Speaking, etc., oral, spoken, unwritten, elocutionary, oratorical, rhetorical, declamatory, outspoken.

(Adverbs) Viva voce; *ore rotundo*; by word of mouth.

583 Imperfect speech.

Stammering *(Substantives)*, inarticulateness, stuttering, impediment in one's speech, titubancy, faltering, hesitation, lisp, drawl, jabber, gibber, sputter, splutter, mumbling, mincing, muttering, mouthing, twang, a broken or cracked voice, broken accents or sentences, tardiloquence, falsetto, a whisper (405), mispronunciation.

(Verbs) to stammer, stutter, hesitate, falter, hem, haw, hum and ha, mumble, lisp, jabber, gibber, mutter, sputter, splutter, drawl, mouth, mince, lisp, croak, speak through the nose, snuffle, clip one's words, mispronounce, missay.

(Phrases) To clip the King's (or Queen's) English; *parler à tort et à travers*; not to be able to put two words together.

(Adjectives) Stammering, etc., inarticulate, guttural, nasal, tremulous.

———

584 Loquacity *(Substantives)*, loquaciousness, talkativeness, garrulity, flow of words, prate, gas, jaw, gab, gabble, jabber, chatter, prattle, cackle, clack, clash, blether (or blather), patter, rattle, twaddle, bibble-babble, gibble-gabble, talkee-talkee, gossip.

Fluency, flippancy, volubility, verbosity, *cacoethes loquendi*, anecdotage.

A chatterer, chatterbox, blatherskite, babbler, wind-bag, gas-bag, rattle, ranter, tub-thumper, sermonizer, proser, driveller, gossip.

Magpie, jay, parrot, poll; Babel.

(Phrases) A twice (or thrice) told tale; a long yarn; the gift of the gab.

(Verbs) To be loquacious, etc., to

585 Taciturnity *(Substantives)*, closeness, reserve, reticence (528), muteness, silence, curtness; aposiopesis; a clam, oyster.

(Phrases) A Quaker meeting; a man of few words.

(Verbs) To be silent, etc. (403), to hold one's tongue, keep silence, hold one's peace, say nothing, hold one's jaw, close one's mouth or lips, fall silent, dry up, shut up, stow it.

To render silent, silence, put to silence, seal one's lips, smother, suppress, stop one's mouth, gag, muffle, muzzle (581).

(Adjectives) Taciturn, silent, close, reserved, mute, sparing of words, buttoned up, curt, short-spoken, close-tongued, tight-lipped, reticent,

prate, palaver, chatter, prattle, jabber, jaw, rattle, twaddle, blether, babble, gabble, gas, out-talk, descant, dilate, dwell on, reel off, expatiate, prose, launch out, yarn, gossip, wag one's tongue, run on.

(Phrases) To din in the ears; to drum into the ear; to spin a long yarn; to talk at random; to bum one's chat; to talk oneself out of breath; to talk nineteen to the dozen.

(Adjectives) Loquacious, talkative, garulous, gassy, gabby, open-mouthed, chatty, chattering, etc.

Fluent, voluble, glib, flippant, long-tongued, long-winded, verbose, the tongue running fast.

(Adverb) Trippingly on the tongue.

586 Allocution *(Substantives)*, address, apostrophe, interpellation, appeal, invocation, alloquialism, salutation, accost, greeting (894).

Feigned dialogue, imaginary conversation; inquiry (461).

(Phrase) A word in the ear.

(Verbs) To speak to, address, accost, buttonhole, apostrophize, appeal to, invoke, hail, make up to, take aside, call to, halloo (or hallo), salute.

(Phrases) To talk with one in private; to break the ice.

(Adjectives) Accosting, etc., alloquial, invocatory, apostrophic.

(Interjections) Hallo! hello! hullo! I say! hoy! oi! hey! what ho! psst!

588 Interlocution *(Substantives)*, collocution, colloquy, conversation, converse, confabulation, confab, talk, discourse, verbal intercourse, dialogue, duologue, logomachy, communication, intercommunication, commerce, debate.

Chat, chit-chat, crack, small talk, table-talk, tattle, gossip, tittle-tattle, babblement, clack, prittle-prattle, idle talk, town-talk, bazaar talk, *on dit*, causerie, *chronique scandaleuse*.

Conference, parley, interview, audience, tête-à-tête, reception, conversazione, palaver, pow-wow; council (686).

A talker, interlocutor, interviewer, gossip, tattler, chatterer, babbler (584), conversationalist, *causeur; dramatis personae*.

(Phrases) 'The feast of reason and the flow of soul'; a heart-to-heart talk.

(Verbs) To talk together, converse, collogue, commune, debate, discourse with, engage in conversation, interview; hold or carry on a conversation; chat, gossip, have a crack, put in a word, chip in, tattle, babble, prate, clack, prattle.

To confer with, hold conference, etc., to parley, palaver, commerce,

secretive, uncommunicative, inconversable.

(Phrases) Not a word escaping one; not having a word to say.

(Interjections) Hush! silence! mum! *chut!* hist! whist! wheesht!

———

587 Response *(Substantives)*, answer, reply (462).

(Verbs) To answer, respond, reply, etc.

(Phrase) To take up one's cue.

(Adjectives) Answering, responding, etc., responsive, respondent.

———

589 Soliloquy *(Substantives)*, monologue, apostrophe, aside.

Soliloquist, monologist, monologuist.

(Verbs) To soliloquize, monologize; to say or talk to oneself, to say aside, to think aloud, to apostrophize.

(Adjectives) Soliloquizing, etc.

———

hold intercourse with, be closeted with, commune with, have speech with, compare notes, intercommunicate.

(Adjectives) Conversing, etc., interlocutory, verbal, colloquial, discursive, chatty, gossiping, etc., conversable, conversational.

3. WRITTEN LANGUAGE

590 Writing *(Substantives)*, chirography, pencraft, penmanship, longhand, calligraphy, quill-driving, pen-pushing, typewriting, typing.

Scribble, scrawl, scratch, cacography, scribbling, etc., jotting, interlineation, palimpsest.

Uncial writing, court hand, cursive writing, picture writing, hieroglyphics, hieroglyph, cuneiform characters, demotic text, hieratic text, ogham, runes.

Pothooks and hangers.

Transcription, inscription, superscription, minute.

Shorthand, stenography, phonography, brachygraphy, tachygraphy, steganography.

Secret writing, writing in cipher, cryptography, polygraphy, stelography; cryptogram.

Automatic writing, planchette.

Composition, authorship, *cacoethes scribendi.*

Manuscript, MS., copy, transcript, rough copy, fair copy, carbon, black, duplicate, flimsy, handwriting, hand, fist, script, autograph, signature, sign-manual, monograph, holograph, endorsement, paraph.

A scribe, amanuensis, scrivener, secretary, clerk, penman, calligraphist, copyist, transcriber, stenographer, typist.

Writer, author, scribbler, quill-driver, ink-slinger, pamphleteer, essayist, critic, reviewer, novelist (593), journalist, editor, subeditor, reporter, pressman, penny-a-liner, hack, free-lance; Grub Street, Fleet Street.

Pen, quill, fountain-pen, stylograph, stylo, ball-point, Biro, pencil, stationery, paper, parchment, vellum, tablet, slate, marble, pillar, table, etc.

(Phrase) A dash or stroke of the pen.

(Verbs) To write, pen, typewrite, type, write out, copy, engross, write out fair, transcribe, scribble, scrawl, scratch, interline; to sign, undersign, countersign, endorse (497), set one's hand to.

To compose, indite, draw up, draft, minute, jot down, dash off, make or take a minute of, put or set down in writing; to inscribe, to dictate.

(Phrases) To take up the pen; to spill ink; to sling ink; set or put pen to paper; put on paper; commit to paper.

(Adjectives) Writing, etc., written, in writing, penned, etc., scriptorial; uncial, cursive, cuneiform, runic, hieroglyphical; editorial, journalistic, reportorial.

(Phrases) Under one's hand; in black and white; pen in hand; *currente calamo.*

591 Printing *(Substantives)*, print, letterpress, text, context, note, page, proof, pull, revise; presswork.

Typography, stereotypography, type, character, black-letter, fount (or font), capitals, majuscules, lower case letters, minuscules, etc.; roman, italic, type; braille.

Folio, quarto, octavo, etc. (593).

Printer, pressman, compositor, corrector of the press, proof-reader, copyholder; printer's devil.

Printing-press, linotype, monotype, etc.

(Verbs) To print, put to press, publish, edit, get out a work, etc.

(Adjectives) Printed, etc.

592 Correspondence *(Substantives)*, letter, epistle, note, line, airgraph, postcard, chit, billet, missive, circular, favour, *billet-doux*, dispatch, bulletin, memorial, rescript, rescription.

Letter-bag, mail, post; postage.

(Verbs) To correspond, write to, send a letter to.

(Phrase) To keep up a correspondence.

(Adjectives) Epistolary, postal.

———

593 Book *(Substantives)*, writing, work, volume, tome, codex, opuscule, tract, manual, pamphlet, chap-book, booklet, brochure, enchiridion, circular, publication, part, issue, number, journal, album, periodical, magazine, digest, serial, ephemeris, annual, yearbook.

Writer, author, publicist, scribbler, pamphleteer, poet, essayist, novelist, fabulist, editor (590).

Book-lover, bibliophile, bibliomaniac, paperback.

Bibliography, *incunabula,* Aldine, Elzevir, etc.; library.

Publisher, bookseller, bibliopole, bibliopolist, librarian.

Folio, quarto, octavo, duodecimo, sextodecimo, octodecimo.

Paper, bill, sheet, leaf, fly-leaf, page, title-page.

Chapter, section, paragraph, passage, clause.

(Adjectives) Auctorial, bookish, bibliographical, etc.

594 Description *(Substantives)*, account, statement, report, return, delineation, specification, particulars, sketch, representation (554), narration, narrative, yarn, relation, recital, rehearsal, annals, chronicle, saga, *adversaria*, journal (551), itinerary, log-book.

Historiography; historicity, historic muse, Clio.

Story, history, memoir, tale, tradition, legend, folk-tale, folk-lore, anecdote, ana, analects (596), fable, fiction, novel, novelette, thriller, whodunit, romance, short story, *conte, nouvelle*, apologue, parable; word-picture; local colour.

Biography, necrology, obituary, life, personal narrative, adventures, autobiography, confessions, reminiscences.

A historian, historiographer, narrator, *raconteur*, annalist, chronicler, biographer, fabulist, novelist, fictionist, story-teller.

(Verbs) To describe, state (535), set forth, sketch, delineate, represent (554), portray, depict, paint, shadow forth, adumbrate.

To relate, recite, recount, sum up, run over, recapitulate, narrate, chronicle, rehearse, tell, give or render an account of, report, draw up a statement, spin a yarn, unfold a tale, novelize, actualize.

To take up or handle a subject; to enter into particulars, detail, etc., to characterize, particularize, detail, retail, elaborate, write up; to descend to particulars; to Boswellize.

(Phrases) To plunge *in medias res*; to fight one's battles over again.

(Adjectives) Descriptive, narrative, graphic, realistic, naturalistic, novelistic, historic, traditional, traditionary, legendary, storied, romantic, anecdotic, Boswellian, described, etc.

595 Dissertation *(Substantives)*, treatise, tract, tractate, thesis, theme, monograph, essay, discourse, article, leading article, leader, leaderette, editorial, feuilleton, criticism, critique, review, memoir, prolusion, disquisition, exposition, exercitation, compilation, sermon, lecture, teach-in, homily, pandect, *causerie*, pamphlet (593).

Commentator, lecturer, critic, leader-writer, pamphleteer.

(Verbs) To dissert, descant, treat of, discuss, write, compile, touch upon ventilate, canvass; deal with, do justice to a subject.

(Adjectives) Discursive, disquisitional, expository, compiled

596 Compendium *(Substantives)*, compend, summary, abstract, précis, epitome, *aperçu*, analysis, digest, sum and substance, *compte rendu, procès verbal*, draft, *exposé*, brief, recapitulation, résumé, conspectus, abridgment, abbreviation, minute, note, synopsis, argument, plot, syllabus, contents, heads, prospectus.

Scrap-book, album, note-book, commonplace-book, compilation, extracts, cuttings, clippings, text-book, analects, *analecta*, excerpts, flowers, anthology, *collectanea*, memorabilia.

(Verbs) To abridge, abstract, excerpt, abbreviate, recapitulate, run over, make or prepare an abstract, etc. (201), epitomize, sum up, summarize, boil down, anthologize.

(Adjectives) Compendious, etc., synoptic, abridged, etc., analectic.

(Phrase) In a nutshell; in substance; in short.

597 Poetry *(Substantives)*, poetics, poesy, the Muse, the Nine, Calliope, Parnassus, Helicon, the Pierian spring.

Verse, metre, measure, foot, numbers, strain, rhyme (or rime), head-rhyme, alliteration, rhythm, heroic verse, Alexandrine, octosyllables, *terza rima,* blank verse, free verse, *vers libre,* sprung rhythm, assonance, versification, macaronics, doggerel, jingle, prosody, orthometry, scansion.

598 Prose *(Substantives)* prose-writer, proser, prosaist.

(Verb) To prose.

(Adjectives) Prosaic, prosaical, prosing, prosy, rhymeless, unrhymed, unpoetical, commonplace, humdrum.

———

Poem, epic, epopee, epic poem, ballad, ode, epode, idyll, lyric, eclogue, pastoral, bucolic, macaronic, dithyramb, anacreontic, sonnet, lay, roundelay, rondeau, rondel, ballade, villanelle, triolet, sestina, rhyme royal, madrigal, canzonet, libretto, posy, anthology; distich, stanza, stave, strophe, antistrophe, couplet, triplet, quatrain, cento, monody, elegy, *vers de société.*

Iambic (or iamb), trochee, spondee, dactyl, anapaest, amphibrach, amphimacer, tribrach, paeon, etc.

A poet, laureate, bard, scald, poetess, rhymer, rhymist, versifier, rhymester, sonneteer, poetaster, minor poet, minnesinger, meistersinger, troubadour, *trouvère.*

(Phrase) Genus irritabile vatum.

(Verbs) To rhyme, versify, sing, make verses, scan, poetize.

(Adjectives) Poetical, poetic, Castalian, Parnassian, Heliconian, lyric, lyrical, metrical, epic, heroic; catalectic, dithyrambic, doggerel, macaronic, leonine; Pindaric, Homeric, Virgilian, Shakespearian, Miltonic, Tennysonian, etc.

599 The Drama *(Substantives)*, stage, theatre, the histrionic art, dramatic art, histrionics, acting; stage effect, *mise en scène*, stage production, setting, scenery; buskin, sock, cothurnus; Melpomene, Thalia, Thespis; play-writing, dramaturgy.

Play, stage-play, piece, tragedy, comedy, tragi-comedy, morality, mystery, melodrama, farce, knock-about farce, comedietta, curtain-raiser, interlude, after-piece, vaudeville, extravaganza, *divertissement,* burletta, burlesque, variety show, revue; opera, grand opera, music-drama, comic opera, *opéra bouffe*, operetta, ballad opera, *singspiel*, musical comedy; ballet, pantomime, harlequinade, charade, wordless play, dumb-show, by-play; monodrama, monologue, duologue; masque, pageant, show; scenario, libretto, book of words, part, role; matinée, benefit; act, scene, prologue, epilogue.

Theatre, playhouse, music-hall, variety theatre; stage, the boards, the footlights, green-room, foyer, proscenium, flies, wings, stalls, box, pit, circle, dress-circle, balcony, amphitheatre, gallery.

An actor, player, stage-player, performer, artiste, comedian, comedienne, tragedian, tragedienne, Thespian, Roscius, clown, harlequin, pantaloon, *buffo*, buffoon, pierrot, pierrette, impersonator, entertainer, etc., strolling player; ballet dancer, *ballerina*, figurant, mime, star; prima donna, *primo tenore*, etc., leading lady, heavy lead, juvenile lead, *ingénue*, soubrette; supernumerary, super, walking, gentleman or lady, chorus girl; *dramatis personae*, cast, company, stock company, touring company, repertory company; a star turn.

Mummer, guiser, masquer; dancer, nautch-girl, bayadère, geisha.

Stage manager, impresario, producer, prompter, stage hands, call-boy, etc.

Dramatic writer, pantomimist, playwright, play-writer, dramatist, dramaturge, librettist.

(Phrase) The profession.

(Verbs) To act, enact, play, perform, personate (554), play or interpret a part, rehearse, spout, rant, gag, star, walk on.

To produce, present, stage, stage-manager.

(Phrases) To strut and fret one's hour on the stage; to tread the boards.

(Adjectives) Dramatic, theatre, theatrical, scenic, histrionic, comic, tragic, buskined, farcical, knock-about, slapstick, tragi-comic, melodramatic, transpontine, stagy, operatic.

599ᴀ Cinema *(Substantives)*, picture theatre, picturedrome, film, motion picture, pictures, movies, flicks, pix, silver screen; silent film, sound film, talkie, flattie; three-dimensional film, 3-D, wide-screen film, deepie; documentary, trailer.

Close-up, flash-back, fade-out.

Scenario, star, vamp; cinema-goer, cinemaddict, film fan.

(Verbs) To feature, screen; dub.

599ʙ Radio *(Substantives)*, wireless, receiving set, transistor, walkie-talkie; broadcast, radio play; teleprompter.

Announcer, listener.

Television, TV., video, telly; telecast, telefilm, newscast, script.

Looker-in, televiewer, viewer.

(Verbs) To broadcast, televise, telecast.

To listen in, look in, view, teleview.

(Phrase) On the air.

(Adjective) Telegenic.

CLASS V

WORDS RELATING TO THE VOLUNTARY POWERS

DIVISION I—INDIVIDUAL VOLITION

SECTION I—VOLITION IN GENERAL

1°. Acts of Volition

600 Will (*Substantives*), volition, voluntariness, velleity, conation, free-will, spontaneity, spontaneousness, freedom (748).

Pleasure, wish, mind, animus, breast, mood, bosom, *petto*, heart, discretion, accord.

Libertarianism.

Determination (604), predetermination (611), intention (620), choice (609).

(*Verbs*) To will, list, think fit, see fit, think proper, determine, etc. (604), settle, choose (609), to take upon oneself, to have one's will, to do as one likes, wishes, or chooses; to use or exercise one's own discretion, to volunteer, lend oneself to.

(*Phrases*) To have a will of one's own; *hoc volo, sic jubeo, stet pro ratione voluntas*; to take the will for the deed; to know one's own mind; to know what one is about; to see one's way; to have one's will; to take upon oneself; to take the law into one's own hands.

(*Adjectives*) Voluntary, volitional, willing, content, minded, spontaneous, free, left to oneself, unconstrained, unfettered, autocratic, bossy, unbidden, unasked, unurged, uncompelled, of one's own accord, gratuitous, of one's own head, prepense, advised, express, designed, intended, calculated, premeditated, preconcerted, predetermined, deliberate.

(*Adverbs*) At will, at pleasure, *à volonté, à discrétion, ad libitum, ad*

601 Necessity (*Substantives*), instinct, blind impulse, necessitation, ἀνάγκη, fate, fatality, destiny, doom, kismet, weird (152), foredoom, destination, election, predestination, preordination, fore-ordination, compulsion (744), subjection (749), inevitability, inevitableness.

Determinism, necessitarianism, fatalism, automatism.

A determinist, necessarian, necessitarian; robot, automaton.

The Fates, Parcae, the Three Sisters, fortune's wheel, the book of fate, the stars, astral influence, spell (152).

(*Phrases*) Hobson's choice; what must be; a blind bargain; a *pis aller*.

(*Verbs*) To lie under a necessity, to be fated, doomed, destined, etc. (152), to need be, have no alternative.

To necessitate, destine, doom, foredoom, predestine, preordain.

To compel, force, constrain, etc. (744), cast a spell, etc. (992).

(*Phrases*) To make a virtue of necessity; to be pushed to the wall; to dree one's weird.

(*Adjectives*) Necessitated, fated, destined, predestined, foreordained, doomed, elect, spellbound.

Compelled, forced, etc., unavoidable, inevitable, irresistible, irrevocable.

Compulsory, involuntary, unintentional, undesigned, unintended, instinctive, automatic, blind, mechanical, impulsive, unconscious, reflex, unwitting, unaware.

arbitrium, spontaneously, freely, of one's own accord, voluntarily, advisedly, designedly, intentionally, expressly, knowingly, determinately, deliberately, pointedly, in earnest, in good earnest, studiously, purposely, *proprio motu, suo motu, ex mero motu; quo animo.*

(Phrases) With one's eyes open; in cold blood.

---

602 Willingness *(Substantives),* voluntariness, disposition, inclination, leaning, *penchant,* humour, mood, vein, bent, bias, propensity, proclivity, aptitude, predisposition, predilection (865), proneness, docility, pliability (324), alacrity, earnestness, readiness, assent (448).

(Phrases) A labour of love; *labor ipse voluptas.*

(Verbs) to be willing, etc., to incline to, lean to, not mind (865), to propend; to volunteer.

(Phrases) To find in one's heart; to set one's heart upon; to make no bones of; have a mind to; have a great mind to; 'Barkis is willin'.'

(Adjectives) Willing, fain, disposed, inclined, minded, bent upon, set upon, forward, predisposed, content, favourable, hearty, ready, wholehearted, cordial, genial, keen, prepense, docile, persuadable, persuasible, facile, tractable, easy-going, easily led.

Free, spontaneous, voluntary, gratuitous, unforced, unasked, unsummoned, unbiased, unsolicited, unbesought, undriven.

(Adverbs) Willingly, freely, readily, lief, heartily, with a good grace, without reluctance, etc., as soon, of one's own accord (600), certainly, be it so (488).

(Phrases) With all one's heart, *con amore;* with heart and soul; with a right good will; with a good grace; *de bon cœur;* by all means; by all manner of means; nothing loth; *ex animo;* to one's heart's content.

Deterministic, necessitarian, fatalistic.

(Phrase) Unable to help it.

(Adverbs) Necessarily, needs, of necessity, perforce, forcibly, compulsorily; on or by compulsion or force, willy-nilly, *nolens volens;* involuntarily, etc., impulsively (612), unwittingly (491).

(Phrases) It must be; it needs must be; it is written; one's fate is sealed; *che sarà sarà;* there is no help for it; there is no alternative; nothing for it but; necessity knows no law; needs must when the devil drives.

603 Unwillingness *(Substantives),* indisposition, indisposedness, backwardness, disinclination, averseness, aversion, reluctance, repugnance, demur, renitence, remissness, slackness, lukewarmness, indifference, nonchalance.

Hesitation, shrinking, recoil, suspense, dislike (867), scrupulousness, scrupulosity, delicacy, demur, scruple, qualm.

A recusant, pococurante.

(Verbs) To be unwilling, etc., to demur, stick at, hesitate (605), waver, hang in suspense, scruple, stickle, boggle, falter, to hang back, hang fire, fight shy of, jib, grudge.

To decline, reject, refuse (764), refrain, keep from, abstain, recoil, shrink, reluct.

(Phrases) To stick in the throat; to set one's face against; to draw the line at; I'd rather not.

(Adjectives) Unwilling, unconsenting, disinclined, indisposed, averse, reluctant, not content, laggard, backward, shy, remiss, slack, indifferent, lukewarm, frigid, scrupulous, repugnant, disliking (867).

Demurring, wavering, etc., refusing (764), grudging.

(Adverbs) Unwillingly, etc., perforce.

(Phrases) Against the grain; *invita Minerva; malgré lui; bon gré, mal gré; nolens volens;* in spite of one's teeth; with a bad grace; not for the world; willy-nilly.

604 Resolution *(Substantives)*, determination, decision, resolve, resolvedness, fixedness, steadiness, constancy, indefatigability, unchangeableness, inflexibility, decision, finality, firmness, doggedness, tenacity of purpose, pertinacity, perseverance, constancy, solidity, stability.

Energy, manliness, vigour, spirit, spiritedness, pluck, bottom, backbone, stamina, gameness, guts, grit, sand, will, iron will; self-reliance; self-mastery; self-control.

A devotee, zealot, extremist, ultra, enthusiast, fanatic, fan; bulldog, British lion.

(Verbs) To be resolved, etc., to have resolution, etc., to resolve, decide, will, persevere, determine, conclude, make up one's mind; to stand, keep, or remain firm, etc., to come to a determination, to form a resolution, to take one's stand, to stand by, hold fast, stick to, abide by, adhere to, keep one's ground, persevere, keep one's course, hold on, hang on, not to fail.

To insist upon, to make a point of.

(Phrases) To determine once for all; to form a resolution; to steel oneself; to pass the Rubicon; take a decisive step; to burn one's boats; to nail one's colours to the mast; to screw one's courage to the sticking-place; to take the bull by the horns; to mean business; to set one's teeth; to keep a stiff upper lip; to keep one's chin up.

(Adjectives) Resolved, resolute, game, firm, steady, steadfast, staunch, constant; solid, manly, stout.

Decided, strong-willed, determined, uncompromising, purposive, self-possessed, fixed, unmoved, unshaken, unbending, unyielding, unflagging, unflinching, inflexible, unwavering, unfaltering, unshrinking, undiverted, undeterred, immovable, not to be moved, unhesitating, unswerving.

Peremptory, inexorable, indomitable, persevering, pertinacious, persistent, irrevocable, irreversible, reverseless, decisive, final.

Strenuous, bent upon, set upon, intent upon, proof against, master of oneself, steeled, staid, serious, stiff, stiff-necked, obstinate (606).

605 Irresolution *(Substantives)*, indecision, indetermination, demur, hesitation, suspense, uncertainty (475), hesitancy, vacillation, unsteadiness, inconstancy, wavering, fluctuation, flickering, changeableness, mutability, fickleness, caprice (608), levity, *légèreté*, trimming, softness, weakness, instability.

A weathercock, trimmer, timeserver, turncoat, shuttlecock, butterfly, harlequin, chameleon.

(Verbs) To be irresolute, etc., to hesitate, hang in suspense, demur, waver, vacillate, quaver, fluctuate, shuffle, boggle, flicker, falter, palter, debate, dilly-dally, shilly-shally, dally with, coquette with, swerve, etc.

(Phrases) To hang fire; to hum and ha; to blow hot and cold; not to know one's own mind; to leave *'ad referendum'*; letting 'I dare not' wait upon 'I would'.

(Adjectives) Irresolute, undecided, unresolved, undetermined, vacillating, wavering, hesitating, faltering, shuffling, etc., half-hearted, double-minded, indecisive.

Unsteady, unsteadfast, fickle, flighty, changing, changeable, versatile, variable, inconstant, mutable, protean, fluctuating, unstable, unsettled, unhinged, unfixed, weak-kneed, spineless.

Weak, feeble-minded, frail, soft, pliant, giddy, capricious, coquettish, volatile, fitful, frothy, freakish, lightsome, light-minded, invertebrate.

Revocable, reversible.

(Phrases) Infirm of purpose; without ballast; waiting to see which way the cat jumps, or the wind blows.

(Adverbs) Irresolutely, etc.; off and on.

(Phrases) Firm as a rock; game to the last; true to oneself; master of oneself; *in utrumque paratus.*

(Adverbs) Resolutely, etc., without fail.

(Phrases) Through thick and thin; through fire and water; at all hazards; sink or swim; *coûte que coûte; fortiter in re*; like grim death.

606 Obstinacy *(Substantives)*, obstinateness, wilfulness, self-will, pertinacity, pertinaciousness, pervicacity, pervicaciousness, tenacity, tenaciousness, inflexibility, immovability, doggedness, stubbornness, steadiness (604), restiveness, contumacy, cussedness, obduracy, obduration, unruliness.

Intolerance, dogmatism, bigotry, opinionatedness, opiniativeness, fanaticism, zealotry, infatuation, monomania, indocility, intractability, intractableness (481), pig-headedness.

An opinionist, *opiniâtre*, crank, diehard, blimp, stickler, enthusiast, monomaniac, zealot, dogmatist, fanatic, mule.

A fixed idea, rooted prejudice, blind side, obsession (481), King Charles's head.

(Phrase) A bee in one's bonnet.

(Verbs) To be obstinate, etc., to persist, stickle, opiniate.

(Phrases) To stick at nothing; to dig in one's heels; not yield an inch.

(Adjectives) Obstinate, opinionative, opinative, opinionated, opinioned, wedded to an opinion, self-opinioned, prejudiced (481), cranky, wilful, self-willed, positive, tenacious.

Stiff, stubborn, stark, rigid, stiff-necked, dogged, pertinacious, restive, pervicacious, dogmatic, arbitrary, bigoted, unpersuadable, mulish, unmoved, uninfluenced, hard-mouthed, unyielding, inflexible, immovable, pig-headed, wayward, intractable, hidebound, headstrong, restive, refractory, unruly, infatuated, *entêté*, wrong-headed, cross-grained, obdurate, contumacious, fanatical, rabid, inexorable, impracticable.

(Phrases) Obstinate as a mule; impervious to reason.

(Adverbs) Obstinately, etc.

(Phrases) Non possumus; vestigia nulla retrorsum.

607 Change of mind, intention, purpose, etc.

Tergiversation *(Substantives)*, retractation, recantation, revocation, revokement, reversal, palinode, volteface, renunciation, disavowal (536), abjuration, abjurement, apostasy, relinquishment (624), repentance (950), vacillation, etc. (605).

A turncoat, rat, Janus, renegade, apostate, pervert, backslider, recidivist, trimmer, time-server, opportunist, Vicar of Bray, deserter, weathercock, etc. (605), Proteus.

(Verbs) To change one's mind, etc., to retract, recant, revoke, forswear, unsay, take back, abjure, renounce, apostatize, relinquish, trim, straddle, veer round, change sides, rat, go over; pass, change, or skip from one side to another; back out, back down, swerve, flinch, balance.

(Phrases) To eat one's words; turn over a new leaf; think better of it; play fast and loose; blow hot and cold; box the compass; swallow the leek; eat dirt.

(Adjectives) Changeful, changeable, mobile, unsteady (605), trimming, double-faced, ambidexter, fast and loose, time-serving, facing both ways.

Fugacious, fleeting (111), revocatory.

608 Caprice *(Substantives)*, fancy, fantasy, humour, whim, crotchet, fad, fike, craze, *capriccio*, quirk, freak, maggot, vagary, whimsy, whim-wham, kink, prank, shenanigans, fit, flim-flam, escapade, ploy, dido, monkey-tricks, rag, monkey-shines, *boutade*, wild-goose chase, freakishness, skittishness, volatility, fancifulness, whimsicality, giddiness, inconsistency, contrariety; a madcap.

(Verb) To be capricious, etc.

(Phrases) To strain at a gnat and swallow a camel; to take it into one's head.

(Adjectives) Capricious, inconsistent, fanciful, fantastic, whimsical, full of whims, etc., erratic, crotchety, faddy, maggoty, fiky, perverse, humoursome, wayward, captious, contrary, contrarious, skittish, fitful.

(Phrases) The head being turned; the deuce being in him; by fits and starts.

609 Choice *(Substantives)*, option, election, arbitrament, adoption, selection, excerption, co-optation, gleaning, eclecticism, lief, preference, predilection, preoption, discretion (600), fancy.

Decision, determination, adjudication, award, vote, suffrage, ballot, poll, plebiscite, referendum, verdict, voice, plumper.

Alternative, dilemma (704).

Excerpt, extract, cuttings, clippings; pick, *élite*, cream (650).

Chooser, elector, voter, constituent; electorate, constituency.

(Verbs) To choose, decide, determine, elect, list, think fit, use one's discretion, fancy, shape one's course, prefer, have rather, have as lief, take one's choice, adopt, select, fix upon, pitch upon, pick out, single out, vote for, plump for, co-opt, pick up, take up, catch at, jump at, cull, glean, pick, winnow.

(Phrases) To winnow the chaff from the wheat; to indulge one's fancy; to pick and choose; to take a decided step; to pass the Rubicon (604); to hold out; offer for choice; commend me to; to swallow the bait; to gorge the hook; to yield to temptation.

(Adjectives) Optional, discretional, eclectic, choosing, etc., chosen, etc., decided, etc., choice, preferential; left to oneself.

(Adverbs) Discretionally, at pleasure, *à plaisir, a piacere*, at discretion, at will, *ad libitum*.

Decidedly, etc., rather; once for all, either the one or the other, for one's money, for choice.

610 Absence of Choice *(Substantives)*, Hobson's choice, necessity (601).

Indifference, indecision (605).

(Phrase) First come, first served.

(Adjectives) Neutral; indifferent, undecided.

(Phrase) To sit on the fence.

Rejection *(Substantives)*, refusal (764); declining, repudiation, exclusion.

(Verbs) To reject, refuse, etc., decline, give up, repudiate, exclude, lay aside, pigeon-hole, refrain, spare (678), abandon, turn down, black-ball; to fail, plough, pluck, spin, cast.

(Phrases) To lay on the shelf; to return to store; to throw overboard; to draw the line at.

(Adjectives) Rejecting, etc., rejected, etc., not chosen, etc.

(Phrases) Not to be thought of; out of the question.

(Adverbs) Neither; neither the one nor the other, nothing to choose between them.

---

611 Predetermination *(Substantives)*, premeditation, predeliberation, foregone conclusion, parti pris.

(Verbs) To predetermine, premeditate, preconcert, resolve beforehand.

(Adjectives) Prepense, premeditated, predetermined, advised, predesigned, aforethought, calculated, studied, designed (620).

612 Impulse *(Substantives)*, sudden thought, improvisation, inspiration, flash, spurt.

Improvisator, improvisatore, improvisatrice, creature of impulse.

(Verbs) To flash on the mind; to improvise, improvisate, make up, extemporize, vamp, ad-lib.

(Adjectives) Extemporaneous, ex-

(Adverbs) Advisedly, deliberately, etc., with the eyes open, in cold blood.

———

temporary, impulsive, unrehearsed, unpremeditated (674), improvised, improvisatorial, improvisatory, un-prompted, instinctive, spontaneous, natural, unguarded, unreflecting, precipitate.

(Adverbs) Extempore, offhand, impromptu, *à l-improviste*, out of hand.
(Phrases) On the spur of the moment, or of the occasion.

613 Habit *(Substantives)*, habitude, wont, rule, routine, jog-trot, groove, rut.

Custom, consuetude, use, usage, practice, trick, run, run of things, way, form, prevalence, observance, fashion (852), etiquette, prescription, convention, *convenances*, red tape, red-tapery, red-tapism, routinism, conventionalism, vogue.

Seasoning, training, hardening, etc. (673), acclimatization, acclimation, acclimatation.

Second nature, *cacoethes,* taking root, diathesis.

A victim of habit, etc., an addict, junkie, *habitué*.

(Verbs) To be habitual, etc., to be in the habit of, be wont, be accustomed to, etc.

To follow, observe, conform to, obey, bend to, comply with, accommodate oneself to, adapt oneself to; fall into a habit, convention, custom, or usage; to addict oneself to, take to, get the hang of.

To become a habit, to take root, to gain or grow upon one, to run in the blood.

To habituate, inure, harden, season, form, train, accustom, familiarize, naturalize, acclimatize, conventionalize, condition.

To acquire a habit, to get into the way of, to learn, etc.

(Phrases) To follow the multitude; go with the current, stream, etc.; run on in a groove; do in Rome as the Romans do.

(Adjectives) Habitual, accustomed, prescriptive, habituated, etc.; in the habit, etc., of; used to, addicted to, attuned to, wedded to, at home in; usual, wonted, customary, hackneyed, commonplace, trite, ordinary, set, stock, established, accepted, stereotyped, received, acknowledged, recognized; groovy, fixed, rooted, permanent, inveterate, ingrained, running in the blood, hereditary, congenital, innate, inborn, besetting, natural, instinctive, etc. (5).

Fashionable, in fashion, in vogue, according to use, routine, conventional, etc.

(Phrases) Bred in the bone; in the blood.

(Adverbs) Habitually; as usual, as the world goes, *more suo, pro more, pro forma,* according to custom, *de rigueur.*

614 Desuetude *(Substantives),* disuse, want of habit or of practice, inusitation, newness to.

Non-observance (773), infraction, vilation, infringement.

(Phrase) 'A custom more honoured in the breach than the observance.'

(Verbs) To be unaccustomed, etc., to be new to; to leave off, wean oneself of, break off, break through, infringe, vilate, etc., a habit, usage, etc.; to disuse, to wear off.

(Adjectives) Unaccustomed, un-used, unusual, unwonted, unpractised, unprofessional, unfashionable, non-observant, lax, disused, weaned.

Unseasoned, uninured, untrained, green.

Unhackneyed, unconventional, Bohemian (83).

———

2°. Causes of Volition

615 Motive (*Substantives*), reason, ground, principle, mainspring, *primum mobile*, account, score, sake, consideration, calculation, *raison d'être*.

Inducement, recommendation, encouragement, attraction, allectation, temptation, enticement, bait, allurement, charm, witchery, bewitchment.

Persuasibility, softness, susceptibility, attractability, impressibility.

Influence, prompting, dictate, instance, impulse, impulsion, incitement, incitation, press, instigation, excitement, provocation, invitation, solicitation, advocacy, call, suasion, persuasion, hortation, exhortation, seduction, cajolery, tantalization, *agacerie*, seducement, fascination, blandishment, inspiration, honeyed words.

Incentive, stimulus, spur, fillip, urge, goad, rowel, provocative, whet, dram, cocktail, pick-me-up, appetizer.

Bribe, graft, sop, lure, decoy, charm, spell, magnetism, magnet, loadstone.

Prompter, tempter, seducer, seductor, siren, Circe, instigator, *agent provocateur*.

(*Phrases*) The pros and cons; the why and wherefore.

The golden apple; a red herring; a sop for Cerberus; the voice of the tempter; the song of the sirens.

(*Verbs*) To induce, move, lead, draw, draw over, carry, bring, to influence, to weigh with, bias, to operate, work upon, engage, incline, dispose, predispose, put up to, prompt, whisper, call, call upon, recommend, encourage, entice, invite, solicit, press, enjoin, entreat (765),

616 Absence of Motive, caprice (608).

(*Adjectives*) Aimless, motiveless, pointless, purposeless (621); uninduced, unmoved, unactuated, uninfluenced, unbiased, unimpelled, unswayed, impulsive, wanton, unprovoked, uninspired, untempted, unattracted.

(*Phrase*) Without rhyme or reason.

Dissuasion (*Substantives*), dehortation, discouragement, remonstrance, expostulation, deprecation (766).

Inhibition, check, restraint, curb (752), bridle, rein, stay, damper, chill; deterrent, disincentive.

Scruple, qualm, demur (867), reluctance, delicacy (868); counter-attraction.

(*Phrase*) A wet blanket.

(*Verbs*) To dissuade, dehort, discourage, disincline, indispose, dispirit, damp, choke off, dishearten, disenchant, disillusion, deter, keep back, put off, render averse, etc.

To withhold, restrain, hold, hold back, check, bridle, curb, rein in, keep in, inhibit, censor, repel (751).

To cool, blunt, calm, quiet, quench slake, stagger, remonstrate, expostulate, warn, deprecate (766).

To scruple, refrain, abstain, etc. (603).

(*Phrases*) To throw cold water on; to turn a deaf ear to.

(*Adjectives*) Dissuading, etc., dissuasive, dehortatory, expostulatory, deprecatory.

Dissuaded, discouraged, etc.

Repugnant, averse, scrupulous, etc. (867), unpersuadable (606).

———

court, plead, advocate, exhort, enforce, dictate, tantalize, bait the hook, tempt, allure, lure, seduce, decoy, draw on, captivate, fascinate, charm, bewitch, conciliate, wheedle, coax, speak fair, carny (or carney), cajole, pat on the back or shoulder, talk over, inveigle, persuade, prevail upon, get to do, bring over, procure, lead by the nose, sway, over-persuade, come over, get round, turn the head, enlist, retain, kidnap, bribe, suborn, tamper with.

To act upon, to impel, excite, suscitate, stimulate, key up, motivate, incite, animate, instigate, provoke, set on, urge, pique, spirit, inspirit, inspire, awaken, buck up, give a fillip, light up, kindle, enkindle, rekindle, quicken, goad, spur, prick, edge, egg on, hurry on, stir up, work up, fan, fire, inflame, set on fire, fan the flame, blow the coals, stir the embers, put on one's mettle, set on, force, rouse, arouse, lash into fury, get a rise out of.

(Phrases) To grease the palm; to gild the pill; to work the oracle.

To follow the bent of; to follow the dictates of; to yield to temptation; to act on principle.

(Adjectives) Impulsive, motive, persuasive, hortative, hortatory, seductive, carnying, suasory, suasive, honey-tongued, attractive, tempting, alluring, piquant, exciting, inviting, tantalizing, etc.

Persuadable, persuasible, suasible, soft, yielding, facile, easily persuaded, etc.

Induced, moved, disposed, led, persuaded, etc., spellbound, instinct with or by.

(Adverbs) Because, for, since, on account of, out of, from; by reason of, for the sake of, on the score of.

As, forasmuch as, therefore, hence, why, wherefore; for all the world.

(Phrase) Hinc illae lacrimae.

617 Ostensible motive, or reason assigned.

Plea *(Substantives)*, allegation, pretext, pretence, excuse, alibi, cue, colour, gloss, salvo, loophole, handle, shift, quirk, guise, stalking-horse, makeshift, white lie, evasion, get-out, special pleading (477), claptrap, advocation, soft sawder, blarney (933), moonshine; a lame excuse or apology.

(Verbs) To make a pretext, etc., of; to use as a plea, etc.; to plead, allege, pretend, excuse, make a handle, etc., of, make capital of.

(Adjectives) Ostensible, colourable, pretended, alleged, etc.

(Phrases) Ad captandum; qui s'excuse s'accuse; playing to the gallery.

3°. *Objects of Volition*

618 Good *(Substantives)*, benefit, advantage, service, interest, weal, boot, gain, profit, velvet, good turn, blessing, boon; behoof, behalf.

Luck, piece of luck, windfall, strike, treasure trove, godsend, bonus, bunce, bonanza, prize; serendipity.

Goodness (648), utility (644), remedy (662).

(Phrases) The main chance; *summum bonum; cui bono?*

(Adjectives) Good, etc. (648), gainful (644).

(Adverbs) Aright, well, favourably, satisfactorily, for the best.

In behalf of, in favour of.

---

619 Evil *(Substantives)*, harm, ill, injury, wrong, scathe, curse, detriment, hurt, damage, disservice, ill-turn, bale, grievance, prejudice, loss, mischief, devilry (or deviltry), gravamen.

Disadvantage, drawback, trouble, vexation (828), annoyance, nuisance, molestation, oppression, persecution, plague, corruption (659).

Blow, dunt, knock (276), bruise, scratch, wound, mutilation, outrage, spoliation, mayhem, plunder, pillage, rapine, destruction (791), dilapidation, havoc, ravage, devastation, inroad, sweep, sack, foray (716), desolation, *razzia*, dragonnade.

Misfortune, mishap, woe, disaster, calamity, affliction, catastrophe, downfall, ruin (735), prostration, curse, wrack, blight, blast, Pandora's box; a plague-spot.

Cause of evil, bane (663).

(Phrases) Bad show; there's the devil to pay.

(Adjectives) Bad, hurtful, etc. (649).

(Adverbs) Amiss, wrong, evil, ill.

SECTION II—PROSPECTIVE VOLITION

1°. *Conceptional Volition*

620 Intention *(Substantives)*, intent, purpose, design, purport, mind, meaning, drift (516), animus, view, set purpose, point, bent, turn, proposal, study, scope, purview.

Final cause, object, aim, end, motive (615), *raison d'être*; destination, mark, point, butt, goal, target, prey, quarry, game, objective; the philosophers' stone.

Decision, determination, resolve, resolution (604), predetermination (611); set purpose.

A hobby, ambition, wish (865).

Study of final causes, teleology; study of final issues, eschatology.

(Verbs) To intend, purpose, plan (626), design, destine, mean, aim at, propose to oneself.

To be at, drive at, be after, point at, level at, take aim, aspire at or after, endeavour after.

To meditate, think of, dream of, premeditate (611), contemplate, compass.

To propose, project, devise, take into one's head.

(Phrases) To have in view; to have an eye to; to take upon oneself; to have to do; to see one's way; to find in one's heart.

(Adjectives) Intended, etc., intentional, deliberate, advised, studied, minded, express, prepense (611), aforethought; set upon, bent upon, intent upon, in view, *in petto*, in prospect; teleological, eschatological.

(Phrases) In the world; *sur le tapis*; on the stocks; in contemplation.

(Adverbs) Intentionally, etc., expressly, knowingly, wittingly, designedly, purposely, on purpose, with a view to, with an eye to, for the

621 Absence of purpose in the succession of events.

Chance *(Substantives)*, fortune, accident, hazard, hap, haphazard (156), lot, fate (601), chance-medley, hit, fluke, casualty, contingency, exigency, fate, adventure, random shot, off chance, toss-up, gamble.

A godsend, luck, a run of luck, a turn of the dice or cards, a break, windfall, etc. (618).

Drawing lots, sortilege, *sortes Virgilianae*.

Wager, bet, flutter, betting, gambling; pitch-and-toss, *roulette, rouge-et-noir*.

(Phrases) A blind bargain; a pig in a poke.

(Verbs) To chance, hap, turn up; to stand a chance.

To risk, venture, hazard, speculate, stake; incur or run the risk; bet, wager, punt, gamble, plunge, raffle.

(Phrases) To take one's chance; to chance it; to chance one's arm; try one's luck; shuffle the cards; put into a lottery; lay a wager; toss up; spin a coin; cast lots; draw lots; stand the hazard.

To buy a pig in a poke; *alea jacta est*; the die being cast; to go nap on; to put one's shirt on.

(Adjectives) Casual, fortuitous, accidental, inadvertent, fluky, contingent, random, hit-or-miss, happy-go-lucky, adventitious, incidental.

Unintentional, involuntary, aimless, driftless, undesigned, undirected; purposeless, causeless, without purpose, etc., unmeditated, unpurposed, indiscriminate, promiscuous.

On the cards, possible (470), at stake.

(Adverbs) Casually, etc., by chance,

purpose of, with the view of, in order to, to the end that, on account of, in pursuance of, pursuant to, with the intent, etc.

(Phrases) In good earnest; with one's eyes open; to all intents and purposes.

622 Purpose in action.

Pursuit *(Substantives)*, pursuance, undertaking, enterprise (676), emprise, adventure, game, hobby, endeavour.

Prosecution, search, angling, chase, venery, quest, hunt, shikar, race, battue, drive, course, direction, wildgoose chase, steeplechase, point-to-point.

Pursuer, huntsman, hunter, Nimrod, shikari, hound, greyhound, foxhound, whippet, bloodhound, sleuth-hound, beagle, harrier.

(Verbs) To pursue, undertake, engage in, take in hand, carry on, prosecute (461), endeavour.

To court, seek, angle, chase, give chase, course, dog, stalk, trail, hunt, drive, follow, run after, hound, bid for, aim at, take aim, make a leap at, rush upon, jump at, quest, shadow, tail, chivy.

(Phrases) Take or hold a course; tread a path; shape one's course; direct or bend one's steps or course; run a race; rush headlong; rush head-foremost; make a plunge; snatch at, etc.; start game; follow the scent; to run or ride full tilt at.

(Adjectives) Pursuing, etc., in hot pursuit; in full cry.

(Adverbs) In order to, in order that, for the purpose of, with a view to, etc. (620); on the scent of.

(Interjections) Yoicks! tally-ho!

by accident, accidentally, etc., at haphazard, at a venture; heads or tails.

(Phrase) As luck would have it.

---

623 Absence of pursuit.

Avoidance *(Substantives)*, forbearance, abstention, abstinence, sparing, refraining.

Flight, escape (671), evasion, elusion.

Motive for avoidance, counter-attraction.

Shirker, slacker, quitter, truant, fugitive, runaway.

(Verbs) To avoid, refrain, abstain; to spare, hold, shun, fly, slope, flee, eschew, run away from, shrink, hold back, draw back (287), recoil from, flinch, blench, shy, elude, evade, shirk, blink, parry, dodge, let alone.

(Phrases) To give the slip or go-by; to part company; to beat a retreat; get out of the way; to give one a wide berth; steer clear of; fight shy of; to take to one's heels.

(Adjectives) Avoiding, etc., elusive, evasive, flying, fugitive, runaway, shy, retiring; unattempted, unsought.

(Adverbs) Lest, with a view to prevent.

(Phrases) *Sauve qui peut*; the devil take the hindmost.

624 Relinquishment *(Substantives)*, dereliction, abandonment (782), renunciation, desertion (607), discontinuance (142).

Dispensation, riddance.

(Verbs) To relinquish, give up (782); lay, set, or put aside; drop, yield, resign, abandon, renounce, discard, shelve, pigeon-hole, waive, desist from, desert, defect, leave, leave off, back out of, quit, throw up, chuck up, give over, forgo, give up, forsake, throw over, forswear, swerve from (279), put away, discontinue (681).

(Phrases) To drop all idea of; to think better of it; to wash one's hands of; to turn over a new leaf; to throw up the sponge; to have other fish to fry; to draw in one's horns; to lay on the shelf; to move the previous question.

To give warning; to give notice; to ask for one's books.

(Adjectives) Relinquishing, etc., relinquished, etc., unpursued.

(Interjections) Hands off! keep off! give over! chuck it!

625 Business *(Substantives)*, affair, concern, matter, task, work, job, job of work, assignment, darg, chore, stint, stunt, errand, agenda, commission, office, charge, part, duty, role; a press of business.

Province, department, beat, round, routine, mission, function, vocation, calling, avocation, profession, occupation, pursuit, cloth, faculty, trade, industry, commerce, art, craft, mystery, walk, race, career, walk of life, *métier*.

Place, post, orb, sphere, field, line, capacity, employment, engagement, exercise, occupation; situation, undertaking (676).

(Verbs) To carry on or run a business, ply one's trade, keep a shop, etc.; to officiate, serve, act, traffic.

(Phrases) To have to do with; have on one's hands; betake oneself to; occupy or concern oneself with; go in for; have on one's shoulders; make it one's business; go to do; act a part; perform the office of or functions of; to enter or take up a profession; spend time upon; busy oneself with, about, etc.

(Adjectives) Business-like, official, functional, professional, workaday, commercial, in hand.

(Adverbs) On hand, on foot, afoot, afloat, going.

(Phrase) In the swim.

626 Plan *(Substantives)*, scheme, device, design, project, proposal, proposition, suggestion.

Line of conduct, game, card course, tactics, strategy, policy, polity (692), craft, practice, campaign, platform, plank, ticket, agenda, orders of the day, gambit.

Intrigue, cabal, plot, conspiracy, complot, racket, machination, *coup d'état*.

Measure, step, precaution, proceeding, procedure, process, system, economy, set-up, organization, expedient, resource, contrivance, invention, artifice, shift, makeshift, gadget, stopgap, manœuvre, stratagem, fetch, trick, dodge, machination, intrigue, stroke, stroke of policy, masterstroke, great gun, trump card.

Alternative, loophole, counterplot, counter-project, side-wind, last resort, *dernier ressort, pis aller*.

Sketch, outline, blue-print, programme, draft (or draught), scenario, *ébauche*, rough draft, skeleton, forecast, prospectus, *carte du pays*, bill of fare, menu.

After-course, after-game, after-thought, *arrière-pensée*, under-plot.

A projector, designer, schemer, contriver, strategist, promoter, organizer, *entrepreneur*, artist, schematist, intriguant.

(Verbs) To plan, scheme, devise, imagine, design, frame, contrive, project, plot, conspire, cabal, intrigue (702), think out, invent, forecast, strike out, work out, chalk out, rough out, sketch, lay out, lay down, cut out, cast, recast, map out, countermine, hit upon, fall upon, arrange, mature, organize, systematize, concert, concoct, digest, pack, prepare, hatch, elaborate, make shift, make do, wangle.

(Phrases) To have many irons in the fire; to dig a mine; to lay a train; to spring a project; to take or adopt a course; to make the best of a bad job; to work the oracle.

(Adjectives) Planned, etc., strategic; planning, scheming, etc.

Well-laid, deep-laid, cunning, well-devised, etc., maturely considered, well-weighed, prepared, organized, etc.

(Adverbs) In course of preparation, under consideration, on the anvil, on the stocks, in the rough, *sur le tapis; faute de mieux*.

627 Way *(Substantives)*, method, manner, wise, form, mode, guise, fashion.

Path, road, gait, route, channel, walk, access, course, pass, ford, ferry, passage, line of way, trajectory, orbit, track, ride, avenue, approach, beaten track, pathway, highway, roadway, causeway, footway, pavement, sidewalk, *trottoir*, footpath, bridle path, corduroy road, cinder-path, turnpike road, high road, arterial road, *autobahn*, clearway, boulevard, the King's (or Queen's) highway, thoroughfare, street, lane, alley, gangway, hatchway, cross-road, crossway, flyover, cut, short cut, royal road, cross-cut, *carrefour*, promenade, subway.

Railway, railroad, tramway, tube, underground, elevated; canal.

Bridge, viaduct, stepping-stone, stair, corridor, aisle, lobby, staircase, moving staircase, escalator, companion-way, flight of stairs, ladder, step-ladder, stile, scaffold, scaffolding, lift, hoist, elevator; speedwalk, travolator.

Indirect way: By-path, by-way, by-walk, by-road, back door, backstairs.

Inlet, gate, door, gateway (260), portal, porch, doorway, adit, conduit, tunnel.

(Phrase) Modus operandi.

(Adverbs) How, in what way, in what manner, by what mode.

By the way, *en passant*, by the by, via, *in transitu, chemin faisant*.

One way or another, somehow, anyhow, by hook or by crook.

(Phrases) All roads lead to Rome; *hae tibi erunt artes*; where there's a will there's a way.

628 Mid-course *(Substantives)*, middle course, middle (68), mean (29), golden mean, *juste milieu, mezzo termine*.

Direct, straight, straightforward, course or path; great-circle sailing.

Neutrality, compromise.

(Verbs) To keep in a middle course, etc.; to compromise, go half-way.

(Adjectives) Undeviating, direct, straight, straightforward.

(Phrases) In medio tutissimus ibis; to sit on the fence.

629 Circuit *(Substantives)*, roundabout way, zigzag, circuition, detour, circumbendibus (311), wandering, deviation (279), divergence (291).

(Verbs) To perform a circuit, etc., to deviate, wander, go round about, meander, etc. (279).

(Phrases) To beat about the bush; to make two bites of a cherry; to lead one a pretty dance.

(Adjectives) Circuitous, indirect, roundabout, tortuous, zigzag, etc.

(Adverbs) By a roundabout way, by an indirect course, etc.

630 Requirement *(Substantives)*, requisition, need, occasion, lack, wants, requisites, necessities, desideratum, exigency, pinch, *sine qua non*, the very thing, essential, must.

Needfulness, essentiality, necessity, indispensability, urgency, call for.

(Phrases) Just what the doctor ordered; a crying need; a long-felt want.

(Verbs) To require, need, want, have occasion for, stand in need of, lack, desire, be at a loss for, desiderate; not to be able to do without or dispense with; to want but little.

To render necessary, to necessitate, to create a necessity for, demand, call for.

(Adjectives) Requisite, required, etc., needful, necessary, imperative, exigent, essential, indispensable, irreplaceable, prerequisite, that cannot be spared or dispensed with, urgent.

2°. *Subservience to Ends*

1. ACTUAL SUBSERVIENCE

631 Instrumentality *(Substantives)*, medium, intermedium, vehicle, channel, intervention, mediation, dint, aid (707), agency (170).

Minister, handmaid; obstetrician, midwife, *accoucheur*.

Key, master-key, passport, safe-conduct, passe-partout, 'open sesame'; a go-between, middleman (758), a cat's-paw, jackal, pander, tool, ghost, mainstay, trump card.

(Phrase) Two strings to one's bow.

(Verbs) To subserve, minister, intervene, mediate, devil, pander to.

(Adjectives) Instrumental, intervening, intermediate, intermediary, subservient, auxiliary, ancillary.

(Adverbs) Through, by, with, by means of, by dint of, *à force de*, along with, thereby, through the medium, etc., of, wherewith, wherewithal.

632 Means *(Substantives)*, resources, wherewithal, appliances, ways and means, convenience, expedients, step, measure (626), aid (707), intermedium, medium.

Machinery, mechanism, mechanics, engineering, mechanical powers, automation, scaffolding, ladder, mainstay.

(Phrases) Wheels within wheels; a shot in the locker.

(Adjectives) Instrumental, accessory, subsidiary, mechanical.

(Adverbs) How, by what means, by all means, by all manner of means, by the aid of, by dint of.

(Phrases) By hook or by crook; somehow or other; for love or money; by fair means or foul; *quocumque modo*.

633 Instrument *(Substantives)*, tool, implement, appliance, contraption, apparatus, utensil, device, gadget, craft, machine, engine, motor, dynamo, generator, mill, lathe.

Equipment, gear, tackle, tackling, rigging, harness, trappings, fittings, accoutrements, paraphernalia, equipage, outfit, appointments, furniture, material, plant, appurtenances.

A wheel, jack, clockwork, wheel-work, spring, screw, turbine, wedge, flywheel, lever, bascule, pinion, crank, winch, crane, capstan, windlass, pulley, hammer, mallet, mattock, mall, bat, racket, sledge-hammer, mace, club, truncheon, pole, staff, bill, crow, crowbar, poleaxe, handspike, crutch, boom, bar, pitchfork, etc.

Organ, limb, arm, hand, finger, claw, paw, talons, tentacle, wing, oar, paddle, pincer, plier, forceps, thimble.

Handle, hilt, haft, shaft, shank, heft, blade, trigger, tiller, helm, treadle, pummel, peg (214, 215), key.

Edge-tool, hatchet, axe, pickaxe, etc. (253), axis (312).

634 Substitute *(Substantives)*, shift, makeshift, succedaneum (147), stop-gap, expedient, *pis aller*, surrogate, understudy, pinch-hitter, stand-in, locum tenens, proxy, deputy (759).

635 Materials *(Substantives)*, material, matter, stuff, constituent, ingredient (56), pabulum, fuel, grist, provender, provisions, food (298).

Supplies, munition, ammunition, reinforcement, relay, contingents.

Baggage, luggage, bag and baggage, effects, goods, chattels, household stuff, equipage, paraphernalia, impedimenta, stock-in-trade, cargo, lading (780).

Metal, stone, ore, brick, clay, wood, timber, composition, compo, plastic.

636 Store (*Substantives*), stock, fund, supply, reserve, relay, budget, quiver, *corps de réserve*, reserve fund, mine, quarry, vein, lode, fountain, well, spring, milch cow.

Collection, accumulation, heap (72), hoard, cache, stockpile, magazine, pile, rick, nest-egg, savings, bank (802), treasury, reservoir, repository, repertory, repertoire, album, depot, depository, treasure, thesaurus, museum, storehouse, promptuary, reservatory, conservatory, menagerie, aviary, aquarium, receptacle, warehouse, godown, *entrepôt*, dock, larder, cellar, garner, granary, store-room, box-room, lumber-room, silo, cistern, well, tank, gasometer, mill-pond, armoury, arsenal, coffer (191).

(*Verbs*) To store, stock, stockpile, treasure up, lay in, lay by, lay up, file, garner, save, husband, hoard, deposit, amass, accumulate (72).

To reserve, keep back, hold back.

(*Phrase*) To husband one's resources.

(*Adjectives*) Stored, etc., in store, in reserve, spare, surplus, extra.

637 Provision (*Substantives*), supply, providing, supplying, sustentation (707), purveyance, purveying, reinforcement, husbanding, commissariat, victualling.

Forage, pasture, food, provender (298).

A purveyor, caterer, contractor, commissary, quartermaster, sutler, victualler, *restaurateur*, feeder, batman; bum-boat.

(*Verbs*) To provide, supply, furnish, purvey, suppeditate, replenish, fill up, feed, stock with, recruit, victual, cater, find, fend, keep, lay in, lay in store, store, stockpile, forage, husband (636), upholster.

(*Phrase*) To bring grist to the mill.

638 Waste (*Substantives*), consumption, expenditure, exhaustion, drain, leakage, wear and tear, dispersion (73), ebb, loss, misuse, prodigality (818), seepage, squandermania.

(*Verbs*) To waste, spend, expend, use, consume, spill, leak, run out, run to waste, disperse (73), ebb, dry up, impoverish, drain, empty, exhaust; to fritter away, squander.

(*Phrases*) To cast pearls before swine; to burn the candle at both ends; to employ a steam-hammer to crack nuts; to break a butterfly on a wheel; to pour water into a sieve.

(*Adjectives*) Wasted, spent, profuse, lavish, etc., at a low ebb.

(*Phrase*) Penny wise and pound foolish.

639 Sufficiency (*Substantives*), adequacy, competence; enough, satiety.

Fullness, fill, plenitude, plenty, abundance, copiousness, amplitude, affluence, richness, fertility, luxuriance, uberty, foison.

Heaps, lots, bags, piles, lashings, oceans, oodles, mobs.

Impletion, repletion, saturation.

Riches (803), mine, store, fund, (636); a bumper, a brimmer, a bellyful, a cart-load, truck-load, ship-load; a plumper; a charge.

640 Insufficiency (*Substantives*), inadequacy, inadequateness, incompetence.

Deficiency, stint, paucity, defect, defectiveness, default, defalcation, deficit, shortcoming, falling short (304), too little, what will not do, scantiness, slenderness, a mouthful, etc. (32).

Scarcity, dearth, shortage, want, need, lack, exigency, inanition, indigence, poverty, penury (804), destitution, dole, pittance, short allowance, short commons, a banian day,

A flood, draught, shower, rain (347), stream, tide, spring tide, flush.

(Phrases) The horn of plenty; the horn of Amalthea; cornucopia; the fat of the land.

(Verbs) To be sufficient, etc., to suffice, serve, pass muster, to do, satisfy, satiate, sate, saturate, make up.

To abound, teem, stream, flow, rain, shower down, pour, swarm, bristle with.

To render sufficient, etc., to make up, to fill, charge, replenish, pour in; swim in, wallow in, roll in.

(Adjectives) Sufficient, enough, adequate, commensurate, what will just do.

Moderate, measured.

Full, ample, plenty, copious, plentiful, plenteous, plenary, wantless, abundant, abounding, flush, replete, laden, charged, fraught; well stocked or provided, liberal, lavish, unstinted, to spare, unsparing, unmeasured; *ad libitum*, wholesale.

Brimful, to the brim, chock-full, saturated, crammed, up to the ears, fat, rich, affluent, full up, luxuriant, lush.

Unexhausted, unwasted, exhaustless, inexhaustible.

(Phrases) Enough and to spare; cut and come again; full as an egg; ready to burst; plentiful as blackberries; flowing with milk and honey; enough in all conscience; enough to go round; *quantum sufficit*.

(Adverbs) Amply, etc., galore.

fast (956), a mouthful, starvation, malnutrition, famine, drought, depletion, emptiness, vacancy, flaccidity, ebbtide, low water.

(Phrase) 'A beggarly account of empty boxes.'

(Verbs) To be insufficient, etc., not to suffice, to come short of, to fall short of, fail, run out of, stop short, to want, lack, need, require (630); caret.

To render insufficient, etc., to stint, grudge, hold back, withhold, starve, pinch, skimp, scrimp, famish.

(Phrase) To live from hand to mouth.

(Adjectives) Insufficient, inadequate, incompetent, too little, not enough, etc., scant, scanty, skimpy, scrimpy, deficient, defective, in default, scarce, empty, empty-headed, devoid, short of, out of, wanting, etc., hard up for.

Destitute, dry, drained, unprovided, unsupplied, unfurnished, unreplenished, unfed, unstored, untreasured, bare, meagre, poor, thin, spare, skimpy, stinted, starved, famished, pinched, fasting, starveling, jejune, without resources (735), shorthanded, undermanned, understaffed, etc.

(Phrases) In short supply; not to be had for love or money; at the end of one's tether; at one's last gasp.

———

641 Redundance *(Substantives)*, superabundance, superfluity, superfluence, glut, exuberance, profuseness, profusion, plethora, engorgement, congestion, surfeit, gorge, load, turgidity, turgescence, dropsy.

Excess, nimiety, overdose, oversupply, overplus, surplus, surplusage, over-flow, inundation, deluge, extravagance, prodigality (818), exorbitance, lavishness, immoderation.

An expletive (908), pleonasm.

(Phrases) *Satis superque*; a drug in the market; the lion's share.

(Verbs) To superabound, overabound, run over, overflow, flow over, roll in, wallow in.

To overstock, overdose, overlay, gorge, engorge, glut, sate, satiate, surfeit, cloy, load, overload, surcharge, overrun, choke, drown, drench, inundate, flood, whelm, deluge.

(Phrases) To go begging; it never rains but it pours; to paint the lily; to carry coals to Newcastle.

(Adjectives) Redundant, superfluous, exuberant, superabundant, immoderate, extravagant, excessive, in excess, *de trop*, needless, unnecessary, uncalled-for, over and above (40), more than enough, buckshee, running to waste, overflowing, running over.

Turgid, gorged, plethoric, dropsical, replete, profuse, lavish, prodigal, supervacaneous, extra, spare, duplicate, supernumerary, supererogatory, expletive, surcharged, overcharged, sodden, overloaded, overladen, overburdened, overrun, overfed, overfull.

(Phrase) Enough and to spare.

(Adverbs) Over, over and above, too much, overmuch, over and enough, too far, without measure, without stint.

(Phrase) Over head and ears.

2. DEGREE OF SUBSERVIENCE

642 Importance *(Substantives)*, consequence, moment, weight, gravity, seriousness, consideration, concern, significance, import, influence (175), pressure, urgency, instancy, stress, emphasis, interest, preponderance, prominence (250), greatness (31).

The substance, essence, quintessence, core, kernel, nub, gist, pith, marrow, soul, point, gravamen.

The principal, prominent, or essential part.

A notability, somebody, personage (875), V.I.P., bigwig, toff, big pot, big gun, his nibs; great doings, *notabilia*, a red-letter day.

(Phrases) A sine qua non; a matter of life and death; no laughing matter.

(Verbs) To be important, or of importance, etc., to signify, import, matter, boot, weigh, count, to be prominent, etc., to take the lead.

To attach, or ascribe importance to; to value, care for, etc. (897); overestimate, etc. (482), exaggerate (549).

To mark, underline, italicize, score, accentuate, emphasize, stress, rub in.

(Phrases) To be somebody; to fill the bill; to make much of; to make a stir, a fuss, a piece of work, a song and dance; set store upon; to lay stress upon; to take *au grand sérieux*.

(Adjectives) Important, of importance, etc., grave, serious, material, weighty, influential, significant, emphatic, momentous, earnest, pressing, critical, preponderating, pregnant, urgent, paramount, essential, vital.

643 Unimportance *(Substantives)*, indifference, insignificance, triflingness, triviality, triteness; paltriness, emptiness, nothingness, inanity, lightness, levity, frivolity, vanity, frivolousness, puerility, child's play.

Poverty, meagreness, meanness, shabbiness, etc. (804).

A trifle, small matter, minutiae, bagatelle, cipher, moonshine, molehill, joke, jest, snap of the fingers, flea-bite, pinch of snuff, old song, *nugae*, fiddlestick, fiddlestick end, bubble, bulrush, nonentity, lay figure, nobody.

A straw, pin, fig, button, rush, feather, farthing, brass farthing, red cent, dime, dam, doit, peppercorn, pebble, small fry.

Trumpery, trash, codswallop, stuff, *fatras*, frippery, chaff, drug, froth, smoke, cobweb.

Toy, plaything, knick-knack, gimcrack, gewgaw, thingumbob, bauble, kickshaw, bric-à-brac, fal-lal, whimwham, whigmaleerie, curio, bibelot.

Refuse, lumber, junk, litter, orts, tares, weeds, sweepings, scourings, offscourings; rubble, debris, dross, scoriae, dregs, scum, flue, dust (653).

(Phrases) 'Leather and prunella'; *peu de chose*; much ado about nothing; much cry and little wood; flotsam and jetsam; a man of straw; a stuffed shirt; a toom tabard.

(Verbs) To be unimportant, to be of little or no importance, etc.; not to signify, not to deserve, merit, or be

Great, considerable, etc. (31), capital, leading, principal, superior, chief, main, prime, primary, cardinal, prominent, salient, egregious, outstanding.

Signal, notable, memorable, remarkable, etc., grand, solemn, eventful, stirring, impressive; not to be despised, or overlooked, etc., unforgettable, worth while.

(Phrases) Being no joke; not to be sneezed at; no small beer.

---

worthy of notice, regard, consideration, etc.

(Phrases) To catch at straws; to make much ado about nothing; to cut no ice; *le jeu ne vaut pas la chandelle.*

(Adjectives) Unimportant, secondary, inferior, immaterial, inconsiderable, inappreciable, insignificant, unessential, non-essential, beneath notice, indifferent; of little or no account, importance, consequence, moment, interest, etc.; unimpressive, subordinate.

Trifling, trivial, trite, banal, mere, common, so-so, slight, slender, flimsy, trumpery, foolish, idle, puerile, childish, infantile, frothy, trashy, catchpenny, fiddling, frivolous, commonplace, contemptible, cheap.

Vain, empty, inane, poor, sorry, mean, meagre, shabby, scrannel, vile, miserable, scrubby, weedy, niggling, beggarly, piddling, peddling, pitiful, pitiable, despicable, paltry, ridiculous, farcical, finical, finicking, finicky, finikin, fiddle-faddle, wishy-washy, namby-pamby, gimcrack, twopenny, twopenny-halfpenny, two-by-four, one-horse, piffling, jerry, jerry built.

(Phrases) Not worth a straw; as light as air; not worth mentioning; not worth boasting about; no great shakes; nothing to write home about; small potatoes; neither here nor there.

(Interjections) No matter! pshaw! pooh! pooh-pooh! shucks! I should worry! fudge! fiddle-de-dee! nonsense! boloney! hooey! nuts! rats! stuff! *n'importe!*

(Adverbs) Meagrely, pitifully, vainly, etc.

---

644 Utility *(Substantives)*, service, use, function, office, sphere, capacity, part, role, task, work.

Usefulness, worth, stead, avail, advantageousness, profitableness, serviceableness, merit, *cui bono*, applicability, adequacy, subservience, subserviency, efficacy, efficiency, help, money's worth.

(Verbs) To be useful, etc., of use, of service.

To avail, serve, subserve, help (707), conduce, answer, profit, advantage, accrue, bedstead.

To render useful, to use (677), to turn to account, to utilize, to make the most of.

(Phrases) To stand in good stead; to do yeoman service; to perform a function; to serve a purpose; to serve a turn.

645 Inutility *(Substantives)*, uselessness, inefficacy, inefficiency, ineptness, ineptitude, inadequacy, inaptitude, unskilfulness, fecklessness, fruitlessness, inanity, worthlessness, unproductiveness, barrenness, sterility, vanity, futility, triviality, paltriness, unprofitableness, unfruitfulness, rustiness, obsoleteness, discommodity, supererogation, obsolescence.

Litter, rubbish, lumber, trash, junk, punk, job lot, orts, weeds (643), bilge, hog-wash.

A waste, desert, Sahara, wild, wilderness.

(Phrases) The labour of Sisyphus; the work of Penelope; a slaying of the slain; a dead loss; a work of supererogation.

(Verbs) To be useless, etc., to be of no avail, use, etc. (644).

(Adjectives) Useful, beneficial, advantageous, serviceable, helpful, gainful, profitable, lucrative, worth while.

Subservient, conducive, applicable, adequate, efficient, efficacious, effective, effectual, seaworthy.

Applicable, available, handy, ready.

(Adverbs) Usefully, etc.; *pro bono publico.*

———

To render useless, etc.; to dismantle, disable, disqualify, cripple.

(Phrases) To use vain efforts; to beat the air; to fish in the air; to lash the waves; to plough the sands.

(Adjectives) Useless, inutile, inefficient, inefficacious, unavailing, inadequate, inoperative, bootless, supervacaneous, unprofitable, unremunerative, unproductive, sterile, barren, unsubservient, supererogatory.

Worthless, valueless, at a discount, gainless, fruitless, profitless, unserviceable, rusty, effete, vain, empty, inane, wasted, nugatory, futile, feckless, inept, withered, good for nothing, wasteful, ill-spent, obsolete, obsolescent, stale, dud, punk, dear-bought, rubbishy.

Unneeded, unnecessary, uncalled-for, unwanted, incommodious, discommodious.

(Phrases) Not worth having; leading to no end; no good; not worth while; of no earthly use; a dead letter.

(Adverbs) Uselessly, etc., to no purpose.

646 Specific subservience.

Expedience *(Substantives)*, expediency, fitness, suitableness, suitability, aptness, aptitude, appropriateness, propriety, pertinence, seasonableness (134), adaptation, congruity, consonance (23), convenience, eligibility, applicability, desirability, seemliness, rightness.

An opportunist, time-server.

(Verbs) To be expedient, etc.

To suit, fit, square with, adapt itself to, agree with, consort with, accord with, tally with, confirm to, go with, do for.

(Adjectives) Expedient, fit, fitting, worth while, suitable, applicable, eligible, apt, appropriate, adapted, proper, advisable, politic, judicious, desirable, pertinent, congruous, seemly, consonant, becoming, meet, due, consentaneous, congenial, well-timed, pat, seasonable, opportune, apropos, befitting, happy, felicitous, auspicious, acceptable, etc., convenient, commodious, right.

(Phrases) Being just the thing; just as well.

648 Capability of producing good.

Goodness *(Substantives)*, excellence, integrity (939), virtue (944),

647 Inexpedience *(Substantives)*, inexpediency, disadvantageousness, unserviceableness, disservice, unfitness, inaptitude, ineptitude, ineligibility, inappropriateness, impropriety, undesirability, unseemliness, incongruity, impertinence, inopportuneness, unseasonableness.

Inconvenience, incommodiousness, incommodity, discommodity, disadvantage.

Inefficacy, inefficiency, inadequacy.

(Verbs) To be inexpedient, etc., to embarrass, cumber, lumber, handicap, be in the way, etc.

(Adjectives) Inexpedient, disadvantageous, unprofitable, unfit, unfitting, unsuitable, undesirable, amiss, improper, unapt, inept, impolitic, injudicious, ill-advised, unadvisable, ineligible, objectionable, inadmissible, unseemly, inopportune, unseasonable, inefficient, inefficacious, inadequate.

Inconvenient, incommodious, cumbrous, cumbersome, lumbering, unwieldy, unmanageable, awkward, clumsy.

649 Capability of producing evil.

Badness *(Substantives)*, hurtfulness, disserviceableness, injurious-

merit, value, worth, price, preciousness, estimation, rareness, exquisiteness.

Superexcellence, superiority, supereminence, transcendence, perfection (650).

Mediocrity (651), innocuousness, harmlessness, inoffensiveness.

Masterpiece, *chef d'œuvre*, flower, pick, cream, *crême de la crême*, *élite*, gem, jewel, treasure; a good man (948).

(Phrases) One in a thousand (or in a million); the salt of the earth.

(Verbs) To be good, beneficial, etc.; to be superior, etc., to excel, transcend, top, vie, emulate (708).

To be middling, etc. (651); to pass, to do.

To produce good, benefit, etc., to benefit, to be beneficial, etc., to confer a benefit, etc., to improve (658).

(Phrases) To challenge comparison; to pass muster; to speak well for.

(Adjectives) Good, beneficial, valuable, estimable, serviceable, advantageous, precious, favourable, palmary, felicitous, propitious.

Sound, sterling, standard, true, genuine, household, fresh, in good condition, unfaded, unspoiled, unimpaired, uninjured, undemolished, undamaged, unravaged, undecayed, natural, unsophisticated, unadulterated, unpolluted, unvitiated.

Choice, select, picked, nice, worthy, meritorious (944), fine, rare, unexceptionable, excellent, admirable, first-rate, splendid, swell, bully, wizard, priceless, smashing, super, topping, top-hole, clipping, ripping, nailing, prime, tiptop, crack, jake, cardinal, superlative, superfine, super-excellent, pukka, gradely, champion, exquisite, high-wrought, inestimable, invaluable, incomparable, transcendent, matchless, peerless, inimitable, unrivalled, *nulli secundus*, second to none, *facile princeps*, spotless, immaculate, perfect (650), *récherché*, first-class, first chop.

Moderately good (651).

Harmless, innocuous, innoxious,

ness, banefulness, mischievousness, noxiousness, malignancy, malignity, malevolence, tender mercies, venomousness, virulence, destructiveness, scathe, curse, pest, plague, bane (663), plague-spot, evil star, ill wind; evildoer (913).

Vileness, foulness, rankness, depravation, depravity; injury, outrage, ill treatment, annoyance, molestation, oppression; sabotage; deterioration (659).

(Phrases) A snake in the grass; a fly in the ointment; a nigger in the woodpile; a thorn in the side; a skeleton in the cupboard.

(Verbs) To be bad, etc.

To cause, produce, or inflict evil; to harm, hurt, injure, mar, damage, damnify, endamage, scathe, prejudice, stand in the light of, worsen.

To wrong, molest (830), annoy, harass, infest, grieve, aggrieve, trouble, oppress, persecute, weigh down, run down, overlay.

To maltreat, abuse, ill use, ill treat, bedevil, bruise, scratch, maul, mishandle, man-handle, strafe, knock about, strike, smite, scourge (972), wound, lame, maim, scotch, cripple, mutilate, hamstring, hough, stab, pierce, etc., crush, crumble, pulverize.

To corrupt, corrode, pollute, etc. (659).

To spoil, despoil, sweep, ravage, lay waste, devastate, dismantle, demolish, level, raze, consume, overrun, sack, plunder, destroy (162).

(Phrases) To play the deuce with; to break the back of; crush to pieces; crumble to dust; to grind to powder; to ravage with fire and sword; to knock the stuffing out of; to queer one's pitch; to let daylight into.

(Adjectives) Bad, evil, ill, wrong, prejudicial, disadvantageous, unprofitable, unlucky, sinister, left-handed, obnoxious, untoward, unadvisable, inauspicious, ill-omened.

Hurtful, harmful, injurious, grievous, detrimental, noxious, pernicious, mischievous, baneful, baleful.

Morbific, rank, peccant, malignant,

unoffending, inoffensive, unobjectionable.

(Phrases) The goods; the stuff to give them; a bit of all right; of the first water; precious as the apple of the eye; *ne plus ultra*; sound as a roach; worth its weight in gold; right as a trivet; up to the mark; an easy winner.

tabid, corroding, corrosive, virulent, cankering, mephitic, narcotic.

Deleterious, poisonous, venomous, envenomed, pestilent, pestilential, pestiferous, destructive, deadly, fatal, mortal, lethal, lethiferous, miasmal.

Vile, sad, wretched, sorry, shabby, scurvy, base, low, low-down (940), scrubby, lousy, stinking, horrid.

Hateful, abominable, loathsome, detestable, execrable, iniquitous, cursed, accursed, confounded, damnable, diabolic, devilish, demoniacal, infernal, hellish, Satanic, villainous, depraved, shocking (898).

(Adverbs) Wrong, wrongly, badly, to one's cost.

(Phrases) Corruptio optimi pessima; if the worst comes to the worst.

650 Perfection *(Substantives)*, perfectness, indefectibility, impeccability, infallibility, unimpeachability, *beau idéal*, summit (210).

Masterpiece, *chef d'ouvre, magnum opus*, classic, model, pattern, mirror, phoenix, *rara avis*, paragon, cream, nonsuch (or nonesuch), nonpareil, *élite*.

Gem, bijou, jewel, pearl, diamond, ruby, brilliant.

A Bayard, a Galahad, an Admirable Crichton.

(Phrases) The philosophers' stone; the flower of the flock; the cock of the roost; the peak or acme of perfection; the pick of the bunch; the *ne plus ultra*.

(Verbs) To be perfect, etc., to excel, transcend, overtop, etc. (33).

To bring to perfection, to perfect, to ripen, mature, etc. (52, 729).

(Phrases) To carry everything before it; to play first fiddle; bear away the bell; to sweep the board.

(Adjectives) Perfect, best, faultless, finished, indeficient, indefectible, immaculate, spotless, impeccable, transcendent, matchless, peerless, unparagoned, etc. (648), inimitable, unimpeachable, superlative, superhuman, divine, classical.

(Phrases) Right as a trivet; sound as a bell; *ad unguem factus; sans peur et sans reproche*.

651 Imperfection *(Substantives)*, imperfectness, unsoundness, faultiness, deficiency, disability, weak point, drawback, inadequacy, inadequateness (645), handicap.

Fault, defect, flaw, lacuna (198), crack, twist, taint, blemish, shortcoming (304), peccancy, vice.

Mediocrity, mean (29), indifference, inferiority.

(Verbs) To be imperfect, middling, etc., to fail, fall short, lie under a disadvantage, be handicapped.

(Phrases) To play second fiddle; barely to pass muster.

(Adjectives) Imperfect, deficient, defective, faulty, dud, inferior, inartistic, inadequate, wanting, unsound, vicious, cracked, warped, lame, feeble, frail, flimsy, sketchy, botched, gimcrack, gingerbread, tottering, wonky, decrepit, rickety, ramshackle, rattletrap, battered, worn out, threadbare, seedy, wormeaten, moth-eaten, played out, used up, decayed, mutilated, unrectified, uncorrected.

Indifferent, middling, mediocre, below par, so-so, *couci-couci*, secondary, second-rate, third-rate, etc., second-best, second-hand.

Tolerable, passable, bearable, pretty well, well enough, rather good, decent, fair, admissible, not bad, not amiss, not so dusty, unobjectionable, respectable, betwixt and between.

(Phrases) having a screw loose; out of order; out of kilter; no great catch; mill and water; no great shakes; nothing to boast of; on its last legs; no class.

652 Cleanness *(Substantives)*, cleanliness, asepsis, purity (960), neatness, tidiness, spotlessness, immaculateness.

Cleaning, purification, mundification, lustration, abstersion, depuration, expurgation, purgation, castration.

Washing, ablution, lavation, elutriation, lixiviation, clarification, defecation, edulcoration, filtration.

Fumigation, ventilation, antisepsis, decontamination, disinfection, soap; detergent, shampoo, antiseptic, disinfectant.

Washroom, wash-house, laundry; washerwoman, laundress, charwoman, cleaner, scavenger, dustman, sweep.

Brush, broom, besom, vacuum-cleaner, duster, handkerchief, napkin, face-cloth, towel, sponge, tooth-brush, nail-brush; mop, sieve, riddle, screen, filter.

(Verbs) To be clean, etc.

To render clean, etc., to clean, to mundify, cleanse, wipe, mop, sponge, scour, swab, scrub, brush, sweep, vacuum, dust, brush up.

To wash, lave, sluice, buck, launder, steep, rinse, absterge, deterge, descale, clear, purify, depurate, defecate, elutriate, lixiviate, edulcorate, clarify, drain, strain, filter, filtrate, fine, fine down.

To disinfect, deodorize, fumigate, delouse, ventilate, purge, expurgate, bowdlerize.

To sift, winnow, pick, screen, weed.

(Phrase) To make a clean sweep of.

(Adjectives) Clean, cleanly, pure, spotless, unspotted, immaculate, unstained, stainless, unsoiled, unsullied, taintless, untainted, sterile, aseptic, uninfected.

Cleansing, etc., detergent, detersive, abstersive, abstergent, purgatory, purificatory, etc., abluent, antiseptic.

Spruce, tidy, washed, swept, etc., cleaned, disinfected, purified, etc.

(Phrases) Clean as a whistle; clean as a new penny; neat as ninepence.

653 Uncleanness *(Substantives)*, immundicity, uncleanliness, soilure, sordidness, foulness, impurity (961), pollution, nastiness, offensiveness, beastliness, muckiness, defilement, contamination, abomination, taint, tainture, corruption, decomposition (49).

Slovenliness, slovenly, untidiness, sluttishness, coarseness, grossness, dregginess, squalor.

Dirt, filth, soil, slop, dust, flue, ooss, cobweb, smoke, soot, smudge, smut, stour, clart, glaur, grime, *sordes*, mess, muck.

Slut, slattern, sloven, frump, mudlark, riff-raff.

Dregs, grounds, sediment, lees, settlement, dross, drossiness, precipitate, scoriae, slag, clinker, scum, sweepings, off-scourings, garbage, *caput mortuum*, residuum, draff, fur, scurf, scurfiness, furfur, dandruff, vermin.

Mud, mire, slush, quagmire, slough, sludge, alluvium, silt, slime, spawn, offal, faeces, excrement, ordure, dung, droppings, guano, manure, compost, dunghill, midden, bog, laystall, sink, cesspool, sump, sough, *cloaca*, latrine, lavatory, water-closet, w.c., toilet, urinal, rear, convenience, privy, jakes, comfort station, heads, thunder-box, drain, sewer; hog-wash, bilge-water,

Sty, pigsty, dusthole, lair, den, slum.

Rottenness, corruption, decomposition, decay, putrefaction, putrescence, putridity, purulence, pus, matter, suppuration, feculence, rankness, rancidity, mouldiness, mustiness, mucidness, mould, mother, must, mildew, dry-rot, fetor (401).

Scatology, coprology.

(Phrases) A sink of corruption; an Augean stable.

(Verbs) To be unclean, dirty, etc., to rot, putrefy, corrupt, decompose, go bad, mould, moulder, fester, etc.

To render unclean, etc., to dirt, dirty, soil, tarnish, begrime, smear, besmear, mess, smirch, besmirch, smudge, besmudge, bemire, spatter, bespatter, splash, bedraggle, bedraggle, daub, bedaub, slobber, beslobber, beslime, to cover with dust.

To foul, befoul, sully, pollute, defile, debase, contaminate, taint, corrupt, deflower, rot.

(Adjectives) Unclean, dirty, soiled, filthy, grimy, clarty, dusty, dirtied, etc., smutty, sooty, smoky, reechy, thick, turbid, dreggy, slimy, filthy, mucky.

Slovenly, untidy, sluttish, blowzy, draggle-tailed, dowdy, frumpish, slipshod, unkempt, unscoured, unswept, unwiped, unwashed, unstrained, unpurified, squalid.

Nasty, foul, impure, offensive, abominable, beastly, lousy.

Mouldy, musty, mildewed, fusty, rusty, mouldering, moth-eaten, reasty, rotten, rotting, tainted, rancid, high, fly-blown, maggoty, putrescent, putrid, putrefied, bad, festering, purulent, feculent, fecal, stercoraceous, excrementitious.

(Phrases) Wallowing in the mire; rotten to the core.

654 Health *(Substantives)*, sanity, soundness, heartiness, haleness, vigour, freshness, bloom, healthfulness, euphoria, incorruption, incorruptibility.

(Phrases) Mens sana in corpore sano; a clean bill.

(Verbs) To be in health, etc., to flourish, thrive, bloom.

To return to health, to recover, convalesce, recruit, pull through, to get the better of.

To restore to health, to cure, recall to life, bring to.

(Phrases) To keep on one's legs; to take a new or fresh lease of life; to turn the corner.

(Adjectives) Healthy, in health, well, sound, healthful, hearty, hale, fresh, whole, florid, staunch, flush, hardy, vigorous, chipper, spry, bobbish, blooming, weather-proof, fit.

Unscathed, uninjured, unmaimed, unmarred, untainted.

(Phrases) Sitting up and taking nourishment; being on one's legs; sound as a bell, or roach; fresh as a daisy or rose; in fine or high feather; in good case; fit as a fiddle; in the pink of condition; in the pink; in good form.

655 Disease *(Substantives)*, illness, sickness, ailment, ailing, indisposition, complaint, disorder, malady, distemper.

Attack, visitation, seizure, stroke, fit.

Sickliness, sickishness, infirmity, diseasedness, tabescence, invalidation, delicacy, weakness, cachexy, witheredness, atrophy, marasmus, incurableness, incurability, palsy, paralysis, decline, consumption, prostration.

Taint, pollution, infection, septicity, epidemic, endemic, murrain, plague, pestilence, virus, pox.

A sore, ulcer, abscess, fester, boil, gathering, issue, rot, canker, cancer, carcinoma, sarcoma, caries, gangrene, mortification, eruption, rash, congestion, inflammation, fever.

A valetudinarian, invalid, patient, case, cripple.

Pathology, aetiology, nosology.

(Verbs) To be ill, etc., to ail, suffer, be affected with, etc., to complain of, to droop, flag, languish, halt, sicken, gasp; to malinger.

(Phrases) To be laid up; to keep one's bed.

(Adjectives) Diseased, ill, taken ill, seized, indisposed, unwell, sick, sickish, seedy, queer, crook, toutie, ailing, suffering, confined, bedridden, invalided.

Unsound, sickly, poorly, delicate, weakly, cranky, healthless, infirm, groggy, unbraced, drooping, flagging, withered, palsied, paralytic, paraplectic, decayed, decrepit, lame, crippled, battered, halting, worn out, used up, run down, off colour, moth-eaten, worm-eaten.

Morbid, tainted, vitiated, peccant, contaminated, tabid, tabescent, mangy, poisoned, immedicable, gasping, moribund (360).

(Phrases) Out of sorts; good for nothing; on the sick-list; on the danger list; in a bad way; *hors de combat*; on one's last legs; at one's last gasp.

656 Salubrity *(Substantives),* healthiness, wholesomeness, innoxiousness.

Preservation of health, prophylaxis, hygiene, sanitation.

A health resort, spa, hydropathic, sanatorium (662).

(Verbs) To be salubrious, etc., to agree with.

(Adjectives) Salubrious, wholesome, healthy, sanitary, hygienic, salutary, salutiferous, healthful, tonic, prophylactic, bracing, benign.

Innoxious, innocuous, harmless, uninjurious, innocent.

Remedial, restorative, sanatory (662), nutritious, alterative (660).

657 Insalubrity *(Substantives),* unhealthiness, unwholesomeness, deadliness, fatality.

Microbe, germ, virus, etc. (663).

(Adjectives) Insalubrious, insanitary, unsanitary, unhealthy, ungenial, uncongenial, unwholesome, morbific, mephitic, septic, deleterious, pestilent, pestiferous, pestilential, virulent, poisonous, toxic, contagious, infectious, catching, epidemic, epizootic, endemic, pandemic, zymotic, deadly, pathogenic, pathogenetic, lowering, relaxing; innutritious (645).

(Phrase) 'There is death in the pot.'

658 Improvement *(Substantives),* melioration, amelioration, betterment, mend, amendment, emendation, advance, advancement, progress, elevation, promotion, preferment, convalescence, recovery, recuperation, curability.

Repair, reparation, cicatrization, correction, reform, reformation, rectification, epuration, purification, etc. (652), refinement, relief, redress, second thoughts.

New edition; *réchauffé, rifacimento,* revision, revise, recension, rehash, redaction.

(Verbs) To be, become, or get better, etc., to improve, mend, advance, progress (282), to get on, make progress, gain ground, make way, go ahead, pick up, rally, recover, get the better of, get well, get over it, pull through, convalesce, recuperate.

To render better, improve, amend, better, meliorate, ameliorate, advance, push on, promote, prefer, forward, enhance.

To relieve, refresh, restore, renew, redintegrate, heal (660); to palliate, mitigate.

To repair, refit, cannibalize,

659 Deterioration *(Substantives),* wane, ebb, debasement, degeneracy, degeneration, degradation, degenerateness, demotion, relegation.

Impairment, injury, outrage, havoc, devastation, inroad, vitiation, adulteration, sophistication, debasement, perversion, degradation, demoralization, corruption, prostitution, pollution, contamination, alloy, venenation.

Decline, declension, declination, going downhill, recession, retrogression, retrogradation (283), caducity, decrepitude, decadence, falling off, pejoration.

Decay, disorganization, damage, scathe, wear and tear, mouldiness, rottenness, corrosion, moth and rust, dry-rot, blight, marasmus, atrophy, emaciation, falling to pieces, *délâbrement.*

(Verbs) To be, or become worse, to deteriorate, worsen, disimprove, wane, ebb, degenerate, fall off, decline, go downhill, sink, go down, lapse, droop, be the worse for, recede, retrograde, revert (283), fall into decay, fade, break, break up, break down, fall to pieces, wither, moulder,

retouch, revise, botch, vamp, tinker, cobble, clout, patch up, touch up, cicatrize, darn, fine-draw, rub up, do up, furbish, refurbish, polish, bolster up, caulk, careen; to stop a gap, to staunch.

To purify, depurate (652), defecate, strain, filter, rack, refine, disinfect, chasten.

To correct, rectify, redress, reform, review, remodel, prune, restore (660), mellow, set to rights, sort, fix, put straight, straighten out, revise.

(Phrases) To turn over a new leaf; to take a new lease of life; to make the most of; to infuse new blood into.

(Adjectives) Improving, etc., improved, etc., progressive, corrective, reparatory, emendatory, revisory, sanatory, advanced.

Curable, corrigible, capable of improvement.

———

rot, rust, crumble, totter, shake, tumble, fall, topple, perish, die (360).

To render less good; to weaken, vitiate, debase, alloy, pervert.

To spoil, embase, defile, taint, infect, contaminate, sophisticate, poison, canker, corrupt, tamper with, pollute, deprave, demoralize, envenom, debauch, prostitute, defile, degrade, downgrade, demote, adulterate, stain, spatter, bespatter, soil, tarnish (653), addle.

To corrode, erode, blight, rot, wear away, wear out, gnaw, gnaw at the root of, sap, mine, undermine, shake, break up, disorganize, dismantle, dismast, lay waste, do for, ruin, confound.

To embitter, acerbate, aggravate.

To wound, stab, maim, lame, cripple, mutilate, disfigure, deface.

To injure, harm, hurt, impair, dilapidate, damage, endamage, damnify, etc. (649).

(Phrases) To go to rack and ruin; to have seen better days; to go to the dogs; to go to pot; to go on from bad to worse; to go farther and fare worse; to run to seed; to play the deuce with; to sap the foundations of.

(Adjectives) Deteriorated, worse, impaired, etc., degenerate, *passé*, on the decline, on the down-grade, deciduous, unimproved, unrecovered, unrestored.

Decayed, etc., moth-eaten, worm-eaten, mildewed, rusty, time-worn, moss-grown, effete, wasted, worn, crumbling, tumbledown, dilapidated, overblown.

(Phrases) Out of the frying-pan into the fire; the worse for wear; worn to a thread; worn to a shadow; reduced to a skeleton; the ghost of oneself; a hopeless case.

660 Restoration *(Substantives)*, restoral, reinstatement, replacement, rehabilitation, instauration, re-establishment, rectification, revendication, redintegration, refection, reconstitution, cure, sanation, refitting, retrieval, refreshment.

Renovation, renewal, reanimation, recovery, resumption, reclamation, reconversion, recure, resuscitation, revivification, reviviscence, revival, renascence, renaissance, rejuvenation, rejuvenescence, regeneration, regeneracy, regenerateness, palingenesis, redemption; a Phoenix.

661 Relapse *(Substantives)*, lapse, falling back, backsliding, retrogression, reaction, set-back, recidivism, retrogradation, etc. (659).

Return to or recurrence of a bad state.

A recidivist, backslider, throw-back.

(Verbs) To relapse, lapse, backslide, fall back, slide back, sink back, go back, return, retrograde.

———

Réchauffé, *rifacimento* (658), recast.

(Phrases) A new lease of life; second youth; new birth; 'Richard's himself again.'

(Verbs) To return to the original state, to right itself, come to, come round, rally, revive, recover.

To restore, replace, re-establish, reinstate, reseat, replant, reconstitute, redintegrate, set right, set to rights, sort, fix, rectify, redress, reclaim, redeem, recover, recoup, recure, retrieve, cicatrize.

To refit, recruit, refresh, refocillate, rehabilitate, reconvert, renew, renovate, revitalize, revivify, reinvigorate, regenerate, rejuvenesce, rejuvenate, resuscitate, reanimate, recast, reconstruct, rebuild, reorganize.

To repair, retouch, revise (658).

To cure, heal, cicatrize, remedy, doctor, physic, medicate.

(Phrases) Recall to life; set on one's legs.

(Adjectives) Restoring, etc., restored, etc., restorative, recuperative, reparative, sanative, remedial, curative (662).

Restorable, sanable, remediable, retrievable, recoverable.

(Adverbs) In statu quo; as you were; Phoenix-like.

662 Remedy *(Substantives)*, help, redress, cure, antidote, counter-poison, vaccine, antitoxin, antibiotic, antiseptic, specific, prophylactic, corrective, restorative, pick-me-up, bracer, sedative, anodyne, opiate, hypnotic, nepenthe, tranquillizer.

Febrifuge, diaphoretic, diuretic, carminative, purgative, laxative, emetic, palliative.

Physic, medicine, drug, tonic, medicament, nostrum, placebo, recipe, prescription, catholicon.

Panacea, elixir, *elixir vitae*, balm, balsam, cordial, cardiac, theriac, ptisan.

Pill, pilule, pellet, tablet, tabloid, pastille, lozenge, powder, draught, lincture, suppository.

Salve, ointment, plaster, epithem, embrocation, liniment, lotion, cataplasm, styptic, poultice, compress, pledget.

Treatment, diet, dieting, regimen.

663 Bane *(Substantives)*, scourge, curse, scathe, sting, fang, gall and wormwood.

Poison, virus, venom, toxin, microbe, germ, bacillus, miasma, mephitis, malaria, pest, rust, canker, cancer, canker-worm.

Hemlock, hellebore, nightshade, henbane, aconite, upas-tree.

Sirocco.

A viper, adder, serpent, cobra, rattlesnake, cockatrice, scorpion, wireworm, torpedo, hornet, vulture, vampire.

Science of poisons, toxicology.

(Adjectives) Poisonous, venomous, virulent, toxic, mephitic, pestilent, pestilential, miasmatic, baneful (649).

———

Pharmacy, pharmacology, materia medica, therapeutics, homoeopathy, allopathy, radiotherapy, actinotherapy, heliotherapy, thalassotherapy, hydrotherapy, hydropathy, osteopathy, dietetics, dietary, chirurgery, surgery, gynaecology, midwifery, obstetrics, paediatrics, geriatrics; psycho-analysis, psychiatry, psychotherapy; faith-healing.

A hospital, infirmary, pest-house, lazaretto, madhouse, asylum, lunatic asylum, mental hospital, *maison de santé*, ambulance, clinic, dispensary, sanatorium, spa, hydropathic, nursing home.

A doctor, physician, general practitioner, G.P., surgeon, anaesthetist, dentist, aurist, oculist, specialist, alienist, psycho-analyst, psychiatrist, psycho-therapist; apothecary, druggist; midwife, nurse.

(Verbs) To dose, physic, attend, doctor, nurse.

(Adjectives) Remedial, medical, medicinal, therapeutic, surgical, chirurgical, sanatory, sanative, curative, salutary, salutiferous, healing, paregoric, restorative, tonic, corroborant, analeptic, balsamic, anodyne, sedative, lenitive, demulcent, emollient, depuratory, detersive, detergent, abstersive, disinfectant, antiseptic, corrective, prophylactic, antitoxic, febrifuge, alterative, expectorant; veterinary.

Dietetic, alexipharmic, nutritious, nutritive, peptic, alimentary.

3. CONTINGENT SUBSERVIENCE

664 Safety *(Substantives)*, security, surety, impregnability, invulnerability, invulnerableness, escape (671).

Safeguard, guard, guardianship, chaperonage, protection, tutelage, wardship, wardenship, safe-conduct, escort, convoy, garrison.

Watch, watch and ward, sentinel, sentry, scout, watchman, patrol, vedette, picket, bivouac.

Policeman, policewoman, police officer, constable, cop, copper, bobby, peeler, slop, bull, dick, rozzer.

Watch-dog, bandog, Cerberus.

Protector, guardian, guard (717), defender, warden, warder, preserver, chaperon, tutelary saint, guardian angel, palladium.

Custody, safe-keeping (751).

Isolation, segregation, quarantine; insurance, assurance; cover.

(Verbs) To be safe, etc.

To render safe, etc., to protect, guard, ward, shield, shelter, flank, cover, screen, shroud, ensconce, secure, fence, hedge in, entrench, house, nestle.

To defend, forfend, escort, convoy, garrison, mount guard, patrol, chaperon, picket.

(Phrases) To save one's bacon; to light upon one's feet; to weather the storm; to bear a charmed life; to make assurance doubly sure; to take no chances.

To play gooseberry.

(Adjectives) Safe, in safety, in security, secure, sure, protected, guarded, etc., snug, fireproof, waterproof, seaworthy, airworthy.

Defensible, tenable; insurable.

665 Danger *(Substantives)*, peril, insecurity, jeopardy, risk, hazard, venture, precariousness, slipperiness.

Liability, exposure (177), vulnerability, vulnerable point, Achilles heel.

Hopelessness (859), forlorn hope, alarm (860), defencelessness.

(Phrases) The ground sliding from under one; breakers ahead; a storm brewing; the sword of Damocles.

(Verbs) To be in danger, etc., to be exposed to, to incur or encounter danger, run the danger of, run a risk.

To place or put in danger, etc., to endanger, expose to danger, imperil, jeopardize, compromise, adventure, risk, hazard, venture, stake.

(Phrases) To sit on a barrel of gunpowder; stand on a volcano; to engage in a forlorn hope.

(Adjectives) In danger, peril, jeopardy, etc., unsafe, insecure, unguarded, unscreened, unsheltered, unprotected, guardless, helpless, guideless, exposed, defenceless, vulnerable, at bay.

Unwarned, unadmonished, unadvised.

Dangerous, perilous, hazardous, parlous, risky, chancy, untrustworthy, fraught with danger, adventurous, precarious, critical, touch-and-go, breakneck, slippery, unsteady, shaky, tottering, top-heavy, harbourless, ticklish, dicky.

Threatening, ominous, alarming, minacious (909).

(Phrases) Not out of the wood; hanging by a thread; neck or nothing; in a tight place; between two fires; out of the frying-pan into the fire;

Invulnerable, unassailable, unattackable, impregnable, inexpugnable.

Protecting, etc., guardian, tutelary.

Unthreatened, unmolested, unharmed, scatheless, unhazarded.

(Phrases) Out of harm's way; safe and sound; under lock and key; on sure ground; under cover; under the shadow of one's wing; the coast being clear; the danger being past; out of the wood; proof against.

(Interjections) All's well! *salva est res!* safety first!

between the devil and the deep sea; between Scylla and Charybdis; on the rocks; hard bested.

---

666 Means of safety.

Refuge *(Substantives)*, asylum, sanctuary, fastness, retreat, ark, hiding-place, dug-out, funk-hole, fox-hole, loophole, shelter, lee, cover.

Roadstead, anchorage, breakwater, mole, groyne, port, haven, harbour, harbour of refuge, pier.

Fort, citadel, fortification, stronghold, strong point, keep, shield, etc. (717).

Screen, covert, wing, fence, rail, railing, wall, dike, ditch, etc. (232).

Anchor, kedge, grapnel, grappling-iron, sheet-anchor, prop, stay, mainstay, jury-mast, lifeboat, lifebuoy, lifebelt, plank, stepping-stone, umbrella, parachute, lightning-conductor, safety-valve, safety curtain, safety-lamp.

667 Source of danger.

Pitfall *(Substantives)*, rocks, reefs, sunken rocks, snags, sands, quicksands, breakers, shoals, shallows, bank, shelf, flat, whirlpool, rapids, current, undertow, precipice, lee shore, air-pocket.

Trap, snare, gin, springe, deadfall, toils, noose, net, spring-net, spring-gun, masked battery, mine.

(Phrases) The sword of Damocles; a snake in the grass; trusting to a broken reed; a lion's den; a hornet's nest; an ugly customer.

---

668 Warning *(Substantives)*, caution, *caveat*, notice, premonition, premonishment, lesson, dehortation, monition, admonition (864); alarm (669).

Beacon, lighthouse, lightship, pharos, watch-tower, signal-post, guide-post (550).

Sentinel, sentry, watch, watchman, patrol, vedette (664); monitor, Cassandra.

(Phrases) The writing on the wall; the yellow flag; a red light; a stormy petrel; gathering clouds.

(Verbs) To warn, caution, forewarn, premonish, give notice, give warning, admonish, dehort, threaten, menace (909).

To take warning, to beware; to be on one's guard (864).

(Phrases) To put on one's guard; to sound the alarm.

(Adjectives) Warning, etc., monitory, premonitory, dehortatory, cautionary, admonitory.

Warned, etc., careful, on one's guard (459).

(Interjections) Beware! look out! mind what you are about! watch your step! let sleeping dogs lie! *foenum habet in cornu!* fore! heads! mind your back! cave!

669 Indication of danger.

Alarm *(Substantives)*, alert, alarum, alarm-bell, horn, siren, maroon, fog-signal, tocsin, tattoo, signal of distress, S O S, hue and cry.

False alarm, cry of wolf, bugbear, bugaboo, bogy.

(Verbs) To give, raise, or sound an alarm, to alarm, warn, ring the tocsin, dial 999; to cry wolf.

(Adjectives) Alarming, etc., threatening.

(Phrases) Each for himself; *sauve qui peut.*

670 Preservation *(Substantives)*, conservation, maintenance (141), support, upkeep, sustentation, deliverance, salvation, rescue, redemption, self-preservation, continuance (143).

Means of preservation, prophylaxis, preservative, preserver.

(Verbs) To preserve, maintain, support, keep, sustain, nurse, save, rescue, file (papers).

To embalm, mummify, dry, dehydrate, cure, kipper, smoke, salt, pickle, marinade, season, kyanize, bottle, pot, can, tin.

(Adjectives) Preserving, conservative, prophylactic, preservatory, hygienic.

Preserved, intact, unimpaired, uninjured, unhurt, unsinged, unmarred.

671 Escape *(Substantives)*, getaway, flight, elopement, evasion, retreat, reprieve, reprieval, deliverance, redemption, rescue.

Narrow escape, hair's-breadth, escape, close shave, close call, narrow squeak.

Means of escape: Bridge, drawbridge, loophole, ladder, plank, stepping-stone, trap-door, fire-escape, emergency exit.

A fugitive, runaway, refugee, evacuee.

(Verbs) To escape, elude, evade, wriggle out of, make or effect one's escape, make off, march off, pack off, skip, skip off, slip away, steal away, slink away, flit, decamp, run away, abscond, levant, skedaddle, scoot, fly, flee, bolt, bunk, scarper, scram, hop it, beat it, vamoose, elope, whip off, break loose, break away, get clear.

(Phrases) To take oneself off; play truant; to beat a retreat; to give one the slip; to slip the collar; to slip through the fingers; to make oneself scarce; to fly the coop; to take to one's heels; to show a clean pair of heels; to take French leave; to do a bunk; to do a guy; to cut one's lucky; to cut and run; to live to fight another day; to run for one's life; to make tracks.

(Interjections) Sauve qui peut! the devil take the hindmost!

(Adjectives) Escaping, etc., escaped, etc., runaway.

(Phrase) The bird having flown.

672 Deliverance *(Substantives)*, extrication, rescue, reprieve, respite, redemption, salvation, riddance, release, liberation (750); redeemableness, redeemability.

(Verbs) To deliver, extricate, rescue, save, redeem, ransom, help out, bring off, *tirer d'affaire*, to get rid, to work off, to rid.

(Phrases) To save one's bacon; to find a hole to creep out of.

(Adjectives) Delivered, saved, etc., scot-free, scatheless.

Extricable, redeemable, rescuable.

3°. *Precursory Measures*

673 Preparation *(Substantives)*, making ready, providing, provision, providence, anticipation, preconcertation, rehearsal, precaution; laying foundations, ploughing, sowing, semination, cooking, brewing, digestion,

674 Non-preparation *(Substantives)*, want or absence of preparation, inculture, inconcoction, improvidence.

Immaturity, crudeness, crudity, greenness, rawness, disqualification.

gestation, hatching, incubation, concoction, maturation, elaboration, predisposition, premeditation (611), acclimatization (613).

Physical preparation, training, drill, drilling, discipline, exercise, exercitation, gymnastics, callisthenics, eurhythmics, athletics, gymnasium, *palaestra*, prenticeship, apprenticeship, qualification, inurement, education, novitiate (537).

Putting or setting in order, putting to rights, clearance, arrangement, disposal, organization, adjustment, adaptation, disposition, accommodation, putting in tune, tuning, putting in trim, dressing, putting in harness, outfit, equipment, accoutrement, armament.

Groundwork, basis, foundation, pedestal, etc. (215), stepping-stone, first stone, scaffold, scaffolding, cradle, sketch (626).

State of being prepared, preparedness, ripeness, maturity, readiness, mellowness.

Preparer, pioneer, avant-courier, sappers and miners.

(Phrases) A stitch in time; clearing decks; a note of preparation; a breather; a trial bout; a practice swing.

(Verbs) To prepare, get ready, make ready, get up, anticipate, forecast, preestablish, preconcert, settle preliminaries, to found.

To arrange, set or put in order, set or put to rights, organize, dispose, cast the parts, mount, adjust, adapt, accommodate, trim, tidy, fit, predispose, inure, elaborate, mature, mellow, season, ripen, nurture, hatch, cook, concoct, brew, tune, put in tune, attune, set, temper, anneal, smelt, undermine, brush up, get up.

To provide, provide against, discount, make provision, keep on foot, take precautions, make sure, lie in wait for (507).

To equip, arm, man, fit out, fit up, furnish, rig, dress, dress up, furbish up, accoutre, array, fettle, vamp up, wind up.

To train, drill, discipline, break in, cradle, inure, habituate, harden, caseharden, season, acclimatize, qualify, educate, teach.

(Phrases) To take steps; prepare the ground; lay or fix the foundations,

Absence of art, state of nature, virgin soil.

An embryo, skeleton, rough copy, draft (626); germ, rudiment (153), raw material, rough diamond.

Tyro, beginner, novice, neophyte, greenhorn, new chum, pommy, recruit, sprog.

(Verbs) To be unprepared, etc., to want or lack preparation.

To improvise, extemporize (612).

To render unprepared, etc., to dismantle, dismount, dismast, disqualify, disable (645), unrig, undress (226).

(Phrases) To put *hors de combat*; to put out of gear; to spike the guns; to remove the sparking-plug.

(Adjectives) Unprepared, rudimentary, immature, embryonic, unripe, raw, green, crude, rough, roughcast, rough-hewn, unformed, unhatched, unfledged, unnurtured, uneducated, unlicked, unpolished, natural, in a state of nature, *au naturel*, unwrought, unconcocted, undigested, indigested, unrevised, unblown, unfashioned, unlaboured, unleavened, fallow, uncultivated, unsown, untilled, untrained, undrilled, unexercised, unseasoned, disqualified, unqualified, out of order, unseaworthy.

Unbegun, unready, unarranged, unorganized, unfurnished, unprovided, unequipped, undressed, in dishabille, dismantled, untrimmed.

Shiftless, improvident, unguarded, happy-go-lucky, feckless, thoughtless, unthrifty.

Unpremeditated, unseen, off-hand (612), from hand to mouth, extempore (111).

(Phrases) Caught on the hop; with their trousers down.

———

the basis, groundwork, etc.; to clear the ground or way or course; clear decks; clear for action; close one's ranks; plough the ground; dress the ground; till the soil; sow the seed; open the way; pave the way; lay a train; dig a mine; prepare a charge; erect the scaffolding; *reculer pour mieux sauter*.

Put in harness; sharpen one's tools; whet the knife; shoulder arms; put the horses to; oil up; crank up; warm up.

To prepare oneself; lay oneself out for; get into harvest; gird up one's loins; buckle on one's armour; serve one's time or apprenticeship; be at one's post; gather oneself together.

To set on foot; to lay the first stone; to break ground.

To erect the scaffold; to cut one's coat according to one's cloth; to keep one's powder dry; to beat up for recruits; to sound the note of preparation.

(Adjectives) Preparing, etc., in preparation, in course of preparation, in hand, in train, brewing, hatching, forthcoming, in embryo, afoot, afloat, on the anvil, on the carpet, on the stocks, *sur le tapis*.

Preparative, preparatory, provisional, in the rough, rough and ready (111).

Prepared, trained, drilled, etc., forearmed, ready, in readiness, ripe, mature, mellow, fledged, ready to one's hand, on tap, cut and dried, annealed, concocted, laboured, elaborated, planned (626).

(Phrases) Armed to the teeth; armed cap-à-pie; booted and spurred; in full feather; *in utrumque paratus*; in working order.

(Adverbs) In preparation, in anticipation of, etc., against.

675 Essay *(Substantives)*, endeavour, try, trial, experiment (463), probation, attempt (676), venture, adventure, tentative, *ballon d'essai*, *coup d'essai*, go crack, whack, slap, shot, speculation.

(Verbs) To try, essay, make trial of, try on, experiment, make an experiment, endeavour, strive, attempt, grope, feel one's way; to venture, adventure, speculate, take upon oneself.

(Phrases) To put out or throw out a feeler; to tempt fortune; to fly a kite; to send up a pilot balloon; to fish for information, compliments, etc.; to have a crack at; to try one's luck; to chance it; to risk it.

(Adjectives) Essaying, etc., experimental, tentative, empirical, on trial, probative, probatory, probationary.

(Adverbs) Experimentally, etc., at a venture.

676 Undertaking *(Substantives)*, enterprise, emprise, quest, mission, endeavour, attempt, move, first move, the initiative, first step.

(Verbs) To undertake, take in hand, set about, go about, set to, fall to, set to work, engage in, launch into, embark in, plunge into, take on, set one's hand to, tackle, grapple with, volunteer, take steps, launch out.

To endeavour, strive, use one's endeavours; to attempt, make an attempt, tempt.

To begin, set on foot, set agoing, take the first step.

(Phrases) To break the neck of the business; take the initiative; to get cracking; to break ground; break the ice; break cover; to pass the Rubicon; to take upon oneself; to take on one's shoulders; to put one's shoulder to the wheel; *ce n'est que le premier pas qui coûte*; well begun is half done.

To take the bull by the horns; to rush *in medias res*; to have too many irons in the fire; to attempt impossibilities.

(Adverbs) Undertaking, attempting, etc.

677 Use *(Substantives)*, employment, employ, application, appliance, adhibition, disposal, exercise, exercitation.

Recourse, resort, avail, service, wear, usage, conversion to use, usufruct, utilization.

Agency (170); usefulness (644).

(Verbs) To use, make use of, utilize, exploit, employ (134), apply, adhibit, dispose of, work, wield, manipulate, handle, put to use; turn or convert to use; avail oneself of, resort to, have recourse to, take up with, betake oneself to.

To render useful, serviceable, available, etc.; to utilize, draw, call forth, tax, task, try, exert, exercise, practise, ply, work up, consume, absorb, expend.

To be useful, to serve one's turn (644).

(Phrases) To take advantage of; to turn to account; to make the most of; to make the best of; to bring to bear upon; to fall back upon; to press or enlist into the service; to make shift with; make a cat's-paw of.

To pull the strings or wires; put in action; set to work; set in motion; put in practice.

(Adjectives) Used, employed, etc., applied, exercised, tried, etc.

---

678 Disuse *(Substantives)*, forbearance, abstinence, dispensation, desuetude (614), relinquishment, abandonment (624, 782).

(Verbs) To disuse, not to use, to do without, to dispense with, neglect, to let alone, to spare, waive.

To lay by; set, put, or lay aside, to discard, dismiss (756); cast off, throw off, turn off, turn out, turn away, throw away, scrap, dismantle, shelve (133), shunt, side-track, get rid of, do away with; to keep back (636).

(Phrases) To lay on the shelf; to lay up in a napkin; to consign to the scrapheap; to cast, heave, or throw overboard; to cast to the winds; to turn out neck and crop; to send to the right-about; to send packing.

(Adjectives) Disused, etc., not used, unused, unutilized, done with, unemployed, unapplied, unspent, unexercised, kept or held back.

Unessayed, untouched, uncalled-for, ungathered, unculled, untrodden.

679 Misuse *(Substantives)*, misusage, misemployment, misapplication, misappropriation, abuse, profanation, prostitution, desecration.

Waste (818), wasting, spilling, exhaustion (638).

(Verbs) To misuse, misemploy, misapply, misappropriate, desecrate, abuse, profane, prostitute.

To waste, spill, fritter away, exhaust, throw or fling away, squander (818).

(Phrases) To waste powder and shot; cut blocks with a razor; cast pearls before swine.

(Adjectives) Misused, etc.

SECTION III—VOLUNTARY ACTION

1°. *Simple Voluntary Action*

680 Action *(Substantives)*, performance, work, operation, execution, perpetration, proceeding, procedure, *démarche*, process, handiwork, handicraft, workmanship, manœuvre, evolution, transaction, bout, turn,

681 Inaction *(Substantives)*, abstinence from action, inactivity (683), non-intervention, non-interference, neutrality, strike, Fabian tactics.

(Verbs) Not to do, to let be, abstain from doing; let or leave alone, refrain,

job, doings, dealings, business, affair.

Deed, act, overt act, touch, move, strike, blow, *coup*, feat, stunt, exploit, passage, measure, step, stroke of policy, *tour de force, coup de main, coup d'état.*

(Verbs) To act, do, work, operate, do or transact business, practise, prosecute, perpetrate, perform, execute (729), officiate, exercise, commit, inflict, strike a blow, handle, take in hand, put in hand, run.

To labour, drudge, toil, ply, set to work, pull the oar, serve, officiate, go about, turn one's hand to, dabble; to have in hand.

(Phrases) To have a finger in the pie; to take or play a part; to set to work; to put into execution (729); to lay one's hand to the plough; to ply one's task; to get on with the job; to discharge an office.

(Adjectives) Acting, etc., in action, in operation, etc., operative, in harness, in play, on duty, on foot, at work, red-handed.

(Interjection) Here goes!

desist, keep oneself from doing; let pass, lie by, let be, wait.

To undo, take down, take or pull to pieces, do away with.

(Phrases) To bide one's time; to let well alone; to cool one's heels; to stay one's hand; to wash one's hands of; to strike work; nothing doing; *nihil fit; dolce far niente.*

(Adjectives) Not doing, not done, let alone, undone, etc.; passive, neutral.

———

682 Activity *(Substantives)*, briskness, quickness, promptness, promptitude, expedition, dispatch, readiness, alertness, smartness, sharpness, nimbleness, agility (274).

Spirit, ardour, animation, life liveliness, vivacity, eagerness, *empressement, brio,* dash, *élan,* abandon, pep, go, alacrity, zeal, push, vim, energy (171), hustle, vigour, intentness.

Wakefulness, pervigilium, insomnia, sleeplessness.

Industry, assiduity, assiduousness, sedulity, sedulousness, diligence; perseverance, persistence, plodding, painstaking, drudgery, busyness, indefatigability, indefatigableness, patience, business habits.

Movement, bustle, commotion, stir, fuss, fluster, bother, pother, ado, fidget, restlessness, fidgetiness.

Officiousness, meddling, interference, interposition, intermeddling, tampering with, intrigue, *tripotage,* supererogation.

A man of action, busy bee, busybody, go-getter, zealot, devotee, meddler, hustler, whizz-kid.

(Phrases) The thick of the action; *in medias res;* too many cooks; new

683 Inactivity *(Substantives)*, inaction (681), idleness, sloth, laziness, indolence, inertness, inertia (172), lumpishness, supineness, sluggishness, segnitude, languor, torpor, quiescence, stagnation, lentor, limpness, listlessness, remissness, slackness.

Dilatoriness, cunctation, procrastination (133), relaxation, truancy, lagging, dawdling, rust, rustiness, want of occupation, resourcelessness.

Somnolence, drowsiness, doziness, nodding, oscitation, sleepiness, hypnosis.

Hypnology.

Sleep, nap, doze, slumber, shut-eye, bye-bye, snooze, dog-sleep, cat-nap, siesta, dream, faint, swoon, coma, trance, hypnotic state, snore, a wink of sleep, lethargy, hibernation, aestivation.

An idler, laggard, truant, do-nothing, lubber, sluggard, sleepy-head, slumberer, faineant, *flâneur,* loafer, drone, dormouse, slow-coach, stick-in-the-mud, lounger, slug, sundowner, bum, Weary Willie, lazybones, lotus-eater, slacker, trifler, dilettante.

brooms sweep clean; too many irons in the fire.

(Verbs) To be active, busy, stirring, etc., to busy oneself in, stir, bestir oneself, bustle, fuss, make a fuss, speed, hasten, push, make a push, go ahead, hustle; to industrialize.

To plod, drudge, keep on, hold on, persist, persevere, fag at, hammer at, peg away, stick to, buckle to, stick to work, take pains; to take or spend time in; to make progress.

To meddle, moil, intermeddle, interfere, interpose, kibitz, tamper with, fool with, get at, nobble, agitate, intrigue.

To overact, overdo, overlay, outdo, ride to death.

(Phrases) To look sharp; to lay about one; to have one's hands full; to kick up a dust; to stir one's stumps; to exert one's energies; to put one's best foot foremost; to do one's best; to do all one can; to leave no stone unturned; to have all one's eyes about one; make the best of one's time; not to let the grass grow under one's feet; to make short work of; to seize the opportunity; to come up to the scratch.

To take time by the forelock; to improve the shining hour; to make hay while the sun shines; to keep the pot boiling; to strike while the iron is hot; to kill two birds with one stone; to move heaven and earth; to go through fire and water; to do wonders; to go all lengths; to stick at nothing; to go the whole hog; to keep the ball rolling; to put one's back into it; to make things hum.

To have a hand in; to poke one's nose in; to put in one's oar; to have a finger in the pie; to mix oneself up with; steal a march upon.

(Adjectives) Active, brisk, quick, prompt, alert, on the alert, stirring, spry, sharp, smart, quick, nimble, agile, light-footed, tripping, ready, awake, broad awake, wide awake, alive, lively, live, animated, vivacious, frisky, forward, eager, strenuous, zealous, expeditious, enterprising, pushing, pushful, spirited, in earnest, up in arms, go-ahead.

Cause of inactivity (174), sedative, hypnotic, knock-out drops, hypnotism; lullaby.

(Phrases) The Castle of Indolence; *dolce far niente*; the Land of Nod; the Fabian policy; *laissez aller; laissez faire*; masterly inactivity; the thief of time.

Sleeping partner; waiter on Providence.

(Verbs) To be inactive, etc., to do nothing, let alone, lie by, lie idle, stagnate, lay to, keep quiet, hang fire, relax, slouch, loll, drawl, slug, dally, lag, dawdle, potter, lounge, loiter, laze, moon, moon about, loaf, hang about, stooge, mouch; to waste, lose, idle away, kill, trifle away, fritter away or fool away time; trifle, footle, dabble, fribble, peddle, fiddle-faddle.

To sleep, slumber, nod, close the eyes, close the eyelids, doze, drowse, fall asleep, take a nap, go off to sleep, hibernate, aestivate, vegetate.

To languish, expend itself, flag, hang fire.

To render idle, etc.; to sluggardize.

(Phrases) To fold one's arms; to let well alone; play truant; while away the time; to rest upon one's oars; to burn daylight; to take it easy; slack off.

To get one's head down; to hit the hay; to have forty winks; to sleep like a top or like a log; to sleep like a dormouse; to swing the lead; to eat the bread of idleness; to twiddle one's thumbs.

(Adjectives) Inactive, unoccupied, unemployed, unbusied, doing nothing (685), resourceless.

Indolent, easy-going, lazy, slothful, idle, thowless, fushionless, slack, inert, torpid, sluggish, languid, supine, heavy, dull, stagnant, lumpish, soulless, listless, moony, limp, languorous, exanimate.

Dilatory, laggard, lagging, tardigrade, drawling, creeping, dawdling, faddling, rusty, lackadaisical, fiddle-faddle, shilly-shally, unpractical, unbusiness-like.

Sleepy, dozy, dopy, dreamy, drowsy, somnolent, dormant, asleep,

Working, on duty, at work, hard at work, intent, industrious, up and coming, assiduous, diligent, sedulous, painstaking, business-like, practical, in harness, operose, plodding, toiling, hard-working, fagging, busy, bustling, restless, fussy, fidgety.

Persevering, indefatigable, untiring, unflagging, unremitting, unwearied, never-tiring, undrooping, unintermitting, unintermittent, unflinching, unsleeping, unslumbering, sleepless, persistent.

Meddling, meddlesome, pushing, intermeddling, tampering, etc., officious, over-officious, intriguing, managing.

(Phrases) Up and doing; up and stirring; busy as a bee; on the *qui vive*; nimble as a squirrel; the fingers itching; no sooner said than done; *nulla dies sine linea*; a rolling stone gathers no moss; the used key is always bright.

(Adverbs) Actively, etc. (684).

(Interjections) Look alive! look sharp! get a move on! get cracking! get busy! hump yourself! get weaving!

lethargic, comatose, napping, somniferous, soporific, soporous, soporose, somnific, hypnotic, narcotic, unawakened.

(Phrases) With folded arms; *les bras croisés*, with the hands in the pockets; at a loose end.

In the arms or lap of Morpheus.

---

684 Haste *(Substantives)*, dispatch, precipitancy, precipitation, precipitousness, impetuosity, post-haste, acceleration, spurt, quickness (274).

Hurry, flurry, drive, bustle, fuss, splutter, scramble, brusquerie, fidget, fidgetiness (682).

(Verbs) To haste, hasten, urge, press on, push on, bustle, hurry, hustle, buck up, precipitate, accelerate; to bustle, scramble, scuttle, scurry, scoot, plunge, rush, dash on, press on, scorch, speed.

(Phrases) To make the most of one's time; to lose not a moment; *festina lente.*

(Adjectives) Hasty, hurried, precipitate, scrambling, etc., headlong, boisterous, impetuous, brusque, abrupt, slapdash, cursory.

(Adverbs) Hastily, etc., headlong, in haste, slapdash, slap-bang, amain, hurry-scurry, helter-skelter, head and shoulders, head over heels, by fits and starts, by spurts.

(Phrases) No sooner said than done; a word and a blow.

685 Leisure *(Substantives)*, leisureliness, spare time, breathing-space, off-time, slack time, holiday, bank holiday, Sunday, sabbath, vacation, recess, red-letter day, relaxation, rest, repose, halt, pause (142), respite.

(Phrases) Otium cum dignitate; time to spare; time on one's hands.

(Verbs) To have leisure, take one's ease, repose (687), pause.

(Phrase) To shut up shop.

(Adjectives) Leisurely, undisturbed, quiet, deliberate, calm, slow (683).

(Adverbs) Leisurely, etc., at leisure.

---

686 Exertion *(Substantives)*, labour, work, toil, fag, exercise, travail, swink, sweat, exercitation, duty, trouble, pains, ado, drudgery, fagging, slavery, operoseness.

Effort, strain, grind, tug, stress,

687 Repose *(Substantives)*, rest, halt, pause, relaxation, breathing-space, respite (685).

Day of rest, *dies non*, sabbath, holiday.

(Verbs) To repose, rest, relax, take

tension, throw, stretch, struggle, spell, heft.

Gymnastics, gym, physical jerks; P.T.

(Phrases) A stroke of work; the sweat of one's brow.

(Verbs) To labour, work, exert oneself, toil, strive, use exertion, fag, strain, drudge, moil, take pains, take trouble, trouble oneself, slave, pull, tug, ply the oar, rough it, sweat, bestir oneself, get up steam, get a move on, fall to work, buckle to, stick to.

(Phrases) To set one's shoulder to the wheel; to strain every nerve; to spare no pains; to do one's utmost or damnedest; to work day and night; to work one's fingers to the bone; to do double duty; to work double tides; to put forth one's strength; to work like a nigger or a horse; to go through fire and water; to put one's best foot forward (682); to do one's level best, grub along; to lay oneself out, lean over backwards.

(Adjectives) Labouring, etc., laborious, toilsome, troublesome, operose, herculean, gymnastic, palaestric.

Hard-working, painstaking, energetic, strenuous (682).

(Adverbs) Laboriously, lustily, roundly.

(Phrases) By the sweat of the brow; with all one's might; *totis viribus*; with might and main; *vi et armis*; tooth and nail; hammer and tongs; through thick and thin; heart and soul.

rest, breathe, take breath, take one's ease, gather breath, recover one's breath, respire, pause, halt, stay one's hand, lay to, lie by, lie fallow, recline, lie down, go to rest, go to bed, go to sleep, etc., unbend, slacken.

(Phrases) To rest upon one's oars, to take a holiday; to shut up shop.

(Adjectives) Reposing, resting, etc., restful, unstrained; sabbatical.

---

688 Fatigue *(Substantives)*, lassitude, weariness (841), tiredness, exhaustion, sweat, collapse, prostration, swoon, faintness, faint, *deliquium*, syncope, yawning, anhelation; overstrain.

(Verbs) To be fatigued, etc., to droop, sink, flag, wilt, lose breath, lose wind, gasp, pant, pech, puff, yawn, drop, swoon, faint, succumb.

To fatigue, tire, weary, fag, irk, jade, harass, exhaust, knock up, prostrate, wear out, strain, overtask, overwork, overburden, overtax, overstrain, drive, sweat.

(Adjectives) Fatigued, tired, unrefreshed, weary, wearied, jaded; wayworn; overworked, hard-driven, toilworn, done up.

Breathless, out of breath, windless, out of wind, blown, winded, broken-winded.

Drooping, flagging, faint, fainting, done up, knocked up, exhausted, sinking, prostrate, spent, overspent, dead-beat, dog-tired, fagged out.

Worn out, played out, battered, shattered, weather-beaten, footsore, *hors de combat*, done for.

Fatiguing, etc., tiresome, irksome, wearisome, trying.

(Phrases) Ready to drop; tired to death; on one's last legs; run off one's legs; all in.

689 Refreshment *(Substantives)*, recovery of strength, recruiting, repair, refection, refocillation, relief, bracing, regalement, bait, restoration, revival; pick-up.

(Phrase) A giant refreshed.

(Verbs) To refresh, recruit, repair, refocillate, give tone, reinvigorate, reanimate, restore, recover.

To recover, regain, renew, etc., one's strength; perk up.

(Adjectives) Refreshing, etc., recuperative, tonic; refreshed, etc., untired, unwearied, etc. (682).

---

690 Agent *(Substantives)*, doer, performer, actor, perpetrator, practitioner, operator, hand, employee, commissionaire, executor, executrix, maker, effector, consignee, steward, broker, factor, middleman, jobber.

Artist, workman, workwoman, charwoman, worker, artisan, artificer, architect, craftsman, handicraftsman, mechanic, roustabout, machinist, machineman, manufacturer, operative, journeyman, labourer, navvy, stevedore, docker, smith, wright, day-labourer, co-worker; *dramatis personae.*

Drudge, hack, fag, man or maid of all work, hired man, hired girl, factotum, handy-man.

(Phrase) Hewers of wood and drawers of water.

691 Workshop *(Substantives)*, laboratory, manufactory, mill, shop, works, factory, mint, forge, smithy, loom, cabinet, office, bureau, studio, atelier, hive, hive of industry, workhouse, nursery, hothouse, hotbed, kitchen, dock, slip, yard, foundry.

Crucible, alembic, cauldron, matrix.

2°. Complex Voluntary Action

692 Conduct *(Substantives)*, course of action, practice, drill, procedure, business (625), transaction, dealing, ways, tactics, policy, polity, generalship, statesmanship, economy, strategy, husbandry, seamanship, stewardship, housekeeping, housewifery, *ménage*, regime, *modus operandi*, economy.

Execution, manipulation, handling, treatment, process, working-out, course, campaign, career, walk.

Behaviour, deportment, comportment, carriage, mien, air, demeanour, bearing, manner, observance.

(Verbs) To conduct, carry on, run, transact, execute, carry out, work out, get through, carry through, go through, dispatch, treat, deal with, proceed with, officiate, discharge, do duty, play a part or game, run a race.

To behave; to comport, acquit, demean, carry, hold, oneself.

(Phrases) To shape one's course; to paddle one's own canoe.

(Adjectives) Conducting, etc., strategical, business-like, practical, executive.

693 Direction *(Substantives)*, management, government, bureaucracy, statesmanship, conduct (692), regulation, charge, agency, senatorship, ministry, ministration, managery, directorate, directorship, chairmanship, guidance, steerage, pilotage, superintendence, stewardship, supervision, surveillance, proctorship, chair, portfolio, statecraft, politics, *haute politique*, kingcraft, cybernetics; council (696).

Helm, rudder, compass, needle, radar.

(Phrase) The reins of government.

(Verbs) To direct, manage, govern, guide, conduct, regulate, order, prescribe, brief, steer, con, pilot, have or take the direction, take the helm, have the charge of, administer, superintend, overlook, supervise, look after, see to, control, boss, run, preside, hold office, hold the portfolio.

To head, lead, show the way, etc.

(Phrase) To pull the wires.

(Adjectives) Directing, etc., managerial, gubernatorial, executive; dirigible.

694 Director *(Substantives)*, manager, executive, master (745), prime minister, premier, governor, statesman, legislator, controller, comptroller, intendent, superintendent, rector, matron, supervisor, president, preses, chairman, headman, supercargo, inspector, moderator, monitor, overseer, overlooker, shopwalker, taskmaster, leader, ringleader, demagogue, conductor, precentor, fugleman, official, jack-in-office, bureaucrat, minister, office-bearer, red-tapist, officer (726).

Conductor, steersman, helmsman, pilot, coxswain, guide, cicerone, guard, driver, engine-driver, motorman, whip, charioteer, coachman, Jehu, muleteer, teamster, chauffeur, postilion, *vetturino*.

Steward, factor, factotum, bailiff, landreeve, foreman, forewoman, gaffer, charge-hand, whipper-in, shepherd, proctor, procurator, housekeeper, major-domo, chef, master of ceremonies, M.C.

695 Advice (*Substantives*), counsel, suggestion, recommendation, advocacy, hortation, exhortation, dehortation, instruction, charge, monition, admonition (668), admonishment, caution, warning, expostulation (616), obtestation, injunction, persuasion.

Guidance, guide, handbook, chart, compass, manual, itinerary, road-book, reference.

An adviser, senator, counsellor, counsel, consultant, specialist, monitor, mentor, Nestor, guide, teacher (540), physician, leech, doctor.

Referee, arbiter, arbitrator, referendary, assessor.

(*Verbs*) To advise, counsel, give advice, recommend, advocate, admonish, submonish, suggest, prompt, caution, warn, forewarn.

To persuade, dehort, exhort, enjoin, expostulate, charge, instruct.

To deliberate, consult together, hold a council, etc., confer, call in, refer to take advice, be closeted with.

(*Phrases*) To lay their heads together; to compare notes; to go into a huddle; to take counsel of one's pillow; to take one's cue from.

(*Adjectives*) Monitory, monitive, admonitory, recommendatory, hortatory, dehortatory, exhortatory, exhortative, warning, etc.

(*Phrases*) A word to the wise; *verb sap.*

(*Interjection*) Go to!

696 Council (*Substantives*), conclave, court, chamber, cabinet, cabinet council, house, committee, subcommittee, board, bench, brains trust, *comitia*, staff.

Senate, *senatus*, parliament, synod, soviet, convocation, convention, congress, consistory, conventicle, chapter, chapel, witenagemot, junta, states-general, diet, Cortes, Riksdag, Thing, Storthing, Reichsrat, Reichstag, Duma, Politburo, Presidium, Comintern, Sobranje, Skupshtina, Tynewald, divan, durbar, kgotla, indala, Areopagus, sanhedrim, directory.

A meeting, assembly, sitting, session, séance, sederunt.

(*Adjectives*) Senatorial, curule.

697 Precept (*Substantives*), direction, instruction, charge, prescript, prescription, recipe, receipt, order (741).

Rule, canon, code, formula, formulary, law, statute, act, rubric, maxim, apophthegm, etc. (496).

698 Skill (*Substantives*), skilfulness, cleverness, ability, talent, genius, ingenuity, calibre, capacity, competence, shrewdness, sagacity, parts, endowment, faculty, gift, forte, strong point, turn, invention, headpiece.

699 Unskilfulness (*Substantives*), inability, incompetence, incompetency, improficience, improficiency, infelicity, inexpertness, indexterity, unaptness, ineptitude, lefthandedness, awkwardness, maladroitness, clumsiness, gaucherie, rawness,

Address, dexterity, adroitness, aptness, aptitude, facility, felicity, knack, expertness, quickness, sharpness, resourcefulness, smartness, readiness, excellence, habilitation, technique, virtuosity, artistry, ambidexterity, ambidextrousness, sleight of hand (545), know-how, knowingness.

Qualification, proficiency, panurgy, accomplishment, attainment, acquirement, craft, mastery, mastership.

Tact, knowledge of the world, *savoir faire*, discretion, finesse, worldly wisdom.

Prudence, discretion (864).

Art, science, management, tactics, manœuvring, sleight, trick, policy, strategy, jobbery, temporization, technology.

A masterstroke, *chef-d'œuvre*, a masterpiece, *tour de force*, a bold stroke, *coup de maître*, a good hit (650).

(*Verbs*) To be skilful, skilled, etc., to excel in, to specialize in, have the trick of, be master of; to temporize, manœuvre.

(*Phrases*) To play one's cards well; to stoop to conquer; to have all one's wits about one; to keep one's hand in; to know your stuff; to cut one's coat according to one's cloth; to know what one is about; to know what's what; to know the ropes.

(*Adjectives*) Skilled, skilful, etc., clever, able, accomplished, talented, versatile, many-sided, resourceful, ingenious, inventive, shrewd, gifted, hard-headed, sagacious, sharp-witted.

Expert, crack, dexterous, scientific, adroit, apt, sharp, handy, deft, fluent, facile, ready, quick, smart, slick, spry, yare, nimble, ambidextrous, neat-handed, fine-fingered.

Conversant, versed, proficient, efficient, capable, competent, qualified, good at, up to, master of, cut out for, at home in, knowing.

Experienced, practised, hackneyed, trained, initiated, prepared, primed, finished, schooled, thoroughbred, masterly, consummate.

slovenliness, greenness, inexperience, disability, disqualification.

Bungling, blundering, etc., blunder (495), *bêtise*; unteachableness, dumbness, dullness, stupidity (499).

Indiscretion, imprudence (863), thoughtlessness, giddiness, wildness, mismanagement, misconduct, maladministration, misrule, misgovernment, misapplication, misdirection.

(*Phrases*) Rule of thumb; a bad show.

(*Verbs*) To be unskilled, unskilful, etc.

To mismanage, bungle, blunder, botch, boggle, fumble, flounder, stumble, muff, foozle, miscue, muddle, murder, mistake, misapply, misdirect, misconduct; stultify.

(*Phrases*) To make a mess or hash of; to begin at the wrong end; to make sad work or a bad job of; to put one's foot in it; to lose or miss one's way; to lose one's balance; to stand in one's own light; to quarrel with one's bread and butter; to pay dear for one's whistle; to cut one's own throat; to kill the goose which lays the golden eggs; to reckon without one's host.

(*Adjectives*) Unskilled, etc., unskilful, bungling, etc., awkward, clumsy, unhandy, unworkmanlike, unscientific, shiftless, lubberly, *gauche*, maladroit, left-handed, hobbling, slovenly, sloppy, slatternly, giddy, gawky, dumb, dull, unteachable, at fault.

Unapt, unqualified, inhabile, incompetent, disqualified, untalented, ill-qualified, inapt, inept, inexpert, inartistic, raw, green, rusty.

Unaccustomed, unused, unhackneyed, unexercised, untrained, unpractised, undisciplined, uneducated, undrilled, uninitiated, unschooled, unconversant, unversed, inexperienced, unstatesmanlike, non-professional.

Unadvised, misadvised, ill-judged, ill-advised, unguided, misguided, foolish, wild, ill-devised, misconducted.

Technical, artistic, workmanlike, business-like, daedalian.

Discreet, politic, tactful, diplomatic, sure-footed, felicitous, strategic.

(Phrases) Up to snuff; sharp as a needle; no flies on him.

(Adverbs) Skilfully, etc., aright.

700 Proficient *(Substantives)*, adept, expert, specialist, genius, dab, crack, whiz, master, *maître*, masterhand, virtuoso, champion, first string, first fiddle, protagonist, ace, artist, tactician, marksman, old stager, veteran, top-sawyer, picked man, cunning man, conjurer, wizard, etc. (994); connoisseur (850); prodigy (872), an Admirable Crichton.

(Phrases) A man of the world; a practised hand; no slouch; a smart customer; an old file; an all-round man.

702 Cunning *(Substantives)*, craft, craftiness, wiliness, artfulness, subtlety, shrewdness, smartness, archness, insidiousness, slyness, opportunism, artificialness, artificiality.

Artifice, stratagem, wile, dodge, subterfuge, evasion, finesse, ruse, diplomacy, jobbery, backstairs influence.

Duplicity, guile, circumvention, chicane, chicanery, sharp practice, Machiavellism, legerdemain, trickery, etc. (545).

Net, toils, trap, etc. (667).

A slyboots, Ulysses, Machiavel, trickster, serpent, fox, intriguer, opportunist, time-server.

(Verbs) To be cunning, etc., to contrive, design, manœuvre, gerrymander, finesse, shuffle, wriggle, wangle, intrigue, temporize, overreach (545), circumvent, get round, nobble, undermine.

(Phrases) To play a deep game; to steal a march on; to know on which side one's bread is buttered.

(Phrases) His fingers are all thumbs; penny wise and pound foolish.

———

701 Bungler *(Substantives)*, blunderer, marplot, greenhorn, lubber, landlubber, fumbler, muddler, duffer, butter-fingers, novice, no conjurer, flat, muff, babe.

(Phrases) A poor hand at; no good at; a fish out of the water; a freshwater sailor; the awkward squad; not likely to set the Thames on fire.

———

703 Artlessness *(Substantives)*, nature, naturalness, simplicity, ingenuousness, *bonhomie*, frankness, naïveté, openness, *abandon*, candour, outspokenness, sincerity, straightforwardness, honesty (939), innocence (946).

(Phrases) Enfant terrible; a rough diamond, a mere babe.

(Verbs) To be artless, etc.

(Phrases) To call a spade a spade; not to mince one's words; to speak one's mind; to wear one's heart upon one's sleeve.

(Adjectives) Artless, natural, native, plain, simple-minded, ingenuous, candid, untutored, unsophisticated, simple, naïve, sincere, frank (543), open, frank-hearted, open-hearted, above-board, downright, unreserved, guileless, inartificial, undesigning, single-minded, honest, straightforward, outspoken, blunt, matter-of-fact.

———

(Adjectives) Cunning, crafty, artful, knowing, wily, sly, fly, pawky, smooth, sharp, smart, slim, feline, subtle, arch, designing, intriguing, contriving, insidious, canny, downy, leery, tricky, deceitful (545), artificial, deep, profound, diplomatic, vulpine, Machiavellian, time-serving.

(Phrases) Cunning as a fox; too clever by half; not born yesterday; not to be caught with chaff.

SECTION IV—ANTAGONISM

1°. *Conditional Antagonism*

704 Difficulty (*Substantives*), hardness, toughness, hard work, up-hill work, hard task, troublesomeness, laboriousness.

Impracticability, infeasibility, intractability, toughness, perverseness (471).

Embarrassment, awkwardness, perplexity, intricacy, intricateness, entanglement, knot, Gordian knot, labyrinth, net, meshes, maze, etc. (248).

Dilemma, nice point, delicate point, knotty point, stumbling-block, snag, vexed question, crux; *pons asinorum*, poser, puzzle, floorer, teaser, nonplus, quandary, strait, pass, critical situation, crisis, trial, pinch, emergency, exigency, scramble.

Scrape, hobble, fix, hole, lurch, contretemps, hitch, how-d'ye-do, slough, quagmire, hot water, pickle, stew, imbroglio, mess, ado, false position, stand, deadlock, encumbrance, cul-de-sac, impasse.

(*Phrases*) A Herculean task; a labour of Sisyphus; a difficult role to play; a sea of troubles; horns of a dilemma; a peck of troubles; a kettle of fish; a pretty state of things; a handful; 'Ay, there's the rub.'

(*Verbs*) To be difficult, etc.

To meet with, experience, labour under, get into, plunge into, be surrounded by, be encompassed with, be entangled by, struggle, contend against or grapple with difficulties.

To come to a stand, to stick fast, to be set fast, to boggle, flounder, get left.

To render difficult, etc., to embarrass, perplex, put one out, bother, pose, puzzle, floor, nonplus, ravel, entangle, gravel, faze, flummox, run hard.

(*Phrases*) To come to a deadlock; to be at a loss; to get into hot water; to get into a mess; to be bunkered; to weave a tangled web; to fish in troubled waters; to buffet the waves;

705 Facility (*Substantives*), practicability, feasibility, practicableness (470).

Ease, easiness, smoothness, tractability, tractableness, ductility, flexibility, malleability, capability, disentanglement, freedom, advantage, vantage-ground.

A cinch, snap, cakewalk, walkover.

(*Phrases*) Plain sailing; smooth water; fair wind; a clear coast; a holiday task; a royal road; child's play; a soft job; a piece of cake.

(*Verbs*) To be easy, etc., to go, flow, swim, or drift with the tide or stream; to do with ease, to throw off.

To render easy, etc., to facilitate, popularize, smooth, ease, lighten, free, clear, disencumber, deobstruct, disembarrass, clear the way, smooth the way, disentangle, unclog, disengage, extricate, unravel, disburden, exonerate, emancipate, free from; to lubricate, etc. (332), relieve (834).

(*Phrases*) To have it all one's own way; to have a walk-over; to win in a canter; to make light (or nothing) of.

To leave a loophole; to open the door to; to pave the way to; to bridge over; to grease the wheels.

(*Adjectives*) Easy, facile, cushy, attainable, handy, practicable, feasible, achievable, performable, possible (470), superable, surmountable, accessible, come-at-able, get-at-able.

Easily managed or accomplished, etc., tractable, manageable, smooth, glib, pliant, yielding, malleable, ductile, flexible, plastic, submissive, docile.

At ease, free, light, unburdened, unencumbered, unloaded, disburdened, disencumbered, disembarrassed, exonerated, unrestrained, unobstructed, unimpeded, untrammelled, at home.

(*Phrases*) The coast being clear; as easy as falling off a log; like taking candy from a child.

to be put to one's shifts; not to know which way to turn; to skate over thin ice.

To lead one a pretty dance; to put a spoke in one's wheel; to leave in the lurch.

(Adjectives) Difficult, not easy, hard, stiff, troublesome, toilsome, formidable, laborious, onerous, operose, awkward, unwieldy, beset with or full of difficulties, Herculean, Sisyphean.

Unmanageable, tough, stubborn, hard to deal with, *difficile*, trying, provoking, ill-conditioned, refractory, perverse, crabbed, intractable, against the grain.

Embarrassing, perplexing, delicate, ticklish, pernickety, complicated, intricate, thorny, spiny, knotty, tricky, critical, pathless, trackless, labyrinthine.

Impracticable, not possible, impossible (471), not practicable, not feasible, unachievable, un-come-at-able, inextricable, impassable, innavigable, desperate, insuperable, insurmountable, unplayable.

In difficulty, perplexed, etc., beset, water-logged, put to it, hard put to it, run hard, hard pressed, thrown out, adrift, at fault, abroad, pushed.

Stranded, aground, stuck fast, at bay.

(Phrases) At a standstill; at a stand; up against it; up a gum-tree; out of one's depth; at the end of one's tether; in a cleft stick; on a wrong scent; driven from pillar to post; things being come to a pretty pass; at a pinch; between two stools; in the wrong box; in a fix; in a hole; in a tight place; in the cart; in the soup.

(Adverbs) With difficulty, hardly, etc., against the stream, against the grain, uphill.

Quite at home; in one's element; in smooth water; on velvet.

(Adverbs) Easily, etc., swimmingly.

———

2°. *Active Antagonism*

706 Hindrance *(Substantives)*, prevention, preclusion, impedance, retardment, retardation.

Obstruction, stoppage, interruption, interclusion, oppilation, interception, restriction, restraint, inhibition, embargo, blockade, embarrassment.

Interference, interposition, obtrusion, discouragement, chill.

An impediment, hindrance, obstacle, obstruction, bunker, hazard, let, stumbling-block, snag, check, impasse, countercheck, *contretemps*, set-back, hitch, bar, barrier, barrage, barricade, turnpike, dead wall, bulkhead, portcullis, etc. (717), dam, weir, broom, turnstile, tourniquet.

Drawback, objection.

An encumbrance, impedimenta, onus, clog, skid, drag, weight, dead weight, lumber, top-hamper, pack, millstone, incubus, nightmare; trammel, etc. (752).

707 Aid *(Substantives)*, assistance, help, succour, support, advocacy, relief, advance, furtherance, promotion.

Coadjuvancy, patronage, interest, championship, countenance, favour, helpfulness.

Sustentation, subvention, subsidy, alimentation, nutrition, nourishment, ministration, ministry, accommodation.

Supplies, reinforcements, succours, contingents, recruits; physical support (215); relief, rescue.

(Phrases) Corn in Egypt; a *deus ex machina*.

(Verbs) To aid, assist, help, succour, support, sustain, uphold, subscribe to, finance, promote, further, abet, advance, foster, cherish, foment; to give, bring, furnish, afford or supply support, etc., to reinforce, recruit, nourish, nurture.

A hinderer, marplot; killjoy, interloper, passenger; opponent (710).

(Phrases) A lion in the path; a millstone round one's neck; a wet blanket; the old man of the sea; *damnosa hereditas*; back to square one.

(Verbs) To hinder, impede, prevent, preclude, retard, slacken, obviate, forefend, avert, turn aside, ward off, draw off, cut off, counteract, undermine.

To obstruct, stop, stay, let, make against, bar, debar, inhibit, scotch, squash, cramp, restrain, check, stonewall, set back, discourage, discountenance, foreclose.

To thwart, traverse, contravene, interrupt, intercept, interclude, frustrate, defeat, disconcert, embarrass, baffle, undo, intercept; to balk, unsight, cushion, stymie, spoil, mar.

To interpose, interfere, intermeddle, obtrude (682).

To hamper, clog, cumber, encumber, saddle with, load with, overload, overlay, lumber, block up, incommode, hustle; to curb, shackle, fetter; to embog.

(Phrases) To lay under restraint; to tie the hands; to keep in swaddling-bands.

To stand in the way of; to take the wind out of one's sails; to break in upon; to run or fall foul of; to put a spoke in the wheel; to throw cold water on; to nip in the bud; to apply the closure.

(Adjectives) Hindering, etc., in the way of, impedimental, inimical, unfavourable, onerous, burdensome, cumbrous, intercipient, obstructive.

Hindered, etc., wind-bound, storm-stayed, water-logged, heavy-laden.

Unassisted, unaided, unhelped, unsupported, single-handed, unbefriended.

(Phrase) Prevention is better than cure.

To favour, countenance, befriend, smile upon, encourage, patronize, make interest for.

To second, stand by, relieve, rescue, back, back up, take part with, side with, to come or pass over to, to join, to rally round, play up to.

To serve, do service, minister to, oblige, humour, cheer, accommodate, work for, administer to, pander to; to tend, attend, take care of, wait on, nurse, dry-nurse, entertain.

To speed, expedite, forward, quicken, hasten, set forward.

(Phrases) To take the part of; consult the wishes of; to take up the cudgels for; to espouse the cause of; to enlist under the banners of; to lend or bear a hand; to hold out a helping hand; to give one a lift; to do one a good turn; to see one through; to take in tow; to pay the piper; to help a lame dog over the stile; to give a leg-up.

(Adjectives) Aiding, helping, assisting, etc., auxiliary, adjuvant, ancillary, accessory, ministrant, subservient, subsidiary, helpful.

Friendly, amicable, favourable, propitious, well-disposed, neighbourly.

(Adverbs) On or in behalf of; in the service of; under the auspices of; hand in hand.

(Interjections) Help! save us! *à moi!*

---

708 Opposition *(Substantives)*, antagonism, oppugnancy, oppugnation, counteraction (179), contravention, impugnment, control, clashing, collision, competition, conflict, rivalry, emulation.

Absence of aid, etc., counterplot (718).

(Phrase) A head wind.

709 Co-operation *(Substantives)*, coadjuvancy, collaboration, concert, collusion, participation, complicity, co-efficiency, concurrence (178).

Alliance, colleagueship, freemasonry, joint-stock, co-partnership, coalition, combine, syndicate (778), amalgamation, federation, confederation (712).

(Verbs) To oppose, antagonize, cross, counteract, control, contravene, countervail, counterwork, contradict, belie, controvert, oppugn, stultify, thwart, counter, countermine, run counter, go against, collide with, clash, rival, emulate, put against, militate against, beat against, stem, breast, encounter, compete with, withstand, to face, face down.

(Phrases) To set one's face against; to make a dead set against; to match (or pit) oneself against; to stand out against; to fly in the face of; to fall foul of; to come into collision with; to be or to play at cross-purposes; to kick against the pricks; to buffet the waves; to cut one another's throats; to join issue.

(Adjectives) Opposing, etc., adverse, antagonistic, opposed, conflicting, contrary, unfavourable, unfriendly, hostile, inimical; competitive, emulous.

(Phrases) Up in arms; at daggers drawn.

(Phrases) A helping hand; a long pull.

(Verbs) To co-operate, combine, concur, conspire, concert, collaborate, draw or pull together, to join with, collude, unite one's efforts, club together, fraternize, be in league, etc., with, be a party to, to side with.

(Phrases) To make common cause; to be in the same boat; to stand shoulder to shoulder; to play into the hands of; to hunt in couples; to hit it off together; to lay their heads together; to play ball.

(Adjectives) Co-operating, etc., co-operative, co-operant, in co-operation, etc., in concert, allied, clannish; favourable (707).

Unopposed, unobstructed, unimpeded.

(Phrase) Wind and weather permitting.

(Adverbs) As one man (488).

(Adverbs) Against, versus, counter to, against the grain; against the stream, tide, wind, etc., in the way of, in spite of, in despite of, in the teeth of, in the face of, *per contra*; single-handed.

Across, athwart, overthwart.

Though, although, (179), even, *quand même*, all the same.

(Phrases) In spite of one's teeth; with the wind in one's teeth.

710 Opponent *(Substantives)*, antagonist, adversary, adverse party, opposition, rival, competitor, pacemaker, enemy, foe (891), assailant; malcontent.

711 Auxiliary *(Substantives)*, assistant, adjuvant, adjunct, adjutant, help, helper, helpmate, helpmeet, colleague, partner, side-kick, *confrère,* coadjutor, co-operator collaborator, co-belligerent, ally, aide-de-camp, accomplice, accessory, stand-in, stooge.

Friend (890), confidant, champion, partisan, right hand, stand-by; adherent, *particeps criminis,* confederate, bottle-holder, second, candle-holder, servant (746); *fidus Achates.*

(Phrase) Deus ex machina.

712 Party *(Substantives)*, side, partnership, fraternity, sodality, company, society, firm, house, establishment, body, corporation, corporate body, union, association, syndicate, guild, tong, joint concern, combine, trust, cartel.

Fellowship, brotherhood, sisterhood, denomination, communion, community, clan, clanship, club, friendly society, clique, junto, coterie, faction, gang, ring, circle, *camarilla,* cabal, league, confederacy, confederation, federation; *esprit de corps*; alliance, partisanship.

Band, staff, crew, team, set, posse, phalanx, *dramatis personae.*

(Verbs) To unite, join, club together, join forces, federate, co-operate, befriend, aid, etc. (707), cement, form a party, league, etc., to be in the same boat.

(Adjectives) In partnership, alliance, etc., federal, federated, bounded, banded, linked, cemented, etc., together, embattled.

---

713 Discord *(Substantives)*, disagreement (24), variance, difference, divergence, dissent, dissension, misunderstanding, jar, jarring, clashing, friction, odds, dissonance, disaccord.

Disunion, schism, breach, falling out, division, split, rupture, disruption, open rupture, *brouillerie*, feud, vendetta, contentiousness, litigiousness, strife, contention (720); emnity (889).

Dispute, controversy, polemics, quarrel, tiff, spat, *tracasserie*, altercation, imbroglio, bickering, snip-snap, chicanery, squabble, row, shemozzle, rumpus, racket, fracas, brawl, bear garden, Donnybrook, debate (476).

Litigation, words, war of words, battle of the books, logomachy, wrangling, wrangle, jangle, breach of the peace, declaration of war (722).

Subject of dispute, ground of quarrel, disputed point, vexed question, bone of contention, apple of discord, *casus belli*.

(Verbs) To be discordant, etc., to differ, dissent, disagree, clash, jar, to misunderstand one another.

To fall out, dispute, controvert, litigate, to quarrel, argue, wrangle, squabble, bicker, spar, jangle, nag, brawl; to break with; to declare war.

To embroil, entangle, disunite, set against, pit against; to sow dissension, disunion, discord, etc. among.

(Phrases) To be at odds with; to fall foul of; to have words with; to have a bone to pick with; to have a crow to pluck with; to have a chip on one's shoulder; to be at variance with; to be at cross purposes; to join issue; to pick a quarrel with; to part brass rags; to chew the fat or rag; to go to the mat with; to live like cat and dog.

To set by the ears; to put the cat among the pigeons; to sow or stir up contention.

(Adjectives) Discordant, disagreeing, differing, disunited, clashing, jarring, discrepant, divergent, dissentient, sectarian, at variance, controversial.

Quarrelsome, disputatious, litigious, litigant, factious, pettifogging, polemic, schismatic; unpacified, unreconciled.

(Phrases) At odds; on bad terms; in hot water; at daggers drawn; up in arms; out of tune; at sixes and sevens; at loggerheads; a house divided against itself; no love lost between them.

714 Concord *(Substantives)*, accord, agreement (23), unison, unity, union, good understanding, quiet, peace, conciliation, unanimity (488), harmony, amity, sympathy (897), *entente cordiale, rapprochement*, alliance.

(Phrases) The bonds of harmony; a happy family; kittens in a basket; a happy band of brothers.

(Verbs) To agree, accord, be in unison, etc., to harmonize with, fraternize, stand in with.

(Phrases) To understand one another; to see eye to eye with; to hit it off; to keep the peace; to pull together.

(Adjectives) Concordant, congenial, agreeing, etc., united, in unison, etc., harmonious, allied, cemented, friendly (888), amicable, fraternal, at peace, peaceful, pacific, tranquil.

(Phrases) At one with; with one voice.

715 Defiance *(Substantives)*, challenge, dare, cartel, daring, war-cry, slogan, college yell, war-whoop.

(Verbs) To defy, challenge, dare, brave, beard, bluster, look big.

(Phrases) To set at naught; snap the fingers at; to cock a snook at; to bid defiance to; set at defiance; to hurl defiance at; to double the fist; to show a bold front; to brave it out; to show fight; to throw down the gauntlet or glove; to call out.

(Adjectives) Defying, etc., defiant.

(Adverbs) In defiance of; with arms akimbo.

(Interjections) Come on! let 'em all come! do your worst!

(Phrase) Nemo me impune lacessit.

716 Attack *(Substantives)*, aggression, offence, assault, charge, onset, onslaught, battue, brunt, thrust, pass, passado, cut, sally, inroad, invasion, irruption, incursion, excursion, sortie, *camisade*, storm, storming, boarding, escalade, foray, raid, air raid, *razzia,* dragonnade (619), siege, investment.

Fire, volley, cannonade, barrage, blitz, broadside, bombardment, stonk, hate, raking fire, platoon-fire, fusillade.

Kick, punch (276), lunge, a run at, a dead set at, carte and tierce, a backhander.

An assailant, aggressor, invader.

(Verbs) To attack, assault, assail, go for, fall upon, close with, charge, bear down upon, set on, have at, strike at, run at, make a run at, butt, tilt at, poke at, make a pass at, thrust, pitch into, kick, buffet, bonnet, beat (972), lay about one, lift a hand against, come on, have a fling at, slap on the face, pelt, throw stones, etc., to round on.

To shoot, shoot at, fire at, fire upon, let fly at, brown, pepper, bombard, shell, bomb, dive-bomb, blitz, strafe, prang.

To beset, besiege, lay siege to, invest, beleaguer, open the trenches, invade, raid, storm, board, scale the walls.

To press one hard, be hard upon, drive one hard.

(Phrases) To draw the sword against; to launch an offensive; take the offensive; assume the aggressive; make a dead set at.

To give the cold steel to; to lay down a barrage; to pour in a broadside; to fire a volley.

717 Defence *(Substantives)*, self-defence, self-preservation, protection, ward, guard, guardianship, shielding, etc., resistance (719), safety (664).

Fence, wall, parapet, dike, ditch, fosse, moat (232), boom, mound, mole, outwork, trench, foxhole, dug-out, shelter, Anderson shelter, Morrison shelter, entrenchment, fortification, embankment, bulwark, barbican, battlement, stockade, laager, zareba, abattis, turret, barbette, casemate, muniment, vallum, circumvallation, contravallation, barbed-wire entanglement, sunk fence, ha-ha, buttress, abutment, breastwork, portcullis, glacis, bastion, redoubt, rampart.

Hold, stronghold, keep, donjon, palladium, fort, fortress, blockhouse, pillbox, hedgehog, sconce, citadel, tower, castle, capitol, fastness, asylum (666).

Anchor, sheet-anchor.

Shield, armour, buckler, aegis, breastplate, coat of mail, cuirass, hauberk, habergeon, *chevaux de frise,* screen, etc. (666), helmet, tin hat, battle bowler, casque, shako, bearskin, gas-mask, panoply; fender, torpedo-net, paravane, cow-catcher, buffer.

Defender, protector, guardian (664), champion, protagonist, knight errant; garrison, picket.

(Verbs) To defend, shield, fend, fence, entrench, guard (664), keep off, keep at bay, ward off, beat off, parry, repel, bear the brunt of, put to flight.

(Phrases) To act on the defensive; to maintain one's ground; to stand

(Adjectives) Attacking, etc., aggressive, offensive, up in arms.

———

loopholed, sandbagged, castellated, panoplied, proof, bullet-proof, bombproof.

at bay; to give a warm reception to.

(Adjectives) Defending, etc., defensive, defended, etc., armed, armoured, armour-plated, iron-clad,

(Phrases) Armed cap-à-pie; armed to the teeth.

(Adverbs) Defensively, on the defence, on the defensive, at bay.

---

718 Retaliation *(Substantives)*, reprisal, retort, come-back, counter-stroke, reciprocation, *tu quoque*, recrimination, retribution, counterplot, counterproject, counterblast, *lex talionis*, revenge (919), compensation (30).

(Phrases) Tit for tat; a *quid pro quo*; a Roland for an Oliver; diamond cut diamond; the biter bit; catching a Tartar; a game two can play at; hoist with his own petard.

(Verbs) To retaliate, retort, cap, reciprocate, recriminate, counter, get even with one, pay off.

(Phrases) To turn the tables; to return the compliment; to pay off old scores; to pay in one's own coin; to give as good as one got.

(Adjectives) Retaliating, retaliatory, retaliative, recriminatory, recriminative.

(Interjection) You're another!

———

719 Resistance *(Substantives)*, stand, oppugnation, reluctation, front, repulse, rebuff, opposition (708), disobedience (742), recalcitration.

Strike, industrial action, lockout, tumult, riot, pronunciamento, *émeute*, mutiny.

Revolt, rising, insurrection, rebellion, *coup d'état, putsch*.

(Verbs) To resist, not to submit, etc., to withstand, stand against, stand firm, make a stand, repugn, reluct, reluctate, confront, grapple with, face down.

To kick, kick against, recalcitrate, lift the hand against (716), repel, repulse, rise, revolt, mutiny.

(Phrases) To show a bold front; to make head against; to stand one's ground; to stand the brunt of; to hold one's own; to keep at bay; to stem the torrent; to champ the bit; to sell one's life dearly.

To fly in the face of; to kick against the pricks; to take the bit between one's teeth.

(Adjectives) Resisting, etc., resistive, resistant, refractory, mutinous, recalcitrant, rebellious, up in arms, out.

Unyielding, unconquered, indomitable.

(Interjections) Hands off! keep off!

---

720 Contention *(Substantives)*, contest, struggle, contestation, debate (476), logomachy, paper war, litigation, high words, rivalry, corrivalry, corrivalship, competition, *concours*, gymkhana, race, heat, match, tie, bickering, strife (713).

Wrestling, jiu-jitsu, pugilism, boxing, fisticuffs, spar, prize-fighting, athletics, sports, gymnastics, set-to, round, fracas, row, shindy, scrap, dust, rumpus, shemozzle, stramash,

721 Peace *(Substantives)*, amity, truce, armistice, harmony (714), tranquillity.

(Phrases) Piping time of peace; a quiet life.

(Verbs) To be at peace, etc., to keep the peace, etc. (714), pacify (723).

(Adjectives) Pacific, peaceable, peaceful, tranquil, untroubled, bloodless, halcyon.

———

outbreak, clash, collision, shock, breach of the peace, brawl, Donnybrook (713).

Conflict, skirmish, rencounter, scuffle, encounter, velitation, tussle, scrimmage, scrummage, broil, fray, affray, *mêlée*, affair, brush, bout, fight, battle, combat, action, engagement, battle royal, running fight, free fight, joust, tournament, tourney, pitched battle, death struggle, Armageddon.

Naval engagement, naumachy, sea-fight; air duel, dogfight.

Duel, satisfaction, monomachy, single combat, passage of arms, affair of honour, a triangular duel.

(Verbs) To contend, contest, struggle, vie with, emulate, rival, race, race with, outvie, battle with, cope with, compete, join issue, bandy words with, try conclusions with, close with, square, buckle with, spar, box, tussle, fence, wrestle, joust, enter the lists, take up arms, take the field, encounter, struggle with, grapple with, tackle, engage with, pitch into, strive with, fall to, encounter, collide with.

(Phrases) Join battle; fall foul of; have a brush with; break the peace; take up the cudgels; unsheathe the sword; break a lance; to run a tilt at; give satisfaction; measure swords; exchange shots; lay about one; cut and thrust; fight without the gloves; go on the warpath.

(Adjectives) Contending, etc., contentious, combative, bellicose (722); pugilistic, agonistic, competitive, rival, polemical (476), rough-and-tumble.

(Phrases) A word and a blow; pull devil, pull baker.

---

722 Warfare *(Substantives)*, war, hostilities, fighting, etc., arms, the sword, open war, *ultima ratio*, war to the knife.

Battle array, campaign, crusade, expedition, operation, mission, war-path.

Warlike spirit, military spirit, militarism, bellicosity.

The art of war, tactics, strategy, military evolutions, arms, service, campaigning, tented field; Mars, Bellona.

War-cry, slogan, fiery cross, trumpet, clarion, bugle, pibroch, war-whoop, beat of drum, tom-tom; mobilization.

(Phrases) The mailed fist; wager of battle.

(Verbs) To arm, fight, set to, spar, scrap, tussle, joust, tilt, box, skirmish, fight hand to hand, fence, measure swords, engage, combat, give battle, go to battle, join battle, engage in battle, raise or mobilize troops, declare war, wage war, go to war, come to blows, break a lance with, appeal to arms, appeal to the sword, give satisfaction, take the

723 Pacification *(Substantives)*, reconciliation, accommodation, arrangement, *modus vivendi*, adjustment, terms, amnesty.

Peace-offering, olive-branch, calumet or pipe of peace, preliminaries of peace.

Pacifism, pacificism, appeasement.

Truce, armistice, suspension of arms, of hostilities, etc., convention, *détente*.

Flag of truce, white flag, cartel.

(Phrases) Hollow truce; cold war; *pax in bello*.

(Verbs) To make peace, pacify, make it up, reconcile, conciliate, propitiate, appease, tranquillize, compose, allay, settle differences, restore harmony, heal the breach.

(Phrases) To put up the sword; to sheathe the sword; to beat swords into ploughshares; to bury the hatchet; to smoke the pipe of peace; to close the temple of Janus; to cry quits.

(Adjectives) Pacified, etc., pacific, conciliatory.

field, keep the field, fight it out, fight to a finish, spill blood, carry on war, carry on hostilities, to fight one's way, to serve, to fight like devils, to sell one's life dearly.

(Phrases) To see service; to smell powder; to go over the top.

(Adjectives) Contending, etc., unpeaceful, unpacific, contentious, belligerent, bellicose, jingo, chauvinistic, martial, warlike, military, militant, soldierly, soldierlike, gladiatorial, chivalrous, in arms, embattled.

(Phrases) Together by the ears; sword in hand.

(Adverbs) Pendente lite, the battle raging, in the cannon's mouth; in the thick of the fray.

(Interjections) To arms! the Philistines be upon thee!

724 Mediation *(Substantives)*, intervention, interposition, interference, intermeddling, intercession, parley, negotiation, arbitration, conciliation, mediatorship, good offices, diplomacy, peace-offering, eirenicon.

A mediator, intermediary, go-between, intercessor, peacemaker, diplomat, diplomatist, negotiator, troubleshooter, ombudsman.

(Verbs) To mediate, intermediate, intercede, interpose, interfere, intervene, negotiate, arbitrate, compromise, meet half-way.

(Phrase) To split the difference.

725 Submission *(Substantives)*, surrender, non-resistance, appeasement, deference, yielding, capitulation, cession.

Homage, obeisance, bow, curtsy, kneeling, genuflexion, prostration, kow-tow.

(Verbs) To surrender, succumb, submit, yield, give in, bend, cringe, crawl, truckle to, knuckle down or under, knock under, capitulate, lay down or deliver up one's arms, retreat, give way, cave in.

(Phrases) Beat a retreat; strike one's flag or colours; surrender at discretion; make a virtue of necessity; to come to terms.

To eat humble pie; to eat dirt; to swallow the pill; to kiss the rod; to turn the other cheek; to lick a person's boots.

(Adjectives) Surrendering, etc., non-resisting, unresisting, submissive, downtrodden.

Undefended, untenable, indefensible.

726 Combatant *(Substantives)*, belligerent, champion, disputant, controversialist, litigant, competitor, rival, corrival, assailant, bully, bruiser, fighter, duellist, fightingman, pugilist, pug, boxer, the fancy, prize-fighter, fighter, duellist, fighting-man, pugilist, buckler, fire-eater, berserker; swordsman, wrestler, Amazon, Paladin, son of Mars; staff, *état-major*, brass hats; militarist.

726A Non-combatant *(Substantives)*, civilian; passive resister, conscientious objector, conchy, Cuthbert, pacifist, pacificist; non-effective.

Quaker, Quirites.

(Adjectives) Non-effective.

Warrior, soldier, campaigner, veteran, man-at-arms, redcoat, man in khaki, Tommy Atkins, tommy, doughboy, G.I., *poilu*, trooper, dragoon, hussar, grenadier, fusilier, guardsman, lifeguard, lancer, cuirassier, spearman, musketeer, carabineer, rifleman, sniper, sharpshooter, *bersagliere*;

ensign, standard-bearer, halberdier; private, subaltern, conscript, recruit, cadet; effectives, line, rank and file, cannon fodder, P.B.I.

Engineer, artilleryman, gunner, cannoneer, bombardier, sapper, miner; archer, bowman.

Paratrooper, aircraftman, erk, pilot, observer, aircrew.

Marine, jolly, leatherneck; seaman, bluejacket, tar, A.B.

Guerrilla, Maquis, partisan, cossack, sepoy, gurkha, spahi, janizary, zouave, bashi-bazouk.

Armed force, the army, the military, regulars, soldiery, infantry, mounted infantry, fencibles, volunteers, territorials, yeomanry, cavalry, artillery, guns, tanks, armour, commando.

Militia, irregulars, *francs-tireurs*, Home Guard, train-band.

Legion, phalanx, myrmidons, squadron, wing, group, troop, cohort, regiment, corps, platoon, battalion, unit, mob, company (72), column, detachment, brigade, division, garrison, battle array, order of battle.

727 Arms *(Substantives)*, weapons, armament, armour, armoury, quiver, arsenal, magazine, armature.

Mail, chain-mail, lorication; ammunition, powder, gunpowder, gun-cotton, dynamite, gelignite, T.N.T., cordite, lyddite, cartridge, cartouche (635).

Artillery, park, ordnance piece, gun, cannon, swivel, howitzer, carronade, culverin, field-piece, machine-gun, Gatling, Maxim, submachine-gun, tommy-gun, mitrailleuse, pom-pom, mortar, grenade, petronel, petard, falconet.

Fire-arms, side-arms, stand of arms, musketry, musket, smooth-bore, muzzle-loader, firelock, match-lock, flint-lock, fowling-piece, rifle, revolver, six-shooter, carbine, blunderbuss, pistol, gat, rod, betsy, automatic pistol, derringer, Winchester, Lee-Metford, Mauser, Bren gun, Bofors, Sten gun, Lewis gun, bazooka.

Bow, arquebus (or harquebus), cross-bow, sling, catapult.

Missile, projectile, shot, round-shot, ball, shrapnel; grape, grape-shot, chain-shot, bullet, stone, shell, gas-shell, bomb, land-mine, block-buster, flying bomb, buzz-bomb, doodlebug, guided missile, V1, V2, atomic bomb, hydrogen bomb, torpedo, rocket, ballistics.

Pike, lance, spear, javelin, assagai, dart, arrow, reed, shaft, bolt, boomerang, harpoon.

Bayonet, sword, sabre, broadsword, cutlass, falchion, scimitar, rapier, skean, toledo, tuck, claymore, kris (or creese), dagger, dirk, hanger, poniard, stiletto, stylet, dudgeon, axe, bill, pole-axe, battle axe, halberd, tomahawk, bowie-knife, snickersnee, yataghan, kukri.

Club, mace, truncheon, staff, bludgeon, cudgel, knobkerrie, life-preserver, knuckle-duster, shillelagh, bat, cosh, sandbag, lathi.

Catapult, battering-ram; tank.

728 Arena *(Substantives)*, field, walk, battle-field, field of battle, lists, palaestra, campus, playing field, recreation ground, playground, course, cinder-track, dirt-track, gridiron, diamond, pitch, links, rink, court, platform, stage, boards, race-course, *corso*, circus, ring, cockpit, bear garden, scene of action, theatre of war, the enemy's camp, amphitheatre, hippodrome, coliseum (or colosseum), proscenium.

SECTION V—RESULTS OF VOLUNTARY ACTION

729 Completion *(Substantives)*, accomplishment, performance, fulfilment, fruition, execution, achievement, dispatch, work done, superstructure, finish, termination, denouement, catastrophe, conclusion, culmination, climax, consummation, *fait accompli*, winding up, the last stroke, finishing stroke, *coup de grâce*, last finish, final touch, crowning touch, coping-stone, end (67), arrival (292), completeness (52).

(Adjectives) To complete, effect, perform, do, execute, go through, accomplish, fulfil, discharge, achieve, compass, effectuate, dispatch, knock off, close, terminate, conclude, finish, end (67), consummate, elaborate, bring about, bring to bear, bring to pass, get through, carry through, bring through, bring off, pull off, work out, make good, carry out, wind up, dispose of, bring to a close, termination, conclusion, etc.

To perfect, bring to perfection, stamp, put the seal to, polish off, crown.

To reach, arrive (292), touch, reach, attain the goal; to run one's race.

(Phrases) To give the last finish or finishing touch; to be through with; to get it over; to deliver the goods; to shut up shop.

(Adjectives) Completing, final, terminal, concluding, conclusive, exhaustive, crowning, etc., done, completed, wrought.

(Phrases) It is all over; *finis coronat opus; actum est.*

(Adverbs) Completely, etc. (52), out of hand, effectually, with a vengeance, with a witness.

730 Non-completion *(Substantives)*, inexecution, shortcoming (304), non-fulfilment, non-performance, neglect; incompleteness (53); a drawn battle or game, a draw, a stalemate.

(Phrases) The web of Penelope; one swallow does not make a summer.

(Verbs) Not to complete, perform, etc., to fall short of, leave unfinished, let slip, lose sight of, neglect, leave undone, etc., draw.

(Phrases) To scotch the snake, not kill it; hang fire; do by halves.

(Adjectives) Not completed, etc., uncompleted, incomplete, unfinished, left undone (53), short, unaccomplished, unperformed, unexecuted.

In progress, in hand, proceeding, going on, on the stocks.

(Adverbs) Re infecta; nihil fit.

---

731 Success *(Substantives)*, successfulness, speed, thrift, advance, luck, good fortune (734), godsend, prize, windfall, trump card, hit, stroke, lucky strike, break; lucky or fortunate hit; bold stroke, master-stroke, *coup de maître*, knock-out blow (698), checkmate.

Continued success, run of luck, time well spent, tide, flood, high tide, heyday.

Advantage over, ascendancy, mastery, conquest, subdual, victory, subjugation, triumph, exultation (884).

732 Failure *(Substantives)*, unsuccess, non-success, disappointment, blow, frustration, inefficacy, discomfiture, abortion, miscarriage, lost trouble; vain, ineffectual, or abortive attempt or effort.

A mistake, error, blunder, fault, miss, oversight, blot, slip, trip, stumble, claudication, breakdown, false step, wrong step, howler, floater, clanger, boner, *faux pas, bêtise*, titubation, scrape, botch, bungle, foozle, mess, washout, stalemate, botchery, fiasco, flop, frost, sad work, bad job, bad show, want of skill.

A conqueror, victor, winner.

(Phrase) A feather in one's cap.

(Verbs) To succeed, to be successful, to come off successful, to be crowned with success, to come or go off well, catch on, to thrive, speed, prosper, bloom, blossom, flourish, go on well, be well off.

To gain, attain, carry, secure, or win a point or object; to triumph, be triumphant, etc.; to surmount, overcome, conquer, master, or get over a difficulty or obstacle; to score, make a hit.

To advance (282), come on, get on, gain ground, make one's way, make progress, progress, worry along, get by.

To bring to bear, to bring about, to effect, accomplish, complete (729), manage, contrive to, make sure; to reap, gather, etc., the benefit of.

To master, get the better of, conquer, subdue, subjugate, quell, reduce, overthrow, overpower, vanquish, get under; get or gain the ascendancy, obtain a victory; to worst, defeat, beat, lick, drub, trim, settle, floor, knock out, put down, trip up, beat hollow, checkmate, non-suit, trip up the heels of, capsize, shipwreck, ruin, kibosh, do for, victimize, put to flight, drown, etc.; to roll in the dust, to trample under foot, to wipe the floor with.

To baffle, disconcert, frustrate, confound, discomfit, dish, foil, outgeneral, outmanœuvre, outflank, outwit, overreach, balk, outvote, circumvent, score off, catch napping.

To answer, succeed, work well, turn out well.

(Phrases) to sail before the wind; to swim with the tide; to stem the torrent; to turn a corner; to weather a point; to fall on one's legs or feet; *se tirer d'affaire*; to take a favourable turn; to turn up trumps; to have the ball at one's feet; to come off with flying colours; to win or gain the day; to win the palm; to win one's spurs; to breast the tape; to bear away the bell.

To get the upper hand; to gain an

Mischance, mishap, misfortune, misadventure, disaster, bad or hard luck (735).

Repulse, rebuff, set-down, defeat, fall, downfall, rout, discomfiture, collapse, smash, crash, wreck, perdition, shipwreck, ruin, subjugation, overthrow, death-blow, quietus, knockout, destruction.

A victim, loser, bankrupt, insolvent (808).

(Phrases) A losing game; a flash in the pan; a wild-goose chase; a mare's-nest; a fool's errand.

(Verbs) To fail, to be unsuccessful etc., to come off badly, go badly, go amiss, abort, go wrong, fall flat, flop, fall through, fizzle out, turn out ill, work ill, lose ground, recede (283), fall short of (304), prang (162, 176).

To miss, miss one's aim; to labour, toil, etc., in vain; to lose one's labour, flounder, limp, miss one's footing, miscarry, abort; to make vain, ineffectual, or abortive efforts; to make a slip; to make or commit a mistake, commit a fault, make a mess of; to botch, make a botch of, bungle, foozle.

To be defeated, overthrown, foiled, worsted, let down, etc.; to break down, sink, drown, founder, go to ruin, etc., fall, slip, tumble, stumble, falter, be capsized, run aground, pack up, crock up, collapse.

(Phrases) To come to nothing; to end in smoke; to slip through one's fingers; to hang fire; to miss fire; to miss stays; to flash in the pan; to split upon a rock; to go to the wall; to have had it; to take a back seat; to get the worst of it; to go to the dogs; to go to pot; to be all up with; to be in the wrong box; to stand in one's own light; to catch a Tartar; to get hold of the wrong sow by the ear; to burn one's fingers; to shoot at a pigeon and kill a crow; to beat the air; to tilt against windmills; to roll the stone of Sisyphus; to fall between two stools; to pull a boner; to come a cropper or mucker.

(Adjectives) Unsuccessful, failing, etc., unfortunate, in a bad way,

advantage; to get the whip-hand of; to have on the hip; to get the start of; to have a run of luck; to make a hit; to make a killing; to score a success; to reap or gather the harvest; to strike oil; to give a good account of oneself; to carry all before one; to put to rout; to cook one's goose; to settle one's hash.

(Adjectives) Succeeding, etc., successful, home and dry, prosperous, felicitous, blooming, etc., set up, triumphant, victorious, cock-a-hoop.

Unfoiled, unbeaten, unsubdued, etc. Effective, well-spent.

(Phrases) Flushed with success; one's star being in the ascendant; the spoilt child of fortune.

(Adverbs) Successfully, etc., triumphantly, with flying colours, in triumph, *à merveille*, to good purpose.

(Phrase) Veni, vidi, vici.

unlucky, luckless, out of luck, ill-fated, ill-starred, disastrous.

Unavailing, abortive, addle, still-born, fruitless, bootless, ineffectual, stickit, unattained, lame, hobbling, impotent, futile.

Aground, grounded, swamped, stranded, cast away, wrecked, on the rocks, foundered, capsized, torpedoed, shipwrecked.

Defeated, overcome, overthrown, overpowered, mastered, worsted, vanquished, conquered, subjugated, routed, silenced, distanced, foiled, unhorsed, baffled, befooled, dished, tossed about, stultified, undone, done for, down and out, ruined, circumvented, planet-struck, nonplussed.

(Phrases) At a loss; wide of the mark; not having a leg to stand upon; ruined root and branch; the sport of fortune; bitched, bothered, and bewildered; hoist by one's own petard; left in the lurch; out of the running.

(Adverbs) Unsuccessfully, etc., in vain, to no purpose, all up with.
(Phrases) The game is up; all is lost.

---

733 Trophy *(Substantives)*, laurel, palm, crown, bays, wreath, garland, chaplet, civic crown, medal, ribbon, cup, scalp, prize, award, oscar, triumphal arch, ovation, triumph (883), flourish of trumpets, flying colours.
(Phrase) A feather in one's cap.

734 Prosperity *(Substantives)*, affluence (803), success (731), thrift, good fortune, welfare, well-being, felicity, luck, good luck, a run of luck, fair weather, sunshine, fair wind, a bed of roses, palmy days, the smiles of fortune, halcyon days, *Saturnia regna*, golden age.

An upstart, parvenu, *nouveau riche*, profiteer, skipjack, mushroom, self-made man.

A made man, a lucky dog.

(Phrase) A roaring trade.

(Verbs) To prosper, thrive, flourish, be well off; to flower, blow, blossom, bloom, fructify.

(Phrases) To feather one's nest; to line one's pockets; to make one's pile; to bask in the sunshine; to rise in the world; to make one's way; to better oneself; to light on one's feet.

735 Adversity *(Substantives)*, bad, ill, evil, adverse, etc., fortune, hap, or luck, tough luck, hard lines, reverse, set-back, come-down, broken fortunes, falling or going down in the world, hard times, iron age, evil day, rainy day.

Fall, ruin, ruination, ruinousness, undoing, mishap, mischance, misadventure, misfortune, disaster, calamity, catastrophe (619), failure (732); a hard life; trouble, hardship, blight, curse, evil star, evil genius, evil dispensation.

(Phrases) The frowns of fortune; the ups and downs of life; a black look-out; the time being out of joint.

(Verbs) To be ill off; to decay, sink, go under, fall, decline, come down in the world, lose caste; to have had it.

(Adjectives) Prosperous, fortunate, lucky, well-off, well-to-do, bein, affluent, solvent (803), thriving, set up, prospering, etc., blooming, palmy, halcyon.

Auspicious, propitious, in a fair way.

(Phrases) Born with a silver spoon in one's mouth; the spoilt child of fortune; in clover; on velvet; in luck's way.

(Adverbs) Prosperously, etc., swimmingly.

(Adjectives) Unfortunate, unlucky, luckless, untoward, ill-off, badly off, decayed, ill-fated, ill-starred, impecunious, necessitous (804), bankrupt (808), unprosperous, adverse, untoward.

Disastrous, calamitous, ruinous, dire, deplorable, etc.

(Phrases) Down on one's luck; in a bad way; in poor shape; having seen better days; born with a wooden ladle in one's mouth; one's star on the wane; from bad to worse; down and out.

736 Mediocrity *(Substantives)*, the golden mean, *aurea mediocritas*, moderation (174), moderate circumstances; the middle classes, bourgeoisie.

(Adjectives) Tolerable, fair, middling, passable, average, so-so, ordinary, mediocre; middle-class, bourgeois.

(Verbs) To keep a middle course, jog on, get along, get by.

(Phrase) Medio tutissimus ibis.

DIVISION II—INTERSOCIAL VOLITION

SECTION I—GENERAL INTERSOCIAL VOLITION

737 Authority *(Substantives)*, influence, patronage, credit, power, prerogative, control, jurisdiction, censorship, authoritativeness, absoluteness, despotism, absolutism, tyranny.

Command, empire, sway, rule, dominion, domination, supremacy, sovereignty, suzerainty, lordship, headship, seigniory, seigniorship, mastery, mastership, office, government, administration, gubernation, empire, body politic, accession.

Hold, grasp, gripe, grip, reach, fang, clutches, talons, helm, reins.

Reign, dynasty, regime, directorship, proconsulship, prefecture, caliphate, seneschalship, magistrature, magistracy, presidency, presidentship, premiership.

Empire, autocracy, monarchy, kinghood, kingship, royalty, regality, kingcraft, aristocracy, oligarchy, feudalism, republic, republicanism, democracy, socialism, demagogy, ochlocracy, mobocracy, mob-rule, dictatorship of proletariat, ergatocracy, collectivism, communism,

738 Absence of authority.

Laxity *(Substantives)*, laxness, licence, licentiousness, relaxation, looseness, loosening, slackness, toleration, *laissez-faire*, remission, liberty (748).

Misrule, anarchy, interregnum.

Deprivation of power, dethronement, deposition, usurpation.

Denial of authority: anarchism, nihilism; insubordination, mutiny (742).

Anarchist, nihilist, usurper, mutineer.

(Phrases) A dead letter; *brutum fulmen.*

(Verbs) To be lax, etc., to hold a loose rein, tolerate, to relax, to misrule.

To dethrone.

(Phrases) To give a loose rein to; to give rope enough.

(Adjectives) Lax, permissive, loose, slack, remiss, relaxed, licensed, reinless, unbridled, anarchic, anarchical, nihilistic.

Unauthorized (925).

Bolshevism, bureaucracy, bumbledom, syndicalism, militarism, stratocracy, *imperium in imperio*, dictatorship, protectorate, protectorship, directorate, directory, executive, raj.

Limited monarchy, constitutional government, representative government, home rule, diarchy (or dyarchy), duumvirate, triumvirate.

Vicarious authority (755, 759).

Gynarchy, gynaecocracy, petticoat government, matriarchy; patriarchy, patriarchism.

(Verbs) To have, hold, possess, or exercise authority, etc.

To be master, etc.; to have the control, etc.; to overrule, override, overawe, dominate.

To rule, govern, sway, command, control, direct, administer, lead, preside over, boss; to dictate, reign, hold the reins; to possess or be seated on the throne; to ascend or mount the throne; to sway or wield the sceptre.

(Phrases) To have the upper hand; to have the whip-hand; to bend to one's will; to have one's own way; to rule the roast; to lay down the law; to be cock of the roost; to have under the thumb; to keep under; to lead by the nose; to wear the breeches; to have the ball at one's feet; to play first fiddle.

(Adjectives) Ruling, etc., regnant, dominant, paramount, supreme, authoritative, executive, gubernatorial, administrative, official.

Imperial, regal, sovereign, royal, royalist, kingly, monarchical, imperatorial, princely, baronial, feudal, seigneurial, seigniorial, aristocratic, democratic, etc.; totalitarian, ultramontane, absolutist.

Imperative, peremptory, arbitrary, absolute, overruling.

(Adverbs) In the name of, by the authority of, in virtue of, at one's command, under the auspices of, under the aegis of, *ex officio, ex cathedra*.

---

739 Severity *(Substantives)*, strictness, rigour, rigidity, rigidness, sternness, stringency, austerity, inclemency, harshness, acerbity, stiffness, rigorousness, inexorability.

Arbitrary power, absolutism, despotism, dictatorship, autocracy, domineering, tyranny; Moloch.

Assumption, usurpation.

A tyrant, disciplinarian, martinet, stickler, despot, oppressor, hard master; King Stork.

(Phrases) Iron rule; reign of terror; mailed fist; martial law; blood and iron; tender mercies; red tape.

740 Lenity *(Substantives)*, mildness, lenience, leniency, gentleness, indulgence, clemency, tolerance, forbearance.

(Verbs) To be lenient, etc., to tolerate, indulge, spoil, bear with, to allow to have one's own way, to let down gently.

(Adjectives) Lenient, mild, gentle, soft, indulgent, tolerant, easy-going, clement.

(Phrase) Live and let live.

(Verbs) To be severe, etc.; to assume, usurp, arrogate, take liberties; to hold or keep a tight hand; to bear or lay a heavy hand on; to be down on; to dictate; to domineer, bully, oppress, override, tyrannize.

(Phrases) To lord it over; to carry matters with a high hand; to ride roughshod over; to rule with a rod of iron; to put on the screw; to deal faithfully with; to keep a person's nose to the grindstone.

(Adjectives) Severe, strict, rigid, stern, stiff, dour, strait-laced, rigorous, exacting, stringent, hard and fast, peremptory, absolute, positive, uncompromising, harsh, austere, arbitrary, haughty, overbearing,

arrogant, autocratic, bossy, dictatorial, imperious, domineering, tyranni-
cal, masterful, obdurate, unyielding, inflexible, inexorable, exigent, inclement, Spartan, Rhadamanthine, Draconian.

(Adverbs) Severely, etc., with a heavy hand.

741 Command *(Substantives)*, order, fiat, bidding, dictum, hest, behest, call,
beck, nod, message, direction, injunction, charge, instructions, appointment,
demand, exaction, imposition, requisition, requirement, claim, reclamation, revendication.

Dictation, dictate, mandate, caveat, edict, decree, decretal, enactment, precept,
prescript, writ, rescript, law, ordinance, ordination, bull, regulation, prescription,
brevet, placet, ukase, firman, warrant, passport, mittimus, mandamus, summons,
subpoena, interpellation, citation, word of command.

(Verbs) To command, to issue a command, order, give order, bid, require,
enjoin, charge, claim, call for, demand, exact, insist on, make a point of, impose,
entail, set, tax, prescribe, direct, brief, appoint, dictate, ordain, decree, enact; to
issue or promulgate a decree, etc.

To cite, summon, call for, call up, send for, requisition, subpoena; to set or prescribe a task, to set to work, to give the word of command, to call to order.

(Phrase) The decree is gone forth.

(Adjectives) Commanding, etc., authoritative, peremptory, decretive, de-
cretory (737).

(Adverbs) By order, with a dash of the pen.

(Phrase) Le roy le veult.

742 Disobedience *(Substantives)*,
non-compliance, insubordination,
contumacy, defection, infringement,
infraction, violation; defiance (715),
resistance (719), non-observance
(773).

Rising, insurrection, revolt, *coup
d'état, putsch,* rebellion, turn-out,
strike, riot, riotousness, mutinous-
ness, mutiny, tumult, sedition, treason,
lese-majesty.

An insurgent, mutineer, rebel, rioter,
traitor, apostate, renegade, seceder,
quisling, fifth columnist; *carbonaro,*
sansculotte, *frondeur*; agitator,
demagogue, Jack Cade, Wat Tyler;
ringleader.

(Verbs) To disobey, violate, infringe,
resist (719), defy (715), turn restive,
shirk, kick, strike, mutiny, rise, rebel,
secede, lift the hand against, turn out,
come out, go on strike.

(Phrases) To champ the bit; to kick
over the traces; to unfurl the red
flag.

(Adjectives) Disobedient, resisting,
rebellious, unruly, unsubmissive, un-

743 Obedience *(Substantives)*, submission, non-resistance, passiveness,
resignation, cession, compliance, surrender (725), subordination, deference, loyalty, devotion, allegiance,
obeisance, homage, fealty, prostration,
kneeling, genuflexion, curtsy, kotow,
salaam, submissiveness, obsequiousness (886), servitorship, subjection (749).

(Verbs) To be obedient, etc.; to obey,
submit, succumb, give in, knock under,
cringe, yield (725), comply, surrender,
follow, give up, give way, resign, bend
to, bear obedience to.

To kneel, fall on one's knees, bend
the knee, curtsy, kowtow, salaam, bow,
pay homage to.

To attend upon, tend; to be under the
orders of, to serve.

(Phrases) To kiss the rod; to do one's
bidding; to play second fiddle; to take it
lying down; to dance attendance on.

(Adjectives) Obedient, submissive,
resigned, passive, complying, compliant, loyal, faithful, devoted, yielding, docile, tractable, amenable,

governable, uncomplying, uncompliant, restive, insubordinate, contumacious, mutinous, riotous, seditious, disaffected, recusant, recalcitrant, refractory, naughty.

Unbidden, unobeyed, a dead letter.

(Phrase) The grey mare being the better horse.

biddable, unresisting, henpecked; restrainable, unresisted.

---

744 Compulsion *(Substantives)*, coercion, coaction, force, constraint, enforcement, press, *corvée,* conscription, levy, duress, brute force, main force, *force majeure,* the sword, club law, *ultima ratio, argumentum baculinum.*

(Verbs) To compel, force, make, drive, coerce, constrain, steam-roller, enforce, put in force, oblige, force upon, press, conscribe, extort, put down, bind, pin down, bind over, impress, commandeer, requisition.

(Phrases) To cram down the throat; to take no denial; to insist upon; to make a point of.

(Adjectives) Compelling, etc., compulsory, compulsatory, obligatory, forcible, coercive, coactive, peremptory, rigorous, stringent, inexorable (739); being fain to do, having to do.

(Adverbs) By force, perforce, under compulsion, *vi et armis,* in spite of one's teeth; *bon gré, mal gré;* willy-nilly, *nolens volens; de rigueur.*

---

745 Master *(Substantives)*, lord, laird, chief, leader, captain, skipper, mate, protagonist, coryphaeus, head, chieftain, commander, commandant, director (694), captain of industry, ruler, potentate, dictator, liege, sovereign, monarch, autocrat, despot, tyrant, *führer, duce,* demagogue, ringleader, boss, big shot, fugleman.

Crowned head, emperor, king, majesty, tetrarch, *imperator,* protector, president, stadtholder, governor.

Caesar, czar, sultan, soldan, caliph, sophy, khan, cacique, inca, lama, mogul, imam, shah, khedive, pasha (or bashaw), dey, cham, judge, aga, hospodar, mikado, shogun, tycoon, exarch.

Prince, seignior, highness, archduke, duke, marquis, earl, viscount, baron (875), margrave, landgrave, palatine, elector, doge, satrap, rajah, maharajah, emir, bey, effendi, nizam, nawab, mandarin, sirdar, ameer, sachem, sagamore.

Empress, queen, czarina, sultana, princess, duchess, marchioness, countess, viscountess, baroness, infanta, ranee, maharanee, margravine, etc.

Military authorities, marshal, field-marshal, *maréchal,* generalissimo,

746 Servant *(Substantives)*, servitor, employee, attaché, secretary, subordinate, clerk, retainer, vassal, protégé, dependant, hanger-on, pensioner, client, emissary, *âme damnée.*

Retinue, cortège, staff, court, train, entourage, clientele, suite.

An attendant, squire, henchman, led captain, chamberlain, follower, usher, page, train-bearer, domestic, help, butler, footman, lackey, flunkey, parlour-man, valet, waiter, *garçon,* equerry, groom, jockey, ostler (or hostler), stable-boy, tiger, buttons, boot-boy, boots, livery servant, hireling, mercenary, underling, menial, gillie, under-strapper, journeyman, whipper-in, bailiff, castellan, seneschal, majordomo, cup-bearer, bottle-washer, scout, gyp.

Serf, villein, slave, galley-slave, thrall, peon, helot, bondsman, *adscriptus glebae,* wage-slave.

A maid, handmaid, abigail, chamber-maid, lady's maid, housekeeper, lady help, soubrette, *fille de chambre,* parlour-maid, housemaid, between-maid, kitchen-maid, nurse, *bonne,* scullion, laundress, bed-maker, skivvy, slavey, daily.

(Verbs) To serve, attend upon, dance attendance, wait upon, squire, valet.

commander-in-chief, admiral, commodore, general, lieutenant-general, major-general, brigadier, colonel, lieutenant-colonel, officer, captain, major, lieutenant, adjutant, midshipman, quartermaster, aide-de-camp, ensign, cornet, cadet, subaltern, non-commissioned officer, drum-major, sergeant-major, sergeant, corporal, air-marshal, group-captain, wing-commander, squadron-leader, flight-lieutenant, centurion, *seraskier*, hetman, subahdar, *condottiere*.

Civil authorities, mayor, prefect, chancellor, provost, magistrate, syndic, alcade (or alcayde), burgomaster, *corregidor*, sheik, seneschal, burgrave, alderman, warden, constable (965), beadle, alguazil, kavass, tribune, consul, proconsul, quaestor, praetor, aedile, archon, polemarch.

Statesman, politician, statist, legislator, lawgiver.

President, chairman, speaker, moderator, vice-president, comptroller, director (694), monitor, monitress.

(Adverbs) In one's pay or employ, in the train of.

———

747 Ensign, or badge of authority.
Sceptre *(Substantives)*, regalia, insigma (550), crown, coronet, rod of empire, orb, mace, *fasces*, wand, baton, truncheon, staff, insignia (550), portfolio.

A throne, chair, divan, dais, woolsack.

Diadem, tiara, ermine, purple, signet, seals, keys, talisman, cap of maintenance, toga, robes of state, decoration.

748 Freedom *(Substantives)*, independence, liberty, licence (760), self-government, autonomy, scope, range, latitude, play, swing, free play, elbow-room, *lebensraum*, margin.

Franchise, immunity, exemption, emancipation (750), naturalization, denizenship.

Freeland, freehold, allodium (780).

A freeman, freedman, denizen.

(Phrases) The four freedoms; *liberté, egalité, fraternité*; a place in the sun; Liberty Hall.

(Verbs) To be free, to have scope, etc.

To render free, etc., to free, to emancipate, enfranchise (750), naturalize.

(Phrases) To have the run of; to have one's own way; to have one's fling; to stand on one's own feet; to stand on one's rights; to have a will of one's own; to paddle one's own canoe; to play a lone hand.

To take a liberty; to make free with; to take the bit between one's teeth.

749 Subjection *(Substantives)*, dependence, thrall, thraldom, subjugation, subordination, bondage, serfdom, servitude, slavery, vassalage, villeinage, service, clientship, liability (177), enslavement, tutelage, constraint (751).

Yoke, harness, collar.

(Verbs) To be subject, dependent, etc., to fall under, obey, serve (743).

To subject, subjugate, enthral, enslave, keep under, control, etc. (751), to reduce to slavery, mediatize, break in.

(Phrases) To drag a chain; not dare to call one's soul one's own; to be led by the nose; to be or lie at the mercy of.

To keep in leading strings.

(Adjectives) Subject, subordinate, dependent, subjected, in subjection to, in thrall to, feudatory, feudal, enslaved, a slave to, at the mercy of, downtrodden, overborne, henpecked, enthralled, controlled, constrained (751).

(Phrases) Under the thumb of; at the feet of; tied to the apron-

(Adjectives) Free, independent, loose, at large, unconstrained, unrestrained, unchecked, unobstructed, unconfined, unsubdued, unsubjugated, self-governed, autonomous, self-supporting, untrammelled, unbound, uncontrolled, unchained, unshackled, unfettered, uncurbed, unbridled, unrestricted, unmuzzled, unbuttoned, unforced, uncompelled, unbiased, spontaneous, unhindered, unthwarted, heart-whole, uncaught, unenslaved, unclaimed, ungoverned, resting.

Free and easy, at ease, *dégagé*, wanton, rampant, irrepressible, unprevented, unvanquished, exempt, freehold, allodial, enfranchised, emancipated, released, disengaged (750), out of hand.

(Phrases) Free as air; one's own master; *sui juris*; a law to oneself; on one's own; a cat may look at a king.

strings of; the puppet, sport, plaything of.

---

750 Liberation *(Substantives)*, disengagement, release, enlargement, emancipation, affranchisement, enfranchisement, manumission, discharge, dismissal.

Escape (671), deliverance (672), redemption, extrication, absolution, acquittance, acquittal (970).

Licence, toleration; parole, ticket of leave.

(Verbs) To gain, obtain, acquire, etc., one's liberty, freedom, etc., to get off, get clear, to deliver oneself from.

To break loose, escape, slip away, make one's escape, cut and run, slip the collar, bolt (671).

To liberate, free, set free, set at liberty, release, loose, let loose, loosen, relax, unloose, untie, unbind, unhand, unchain, unshackle, unfetter, unclog, disengage, unharness (44).

To enlarge, set clear, let go, let out, disenchain, disimprison, unbar, unbolt, uncage, unclose, uncork, discharge, disenthral, dismiss, deliver, extricate, let slip, enfranchise, affranchise, manumit, denizen, emancipate, assoil (748).

To clear, acquit, redeem, ransom, get off.

(Phrases) To throw off the yoke; to burst one's bonds; to break prison.

To give one one's head.

(Adjectives) Liberated, freed, etc.

---

751 Restraint *(Substantives)*, constraint, coercion, cohibition, repression, clamp down, control, discipline.

Confinement, durance, duress, detention, imprisonment, incarceration, prisonment, internment, blockade, quarantine, coarctation, mancipation, entombment, 'durance vile,' limbo, captivity, penal servitude.

Arrest, arrestation, custody, keep, care, charge, ward.

Prison, fetter (752); *lettre de cachet*.

(Verbs) To be under restraint or arrest, to be coerced, etc.

To restrain, constrain, coerce, check, trammel, curb, cramp, keep under, enthral, put under restraint, restrict, repress, cohibit, detain, debar; to chain, enchain, fasten, tie up (43), picket, fetter, shackle, manacle, handcuff, bridle, muzzle, gag, suppress, pinion, pin down, tether, hobble.

To confine, shut up, shut in, clap up, lock up, cage, encage, impound, pen, coop, hem in, jam in, enclose, bottle up, cork up, seal up, mew, wall in, rail in, cloister, bolt in, close the door upon, imprison, incarcerate, immure, entomb, seclude, corral.

To take prisoner, lead captive, send or commit to prison, give in charge or in custody, arrest, commit, run in, lag; recommit, remand.

(Phrases) To put in irons; to clap under hatches; to put in a strait-waistcoat.

(Adjectives) Restrained, coerced, etc., sewn up, pent up.

Held up, wind-bound, weather-bound, storm-stayed.

Coactive, stiff, restringent, strait-laced, hide-bound.

(Phrases) In limbo; under lock and key; laid by the heels; 'cabined, cribbed, confined'; in quod; in durance vile; doing time; bound hand and foot.

752 Means of restraint.

Prison *(Substantives)*, jail (or gaol), prison-house, house of detention, lock-up, the cells, clink, glasshouse, brig, jug, quod, cooler, choky, stir, calaboose, cage, coop, den, cell, stronghold, fortress, keep, dungeon, bastille, oubliette, bridewell, tollbooth, panopticon, hulks, galleys, penitentiary, guard-room, hold, round-house, blackhole, station, enclosure, concentration camp, pen, fold, pound, paddock, stocks, bilboes, nick.

Newgate, King's Bench, Fleet, Marshalsea, Pentonville, Holloway, Dartmoor, Portland, Peterhead, Broadmoor, Sing Sing, the Bastille.

Fetter, shackle, trammel, bond, chain, irons, collar, cangue, pinion, gyve, fetterlock, manacle, handcuff, darbies, strait waistcoat; yoke, halter, harness, muzzle, gag, bridle, curb, bit, snaffle, rein, martingale, leading-strings, swaddling-bands, tether, hobble, picket, band, brake.

Bolt, bar, lock, padlock, rail, wall, paling, palisade (232), fence, corral, barrier, barricade.

753 Keeper *(Substantives)*, custodian, *custos*, warder, jailer (or gaoler), turnkey, castellan, guard, ranger, gamekeeper, watch, watchman, watch and ward, sentry, sentinel, coastguard, convoy, escort, *concierge*, caretaker, watch-dog.

Guardian, duenna, nurse, ayah, chaperon.

755 Vicarious authority.

Commission *(Substantives)*, delegation, consignment, assignment, devolution, procuration, deputation, legation, mission, agency, clerkship, agentship; power of attorney; errand, embassy, charge, brevet, diploma, exequatur, committal, commitment.

Appointment, nomination, ordination, installation, inauguration, return, accession, investiture, coronation.

Viceregency, regency, regentship.

Deputy (759).

(Verbs) To commission, delegate, depute, devolve, send out, assign, consign, charge, encharge, entrust with, commit to, enlist.

To appoint, name, nominate, accredit, engage, bespeak, ordain, install, induct, inaugurate, invest, crown, return, enrol.

754 Prisoner *(Substantives)*, prisoner-of-war, P.O.W., kriegie, captive, *détenu*, convict, jail-bird, lag; ticket-of-leave man.

(Adjectives) In custody, in charge, imprisoned, locked up, incarcerated, pent.

756 Abrogation *(Substantives)*, annulment, cancel, cancellation, revocation, repeal, rescission, rescinding, deposal, deposition, dethronement, defeasance, dismissal, sack, *congé*, demission, disestablishment, disendowment.

Abolition, abolishment, counterorder, countermand, repudiation, nullification, recantation, palinode, retractation (607).

(Verbs) To abrogate, annul, cancel, revoke, repeal, rescind, reverse, override, overrule, abolish, disannul, dissolve, quash, repudiate, nullify, retract, recant, recall, countermand, counter-order, break off, disclaim, declare null and void, disestablish, disendow, deconsecrate, set aside, do away with.

To dismiss, send off, send away, discard, turn off, turn away, cashier,

Employ, empower, set over.

To be commissioned, to represent.

(Adverbs) Per procurationem, per pro., p.p.

sack, fire, bounce, oust, unseat, unthrone, dethrone, depose, uncrown, unfrock, disbar, disbench.

(Phrases) Send about one's business; put one's nose out of joint; give one the mitten, the chuck, the sack, the boot, the push.

To get one's books or cards; to get the key of the street.

(Adjectives) Abrogated, etc.; *functus officio.*

(Interjections) Get along with you! clear out! be off! beat it!

757 Resignation *(Substantives)*, retirement, abdication, renunciation, abjuration.

(Verbs) To resign, give up, throw up, retire, abdicate, lay down, abjure, renounce, forgo, disclaim, retract (756); to tender one's resignation, send in one's papers.

(Phrases) To swallow the anchor; to be given one's bowler.

(Adjective) Emeritus.

(Phrase) 'Othello's occupation's gone.'

758 Consignee *(Substantives)*, delegate, commissary, commissioner, vice-regent, legate, representative, secondary, nominee, surrogate, functionary, trustee, assignee.

Corps diplomatique, plenipotentiary, emissary, embassy, ambassador, diplomat(ist), consul, resident, nuncio, internuncio.

Agent, factor, attorney, broker, factotum, bailiff, man of business, go-between, intermediary, middleman, salesman, commission agent, commercial traveller, bagman, drummer, colporteur, commissionaire, employee, attaché, curator, clerk, placeman.

759 Deputy *(Substantives)*, substitute, vice, proxy, locum tenens, baby-sitter, *chargé d'affaires*, delegate, representative, *alter ego*, surrogate, understudy, stooge, stand-in, stopgap, pinch-hitter.

Regent, viceroy, viceregent, vicar, satrap, exarch, vizier, minister, premier, commissioner, chancellor, prefect, warden, lieutenant, proconsul, legate.

(Verbs) To deputize; to be deputy, etc., for; to appear for; to understudy; to take duty for.

(Phrase) To hold a watching brief for.

(Adjectives) Acting, deputizing, etc.

(Adverbs) In place of, vice.

SECTION II—SPECIAL INTERSOCIAL VOLITION

760 Permission *(Substantives)*, leave, allowance, sufferance, tolerance, toleration, liberty, law, licence, concession, grant, vouchsafement, authorization, sanction, accordance, admission, favour, dispensation, exemption, connivance.

A permit, warrant, brevet, precept, authority, firman, pass, passport,

761 Prohibition *(Substantives)*, inhibition, veto, disallowance, interdiction, estoppage, hindrance (706), restriction, restraints (751), embargo, an interdict, ban, injunction, taboo, proscription; *index librorum prohibitorum.*

(Verbs) To prohibit, forbid, inhibit, disallow, bar, debar, interdict, ban,

furlough, ticket, licence, charter, patent, *carte blanche*, exeat.

(*Verbs*) To permit; to give leave or permission; to let, allow, admit, suffer, tolerate, concede, accord, vouchsafe, humour, indulge, to leave it to one; to leave alone; to grant, empower, charter, sanction, authorize, warrant, license; to give licence; to give a loose to.

To let off, absolve, exonerate, dispense with, favour, wink, connive at.

(*Phrases*) To give *carte blanche*; to give rein to; to stretch a point; leave the door open; to let one have a chance; to give one a fair show.

To take a liberty; to use a freedom; to make so bold; to beg leave.

(*Adjectives*) Permitting, etc., permissive, conceding, indulgent.

Allowable, permissible, lawful, legitimate, legal.

Unforbid, unforbidden, unconditional.

estop, veto, keep in, hinder, restrain (751), restrict, withhold, limit, circumscribe, keep within bounds.

To exclude, shut out, proscribe.

(*Phrases*) To clip the wings of; to forbid the banns.

(*Adjectives*) Prohibitive, restrictive, exclusive, prohibitory, forbidding, etc.

Not permitted, prohibited, etc., unlicensed, contraband, unauthorized.

(*Phrases*) Under the ban of; on the Index.

(*Interjections*) Hands off! keep off! God forbid!

———

762 Consent (*Substantives*), compliance, acquiescence, assent (488), agreement, concession, yieldingness, acknowledgment, acceptance.

Settlement, ratification, confirmation.

(*Verbs*) To consent, give consent, assent, comply with, acquiesce, agree to, subscribe to, accede, accept.

To concede, yield, satisfy, grant, settle, acknowledge, confirm, homologate, ratify, deign, vouchsafe.

(*Phrase*) To take at one's word.

(*Adjectives*) Consenting, etc., having no objection, unconditional.

(*Adverbs*) Yes (488); if you please, as you please, by all means, by all manner of means, so be it, of course, certainly, sure, O.K.

(*Phrases*) Suits me; all right by me.

———

763 Offer (*Substantives*), proffer, tender, present, overture, proposition, motion, proposal, invitation, candidature, presentation, offering, oblation, bid, bribe.

Sacrifice, immolation.

(*Verbs*) To offer, proffer, tender, present, invite, volunteer, propose, move, make a motion, start, press, bid, hold out, hawk about.

To sacrifice, immolate.

(*Phrases*) To be a candidate; to go a-begging.

(*Adjectives*) Offering, etc., in the market, for sale, on hire.

764 Refusal (*Substantives*), rejection, declining, non-compliance, declension, dissent (489), denial, repulse, rebuff, discountenance.

Disclaimer, recusancy, abnegation, protest.

Revocation, violation, abrogation (756), flat refusal, peremptory denial.

(*Verbs*) To refuse, reject, deny, decline, disclaim, repudiate, protest, resist, repel, veto, refuse or withhold one's assent; to excuse oneself, to negative, turn down, rebuff, snub, spurn, resist, cross, grudge, begrudge.

To discard, set aside, rescind, revoke, discountenance, forswear.

(*Phrases*) To turn a deaf ear to; to shake the head; not to hear of;

to send to the right-about; to hang fire; to wash one's hands of; to declare off.

(Adjectives) Refusing, etc., recusant, restive, uncomplying, unconsenting.

Refused, etc., out of the question, not to be thought of.

(Adverbs) No, by no means, etc. (489).

(Phrases) Excuse me; nix on that; not on your life; nothing doing.

765 Request *(Substantives)*, requisition, asking, petition, demand, suit, solicitation, craving, entreaty, begging, postulation, adjuration, canvass, candidature, prayer, supplication, impetration, imploration, instance, obsecration, obtestation, importunity, application, address, appeal, motion, invitation, overture, invocation, interpellation, apostrophe, orison, incantation, imprecation, conjuration.

Mendicancy, begging letter, round robin.

Claim, reclamation, revendication.

(Verbs) To request, ask, sue, beg, cadge, crave, pray, petition, solicit, beg a boon, demand, prefer a request or petition, ply, apply to, make application, put to, make bold to ask, invite, beg leave, put up a prayer.

To beg hard, entreat, beseech, supplicate, implore, plead, conjure, adjure, invoke, evoke, kneel to, fall on one's knees, impetrate, imprecate, appeal to, apply to, put to, address, call for, press, urge, beset, importune, dun, tax, besiege, cry to, call on.

To bespeak, canvass, tout, make interest, court; to claim, reclaim.

(Phrases) To send the hat round; to beg from door to door.

(Adjectives) Requesting, asking, beseeching, etc., precatory, suppliant, supplicatory, postulant, importunate.

(Phrases) Cap in hand; on one's knees.

(Adverbs) Do, please, kindly, be good enough, pray, prithee, be so good as, have the goodness, vouchsafe.

For heaven's sake, for goodness' sake, for God's sake, for the love of Mike.

766 Negative request.

Deprecation *(Substantives)*, expostulation, intercession, mediation.

(Verbs) To deprecate, protest, expostulate; to enter a protest; to intercede for.

(Adjectives) Deprecating, etc., deprecatory, expostulatory, intercessory; deprecated, protested.

Unsought, unbesought.

(Interjections) God forbid! forbid it heaven! *absit omen!*

767 Petitioner *(Substantives)*, solicitor, applicant, suppliant, supplicant, mendicant, beggar, mumper, suitor, candidate, aspirant, claimant, postulant, canvasser, tout, cadger, sponger.

SECTION III—CONDITIONAL INTERSOCIAL VOLITION

768 Promise *(Substantives)*, word, troth, plight, profession, pledge, parole, word of honour, assurance, vow, oath.

Engagement, guarantee, undertaking, insurance, contract (769), obligation; affiance, betrothal, betrothment.

768A Release from engagement, disengagement, liberation (750).

(Adjectives) Absolute, unconditional, uncovenanted, unsecured.

(Verbs) To promise, give a promise, undertake, engage, assure; to give, pass, pledge or plight one's word, honour, credit, faith, etc.; to covenant, warrant, guarantee (467); to swear, vow, be sworn; take oath, make oath, kiss the book; to attest, adjure; to betroth, plight troth, affiance.

To answer for, be answerable for, secure, give security (771).

(Phrases) To enter on, make or form an engagement, take upon oneself; to bind, tie, commit, or pledge oneself; to be in for it; to contract an obligation; to be bound; to hold out an expectation.

To call heaven to witness; to swear by bell, book, and candle; to put on one's oath; to swear a witness.

(Adjectives) Promising, etc., promised, pledged, sworn, etc.; votive, promissory.

(Phrases) Under one's hand and seal; as one's head shall answer for.

(Interjection) So help me God!

769 Compact *(Substantives)*, contract, agreement, understanding, bargain, bond, deal, pact, paction, stipulation, covenant, settlement, convention, cartel, protocol, charter, treaty, indenture, concordat, *zollverein*.

Negotiation, transaction, bargaining, haggling, chaffering; diplomacy.

Ratification, settlement, signature, endorsement, seal, signet.

A negotiator, diplomatist, diplomat, agent, contractor, underwriter, attorney, broker (758).

(Verbs) To contract, covenant, agree for, strike a bargain, engage (768); to underwrite.

To treat, negotiate, bargain, stipulate, haggle (or higgle), chaffer, stick out for, insist upon, make a point of, compound for.

To conclude, close, confirm, ratify, endorse, clench, come to an understanding, take one at one's word, come to terms.

To subscribe, sign, seal, indent, put the seal to, sign and seal.

(Phrase) Caveat emptor.

770 Conditions *(Substantives)*, terms, articles, articles of agreement, clauses, proviso, provisions, salvo, covenant, stipulation, obligation, ultimatum, *sine qua non*.

(Verbs) To make it a condition, make terms; to stipulate, insist upon; to tie up.

(Adjectives) Conditional, provisional, guarded, fenced, hedged in.

(Adverbs) Conditionally, on the understanding; provided (469).

(Phrases) With a string tied to it; wind and weather permitting; God willing; D.V.; *Deo volente*.

771 Security *(Substantives)*, surety, guaranty, guarantee, mortgage, warranty, bond, debenture, pledge, tie, plight, pawn, lien, caution, sponsion, hostage, sponsor, bail, parole.

Deed, instrument, deed-poll, indenture, warrant, charter, cartel, protocol, recognizance; verification, acceptance, endorsement, signature, execution, seal, stamp, I O U.

Promissory note, bill of exchange, bill.

Stake, deposit, pool, kitty, jack-pot, earnest, handsel.

Docket, certificate, voucher, verification, authentication.

(Verbs) To give security, go bail, pawn (787); guarantee, warrant, accept, endorse, underwrite, insure; execute, stamp.

To hold in pledge.

772 Observance *(Substantives)*, performance, fulfilment, satisfaction, discharge, compliance, acquittance, quittance, acquittal, adhesion, acknowledgment, fidelity (939).

(Verbs) To observe, perform, keep, fulfil, discharge, comply with, make good, meet, satisfy, respect, abide by, adhere to, be faithful to, act up to, acquit oneself.

(Phrase) To redeem one's pledge.

(Adjectives) Observant, faithful, true, honourable (939), strict, rigid, punctilious.

(Adverb) Faithfully, etc., to the letter.

(Phrase) As good as one's word.

773 Non-observance *(Substantives)*, inobservance, evasion, omission, failure, neglect, laches, laxity, infringement, infraction, violation, forfeiture, transgression.

Retractation, repudiation, nullification, protest.

Informality, lawlessness, disobedience, bad faith (742).

(Verbs) To break, violate, fail, neglect, omit, skip, cut, forfeit, infringe, transgress.

To retract, discard, protest, go back upon or from one's word, repudiate, nullify, ignore, set at naught, wipe off, cancel, etc. (552), to fob off, palter, elude, evade.

(Phrases) To wash out; to shut one's eyes to; to drive a coach and six through.

(Adjectives) Violating, etc., elusive, evasive, transgressive, unfulfilled; compensatory (30).

774 Compromise *(Substantives)*, composition, middle term, *mezzo termine, modus vivendi*; bribe, hush-money.

(Verbs) To compromise, compound, commute, adjust, take the mean, split the difference, come to terms, come to an understanding, meet one half-way, give and take, submit to arbitration.

SECTION IV—POSSESSIVE RELATIONS

1°. *Property in general*

775 Acquisition *(Substantives)*, obtainment, gaining, earning, procuration, procuring, procurement, gathering, gleaning, picking, collecting, recovery, retrieval, totting, salvage, find.

Book-collecting, book-hunting, etc., philately, cartophily, phillumeny.

Gain, profit, benefit, emolument, the main chance, pelf, lucre, loaves and fishes, produce, product, proceeds, return, fruit, crop, harvest, scoop, takings, winnings.

Inheritance, bequest, legacy.

Fraudulent acquisition, subreption, stealing (791).

Profiteering, pot-hunting.

A collector, book-collector, etc., bird-fancier, etc., philatelist,

776 Loss *(Substantives)*, perdition, forfeiture, lapse.

Privation, bereavement, deprivation (789), dispossession, riddance.

(Verbs) To lose; incur, experience, or meet with a loss; to miss, mislay, throw away, forfeit, drop, let slip, allow to slip through the fingers; to get rid of (782), to waste (638, 679).

To be lost, lapse.

(Phrase) To throw good money after bad.

(Adjectives) Losing, etc., lost, etc.

Devoid of, not having, unobtained, unpossessed, unblest with.

Shorn of, deprived of, bereaved of, bereft of, rid of, quit of, dispossessed, denuded, out of pocket, minus, cut off.

cartophilist, phillumenist; a profiteer, money-grubber, pot-hunter.

(Verbs) To acquire, get, gain, win, earn, realize, regain, receive (785), take (789), obtain, procure, derive, secure, collect, reap, gather, glean, come in for, step into, inherit, come by, rake in, scrape together, get hold of, scoop, pouch.

To profit, make profit, turn to profit, make money by, obtain a return, make a fortune, coin money, profiteer.

To be profitable, to pay, to answer.

To fall to, come to, accrue.

(Phrases) To turn an honest penny; to earn an honest crust; to bring grist to the mill; to raise the wind; to line one's pockets; to feather one's nest; to reap or gain an advantage; to keep the wolf from the door; to keep the pot boiling.

(Adjectives) Acquisitive, acquiring, acquired, etc., profitable, lucrative, remunerative, paying.

(Phrase) On the make.

Irrecoverable, irretrievable, irremediable, irreparable.

(Interjections) Farewell to! adieu to!

———

777 Possession *(Substantives)*, ownership, proprietorship, tenure, tenancy, seisin, occupancy, hold, holding, preoccupancy.

Exclusive possession, impropriation, monopoly, inalienability.

Future possession, heritage, heirship, inheritance, reversion.

(Phrases) A bird in the hand; nine points of the law; the haves and the have-nots.

(Verbs) To possess, have, hold, own, be master of, be in possession of, enjoy, occupy, be seised of, be worth, to have in hand or on hand; to inherit (775).

To engross, monopolize, corner, forestall, absorb, preoccupy.

To be the property of, belong to, appertain to, pertain to, be in the hands of, be in the possession of.

(Adjectives) Possessing, etc., possessed of, seised of, worth, endowed with, instinct with, fraught, laden with, charged with.

Possessed, etc., proprietary, proprietorial; on hand, in hand, in store, in stock, unsold, unshared; inalienable.

778 Joint possession.

Participation *(Substantives)*, joint stock, common stock, partnership, copartnership, possession in common, communion, community of possessions or goods, socialism, collectivism, communism, syndicalism.

Bottle party, share-out, picnic.

A syndicate, ring, corner, combine, cartel, trust, monopoly, pool.

A partner, co-partner, shareholder; co-tenant, co-heir; a communist, socialist.

(Verbs) To participate, partake, share, communicate, go snacks, go halves, share and share alike; to have or possess, etc., in common; to come in for a share, to stand in with, to socialize, to pool.

(Adjectives) Partaking, etc.; socialist, socialistic, communist.

(Adverbs) Share and share alike, fifty-fifty, even Stephen.

———

779 Possessor *(Substantives)*, owner, holder, proprietor, proprietress, proprietary, master, mistress, heritor, occupier, occupant, landlord, landlady, landowner, lord of the manor, squire, laird, landed gentry; tenant, renter, lessee, lodger.

Future possessor, heir, heiress, inheritor.

780 Property *(Substantives)*, possession, ownership, proprietorship, seisin, tenancy, tenure, lordship, title, claim, stake, legal estate, equitable estate, fee simple, fee tail, *meum et tuum*, occupancy.

Estate, effects, assets, resources, means, belongings, stock, goods, chattels, fixtures, plant, movables, furniture, things, traps, trappings, paraphernalia, luggage, baggage, bag and baggage, cargo, lading.

Lease, term, settlement, remainder, reversion, dower, jointure, apanage, heritage, inheritance, patrimony, heirloom.

Real property, land, landed estate, manor, demesne, domain, tenement, holding, hereditament, household, freehold, farm, ranch, *hacienda, estancia*, fief, feoff, seigniority, allodium.

Ground, acres, field, close.

State, realm, empire, kingdom, principality, territory, sphere of influence.

(Adjectives) Predial, manorial, freehold, etc., copyhold, leasehold.

781 Retention *(Substantives)*, keep, holding, keeping, retaining, detention, custody, grasp, gripe, grip, tenacity.

Fangs, teeth, clutches, hooks, tentacles, claws, talons, nails.

Forceps, pincers, pliers, tongs, vice.

Incommunicableness, incommunicability.

(Phrase) A bird in the hand.

(Verbs) To retain, keep, keep in hand, secure, detain, hold fast, grasp, clutch, clench, cinch, gripe, grip, hug, withhold, keep back.

(Adjectives) Retaining, etc., retentive, tenacious.

Unforfeited, undeprived, undisposed, uncommunicated, incommunicable, inalienable, not transferable.

782 Relinquishment *(Substantives)*, cession, abandonment (624), renunciation, surrender, dereliction, rendition, riddance (776), resignation (758).

(Verbs) To relinquish, give up, let go, lay aside, resign, forgo, drop, discard, dismiss, waive, renounce, surrender, part with, get rid of, lay down, abandon, cede, yield, dispose of, divest oneself of, spare, give away, throw away, cast away, fling away, maroon, jettison, chuck up, let slip, make away with, make way for.

(Phrases) To lay on the shelf; to throw overboard.

(Adjectives) Relinquished, etc., derelict, left, residuary (40), unculled.

2°. *Transfer of Property*

783 Transfer *(Substantives)*, interchange, exchange, transmission, barter (794), conveyance, assignment, alienation, abalienation, demise, succession, reversion; metastasis.

(Verbs) To transfer, convey, assign, consign, make over, pass, transmit, interchange, exchange (148).

To change hands, change from one to another, alienate, devolve.

To dispossess, abalienate, disinherit.

(Adjectives) Alienable, negotiable, transferable.

784 Giving (*Substantives*), bestowal, donation, accordance, presentation, oblation, presentment, delivery, award, investment, granting.

Cession, concession, consignment, dispensation, benefaction, charity, liberality, generosity, munificence, almsgiving.

Gift, donation, bonus, boon, present, testimonial, presentation, fairing, benefaction, grant, subsidy, subvention, offering, contribution, subscription, whip-round, donative, meed, tribute, gratuity, tip, Christmas box, handsel, trinkgeld, *douceur, pourboire*, baksheesh, cumshaw, dash, bribe, free gift, favour, bounty, largess, allowance, endowment, charity, alms, dole, peace-offering, payment (807).

Bequest, legacy, demise, dotation.

Giver, grantor, donor, benefactor.

(*Phrase*) Panem et circenses.

(*Verbs*) To give, bestow, accord, confer, grant, concede, present, give away, deliver, deliver over, make over, consign, entrust, hand, tip, render, impart, hand over, part with, fork out, yield, dispose of, put into the hands of, vest in, assign, put in possession, settle upon, endow, subsidize.

To bequeath, leave, demise, devise.

To give out, dispense, deal, deal out, dole out, mete out.

To contribute, subscribe, put up a purse, send round the hat, pay (807), spend (809).

To furnish, supply, administer, afford, spare, accommodate with, indulge with, shower upon, lavish.

To bribe, suborn, grease the palm, square.

(*Adjectives*) Giving, etc., given, etc., charitable, eleemosynary, tributary.

(*Phrase*) Bis dat qui cito dat.

785 Receiving (*Substantives*), acquisition (775), reception, acceptance, admission.

A recipient, donee, assignee, legatee, grantee, stipendiary, beneficiary, pensioner, almsman.

(*Verbs*) To receive, take (789), accept, pocket, pouch, admit, catch, catch at, jump at, take in.

To be received, etc.; to accrue, come to hand.

(*Adjectives*) Receiving, etc., recipient, pensionary, stipendiary.

---

786 Apportionment (*Substantives*), distribution, dispensation, allotment, assignment, consignment, partition, division, deal, share-out.

Dividend, portion, contingent, share, whack, meed, allotment, lot, measure, dole, pittance, quantum, ration, quota, modicum, allowance, appropriation.

(*Phrase*) Cutting up the melon.

(*Verbs*) To apportion, divide, distribute, administer, dispense, billet, allot, cast, share, mete, parcel out, serve out, deal, partition, appropriate, assign.

(*Adjectives*) Apportioning, etc., respective.

(*Adverbs*) Respectively, severally.

787 Lending (*Substantives*), loan, advance, mortgage, accommodation, lease-lend, subsistence money, sub, pawn, pignoration, hypothecation, investment; pawnshop, *mont de piété*.

Lender, pawnbroker, uncle.

788 Borrowing (*Substantives*), pledging, replevin, borrowed plumes, plagiarism, plagiary; a touch.

(*Verbs*) To borrow, hire, rent, farm, raise money, raise the wind; to plagiarize.

(Verbs) to lend, loan, advance, mortgage, invest, pawn, impawn, pop, hock, hypothecate, impignorate, place or put out to interest, entrust, accommodate with.

(Adjectives) Lending, etc., lent, etc., unborrowed.

(Adverb) In advance; up the spout.

(Adjectives) Borrowing, etc., borrowed, second-hand.

(Phrases) To borrow of Peter to pay Paul; to run into debt.

———

789 Taking *(Substantives)*, appropriation, prehension, capture, seizure, abduction, ablation, catching, seizing, apprehension, arrest, kidnapping, round-up.

Abstraction, subtraction, deduction, subduction.

Dispossession, deprivation, deprival, bereavement, divestment, sequestration, confiscation, disendowment.

Resumption, reprise, reprisal, recovery (775).

Clutch, swoop, wrench, catch, take, haul.

(Verbs) To take, capture, lay one's hands on; lay, take, or get hold of; to help oneself to; to possess oneself of, take possession of, make sure of, make free with.

790 Restitution *(Substantives)*, return, reddition, rendition, restoration, rehabilitation, remission, reinvestment, reparation, atonement.

Redemption, recovery, recuperation, release, replevin.

(Verbs) To return, restore, give back, bring back, derequisition, denationalize, render, refund, reimburse, recoup, remit, rehabilitate, repair, reinvest.

To let go, disgorge, regorge, regurgitate.

(Adjectives) Restoring, etc., recuperative.

(Phrase) Suum cuique.

———

To appropriate, impropriate, pocket, put into one's pocket, pouch, bag; to ease one of.

To pick up, gather, collect, round up, net, absorb (296), reap, glean, crop, get in the harvest, cull, pluck; intercept, tap.

To take away, carry away, carry off, bear off, hurry off with, abduct, kidnap, crimp, shanghai.

To lay violent hands on, fasten upon, pounce upon, catch, seize, snatch, nip up, whip up, jump at, snap at, hook, claw, clinch, grasp, gripe, grip, grab, clutch, wring, wrest, wrench, pluck, tear away, catch, nab, capture, collar, throttle.

To take from, deduct, subduct (38), subtract, curtail, retrench, abridge of, dispossess, expropriate, take away from, abstract, deprive of, bereave, divest, disendow, despoil, strip, fleece, shear, impoverish, levy, distrain, confiscate, sequester, sequestrate, commandeer, requisition, oust, extort, usurp, suck, squeeze, drain, bleed, milk, gut, dry, exhaust.

(Phrases) To suck like a leech; to be given an inch and take an ell; to sweep the board; to scoop the pool.

(Adjectives) Taking, etc., privative, prehensile, predatory, rapacious, raptorial, predial, ravenous.

———

791 Stealing *(Substantives)*, theft, thieving, thievery, abstraction, appropriation, plagiarism, depredation, pilfering, rape, larceny, robbery, shoplifting, burglary, house-breaking, abaction (of cattle), cattle-lifting, kidnapping.

Spoliation, plunder, pillage, sack, rapine, brigandage, foray, raid, hold-up, dragonnade, marauding.

Peculation, embezzlement, swindling (545), blackmail, *chantage*, smuggling, black market; thievishness, rapacity, kleptomania; den of thieves, Alsatia.

Licence to plunder, letter of marque.

(Verbs) To steal, thieve, rob, abstract, appropriate, filch, pilfer, purloin, nab, nim, prig, grab, bag, lift, pick, pinch, knock off.

To convey away, carry off, make off with, run or walk off with, abduct, spirit away, kidnap, crimp, seize, lay violent hands on, etc. (789), abact, rustle (of cattle), shanghai.

To scrounge, wangle, win, crib, sponge, rook, bilk, diddle, swindle (545), peculate, embezzle, fiddle, flog, poach, run, smuggle, hijack.

To plunder, pillage, rifle, sack, ransack, burgle, spoil, spoliate, despoil, hold up, stick up, bail up, strip, fleece, gut, loot, forage, levy blackmail, pirate, plagiarize.

(Phrases) To live by one's wits; to rob Peter to pay Paul; to obtain under false pretences; to set a thief to catch a thief.

(Adjectives) Stealing, etc., thievish, light-fingered, larcenous, stolen, furtive, piractical, predaceous.

792 Thief *(Substantives)*, robber, spoiler, pickpocket, cutpurse, dip, depredator, yegg, yeggman, footpad, highwayman, burglar, house-breaker, larcener, larcenist, pilferer, filcher, sneak-thief, shop-lifter, poacher, rustler; swell mob; the light-fingered gentry; kleptomaniac.

Swindler, crook, spiv, welsher, smuggler, bootlegger, hijacker, gangster, cracksman, magsman, mobsman, sharper, blackleg, shark, trickster, harpy, *chevalier d'industrie*, peculator, plagiarist, blackmailer; receiver, fence.

Brigand, freebooter, bandit, pirate, viking, corsair, buccaneer, thug, dacoit, picaroon, moss-trooper, rapparee, maurauder, filibuster, wrecker, bushranger; Autolycus, Turpin, Macheath, Bill Sikes, Jonathan Wild.

(Phrases) A snapper-up of unconsidered trifles; *homo triarum literarum*.

793 Booty *(Substantives)*, spoil, plunder, swag, loot, boodle, prey, pickings, grab, forage, blackmail, graft, prize.

3°. *Interchange of Property*

794 Barter *(Substantives)*, exchange, truck, swop (or swap), chop, interchange, commutation.

Traffic, trade, commerce, dealing, business, custom, negotiation, transaction, jobbing, agiotage, bargain, deal, package deal, commercial enterprise, speculation, brokery.

(Phrases) A Roland for an Oliver; a *quid pro quo*; payment in kind.

(Verbs) To barter, exchange, truck, interchange, commute, swap (or swop), traffic, trade, speculate, transact, or do business with, deal with, have dealings with; open or keep an account with; to carry on a trade; to rig the market.

To bargain; drive, make, or strike a bargain; negotiate, bid for, haggle (or higgle), chaffer, dicker, stickle, cheapen, compound for, beat down, outbid, underbid, outbargain, come to terms, do a deal, quote, underquote.

(Phrase) To throw a sprat to catch a whale.

(Adjectives) Commercial, mercantile, trading, interchangeable, marketable, negotiable; wholesale, retail.

795 Purchase *(Substantives)*, emption, buying, purchasing, shopping, hire-purchase, never-never; pre-emption, bribery, co-emption.

A buyer, purchaser, customer, emptor, shopper, patron, client, clientele.

(Verbs) To buy, purchase, procure, hire, rent, farm, pay, fee, repurchase, buy in, keep in one's pay; pre-empt; bribe, suborn, square, buy over; shop, market.

(Adjectives) Purchased, etc.

(Phrase) Caveat emptor.

796 Sale *(Substantives)*, disposal, custom.

Auction, Dutch auction, roup.

Lease, mortgage.

Vendibility, salability.

A vendor, seller (797).

To sell, vend, dispose of, retail, dispense, auction, auctioneer, hawk, peddle, undersell.

To let, sublet, lease, mortgage.

(Phrases) Put up to sale or auction; bring under the hammer.

(Adjectives) Vendible, marketable, salable; unpurchased, unbought, on one's hands, unsalable.

---

797 Merchant *(Substantives)*, trader, dealer, tradesman, buyer and seller, vendor, monger, chandler, shopkeeper, shopman, salesman, saleswoman, changer.

Retailer, chapman, hawker, huckster, regrater, higgler, pedlar, cadger, sutler, bumboatman, middleman, coster, costermonger; auctioneer, broker, money-broker, bill-broker, money-changer, jobber, factor, go-between, cambist, usurer, money-lender.

House, firm, concern, partnership, company, guild, syndicate.

798 Merchandise *(Substantives)*, ware, mercery, commodity, effects, goods, article, stock, stock-in-trade, cargo (190), produce, freight, lading, ship-load, staple commodity.

799 Mart *(Substantives)*, market, change (or 'change), exchange, bourse, market-place, fair, hall, staple, bazaar, guildhall, tollbooth (or tolbooth), custom-house.

Office, shop, counting-house, bureau, counter, stall, booth, chambers.

Warehouse, depot, store (636), *entrepôt*, emporium, godown.

4°. *Monetary Relations*

800 Money *(Substantives)*, funds, treasure, capital, stock, proceeds, assets, cash, bullion, ingot, nugget; sum, amount, balance.

Currency, soft currency, hard currency, circulating medium, legal tender, specie, coin, hard cash, sterling, pounds shillings and pence, L.S.D.

Ready, rhino, blunt, oof, lolly, splosh, chink, dibs, plunks, bucks, bones, siller, dust, tin, dough, jack, spondulicks, simoleons, mazuma, ducats, the needful, the wherewithal.

Gold, silver, copper, nickel, rouleau, dollar, etc.

Finance, gold standard, monometallism, bimetallism.

Pocket-money, pin money, chicken feed, petty cash, change, small coin; doit, farthing, bawbee, penny, shilling, stiver, mite, sou; plum, grand, monkey, pony, tenner, fiver, quid, wheel, bob, tanner, two bits.

Sum, amount, balance.

Paper money, note, bank-note, treasury note, greenback, note of hand, promissory note, I O U.

Cheque (or check), bill, draft (or draught), order, remittance, postal order, money order, warrant, coupon, debenture, bill of exchange, exchequer bill, treasury bill, assignat.

A drawer, a drawee.

False money, base coin, flash note, kite, stumer.

Science of coins, numismatics.

(*Phrases*) The sinews of war; the almighty dollar.

(*Verbs*) To draw, draw upon, endorse, issue, utter; to amount to, come to.

(*Adjectives*) Monetary, pecuniary, fiscal, financial, sumptuary; monometallic, bimetallic; numismatical.

(*Phrases*) To touch the pocket; *argumentum ad crumenam*.

801 Treasurer (*Substantives*), purse-bearer, purser, bursar, banker, moneyer, paymaster, cashier, teller, accountant, steward, trustee, almoner.

Chancellor of the Exchequer, minister of finance, Queen's Remembrancer.

802 Treasury (*Substantives*), bank, savings-bank, exchequer, coffer, chest, money-box, money-bag, strong-box, strong-room, safe, bursary, till, notecase, wallet, purse, *purse-monnaie*, purse-strings, pocket, fisc.

Consolidated fund, sinking fund, the funds, consols, government securities, war loan, savings certificates.

803 Wealth (*Substantives*), fortune, riches, opulence, affluence, independence, solvency, competence, easy circumstances, command of money; El Dorado, Golconda, plutocracy.

Means, provision, substance, resources, capital, revenue, income, alimony, livelihood, subsistence, loaves and fishes, pelf, mammon, lucre, dower (810), pension, superannuation, annuity, unearned increment, pin-money.

A rich man, capitalist, plutocrat, financier, money-bags, millionaire, a Nabob, Dives, Croesus, Midas; *rentier*.

(*Phrases*) The golden calf; a well-lined purse; the purse of Fortunatus; a mint or pot of money.

(*Verbs*) To be rich, etc., to afford.

To enrich, fill one's coffers, etc.; to capitalize.

(*Phrases*) To roll in riches; to wallow in wealth; to make one's pile; to feather one's nest; to line one's pockets; to keep one's head above water.

(*Adjectives*) Wealthy, rich, well-off, affluent, opulent, flush, oofy, solvent (734), moneyed, plutocratic.

(*Phrases*) Made of money; in

804 Poverty (*Substantives*), indigence, penury, pauperism, destitution, want, need, lack, necessity, privation, distress, an empty purse; bad, reduced, or straitened circumstances; narrow means, straits, insolvency, impecuniosity, beggary, mendicancy, mendicity.

A poor man, pauper, mendicant, beggar, tramp, bum, vagabond, gangrel, starveling; the proletariat; *un pauvre diable*.

Poorhouse, workhouse, the institution.

(*Phrases*) *Res angusta domi*; the wolf at the door.

(*Verbs*) To be poor, etc., to want, lack, starve.

To render poor, etc., to reduce, to impoverish, reduce to poverty, depauperate, ruin; to pauperize.

(*Phrases*) To live from hand to mouth; come upon the parish; not to have a penny; to have seen better days; to beg one's bread.

(*Adjectives*) Poor, indigent, penniless, moneyless, impecunious, short of money, out of money, out of dash, out of pocket, needy, destitute, necessitous, distressed, hard up, in need, in want, poverty-stricken,

funds; rich as Croesus; rolling in riches; one's ship come home.

———

badly off, in distress, pinched, straitened, dowerless, fortuneless, reduced, insolvent (806), bereft, bereaved, fleeced, stripped, stony broke, stony stumped.

(Phrases) Unable to make both ends meet; out at elbows; in reduced circumstances; not worth a sou; poor as Job; poor as a church mouse; down at heels; on one's uppers; on the rocks.

———

805 Credit *(Substantives)*, trust, tick, score, account.

Letter of credit, duplicate, traveller's cheque (or check); mortgage, lien, debenture.

A creditor, lender, lessor, mortgagee, debenture-holder; a dun, usurer, gombeen-man, Shylock.

(Verbs) To keep an account with, to credit, accredit.

To place to one's credit or account, give credit.

(Adjective) Crediting.

(Adverbs) On credit, on tick, on account, to pay, unpaid-for.

———

806 Debt *(Substantives)*, obligation, liability, debit, indebtment, arrears, deficit, default, insolvency.

Interest, usance, usury.

Floating debt, bad debt, floating capital, debentures; deferred payment, hire system, never-never system.

A debtor, debitor, borrower, lessee, mortgagor; a defaulter (808).

(Verbs) To be in debt, to owe, to answer for, to incur a debt, borrow (788).

(Phrases) To run up a bill; to go on tick; to outrun the constable.

(Adjectives) In debt, indebted, owing, due, unpaid, outstanding, in arrear, being minus, out of pocket, encumbered, involved, in difficulties, liable, chargeable, answerable for, insolvent, in the red.

Unrequited, unrewarded.

———

807 Payment *(Substantives)*, defrayment, discharge, quittance, acquittance, settlement, clearance, liquidation, satisfaction, remittance, instalment, stake, reckoning, arrangement, composition, acknowledgment, release.

Repayment, reimbursement, retribution, reward (973).

Bill, cheque, cash, ready money (800).

(Phrase) A *quid pro quo*.

(Verbs) To pay, defray, discharge, settle, quit, acquit oneself of, reckon with, remit, clear, liquidate, release; repay, refund, reimburse.

(Phrases) To honour a bill; to strike a balance; to settle, balance, or square accounts with; to be even with; to wipe off old scores; to satisfy all demands; to pay one's way or shot; to pay in full.

808 Non-payment *(Substantives)*, default, defalcation, repudiation, protest.

Insolvency, bankruptcy, failure, whitewashing, application of the sponge.

Waste paper, dishonoured bills.

A defaulter, bankrupt, welsher, levanter, insolvent debtor, man of straw, lame duck.

(Verbs) Not to pay, to fail, break, become insolvent or bankrupt, default, defalcate.

To protest, dishonour, repudiate, nullify; hammer.

(Phrases) To run up bills; to tighten the purse-strings.

(Adjectives) Not paying, in debt, behindhand, in arrear, insolvent, bankrupt, gazetted.

(Phrases) Being minus or worse

(Adjectives) Paying, etc., paid, owing nothing, out of debt.

(Adverbs) On the nail, money down, C.O.D.

809 Expenditure *(Substantives)*, money going out; outgoings, expenses, disbursements, outlay.

Pay, payment, fee, hire, wages, perquisites, vails, allowance, stipend, salary, screw, dividend, tribute, subsidy, batta, bat-money, shot, scot.

Remuneration, recompense, reward (973), tips, *pourboire*, largess, honorarium, refresher, bribe, *douceur*, hush-money, extras, commission, rake-off.

Advance, subsistence money, sub, earnest, handsel, deposit, prepayment, entrance fee, entrance.

Contribution, donation, subscription, deposit, contingent, dole, quota.

Investment, purchase (795), alms (748).

(Verbs) To expend, spend, pay, disburse, lay out, lay or pay down, to cash, to come down with, brass up, shell out, fork out, bleed, make up a sum, to invest, sink money, prepay, tip.

(Phrases) To unloose the purse-strings; to pay the piper; to pay through the nose.

(Adjectives) Expending, etc., expended, etc., sumptuary.

than nothing; plunged or over head and ears in debt; in the gazette; in Queer Street.

810 Receipt *(Substantives)*, money coming in, incomings.

Income, revenue, earnings (775), rent, rental, rent-roll, rentage, return, proceeds, premium, bonus, gate-money, royalty.

Pension, annuity, tontine, jointure, dower, dowry, dot, alimony, compensation.

Emoluments, perquisites, recompense (809), sinecure.

(Verbs) To receive, pocket (789), to draw from, derive from.

To bring in, yield, return, afford, pay, accrue.

(Phrases) To get what will make the pot boil; keep the wolf from the door; bring grist to the mill.

(Adjectives) Receiving, etc., received, etc.

Gainful, profitable, remunerative, lucrative, advantageous (775).

811 Accounts *(Substantives)*, money matters, finance, budget, bill, score, reckoning, balance-sheet, books, account-books, ledger, day-book, cash-book, cash account, current account, deposit account, pass-book.

Book-keeping, audit, double entry.

An accountant, C.A., auditory, actuary, book-keeper.

(Verbs) To keep accounts, to enter, post, credit, debit, tot up, carry over; balance, make up accounts, take stock, audit.

To falsify, garble, cook, or doctor accounts.

812 Price *(Substantives)*, cost, expense, amount, figure, charge, demand, damage, fare, hire.

Dues, duty, toll, tax, supertax, pay-as-you-earn, P.A.Y.E., rate, impost, cess, levy, gabelle, octroi, assessment, benevolence, custom, tithe, exactment, ransom, salvage, excise, tariff, brokerage, demurrage.

Bill, account, score, reckoning.

Worth, rate, value, valuation,

813 Discount *(Substantives)*, abatement, reduction, deduction, depreciation, allowance, drawback, poundage, *agio*, percentage, rebate, set-off, backwardation, contango, tare and tret, salvage.

(Verbs) To discount, bate, abate, rebate, reduce, take off, allow, give, discount, tax.

(Adjectives) Discounting, etc.

(Adverb) At a discount.

evaluation, appraisement, market price, quotation; money's worth, pennyworth; price-current, price list.

(Verbs) To set or fix a price, appraise, assess, value, evaluate, price, charge, demand, ask, require, exact.

To fetch, sell for, cost, bring in, yield, make, change hands for, go for, realize, run into, stand one in; afford.

(Phrases) To run up a bill; to amount to; to set one back.

(Adjectives) Priced, charged, etc., to the tune of, *ad valorem*; mercenary, venal.

(Phrases) No penny, no paternoster; *point d'argent, point de Suisse*.

814 Dearness *(Substantives)*, costliness, high price, expensiveness, rise in price, overcharge, surcharge, extravagance, exorbitance, extortion.

(Phrase) A pretty penny.

(Verbs) To be dear, etc., to cost much, to come expensive; to overcharge, surcharge, bleed, fleece (791).

To pay too much, to pay through the nose.

(Adjectives) Dear, high, high-priced, expensive, costly, dear-bought, precious, unreasonable, extortionate, extravagant, exorbitant, steep, stiff.

(Adverbs) Dear, at great cost, at a premium.

815 Cheapness *(Substantives)*, low price, inexpensiveness, drop in price, undercharge, bargain; absence of charge, gratuity, free admission.

(Phrases) A labour of love; the run of one's teeth; a drug in the market.

(Verbs) To be cheap, etc., to cost little, to come down or fall in price, to cut prices.

(Phrase) To have one's money's worth.

(Adjectives) Cheap, low, moderate, reasonable, inexpensive, unexpensive, low-priced, dirt-cheap, worth the money, half-price; catchpenny.

Gratuitous, gratis, free, for nothing, given away, free of cost, without charge, not charged, untaxed, scot-free, shot-free, expenseless, free of expense, free of all demands, honorary, unpaid.

(Phrases) Cheap as dirt; for a mere song; given away with a pound of tea; at cost price; at a reduction; at a sacrifice.

816 Liberality *(Substantives)*, generosity (942), bounty, munificence, bounteousness, bountifulness, charity (906), hospitality.

(Verbs) To be liberal, etc., spend freely, lavish, shower upon.

(Phrases) To loosen one's purse-strings; to give *carte blanche*; to spare no expense.

(Adjectives) Liberal, free, generous, charitable, hospitable, bountiful, bounteous, handsome, lavish, ungrudging, free-handed, open-handed, open-hearted, free-hearted, munificent, princely.

Overpaid.

817 Economy *(Substantives)*, frugality, thrift, thriftiness, care, husbandry, good housewifery, austerity, retrenchment; parsimony (819).

(Verbs) To be economical, etc., to save, economize, skimp, scrimp, scrape, meet one's expenses, retrench; to lay by, put by, save up, invest, bank, hoard, accumulate.

(Phrases) To cut one's coat according to one's cloth; to make ends meet; to pay one's way; to look at both sides of a shilling; to provide for a rainy day.

(Adjectives) Economical, frugal, thrifty, canny, careful, saving, chary, spare, sparing, cheese-paring.

(Phrase) Take care of the pence and the pounds will take care of themselves.

818 Prodigality *(Substantives)*, unthriftiness, thriftlessness, unthrift, waste, profusion, profuseness, extravagance, dissipation, squandering, squandermania, malversation.

A prodigal, spendthrift, squanderer, waster, wastrel.

(Verbs) To be prodigal, etc., to squander, lavish, waste, dissipate, exhaust, run through, spill, misspend, throw away money, drain.

(Phrases) To burn the candle at both ends; to make ducks and drakes of one's money; to spend money like water; to outrun the constable; to fool away, potter, muddle away, fritter away, etc., one's money; to pour water into a sieve; to go the pace.

(Adjectives) Prodigal, profuse, improvident, thriftless, unthrifty, wasteful, extravagant, lavish, dissipated.

(Phrases) Penny wise and pound foolish; money burning a hole in one's pocket.

———

819 Parsimony *(Substantives)*, parsimoniousness, stint, stinginess, niggardliness, cheese-paring, extortion, illiberality, closeness, penuriousness, avarice, tenacity, covetousness, greediness, avidity, rapacity, venality, mercenariness, cupidity.

A miser, niggard, churl, screw, skinflint, money-grubber, codger, muckworm, hunks, curmudgeon, harpy.

(Phrase) Auri sacra fames.

(Verbs) To be parsimonious, etc., to grudge, begrudge, stint, pinch, screw, dole out.

(Phrases) To skin a flint; to drive a hard bargain; to tighten one's purse-strings.

(Adjectives) Parsimonious, stingy, miserly, mean, mingy, penurious, shabby, near, niggardly, cheese-paring, close, close-fisted, close-handed, chary, illiberal, ungenerous, churlish, sordid, mercenary, venal, covetous, avaricious, greedy, grasping, griping, pinching, extortionate, rapacious.

(Phrases) Having an itching palm; with a sparing hand.

CLASS VI

WORDS RELATING TO THE SENTIENT AND MORAL POWERS

SECTION I—AFFECTIONS IN GENERAL

820 Affections *(Substantives)*, character, qualities, disposition, nature, spirit, mood, tone, temper, temperament; cast or frame of mind or soul; turn, bent, idiosyncrasy, bias, turn of mind, predisposition, diathesis, predilection, propensity, proneness, proclivity, vein, humour, grain, mettle.

Soul, heart, breast, bosom, the inner man, inmost heart, heart's core, heart-strings, heart's-blood, heart of hearts, *penetralia mentis*.

Passion, pervading spirit, ruling passion, master-passion.

(Phrases) Flow of soul; fullness of the heart; the cockles of one's heart; flesh and blood.

(Verbs) To have or possess affections, etc.; be of a character, etc.; to breathe.

(Adjectives) Affected, characterized, formed, moulded, cast, tempered, attempered, framed, disposed, predisposed, prone, inclined, having a bias, etc., imbued or penetrated with; inbred, inborn, engrained (or ingrained).

821 Feeling *(Substantives)*, endurance, suffering, tolerance, sufferance, experience, sensibility (822), passion (825).

Impression, sensation, affection, response, emotion, pathos, warmth, glow, fervour, fervency, heartiness, effusiveness, effusion, gush, cordiality, ardour, exuberance, zeal, eagerness, *empressement, élan*, enthusiasm, verve, inspiration.

Blush, suffusion, flush, tingling, thrill, kick, excitement (824), turn, shock, agitation (315), heaving, flutter, flurry, fluster, twitter, stew, tremor, throb, throbbing, panting, palpitation, trepidation, perturbation, hurry of spirits, the heart swelling, throbbing, thumping, pulsating, melting, bursting; transport, rapture, ecstasy, ravishment (827).

(Verbs) To feel, receive, an impression, etc.; to be impressed with, affected with, moved with, touched with, keen on.

To bear, bear with, suffer, endure, brook, tolerate, stomach, stand, thole, experience, taste, meet with, go through, put up with, prove; to harbour, cherish, support, abide, undergo.

To blush, change colour, mantle, tingle, twitter, throb, heave, pant, palpitate, go pit-a-pat, agitate, thrill, tremble, shake, quiver, wince, simmer, burble.

To swell, glow, warm, flush, redden, look blue, look black, catch the flame, catch the infection, respond, enthuse.

To possess, pervade, penetrate, imbue, absorb, etc., the soul.

(Phrases) To bear the brunt of; to come home to one's feelings or bosom; to strike a chord.

(Adjectives) Feeling, suffering, enduring; sentient, emotive, emotional.

Impressed, moved, touched, affected with, etc., penetrated, imbued.

Warm, quick, lively, smart, strong, sharp, keen, acute, cutting, incisive, piercing, pungent, racy, piquant, poignant, caustic.

257

Deep, profound, indelible, ineffaceable, impressive, effective, deep-felt, home-felt, heart-felt, warm-hearted, hearty, cordial, swelling, thrilling, rapturous, ecstatic, soul-stirring, emotive, deep-mouthed, heart-expanding, electric.

Earnest, hearty, eager, exuberant, gushing, effusive, breathless, glowing, fervent, fervid, ardent, soulful, burning, red-hot, fiery, flaming, boiling, boiling over, zealous, pervading, penetrating, absorbing, hectic, rabid, fanatical; the heart being big, full, swelling, overflowing, bursting.

Wrought up, excited, passionate, enthusiastic (825).

(Phrase) Struck all of a heap.

(Adverbs) Heartily, cordially, earnestly, etc.

(Phrases) From the bottom of one's heart; *de profundis*; heart and soul; over head and ears.

---

822 Sensibility *(Substantives)*, impressibility, sensibleness, sensitiveness, hyperaesthesia (825), responsiveness, affectibility, susceptibleness, susceptibility, susceptivity, excitability, mobility, vivacity, vivaciousness, tenderness, softness, sentimentality, sentimentalism, schmalz.

Physical sensibility (375).

(Verbs) To be sensible, etc., to shrink, have a tender heart.

(Phrases) To be touched to the quick; to feel where the shoe pinches; to take it hard; to take to heart.

(Adjectives) Sensible, sensitive, impressible, impressionable, susceptive, susceptible, responsive, excitable, mobile, thin-skinned, touchy, alive, vivacious, lively, mettlesome, high-strung, intense, emotional, tender, soft, sentimental, maudlin, sloppy, romantic, enthusiastic, neurotic.

(Adverbs) Sensibly, etc., to the quick.

---

823 Insensibility *(Substantives)*, insensibleness, inertness, insensitivity, impassibility, impassibleness, impassivity, apathy, phlegm, dullness, hebetude, coolness, coldness, supineness, stoicism, insouciance, nonchalance, indifference, lukewarmness, frigidity, cold blood, sang-froid, dry eyes, cold heart, deadness, torpor, torpidity, ataraxia, pococurantism.

Lethargy, coma, trance, stupor, stupefaction, amnesia, paralysis, palsy, catalepsy, suspended animation, hebetation, anaesthesia (381), stock and stone, neutrality.

Physical insensibility (376).

(Verbs) To disregard, be insensible, not to be affected by, not to mind, to vegetate, *laisser aller*, not to care; to take it easy.

To render insensible (376), numb, benumb, paralyse, deaden, render callous, sear, inure, harden, steel, case-harden, stun, daze, stupefy, brutalize, hebetate.

(Phrases) To turn a deaf ear to; not care a straw (or a fig).

(Adjectives) Insensible, unconscious, impassive, unsusceptible, insusceptible, impassible, unimpressionable, unresponsive, unfeeling, blind to, deaf to, dead to, passionless, spiritless, soulless, apathetic, listless, phlegmatic, callous, hard-boiled, thick-skinned, pachydermatous, obtuse, proof against, case-hardened, inured, steeled against, stoical, dull, frigid, cold, cold-blooded, cold-hearted, flat, inert, bovine, supine, sluggish, torpid, languid, tame, tepid, numb, numbed, sleepy, yawning, comatose, anaesthetic.

Indifferent, insouciant, lukewarm, careless, mindless, regardless, disregarding, nonchalant, unconcerned, uninterested, pococurante; taking no interest in.

Unfelt, unaffected, unruffled, unimpressed, unmoved, unperturbed, uninspired, untouched, etc.; platonic, imperturbable, vegetative, automatic.

(Adverbs) Insensibly, etc., *aequo animo*, with dry eyes, with withers unwrung.

(Phrases) No matter; never mind; *n'importe*; it matters not; it does not signify; it is of no consequence or importance (643); it cannot be helped; nothing coming amiss; it is all the same or all one to; what's the odds? *nichevo*.

824 Excitation *(Substantives)*, of feeling, excitement, galvanism, stimulation, provocation, calling forth, infection, animation, inspiration, agitation, perturbation, subjugation, fascination, intoxication, enravishment, unction; a scene, sensation, tableau, shocker, thriller.

(Verbs) To excite, affect, touch, move, stir, wake, awaken, raise, raise up, evoke, call up, summon up, rake up.

To impress, strike, hit, quicken, swell, work upon.

To warm, kindle, stimulate, pique, whet, animate, hearten, inspire, impassion, inspirit, spirit, provoke, irritate, infuriate, sting, rouse, work up, hurry on, ginger up, commove.

To agitate, ruffle, flutter, fluster, flush, shake, thrill, penetrate, pierce, cut; to work oneself up, to simmer, bubble, burble.

To soften, subdue, overcome, master, overpower, overwhelm, bring under.

To shock, stagger, jar, jolt, stun, astound, electrify, galvanize, give one a shock, petrify.

To madden, intoxicate, fascinate, transport, ravish, enrapture, enravish, entrance, send.

(Phrases) To come home to one's feelings; to make a sensation; to prey on the mind; to give one a turn; to cut to the quick; to go through one; to strike one all of a heap; to make one's blood boil; to lash to a fury; to make one sit up.

(Adjectives) Excited, affected (825), wrought up, worked up, strung up, lost, *éperdu*, wild, haggard, feverish, febrile.

Exciting, etc., impressive, pathetic, sensational, provocative, piquant, aphrodisiac, dramatic, warm, glowing, fervid, swelling.

(Phrases) Being all of a twitter; all of a flutter; the head being turned.

---

825 Excess of sensitiveness.

Excitability *(Substantives)*, intolerance, impatience, wincing, perturbation, trepidation, disquiet, disquietude, restlessness, fidgets, fidgetiness, fuss, hurry, agitation, flurry, fluster, flutter, irritability (901), hypersensitiveness, hyperaesthesia.

Passion, excitement, vehemence, impetuosity, flush, heat, fever, fire, flame, fume, wildness, turbulence, boisterousness, tumult, effervescence, ebullition, boiling, boiling over, whiff, gust, storm, tempest, outbreak, outburst, burst, explosion, fit, paroxysm, brain-storm, the blood boiling.

Fierceness, rage, fury, furore, tantrum, hysteria, hysterics, raving, delirium, frenzy, intoxication, fascination, infection, infatuation, fanaticism, Quixotism, *la tête montée*.

826 Absence of excitability.

Inexcitability *(Substantives)*, hebetude, tolerance, patience.

Coolness, composure, calmness, imperturbability, sang-froid, collectedness, tranquillity, quiet, quietude, quietness, sedateness, soberness, poise, staidness, gravity, placidity, sobriety, philosophy, stoicism, demureness, meekness, gentleness, mildness.

Submission, resignation, sufferance, endurance, longanimity, longsufferance, forbearance, fortitude, equanimity.

Repression, restraint (174), hebetation, tranquillization.

(Phrases) Patience of Job; even temper; cool head; Spartan endurance; a sober-sides.

(Verbs) To be composed, etc., to

(Verbs) To be intolerant, etc., not to bear, to bear ill, wince, chafe, fidget, fuss, not to be able to bear, stand, tolerate, etc.

To break out, fly out, burst out, explode, run riot, boil, boil over, fly off, flare up, fire, take fire, fume, rage, rampage, rave, run mad, run amuck, raise Cain.

(Phrases) To fly off at a tangent; to be out of all patience; to go off the deep end; to get the wind up; to make a scene; to go up in a blue flame.

(Adjectives) Excitable, etc., excited, etc.

Intolerant, impatient, unquiet, restless, restive, fidgety, irritable, mettlesome, chafing, wincing, etc.

Vehement, boisterous, impetuous, demonstrative, fierce, fiery, flaming, boiling, ebullient, over-zealous, passionate, impassioned, enthusiastic, rampant, mercurial, high-strung, skittish, overwrought, overstrung, hysterical, hot-headed, hurried, turbulent, furious, fuming, boiling, raging, raving, frantic, phrenetic, rampageous, wild, heady, delirious, intoxicated, demoniacal; hypersensitive.

Overpowering, overwhelming, uncontrolled, madcap, reckless, stanchless, irrepressible, ungovernable, uncontrollable, inextinguishable, volcanic.

(Phrases) More than flesh and blood can stand; stung to the quick; all hot and bothered.

(Interjections) Pish! pshaw! botheration!

bear, to bear well, tolerate, put up with, bear with, stand, bide, abide, aby, take easily, rub on, rub along, make the best of, acquiesce, submit, yield, bow to, resign oneself, suffer, endure, support, go through, reconcile oneself to, bend under; subside, calm down, pipe down.

To brook, digest, eat, swallow, pocket, stomach, brave, make light of.

To be borne, endured, etc., to go down.

To allay, compose, calm, still, lull, pacify, placate, quiet, tranquillize, hush, smooth, appease, assuage, mitigate, soothe, soften, temper, chasten, alleviate, moderate, sober down, mollify, lenify, tame, blunt, obtund, dull, deaden (823), slacken, damp, repress, restrain, check, curb, bridle, rein in, smother (174).

(Phrases) To take things as they come; to submit with a good grace; to shrug the shoulders.

To set one's heart at rest or at ease.

(Adjectives) Inexcitable, unexcited, calm, cool, temperate, composed, collected, placid, quiet, tranquil, unstirred, undisturbed, unruffled, serene, demure, sedate, staid, sober, dispassionate, unimpassioned, passionless, good-natured, easy-going, platonic, philosophic, stoical, imperturbable, cold-blooded, insensible (823).

Meek, tolerant, patient, submissive, unoffended, unresenting, content, resigned, subdued, bearing with, long-suffering, gentle, mild, sober-minded, cool-headed.

(Phrases) Gentle or meek as a lamb; mild as milk; patient as Job; armed with patience; cool as a cucumber.

SECTION II—PERSONAL AFFECTIONS

1°. *Passive Affections*

827 Pleasure *(Substantives)*, gratification, delectation, enjoyment, fruition, relish, zest, gusto, kick.

Well-being, satisfaction, complacency, content (831), ease, comfort, bed of roses, bed of down, velvet.

828 Pain *(Substantives)*, suffering; physical pain (378).

Displeasure, dissatisfaction, discontent, discomfort, discomposure, malaise.

Uneasiness, disquiet, inquietude,

Joy, gladness, delight, glee, cheer, sunshine.

Physical pleasure (377).

Treat, refreshment, feast, luxury, voluptuousness, clover.

Happiness, felicity, bliss, beatitude, beatification, enchantment, transport, rapture, ravishment, ecstasy, heaven, *summum bonum*, paradise, Eden, Arcadia, nirvana, elysium, empyrean (981).

Honeymoon, palmy days, halcyon days, golden age, *Saturnia regna*.

(Verbs) To be pleased, etc., to feel, receive, or derive pleasure, etc.; to take pleasure or delight in; to delight in, joy in, rejoice in, relish, like, enjoy, take to, take in good part.

To indulge in, treat oneself, solace oneself, revel, riot, luxuriate in, gloat over; to be on velvet, in clover, in heaven, etc.; to enjoy oneself; to congratulate oneself, hug oneself.

(Phrases) To slake the appetite; to bask in the sunshine; to tread on enchanted ground; to have a good time; to make whoopee.

(Adjectives) Pleased, enjoying, relishing, liking, gratified, glad, gladdened, rejoiced, delighted, overjoyed, charmed.

Cheered, enlivened, flattered, tickled, indulged, regaled, treated.

Comfortable, at ease, easy, cosy, satisfied, content (831), luxurious, on velvet, in clover, on a bed of roses, *sans souci*.

Happy, blest, blessed, blissful, overjoyed, enchanted, captivated, fascinated, transported, raptured, rapt, enraptured, in raptures, in ecstasies, in a transport, beatified, in heaven, in the seventh heaven, in paradise.

(Phrases) With a joyful face; with sparkling eyes; happy as a king; pleased as Punch; in the lap of luxury; happy as the day is long; *ter quaterque beatus*.

(Adverbs) Happily, etc.

———

weariness (841), dejection (837).

Annoyance, irritation, plague, bore, bother, botheration, worry, infliction, stew.

Care, anxiety, concern, mortification, vexation, chagrin, trouble, trial, solicitude, cark, dole, dule, load, burden, fret.

Grief, sorrow, distress, affliction, woe, bitterness, heartache, a heavy heart, a bleeding heart, a broken heart, heavy affliction.

Unhappiness, infelicity, misery, wretchedness, desolation, tribulation.

Dolour, sufferance, ache, aching, hurt, smart, cut, twitch, twinge, stitch, cramp, spasm, nightmare, convulsion, throe, angina.

Pang, anguish, agony, torture, torment, rack, crucifixion, martyrdom, purgatory, hell (982).

A sufferer, victim, prey, martyr.

(Phrases) Vexation of spirit; a peck of troubles; a sea of troubles; the ills that flesh is heir to; *mauvais quart d'heure*; the iron entering the soul.

(Verbs) To feel, suffer, or experience pain, etc.; to suffer, ache, smart, ail, bleed, twinge, tingle, gripe, wince, writhe.

To grieve, fret, pine, mourn, bleed, worry oneself, chafe, yearn, droop, sink, give way, despair (859).

(Phrases) To sit on thorns; to be on pins and needles; to labour under afflictions; to have a bad or thin time; to drain the cup of misery to the dregs; to fall on evil days.

(Adjectives) In pain; feeling, suffering, enduring, etc., pain; in a state of pain, of suffering, etc., sore, aching, suffering, ailing, etc., pained, hurt, stung (830).

Displeased, annoyed, dissatisfied, discontented, weary (832), uneasy, ungratified, uncomfortable, ill at ease.

Crushed, stricken, victimized, ill-used.

Concerned, afflicted, in affliction, sorry, sorrowful, in sorrow, cut up, bathed in tears (839).

Unhappy, unfortunate, hapless, unblest, luckless, unlucky, ill-fated, ill-starred, fretting, wretched, miserable, careworn, disconsolate, inconsolable, woebegone, poor, forlorn, comfortless, a prey to grief, etc., despairing, in despair (859), heart-broken, broken-hearted, the heart bleeding, doomed, devoted, accursed, undone.

829 Capability of giving pleasure.

Pleasurableness (*Substantives*), pleasantness, gratefulness, welcomeness, acceptableness, acceptability, agreeableness, delectability, deliciousness, daintiness, sweetness, luxuriousness, lusciousness, voluptuousness, eroticism.

Charm, attraction, attractiveness, sex-appeal, S.A., It, oomph, fascination, witchery, prestige, loveliness, takingness, winsomeness, likableness, invitingness, glamour.

A treat, dainty, titbit, bonbon, *bonne bouche*, sweet, sweetmeat, sugar-plum, nuts, *sauce piquante*.

(*Verbs*) To cause, produce, create, give, afford, procure, offer, present, yield, etc., pleasure, gratification, etc.

To please, take, gratify, satisfy, indulge, flatter, tickle, humour, regale, refresh, interest.

To charm, rejoice, cheer, gladden, delight, enliven (836), to transport, captivate, fascinate, enchant, entrance, bewitch, ravish, enrapture, enravish, beatify, enthral, imparadise.

(*Phrases*) To do one's heart good; to tickle one to death; to take one's fancy.

(*Adjectives*) Causing or giving pleasure, etc., pleasing, agreeable, grateful, gratifying, pleasant, pleasurable, acceptable, welcome, glad, gladsome, comfortable.

Sweet, delectable, nice, jolly, palatable, dainty, delicate, delicious, dulcet, savoury, toothsome, tasty, luscious, luxurious, voluptuous, genial, cordial, refreshing, comfortable, scrumptious.

Fair, lovely, favourite, attractive, engaging, winsome, winning, taking, prepossessing, inviting, captivating, bewitching, fascinating, magnetic, seductive, killing, stunning, ripping, smashing, likable.

Charming, delightful, exquisite, enchanting, enthralling, ravishing,

830 Capability of giving pain.

Painfulness (*Substantives*), disagreeableness, unpleasantness, irksomeness, displeasingness, unacceptableness, bitterness, vexatiousness, troublesomeness.

Trouble, care, cross, annoyance, burden, load, nuisance, pest, plague, bore, bother, botheration, vexation, sickener, pin-prick.

Scourge, bitter pill, worm, canker, cancer, ulcer, curse, gall and wormwood, sting, pricks, scorpion, thorn, brier, bramble, hornet, whip, lash, rack, wheel.

A mishap, misadventure, mischance, pressure, infestation, grievance, trial, crosses, hardship, blow, stroke, affliction, misfortune, reverse, infliction, dispensation, visitation, disaster, undoing, tragedy, calamity, catastrophe, adversity (735).

Provocation, infestation, affront, aggravation, indignity, outrage (900, 929).

(*Phrases*) A thorn in one's side; a fly in the ointment; a sorry sight; a bitter pill; a crumpled rose-leaf.

(*Verbs*) To cause, produce, give, etc., pain, uneasiness, suffering, etc.

To pain, hurt, wound, sting, pinch, grate upon, irk, gall, jar, chafe, gnaw, prick, lacerate, pierce, cut, cut up, stick, gravel, hurt one's feelings, mortify, horrify, shock, twinge, gripe.

To wring, harrow, torment, torture, rack, scarify, cruciate, crucify, convulse, agonize.

To displease, annoy, incommode, discompose, trouble, disquiet, grieve, cross, tease, rag, josh, bait, tire, vex, worry, try, plague, fash, faze, fret, haunt, obsess, bother, pester, bore, gravel, flummox, harass, importune, tantalize, aggravate.

To irritate, provoke, nettle, pique, rile, ruffle, aggrieve, enchafe, enrage.

rapturous, heart-felt, thrilling, beatific, heavenly, celestial, elysian, empyrean, seraphic, ideal.

Palmy, halcyon, Saturnian, Arcadian.

(Phrases) To one's heart's content; to one's taste.

———

To maltreat, bite, assail, badger, infest, harry, persecute, haze, roast.

To sicken, disgust, revolt, turn the stomach, nauseate, disenchant, repel, offend, shock.

To horrify, prostrate.

(Phrases) To barb the dart; to set the teeth on edge; to stink in the nostrils; to stick in one's throat; to add a nail to one's coffin; to plant a dagger in the breast; to freeze the blood; to make one's flesh creep; to make one's hair stand on end; to break or wring the heart.

(Adjectives) Causing, occasioning, giving, producing, creating, inflicting, etc., pain, etc., hurting, etc.

Painful, dolorific, dolorous, unpleasant, unpleasing, displeasing, unprepossessing, disagreeable, distasteful, uncomfortable, unwelcome, unsatisfactory, unpalatable, unacceptable, thankless, undesirable, untoward, unlucky, undesired, obnoxious.

Distressing, bitter, afflicting, afflictive, cheerless, joyless, comfortless, depressing, depressive, mournful, dreary, dismal, bleak, melancholy, grievous, pathetic, woeful, disastrous, calamitous, ruinous, sad, tragic, tragical, deplorable, dreadful, frightful, lamentable, ill-omened.

Irritating, provoking, provocative, stinging, biting, vexatious, annoying, unaccommodating, troublesome, fashious, wearisome, tiresome, irksome, plaguing, plaguy, teasing, pestering, bothering, bothersome, carking, mortifying, galling, harassing, worrying, tormenting, aggravating, racking, importunate, insistent.

Intolerable, insufferable, insupportable, unbearable, unendurable, shocking, frightful, terrific, grim, appalling, dire, heart-breaking, heart-rending, heart-wounding, heart-corroding, dreadful, horrid, harrowing, horrifying, horrific, execrable, accursed, damnable.

Odious, hateful, unpopular, repulsive, repellent, uninviting, offensive, nauseous, disgusting, sickening, nasty, execrable, revolting, shocking, vile, foul, abominable, loathsome, rotten.

Sharp, acute, sore, severe, grave, hard, harsh, bitter, cruel, biting, caustic, corroding, consuming, racking, excruciating, grinding, agonizing.

(Phrase) More than flesh and blood can bear.

(Adverbs) Painfully, etc.

---

831 Content *(Substantives)*, contentment, contentedness, satisfaction, peace of mind, complacency, serenity, sereneness, ease.

Comfort, snugness, well-being.

Moderation, patience (826), endurance, resignation, reconciliation.

(Verbs) To be content, etc.; to rest satisfied, to put up with; to take up with; to be reconciled to.

To render content, etc., to set at ease, to conciliate, reconcile, disarm, propitiate, win over, satisfy, indulge, slake, gratify.

832 Discontent *(Substantives)*, discontentment, dissatisfaction, disappointment, mortification.

Repining, taking on, inquietude, heart-burning, regret (833).

Nostalgia, home-sickness, *maladie du pays*.

Grumbler, grouser, croaker.

(Verbs) To be discontented, dissatisfied, etc.; to repine, regret (833), grumble (839).

To cause discontent, etc., to disappoint, dissatisfy, mortify.

(Phrases) To take in bad part; to

(Phrases) To make the best of; to let well alone; to take in good part; to set one's heart at ease or at rest.

(Adjectives) Content, contented, satisfied, at ease, easy, snug, comfortable, cosy.

Patient, resigned to, reconciled to, unrepining; disarming, conciliatory.

Unafflicted, unvexed, unmolested, unplagued, etc., serene, at rest, *sine cura, sans souci.*

(Phrases) To one's heart's content; like patience on a monument.

(Interjections) Very well, all right, suits me.

833 Regret *(Substantives)*, bitterness, repining; lamentation (839); self-reproach, penitence (950).

(Verbs) To regret, deplore, repine, lament, rue, repent (950).

(Phrase) To rue the day.

(Adjectives) Regretting, etc., regretful, regretted, regrettable, lamentable.

(Phrase) What a pity!

835 Aggravation *(Substantives)*, heightening, exacerbation, exasperation.

(Verbs) To aggravate, render worse, heighten, intensify, embitter, sour, acerbate, envenom, exacerbate, exasperate.

(Phrase) To add fuel to the flame.

(Adjectives) Aggravating, etc., aggravated, etc., unrelieved; aggravable.

(Phrases) Out of the frying-pan into the fire; from bad to worse.

836 Cheerfulness *(Substantives)*, gaiety, cheer, spirits, high spirits, high glee, light-heartedness, joyfulness, joyousness, good humour, geniality, hilarity, exhilaration, liveliness, sprightliness, briskness, vivacity, buoyancy, sunniness, jocundity, joviality, levity, sportiveness, playfulness, jocularity.

Mirth, merriment, merrymaking, laughter (838), amusement (840); nepenthe, Euphrosyne.

Gratulation, rejoicing, exultation,

have the hump; to quarrel with one's bread and butter.

(Adjectives) Discontented, dissatisfied, unsatisfied, malcontent, mortified, disappointed, cut up.

Repining, glum, grumbling, grousing, grouchy, exigent, *exigeant*, exacting; nostalgic, home-sick; disgruntled.

Disappointing, unsatisfactory.

(Phrases) Out of humour; in the dumps; in high dudgeon; down in the mouth.

———

834 Relief *(Substantives)*, easement, alleviation, mitigation, palliation, solace, consolation, comfort, encouragement, refreshment (689), lullaby; deliverance, delivery.

Lenitive, balm, oil, restorative, cataplasm (662); cushion, pillow, bolster (215).

(Phrases) A crumb of comfort; balm in Gilead.

(Verbs) To relieve, ease, alleviate, mitigate, palliate, soften, soothe, assuage, allay, cheer, comfort, console, encourage, bear up, refresh, restore, remedy, cure.

(Phrases) To dry the tears; to pour balm into; to lay the flattering unction to one's soul; to temper the wind to the shorn lamb; to breathe again; to breathe freely.

(Adjectives) Relieving, etc., consolatory; balmy, balsamic, soothing, lenitive, anodyne (662), remedial, curative; easeful.

837 Dejection *(Substantives)*, depression, low spirits, lowness or depression of spirits, dejectedness, sadness.

Heaviness, dullness, infestivity, joylessness, gloom, dolefulness, dolesomeness, weariness (841), heaviness of heart, heart-sickness.

Melancholy, melancholia, dismals, mumps, dumps, doldrums, blues, mulligrubs, blue devils, megrims, vapours, accidie, spleen, hypochondria; *taedium vitae; maladie du pays.*

jubilation, jubilee, triumph, paean, Te Deum, heyday; joy-bells.

(Verbs) To be cheerful, etc.; to be of good cheer, to cheer up, perk up, brighten up, light up; take heart, bear up.

To rejoice, make merry, exult, congratulate oneself, triumph, clap the hands, crow, sing, carol, lilt, frisk, prance, galumph, rollick, maffick, frivol.

To cheer, enliven, elate, exhilarate, entrance, inspirit, animate, gladden, buck up, liven up.

(Phrases) To drive dull care away; to make whoopee; to keep up one's spirits; care killed the cat; *ride si sapis*; laugh and grow fat.

(Adjectives) Cheerful, gay, blithe, cheery, jovial, genial, gleeful, of good cheer, in spirits, in good or high spirits, *allegro*, light, lightsome, buoyant, debonair, bright, glad, light-hearted, hearty, free and easy, airy, jaunty, canty, perky, spry, chipper, saucy, sprightly, lively, vivacious, sunny, breezy, chirpy, hopeful (858).

Merry, joyous, joyful, jocund, playful, waggish, frisky, frolicsome, sportive, gamesome, jokesome, joky, jocose, jocular, jolly, frivolous.

Rejoicing, elated, exulting, jubilant, hilarious, flushed, rollicking, cock-a-hoop.

(Phrases) In high feather; walking on air; with one's head in the clouds; gay as a lark; happy as a king or as the day is long; playful as a kitten; jolly as a sandboy; merry as a grig; full of beans.

(Adverbs) Cheerfully, cheerily, cheerly, etc.

(Interjections) Cheer up! never say die! hurrah! huzza!

———

Despondency, despair, pessimism, disconsolateness, prostration; the Slough of Despond (859).

Demureness, seriousness, gravity, solemnity, solemnness, sullenness.

A hypochondriac, self-tormentor, *malade imaginaire,* kill-joy, Job's comforter, wet blanket, pessimist, futilitarian.

(Verbs) To be dejected, sad, etc.; to grieve, take on, take to heart, give way, droop, sink, lour, look downcast, mope, mump, pout, brood over, fret, pine, yearn, frown, despond (859).

To depress, discourage, dishearten, dispirit, dull, deject, lower, sink, dash, unman, prostrate, over-cloud.

(Phrases) To look blue; to hang down the head; to wear the willow; to laugh on the wrong side of the mouth; to get the hump.

To prey on the mind or spirits; to dash one's hopes.

(Adjectives) Cheerless, unmirthful, mirthless, joyless, dull, glum, flat, dispirited, out of spirits, out of sorts, out of heart, in low spirits, spiritless, lowering, frowning, sulky.

Discouraged, disheartened, downhearted, downcast, cast down, depressed, chap-fallen, crest-fallen, dashed, drooping, sunk, heart-sick, dumpish, mumpish, desponding, pessimistic.

Dismal, melancholy, sombre, tristful, *triste*, pensive, *penseroso*, mournful, doleful, moping, splenetic, gloomy, lugubrious, funereal, woebegone, comfortless, forlorn, overcome, prostrate, cut up, care-worn, care-laden.

Melancholic, hipped, hypochondriacal, bilious, jaundiced, atrabilious, atrabiliar, saturnine, adust.

Disconsolate, inconsolable, despairing, in despair (859).

Grave, serious, sedate, staid, sober, solemn, grim, grim-faced, grim-visaged (846), rueful, sullen.

Depressing, preying upon the mind (830).

(Phrases) Down in the mouth; down on one's luck; sick at heart; with a long face; a prey to melancholy; dull as a beetle; dull as ditchwater; as melancholy as a gib-cat; grave as a judge.

838 Expression of pleasure.

Rejoicing (*Substantives*), exultation, heyday, triumph, jubilation, jubilee (840), paean (990).

Smile, simper, smirk, grin, broad grin.

Laughter, giggle, titter, snigger, crow, cheer, chuckle, guffaw, shout, hearty laugh, horse-laugh, cachinnation; a shout, burst, or peal of laughter. Derision, risibility (856).

Momus, Democritus the Abderite.

(*Verbs*) To rejoice, exult, triumph (884), hug oneself, sing, carol, dance with joy.

To smile, simper, smirk, grin, mock; to laugh, giggle, titter, snigger, chuckle, chortle, burble, crow, cackle; to burst out, shout, guffaw.

To cause, create, occasion, raise, excite, or produce laughter, etc.; to tickle, titillate.

(*Phrases*) To clap one's hands; to fling up one's cap; to laugh in one's sleeve; to shake one's sides; to hold both one's sides; to split one's sides; to die with laughter.

To tickle one's fancy; to set the table in a roar; to convulse with laughter; to be the death of one.

(*Adjectives*) Laughing, rejoicing, etc.; jubilant (836), triumphant.

Laughable, risible, ludicrous (853), side-splitting.

(*Phrases*) Ready to burst or split oneself; 'Laughter holding both his sides.'

(*Interjections*) Hurrah! three cheers!

---

839 Expression of pain.

Lamentation (*Substantives*), complaint, murmur, mutter, plaint, lament, wail, sigh, suspiration, heaving.

Cry, whine, whimper, sob, tear, moan, snivel, grumble, groan.

Outcry, scream, screech, howl, whoop, yell, roar (414).

Weeping, crying, etc.; lachrymation, complaining, frown, scowl, sardonic grin or laugh.

Dirge (363), elegy, requiem, monody, threnody, jeremiad; coronach, wake, keen, keening.

Plaintiveness, querimoniousness, languishment, querulousness.

Mourning, weeds, willow, cypress, crape, sackcloth and ashes.

A grumbler, grouser, croaker, drip; Heraclitus, Niobe.

(*Phrases*) The melting mood; wringing of hands; weeping and gnashing of teeth.

(*Verbs*) To lament, mourn, grieve, keen, complain, murmur, mutter, grumble, grouse, belly-ache, beef, squawk, sigh; give, fetch, or heave a sigh.

To cry, weep, sob, greet, blubber, blub; snivel, whimper; to shed tears; pule, take on, pine.

To grumble, groan, grunt, croak, whine, moan, bemoan, wail, bewail, frown, scowl.

To cry out, growl, mew, mewl, squeak, squeal, sing out, scream, cry out lustily, screech, skirl, bawl, howl, holloa, bellow, yell, roar, yammer.

(*Phrases*) To melt or burst into tears; to cry oneself blind; to cry one's eyes out; to beat one's breast; to wring one's hands; to gnash one's teeth; to tear one's hair; to cry before one is hurt; to laugh on the wrong side of one's mouth.

(*Adjectives*) Lamenting, complaining, etc.; mournful, doleful, sad, tearful, lachrymose, plaintive, plaintful, querulous, querimonious, elegiac.

(*Phrases*) With tears in one's eyes; bathed or dissolved in tears; the tears starting from the eyes.

(*Interjections*) O dear! ah me! alas! alack! heigh-ho! ochone! well-a-day! well-a-way! alas the day! woe worth the day! *O tempora, O mores!*

---

840 Amusement (*Substantives*), diversion, entertainment, sport, divertissement, recreation, relaxation, distraction, avocation, pastime.

841 Weariness (*Substantives*), tedium, ennui, boredom, lassitude, fatigue (688), dejection (837).

Disgust, nausea, loathing, sickness,

Fun, frolic, pleasantry, drollery, jollity, joviality, jovialness, jocoseness, laughter (838).

Play, game, gambol, romp, prank, quip, quirk, rig, lark, fling, bat, spree, burst, binge, razzle-dazzle, escapade, dido, monkey-shines, ploy, jamboree.

Dance (309), ball, ballet (599), hop, shindig, jig, fling, reel, strathspey, cotillion, quadrille, lancers, rigadoon, saraband, lavolta, pavane, galliard, hornpipe, can-can, tarantella, cachucha, fandango, bolero, minuet, gavotte, polka, mazurka, schottische, waltz (or valse), fox-trot, tango, maxixe, rumba, samba, blues, two-step, one-step; folk-dance, morris-dance, square dance, round dance, country dance, step-dance, clog-dance, sword-dance, egg-dance, cake-walk, break-down.

Festivity, festival, jubilee, party (892), merrymaking, rejoicing, fête, gala, ridotto, revelry, revels, carnival, corroboree, saturnalia, high jinks, night out.

Feast, banquet, entertainment, carousal, bean-feast, beano, wayz-goose, jollification, junketing, junket, wake, field-day, regatta, fair, kermess, *fête champêtre*, symposium, wassail.

Buffoonery, mummery, tomfoolery, raree-show, puppet-show, masquerade.

Bonfire, fireworks, *feu de joie*.

A holiday, gala day, red-letter day.

A place of amusement, theatre, music-hall, concert-hall, cinema, circus, hippodrome, ballroom, dance hall, arena, auditorium, recreation ground, playground, playing field, park.

Toy, plaything, bauble, doll, puppet, teddy-bear.

A master of ceremonies, or revels; a sportsman, sportswoman, gamester, reveller; devotee, votary, enthusiast, fan.

(Phrases) A round of pleasure; a short life and a merry one; high days and holidays.

(Verbs) To amuse, divert, entertain, rejoice, cheer, recreate, enliven, solace; to beguile or while away the time; to drown care.

To play, sport, disport, make merry, take one's pleasure, make holiday, keep holiday; to game, gambol, revel, frisk, frolic, romp, jollify, skylark, dally; to dance, hop, foot it, jump, caper, cut capers, skip.

To treat, feast, regale, carouse, banquet.

(Phrases) To play the fool; to jump over the moon; to make a night of it; to make whoopee; to go on the bust; to have one's fling; *desipere in loco*.

disgust of life, *taedium vitae, Weltschmerz*.

Wearisomeness, irksomeness, tiresomeness, monotony, sameness, treadmill, grind.

A bore, a buttonholer, proser, fossil, wet blanket.

(Phrases) A twice-told tale; time hanging heavily on one's hands; a thin time.

(Verbs) To tire, weary, fatigue, fag, jade, bore; set to sleep, send to sleep.

To sicken, disgust, nauseate.

(Phrases) To harp on the same string; to bore to tears; never hear the last of.

(Adjectives) Wearying, etc., wearisome, tiresome, irksome, uninteresting, devoid of interest, monotonous, humdrum, pedestrian, mortal, flat, tedious, prosy, prosing, slow, soporific, somniferous.

Disgusting, sickening, nauseating.

Weary, tired, etc.; aweary, uninterested, sick of, flagging, used up, blasé, bored, stale, fed up, browned off, brassed off, cheesed off, chokka, weary of life; drowsy, somnolent, sleepy (683).

(Adverbs) Wearily, etc.

(Phrase) Ad nauseam.

(Adjectives) Amusing, amusive, diverting, entertaining, etc., amused, etc.
Sportive, jovial, festive, jocose, tricksy, rompish.
(Phrases) On with the dance! *vogue la galère! vive la bagatelle!*

842 Wit *(Substantives)*, humour, comicality, imagination (515), fancy, fun, drollery, whim, jocularity, jocosity, facetiousness, waggery, waggishness, wittiness, salt, Atticism, Attic wit, Attic salt, *esprit*, smartness, banter, chaff, persiflage, badinage, farce, *espièglerie*.

Jest, joke, jape, conceit, quip, quirk, quiddity, crank, wheeze, side-splitter, *concetto*, witticism, gag, wisecrack, repartee, retort, comeback, *mot, bon mot*, pleasantry, funniment, flash of wit, happy thought, sally, point, dry joke, idle conceit, epigram, quibble, play upon words, pun (563), conundrum, anagram (533), quodlibet, *jeu d'esprit, facetiae*; a chestnut, a Joe Miller; an absurdity (497).

A practical joke, a rag.
(Phrases) The cream of the jest; the joke of it; *le mot pour rire.*

843 Dullness *(Substantives)*, heaviness, stolidity, stolidity, dumbness, stupidity (499), flatness, prosiness, gravity (837), solemnity; prose, matter of fact, platitude, commonplace, bromide.

(Verbs) To be dull, prose, fall flat.
To render dull, etc., damp, depress.
(Phrase) To throw cold water on.

(Adjectives) Dull, prosaic, prosing, prosy, unentertaining, dismal (837), uninteresting, boring, flat, pointless, stolid, humdrum (841), pedestrian, literal, unimaginative, matter-of-fact, commonplace.

Slow, stupid, dumb, plodding, Boeotian.

(Phrases) Dull as ditch-water; *Davus sum, non Oedipus; aliquando bonus dormitat Homerus.*

(Verbs) To joke, jest, jape, retort; to cut jokes, crack a joke, perpetrate a joke or pun.
To laugh at, banter, rally, chaff, josh, jolly, jeer (856), rag, guy, kid; to make fun of, make merry with.
(Phrase) To set the table in a roar.
(Adjectives) Witty, facetious, humorous, fanciful, quick-witted, ready-witted, nimble-witted, imaginative (515), sprightly, *spirituel*, smart, jocose, jocular, waggish, comic, comical, laughable, droll, ludicrous, side-splitting, killing, funny, risible, farcical, roguish, sportive, pleasant, playful, sparkling, entertaining, arch.
(Adverbs) In joke, in jest, in sport, for fun.

844 A Humorist *(Substantives)*, wag, wit, funny man, caricaturist, cartoonist, epigrammatist, *bel esprit*, jester, joker, punster, wise-cracker.
A buffoon (599), comedian, *farceur*, merry-andrew, jack-pudding, tumbler, mountebank, harlequin, punch, punchinello, scaramouch, clown, pantaloon.
(Phrase) The life and soul of the party.

2°. Discriminative Affections

845 Beauty *(Substantives)*, handsomeness, beauteousness, beautifulness, pulchritude, aesthetics.
Form, elegance, grace, symmetry, *belle tournure*; good looks.

846 Ugliness *(Substantives)*, deformity, inelegance, plainness, homeliness, uncomeliness, ungainliness, uncouthness, clumsiness, stiffness, disfigurement, distortion, contortion.

Comeliness, seemliness, shapeliness, fairness, prettiness, neatness, spruceness, attractiveness, loveliness, quaintness, speciousness, polish, gloss, nattiness; a good effect.

Bloom, brilliancy, radiance, splendour, magnificence, sublimity.

Concinnity, delicacy, refinement, charm, style.

A beautiful woman, belle, charmer, enchantress, goddess; Helen of Troy, Venus, Hebe, the Graces, Peri, Houri; Cupid, Apollo, Hyperion, Adonis, Antinous, Narcissus.

Peacock, butterfly, flower, rose, lily; the flower of, the pink of, etc.; a garden, a picture.

(Phrases) Je ne sais quoi; le beau idéal; a sight for sore eyes.

(Verbs) To be beautiful; to shine, beam, bloom.

To render beautiful, etc., to beautify, embellish, adorn, deck, bedeck, decorate, set out, set off, ornament (847), dight, bedight, array, garnish, furbish, smarten, trick out, rig out, fig out, dandify, dress up, prank, prink, perk, preen, trim, embroider, emblazon, adonize.

To polish, burnish, gild, varnish, japan, enamel, lacquer.

To powder, rouge, make up, doll up, titivate.

(Adjectives) Beautiful, handsome, good-looking, fine, pretty, lovely, graceful, elegant, delicate, refined, fair, personable, comely, seemly, bonny, braw, well-favoured, proper, shapely, well-made, well-formed, well-proportioned, symmetrical, sightly, becoming, goodly, neat, dapper, tight, trig, spruce, smart, stylish, chic, dashing, swagger, dandified, natty, sleek, quaint, jaunty, bright-eyed, attractive, seductive, stunning.

Blooming, rosy, brilliant, shining, beaming, splendid, resplendent, dazzling, gorgeous, superb, magnificent, sublime, grand.

Picturesque, statuesque, artistic, aesthetic, decorative, photogenic, well-composed, well-grouped.

malformation, monstrosity, misproportion, inconcinnity, want of symmetry, roughness, repulsiveness, squalor, hideousness, unsightliness, odiousness.

An eyesore, object, figure, sight, fright, guy, spectre, scarecrow, hag, harridan, satyr, sibyl, toad, baboon, monster, gorgon, Caliban, Hecate.

(Phrases) A forbidding countenance; a wry face; a blot on the landscape; no oil-painting; *'monstrum horrendum, informe, ingens, cui lumen ademptum.'*

(Verbs) To be ugly, etc.

To render ugly, etc., to deform, deface, distort, disfigure (241), disfeature, misshape, blemish, spot, stain, distain, soil, tarnish, discolour, sully, blot, daub, bedaub, begrime, blur, smear, besmear (653), bespatter, maculate, denigrate, uglify.

(Phrase) To make faces.

(Adjectives) Ugly, plain, homely, unsightly, unornamental, unshapely, unlovely, ill-looking, ordinary, unseemly, ill-favoured, hard-favoured, evil-favoured, hard-featured, hard-visaged, ungainly, uncouth, gawky, hulking, lumbering, slouching, ungraceful, clumsy, graceless, rude, rough, rugged, homespun, gaunt, raw-boned, haggard, scraggy.

Misshapen, shapeless, misproportioned, ill-proportioned, deformed, ill-made, ill-shaped, inelegant, disfigured, distorted, unshapen, unshapely, hump-backed, crooked, bandy, stumpy, dumpy, squat, stubby, bald, rickety.

Squalid, grim, grisly, gruesome, grooly, macabre, grim-faced, grim-visaged, ghastly, ghost-like, death-like, cadaverous, repellent, repulsive, forbidding, grotesque.

Frightful, odious, hideous, horrid, shocking, monstrous, unprepossessing.

Foul, soiled, tarnished, stained, distained, sullied, blurred, blotted, spotted, maculated, spotty, splashed, smeared, begrimed,

Passable, presentable, not amiss, undefaced, spotless, unspotted.

(Phrases) Easy to look at; dressed up to kill.

847 Ornament *(Substantives)*, ornamentation, adornment, decoration, embellishment, enrichment, illustration, illumination, ornature, ornateness, flamboyancy.

Garnish, polish, varnish, gilding, japanning, enamel, lacquer, ormolu.

Cosmetic, rouge, powder, lipstick, mascara, hair-oil, brilliantine.

Jewel, jewellery, bijouterie, spangle, trinket, locket, bracelet, bangle, anklet, necklace, earring, brooch, chain, chatelaine, carcanet, tiara, coronet, diadem.

Gem, precious stone, diamond, brilliant, emerald, sapphire, ruby, agate, garnet, beryl, onyx, topaz, amethyst, opal; pearl, coral.

Embroidery, broidery, brocade, galloon, lace, fringe, trapping, trimming, edging, border, chiffon, hanging, tapestry, arras.

Wreath, festoon, garland, lei, chaplet, tassel, knot, epaulette, frog, star, rosette, bow.

Feather, plume, *panache*, aigrette.

Nosegay, bouquet, posy, buttonhole.

Tracery, moulding, arabesque.

Frippery, finery, bravery, gewgaw, gaud, fal-lal, tinsel, spangle, clinquant, bric-à-brac, knick-knack.

Trope, flourish, flowers of rhetoric, purple patches (577).

Excess of ornament, tawdriness (851).

(Verbs) To ornament, embellish, illustrate, illuminate, enrich, decorate, adorn, beautify, garnish, polish, gild, varnish, enamel, paint, white-wash, stain, japan, lacquer, fume, grain; bespangle, bedeck, bedizen (845), embroider, work, chase, emboss, fret, tool; emblazon, illuminate.

(Adjectives) Ornamented, etc., beautified, rigged out, figged out, wellgroomed, dolled up, ornate, showy, dressy, gaudy (851), garish, gorgeous, fine, gay, rich.

(Phrases) Fine as fivepence; in full fig; in one's Sunday best; dressed up to the nines.

850 Good taste.

Taste *(Substantives)*, delicacy, refinement, gust, gusto, *goût*, virtuosity, virtuosoship, nicety, finesse, grace, culture, virtu, τὸ πρέπον, polish, elegance.

spattered, bedaubed, besmeared; ungarnished.

(Phrases) Ugly as sin; not fit to be seen.

848 Blemish *(Substantives)*, disfigurement, defacement, deformity, eyesore, defect, fault, deficiency, flaw, fleck.

Stain, blot, spot, speck, mote, blur, macula, blotch, speckle, spottiness; soil, tarnish, smudge, smut, dirt, soot (653); freckle, birthmark.

Excrescence, pimple, pustule (250).

(Verbs) To blemish, disfigure, deface (846).

(Adjectives) Blemished, disfigured, etc.; spotted, speckled, freckled, pitted.

849 Simplicity *(Substantives)*, plainness, undress, chastity, chasteness; freedom from ornament or affectation, homeliness.

(Phrase) Simplex munditiis.

(Verbs) To be simple, etc., to render simple, etc., to simplify.

(Adjectives) Simple, plain, ordinary, household, homely, homespun, chaste, unaffected, severe, primitive.

Unadorned, unornamented, undecked, ungarnished, unarrayed, untrimmed, unsophisticated, in dishabille.

———

851 Bad taste.

Vulgarity *(Substantives)*, vulgarism, barbarism, Vandalism, Gothicism, *mauvais goût*, sensationalism, flamboyance.

Coarseness, grossness, indecorum,

Science of taste, aesthetics.

A man of taste, connoisseur, judge, critic, *cognoscente*, virtuoso, dilettante, amateur, aesthete, purist, precisian; an Aristarchus, Corinthian, *arbiter elegantiarum*.

(*Phrase*) Caviare to the general.

(*Verbs*) To appreciate, judge, discriminate, criticize (465).

(*Adjectives*) In good taste, tasteful, unaffected, pure, chaste, classical, attic, refined, aesthetic, cultivated, cultured, artistic, elegant.

(*Adverb*) Elegantly, etc.

(*Phrases*) To one's taste or mind; after one's fancy; *comme il faut*.

852 Fashion (*Substantives*), style, tonishness, *ton, bon ton*, mode, vogue, craze, rage, fad.

Manners, breeding, politeness, gentlemanliness, courtesy (894), decorum, *bienséance, savoir faire, savoir vivre*, punctilio, convention, conventionality, propriety, the proprieties, Mrs. Grundy, form, formality, etiquette, custom, demeanour, air, port, carriage, presence.

Show, equipage, turn-out (882).

The world, the fashionable world, the smart set, the *beau monde*, high life, society, town, court, gentility (875), civilization, civilized life, the *élite*.

(*Phrases*) The height of fashion; *dernier cri*; the latest thing.

(*Verbs*) To be fashionable, etc.

(*Phrases*) To cut a dash; to be in the swim.

(*Adjectives*) Fashionable, in fashion, in vogue, *à la mode*, modish, tony, tonish, stylish, smart, courtly, *recherché*, genteel, aristocratic, conventional, punctilious, *comme il faut*, well-bred, well-mannered, polished, gentlemanlike, ladylike, well-spoken, civil, presentable, *distingué*, refined, thorough-bred, county, *dégagé*, jaunty, swell, swagger, posh, dashing, unembarrassed; trendy.

(*Phrases*) Having a run; all the go.

(*Adverbs*) Fashionably, in fashion.

lowness, low life, *mauvais ton*, bad form, ribaldry, clownishness, rusticity, boorishness, brutishness, brutality, rowdyism, ruffianism, awkwardness, *gaucherie*, want of tact, tactlessness.

Excess of ornament, false ornament, tawdriness, loudness, gaudiness, flashiness, ostentation.

A rough diamond, a hoyden, tomboy, slattern, sloven, dowdy, frump, cub, unlicked cub, clown, cad, guttersnipe, ragamuffin (876); a Goth, Vandal.

(*Verbs*) To be vulgar, etc., to misbehave.

(*Adjectives*) In bad taste, vulgar, coarse, unrefined, gross, ribald, heavy, rude, unpolished, indecorous, homespun, clownish, uncouth, awkward, *gauche*, ungraceful, slovenly, slatternly, dowdy, frumpish.

Ill-bred, ungenteel, impolite, ill-mannered, uncivil, tactless, underbred, caddish, ungentlemanly, unladylike, unfeminine, unmaidenly, unseemly, unpresentable, unkempt, uncombed.

Rustic, countrified, boorish, provincial, barbarous, barbaric, brutish, blackguardly, rowdy, raffish, Gothic, unclassical, heathenish, outlandish, untamed (876).

Obsolete, out of fashion, *démodé*, out of date, unfashionable, antiquated, fossil, old-fashioned, old-world, gone by.

New-fangled, odd, fantastic, grotesque, ridiculous (853), affected, meretricious, extravagant, sensational, monstrous, shocking, horrid, revolting.

Gaudy, tawdry, tinsel, bedizened, flamboyant, baroque, tricked out, gingerbread, loud, flashy, showy.

(*Phrase*) A back number.

853 Ridiculousness *(Substantives)*, ludicrousness, risibility.

Oddness, oddity, whimsicality, comicality, drollery, grotesqueness, fancifulness, quaintness, frippery, gawkiness, preposterousness, extravagance, monstrosity, absurdity (497).

Bombast, bathos, fustian, doggerel, nonsense verse, amphigouri, extravaganza, clerihew, bull, Irish bull, spoonerism.

(Adjectives) Ridiculous, absurd, extravagant, *outré*, monstrous, preposterous, irrational, nonsensical.

Odd, whimsical, quaint, queer, rum, droll, grotesque, fanciful, eccentric, bizarre, strange, out-of-the-way, outlandish, fantastic, baroque, rococo.

Laughable, risible, ludicrous, comic, serio-comic, mock-heroic, comical, funny, derisive, farcical, burlesque, *pour rire*, quizzical, bombastic, inflated, stilted.

Awkward, gawky, lumbering, lumpish, hulking, uncouth.

854 Fop *(Substantives)*, dandy, exquisite, swell, toff, dude, nut, masher, lady-killer, coxcomb, beau, macaroni, blade, blood, buck, spark, dog, popinjay, puppy, *petit-maître*, jackanapes, jack-a-dandy, tailor's dummy, man-milliner, man about town.

855 Affectation *(Substantives)*, mannerism, pretension, airs, dandyism, coxcombry, frills, side, swank, dog, conceit, foppery, affectedness, preciosity, euphuism, charlatanism, quackery, foppishness, pedantry, acting a part, pose, gush.

Prudery, Grundyism, demureness, coquetry, *minauderie*, sentimentality, lackadaisicalness, stiffness, formality, buckram, mock modesty, *mauvaise honte*.

Pedant, precisian, prig, square, bluestocking, *bas bleu*, formalist, *poseur*, mannerist, *précieuse ridicule*; prude, Mrs. Grundy.

(Phrases) A lump of affectation; prunes and prisms.

(Verbs) To affect, to give oneself airs, put on side or frills, to swank, simper, mince, to act a part, overact, attitudinize, gush, pose.

(Adjectives) Affected, conceited, precious, pretentious, stilted, pedantic, pragmatical, priggish, smug, puritanical, prim, prudish, starchy, up-stage, high-hat, stiff, formal, demure, goody-goody.

Foppish, namby-pamby, slip-slop, coxcombical, slipshod, simpering, mincing, niminy-piminy, la-di-da, sentimental, lackadaisical.

Exaggerated (549), overacted, overdone, high-falutin, gushing, stagy, theatrical.

856 Ridicule *(Substantives)*, derision, mockery, quiz, banter, chaff, badinage, irony, persiflage, raillery, send-up.

Jeer, gibe, quip, taunt, satire, scurrility, scoffing.

A parody, burlesque, travesty, skit, farce, comedy, tragi-comedy, doggerel, blunder, bull, *lapsus linguae*, slip of the tongue, malapropism, spoonerism, anticlimax.

Buffoonery, vagary, antic, mummery, tomfoolery, grimace, monkey-trick, escapade, prank, gambade, extravaganza, practical joke, booby-trap.

(Verbs) To ridicule, deride, laugh at (929), laugh down, scoff, mock, jeer, banter, quiz, rally, fleer, flout, rag, rot, chaff, josh, guy, rib, razz, roast, twit, taunt, point at, grin at.

To parody, caricature, burlesque, travesty, pillory, take off.

(Phrases) To raise a smile; to set the table in a roar; to make fun of; to poke fun at; to make merry with; to make a fool of; to make an ass of; to make game of; to make faces at; to make mouths at; to lead one a dance;

to run a rig upon; to make an April fool of; to laugh out of court; to laugh in one's sleeve; to take the micky out of.

(Adjectives) Derisory, derisive, sarcastic, ironical, quizzical, mock, scurrilous, burlesque, Hudibrastic.

857 Object and cause of ridicule.

Laughing-stock *(Substantives)*, gazing-stock, butt, stooge, target, quiz; an original, guy, oddity, card, crank, eccentric, monkey, buffoon, jester (844), mime, mimer (599), scaramouch, punch, punchinello, mountebank, golliwog.

(Phrases) A figure of fun; a queer fish; fair game.

3°. *Prospective Affections*

858 **Hope** *(Substantives)*, trust, confidence, reliance, faith, assurance, credit, security, expectation, affiance, promise, assumption, presumption.

Hopefulness, buoyancy, reassurance, optimism, enthusiasm, aspiration.

A reverie, day-dream, pipe-dream, Utopia, millennium.

Anchor, mainstay, sheet-anchor, staff (215).

(Phrases) Castles in the air; castles in Spain; a ray, gleam, or flash of hope; the silver lining of the cloud.

(Verbs) To hope; to feel, entertain, harbour, cherish, feed, nourish, encourage, foster, etc., hope or confidence; to promise oneself.

To trust, confide, rely on, build upon, feel or rest assured, confident, secure, etc.; to flatter oneself, expect, aspire, presume, be reassured.

To give or inspire hope; to augur well, shape well, bid fair, be in a fair way; to encourage, assure, promise, flatter, buoy up, reassure, embolden, raise expectations.

(Phrases) To see daylight; to live in hopes; to look on the bright side; to pin one's hope or faith upon; to catch at a straw; to hope against hope.

(Adjectives) Hoping, etc., in hopes, hopeful, confident, secure, buoyant, buoyed up, in good heart, sanguine, optimistic, enthusiastic, utopian.

Fearless, unsuspecting, unsuspicious; free or exempt from fear, suspicion, distrust, etc., undespairing.

Auspicious, promising, propitious, bright, rose-coloured, rosy, of good omen, reassuring.

859 Absence, want, or loss of hope.

Hopelessness *(Substantives)*, despair, desperation, despondency, pessimism (837); forlornness, a forlorn hope, the Slough of Despond.

(Phrases) A black look-out; a bad business.

(Verbs) To despair, despond, give up, be hopeless; to lose, give up, abandon, relinquish, etc., all hope; to yield to despair.

To inspire or drive to despair; to dash, crush, or destroy one's hopes.

(Phrases) To trust to a broken reed; *'lasciate ogni speranza voi ch'entrate.'*

(Adjectives) Hopeless, having lost or given up hope, losing, etc., hope, past hope, despondent, pessimistic, forlorn, desperate, despairing.

Incurable, irremediable, irreparable, irrevocable, incorrigible, beyond remedy.

Inauspicious, unpropitious, unpromising, threatening, ill-omened.

860 **Fear** *(Substantives)*, cowardice (862), timidity, diffidence, nervousness, restlessness, inquietude, disquietude, solicitude, anxiety, care, distrust, mistrust, hesitation, misgiving, suspicion, qualm, want of confidence, nerves.

Apprehension, flutter, trepidation, tremor, shaking, trembling, palpitation, jitters, the jumps, the creeps, the needle, ague-fit, fearfulness, despondency; stage fright, cold feet, wind up.

Fright, affright, alarm, dread, awe, terror, horror, dismay, obsession,

(Phrases) Nil desperandum; while there's life there's hope; *dum spiro spero*; never say die; all for the best.

panic, funk, flap, stampede, scare, consternation, despair (859).

Intimidation, terrorism, reign of terror; an alarmist, scaremonger.

Object of fear, bugbear, bugaboo, bogy, scarecrow, goblin (980), *bête noire*, nightmare, Gorgon, ogre.

(Phrases) Raw head and bloody bones; fee-faw-fum; butterflies in the stomach.

(Verbs) To fear, be afraid, etc., to distrust, hesitate, have qualms, misgiving, suspicions.

To apprehend, take alarm, start, wince, boggle, skulk, cower, crouch, tremble, shake, quake, quaver, quiver, shudder, quail, cringe, turn pale, blench, flutter, flinch, funk.

To excite fear, raise apprehensions, to give, raise, or sound an alarm, to intimidate, put in fear, frighten, fright, affright, alarm, startle, scare, haunt, obsess, strike terror, daunt, terrify, unman, awe, horrify, dismay, petrify, appal.

To overawe, abash, cow, browbeat, bully, deter, discourage.

(Phrases) To shake in one's shoes; to shake like an aspen leaf; to stand aghast; to eye askance.

To fright from one's propriety; to strike all of a heap; to make the flesh creep; to give one the creeps; to cause alarm and despondency.

(Adjectives) Fearing, timid, timorous, faint-hearted, tremulous, fearful, nervous, nervy, jumpy, funky, diffident, apprehensive, restless, haunted with the fear, apprehension, dread, etc., of.

Frightened, afraid, cowed, pale, alarmed, scared, terrified, petrified, aghast, awestruck, dismayed, horror-struck, horrified, appalled, panic-stricken.

Inspiring fear, fearsome, alarming, formidable, redoubtable, portentous, perilous (665), ugly, fearful, dreadful, dire, shocking, terrible, tremendous, horrid, horrible, horrific, ghastly, awful, awesome, horripilant, hair-raising, creepy, crawly.

(Phrases) White as a sheet; afraid of one's shadow; the hair standing on end; letting 'I dare not' wait upon 'I would'; more frightened than hurt; frightened out of one's senses or wits; in a blue funk.

861 Absence of fear.

Courage *(Substantives)*, bravery, value, boldness, spirit, moral fibre, spiritedness, daring, gallantry, intrepidity, contempt of danger, self-reliance, confidence, fearlessness, audacity.

Manhood, manliness, nerve, pluck, grit, guts, sand, mettle, gameness, heart, spunk, smeddum, virtue, hardihood, fortitude, firmness, resolution, sportsmanship.

Prowess, derring-do, heroism, chivalry.

A hero, heroine, ace, paladin, *preux chevalier,* Hector, Hotspur, Amazon, Joan of Arc, *beau sabreur,* fire-eater (863).

862 Excess of fear.

Cowardice *(Substantives)*, fear (860), pusillanimity, cowardliness, timidity, fearfulness, spiritlessness, faint-heartedness, softness, effeminacy, funk.

Poltroonery, baseness, dastardliness, yellow streak, a faint heart.

A coward, poltroon, dastard, recreant, funk, mollycoddle, milksop, cry-baby, 'fraid-cat, chicken, cowardy custard.

A runaway, fugitive, deserter, quitter.

(Verbs) To be cowardly, etc.; to quail (860), to flinch, fight shy, shy, turn tail, run away, cut and run, fly for one's life, stampede.

A lion, tiger, bulldog, gamecock, fighting-cock, sportsman.

(Verbs) To be courageous, etc., to face, front, affront, confront, despise, brave, defy, etc., danger; to take courage; to summon up, muster up, or pluck up courage; to rally.

To venture, make bold, face, dare, defy, brave (715), beard, hold out, bear up against, stand up to.

To give, infuse, or inspire courage; to encourage, embolden, inspirit, cheer, nerve.

(Phrases) To take the bull by the horns; to come up to the scratch; to face the music; to 'screw one's courage to the sticking-place'; to die game.

To pat on the back; to make a man of.

(Adjectives) Courageous, brave, valiant, valorous, gallant, intrepid.

Spirited, high-spirited, high-mettled, mettlesome, plucky, manly, manful, resolute, stout, stout-hearted, lion-hearted, heart of oak, firm, indomitable, game, sportsmanlike.

Bold, daring, audacious, fearless, unfearing, dauntless, undaunted, indomitable, unappalled, undismayed, unawed, unabashed, unalarmed, unflinching, unshrinking, unblenching, unblenched, unapprehensive, confident, self-reliant.

Enterprising, venturous, adventurous, venturesome, dashing, chivalrous, heroic, fierce, warlike (722).

Unfeared, undreaded, etc.

(Phrases) One's blood is up; brave as a lion; bold as brass; full of beans.

863 Rashness *(Substantives)*, temerity, audacity, presumption, precipitancy, precipitation, impetuosity, recklessness, overboldness, foolhardiness, desperation, knight-errantry, Quixotism; carelessness (460), want of caution, overconfidence.

Imprudence, indiscretion.

A desperado, madcap, bravo, daredevil, *enfant perdu*, gambler, adventurer, knight errant; Hotspur, Don Quixote, Icarus.

(Phrases) A leap in the dark; a blind bargain; a wild-cat scheme.

(Verbs) To be rash, incautious, etc.

(Phrases) To buy a pig in a poke; to go on a forlorn hope; to go at it baldheaded; to play with fire; to tempt providence.

(Adjectives) Rash, temerarious,

(Phrases) To show the white feather; to be in a sweat.

(Adjectives) Coward, cowardly, yellow, pusillanimous, shy, fearful, timid, skittish, timorous, poor-spirited, spiritless, weak-hearted, faint-hearted, chicken-hearted, white-livered.

Dastard, dastardly, base, craven, recreant, unwarlike, unheroic, unsoldierly, unmanly, womanish.

(Phrase) 'In face a lion, but in heart a deer.'

(Interjections) Sauve qui peut! the devil take the hindmost!

---

864 Caution *(Substantives)*, cautiousness, discretion, prudence, reserve, wariness, heed, circumspection, calculation, deliberation (459).

Coolness, self-possession, aplomb, presence of mind, sang-froid, self-command, steadiness, the Fabian policy.

(Phrases) The better part of valour; masterly inactivity.

(Verbs) To be cautious, etc., to beware, take care, have a care, take heed, ca' canny, be on one's guard, look about one, take no chances.

(Phrases) To look before one leaps; to think twice; to let sleeping dogs lie; to see which way the wind blows; to see how the land lies; to feel one's way; to count the cost; to be on the safe side; steady as she goes.

headstrong, insane, foolhardy, slap-dash, dare-devil, devil-may-care, overbold, wild, reckless, desperate, hot-headed, hare-brained, headlong, hot-blooded, over-confident, precipitate, impetuous, venturesome, impulsive, Quixotic.

Imprudent, indiscreet, uncalculating, incautious, improvident.

(Phrases) Without ballast; neck or nothing.

(Interjections) Vogue la galère! come what may!

865 Desire (Substantives), wish, mind, inclination, leaning, bent, fancy, partiality, penchant, predilection, liking, love, fondness, relish.

Want, need, exigency.

Longing, hankering, solicitude, anxiety, yearning, yen, coveting, eagerness, zeal, ardour, aspiration, ambition, over-anxiety.

Appetite, appetence, appetency, the edge of appetite, keenness, hunger, stomach, thirst, thirstiness, drouth, mouth-watering, dipsomania, itch, itching, prurience, lickerishness, *cacoethes*, cupidity, lust, libido, concupiscence, greed.

Avidity, greediness, covetousness, craving, voracity, bulimia, rapacity.

Passion, rage, furore, mania, kleptomania, inextinguishable desire, vaulting ambition, impetuosity.

A gourmand, gourmet, glutton, cormorant (957).

An amateur, votary, devotee, fan, aspirant, solicitant, candidate.

Object of desire, desideratum, attraction, lure, allurement, fancy, temptation, magnet, loadstone, whim, whimsy (608), maggot, hobby, hobby-horse, pursuit.

(Phrases) The height of one's ambition; *hoc erat in votis*; the wish being father to the thought; the torments of Tantalus.

(Verbs) To desire, wish, long for, fancy, affect, like, have a mind to, be glad of, want, miss, need, feel the want of, would fain have, to care for.

To hunger, thirst, crave, lust after; to hanker after, itch for.

(Adjectives) Cautious, wary, careful, heedful, cautelous, chary, canny, cagey, circumspect, prudent, prudential, reserved, discreet, politic, non-committal.

Unenterprising, unadventurous, cool, steady, self-possessed.

(Phrases) Safety first; better be sure than sorry.

———

866 Indifference (Substantives), coldness, coolness, unconcern, nonchalance, insouciance, inappetency, listlessness, lukewarmness, neutrality, impartiality; apathy (823), supineness (683), disdain (930).

(Verbs) To be indifferent, etc.; to have no desire, wish, taste, or relish for; to care nothing about, take no interest in, not mind, make light of; to disdain, spurn (930).

(Phrase) Couldn't care less.

(Adjectives) Indifferent, undesirous, cool, cold, frigid, unconcerned, insouciant, unsolicitous, unattracted, lukewarm, half-hearted, listless, lackadaisical, unambitious, unaspiring, phlegmatic.

Unattractive, unalluring, uninviting, undesired, undesirable, uncared-for, unwished, uncoveted, unvalued.

Vapid, tasteless, insipid (391), wersh, unappetizing, mawkish, namby-pamby, flat, stale, vain.

(Phrases) Never mind; all one to Hippocleides.

867 Dislike (Substantives), distaste, disrelish, disinclination, reluctance, backwardness, demur (603).

Repugnance, disgust, queasiness, turn, nausea, loathing, averseness, aversion, abomination, antipathy, abhorrence, horror, hatred, detestation (898), resentment (900); claustrophobia, agoraphobia, Anglophobia, Gallophobia.

(Verbs) To dislike, mislike, disrelish, mind, object to.

To desiderate; covet; to sigh, cry, gasp, pine, pant, languish, yearn for; to aspire after, catch at, jump at.

To woo, court, solicit, ogle, fish for.

To cause, create, raise, excite, or provoke, desire; to allure, attract, solicit, tempt, hold out temptation or allurement, to tantalize, appetize.

To gratify desire, slake, satiate (827).

(Phrases) To have at heart; to take a fancy to; to set one's heart upon; to make eyes at; to set one's cap at; to run mad after.

To whet the appetite; to make one's mouth water.

(Adjectives) Desirous, inclined, fain, keen, wishful, wishing, optative, desiring, wanting, needing, hankering after, dying for, partial to.

Craving, hungry, esurient, sharp-set, keen-set, peckish, thirsty, athirst, dry, drouthy.

Greedy, voracious, lickerish, open-mouthed, agog, covetous, ravenous, rapacious, extortionate; unsated, un-slaked, insatiable, insatiate, omnivorous.

Eager, ardent, avid, fervent, bent on, intent on, aspiring, ambitious.

Desirable, desired, desiderated (829).

(Phrases) Pinched or perished with hunger; hungry as a hunter; parched with thirst; having a sweet tooth; nothing loth.

(Interjections) O for! would that!

———

To shun, avoid, eschew, withdraw from, shrink from, shrug the shoulders at, recoil from, shudder at.

To loathe, nauseate, abominate, detest, abhor, hate (898).

To cause or excite dislike; to disincline, repel, sicken, render sick, nauseate, disgust, shock, pall.

(Phrases) Not to be able to bear or endure or stand; to have no taste for; to turn up one's nose at; to look askance at.

To go against the grain; to turn one's stomach; to stink in the nostrils; to stick in one's throat; to make one's blood run cold.

(Adjectives) Disliking, disrelishing, etc., averse to, adverse, shy of, sick of, fed up with, queasy, disinclined.

Disliked, disagreeable, unpalatable, unpopular, offensive, loathsome, loathly, sickening, nauseous, nauseating, repulsive, disgusting, detestable, execrable, abhorrent, abhorred (830), disgustful.

(Adverbs) Disagreeably, etc.

(Phrase) Usque ad nauseam.

(Interjections) Faugh! Ugh!

868 Fastidiousness *(Substantives)*, nicety, daintiness, squeamishness, niceness, particularity, finicality, meticulosity, difficulty in being pleased, epicurism.

Excess of delicacy, prudery.

Epicure, gourmet, gourmand, *bon vivant,* gastronomer.

(Verbs) To be fastidious, etc., to discriminate, differentiate, disdain.

(Phrases) To split hairs; to mince one's words; to see spots in the sun.

(Adjectives) Fastidious, nice, difficult, dainty, delicate, finicky, lickerish, pernickety, squeamish, queasy, difficult to please, particular, choosy, punctilious, fussy, hypercriticial; prudish, strait-laced.

———

869 Satiety *(Substantives)*, fullness, repletion, glut, saturation, surfeit.

A spoilt child; too much of a good thing.

(Verbs) To sate, satiate, satisfy, saturate, quench, slake, pall, glut, overfeed, gorge, surfeit, cloy, tire, spoil, sicken.

(Adjectives) Satiated, sated, blasé, used up, fed up, browned off, brassed off, cheesed off, chokka, sick of.

(Phrases) Enough is enough; *Toujours perdrix.*

(Interjections) Enough! that'll do!

4°. Contemplative Affections

870 Wonder *(Substantives)*, surprise, marvel, astonishment, amazement, amazedness, wonderment, admiration, awe, bewilderment, stupefaction, fascination, thaumaturgy (992).

(Verbs) To wonder, marvel, be surprised, admire; to stare, gape, start.

To surprise, astonish, amaze, astound, dumbfound, dumbfounder, strike, dazzle, startle, take by surprise, take aback, strike with wonder, electrify, stun, petrify, flabbergast, confound, stagger, stupefy, bewilder, fascinate, boggle.

To be wonderful, etc.

(Phrases) To open one's mouth or eyes; to look blank; to stand aghast; not to believe one's eyes; not to account for; not to know whether one stands on one's head or one's heels.

To make one sit up; to take one's breath away.

To beggar description; to stagger belief; imagination boggles at it.

(Adjectives) Surprised, astonished, amazed, astounded, struck, startled, taken by surprise, taken aback, struck dumb, awestruck, aghast, agape, dumbfounded, flabbergasted, thunder-struck, planet-struck, stupefied, open-mouthed, petrified.

Wonderful, wondrous, surprising, astonishing, amazing, astounding, startling, stunning, unexpected, unforeseen, strange, uncommon, unheard-of, unaccountable, incredible, inexplicable, indescribable, inexpressible, ineffable, unutterable, unspeakable, monstrous, prodigious, stupendous, marvellous, miraculous, passing strange, uncanny, weird, phenomenal.

(Phrases) Struck all of a heap; lost in wonder; like a dying duck in a thunder-storm; you could have knocked me down with a feather.

(Adverbs) Wonderingly, wonderfully, etc., with gaping mouth, all agog; *mirabile dictu.*

(Interjections) What! indeed! really! hallo! humph! you don't say so! my stars! good heavens! my goodness! good gracious! bless my soul! bless my heart! my word! O gemini! great Scott! gee! *wunderbar!* dear me! well, I'm damned! well, I never! lo! heyday! who'd have thought it!

871 Absence of wonder.

Expectance *(Substantives)*, expectancy, expectation (507).

(Verbs) To expect, not to be surprised, not to wonder, etc., *nil admirari.*

(Phrase) To think nothing of.

(Adjectives) Expecting, etc., unamazed, astonished at nothing, blasé (841).

Common, ordinary (82); foreseen.

---

872 Prodigy *(Substantives)*, phenomenon, wonder, cynosure, marvel, miracle, monster (83), unicorn, phoenix, gazing-stock, curiosity, *rara avis*, lion, sight, spectacle, wonderment, sign, portent (512), eye-opener; wonderland, fairyland.

Thunderclap, thunderbolt, bursting of a shell or bomb, volcanic eruption.

(Phrases) A nine days' wonder; *annus mirabilis.*

5°. Extrinsic Affections

873 Repute *(Substantives)*, distinction, note, notability, name, mark, reputation, figure, *réclame*, *éclat*, celebrity, vogue, fame, famous-

874 Disrepute *(Substantives)*, discredit, ingloriousness, derogation, abasement, degradation, odium, notoriety.

ness, popularity, renown, memory, immortality.

Glory, honour, credit, prestige, kudos, account, regard, respect, reputableness, respectability, respectableness, good name, illustriousness, gloriousness.

Dignity, stateliness, solemnity, grandeur, splendour, nobility, nobleness, lordliness, majesty, sublimity.

Greatness, highness, eminence, supereminence, pre-eminence, primacy, importance (642).

Elevation, ascent (305), exaltation, superexaltation, aggrandisement.

Rank, standing, condition, precedence, *pas*, station, place, status, order, degree, *locus standi*.

Dedication, consecration, enshrinement, glorification, beatification, canonization, deification, posthumous fame.

Chief, leader (745), hero, celebrity, notability, somebody, lion, cock of the roost, cock of the walk, man of mark, pillar of the state, prima donna.

A star, sun, constellation, galaxy, flower, pearl, paragon (650); honour, ornament, aureole.

(Phrases) A halo of glory; a name to conjure with; blushing honours; a feather in one's cap; the top of the tree; a niche in the temple of fame.

(Verbs) To glory in, to be proud of (878), to exult (884), to be vain of (880).

To be glorious, distinguished, etc., to shine, to figure, to make or cut a figure, dash, or splash; to rival, outrival, surpass, emulate, outvie, eclipse, outshine, overshadow, throw into the shade.

To live, flourish, glitter, flaunt.

To honour, lionize, dignify, glorify, ennoble, nobilitate, exalt, enthrone, signalize, immortalize, deify.

To consecrate, dedicate to, devote to, to enshrine.

To confer or reflect honour, etc., on; to do, pay, or render honour to; to redound to one's honour.

(Phrases) To acquire or gain honour, etc.; to bear the palm; to bear the bell; to take the cake; to

Dishonour, shame, disgrace, disfavour, disapprobation (932), slur, scandal, obloquy, opprobrium, ignominy, baseness, turpitude, vileness, infamy.

Tarnish, taint, defilement, pollution.

Stain, blot, spot, blur, stigma, brand, reproach, imputation, slur, black mark.

(Phrases) A burning shame; *scandalum magnatum*; a badge of infamy; the bar sinister; a blot on the scutcheon; a byword of reproach; a bad reputation.

(Verbs) To be conscious of shame, to feel shame, to blush, to be ashamed, humiliated, humbled (879, 881).

To cause shame, etc.; to shame, disgrace, put to shame, dishonour; to throw, cast, fling, or reflect shame, etc., upon; to be a reproach to, to derogate from.

To tarnish, stain, blot, sully, taint, discredit, degrade, debase, defile.

To impute shame to, to brand, stigmatize, vilify, defame, slur, run down, knock.

To abash, humiliate, humble, dishonour, discompose, disconcert, shame, show up, put out, put down, snub, confuse, mortify; to obscure, eclipse, outshine.

(Phrases) To feel disgrace; to cut a poor figure; to hide one's face; to look foolish; to hang one's head; to laugh on the wrong side of the mouth; not to dare to show one's face; to hide one's diminished head; to lose caste; to be in one's black books.

To put to the blush; to put out of countenance; to put one's nose out of joint; to cast into the shade; to take one down a peg; to take the shine out of; to tread or trample under foot; to drag through the mud.

(Adjectives) Feeling shame, disgrace, etc.; ashamed, abashed, disgraced, blown upon, branded, tarnished.

Inglorious, mean, base (940), shabby, nameless, unnoticed, unnoted, unhonoured.

Shameful, disgraceful, despicable, discreditable, unbecoming, degrading,

win laurels; to make a noise in the world; to go far; to make a sensation; to be all the rage; to have a run; to catch on.

To exalt one's horn; to leave one's mark; to exalt to the skies.

(Adjectives) Distinguished, *distingué*, noted, notable, respectable, reputable, celebrated, famous, famed, far-famed, honoured, renowned, popular, deathless, imperishable, immortal (112).

Illustrious, glorious, splendid, bright, brilliant, radiant, full-blown, heroic.

Eminent, prominent, conspicuous, kenspeckle, high, pre-eminent, peerless, signalized, exalted, dedicated, consecrated, enshrined.

Great, dignified, proud, noble, worshipful, lordly, grand, stately, august, imposing, transcendent, majestic, kingly, queenly, princely, sacred, sublime, commanding.

(Phrases) Redounding to one's honour; one's name living for ever; *sic itur ad astra*.

(Interjections) Hail! all hail! *vive! viva!* glory be to! honour be to!

humiliating, unworthy, disreputable, derogatory, vile, ribald, dishonourable, abject, scandalous, infamous, notorious.

(Phrases) Unwept, unhonoured, and unsung; shorn of its beams; unknown to fame; in bad odour; under a cloud; down in the world.

(Interjections) Fie! shame! for shame! *O tempora! O mores!*

---

875 Nobility *(Substantives)*, noblesse, aristocracy, peerage, gentry, gentility, quality, rank, blood, birth, donship, fashionable world (852), the *haute monde*, high life, the upper classes, the upper ten, the four hundred.

A personage, notability, celebrity, man of distinction, rank, etc.; a nobleman, noble, lord, peer, grandee, magnate, magnifico, hidalgo, don, gentleman, squire, patrician, lordling, nob, swell, dignitary, bigwig, big gun.

House of Lords, Lords Spiritual and Temporal.

Gentlefolk, landed proprietors, squirearchy, *optimates*.

Prince, duke, marquis, earl, viscount, baron, thane, banneret, baronet, knight, count, armiger, laird, esquire; nizam, maharajah, rajah, nawab, sultan, emir (or ameer), effendi, sheik, pasha.

Princess, duchess, marchioness, marquise, countess, viscountess, baroness, lady, dame, maharanee, ranee, sultana, begum.

(Verbs) To be noble, etc.

(Adjectives) Noble, exalted, titled,

876 Commonalty *(Substantives)*, the lower classes or orders, the vulgar herd, the crowd, the people, the commons, the proletariat, the multitude, Demos, οἱ πολλοί, the populace, the million, the masses, the mobility, the peasantry.

The middle classes, bourgeoisie.

The mob, rabble, rabble-rout, ruck, *canaille*, the underworld, riff-raff, *profanum vulgus*.

A commoner, one of the people, a proletarian, *roturier*, plebeian; peasant, yeoman, crofter, boor, carle, churl, serf, kern, tyke (or tike), chuff, ryot, fellah, cottar.

A swain, clown, hind, clodhopper, bog-trotter, chaw-bacon, hodge, joskin, yokel, bumpkin, hayseed, rube, hick, ploughman, plough-boy, gaffer, loon, looby, lout, *gamin*, street arab, guttersnipe, mudlark, slubberdegullion.

A beggar, tramp, vagrant, gangrel, gaberlunzie, bum, hobo, sundowner, panhandler, pariah, muckworm, sansculotte, raff, tatterdemalion, ragamuffin.

A Goth, Vandal, Hottentot, savage,

patrician, aristocratic, high-born, well-born, genteel, *comme il faut*, gentlemanlike, ladylike, princely, courtly, fashionable (852).

(Phrases) Noblesse oblige; born in the purple.

877 Title *(Substantives)*, honour, princedom, principality, dukedom, marquisate, earldom, viscounty, baronetcy, lordship, knighthood.

Highness, excellency, grace, worship, reverence, esquire, sir, master, sahib, Mr., monsieur, signor, señor, Herr.

Decoration, laurel, palm, wreath, medal, gong, ribbon, cross, star, garter, feather, crest, epaulette, colours, cockade, livery; order, arms, shield, scutcheon.

(Phrase) A handle to one's name.

878 Pride *(Substantives)*, haughtiness, loftiness, hauteur, stateliness, pomposity, vainglory, superciliousness, assumption, lordliness, stiffness, primness, arrogance, *morgue*, starch, starchiness, side, swank, uppishness; self-respect, dignity.

A proud man, etc., a highflier.

(Verbs) To be proud, etc., to presume, assume, swagger, strut, prance, peacock, bridle.

To pride oneself on, glory in, pique oneself, plume oneself, preen oneself.

(Phrases) To look big; give oneself airs; to ride the high horse; to put on side; to put on dog; to hold up one's head; to get one's tail up.

To put a good face upon.

(Adjectives) Proud, haughty, lofty, high, mighty, high-flown, high-minded, high-mettled, puffed up, flushed, supercilious, patronizing, condescending, disdainful, overweening, consequential, on stilts, swollen, arrogant, pompous.

Stately, dignified, stiff, starchy, prim, perked up, buckram, strait-laced, vainglorious, lordly,

barbarian, yahoo, rough diamond, unlicked cub.

An upstart, parvenu, skipjack, *novus homo, nouveau riche,* outsider, vulgarian, snob, mushroom.

Barbarousness, barbarism.

(Phrases) The man in the street; the submerged tenth; ragtag and bobtail; the swinish multitude; hewers of wood and drawers of water; the great unwashed.

(Verbs) To be ignoble, etc.

(Adjectives) Ignoble, common, mean, low, plebeian, proletarian, vulgar, bourgeois, untitled, homespun, homely, Gorblimey.

Base, base-born, low-bred, beggarly, earth-born, rustic, agrestic, countrified, provincial, parochial; banausic, menial, sorry, scrubby, mushroom, dunghill, sordid, vile, uncivilized, loutish, boorish, churlish, rude, brutish, raffish, unlicked, barbarous, barbarian, barbaric.

879 Humility *(Substantives)*, humbleness, meekness, lowness, lowliness, abasement, self-abasement, self-contempt, humiliation, submission, resignation, verecundity, modesty (881).

(Verbs) To be humble, etc.; to deign; vouchsafe, condescend; to humble or demean oneself; stoop, submit, knuckle under, look foolish, feel small.

To render humble; to humble, humiliate, set down, abash, abase, shame, mortify, crush, take down, snub.

(Phrases) To sing small; to pipe down; to draw in one's horns; to hide one's diminished head; to eat humble-pie; to eat dirt; to kiss the rod; to pocket an affront; to stoop to conquer.

To throw into the shade; to put out of countenance; to put a person in his place; to put to the blush; to take down a peg, cut down to size; to send away with a flea in one's ear.

(Adjectives) Humble, lowly, meek, sober-minded, submissive (725), resigned, self-contemptuous, under correction.

magisterial, purse-proud, stand-offish, up-stage, toffee-nose.

Unabashed (880).

(Phrases) High and mighty; proud as a peacock; proud as Lucifer.

(Adverbs) Proudly, haughtily, arrogantly, etc.

Humbled, humiliated, abashed, ashamed, chapfallen, crestfallen.

(Phrases) Out of countenance; on one's bended knees; humbled in the dust; not having a word to say for oneself.

(Adverbs) Humbly, meekly, etc.

880 Vanity *(Substantives)*, conceit, conceitedness, self-conceit, self-confidence, self-sufficiency, self-esteem, self-approbation, self-importance, self-praise, self-laudation, self-admiration, complacency, self-complacency, swelled head, megalomania, *amour-propre*.

Pretensions, airs, mannerism, egotism, egoism, egomania, priggishness, coxcombry, gaudery, vainglory (943), elation, ostentation (882).

A coxcomb (854).

(Verbs) To be vain, etc., to egotize.

To render vain, etc., to puff up, to inspire with vanity, turn one's head.

(Phrases) To have a high or overweening opinion of oneself; to think no small beer of oneself; to thrust oneself forward; to give oneself airs; to show off; to fish for compliments.

(Adjectives) Vain, conceited, overweening, forward, vainglorious, puffed up, high-flown, inflated, flushed, stuck-up.

Self-satisfied, self-confident, self-sufficient, self-flattering, self-admiring, self-applauding, self-opinionated, self-centred, egocentric, egoistic, egoistical, egotistic, egotistical, complacent, self-complacent, pretentious, priggish.

Unabashed, unblushing, unconstrained, unceremonious, free and easy.

(Phrases) Vain as a peacock; wise in one's own conceit.

(Adverbs) Vainly, etc., ostentatiously (882).

881 Modesty *(Substantives)*, humility (879), diffidence, timidity, bashfulness, shyness, coyness, sheepishness, *mauvaise honte*, shamefacedness, verecundity, self-consciousness.

Reserve, constraint, demureness.

(Verbs) To be modest, humble, etc.; to retire, keep in the background, keep private, reserve oneself.

(Phrases) To hide one's light under a bushel; to take a back seat.

(Adjectives) Modest, diffident, humble (879), timid, bashful, timorous, shy, skittish, coy, sheepish, shamefaced, blushing, self-conscious.

Unpretending, unpretentious, unassuming, unostentatious, unboastful, unaspiring.

Abashed, ashamed, dashed, out of countenance, crestfallen (879).

Reserved, constrained, demure, undemonstrative.

(Adverbs) Modestly, diffidently, quietly, privately, unostentatiously.

882 Ostentation *(Substantives)*, display, show, flourish, parade, pomp, state, solemnity, pageantry, dash, splash, splurge, glitter, veneer, tinsel, magnificence, pomposity, showing off, swank, swagger, strut, *panache, coup de théâtre*, stage effect.

Flourish of trumpets, fanfare, salvo of artillery, salute, fireworks, *feu de joie*.

Pageant, spectacle, procession, march-past, review, promenade, turn-out, set-out, build-up, fête, gala, regatta, field-day.

Ceremony, ceremonial, mummery; formality, form, etiquette, ritual, protocol, punctilio, punctiliousness.

(Verbs) To be ostentatious, etc.; to display, exhibit, posture, attitudinize,

show off, swank, come forward, put oneself forward, flaunt, emblazon, prink, glitter; make or cut a figure, dash, or splash.

To observe or stand on ceremony, etiquette, etc.

(*Adjectives*) Ostentatious, showy, gaudy, garish, flashy, dashing, pretentious, flaunting, jaunty, glittering, sumptuous, spectacular, ceremonial, stagy, theatrical, histrionic.

Pompous, solemn, stately, high-sounding, formal, stiff, ritualistic, ceremonious, punctilious.

(*Phrases*) With flourish of trumpets; with beat of drum; with flying colours; in one's Sunday best; in one's best bib and tucker.

883 Celebration (*Substantives*), jubilee, jubilation, commemoration, festival, feast, solemnization, ovation, paean, triumph.

Triumphal arch, bonfire, illuminations, fireworks, salute, salvo, *feu de joie*, flourish of trumpets, fanfare.

Inauguration, installation, presentation, coronation, fête (882).

Anniversary, silver wedding, golden wedding, diamond wedding, diamond jubilee, centenary, bicentenary, tercentenary, quatercentenary, quingentenary (or quincentenary), sexcentenary, etc., millenary.

(*Verbs*) To celebrate, keep, signalize, do honour to, pledge, drink to, toast, commemorate, solemnize.

To inaugurate, install.

(*Phrase*) To paint the town red.

(*Adjectives*) Celebrating, etc., in honour of, in commemoration of, in memoriam.

(*Interjections*) Hail! all hail! 'See the conquering hero comes.' 'For he's a jolly good fellow.'

884 Boasting (*Substantives*), boast, vaunt, vaunting, brag, bounce, *blague*, swank, bluff, puff, puffing, puffery, flourish, fanfaronade, gasconade, braggadocio, bravado, tall talk, heroics, vapouring, rodomontade, bombast, exaggeration (549), self-advertisement, *réclame*; jingoism, Chauvinism, spread-eagleism.

Exultation, triumph, flourish of trumpets (883).

A boaster, braggart, braggadocio, Gascon, peacock; a pretender, charlatan.

(*Verbs*) To boast, make a boast of, brag, vaunt, puff, flourish, vapour, blow, strut, swagger, swank, skite, gas.

To exult, crow, chuckle, triumph, gloat, glory.

(*Phrases*) To talk big; to shoot a line; to blow one's own trumpet.

(*Adjectives*) Boasting, vaunting, etc., thrasonical, vainglorious, braggart, jingo, jingoistic, chauvinistic.

Elate, elated, flushed, jubilant.

(*Phrases*) On stilts; cock-a-hoop; in high feather.

885 Undue assumption of superiority.

Insolence (*Substantives*), haughtiness, arrogance, imperiousness, contumeliousness, superciliousness, bumptiousness, bounce, swagger, swank.

Impertinence, sauciness, pertness, flippancy, petulance, malapertness.

Assumption, presumption, presumptuousness, forwardness, impudence, assurance, front, face, neck, cheek, lip, side, brass, shamelessness,

886 Servility (*Substantives*), obsequiousness, suppleness, fawning, slavishness, abjectness, prostration, prosternation, genuflexion (900), abasement, subjection (749).

Fawning, mealy-mouthedness, sycophancy, flattery (833), humility (879).

A sycophant, parasite, gate-crasher, toad-eater, toady, spaniel, bootlicker, lickspittle, flunkey, sponger, snob, hanger-on, tuft-hunter, time-server, reptile, cur (941); Uriah Heep.

hardihood, a hardened front, effrontery, audacity, procacity, self-assertion, nerve, gall, crust.

(Verbs) To be insolent, etc.; to bluster, vapour, swagger, swank, swell, roister, arrogate, assume, bluff.

To domineer, bully, beard, snub, huff, outface, outlook, outstare, outbrazen, bear down, beat down, trample on, tread under foot, outbrave, hector.

To presume, take liberties or freedoms.

(Phrases) to give oneself airs; to lay down the law; to put on side; to ride the high horse; to lord it over; *traiter, ou regarder de haut en bas*; to ride roughshod over; to carry with a high hand; to throw one's weight about; to carry it off; to brave it out.

(Verbs) To cringe, bow, stoop, kneel, fall on one's knees, etc.

To sneak, crawl, crouch, cower, truckle to, grovel, fawn.

(Phrases) To pay court to; to dance attendance on; to do the dirty work of; to lick the boots of.

To go with the stream; to worship the rising sun; to run with the hare and hunt with the hounds.

(Adjectives) Servile, subservient, obsequious, sequacious, soapy, oily, unctuous, supple, mean, crouching, cringing, fawning, slavish, grovelling, snivelling, beggarly, sycophantic, parasitical, abject, prostrate.

(Adverb) Cap in hand.

———

(Adjectives) Insolent, etc.; haughty, arrogant, imperious, dictatorial, high-handed, contumelious, supercilious, snooty, uppish, self-assertive, bumptious, overbearing, intolerant, assumptive.

Flippant, pert, perky, cavalier, saucy, cheeky, fresh, forward, impertinent, malapert.

Blustering, swaggering, swanky, vapouring, bluff, roistering, rollicking, high-flown, assuming, presuming, presumptuous, self-assertive, impudent, free, brazen, brazen-faced, barefaced, shameless, unblushing, unabashed.

887 Blusterer (Substantives), bully, swaggerer, braggart (884), fire-eater, daredevil, roisterer, puppy, sauce-box, hussy, minx, malapert, jackanapes, jack-in-office, jingo, Drawcansir, Captain Bobadil, Sir Lucius O'Trigger, Bombastes Furioso, Hector, Thraso, Bumble.

(Phrases) The great Panjandrum himself; a cool hand.

SECTION III—SYMPATHETIC AFFECTIONS

1°. Social Affections

888 Friendship (Substantives), amity, amicableness, amicability, friendliness, friendly regard, affection (897), goodwill, favour, brotherhood, ˙fraternity, sodality, comradeship, *camaraderie*, confraternity, fraternization, cordiality, harmony, good understanding, concord (714), *entente cordiale*.

Acquaintance, introduction, intimacy, familiarity, fellowship, fellow-feeling, sympathy, welcomeness, partiality, favouritism.

889 Enmity (Substantives), hostility, unfriendliness, antagonism, animosity, hate (898), dislike (867), malevolence (907), ill will, ill feeling, spite, bad blood, aversion, antipathy, alienation, estrangement; umbrage, pique.

(Verbs) To be inimical, etc.; to estrange, to fall out, alienate.

(Phrases) To keep at arm's length; to bear malice; to set by the ears.

(Adjectives) Inimical, unfriendly, hostile, antagonistic, adverse, at

(Verbs) To be friends, to be friendly, etc., to fraternize, sympathize with (897), to be well with, to be thick with, to befriend (707), to be in with, to keep in with.

To become friendly, to make friends with, to chum up with.

(Phrases) To take in good part; to hold out the right hand of fellowship; to break the ice; to scrape acquaintance with.

(Adjectives) Friendly, amical, amicable, brotherly, fraternal, harmonious, cordial, social, chummy, pally, neighbourly, on good terms, on a friendly footing, on friendly terms, well-affected, well-disposed, favourable.

Acquainted, familiar, intimate, thick, hand and glove, welcome.

Firm, staunch, intimate, familiar, bosom, cordial, devoted.

(Phrases) In one's good books; hail fellow well met.

(Adverbs) friendly, amicably, etc., *sans cérémonie*.

variance, at loggerheads, at daggers drawn, on bad terms.

Estranged, alienated, irreconcilable.

---

890 Friend *(Substantives)*, well-wisher, *amicus curiae, alter ego*, bosom friend, *fidus Achates*, partner (711); *persona grata*.

Partisan, sympathizer, ally, backer, patron, good genius, fairy godmother.

Neighbour, acquaintance, associate, compeer, comrade, companion, *confrère, camarade*, mate, messmate, shopmate, shipmate, crony, cummer, confidant, chum, pal, buddy, side-kick, boon companion, pot-companion, schoolfellow, playfellow, playmate, bed-fellow, bed-mate, bunkie, room-mate.

Arcades ambo, Pylades and Orestes, Castor and Pollux, Nisus and Euryalus, Damon and Pythias, David and Jonathan, *par nobile fratrum*.

Host, guest, visitor, *habitué*, protégé.

891 Enemy *(Substantives)*, foe, opponent (710), antagonist.

Public enemy, enemy to society, anarchist, terrorist, Ishmael.

---

892 Sociality *(Substantives)*, sociability, sociableness, social intercourse, companionship, companionableness, consortship, intercommunication, intercommunion, consociation.

Conviviality, good fellowship, hospitality, heartiness, welcome, the glad hand, joviality, jollity, *savoir vivre*, festivity, merrymaking.

Society, association, union, co-partnership, fraternity, sodality, coterie, clan, club (72), circle, clique, knot.

Assembly-room, casino, clubhouse, common-room.

Esprit de corps, nepotism (11).

An entertainment, party, social gathering, reunion, gaudy, levee, soirée, conversazione, rout, *ridotto*,

893 Seclusion *(Substantives)*, privacy, retirement, withdrawal, reclusion, recess, retiredness, rustication.

Solitude, singleness, estrangement from the world, loneliness, lonesomeness, retiredness, isolation; hermitage, cloister, nunnery (1000); study, den; ivory tower, Shangri-la.

Wilderness, depopulation, desolation.

Agoraphobia, claustrophobia.

Exclusion *(Substantives)*, excommunication, banishment, expatriation, exile, ostracism, cut, cut direct, dead cut, inhospitality, inhospitableness, unsociability.

A recluse, hermit, cenobite, anchoret (or anchorite), stylite, santon,

at-home, house-warming, bee, tea-party, bunfight, picnic, garden-party, festival (840), interview, assignation, appointment, date, tryst, call, visit, visiting, reception (588).

A good fellow, good scout, boon companion, good mixer, *bon vivant*.

(Verbs) To be sociable, etc., to associate with, keep company with, to club together, sort with, hobnob with, consort, make advances, fraternize, make the acquaintance of.

To visit, pay a visit, interchange visits or cards, call upon, leave a card.

To entertain, give a party, dance, etc.; to keep open house; to receive, to welcome.

(Phrases) To make oneself at home; to crack a bottle with.

To be at home to; to do the honours; to receive with open arms; to give a warm reception to; to kill the fatted calf.

(Adjectives) Sociable, social, companionable, neighbourly, gregarious, clannish, clubbable, conversable, affable, accessible, familiar, on visiting terms, welcome, hospitable, convivial, jovial, festive.

(Phrases) Free and easy; hail fellow well met.

(Adverbs) En famille; in the family circle; in the social whirl; sans façon; sans cérémonie; sans gêne.

---

894 Courtesy (*Substantives*), good manners, good breeding, good form, mannerliness, manners, *bienséance*, urbanity, civilization, polish, politeness, gentility, comity, civility, amenity, suavity, discretion, diplomacy, good temper, easy temper, gentleness, mansuetude, graciousness, gallantry, affability, obligingness, *prévenance*, amiability, good humour,

Compliment, fair words, soft words, sweet words, honeyed phrases, attentions, *petits soins*, salutation, reception, presentation, introduction, *accueil*, greeting, regards, remembrances, welcome, *abord*, respect, devoir.

troglodyte, solitary, ruralist; displaced person, outcast, pariah; foundling, waif, wastrel, castaway; Timon of Athens, Simon Stylites.

(Phrase) 'A lone lorn creetur.'

(Verbs) To be secluded, etc., to retire, to live retired, secluded, etc.; to keep aloof, keep snug, shut oneself up, deny oneself.

To cut, refuse to associate with or acknowledge; repel, cold-shoulder, blackball, outlaw, proscribe, excommunicate, boycott, exclude, banish, exile, ostracize, rusticate, send down, abandon, maroon.

To depopulate, dispeople, unpeople.

(Phrases) To retire from the world; to take the veil; to sport one's oak.

To send to Coventry; to turn one's back upon; to give one the cold shoulder.

(Adjectives) Secluded, sequestered, retired, private, snug, domestic, claustral.

Unsociable, unsocial, aloof, eremitical, offish, stand-offish, unclubbable, inhospitable, cynical, inconversible, retiring, unneighbourly, exclusive, unforthcoming.

Solitary, lonely, lonesome, isolated, single, estranged, unfrequented, uninhabited, unoccupied, tenantless.

Unvisited, cut, blackballed, uninvited, unwelcome, friendless, deserted, abandoned, derelict, lorn, forlorn, homeless, out of it.

(Phrase) Left to shift for oneself.

---

895 Discourtesy (*Substantives*), ill-breeding; ill, bad, or ungainly manners; rusticity, inurbanity, impoliteness, ungraciousness, uncourtliness, insuavity, rudeness, incivility, tactlessness, disrespect, impertinence, impudence, cheek, barbarism, misbehaviour, *grossièreté*, brutality, blackguardism, roughness, ruggedness, brusqueness, brusquerie, bad form.

Bad or ill temper, churlishness, crabbedness, tartness, crossness, peevishness, moroseness, sullenness, sulkiness, grumpiness, grouchiness, acrimony, sternness, austerity, moodi-

Obeisance, reverence, bow, curtsy, scrape, salaam, kowtow, capping, shaking hands, embrace, hug, squeeze, accolade, salute, kiss, buss, kissing hands, genuflexion, prostration, obsequiousness.

Mark of recognition, nod, wave, valediction (293).

(Verbs) To be courteous, civil, etc., to show courtesy, civility, etc., to speak one fair; to make oneself agreeable; to unbend, thaw.

To visit, wait upon, present oneself, pay one's respects, kiss hands.

To receive, do the honours, greet, welcome, bid welcome, usher in, bid God speed; hold or stretch out the hand; shake, press, or squeeze the hand.

To salute, kiss, embrace, hug, drink to, pledge, hobnob; to wave to, nod to, smile upon, bow, curtsy, scrape, uncover, cap, present arms, take off the hat.

To pay homage or obeisance, kneel, bend the knee, prostrate oneself, etc.

To render polite, etc., to polish, civilize, humanize.

(Phrases) To mind one's p's and q's; to do the polite; to greet with open arms; to speed the parting guest.

(Adjectives) Courteous, courtly, civil, civilized, polite, Chesterfieldian, genteel, well-bred, well-mannered, mannerly, urbane, gentlemanly, ladylike, refined (850), polished, genial.

Gracious, affable, familiar, well-spoken, fair-spoken, soft-spoken, fine-spoken, suave, bland, mild, conciliatory, winning, obsequious, obliging, open-armed.

(Phrases) With a good grace; *suaviter in modo; à bras ouverts.*

(Interjections) Hail! welcome! good morning! good day! good afternoon! good evening! good night! well met! *pax vobiscum!*

ness, asperity, captiousness, sharpness, snappishness, perversity, cussedness, irascibility (901).

Sulks, dudgeon, mumps, scowl, frown, hard words, black looks.

A bear, brute, boor, blackguard, beast, cross-patch, grouch, sorehead.

(Verbs) To be rude, etc., frown, scowl, glower, lour, pout, snap, snarl, growl, nag; to cut, insult, etc.

To render rude, etc., to brutalize, decivilize, dehumanize.

(Phrases) To turn one's back upon; to turn on one's heel; to look black upon; to give one the cold shoulder, or the frozen face, or the frozen mitt; to take liberties with.

(Adjectives) Discourteous, uncourteous, uncourtly, ill-bred, ill-mannered, ill-behaved, unmannerly, mannerless, impolite, unpolished, ungenteel, ungentlemanly, unladylike, uncivilized.

Uncivil, rude, ungracious, cool, chilly, distant, stand-offish, offish, icy, repulsive, uncomplaisant, unaccommodating, ungainly, unceremonious, ungentle, rough, rugged, bluff, blunt, gruff, churlish, boorish, bearish, brutal, brusque, blackguardly, vulgar, stern, harsh, austere, cavalier.

Ill-tempered, out of temper or humour, cross, crusty, tart, sour, crabbed, sharp, short, snappish, testy, peevish, waspish, captious, grumpy, snarling, caustic, acrimonious, ungenial, petulant, pettish, pert.

Perverse, cross-grained, ill-conditioned, wayward, humoursome, naughty, cantankerous, intractable, curst, nagging, froward, sulky, glum, grim, morose, scowling, grouchy, glowering, surly, sullen, growling, splenetic, spleenful, spleeny, spleenish, moody, dogged, ugly.

(Phrases) Cross as two sticks; sour as a crab; surly as a bear.

(Adverbs) With a bad grace, grudgingly.

---

896 Congratulation *(Substantives)*, felicitation, wishing joy, the compliments of the season, good wishes.

(Verbs) To congratulate, felicitate, give or wish joy, tender or offer one's congratulations.

(Adjectives) Congratulatory, etc.
(Phrases) Many happy returns of the day! merry Christmas! happy New Year!

897 Love *(Substantives)*, fondness, liking, inclination (865), regard, good graces, partiality, benevolence (906), admiration, fancy, tenderness, leaning, penchant, predilection; amativeness, amorousness.

Affection, sympathy, fellow-feeling, heart, affectionateness.

Attachment, yearning, amour, romance, gallantry, love-affair, *affaire de cœur*, passion, tender passion, *grande passion*, flame, pash, crush, rave, devotion, enthusiasm, fervour, enchantment, infatuation, adoration, idolatry, idolization.

Eros, Cupid, Aphrodite, Venus, Freya, the myrtle.

Maternal love, στοργή.

Attractiveness, etc., popularity.

Abode of love, love-nest, agapemone.

A lover, suitor, follower, admirer, adorer, wooer, beau, fiancé, gallant, young man, boy friend, sweetheart, flame, love, true-love, leman, paramour, amorist, *amoroso, cavaliere servente, cicisbeo*; turtle-doves.

Girl friend, lady-love, fiancée, sweetie, cutie, mistress, *inamorata*, idol, doxy, dona, Dulcinea, goddess.

Betrothed, affianced.

(Verbs) To love, like, affect, fancy, care for, regard, revere, cherish, admire, dote on, adore, idolize, fall for, hold dear, prize.

To bear love to; to take to; to be in love with; to be taken, smitten, etc., with; to have, entertain, harbour, cherish, etc., a liking, love, etc., for; to be fond of, be gone on.

To excite love; to win, gain, secure, etc., the love, affections, heart, etc.; to take the fancy of, to attract, attach, seduce, charm, fascinate, captivate, enamour, enrapture.

To get into favour; to ingratiate oneself, insinuate oneself, curry favour with, pay one's court to, *faire l'aimable*.

(Phrases) To take a fancy to; to

898 Hate *(Substantives)*, hatred, disaffection, disfavour, alienation, estrangement, odium, dislike (867), enmity (899), animus, animosity (900).

Umbrage, pique, grudge, dudgeon, spleen, bitterness, ill feeling, acrimony, acerbity, malice (907), implacability.

Disgust, repugnance, aversion, averseness, loathing, abomination, horror, detestation, antipathy, abhorrence.

Object of hatred, abomination, *bête noir*.

(Verbs) To hate, dislike, disrelish (867), loathe, nauseate, execrate, detest, abominate, shudder at, recoil at, abhor, shrink from.

To excite hatred, estrange, incense, envenom, antagonize, rile, alienate, disaffect, set against; to be hateful, etc.

(Phrases) To make one's blood run cold; to have a down on; to hate one's guts.

To sow dissension among; to set by the ears.

(Adjectives) Hating, etc., averse to, set against.

Unloved, disliked, unwept, unlamented, undeplored, unmourned, unbeloved, uncared-for, unvalued.

Crossed in love, forsaken, jilted, rejected, lovelorn.

Obnoxious, hateful, abhorrent, odious, repulsive, offensive, shocking, loathsome, sickening, nauseous, disgusting, abominable, horrid (830).

Invidious, spiteful, malicious (907), spleenful, disgustful.

Insulting, irritating, provoking.

(Phrases) Not on speaking terms; there being no love lost between them; at daggers drawn.

make a fuss of; to look sweet upon; to cast sheep's eyes at; to fall in love with; to set one's affections on; to lose one's heart to.

To set one's cap at; to turn one's head.

(Adjectives) Loving, liking, etc., attached to, fond of, taken with, struck with, gone on, sympathetic, sympathizing with, charmed, captivated, fascinated, smitten, bitten, *épris*, enamoured, lovesick, love-lorn.

Affectionate, tender, sweet upon, loving, lover-like, loverly, amorous, amatory, amative, spoony, erotic, uxorious, motherly, ardent, passionate, devoted, amatorial.

Loved, beloved, etc., dear, precious, darling, favourite (899), pet, popular.

Lovely, sweet, dear, charming, engaging, amiable, winning, winsome, lovesome, attractive, adorable, enchanting, captivating, fascinating, bewitching, taking, seductive (829).

(Phrases) Head over ears in love; to one's mind, taste, or fancy; in one's good graces; nearest to one's heart.

899 Favourite *(Substantives)*, pet, cosset, dear, darling, honey, duck, moppet, jewel, idol, minion, spoilt child, blue-eyed boy, *persona grata*.

(Phrases) The apple of one's eye; a man after one's own heart; the idol of the people; the answer to the maiden's prayer.

900 Resentment *(Substantives)*, displeasure, animus, animosity, anger, wrath, indignation.

Pique, umbrage, huff, miff, soreness, dudgeon, moodiness, acerbity, bitterness, asperity, spleen, gall, heart-burning, heart-swelling, rankling; temper (901), bad blood, ill blood, ill humour.

Excitement, irritation, exasperation, warmth, bile, choler, ire, fume, dander, passion, fit, tantrum, burst, explosion, paroxysm, storm, rage, wax, fury, desperation.

Temper, petulance, procacity, angry mood, taking, snappishness.

Cause of umbrage, affront, provocation, offence, indignity, insult (929).

The Furies; the Eumenides.

(Phrases) The blood being up or boiling; a towering passion; the vials of wrath; fire and fury.

A sore subject; a rap on the knuckles; *casus belli*.

(Verbs) To resent, take amiss, take offence, take umbrage, take huff, bridle up, bristle up, frown, scowl, lour, snarl, growl, gnash, snap.

To chafe, mantle, redden, colour, fume, froth up, kindle; get, fall, or fly into a passion, rage, etc.; fly out, take fire, fire up, flare up, boil, boil over, rage, storm, foam.

To cause or raise anger; to affront, offend, give offence or umbrage; hurt the feelings; discompose, fret, ruffle, nettle, excite, irritate, provoke, rile, chafe, wound, sting, incense, inflame, enrage, aggravate, embitter, exasperate, rankle, infuriate, peeve.

(Phrases) To take in bad part; to take it ill; to take exception to; to stick in one's gizzard; to take in dudgeon; to have a bone (or crow) to pick with one; to get up on one's hind legs; to show one's teeth; to lose one's temper; to stamp, quiver, swell, or foam with rage; to see red; to look as black as thunder; to breathe revenge; to cut up rough; to pour out the vials of one's wrath; to blaze up; to blow one's top; to go up in a blue flame; to go on the war-path; to raise Cain.

To put out of humour; to stir up one's bile; to raise one's dander or choler; to work up into a passion; to make one's blood boil; to lash into a fury; to drive one mad; to put one's monkey up; to get one's goat.

(Adjectives) Angry, wroth, irate, ireful, warm, boiling, fuming, raging, etc.,

nettled, sore, bitter, riled, ruffled, chafed, exasperated, wrought up, worked up, snappish.

Fierce, wild, rageful, furious, infuriate, mad, fiery, savage, rabid, waxy, shirty, boiling over, rankling, bitter, virulent, set against.

Relentless, ruthless, implacable, unpitying, pitiless (919), inexorable, remorseless, stony-hearted, immitigable.

(Phrases) One's back being up; up in arms; in a stew; the gorge rising; in the height of passion.

(Interjections) Hell's bells! zounds! damme! For crying out loud!

901 Irascibility *(Substantives)*, susceptibility, excitability, temper, bad temper, procacity, petulance, irritability, fretfulness, testiness, grouchiness, tetchiness, touchiness, frowardness, peevishness, snappishness, hastiness, tartness, huffiness, resentfulness, vindictiveness, acerbity, protervity, aggressiveness, pugnacity (895).

A shrew, vixen, termagant, virago, scold, spitfire, Xanthippe; a tartar, fire-eater, fury; *genus irritabile.*

(Verbs) To be irascible, etc.; to take fire, fire up, flare up (900).

(Adjectives) Irascible, susceptible, excitable, irritable, fretful, fretty, on the fret, fidgety, peevish, hasty, over-hasty, quick, warm, hot, huffish, huffy, touchy, testy, tetchy (or techy), grouchy, restive, pettish, waspish, snappish, petulant, peppery, fiery, passionate, choleric, short-tempered.

Ill-tempered, bad-tempered, cross, churlish, sour, crabbed, cross-grained, sullen, sulky, grumpy, fractious, splenetic, spleenful, froward, shrewish.

Quarrelsome, querulous, disputatious, contentious, cranky, cantankerous, sarcastic (932), resentful, vindictive, pugnacious, aggressive.

(Phrases) Like touchwood or tinder; a word and a blow; as cross as two sticks.

902 Expression of affection or love.

Endearment *(Substantives)*, caress, blandishment, fondling, billing and cooing, petting, necking, embrace, salute, kiss, buss, smack, osculation, deosculation.

Courtship, wooing, suit, addresses, attentions, *petits soins,* flirtation, coquetry, philandering, gallivanting, serenading, œillade, ogle, the glad eye, sheep's eyes, goo-goo eyes.

Love-tale, love-token, love-letter, *billet-doux,* valentine.

Flirt, coquette, gold digger, vamp; male flirt, masher, philanderer, lady killer, wolf, lounge lizard, cake eater, sheik.

(Verbs) To caress, fondle, wheedle, dandle, dally, cuddle, cockle, cosset, nestle, nuzzle, snuggle, clasp, hug, embrace, kiss, salute, bill and coo.

To court, woo, flirt, coquette, philander, spoon, canoodle, mash, spark, serenade.

(Phrases) To make much of; to smile upon; to make eyes at; to chuck under the chin; to pat on the cheek; to make love; to pay one's court or one's addresses to; to set one's cap at; to pop the question.

To win the heart, affections, love, etc., of

(Adjectives) Caressing, etc., caressed, etc., flirtatious, spoony.

903 Marriage *(Substantives)*, matrimony, wedlock, union, bridal, match, intermarriage, coverture, cohabitation, bed, the marriage bond, the nuptial tie.

Wedding, nuptials, Hymen, spousals, espousals; leading to the altar;

904 Celibacy *(Substantives)*, singleness, misogamy; bachelorhood, bachelorship; virginity, maidenhood, maidenhead.

An unmarried man, bachelor, celibate, misogamist, misogynist.

An unmarried woman, spinster,

the torch of Hymen; nuptial benediction, marriage song, epithalamium.

Bride, bridegroom, groom, bridesmaid, maid of honour, matron of honour, bridesman, groomsman, best man.

Honeymoon, honeymooner.

A married man, a husband, spouse, benedick (or benedict), consort, goodman, lord and master, hubby.

A married woman, a wife, lady, matron, mate, helpmate, helpmeet, rib, better half, *femme couverte* (or *feme coverte*), squaw.

A married couple, wedded pair, Darby and Joan, man and wife.

A monogamist, bigamist, polygamist, a much-married man, a Turk, a Bluebeard, a Mormon.

Monogamy, bigamy, digamy, deuterogamy, trigamy, polygamy, polygyny, polyandry, endogamy, exogamy.

A morganatic marriage, left-handed marriage, marriage of convenience, *mariage de convenance*, companionate marriage, trial marriage, misalliance, *mésalliance*.

(Verbs) To marry, wed, espouse, wive.

To join, give away, handfast, splice.

(Phrases) To lead to the altar; to take to oneself a wife; to take for better for worse; to give one's hand to; to get spliced.

To tie the nuptial knot; to give in marriage.

(Adjectives) Matrimonial, conjugal, connubial, nuptial, wedded, hymeneal, spousal, bridal, marital, epithalamic.

Monogamous, bigamous, polygamous, etc.

maid, maiden, old maid, virgin, *femme sole*, bachelor girl.

(Phrase) Single blessedness.

(Verb) To live single.

(Adjectives) Unwedded, unmarried, single, celibate, wifeless, spouseless, lone.

---

905 Divorce *(Substantives)*, dissolution of marriage, separation, divorcement.

A divorcee, co-respondent, cuckold.

(Verbs) To live separate, divorce, put away.

Widowhood, viduity, weeds.

Widow, relict, dowager, jointress, grass widow; widower, grass widower.

2°. Diffusive Sympathetic Affections

906 Benevolence *(Substantives)*, goodwill, good nature, kindness, kindliness, benignity, brotherly love, beneficence, charity, humanity, fellow-feeling, sympathy, good feeling, kindheartedness, amiability, complaisance, loving-kindness; toleration, consideration, generosity.

Charitableness, bounty, bounteousness, bountifulness, almsgiving, philanthropy (910), unselfishness (942).

Acts of kindness, a good turn, good works, kind offices, attentions, good treatment.

(Phrases) The milk of human kindness; the good Samaritan.

(Verbs) To be benevolent, etc., to do good to, to benefit, confer a benefit, be of use, aid, assist (707),

907 Malevolence *(Substantives)*, ill will, unkindness, ill nature, malignity, malice, maliciousness, spite, spitefulness, despite, despitefulness.

Uncharitableness, venom, gall, rancour, rankling, bitterness, acerbity, harshness, mordacity, acridity, virulence, *acharnement*, misanthropy (911).

Cruelty, hardness of heart, obduracy, cruelness, brutality, brutishness, hooliganism, savageness, savagery, ferocity, barbarity, bloodthirstiness, immanity, pitilessness, truculence, devilry (or deviltry), devilment.

An ill turn, a bad turn, outrage, atrocity, affront (929).

(Phrases) A heart of stone; the evil eye; the cloven hoof.

render a service, treat well, to sympathize with.

(Phrases) To have one's heart in the right place; to enter into the feelings of others; to do a good turn to; to do as one would be done by.

(Adjectives) Benevolent, well-meaning, kind, obliging, accommodating, kind-hearted, tender-hearted, charitable, generous, beneficent, bounteous, bountiful, humane, clement, benignant, benign, considerate.

Good-natured, *bon enfant, bon diable,* a good sort, sympathizing, sympathetic, responsive, complaisant, accommodating, amiable, gracious.

Kindly, well-meant, well-intentioned, brotherly, fraternal, friendly (888).

(Adverbs) With a good intention, with the best intentions.

(Interjections) Good luck! God speed!

_____

(Verbs) To be malevolent, etc.; to injure, hurt, harm, molest, disoblige, do harm to, ill treat, maltreat (649), do an ill office or turn to (830), to wrong.

To worry, harass, bait, oppress, grind, haze, persecute, hunt down, dragoon, hound.

(Phrases) To wreak one's malice on; to bear or harbour malice against; to do one's worst.

(Adjectives) Malevolent, malicious, ill-disposed, evil-minded, ill-intentioned, maleficent, malign, malignant.

Ill-natured, disobliging, inofficious, unfriendly, unsympathetic, unkind, uncandid, unaccommodating, uncharitable, ungracious, unamiable.

Surly, churlish (895), grim, spiteful, despiteful, ill-conditioned, foul-mouthed, acrid, rancorous, caustic, bitter, acrimonious, mordacious, vitriolic, venomous.

Cold, cold-blooded, cold-hearted, hard-hearted, iron-hearted, flint-hearted, marble-hearted, stony-hearted.

Pitiless, unpitying, uncompassionate, without bowels, ruthless, merciless, unmerciful, inexorable, relentless, unrelenting, virulent, dispiteous.

Cruel, brutal, savage, ferocious, atrocious, untamed, ferine, inhuman, barbarous, fell, Hunnish, bloody, blood-stained, bloodthirsty, bloody-minded, sanguinary, truculent (919), butcherly.

Fiendish, fiendlike, infernal, demoniacal, diabolical, devilish, hellish.

(Adverbs) Malevolently, etc., with bad intent or intention, despitefully.

908 Malediction *(Substantives)*, curse, malison, imprecation, denunciation, execration, anathema, ban, proscription, excommunication, commination, fulmination, *maranatha.*

Cursing, scolding, revilement, vilification, vituperation, invective, flyting, railing, Billingsgate, expletive, oath, bad language, unparliamentary language, ribaldry, scurrility.

(Verbs) To censure, curse, imprecate, damn, scold, swear at, flyte on, rail at or against, execrate.

To denounce, proscribe, excommunicate, fulminate against, anathematize, blaspheme.

(Phrases) To devote to destruction; to invoke or call down curses on one's head; to swear like a trooper; to rap out an oath; to curse with bell, book and candle.

(Adjectives) Cursing, etc., accursed, cursed, etc., blue-pencil, asterisk; maledictory, imprecatory, blasphemous.

(Interjections) Curse! damn! blast! devil take it! hang! blow! confound! plague on it! woe to! beshrew! *ruat coelum!* ill betide!

909 Threat *(Substantives)*, menace, defiance (715), abuse, minacity, intimidation, commination.

(Verbs) To threaten, threat, menace, fulminate, thunder, bluster, defy, snarl; growl, gnarl, mutter; to intimidate (860).

(Phrases) To hurl defiance; to throw down the gauntlet; to look daggers; to show one's teeth; to shake the fist at.

(Adjectives) Threatening, menacing, minatory, comminatory, minacious, abusive, sinister, ominous, louring, defiant (715).

(Interjections) Let them beware! You have been warned!

910 Philanthropy *(Substantives)*, humanity, humanitarianism, altruism, public spirit.

Patriotism, civicism, nationality, nationalism, love of country, *amor patriae*, sociology, socialism, utilitarianism.

A philanthropist, humanitarian, utilitarian, Benthamite, socialist, cosmopolitan, cosmopolite, citizen of the world, patriot, nationalist, lover of mankind.

(Adjectives) Philanthropic, philanthropical, humanitarian, humane, utilitarian, patriotic, altruistic, public-spirited.

(Phrases) 'Humani nihil a me alienum puto'; pro bono publico; the greatest happiness of the greatest number.

911 Misanthropy *(Substantives)*, egotism, egoism, incivism, want of patriotism, moroseness, selfishness (943); misogynism.

A misanthrope, egotist, cynic, man-hater, Timon, Diogenes.

Woman-hater, misogynist.

(Adjectives) Misanthropic, misanthropical, antisocial, unpatriotic, fish, egotistical, morose, sullen, maladjusted.

912 Benefactor *(Substantives)*, saviour, good genius, tutelary saint, guardian angel, fairy godmother, good Samaritan.

(Phrase) Deus ex machina.

913 Maleficent being.

Evildoer *(Substantives)*, wrongdoer, mischief-maker, marplot, anarchist, nihilist, terrorist, firebrand, incendiary, evil genius (980).

Frankenstein's monster.

Savage, brute, ruffian, blackguard, villain, scoundrel, cutthroat, barbarian, caitiff, desperado, jail-bird, hooligan, tough, rough, teddy boy, larrikin, hoodlum, gangster, crook, yegg, apache (949).

Fiend, tiger, hyena, bloodhound, butcher, blood-sucker, vampire, ogre, ghoul, serpent, snake, adder, viper, rattlesnake, scorpion, hellhound, hag, hellbag, beldam, harpy, siren, fury, Jezebel.

Monster, demon, imp, devil (980), anthropophagi, Attila, vandal, Hun, Goth.

(Phrases) A snake in the grass; a scourge of the human race; a fiend in human shape; worker of iniquity.

3°. Special Sympathetic Affections

914 Pity *(Substantives)*, compassion, commiseration, sympathy, fellow-feeling, tenderness, yearning.

Forbearance, mercy, humanity, clemency, leniency, ruth, long-suffering, quarter.

(Phrases) The melting mood; *coup de grâce*; bowels of compassion; *argumentum ad misericordiam*.

(Verbs) To pity, commiserate, compassionate, sympathize, feel for, yearn for, console, enter into the feelings of, have or take pity; show or have mercy; to forbear, relent, thaw, spare, relax, give quarter.

To excite pity, touch, soften, melt, propitiate, disarm.

To ask for pity, mercy, etc.; to supplicate, implore, deprecate, appeal to, cry for quarter, etc.; beg one's life, kneel, fall on one's knees, etc.

(Phrase) To put one out of one's misery.

(Adjectives) Pitying, commiserating, etc.

Pitiful, compassionate, tender, clement, merciful, lenient, relenting, etc.; soft-hearted, sympathetic, touched, weak, soft, melting, unhardened (740).

Piteous, pitiable, sorry, miserable.

(Phrases) Tender as a woman; one's heart bleeding for.

(Interjections) For pity's sake! mercy! God help you! poor thing! poor fellow!

915 Condolence *(Substantives)*, lamentation, lament (839), sympathy, consolation.

(Verbs) To condole with, console, solace, sympathize; express, testify, etc., pity; to afford or supply consolation, grieve for, lament with, weep with (839).

4°. Retrospective Sympathetic Affections

916 Gratitude *(Substantives)*, gratefulness, thankfulness, feeling of obligation.

Acknowledgment, recognition, thanksgiving, giving thanks.

Thanks, praise, benediction, grace, paean, Te Deum (990).

Requital, thank-offering.

(Verbs) To be grateful, etc.; to thank, to give, render, return, offer, tender thanks, acknowledgments, etc.; to acknowledge, appreciate, requite.

To lie under an obligation, to be obliged, beholden, etc.

(Phrases) To overflow with gratitude; to thank one's stars; never to forget.

(Adjectives) Grateful, thankful, obliged, beholden, indebted to, under obligation.

917 Ingratitude *(Substantives)*, ungratefulness, thanklessness, oblivion of benefits.

(Phrases) 'Benefits forgot'; a thankless task.

(Verbs) To be ungrateful, etc.; to forget benefits.

(Phrases) To look a gift-horse in the mouth; to bite the hand that fed one.

(Adjectives) Ungrateful, unmindful, unthankful, thankless, ingrate, inappreciative.

Forgotten, unacknowledged, unthanked, unrequited, unrewarded, ill-requited.

(Phrase) Thank you for nothing.

(Interjections) Thanks! many thanks! ta! *merci!* gramercy! much obliged! thank heaven! heaven be praised!

918 Forgiveness *(Substantives)*, pardon, condonation, grace, remission, absolution, amnesty, indemnity, oblivion, indulgence, reprieve.

Reconcilement, reconciliation, appeasement, mollification, shaking of hands, pacification (723).

919 Revenge *(Substantives)*, vengeance, revengement, avengement, vendetta, feud, retaliation.

Rancour, vindictiveness, implacability.

Revenger, avenger, vindicator, Nemesis, Furies.

Excuse, exoneration, quittance, acquittal, propitiation, exculpation.

Longanimity, forbearance, placability.

(Verbs) To forgive, pardon, excuse, pass over, overlook, bear with, condone, absolve, pass, let off, remit, reprieve, exculpate, exonerate.

To allow for; to make allowance for.

To conciliate, propitiate, pacify, appease, placate, reconcile.

(Phrases) To make it up; to forgive and forget; to shake hands; to heal the breach; to kiss and be friends; to bury the hatchet; to wipe the slate clean; to let bygones be bygones.

(Adjectives) Forgiving, etc., unreproachful, placable, conciliatory.

Forgiven, etc., unresented.

(Verbs) To revenge, take revenge, avenge.

(Phrases) To wreak one's vengeance; to visit the sins on; to breathe vengeance; to have a bone to pick with; to have accounts to settle; to have a rod in pickle; to get one's knife into; to take one's change out of.

To harbour vindictive feelings; to rankle in the breast.

(Adjectives) Revengeful, revanchist, vindictive, vengeful, rancorous, unforgiving, pitiless, ruthless, remorseless, unrelenting, relentless, implacable, rigorous.

---

920 Jealousy (Substantives), jealousness, heartburning.

(Phrases) A jaundiced eye; the green-eyed monster.

(Verbs) To be jealous, etc.; to view with jealousy.

(Adjectives) Jealous, jaundiced, yellow-eyed.

(Phrase) Eaten up with jealousy.

921 Envy (Substantives), rivalry, emulation, covetousness; a Thersites, Zoilus.

(Verbs) To envy, rival, emulate, covet.

(Adjectives) Envious, invidious, covetous.

(Phrase) Bursting with envy.

SECTION IV—MORAL AFFECTIONS

1°. Moral Obligation

922 Right (Substantives), what ought to be, what should be; goodness, virtue (944), rectitude, probity (939).

Justice, equity, equitableness, fitness, fairness, fair play, impartiality, reasonableness, propriety.

Astraea, Themis.

(Phrases) The scales of justice; even-handed justice; suum cuique; a fair field and no favour; lex talionis; 'Fiat justitia, ruat coelum.'

Morality, morals, ethics, duty (926).

(Verbs) To stand to reason; to be right, just, etc.

To deserve, merit; to be worthy of, to be entitled to (924).

923 Wrong (Substantives), what ought not to be, badness, evil (945), turpitude, improbity (940).

Injustice, unfairness, inequity, foul play, partiality, favour, favouritism, leaning, bias, party spirit, undueness (925), unreasonableness, tort, unlawfulness (964), encroachment, imposition.

(Verbs) To be wrong, unjust, etc.; to favour, lean towards, show partiality, to encroach, impose upon.

(Phrase) To rob Peter to pay Paul.

(Adjectives) Wrong, wrongful, bad, unjust, unfair, undue, inequitable, unequal, partial, invidious, one-sided, improper, unreasonable, iniquitous, unfit, immoral (945).

(Phrases) To do justice to; to see justice done; to hold the scales even; to see fair play; to see one righted; to serve one right; to give the devil his due; to give and take; *audire alteram partem*.

(Adjectives) Right, just, equitable, fair, equal, even-handed, impartial, judicial, legitimate, justifiable, rightful, reasonable, fit, proper, becoming, decorous, decent (926).

Deserved, merited, condign (924).

(Adverbs) Rightly, in justice, in equity, fairly, etc., in reason, without distinction, without respect of persons.

(Phrases) En règle; de jure.

Unjustified, unjustifiable, unwarranted, unauthorized, unallowable, unwarrantable.

(Phrases) In the wrong; in the wrong box.

(Adverbs) Wrongly, unjustly, etc., amiss.

(Phrase) It won't do.

———

924 Dueness *(Substantives)*, due.

Right, privilege, prerogative, title, claim, qualification, pretension, birthright, prescription, immunity, exemption, licence, liberty, franchise, enfranchisement, vested interest.

Sanction, authority, warranty, tenure, bond, security, lien, constitution, charter, warrant (760), patent, letters patent, copyright, *imprimatur*.

A claimant, pretender, appellant, plaintiff (938).

Women's rights, feminism; feminist, suffragist, suffragette.

(Verbs) To be due, etc., to.

To have a right to, to be entitled to, to be qualified for, to have a claim upon, a title to, etc.; to deserve, merit, be worthy of.

To demand, claim, call upon, exact, insist on, challenge, to come upon one for, to revendicate, make a point of, enforce, put in force, use a right.

To appertain to, belong to, etc. (777).

To lay claim to, assert, assume, arrogate, make good, substantiate; to vindicate a claim, etc., to make out a case.

To give or confer a right; to entitle, authorize, warrant, sanction, sanctify, privilege, enfranchise, license, legalize, ordain, prescribe, allot.

(Adjectives) Having a right to, a claim to, etc.; due to, entitled to, deserving, meriting, worthy of, claiming, qualified.

925 Absence of right.

Undueness *(Substantives)*, unlawfulness, impropriety, unfitness, illegality (964).

Falseness, spuriousness, emptiness or invalidity of title, illegitimacy.

Loss of right, forfeiture, disfranchisement.

Usurpation, violation, breach, encroachment, stretch, imposition, relaxation.

(Verbs) Not to be due, etc., to; to be undue, etc.

To infringe, encroach, violate, do violence to; to stretch or strain a point; to trench on, usurp.

To disfranchise, disentitle, disfrock, unfrock; to disqualify, invalidate, relax.

To misbecome, misbehave (945).

(Adjectives) Undue, unlawful, illicit, unconstitutional.

Unauthorized, unwarranted, unsanctioned, unjustified, unprivileged, illegitimate, bastard, spurious, supposititious, false, usurped, unchartered, unfulfilled, unofficial, unauthorized.

Unentitled, disentitled, unqualified, underprivileged; disfranchised, forfeit.

Undeserved, unmerited, unearned.

Improper, unmeet, unbecoming, unfit, misbecoming, unseemly, preposterous.

(Phrases) Not the thing; out of the question; not to be thought of; out of court.

Privileged, allowed, sanctioned, warranted, authorized, permitted, licit, ordained, prescribed, chartered, enfranchised, constitutional, official.

Prescriptive, presumptive, absolute, indefeasible, unalienable, inalienable, imprescriptible, inviolable, unimpeachable, unchallenged, sacred, sacrosanct.

Condign, merited, deserved.

Allowable, permissible, lawful, legitimate, legal, legalized (963), proper, square, equitable, unexceptionable, reasonable (922), right, correct, meet, fitting (926).

(Adverbs) Duly, by right, by divine right, *ex officio, Dei gratia, de jure*.

---

926 Duty *(Substantives)*, what ought to be done; moral obligation, accountableness, accountability, liability, onus, responsibility, bounden duty; dueness (924).

Allegiance, fealty, tie, office, function, province, post, engagement (768).

Morality, morals, conscience, accountableness, conscientiousness; the Decalogue, the Ten Commandments.

Dueness, propriety, fitness, decency, seemliness, decorum.

Observance, fulfilment, discharge, performance, acquittal, satisfaction, redemption, good behaviour.

Science of morals, ethics, deontology; moral or ethical philosophy, casuistry.

(Phrases) The thing; the proper thing; a case of conscience; the still small voice.

(Verbs) To be the duty of, to be due to, to be up to; ought to be; to be incumbent on, to behove, befit, become, beseem, belong to, pertain to, devolve on, to be on one's head; to be, or stand, or lie under an obligation; to have to answer for, to be accountable for, to owe it to oneself, to be in duty bound, to be committed to, to be on one's good behaviour.

To impose a duty or obligation; to enjoin, require, exact, bind, pin down, saddle with, prescribe, assign, call upon, look to, oblige.

To do one's duty, to enter upon a duty; to perform, observe, fulfil, discharge, adhere to; acquit oneself of an obligation.

(Phrases) To be at one's post; to redeem one's pledge; to toe the mark or line.

(Adjectives) Dutiful, duteous, docile, obedient, compliant, tractable.

927 Dereliction of duty *(Substantives)*, guilt (947), sin (945), neglect, evasion, dead letter.

(Verbs) To violate, break, break through, infringe, set at naught, slight, neglect, trample on, evade, contravene, disregard, renounce, repudiate, quit, forswear, fail, transgress.

(Phrase) To wash one's hands of.

927A Exemption *(Substantives)*, freedom, irresponsibility, immunity, liberty, licence, release, exoneration, excuse, dispensation, absolution, franchise, renunciation, discharge.

(Verbs) To be exempt, free, at liberty, released, excused, exonerated, absolved, etc.

To exempt, release, excuse, exonerate, absolve, acquit, free, set at liberty, discharge, set aside, let off, remit, pass over, spare, excuse, license, dispense with; to give dispensation.

(Phrase) To stretch a point.

(Adjectives) Exempt, free, released, at liberty, absolved, exonerated, excused, let off, discharged, licensed, acquitted, unencumbered, dispensed, scot-free, immune.

Irresponsible, unaccountable, unanswerable, unbound.

Obligatory, binding, imperative, peremptory, mandatory, behoving, incumbent on, chargeable on, meet, due to.

Being under obligation, under obedience, obliged by, beholden to, bound by, tied by, saddled with, indebted to.

Amenable, liable, accountable, responsible, answerable.

Right, proper, fit, due, correct, seemly, fitting, befitting, decent, meet.

Moral, ethical, casuistical, conscientious.

(Adverbs) Conscientiously, with a safe conscience; as in duty bound; on one's own responsibility.

2°. *Moral Sentiments*

928 Respect *(Substantives)*, deference, reverence, regard, consideration, attention, honour, esteem, estimation, distance, decorum, veneration, admiration.

Homage, fealty, obeisance, genuflexion, kneeling, salaam, kowtow, presenting arms (896), prostration, obsequiousness, devotion, worship (990).

(Verbs) To respect, honour, reverence, regard, defer to; pay respect or deference to, render honour to, look up to, esteem, revere, think much of, think highly of, venerate, hallow.

To pay homage to, bow to, take off one's hat to, kneel to, bend the knee to, present arms, fall down before, prostrate oneself.

To command or inspire respect; to awe, overawe, dazzle.

(Phrases) To keep one's distance; to make way for; to observe due decorum.

(Adjectives) Respecting, etc., respectful, considerate, polite, attentive, reverential, obsequious, ceremonious, bare-headed, cap in hand, on one's knees, prostrate.

Respected, esteemed, honoured, hallowed, venerable, emeritus.

(Phrases) Saving your presence; begging your honour's pardon.

---

929 Disrespect *(Substantives)*, irreverence, dishonour, disparagement, slight, neglect, disesteem, disestimation, superciliousness, contumely, indignity, insult, rudeness.

Ridicule (856), sarcasm, derision, scurrility, mockery, scoffing, sibilation.

A jeer, gibe, taunt, scoff, sneer (930), hiss, hoot, fling, flout.

(Verbs) To treat with disrespect, etc., to disparage, dishonour, misprise, vilipend, slight, insult, affront, disregard, make light of, hold in no esteem, esteem of no account, set at naught, speak slightingly of, set down, pass by, overlook, look down upon, despise (930).

To deride, scoff, sneer at, laugh at, ridicule (856), roast, guy, rag, mock, jeer, taunt, twit, flout, gibe, hiss, hoot, boo.

(Phrases) To make game of; to point the finger at; to make a fool of; to turn into ridicule; to laugh to scorn; to turn one's back upon.

(Adjectives) Disrespectful, slighting, disparaging (934), dishonouring, scornful (940), irreverent, supercilious, contumelious, scurrilous, deriding, derisive, derisory.

Unrespected, unworshipped, unregarded, disregarded, ignored.

(Adverbs) Disrespectfully, cavalierly, etc.

---

930 Contempt *(Substantives)*, disdain, scorn, contumely, despisal, slight, sneer, spurn, sniff; a byword.

Scornfulness, disdainfulness, haughtiness, contemptuousness, superciliousness, derision (929).

The state of being despised, despisedness.

(Verbs) To despise, contemn, scorn, disdain, scout, spurn, look down upon,

disregard, slight, make light of, not mind, hold cheap, hold in contempt, pooh-pooh, sneeze at, sniff at, whistle at, hoot, flout, trample upon.

(Phrases) Not to care a straw, fig, button, etc., for (643); to turn up one's nose at; to shrug one's shoulders; to snap one's fingers at; to take no account of; to laugh to scorn; to make light of; to tread or trample under foot; to set at naught; to point the finger of scorn at.

(Adjectives) Contemptuous, disdainful, scornful, contumelious, cavalier, derisive, supercilious, toplofty, upstage, sniffy, sardonic.

Contemptible, despicable, poor, paltry (643), downtrodden, unenvied.

(Interjections) A fig for! hoots! bah! pshaw! pish! shucks! pooh-pooh! fiddlestick! fiddle-de-dee! tush! tut!

931 Approbation *(Substantives)*, approval, approvement, endorsement, sanction, esteem, admiration, estimation, good opinion, appreciation, regard, account, popularity, kudos.

Commendation, praise, laud, laudation, advocacy, good word; meed or tribute of praise, encomium, eulogium, eulogy, *éloge*, panegyric, puff, blurb, homage.

Applause, plaudit, cheer, clap, clapping, clapping of hands, acclamation; paean, benediction, blessing, benison, hosanna; claque.

(Phrases) A peal, shout, or chorus of applause; golden opinions; *succès d'estime*.

(Verbs) To approve, think well or highly of, esteem, appreciate, value, prize, admire, countenance, endorse.

To commend, speak well of, recommend, advocate, praise, laud, belaud, compliment, bepraise, clap, clap hands, applaud, cheer, panegyrize, celebrate, eulogize, cry up, root for, crack up, write up, extol, glorify, magnify, puff, boom, boost, exalt, swell, bless, give a blessing to.

To deserve praise, etc., to be praised, etc.

(Phrases) To set great store by; to sing the praises of; to extol to the skies; to applaud to the echo; to stick up for; to say a good word for; to pat on the back.

To redound to the honour or praise of; to do credit to.

To win golden opinions; to be in high favour; to bring down the house.

(Adjectives) Approving, etc., commendatory, complimentary, benedictory, laudatory, panegyrical, eulo-

932 Disapprobation *(Substantives)*, disapproval, dislike (867), blame, censure, reprobation, obloquy, dispraise, contumely, odium, disesteem, depreciation, detraction (934), condemnation, ostracism.

Reprobation, exprobation, insinuation, innuendo, animadversion, reflection, stricture, objection, exception, criticism, critique, correction, discommendation.

Satire, sneer, fling, gibe, skit, squib, quip, taunt, sarcasm, lampoon, cavil, pasquinade, recrimination, castigation.

Remonstrance, reprehension, reproof, admonition, expostulation, reproach, rebuke, reprimand, talking-to, telling-off.

Evil speaking, hard words, foul language, personalities, ribaldry, Billingsgate, unparliamentary language.

Upbraiding, abuse, invective, vituperation, scolding, wigging, dressing-down, objurgation, jaw, railing, jobation, nagging, reviling, contumely, execration (908).

A set-down, trimming, rating, slap, snub, frown, scowl, black look.

A lecture, curtain lecture, diatribe, jeremiad, tirade, philippic; clamour, outcry, hue and cry, hiss, hissing, sibilation, cat-call.

(Phrases) A rap on the knuckles; a slap in the face; a left-handed compliment.

(Verbs) To disapprove, dislike (867), dispraise, find fault with, criticize, glance at, insinuate, cut up, carp at, cavil, point at, peck at, nibble at, object to, take exception

gistic, encomiastic.

Approved, praised, uncensured, unimpeached, admired, popular, deserving or worthy of praise, praiseworthy, commendable, estimable, plausible, meritorious.

(Phrases) Lavish of praise; lost in admiration.

(Interjections) Well done! good man! stout fellow! good show! attaboy! bravo! bravissimo! *euge!* that's the stuff! hear, hear!

———

to, animadvert upon, protest against, frown upon, bar.

To disparage, depreciate, deprecate, crab, knock, traduce, smear, speak ill of, decry, vilify, vilipend, defame, detract (934), revile, satirize, sneer, gibe, lampoon, inveigh against, write down, scalp.

To blame; to lay or cast blame upon, reflect upon, cast a slur upon, censure, pass censure on, impugn, show up, denounce, censure, brand, stigmatize, reprobate, improbate.

To reprehend, reprimand, admonish, remonstrate, expostulate, reprove, pull up, take up, set down, snub, twit, taunt, reproach, load with reproaches, rebuke, come down upon, sit on, pitch into, get on to, tell off, tick off.

To chide, scold, wig, rate, objurgate, upbraid, vituperate, recriminate, anathematize, abuse, call names, exclaim against, jaw, mob, trounce, trim, rail at, nag, nag at, bark at, blackguard, revile, ballyrag, rag, natter, blow up, roast, lecture; castigate, chastise, correct, lash, flay; to fulminate against, fall foul of.

To cry out against, cry down, run down, clamour, hiss, hoot; to accuse (938), to find guilty, ostracize, blacklist, blackball.

To scandalize, shock, revolt, incur blame, excite disapprobation.

(Phrases) To set one's face against; to shake the head at; to take a poor or dim view of; to view with dark or jaundiced eyes; to pick holes in; to give a thing the bird; to damn with faint praise; to pluck a crow with; to have a fling at; to read a lecture; to put on the carpet (or mat); to take to task; to bring to book; to haul over the coals; to tear one off a strip; to shoot down in flames; to pull to pieces; to cut up; to cast in one's teeth; to abuse like a pickpocket; to speak or look daggers; to rail in good set terms; to give it one hot; to throw mud; to give a person the rough side of one's tongue.

To forfeit the good opinion of; to catch it; to be under a cloud; to carry the can; to stand corrected.

(Adjectives) Disapproving, disparaging, etc., condemnatory, damnatory, denunciatory, reproachful, abusive, objurgatory, clamorous, vituperative, dyslogistic.

Censorious, critical, carping, satirical, sarcastic, sardonic, cynical, dry, hypercritical, captious; sharp, cutting, mordant, biting, withering, trenchant, caustic, severe, scathing; squeamish, fastidious, strait-laced (868).

Disapproved, chid, unapproved, blown upon, unblest, unlamented, unbewailed.

Blameworthy, uncommendable, exceptionable (649, 945).

(Phrases) Hard upon one; weighed in the balance and found wanting; not to be thought of.

(Interjections) Bad show! shame!

933 Flattery *(Substantives)*, adulation, sycophancy, blandishment, cajolery, fawning, wheedling, coaxing,

934 Detraction *(Substantives)*, obloquy, scurrility, scandal, vilification, smear, defamation, aspersion,

flunkeyism, toad-eating, toadyism, tuft-hunting, back-scratching, blandiloquence, schmalz.

Incense, honeyed words, flummery, soft sawder, soft soap, butter, applesauce, blarney, malarkey; mouth-honour, lip-service.

(Verbs) To flatter, wheedle, cajole, fawn upon, coax (615), humour, gloze, butter, toady, sugar, bespatter, beslaver, earwig, jolly, flannel, truckle to, pander to, court, pay court to.

(Phrases) To curry favour with; to lay it on thick; to lay it on with a trowel; to ingratiate oneself with; to fool to the top of one's bent.

(Adjectives) Flattering, adulatory, mealy-mouthed, smooth, honeyed, candied, soapy, oily, unctuous, fair-spoken, plausible, servile, sycophantic, fulsome; courtier-like.

935 Flatterer *(Substantives)*, adulator, eulogist, encomiast, whitewasher, toady, sycophant, toad-eater, *prôneur*, touter, booster, *claqueur*, spaniel, back-scratcher, flunkey, lickspittle, pick-thank, earwig, tuft-hunter, hanger-on, courtier, parasite, doer of dirty work, *âme damnée, Graeculus esuriens.*

937 Vindication *(Substantives)*, justification, exoneration, exculpation, acquittal, whitewashing.

Extenuation, palliation, mitigation, softening; extenuating circumstances.

Plea, excuse, apology, defence, gloss, varnish, salvo (617).

Vindicator, apologist, justifier, defender.

(Verbs) To vindicate, justify, warrant, exculpate, acquit, clear, set right, exonerate, disculpate, whitewash.

To extenuate, palliate, excuse, soften, apologize, varnish, slur, gloze, gloss over, bolster up.

To plead, advocate, defend, stand up for, stick up for, speak for, make good, bear out, say in defence, contend for.

traducement, slander, calumny, backbiting, criticism, slating, personality, evil-speaking, disparagement, depreciation (932).

Libel, lampoon, skit, squib, sarcasm.

(Verbs) To detract, criticize, asperse, depreciate, derogate, disparage, cheapen, blow upon, bespatter, blacken, denigrate, defame, brand, malign, decry, vilify, vilipend, backbite, libel, slate, lampoon, traduce, slander, calumniate, run down, write down.

(Phrases) To speak ill of one behind one's back; to damn with faint praise; to sell oneself short.

(Adjectives) Detracting, disparaging, libellous, scurrilous, abusive, cynical (932), foul-tongued, foulmouthed, slanderous, defamatory, calumnious, calumniatory.

936 Detractor *(Substantives)*, disapprover, critic, censor, caviller, carper, knocker, *frondeur*, defamer, backbiter, slanderer, traducer, libeller, calumniator, lampooner, satirist, candid friend, Thersites.

———

938 Accusation *(Substantives)*, charge, imputation, inculpation, exprobation, delation, crimination, recrimination, invective, jeremiad (932).

Denunciation, denouncement, challenge, indictment, libel, delation, citation, arraignment, impeachment, appeachment, bill of indictment, true bill, condemnation (971), scandal (934), *scandalum magnatum.*

Accuser, prosecutor, plaintiff, pursuer, informer, appellant, complainant.

Accused, defendant, prisoner, panel, respondent.

(Phrases) The gravamen of a charge; *argumentum ad hominem.*

(Verbs) To accuse, charge, tax, impute, twit, taunt with, slur, reproach, brand with, stigmatize, criminate,

(Phrases) To put in a good word for; to plead the cause of; to put a good face upon; to keep in countenance; to make allowance for.

(Adjectives) Vindicatory, vindicative, palliative, exculpatory; vindicating, etc.

Excusable, defensible, pardonable, venial, specious, plausible, justifiable, warrantable.

(Phrases) 'Honi soit qui mal y pense'; qui s'excuse s'accuse.

———

incriminate, inculpate (932), implicate, saddle with.

To inform against; to indict, denounce, arraign, impeach, challenge, show up, pull up, cite, prosecute, summon.

(Phrases) To lay to one's door; to lay to one's charge; bring home to; to call to account; to bring to book; to take to task; to trump up a charge; to brand with reproach.

(Adjectives) Accusing, etc., accusatory, accusative, imputative, denunciatory, criminative, criminatory, incriminatory, accusable, imputable.

Indefensible, inexcusable, unpardonable, unjustifiable (945).

3°. Moral Conditions

939 Probity *(Substantives)*, integrity, uprightness, honesty, virtue (944), rectitude, faith, good faith, bona fides, fairness, honour, fair play, justice, principle, constancy, fidelity, incorruptibility.

Trustworthiness, trustiness, reliability, dependableness, grace, uncorruptedness, impartiality, equity, candour, veracity (545), straightforwardness, truth, equitableness, singleness of heart.

Conscientiousness, punctiliousness, nicety, scrupulosity, delicacy, sense of decency, strictness, punctuality.

Dignity, respectability, reputableness (873).

A man of honour, a gentleman, a man of his word, a sportsman, white man, trump, brick, *preux chevalier*.

(Phrases) The court of honour; a fair field and no favour; 'a verray parfit gentil knight.'

(Verbs) To be honourable, etc.; to keep one's word, to give and take, to deal honourably, squarely, impartially, fairly.

(Phrases) To hit straight from the shoulder; to play the game.

(Adjectives) Upright, honest, virtuous (944), honourable, fair, right, just, equitable, impartial, evenhanded, square, constant, faithful, loyal, staunch, straight.

940 Improbity *(Substantives)*, wickedness (945), bad faith, unfairness, infidelity, faithlessness, want of faith, dishonesty, disloyalty, falseness, falsity, one-sidedness, disingenuousness, shabbiness, littleness, meanness, caddishness, baseness, villainy, roguery, rascality, vileness, abjectness, turpitude, unreliability, untrustworthiness, insidiousness, knavery, knavishness, fraud (545), falsehood (544), shenanigans.

Disgrace, ignominy, infamy, tarnish, blot, stain, spot, slur, pollution, derogation, degradation (874).

Perfidy, perfidiousness, treason, high treason, perjury, apostasy (607), backsliding, breach of faith, defection, disloyalty, disaffection, foul play, sharp practice, graft, double-dealing, betrayal, treacherousness, treachery.

(Phrases) The kiss of Judas; divided allegiance; Punic faith.

(Verbs) To be of bad faith, dishonest, etc.; to play false, break one's word or faith, betray, forswear, shuffle (545).

To disgrace oneself, derogate, stoop, demean oneself, lose caste, dishonour oneself, sneak, crawl, grovel.

(Phrases) To seal one's infamy; to sell oneself; to go over to the enemy.

Trustworthy, trusty, reliable, dependable, tried, incorruptible, straightforward, ingenuous (703), frank, open-hearted, candid.

Conscientious, tender-conscienced, high-principled, high-minded, high-toned, scrupulous, strict, nice, punctilious, correct, punctual, inviolable, inviolate, unviolated, unbroken, unbetrayed.

Chivalrous, gentlemanlike, respectable, unbought, unbribed, unstained, stainless, untarnished, unsullied, untainted, unperjured, innocent (946).

(Phrases) Jealous of honour; as good as one's word; true to one's colours; *sans peur et sans reproche; integer vitae scelerisque purus.*

(Adverbs) Honourably, etc., bona fide; on the square; on the up and up.

(Adjectives) Dishonest, unfair, one-sided, fraudulent (545), bent, knavish, wicked (945), false, faithless, unfaithful, foul, disingenuous, trothless, trustless, untrustworthy, unreliable, slippery, double-faced, double-tongued, crooked, tortuous, unscrupulous, insidious, treacherous, perfidious, false-hearted, perjured, rascally.

Base, vile, grovelling, dirty, scurvy, scabby, low, low-down, abject, shabby, caddish, mean, paltry, pitiful, inglorious, scrubby, beggarly, putid, unworthy, disgraceful, dishonourable, derogatory, low-thoughted, disreputable, unhandsome, unbecoming (925), unbefitting, ungentlemanly, unmanly, unwomanly, undignified, base-minded, recreant, low-minded, blackguard, pettifogging, underhand, underhanded, unsportsmanlike.

(Phrases) Lost to shame; dead to honour.

(Adverbs) Dishonestly, etc., *mala fide*, on the crook.

941 Knave *(Substantives)*, bad man (949), rogue, rascal, scoundrel, villain, spiv, sharper, shyster, blackleg, scab, trimmer, time-server, timist, turncoat, badmash, Vicar of Bray, Judas (607).

Apostate, renegade, pervert, black sheep, traitor, arch-traitor, quisling, fifth columnist, deviationist, betrayer, recreant, miscreant, cullion, outcast, mean wretch, slubberdegullion, snake in the grass, wolf in sheep's clothing.

942 Unselfishness *(Substantives)*, selflessness, disinterestedness, generosity, highmindedness, nobleness, elevation, liberality, greatness, loftiness, exaltation, magnanimity, chivalry, chivalrous spirit, heroism, sublimity, altruism, self-forgetfulness, unworldliness.

Self-denial, self-abnegation, self-sacrifice, self-restraint, self-control, devotion, stoicism.

(Phrases) To put oneself in the background, in the place of others; to do as one would be done by.

(Adjectives) Unselfish, selfless, self-forgetful, handsome, generous, liberal, noble, princely, great, high, high-minded, elevated, lofty, exalted, spirited, stoical, self-denying, self-sacrificing, self-devoted, magnani-

943 Selfishness *(Substantives)*, egotism, egoism, self-regard, self-love, self-indulgence, worldliness, worldly-mindedness, earthly-mindedness, self-interest, opportunism.

Illiberality, meanness, baseness.

A time-server, tuft-hunter, fortune-hunter, gold-digger, jobber, worldling, self-seeker, opportunist, hog, road-hog.

(Phrase) A dog in the manger.

(Verbs) To be selfish, etc., to indulge oneself, coddle oneself.

(Phrases) To look after one's own interest; to take care of number one; to have an eye for the main chance.

(Adjectives) Selfish, egotistical, egoistical, self-indulgent, apolaustic, self-regarding, self-centred, illiberal, self-seeking, mercenary, venal, mean, ungenerous, interested.

mous, chivalrous, heroic, sublime, unworldly.

Unbought, unbribed, pure, uncorrupted, incorruptible.

(Adverb) En prince.

Worldly, earthly, mundane, time-serving, worldly-minded.

(Phrases) To serve one's private ends; from interested motives; charity begins at home; I'm all right, Jack.

944 Virtue *(Substantives)*, virtuousness, goodness, righteousness, morals, morality (926), rectitude, correctness, dutifulness, conscientiousness, integrity, probity (939), uprightness, nobleness, nobility; innocence (946).

Merit, worth, worthiness, desert, excellence, credit, self-control, self-conquest, self-government, self-respect.

Well-doing, good actions, good behaviour, a well-spent life.

(Verbs) To be virtuous, etc.; to act well; to do, fulfil, perform, or discharge one's duty, to acquit oneself well, to practise virtue; to command or master one's passions (926).

(Phrases) To have one's heart in the right place; to keep in the right path; to fight the good fight; to set an example; to be on one's good behaviour.

(Adjectives) Virtuous, good, innocent (946), meritorious, deserving, worthy, correct, dutiful, duteous (926), moral, ethical, righteous, right-minded (939), laudable, well-intentioned, creditable, commendable, praiseworthy, excellent, admirable, sterling, pure, noble, well-conducted, well-behaved.

Exemplary, matchless, peerless, saintly, saint-like, heaven-born, angelic, seraphic, godlike.

(Phrase) Mens sibi conscia recti.

(Adverb) Virtuously, etc.

---

945 Vice *(Substantives)*, evildoing, wrongdoing, wickedness, sin, iniquity, unrighteousness, demerit, unworthiness, worthlessness, badness.

Immorality, impropriety, indecorum, laxity, looseness of morals, want of principle, obliquity, backsliding, recidivism, gracelessness, infamy, demoralization, pravity, depravity, depravation, obduracy, hardness of heart, brutality (907), corruption, pollution, dissoluteness, debauchery, grossness, baseness, knavery, roguery, rascality, villainy (940), profligacy, abandonment, flagrancy, atrocity, devilry (or deviltry), criminality, guilt (947).

Infirmity, weakness, feebleness, frailty, imperfection, error, weak side or point, blind side, foible, failing, failure, defect, deficiency, indiscretion, peccability.

(Phrases) The cloven hoof; the old Adam; the lowest dregs of vice; a sink of iniquity; the primrose path.

(Verbs) To be vicious, etc.; to sin, commit sin, do amiss, misdo, err, transgress, go astray, misdemean or misconduct oneself, misbehave; to fall, lapse, slip, trip, offend, trespass.

To render vicious, etc., to demoralize, corrupt, seduce, debauch, debase, vitiate.

(Phrases) To deviate from the line of duty or from the paths of virtue, rectitude, etc.; to blot one's copybook; to hug a sin or fault; to sow one's wild oats.

(Adjectives) Vicious, bad, sinful, wicked, evil, evil-minded, immoral, iniquitous, unprincipled, demoralized, unconscionable, worthless, unworthy, good for nothing, graceless, heartless, virtueless, undutiful, unrighteous, unmoral, amoral, guilty (947).

Wrong, culpable, naughty, incorrect, indictable, criminal, dissolute, debauched, disorderly, raffish, corrupt, profligate, depraved, degenerate, abandoned, graceless, shameless, recreant, villainous, sunk, lost, obdurate, reprobate, incorrigible, irreclaimable, ill-conditioned.

Weak, frail, lax, infirm, spineless, invertebrate, imperfect, indiscreet, erring, transgressing, sinning, etc., peccable, peccant.

Blamable, reprehensible, blameworthy, uncommendable, discreditable, disreputable, shady, exceptionable.

Indecorous, unseemly, improper, sinister, base, ignoble, scurvy, foul, gross, vile, black, felonious, nefarious, scandalous, infamous, villainous, heinous, grave, flagrant, flagitious, atrocious, satanic, satanical, diabolic, diabolical, hellish, infernal, stygian, fiendlike, fiendish, devilish, miscreatèd, misbegotten, hell-born, demoniacal.

Unpardonable, unforgivable, indefensible, inexcusable, irremissible, inexpiable.

(Phrases) Past praying for; of the deepest dye; not having a word to say for oneself; weighed in the balance and found wanting; *in flagrante delicto*.

(Adverbs) Wrongly, etc.; without excuse, too bad.

---

946 Innocence *(Substantives)*, guiltlessness, harmlessness, innocuousness, incorruption, impeccability, inerrability, blamelessness, sinlessness.

A newborn babe, lamb, dove.

(Phrases) Clean hands; a clear conscience.

(Verbs) To be innocent, etc.

(Adjectives) Innocent, guiltless, not guilty, faultless, sinless, clear, spotless, stainless, immaculate, unspotted, innocuous, unblemished, untarnished, unsullied, undefiled.

Inculpable, unblamed, blameless, unblamable, clean-handed, irreproachable, unreproached, unimpeachable, unimpeached, unexceptionable, inerrable, unerring.

Harmless, inoffensive, unoffending, dovelike, lamblike, pure, uncorrupted, undefiled, undepraved, undebauched, chaste, unhardened, unsophisticated, unreproved.

(Phrases) Innocent as an unborn babe; in the clear; above suspicion; more sinned against than sinning.

(Adverbs) Innocently, etc.

947 Guilt *(Substantives)*, sin, guiltiness, culpability, criminality, criminousness, sinfulness.

Misconduct, misbehaviour, misdoing, malpractice, malefaction, malfeasance, misprision, dereliction, *corpus delicti*.

Indiscretion, peccadillo, lapse, slip, trip, *faux pas*, fault, error, flaw, blot, omission, failure.

Misdeed, offence, trespass, transgression, misdemeanour, delinquency, felony, sin, crime, enormity, atrocity.

Science of crime, criminology.

(Phrases) Besetting sin; deviation from rectitude; a deed without a name.

---

948 Good man *(Substantives)*, trump, brick, worthy, example, pattern, mirror, model, paragon, phoenix (650), superman, hero, demigod, seraph, angel, saint (987).

A good fellow, good sort, sportsman, white man.

(Phrases) One of the best; one in a million; the salt of the earth.

949 Bad man *(Substantives)*, wrongdoer, evildoer, culprit, delinquent, criminal, recidivist, malefactor, outlaw, felon, convict, lag, outcast, sinner (988).

Knave, rogue, rascal, scoundrel, spiv, scamp, scapegrace, black sheep, scallywag, spalpeen, varlet, *vaurien*, blighter, rotter, good-for-nothing, twerp, heel, jerk, creep, goon, son of a gun, dastard, blackguard, sweep, loose fish, bad egg, bad lot, hard case, lost soul, vagabond, bum, *mauvais sujet*, cur, sad dog, rip, rascallion, rap-scallion, slubberdegullion, cullion, roisterer.

Mohock, rowdy, hooligan, larrikin, teddy boy, apache, thug, reprobate, *roué*, recreant, jail-bird, crook, tough, rough, roughneck, gangster, gunman, hoodlum, yegg, villain, ruffian, miscreant, caitiff, wretch, *âme damnée*, castaway, monster, Jonathan Wilde, Jack Sheppard, Lazarillo de Tormes, Scapin (941).

Cur, dog, hound, skunk, swine, rat, viper, serpent, cockatrice, basilisk, reptile, urchin, tiger, imp, demon, devil, devil incarnate, Mephistopheles (978), hellhound, son of Belial, cut-throat, *particeps criminis*, incendiary.

Bad woman, hellcat, hellhag, bitch, witch, hag, harridan, trollop, jade, drab, hussy, minx, Jezebel.

Riff-raff, rabble, ragtag and bobtail, *canaille*.

(Phrases) A fiend in human shape; scum of the earth; poor white trash.

(Interjection) Sirrah!

950 Penitence *(Substantives)*, contrition, compunction, regret (833), repentance, remorse.

Self-reproach, self-reproof, self-accusation, self-condemnation.

Confession, acknowledgment, shrift, apology, recantation (607).

A penitent, prodigal, Magdalen.

(Phrases) The stool of repentance; the cutty-stool; sackcloth and ashes; qualms or prickings of conscience; a sadder and a wiser man.

(Verbs) To repent, regret, rue, repine, deplore, be sorry for.

To confess (529), acknowledge, apologize, shrive oneself, humble oneself, reclaim, turn from sin.

(Phrases) To have a weight on one's mind; to plead guilty; to sing small; to cry *peccavi*; to eat humble pie; to turn over a new leaf; to stand in a white sheet.

(Adjectives) Penitent, repentant, contrite, repenting, remorseful, regretful, sorry, compunctious, self-reproachful, self-accusing, self-convicted, conscience-stricken, conscience-smitten.

Not hardened, unhardened, reclaimed.

(Adverb) Meâ culpâ.

951 Impenitence *(Substantives)* obduracy, recusance, irrepentance, hardness of heart, a seared conscience, induration.

(Verbs) To be impenitent, etc.; to steel or harden the heart.

(Phrases) To make no sign; to die game.

(Adjectives) Impenitent, uncontrite, obdurate, hard, callous, unfeeling, hardened, seared, recusant, relentless, unrepentant, graceless, shiftless, lost, incorrigible, irreclaimable, irredeemable, unatoned, unreclaimed, unreformed, unrepented.

---

952 Atonement *(Substantives)*, reparation, compromise, composition, compensation (30), quittance, quits; propitiation, expiation, redemption, conciliation.

Amends, *amende honorable*, apology, satisfaction, peace-offering, olive branch, sin-offering, scapegoat, sacrifice, burnt-offering.

Penance, fasting, maceration, flagellation, sackcloth and ashes, white sheet, lustration, purgation, purgatory.

(Verbs) To atone, expiate, propitiate, make amends, redeem, make good, repair, ransom, absolve, do penance, apologize, purge, shrive, give satisfaction.

(Phrases) To purge one's offence; to pay the forfeit or penalty.

(Adjectives) Propitiatory, piacular, expiatory, expiational.

4°. *Moral Practice*

953 Temperance (*Substantives*), moderation, forbearance, abnegation, self-denial, self-conquest, self-control, self-command, self-discipline, sobriety, frugality, vegetarianism.

Abstinence, abstemiousness, teetotalism, prohibition, asceticism (955), gymnosophy, system of Pythagoras.

An abstainer, ascetic, gymnosophist, vegetarian, teetotaller, Pythagorean.

(*Phrases*) The simple life; the blue ribbon.

(*Verbs*) To be temperate, etc.; to abstain, forbear, refrain, deny oneself, spare.

(*Phrases*) To sign the pledge; to go on the water wagon.

(*Adjectives*) Temperate, moderate, sober, frugal, sparing, abstemious, abstinent, Pythagorean, vegetarian, teetotal, dry.

—

954 Intemperance (*Substantives*), excess, immoderation, unrestraint; epicurism, epicureanism, hedonism, sensuality, luxury, luxuriousness, animalism, carnality, effeminacy; the lap of pleasure or luxury; indulgence, self-indulgence, voluptuousness; drunkenness (959).

Dissipation, licentiousness, debauchery, dissoluteness, crapulence, brutishness.

Revels, revelry, carousal, orgy, spree, jag, toot, drinking bout, debauch, jollification, saturnalia.

A sensualist, epicure, epicurean, voluptuary, rake, rip, *roué*, sybarite, drug addict, dope fiend, hophead.

(*Phrases*) The Circean cup; a fast life; wine, women, and song.

(*Verbs*) To be intemperate, sensual, etc.

To indulge, exceed, revel, dissipate; give a loose to indulgence, live hard.

To debauch, pander to, sensualize, animalize, brutalize.

(*Phrases*) To wallow in voluptuousness, luxury, etc.; to plunge into dissipation; to paint the town red; to live on the fat of the land; to sow one's wild oats.

(*Adjectives*) Intemperate, sensual, pampered, self-indulgent, fleshly, inabstinent, licentious, wild, dissolute, dissipated, fast, rakish, debauched, brutish, crapulous, hedonistic, epicurean, sybaritical, Sardanapalian, voluptuous, apolaustic, orgiastic, swinish, piggish, hoggish; indulged, pampered.

955 Asceticism (*Substantives*), austerity, puritanism, mortification, maceration, sackcloth and ashes, flagellation, martyrdom, yoga.

An ascetic, anchoret, yogi, martyr; a recluse, hermit (893); puritan, Cynic.

(*Adjectives*) Ascetic, ascetical, austere, puritanical.

956 Fasting (*Substantives*), fast, spare diet, meagre diet, Lent, Quadragesima, a lenten entertainment, famishment, starvation, banian day, Ramadan.

(*Phrases*) A Barmecide feast; a hunger strike; short commons.

(*Verbs*) To fast, starve, clem, famish.

(*Phrases*) To dine with Duke Humphrey; to perish with hunger.

957 Gluttony (*Substantives*), epicurism, greediness, good cheer, high living, edacity, voracity, gulosity, crapulence, hoggishness, piggishness.

Gastronomy; feast, banquet, good cheer, blow-out.

A glutton, epicure, *bon vivant*, cormorant, gourmand, gourmet, bellygod, pig, hog, Apicius, gastronome, gastronomer, gastronomist.

(Adjectives) Fasting, etc., unfed, famished, starved; lenten, Quadragesimal.

———

(Verbs) To gormandize, gorge, cram, stuff, guzzle, bolt, devour, gobble up, pamper.

(Phrases) To eat out of house and home; to have the stomach of an ostrich; to play a good knife and fork.

(Adjectives) Gluttonous, greedy, gormandizing, edacious, voracious, crapulent, swinish, piggish, hoggish, pampered, overfed; gastronomical.

---

958 Sobriety *(Substantives)*, teetotalism, total abstinence, temperance (953).

Compulsory sobriety, prohibition.

A water-drinker, teetotaller, abstainer, total abstainer, blue-ribbonite, Rechabite, Band of Hope; prohibitionist.

(Verbs) To abstain, to take the pledge.

(Adjectives) Sober, abstemious, teetotal.

(Phrases) Sober as a judge; on the water wagon.

———

959 Drunkenness *(Substantives)*, insobriety, ebriety, inebriety, inebriation, intoxication, ebriosity, bibacity, drinking, toping, tippling, sottishness, tipsiness, bacchanals, compotation, intemperance (954); dipsomania, alcoholism, delirium tremens, D.T.

A drunkard, sot, toper, tippler, hard drinker, winebag, winebibber, dram-drinker, soak, soaker, sponge, tun, tosspot, pub-crawler, reveller, carouser, Bacchanal, Bacchanalian, Bacchant, a devotee to Bacchus; a dipsomaniac.

Drink, hard drinks, intoxicant, alcohol, liquor, spirits, booze, blue ruin, grog, cocktail, highball, dram, peg, stirrup-cup, doch-an-doris.

(Phrases) The flowing bowl; one for the road.

(Verbs) To drink, tipple, tope, booze; to guzzle, swill, soak, swig, get or be drunk, etc.; to take to drinking, drink hard, drink deep.

To inebriate, intoxicate, fuddle.

(Phrases) To liquor up; to wet one's whistle; to crack a bottle; to have a bucket; to look on the wine when it is red; to take a drop too much; to drink like a fish; to splice the main-brace; to crook or lift the elbow.

(Adjectives) Drunk, drunken, tipsy, intoxicated, in liquor, inebriated, fuddled, mellow, boozy, high, fou, boiled, tiddly, stinko, blotto, lit up, groggy, top-heavy, pot-valiant, glorious, overcome, overtaken, elevated, whiffled, sozzled, screwed, corned, raddled, sewed up, lushy, squiffy, muddled, oiled, canned, muzzy, maudlin, dead-drunk, disguised, tight, beery.

Bibacious, bibulous, sottish, Bacchanal, Bacchanalian.

(Phrases) In one's cups; *inter pocula*; the worse for liquor; half-seas-over; three sheets in the wind; under the table; drunk as a piper, as a fiddle, as a lord, as an owl, as David's sow; stewed to the eyebrows; pickled to the gills; one over the eight.

(Interjections) Cheers! here's to you! down the hatch! mud in your eye! skin off your nose! *prosit! slainte! skoal!*

---

960 Purity *(Substantives)*, modesty, decency, decorum, delicacy, continence, chastity, honesty, pudency, virtue, virginity.

961 Impurity *(Substantives)*, immodesty, grossness, coarseness, indelicacy, impropriety, impudicity, indecency, obscenity, obsceneness,

A virgin, maiden, maid, vestal; Joseph, Hippolytus, Lucrece.

(Phrase) The white flower of a blameless life.

(Adjectives) Pure, immaculate, undefiled, modest, delicate, decent, decorous.

Chaste, continent, honest, virtuous; Platonic.

———

ribaldry, smut, smuttiness, bawdiness, bawdry, *double entendre*, equivoque, pornography.   .

Concupiscence, lust, carnality, flesh, salacity, lewdness, prurience, lechery, lasciviousness, voluptuousness, lubricity.

Incontinence, intrigue, gallantry, debauchery, libertinism, libertinage, fornication, liaison, wenching, whoring, whoredom, concubinage, hetaerism.

Seduction, defloration, violation, rape, adultery, defilement, *crim. con.*, incest, harlotry, stupration, procuration, white slave traffic.

A seraglio, harem, brothel, bagnio, stew, bawdy-house, disorderly house, house of ill fame, red lamp district, Yoshiwara.

(Phrases) The morals of the farmyard; the oldest profession.

(Verbs) To intrigue, debauch, defile, seduce, abuse, violate, force, rape, ravish, deflower, ruin, prostitute, procure.

(Adjectives) Impure, immodest, indecorous, indelicate, unclean, unmentionable, unseemly, improper, suggestive, indecent, loose, coarse, gross, broad, equivocal, risky, *risqué*, high-seasoned, nasty, smutty, scabrous, ribald, obscene, bawdy, lewd, pornographic, Rabelaisian, Aristophanic.

Concupiscent, prurient, lickerish, rampant, carnal, fleshy, sensual, lustful, lascivious, lecherous, libidinous, goatish, erotic, ruttish, salacious.

Unchaste, light, wanton, debauched, dissolute, carnal-minded, licentious, frail, riggish, incontinent, meretricious, rakish, gallant, dissipated, adulterous, incestuous, bestial.

(Phrases) On the streets; of easy virtue; no better than she should be. Near the knuckle; not for ears polite; four-letter words.

962 A Libertine *(Substantives)*, voluptuary, man of pleasure, sensualist (954), rip, rake, *roué*, debauchee, loose fish, intriguant, gallant, seducer, fornicator, lecher, satyr, whoremonger, *paillard*, adulterer, a gay deceiver, Lothario, Don Juan, Bluebeard.

A prostitute, courtesan, tart, call-girl, strumpet, harlot, whore, punk, *fille de joie, cocotte, lorette*, woman of the town, streetwalker, pick-up, piece, the frail sisterhood, the *demi-monde*, soiled dove, demirep, wench, trollop, trull, baggage, hussy, drab, jade, quean, slut, harridan, an unfortunate, Jezebel, Messalina, Delilah, Thais, Aspasia, Phryne, Lais.

Concubine, odalisque, mistress, doxy, kept woman, *petite amie*, hetaera.

Pimp, pander, ponce, *souteneur*, bawd, procuress.

5°. Institutions

963 Legality *(Substantives)*, legitimateness, legitimacy, justice (922).

Law, legislature, code, constitution, pandect, enactment, edict, statute, charter, rule, order, ordinance, injunction, institution, precept, regulation, by-law, decree, firman, bull, ukase, decretal.

964 Absence or violation of law.

Illegality *(Substantives)*, lawlessness, arbitrariness, antinomy, violence, brute force, despotism, outlawry.

Mob law, lynch law, club law, martial law.

Legal process, form, formula, formality, rite.

Science of law, jurisprudence, legislation, codification.

Equity, common law, *lex non scripta*, unwritten law, law of nations, international law, *jus gentium*, civil law, canon law, statute law, *lex mercatoria*, ecclesiastical law.

(Phrase) The arm of the law.

(Verbs) To legalize, enact, ordain, enjoin, prescribe, order, decree (741); to pass a law, issue an edict or decree; to legislate, codify.

(Adjectives) Legal, lawful, according to law, legitimate, constitutional, chartered, vested.

Legislative, statutable, statutory.

(Adverbs) Legally, etc.

(Phrases) In the eye of the law; *de jure*.

_____

Camorra, Ku Klux Klan, Judge Lynch.

Informality, unlawfulness, illegitimacy, bastardy, the baton or bar sinister.

Smuggling, poaching, bootlegging; black market, grey market.

(Verbs) To smuggle, run, poach.

To invalidate, annul, illegalize, abrogate, void, nullify, quash.

(Phrases) To take the law into one's own hands; to set the law at defiance; to drive a coach and six through the law.

(Adjectives) Illegal, unlawful, illicit, illegitimate, injudicial, unofficial, lawless, unauthorized, unchartered, unconstitutional, informal, contraband, hot.

Arbitrary, extrajudicial, despotic, autocratic, irresponsible, unanswerable, unaccountable.

(Adverbs) Illegally, with a high hand.

965 Jurisdiction *(Substantives)*, judicature, soc (or soke), administration of justice.

Inquisition, inquest, coroner's inquest.

The executive, municipality, corporation, magistracy, police, police force, constabulary, posse, *gendarmerie*.

Lord lieutenant, sheriff, sheriff-substitute, deputy, officer, constable, policeman, state trooper, traffic warden, bailiff, tipstaff, bum-bailiff, catchpoll, beadle; *gendarme*, lictor, mace-bearer.

(Adjectives) Juridical, judicial, forensic, municipal, executive, administrative, inquisitorial, causidical.

(Phrases) Coram judice; ex cathedra.

966 Tribunal *(Substantives)*, court, guild, board, bench, judicatory, senate-house, court of law, court of justice, criminal court, police-court, Court of Chancery, of King's Bench; Probate, Divorce, Admiralty Court, court of appeal, justice-seat, judgment-seat, mercy-seat, Star Chamber, Judicial Committee of the Privy Council, U.S. Supreme Court, durbar.

City hall, town hall, theatre, bar, dock, forum, hustings, drum-head, woolsack, jury-box, witness-box.

Assize, sessions, quarter sessions, petty sessions, eyre, court-martial, ward-mote.

967 Judge *(Substantives)*, justice, justiciar, justiciary, chancellor, magistrate, beak, recorder, common serjeant, stipendiary, coroner, arbiter, arbitrator, umpire, referee, jury, Justice of the Peace, J.P., Lord Chancellor, Lord Chief Justice, Master of the Rolls.

Mullah, ulema, mufti, cadi (or kadi), kavass.

Prosecutor, plaintiff, accuser, appellant, pursuer.

Defendant, panel, prisoner, the accused.

(Verbs) Judge, try, pass judgment, give verdict.

968 Lawyer (*Substantives*), the bar, advocate, counsellor, counsel, queen's or king's counsel, Q.C., K.C., pleader, special pleader, conveyancer, bencher, proctor, civilian, barrister, barrister-at-law, jurist, jurisconsult, publicist, draughtsman, notary, notary public, scrivener, attorney, solicitor, legal adviser, writer to the signet, writer, marshal, pundit; pettifogger.

(*Phrases*) The gentlemen of the long robe; the learned in the law; a limb of the law.

(*Verbs*) To practise law, plead.

(*Phrases*) To be called to the bar; to take silk.

969 Lawsuit (*Substantives*), suit, action, case, cause, trial, litigation.

Denunciation, citation, arraignment, prosecution, indictment, impeachment, apprehension, arrest, committal, imprisonment (751).

Pleadings, writ, summons, subpoena, plea, bill, affidavit, libel; answer, counterclaim, demurrer, rebutter, rejoinder, surrebutter, surrejoinder.

Verdict, sentence, judgment, finding, decree, arbitrament, adjudication, award, decision, precedent.

(*Verbs*) To denounce, cite, apprehend, sue, writ, arraign, summons, prosecute, indict, contest, impeach, attach, distrain; to commit.

To try, hear a cause, sit in judgment.

To pronounce, find, judge, adjudge, sentence, give judgment; bring in a verdict; to doom, arbitrate, adjudicate, award, report.

(*Phrases*) To go to law; to appeal to the law; to file a claim; to inform against; to lodge an information; to serve with a writ; to bring an action against; to bring to trial or the bar; to give in charge or custody; to throw into prison; to clap in jail.

(*Adjectives*) Litigious, litigant, litigatory.

(*Adverbial phrase*) Sub judice; pendente lite.

970 Acquittal (*Substantives*), acquitment, absolution, exculpation, quietus, clearance, discharge, release, reprieve (918), respite, compurgation.

Exemption from punishment, impunity.

(*Verbs*) To acquit, absolve, whitewash, extenuate, exculpate, exonerate, clear, assoil, discharge, release, reprieve, respite.

(*Adjectives*) Acquitted, etc.

Uncondemned, unpunished, unchastised.

971 Condemnation (*Substantives*), conviction, proscription, damnation, death-warrant.

Attainder, attainture, attaintment.

(*Verbs*) To condemn, convict, cast, find guilty, proscribe, ban, outlaw, attaint, damn, doom, sentence, confiscate, sequestrate, non-suit.

(*Adjectives*) Condemnatory, damnatory, condemned; self-convicted.

972 Punishment (*Substantives*), punition, chastisement, castigation, correction, chastening, discipline, infliction.

Retribution, requital (973), penalty (974), reckoning, Nemesis.

Imprisonment (751), transportation, exile (297), cucking-stool, ducking-stool, treadmill, crank, hulks, galleys, penal servitude, preventive detention.

A blow, slap, spank, skelp, swish, hit, knock, rap, thump, bang, buffet, stripe, stroke, cuff, clout, kick, whack, thwack, box, punch, pummel.

Beating, lash, flagellation, flogging, etc., dressing, lacing, tanning, knockout, fustigation, leathering, lathering, jacketing, strap-oil, gruelling, spiflication, bastinado, strappado, pillory (975), running the gauntlet, *coup de grâce, peine forte et dure.*

Execution, capital punishment, hanging, beheading, decollation, decapitation, electrocution, guillotine, garrotte, *auto da fé*, *noyade*, crucifixion, impalement, *hara-kiri*, martyrdom.

(Verbs) To punish, chastise, castigate, chasten, correct, inflict punishment, pay, do for, serve out, pay out, visit upon, give it to, strafe, spiflicate.

To strike, hit, smite, knock, slap, flap, rap, bang, thwack, whack, thump, kick, punch, pelt, beat, buffet, thrash, swinge, pummel, clapper-claw, drub, trounce, baste, belabour, lace, strap, comb, lash, lick, whip, flog, scourge, knout, swish, spank, skelp, birch, tan, larrup, lay into, knock out, wallop, leather, flagellate, horsewhip, bastinado, lapidate, stone.

To execute, hang, behead, decapitate, decollate, electrocute, guillotine, garrotte, shoot, gibbet; to hang, draw, and quarter; break on the wheel; crucify, impale, torture, flay, keelhaul; lynch.

To banish, exile, transport, deport, expel, drum out, disbar, disbench, unfrock.

To be hanged, etc., to be spread-eagled.

(Phrases) To make an example of; to serve one out; to give it one; to dust one's jacket; to tweak or pull the nose; to box the ears; to beat to a jelly; to tar and feather; to give a black eye; to lay it on.

To come to the gallows; to swing for it; to go to the chair; to die in one's shoes.

(Adjectives) Punishing, etc., punitory, punitive, inflictive, penal, disciplinary, castigatory, borstal.

(Interjection) A la lanterne!

---

973 Reward *(Substantives)*, recompense, remuneration, meed, guerdon, premium, indemnity, indemnification, compensation, reparation, requital, retribution, quittance, hush-money, acknowledgment, amends, solatium, sop, atonement, redress, consideration, return, tribute, honorarium, perquisite, tip, vail; salvage.

Prize, purse, crown, laurel, bays, cross, medal, ribbon, decoration (877).

(Verbs) To reward, recompense, repay, requite, recoup, remunerate, compensate, make amends, indemnify, atone, satisfy, acknowledge, acquit oneself.

(Phrase) To get for one's pains.

(Adjectives) Remunerative, munerary, compensatory, retributive, reparatory.

974 Penalty *(Substantives)*, punishment (972), pain, penance.

Fine, mulct, amercement, forfeit, forfeiture, escheat, damages, deodand, sequestration, confiscation.

(Phrases) Pains and penalties; the devil to pay.

(Verbs) To fine, mulct, amerce, sconce, confiscate, sequester, sequestrate, escheat, estreat.

975 Instrument of punishment.

Scourge *(Substantives)*, rod, cane, stick, rattan, switch, ferule, birch, cudgel.

Whip, lash, strap, thong, knout, cowhide, cat, cat-o'-nine-tails, sjambok, rope's end.

Pillory, stocks, cangue, whipping-post, ducking-stool, triangle, wooden horse, boot, thumbscrew, rack, wheel, treadmill.

Stake, tree, block, scaffold, gallows, halter, bowstring, gibbet, axe, maiden, guillotine, garrotte, electric chair, hot squat, lethal chamber.

Executioner, hangman, electrocutioner, firing squad, headsman, Jack Ketch.

SECTION V—RELIGIOUS AFFECTIONS

1°. *Superhuman Beings and Objects*

976 Deity (*Substantives*), Divinity, Godhead, Omnipotence, Omniscience, Providence.

Quality of being divine, divineness, divinity.

God, Lord, Jehovah, The Almighty; The Supreme Being; The First Cause, *Ens Entium*; The Author of all things, The Infinite, The Eternal, The All-powerful, The All-wise, The All-merciful, The All-holy.

Attributes and perfections: infinite power, wisdom, goodness, justice, mercy, omnipotence, omniscience, omnipresence, unity, immutability, holiness, glory, majesty, sovereignty, infinity, eternity.

The Trinity, The Holy Trinity, The Trinity in Unity, The Triune God.

God the Father, The Maker, The Creator.

Functions: creation, preservation, divine government, theocracy, thearchy, providence; the ways, dispensations, visitatiohs of Providence.

God the Son, Christ, Jesus, The Messiah, The Anointed, The Saviour, The Redeemer, The Mediator, The Intercessor, The Advocate, The Judge, The Son of Man, The Lamb of God, The Word, The Logos, Emmanuel, The King of Kings and Lord of Lords, The King of Glory, The Prince of Peace, The Good Shepherd, The Way of Truth and Life, The Bread of Life, The Light of the World, The Sun of Righteousness, the Incarnation, the Word made Flesh.

Functions: salvation, redemption, atonement, propitiation, mediation, intercession, judgment.

God the Holy Ghost, The Holy Spirit, Paraclete, The Comforter, The Spirit of Truth, The Dove.

Functions: inspiration, unction, regeneration, sanctification, consolation.

(*Verbs*) To create, uphold, preserve, govern.

To atone, redeem, save, propitiate, mediate.

To predestinate, elect, call, ordain, bless, justify, sanctify, glorify.

(*Adjectives*) Almighty, all-powerful, omnipotent, omnipresent, omniscient, all-wise, holy, hallowed, sacred, divine, heavenly, celestial.

Superhuman, ghostly, spiritual, supernatural, theocratic.

977 Beneficent spirits.

Angel (*Substantives*), archangel.

The heavenly host; ministering spirits; the choir invisible.

Madonna, saint.

Seraphim, cherubim, thrones, principalities, powers, dominions.

(*Adjectives*) Angelic, angelical, seraphic, cherubic, celestial, heavenly, saintly.

978 Maleficent spirits.

Satan (*Substantives*), the Devil, Lucifer, Beelzebub, Belial, Mephistopheles, Mephisto, Abaddon, Apollyon, the Prince of Devils.

His Satanic Majesty, the tempter, the evil one, the wicked one, the old Serpent, the Prince of darkness, the father of lies, the fôul fiend, the arch-fiend, the common enemy, Old Harry, Old Nick, the Old Scratch, the Old Gentleman, Old Horny.

Diabolism, devilism, devilship; Satanism, the cloven hoof, the black mass.

Fallen angels, unclean spirits, devils, the powers of darkness, inhabitants of Pandemonium.

(*Adjectives*) Satanic, diabolic, devilish.

Gods of other Religions and Mythological Beings

979 Great spirit *(Substantives)*, deity, numen, god, goddess; Allah, Brahma, Vishnu, Siva, Krishna, Buddha, Mithra, Ormuzd, Isis, Osiris, Moloch, Baal, Asteroth.

Jupiter, Jove, Juno, Minerva, Apollo, Diana, Venus, Vulcan, Mars, Mercury, Neptune, Pluto; Zeus, Hera, Athena, Artemis, Aphrodite, Hephaestus, Ares, Hermes, Poseidon.

Odin or Woden, Frigga, Thor.

Good genius, demiurge, familiar; fairy, fay, sylph, peri, kelpie, nymph, nereid, dryad, hamadryad, naiad, merman, mermaid (341), undine; Oberon, Mab, Titania, Puck, Robin Goodfellow; the good folk, the little people.

(Adjectives) Fairy, faery, fairy-like, sylph-like, sylphine.

Mythical, mythological, fabulous, legendary.

981 Heaven *(Substantives)*, the kingdom of heaven; the kingdom of God, the heavenly kingdom; the throne of God, the presence of God.

Paradise, Eden, Zion, the Celestial City, the New Jerusalem, the abode of the blessed; celestial bliss or glory.

Mythological heaven, Olympus; mythological paradise, Elysium, the Elysian Fields, the garden of the Hesperides; Valhalla, Nirvana, happy hunting grounds.

Translation, apotheosis, deification, resurrection.

(Adjectives) Heavenly, celestial, supernal, unearthly, from on high, paradisaical, paradisical, paradisial, Elysian, beatific.

980 Demon *(Substantives)*, evil genius, fiend, unclean spirit, caco-demon, incubus, succubus, succuba, flibbertigibbet; fury, harpy, siren, faun, satur, Eblis, Demogorgon.

Vampire, werewolf, ghoul, afreet (or afrite), ogre, ogress, gnome, djinn, imp, genie (or jinnee), lamia, bogy, bogle, nix, nixie, kobold, brownie, leprechaun, elf, pixy, troll, sprite, gremlin, spandule.

Supernatural appearance, ghost, spectre, apparition, shade, vision, goblin, hobgoblin, banshee, spook, wraith, *revenant, doppelgänger*, polter-geist.

(Phrase) The powers of darkness.

(Adjectives) Supernatural, ghostly, apparitional, elfin, elfish, unearthly, uncanny, eerie, weird, spectral, spook-ish, spooky, ghostlike, fiendish, fiend-like, impish, demoniacal, haunted.

982 Hell *(Substantives)*, bottom-less pit, place of torment; the habita-tion of fallen angels, Pandemonium, Domdaniel.

Hell-fire, everlasting fire, the lake of fire and brimstone.

Purgatory, limbo, abyss.

Mythological hell, Tartarus, Hades, Pluto, Avernus, Styx, the Stygian creek, Acheron, Cocytus, Phlegethon, Lethe, Erebus, Tophet, Gehenna.

(Phrases) The fire that is never quenched; the worm that never dies.

The infernal or nether regions; the shades below; the realms of Pluto.

(Adjectives) Hellish, infernal, stygian, Tartarean, Plutonian.

2°. Religious Doctrines

983 Religious knowledge.

Theology (natural and revealed) *(Substantives)*, divinity, religion, monotheism, hagiology, hagiography, hierography, theosophy; comparative religion, compara-tive mythology.

Creed, belief, faith, persuasion, tenet, dogma, articles of faith, declaration, profession or confession of faith.

Theologian, divine, schoolman, the Fathers.

(Adjectives) Theological, religious, patristic, ecumenical, denominational, sectarian.

983A Christian Religion *(Substantives)*, true faith, Christianity, Christianism, Christendom, Catholicism, orthodoxy.

A Christian, a true believer.

The Church, the Catholic or Universal Church, the Church of Christ, the body of Christ, the Church Militant.

The members of Christ, the disciples or followers of Christ, the Christian community.

Protestant, Church of England, Anglican, Church of Scotland; Church of Rome, Roman Catholic; Greek Church, Orthodox Church.

(Adjectives) Christian, Catholic, orthodox, sound, faithful, true, scriptural, canonical, schismless.

984 Other religions *(Substantives)*, paganism, heathenism, ethnicism, polytheism, ditheism, tritheism, pantheism, hylotheism.

Judaism, Gentilism, Mohammedanism (or Mahometanism), Islam, Buddhism, Hinduism, Taoism, Confucianism, Shintoism, Sufism.

A pagan, heathen, paynim, infidel, unbeliever, pantheist, etc.

A Jew, Mohammedan (or Mahometan), Mussulman, Moslem, Brahmin (or Brahman), Parsee, Sufi, Magus, Gymnosophist, Fire-worshipper, Buddhist, Rosicrucian.

(Adjectives) Pagan, heathen, ethnic, gentile, pantheistic, etc.

Judaical, Mohammedan, Brahminical, Buddhistic.

984A Heresy *(Substantives)*, heterodoxy, false doctrine, schism, schismaticalness, latitudinarianism, recusancy, apostasy, backsliding, quietism, adiaphorism.

Bigotry, fanaticism, iconoclasm, bibliolatry, fundamentalism, puritanism, sabbatarianism.

Dissent, sectarianism, non-conformity, secularism, syncretism.

A heretic, deist, unitarian.

(Adjectives) Heretical, heterodox, unorthodox, unscriptural, uncanonical, schismatic, sectarian, nonconformist, recusant, latitudinarian.

Credulous, bigoted, fanatical, idolatrous, superstitious, visionary.

985 Christian revelation *(Substantives)*, Word, Word of God, Scripture, the Scriptures, Holy Writ, the Bible, the Holy Book.

Old Testament: Septuagint, Vulgate, Pentateuch, Hagiographa, the Law, the Prophets, the Apocrypha.

New Testament: the Gospel, the Evangelists, the Epistles, the Apocalypse, Revelation.

Talmud, Mishna, Masorah, Torah.

A prophet, seer, evangelist, apostle, disciple, saint, the Fathers.

(Adjectives) Scriptural, biblical, sacred, prophetic, evangelical, apostolic, apostolical, inspired, theopneustic, apocalyptic.

986 Other sacred books *(Substantives)*, the Koran (or Alcoran), Vedas, Upanishads, Puranas, Zend-Avesta.

Religious founders: Buddha (or Gautama), Zoroaster (or Zarathustra), Confucius, Lao-Tsze, Mohammed (or Mahomet).

Idols: Golden calf, Baal, Moloch, Dagon.

(Adjectives) Anti-scriptural, anti-christian, profane, idolatrous, pagan, heathen, heathenish.

3°. Religious Sentiments

987 Piety *(Substantives)*, religion, theism, faith, religiousness, godliness, reverence, humility, veneration, devoutness, devotion, spirituality, grace, unction, edification, unworldliness, other-worldliness; holiness, sanctity, sanctitude, sacredness, consecration; virtue (944).

Theopathy, beatification, adoption, regeneration, conversion, justification, salvation, inspiration.

A believer, convert, theist, Christian, saint, one of the elect, a devotee.

The good, righteous, faithful, godly, elect, just.

(Phrases) The odour of sanctity; the beauty of holiness; spiritual existence.

The children of God, of light.

(Verbs) To be pious, etc., to believe, have faith; to convert, edify, sanctify, hallow, beatify, regenerate, inspire; to consecrate, enshrine.

(Phrases) To work out one's salvation; to stand up for Jesus; to fight the good fight.

(Adjectives) Pious, religious, devout, reverent, reverential, godly, humble, heavenly-minded, pure, holy, spiritual, saintly, saint-like, unworldly, other-worldly.

Believing, faithful, Christian.

Sanctified, regenerated, born again, justified, adopted, elected, inspired, consecrated, converted, unearthly, sacred, solemn, not of the earth.

---

988 Impiety *(Substantives)*, irreverence, profaneness, profanity, blasphemy, desecration, sacrilege, sacrilegiousness, sin (945); scoffing, ribaldry, reviling.

Assumed piety, hypocrisy, cant, pietism, lip-devotion, lip-service, lip-reverence, formalism, sanctimony, sanctimoniousness, pharisaism, precisianism, sabbatism, sabbatarianism, sacerdotalism, religiosity, religionism, *odium theologicum*.

Hardening, backsliding, declension, reprobation, perversion.

Sinner, outcast, castaway, lost sheep, reprobate.

A scoffer, hypocrite, pietist, pervert, religionist, precisian, formalist; son of darkness, son of Belial, blasphemer, Pharisee; bigot, devotee, fanatic, sabbatarian.

The wicked, unjust, ungodly, unrighteous.

(Phrase) The unco guid.

(Verbs) To be impious, etc., to profane, desecrate, blaspheme, revile, scoff, commit sacrilege.

To play the hypocrite, cant.

(Adjectives) Impious, profane, irreverent, sacrilegious, desecrating, blasphemous; unhallowed, unsanctified, hardened, perverted, reprobate.

Bigoted, priest-ridden, fanatical, churchy.

Hypocritical, canting, pietistical, sanctimonious, unctuous, pharisaical, over-righteous, righteous overmuch.

(Phrases) Under the mask, cloak, or pretence of religion.

---

989 Irreligion *(Substantives)*, ungodliness, unholiness, gracelessness, impiety (988).

Scepticism, doubt, unbelief, disbelief, incredulity, incredulousness, faithlessness, want of faith or belief (485, 487).

Atheism, hylotheism, materialism, positivism.

Deism, infidelity, freethinking, rationalism, agnosticism, unchristianness, antichristianity, antichristianism.

An atheist, sceptic, unbeliever, deist, freethinker, rationalist, agnostic, nullifidian, infidel, alien, giaour, heathen.

(Verbs) To be irreligious, disbelieve, lack faith, doubt.

To dechristianize, rationalize.

(Adjectives) Irreligious, undevout, godless, atheistic, atheistical, ungodly, unholy, unhallowed, unsanctified, graceless, without God, carnal-minded.

Sceptical, unbelieving, freethinking, agnostic, rationalistic, incredulous, unconverted, faithless, lacking faith.

Deistical, antichristian, unchristian, worldly-minded, mundane, carnal, earthly-minded.

(Adverbs) Irreligiously, etc.

4°. Acts of Religion

990 Worship *(Substantives)*, adoration, devotion, cult, homage, service, humiliation, kneeling, genuflexion, prostration.

Prayer, invocation, supplication, rogation, petition, orison, litany, the Lord's prayer, paternoster, collect.

Thanksgiving, giving or returning thanks, praise, glorification, benediction, doxology, hosanna, hallelujah, paean, Te Deum, Magnificat, Ave Maria, De Profundis, Nunc dimittis, Non nobis, Domine.

Psalmody, psalm, hymn, plainsong, chant, antiphon, response, anthem, motet.

Oblation, sacrifice, incense, libation, burnt-offering, votive offering; offertory, collection.

Discipline, self-discipline, self-examination, self-denial, fasting.

Divine service, religious service, office, duty, prime, terce, sext, matins, mass (998), angelus, nones, evensong, vespers, vigils, lauds, compline; prayer meeting, revival.

Worshipper, congregation, communicant, celebrant.

(Verbs) To worship, adore, reverence, venerate, do service, pay homage, humble oneself, bow down, kneel, bend the knee, prostrate oneself.

To pray, invoke, supplicate, petition, put up prayers or petitions; to ask, implore (765).

To return or give thanks; to say grace; to bless, praise, laud, glorify, magnify, sing praises, lead the choir, pronounce benediction.

To propitiate, offer sacrifice, fast, deny oneself; vow, offer vows, give alms.

(Phrases) To lift up the heart; to say one's prayers; to tell one's beads; to go to church; to attend divine service.

(Adjectives) Worshipping, etc., devout, solemn, devotional, reverent, pure, fervent, prayerful.

(Interjections) Hallelujah! alleluia! hosanna! glory be to God! *sursum corda!*

991 Idolatry *(Substantives)*, idol-worship, idolism, demonism, demonolatry, fire-worship, devil-worship, fetishism.

Sacrifices, hecatomb, holocaust; human sacrifices, immolation, mactation, infanticide, self-immolation, suttee.

Idol, image, fetish, ju-ju, Mumbo-Jumbo, Juggernaut, joss.

(Verbs) To worship idols, pictures, relics, etc.; to idolize, idolatrize.

(Adjectives) Idolatrous, fetishistic.

992 Occult arts *(Substantives)*, occultism, sorcery, magic, the black art, black magic, necromancy, theurgy, thaumaturgy, psychomancy, *diablerie*, bedevilment, witchcraft, witchery, bewitchment, wizardry, glamour, fetishism, vampirism, shamanism, voodooism, obeah (or obi), sortilege, conjuration, exorcism, fascination, mesmerism, hypnotism, animal magnetism, clairvoyance, telegnosis, telekinesis, psychokinesis, mediumship, spiritualism, extra-sensory perception, telepathy, parapsychology, second sight, spirit-rapping, table-turning, psychometry, crystal-gazing, divination, enchantment, hocus-pocus (545).

(Verbs) To practise sorcery, etc.; to conjure, exorcize, charm, enchant, bewitch, bedevil, hoodoo, entrance, mesmerize, hypnotize, fascinate; to taboo, wave a wand, cast a spell, call up spirits.

(Adjectives) Magic, magical, cabbalistic, talismanic, phylacteric, necromantic, incantatory, occult, mediumistic, charmed, exorcized, etc.

993 Spell *(Substantives)*, charm, fascination, incantation, exorcism, weird, cabbala, exsufflation, cantrip, runes, abracadabra, open sesame, mumbo-jumbo, taboo, counter-charm, evil eye, jinx, hoodoo, Indian sign.

Talisman, amulet, mascot, periapt, phylactery, philtre, fetish, wishbone, merrythought.

Wand, caduceus, rod, divining-rod, the lamp of Aladdin, magic ring, wishing-cap, seven-league boots.

994 Sorcerer *(Substantives)*, sorceress, magician, conjurer, necromancer, enchanter, enchantress, thaumaturgist, occultist, adept, Mahatma, seer, wizard, witch, warlock, charmer, exorcist, mage, archimage, soothsayer (513), shaman, medicine-man, witch-doctor, mesmerist, hypnotist, medium, spiritualist, clairvoyant; control.

(Phrase) Deus ex machina.

5°. *Religious Institutions*

995 Churchdom *(Substantives)*, ministry, apostleship, priesthood, prelacy, hierarchy, church government, Christendom, church; clericalism, sacerdotalism, priestcraft, theocracy, popery, papistry.

Monachism, monasticism, monkdom, monkhood, monkery.

Ecclesiastical offices and dignities: Pontificate, papacy, primacy, archbishopric, archiepiscopacy, bishopric, bishopdom, episcopate, episcopacy, see, diocese, prelacy, deanery, stall, canonry, canonicate, prebend, prebendaryship; benefice, incumbency, advowson, living, cure, rectorship, vicarship, vicariate, deaconry, deaconship, curacy, chaplaincy, chaplainship; cardinalate, abbacy.

Holy orders, ordination, institution, consecration, induction, preferment, translation.

Council, conclave, sanhedrim, synod, presbytery, consistory, chapter, vestry (696).

(Verbs) To call, ordain, induct, install, prefer, translate, consecrate, canonize, beatify; to take the veil, to take vows.

(Adjectives) Ecclesiastical, clerical, sacerdotal, priestly, prelatical, hierarchical, pastoral, ministerial, capitular, theocratic.

Pontifical, papal, episcopal, archidiaconal, diaconal, canonical; monastic, monachal, monkish; levitical, rabbinical.

996 Clergy *(Substantives)*, ministry, priesthood, presbytery.

A clergyman, cleric, parson, divine, ecclesiastic, churchman, priest, presbyter, hierophant, pastor, father, shepherd, minister, father in Christ, patriarch, padre, abbé, curé; sky-pilot, holy Joe, devil-dodger.

Dignitaries of the church: Primate, archbishop, bishop, prelate,

997 Laity *(Substantives)*, flock, fold, congregation, assembly, brethren, people.

Temporality, secularization.

A layman, parishioner.

(Verb) To secularize.

(Adjectives) Secular, lay, laical, civil, temporal, profane.

diocesan, suffragan; dean, subdean, archdeacon, prebendary, canon, capitular, residentiary, beneficiary; rector, vicar, incumbent, chaplain, curate, deacon, sub-deacon, preacher, reader, evangelist, revivalist, missionary, missioner.

Churchwarden, sidesman; clerk, precentor, choir, chorister, almoner, verger, beadle, sexton, sacrist, sacristan, acolyte.

Roman Catholic priesthood: Pope, pontiff, cardinal, confessor, spiritual director.

Cenobite, conventual, abbot, prior, father superior, monk, oblate, friar, lay brother, mendicant, Franciscan (or Grey Friars, Friars minor, Minorites), Observant, Capuchin, Dominican (or Black Friars), Carmelite (or White Friars), Augustin (or Austin Friars), Crossed or Crutched Friars, Benedictine, Jesuit (or Society of Jesus).

Abbess, prioress, canoness, mother, mother superior, *religieuse*, nun, novice, postulant.

Greek Church: Patriarch, metropolitan, archimandrite, pope.

Under the Jewish dispensation: Prophet, priest, high-priest, Levite, rabbi (or rabbin), scribe.

Moslem: Imam, mullah, mufti, dervish, fakir, santon, hadji; muezzin.

Hindu: Brahmin, pundit, guru, yogi.

Buddhist: Lama, bonze.

(Phrase) The cloth.

(Adjectives) Reverend, ordained, in orders.

998 Rite *(Substantives)*, ceremony, ordinance, observance, cult, duty, form, formulary, ceremonial, solemnity, sacrament.

Baptism, immersion, christening, chrism, baptismal regeneration.

Confirmation, imposition or laying on of hands, ordination (995), consecration.

The Eucharist, the Lord's Supper, the communion, the sacrament, consubstantiation, celebration, consecrated elements, bread and wine.

Matrimony (903), burial (363), visitation of the sick, offertory.

Roman Catholic rites and ceremonies: Mass, high mass, low mass, dry mass; the seven sacraments, transubstantiation, impanation, extreme unction, viaticum, invocation of saints, canonization, transfiguration, auricular confession, maceration, flagellation, penance (952), telling of beads.

Relics, rosary, beads, reliquary, pyx (or pix), host, crucifix, *Agnus Dei*, thurible, censer, patera.

Liturgy, ritual, euchology, book of common prayer, litany, etc.; rubric, breviary, missal, ordinal; psalter, psalm book, hymn book, hymnal.

Service, worship (990), ministration, psalmody; preaching, predication; sermon, homily, lecture, discourse, exhortation, address.

Ritualism, ceremonialism, liturgics, liturgiology.

(Verbs) To perform service, do duty, minister, officiate; to baptize, dip, sprinkle; to confirm, lay hands on; to give or administer the sacrament; to take or receive the sacrament, communicate.

To preach, sermonize, predicate, lecture, harangue, hold forth, address the congregation.

(Adjectives) Ritual, ceremonial, baptismal, eucharistical, pastoral, liturgical.

999 Vestments *(Substantives)*, canonicals, robe, gown, pallium, surplice, cassock, alb, scapular (or scapulary), dalmatic, cope, soutane, chasuble, tonsure, cowl, hood, amice, calotte, bands, apron, biretta.

Mitre, tiara, triple crown, crosier.

1000 Place of worship, house of God.

Temple *(Substantives)*, cathedral, pro-cathedral, minster, church, kirk, chapel, meeting-house, tabernacle, conventicle, bethesda, little Bethel, basilica, fane, holy place, chantry, oratory.

Synagogue, mosque, pantheon, pagoda, joss-house, dagobah, tope.

Parsonage, rectory, vicarage, presbytery, deanery, bishop's palace, the Vatican.

Altar, shrine, sanctuary, *sanctum sanctorum,* the Holy of Holies, sacristy, communion table, holy table, table of the Lord; piscina, baptistery, font, aumbry.

Chancel, choir, nave, aisle, transept, vestry, crypt, apse, belfry, stall, pew, pulpit, ambo, lectern, reading-desk, confessional, prothesis, credence.

Monastery, priory, abbey, convent, nunnery, cloister.

(Adjectives) Claustral, monastic, monasterial, conventual.

INDEX

N.B. – The numbers refer to the headings under which the words occur. The headings or related words are given in italics, not to explain the meaning of the words, but to assist in the required reference. Words borrowed from another language have an asterisk prefixed to them.

A

Accord, *concord*, 714
 melody, 413
 give, 784
 grant, 760
 spontaneous, 600
According to, *relation*, 9
 conformably, 15
 evidence, 467
Accordingly, *reasoning*, 476
Accordion, *musical instrument*, 417
Accost, *allocation*, 586
*Accoucheur, *instrument*, 631
Account, *money*, 811
 bill, 812
 computation, 85
 list, 86
 record, 551
 description, 594
 value, 644
 estimation, 484
 judgment, 480
 approbation, 931
 fame, 873
 sake, 615
Account for, *attribution*, 155
Accountable, *duty*, 926
 liability, 177
Accountant, *accounts*, 811
 treasurer, 801
Accouplement, *junction*, 43
Accoutre, *dress*, 225
 equip, 673
Accoutrement, *equipment*, 633
Accredit, *money* , 805
 honour, 873
 commission, 755
Accretion, *coherence*, 46
 increase, 35
Accrue, *result*, 154
 add, 37
 acquire, 775
 receive, 785, 810
 benefit, 644
*Accueil, *courtesy*, 894
Accumulate, *collect*, 72
 store, 636
Accurate, *exact*, 494
 likeness, 17
Accursed, *undone*, 828
 painful, 830
 disastrous, 649
 cursed, 908
Accuse, *charge*, 938
 disapprove, 932
Accuser, *judge*, 967
Accustom, *habituate*, 613
 usual, 82
Ace, *unit*, 87
 small in quantity, 32
 small in size, 193
 courage, 861
Acerbate, *embitter*, 659
 aggravate, 835
Acerbity, *sourness*, 397

Acerbity, *harshness*, 739
 spleen, 898, 900, 901
 malevolence, 907
Acervate, *assemblage*, 72
Acetic, *sour*, 397
Acetous, *sour*, 397
Ache, *physical pain*, 378
 moral pain, 828
Acheron, *hell*, 982
Achievable, *possible*, 470
 easy, 705
Achieve, *accomplish*, 729
 end, 67
Achievement, *escutcheon*, 551
Achromatism, *achromatic*, 429
*Achtung, *attention*, 457
Acicular, *sharpness*, 253
Acid, *sourness*, 397
Acknowledge, *avow*, 535
 disclose, 529
 assent, 488
 consent, 762
 reward, 973
 repent, 950
 answer, 462
 observe, 772
 receive, 82
Acknowledged, *habitual*, 613
Acme, *summit*, 210
 highest degree, 33
 perfection, 650
Acolyte, *clergy*, 996
Aconite, *bane*, 663
Acoustics, *sound*, 402
Acquaint, *information*, 527
Acquaintance, *knowledge*, 490
 friendship, 888
 friend, 890
Acquiesce, *assent*, 488
 consent, 762
Acquire, *acquisition*, 775
Acquirement, *knowledge*, 490
 learning, 539
 talent, 698
Acquisition, *gain*, 775
 knowledge, 490
Acquit, *absolve*, 970
 exempt, 927A
 vindicate, 937
 liberate, 750
Acquit oneself, *of a duty*, 926
 of an agreement, 772
Acquittance, *payment*, 807
Acres, *property*, 780
Acrid, *unsavouriness*, 395
Acrimony, *taste*, 395
 hatred, 898
 malevolence, 907
 discourtesy, 895
Acrobat, *athlete*, 159
Across, *transverse*, 219
 opposition, 708
Acrostic, *neology*, 563
 puzzle, 533

Act, *physical*, 170
 voluntary, 680
 law, 697
 to feign, 544
 to personate, 599
 deputize, 759
 business, 625
 to imitate, 19
Actinotherapy, *remedy*, 662
Action, *physical*, 170
 voluntary, 680
 battle, 720
 at law, 969
Activity, *physical*, 171
 voluntary, 682
Actor, *impostor*, 548
 player, 599
 doer, 690
Actual, *existing*, 1
 real, 494
 present, 118
Actualize, *describe*, 594
 materialize, 3
Actuality, *truly*, 31
Actuary, *accounts*, 811
Actuate, *motive*, 615
*Actum est, *completion*, 729
Acuity, *sharpness*, 253
Aculeated, *sharpness*, 253
Acumen, *wisdom*, 494
Acuminated, *sharpness*, 253
Acupuncture, *opening*, 260
Acute, *pointed*, 253
 violent (physically), 173
 sensible (physically), 375
 painful (morally), 830
 strong feeling, 820
 musical tone, 410
 perspicacious, 498
Acutely, *much*, 31
*Ad arbitrium, *will*, 600
*Ad captandum, *plea*, 617
 deception, 545
*Ad captandum vulgus, *ostentation*, 852
*Ad eundem, *equality*, 27
*Ad infinitum, *infinity*, 105
*Ad interim, *duration*, 106
Ad-lib, *improvise*, 612
*Ad libitum, *will*, 600
 choice, 609
 sufficiency, 639
*Ad rem, *reasoning*, 473
*Ad unguem, *perfection*, 650
*Ad valorem, *price*, 812
Adage, *maxim*, 496
*Adagio, *slowness*, 275
 music, 415
Adamant, *hard*, 323
 strong, 159
Adapt, *fit*, 646
 adjust, 673
 agree, 23
Add, *addition*, 37
 increase, 35

Add, *numerically,* 85
Addendum, *adjunct,* 39
Adder, *viper,* 663
   maleficent being, 913
Addict, *habit,* 613
Addition, *adjunction,* 37
   thing added, 39
   arithmetical, 85
Addle, *barren,* 169
   abortive, 732
   to spoil, 659
Addle-headed, *imbecile,* 499
Address, *speak to,* 586
   skill, 698
   request, 765
   residence, 189
   direction, 550
   lecture, 582
   preach, 998
Addresses, *courtship,* 902
Adduce, *bring to,* 288
   evidence, 467
Adept, *proficient,* 700
   sorcerer, 994
Adequate, *sufficient,* 639
   power, 157
   strength, 159
   for a purpose, 644
Adhere, *stick,* 46
   fidelity, 772
   resoluteness, 604
Adherent, *follower,* 711
Adhesive, *coherence,* 46
   connective, 45
Adhibit, *use,* 677
Adiaphorism, *heresy,* 984A
Adieu, *departure,* 293
Adipose, *unctuous,* 355
Adiposity, *corpulence,* 192
Adit, *conduit,* 350
   orifice, 260
   way, 627
Adjacent, *nearness,* 197
Adjection, *addition,* 37
Adjective, *adjunct,* 39
Adjoin, *nearness,* 197
   contiguity, 199
Adjourn, *lateness,* 133
Adjudge, *lawsuit,* 969
Adjudication, *choice,* 609
   judgment, 480
   lawsuit, 969
Adjunct, *thing added,* 39
   accompaniment, 88
   aid, 707
Adjuration, *affirmation,* 535
Adjure, *request,* 765
   promise, 768
Adjust, *fit,* 27
   preface, 673
   settle, 723
   compromise, 774
Adjutage (or ajutage), *pipe,* 350
   opening, 260
Adjutant, *auxiliary,* 711

Adjutant, *military,* 745
Adjuvant, *helper,* 707, 711
Admeasurement, *measure-*
   ment, 466
Administer, *give,* 784
   apportion, 786
   manage, 693
   govern, 737
Administration, *of justice,* 965
Admirable, *excellent,* 648
   virtuous, 944
Admiral, *master,* 745
Admire, *approve,* 931
   love, 897
   wonder, 870
Admissible, *tolerable,* 651
Admission, *ingress,* 294, 296
   inclusion, 76
Admit, *let in,* 296
   accept, 785
   include, 76
   composition, 54
   concede in argument, 467
   disclose, 529
   allow, 760
   assent, 488
Admit of, *possibility,* 470
Admixture, *mixture,* 41
Admonish, *advise,* 695
   warn, 668
   reprove, 932
   predict, 511
Ado, *exertion,* 686
   activity, 682
   difficulty, 704
Adolescence, *youth,* 131
Adonis, *beauty,* 845
Adopt, *choice,* 609
Adore, *love,* 897
   worship, 990
Adorn, *beauty,* 845
Adown, *lowness,* 207
Adrift, *unrelated,* 10
   dispersed, 73
   at fault, 704
Adroit, *skill,* 698
Adscititious, *extrinsic,* 6
   added, 37
   supplementary, 52
Adscriptus glebæ, servant, 746
Adulation, *flattery,* 933
Adulator, *flatterer,* 935
Adult, *adolescence,* 131
Adulterate, *mix,* 41
   deteriorate, 659
   falsify, 495
Adulterer, *libertine,* 962
Adultery, *impurity,* 961
Adumbrate, *sketch,* 594
   representation, 554
   painting, 556
   faint likeness, 21
   imitate, 19
   personify, 521
Adust, *burnt,* 384

Adust, *gloomy,* 837
Advance, *progress,* 282, 731
   to promote, 658
   forward, 707
   increase, 35
   lend, 787
   expenditure, 809
   assert, 535
Advanced, *progressive,* 658
   modern, 123
Advantage, *good,* 618
   utility, 644
   goodness, 648
   superiority, 33
   inequality, 28
   success, 705, 731
Advene, *addition,* 37
Advent, *arrival,* 292
   event, 151
   futurity, 121
Adventitious, *extrinsic,* 6
   casual, 156, 621
Adventure, *event,* 151
   chance, 156, 621
   pursuit, 622
   trial, 675
Adventurer, *deceiver,* 548
   rashness, 863
Adventurous, *courageous,* 861
   dangerous, 665
Adversaria, register, 551
   chronicle, 594
Adversary, *opponent,* 710
Adverse, *opposed,* 708
   enmity, 889
   disliking, 867
   unprosperous, 735
Adversity, *adversity,* 735
Advert, *attention,* 457
Advertise, *publication,* 531
Advertisement, *preface,* 64
   information, 527
Advice, *counsel,* 695
   notice, 527; *news,* 532
Advisable, *expediency,* 646
Advise, *inform,* 527
   counsel, 695
   predict, 511
Advised, *voluntary,* 600
   intentional, 620
Adviser, *counsellor,* 695
   teacher, 540
Advocacy, *aid,* 707
Advocate, *counsellor,* 968
   advise, 695
   to prompt, 615
   commend, 931
   to vindicate, 937
   Saviour, 967
Advocatus diaboli, soph-
   istry, 477
Advowson, *churchdom,* 995
Adytum, *secret place,* 530
   room, 191
   prediction, 511

Agony, *physical*, 378
  mental, 828
Agoraphobia, *seclusion*, 893
  dislike, 866
Agrarian, *agriculture*, 371
Agree, *accord*, 23
  concur, 178
  assent, 488
  consent, 762
  concord, 714
Agreeable, *pleasant*, 377, 829
Agreeably, *conformably*, 82
Agreement, *bargain*, 769
Agrestic, *rural*, 371
  uncouth, 876
Agriculture, *agriculture*, 371
Agronomy, *agriculture*, 371
Aground, *stranded*, 265, 704
  fixed, 150
  failure, 732
Ague-fit, *fear*, 860
Aguish, *cold*, 383
Ahead, *in front*, 62, 234, 280
Ahead (go), *progression*, 282
  to improve, 658
Aid, *to help*, 707, 712
  charity, 606
Aide-de-camp, *auxiliary*, 711
  officer, 745
Aide-memoire, *memory*, 505
Aigrette, *ornament*, 847
Aiguille, *sharp*, 253
Ail, *sick*, 655
  in pain, 828
Ailment, *disease*, 655
Aim, *direction*, 278
  purpose, 620
Aimless, *chance*, 621
  motiveless, 616
Air, *gas*, 334
  atmospheric, 338
  wind, 349
  tune, 415
  appearance, 448
  conduct, 692
  unsubstantial, 4
  fashion, 852
  affectation, 855
  vanity, 880
Air-balloon, *aircraft*, 273A
Air-built, *imagination*, 515
Air-condition, *air*, 338
Air drop, *transference*, 270
Air lift, *transference*, 270
Air-liner, *aircraft*, 273A
Air Marshal, *master*, 745
Air-pipe, *air-pipe*, 351
Air-pocket, *pitfall*, 667
Air-raid, *attack*, 716
Air-tight, *closed*, 261
Airborne, *locomotion*, 267
  aircraft, 273A
  lightness, 320
Aircraft, *aeroplane*, 273A
Aircraft-carrier, *ship*, 273

Aircraftman, *fighter*, 726
Aircrew, *fighter*, 726
Airfield, *arrival*, 292
Airgraph, *news*, 532; *letter*, 592
Airiness, *levity*, 320
Airing, *journey*, 266
Airman, *navigation*, 269
Airport, *arrival*, 292
Airship, *aircraft*, 273A
Airstop, *arrival*, 292
Airstrip, *arrival*, 292
Airworthy, *safe*, 664
Airy, *atmosphere*, 338
  gay, 836
Aisle, *passage*, 260, 627
  church, 1000
Ajutage, *see* Adjutage
Akimbo, *angular*, 244
Akin, *consanguinity*, 11
Alabaster, *whiteness*, 430
Alack! *lamentation*, 839
Alacrity, *activity*, 682
  cheerfulness, 836
Alarm, *fear*, 860
  notice of danger, 669
  signal, 550
  threatening, 665
Alarmist, *newsmonger*, 532
Alarum, *warning*, 669
  signal, 550; *loudness*, 404
Alas! *lamentation*, 839
Alb, *dress*, 225
  vestments, 999
Albeit, *counteraction*, 179
  counter-evidence, 468
  compensation, 30
Albescent, *white*, 430
Albification, *white*, 430
Albinism, *achromatism*, 429
Albino, *dim-sightedness*, 443
Album, *book*, 553
  compendium, 596
  repertoire, 636
Albuminous, *semiliquidity*, 352
Alcade, *master*, 745
Alchemy, *conversion*, 144
Alcohol, *drunkenness*, 959
Alcoran, *sacred books*, 986
Alcove, *cave*, 252
  dwelling, 189
Alderman, *master*, 745
Alembic, *vessel*, 191
  laboratory, 691
*Alentours, *nearness*, 197
Alert, *active*, 682
  watchful, 459
  alarm, 669
  signal, 550
Alexandrine, *verse*, 597
Alexipharmic, *remedy*, 662
Alfresco, *exterior*, 220
  air, 338
Algebra, *numeration*, 85
Algid, *cold*, 383
Algorism, *numeration*, 85

Alias, *misnomer*, 565
Alibi, *absence*, 187
Alien, *irrelevant*, 10
  foreign, 57
Alienate, *transfer*, 783
  estrange, 889
  set against, 898
Alienation (mental), *insanity*, 503
*Alieni appetens, *desire*, 865
  jealousy, 920
Alienist, *doctor*, 662
Alight; *descend*, 306
  stop, 265
  arrive, 292
  light, 420
  hot, 382
Align, *arrange*, 60
  trend, 278
Alike, *similarity*, 17
Aliment, *food*, 298, 707
Alimentation, *aid*, 707
Alimony, *dowry*, 810
  provision, 803
Aline, *see* Align
Aliquot, *part*, 51
Alive, *living*, 359
  attentive, 457
  sensitive, 822
  active, 682
Alkahest, *solution*, 335
All, *whole*, 50
  complete, 52
  general, 78
All-clear, *signal*, 550
All-embracing, *inclusive*, 76
All hands, *generality*, 78
All in, *exhausted*, 160
All-inclusive, *generality*, 78
All-pervading, *generality*, 78
Allah, *great spirit*, 979
Allay, *moderate*, 174
  pacify, 723
  repress excitement, 826
  relieve, 834
Allege, *evidence*, 467
  assert, 535
  plea, 617
Allegiance, *duty*, 743, 926
Allegory, *comparison*, 464, 521
*Allegresse, *cheerfulness*, 836
*Allegretto, *music*, 415
*Allegro, *cheerfulness*, 836
  music, 415
Alleluia, *worship*, 990
Allemande, *dance*, 840
Allergy, *sensitiveness*, 375
Alleviate, *moderate*, 174
  allay, 826
  relieve, 834
Alley, *passage*, 260
  way, 627
  court, 189
*Allez-vous-en, *repulse*, 297
Alliance, *relation*, 9

Amnesty, *pacification*, 723
Amoebean, *sequence*, 63
Among, *interjacence*, 228
   mixture, 41
Amorist, *love*, 897
*Amoroso, *love*, 897
Amorous, *love*, 897
Amorphous, *formless*, 241
   irregular, 83
Amount, *quantity*, 25
   whole, 50
   numeration, 85
   sum of money, 800
   price, 812
Amour, *love*, 897
*Amour-propre, *vanity*, 880
Amphibian, *aircraft*, 273A
Amphibious, *unconformity*, 83
Amphibology, *equivocality*, 520
Amphibrach, *verse*, 597
Amphigouri, *ridiculous*, 853
   absurdity, 497
Amphimacer, *verse*, 597
Amphitheatre, *arena*, 728
   theatre, 599
   prospect, 441
   school, 542
Ample, *much*, 31
   copious, 639
   large, 192
   broad, 202
   spacious, 180
Amplify, *enlarge*, 35
   loudness, 404
   dilate, 194
   expatiate, 573
   exaggerate, 549
Amplitude, *degree*, 26
   space, 180
   size, 192
   breadth, 202
Amputate, *subduction*, 38
Amtrac, *vehicle*, 272
Amuck, run, *violence*, 173
   insanity, 503
   excitability, 825
Amulet, *spell*, 993
Amuse, *amusement*, 840
Amylaceous, *semiliquidity*, 352
An, *if*, 514
Ana, *description*, 594
Anachronism, *anachronism*, 115
Anacoluthon, *discontinuity*, 70
Anacreontic, *poetry*, 597
Anaemia, *pallor*, 429
   weakness, 160
   feebleness, 575
Anaesthesia, *insensibility*,
           376, 381, 823
Anaesthetist, *doctor*, 662
Ἀνάγκη, *necessity*, 601
Anaglyph, *sculpture*, 557
Anagogic, *concealment*, 528
Anagram, *letter*, 561
   double meaning, 520

Anagram, *puzzle*, 533, 842
*Analecta, *description*, 594
Analeptic, *remedy*, 662
Analgesia, *insensibility*, 376
Analogy, *relation*, 9
   similarity, 17
   comparison, 464
Analysis, *decomposition*, 49
   arrangement, 60
   compendium, 596
   grammar, 567
   algebra, 85
   inquiry, 461
   reasoning, 476
Anamnesis, *memory*, 505
Anamorphosis, *optical*, 443
   misrepresentation, 555
Anapaest, *verse*, 597
Anarchist, *enemy*, 891
   evildoer, 913
Anarchy, *disorder*, 59
   social, 738
Anastomosis, *junction*, 43
   crossing, 219
Anastrophe, *inversion*, 218
Anathema, *malediction*, 908
   disapproval, 932
Anatomy, *dissection*, 44
   skeleton, 329
   inquiry, 461
Ancestor, *paternity*, 166
Anchor, *safeguard*, 666
   hope, 858
   fastening, 45, 150
Anchorage, *roadstead*, 189, 265
Anchoret, *asceticism*, 955
Anchylosis, *immutability*, 150
Ancient, *oldness*, 124
Ancillary, *aid*, 707
   intermediate, 631
And, *addition*, 37
*Andante, *music*, 415
*Andantino, *music*, 415
Anderson, *shelter*, 717
Androgynous, *unconformity*, 83
Anecdotage, *loquacity*, 584
   old age, 128
Anecdote, *description*, 594
Anemometer, *wind*, 349
Anent, *relation*, 9
Aneroid, *measurement*, 466
   air, 338
Anew, *newness*, 123
Anfractuosity, *angle*, 244
   convolution, 248
Angel, *supernatural being*, 977
   object of love, 948
Angelic, *virtue*, 944
Angelus, *worship*, 990
Anger, *resentment*, 900
Angina, *pain*, 828
Angle, *angularity*, 244
   pursuit, 622
   explore, 463
Anglic, *language*, 560

Anglophobia, *dislike*, 867
Anguilline, *narrow*, 203
   serpentine, 248
Anguish, *physical*, 378
   moral, 828
Angular, *angularity*, 244
Anhelation, *fatigue*, 688
Anhydrous, *dryness*, 340
Anility, *age*, 128
   silliness, 499
Animadvert, *reprehend*, 932
   consider, 451
Animal, *animal*, 366
Animal cries, *ululation*, 412
Animalcule, *minute*, 193
Animalism, *sensuality*, 954
Animality, *animality*, 364
Animate, *excite*, 824
   cheer, 836
   stimulate, 615
   living beings, 357
Animation, *life*, 359
   animality, 364
   activity, 682
   excitation, 824
Animosity, *enmity*, 889
   hatred, 898
   anger, 900
Animus, *will*, 600
   intention, 620
   animosity, 898, 900
Anklet, *ornament*, 847
   roundness, 247
Annalist, *recorder*, 114, 553
Annals, *record*, 551
   history, 114
   account, 551
Anneal, *harden*, 323
Annex, *add*, 37
   adjunct, 39
   join, 43
Annihilate, *extinguish*, 2
   destroy, 162
Anniversary, *period*, 138
   celebration, 883
Anno Domini, *period*, 108
Annotation, *note*, 550
   glossary, 522
Annotator, *interpreter*, 524
Announce, *inform*, 527
   publish, 531
   predict, 511
   assert, 535
Announcement, *programme*, 510
Announcer, *radio*, 599B
Annoyance, *pain*, 828
   painfulness, 830
   evil, 619
   badness, 649
Annual, *year*, 108
   periodic, 138
   book, 593
Annuity, *wealth*, 803, 810
Annul, *abrogation*, 756, 964
Annular, *circularity*, 247

INDEX

Attachment, *see* Attach
Attack, *attack*, 716
   disease, 655
Attain, *arrive*, 292
   succeed, 731
Attainable, *possible*, 470
   easy, 705
Attainder, *condemnation*, 971
Attainment, *learning*, 539
   knowledge, 490
   skill, 698
Attar, *fragrance*, 400
Attemper, *mix*, 41
   moderate, 174
Attempt, *undertaking*, 676
   try, 675
Attend, *accompany*, 88
   follow, 281
   treat, 662
   apply the mind, 457
   frequent, 136
   be present, 186
Attendant, *servant*, 746
Attention, *attention*, 451, 457
   respect, 928
Attentions, *courtesy*, 894
   courtship, 902
   kindness, 906
Attenuate, *lessen*, 36
   rarefy, 322
   contract, 195
   narrow, 203
Attest, *bear testimony*, 467
   indicate, 550
   adjure, 768
Attestation, *record*, 551
Attic, *garret*, 191
   high, 206
   elegant, 578
   wit, 842
   taste, 850
Atticism, *wit*, 842
Attila, *evildoer*, 913
Attire, *vestment*, 225
Attitude, *posture*, 183, 240
   circumstance, 8
Attitudinize, *affectation*, 855
   ostentation, 882
Attorney, *consignee*, 758, 769
   in law, 968
Attract, *bring towards*, 288
   please, 829
   allure, 865
Attractability, *motive*, 615
Attractive, *beautiful*, 845
   pleasing, 829
   lovely, 897
   alluring, 615
Attrahent, *attraction*, 288
Attributable, *effect*, 154
Attribute, *power*, 157
Attribution, *attribution*, 155
Attrition, *friction*, 331
*Attroupement, *assemblage*, 72
Attune, *music*, 415

Attune, *prepare*, 673
*Au courant, *knowledge*, 490
*Au fait, *knowledge*, 490
*Au fond, *truth*, 494
   inbeing, 5
*Au pied de la lettre, *truth*, 494
   meaning, 516
*Au revoir, *departure*, 293
Aubade, *music*, 415
Auburn, *brown*, 433
Auction, *sale*, 796
Auctorial, *book*, 593
Audacity, *courage*, 861
   insolence, 863, 885
*Audi alteram partem, *evidence*,
               468
   right, 922
Audible, *sound*, 402
Audience, *hearing*, 418
   conversation, 588
Audiometer, *hearing*, 418
Audiphone, *hearing*, 418
Audit, *accounts*, 811
   numeration, 85
Audition, *hearing*, 418
Auditor, *hearer*, 418
   accounts, 811
Auditorium, *amusement*, 840
Auditory, *hearing*, 418
*Auf wiedersehen, *departure*, 293
Auger, *perforation*, 262
Augment, *to increase*, 35
   thing added, 39
Augmentation, *expansion*, 194
Augur, *predict*, 507, 511
   soothsayer, 513
Augury, *prediction*, 511, 512
August, *repute*, 873
Augustine, *clergy*, 996
Aura, *touch*, 380
   emanation, 295
Aureate, *yellowness*, 436
Aureole, *light*, 420
Aureolin, *orange*, 439
Auricular, *hearing*, 418
Aurist, *doctor*, 662
Aurora, *light*, 423
   dawn, 125
Auroral, *rosy*, 434
Auscultation, *hearing*, 418
Auspices, *patronage*, 175
   prediction, 511
Auspicious, *hopeful*, 858
   prosperous, 734
   expedient, 646
   opportune, 134
Auster, *wind*, 349
Austere, *harsh taste*, 395
   severe, 739
   discourteous, 895
   ascetic, 955
Austerity, *economy*, 817
Authentic, *truth*, 494
   certain, 474
   existence, 1

Authenticate, *record*, 551
   evidence, 467
   security, 771
Author, *producer*, 164
   cause, 153
   writer, 590
Authoritative, *certain*, 474
   peremptory, 741
Authority, *power*, 157, 737
   command, 741
   right, 924
   permission, 760
   testimony, 467
   sign, 500
*Auto da fé, *burning*, 384
   execution, 972
*Autobahn, *way*, 627
Autobiography, *description*, 594
Autobus, *vehicle*, 272
Autocar, *vehicle*, 272
Autochrome, *photograph*, 556
Autochthonous, *inhabitant*, 188
Autocracy, *severity*, 739
   authority, 737
Autocrat, *master*, 745
Autocrat, *arbitrary*, 739, 964
   will, 600
Autocycle, *vehicle*, 272
Autogiro, *aircraft*, 273A
Autograph, *warranty*, 467
   signature, 550
   writing, 590
Autolycus, *thief*, 792
Automatic, *mechanical*, 601
   insensible, 823
Automation, *means*, 632
Automobile, *vehicle*, 272
Autonomy, *freedom*, 748
Autopsy, *vision*, 441
   disinter, 363
Autotype, *copy*, 21
*Aux abois, *death*, 360
*Aux aguets, *care*, 459
Auxiliary, *aid*, 707
   helper, 711
   intermediary, 631
Avail, *use*, 677
   utility, 644
Avalanche, *fall*, 306
   debacle, 348
Avant-courier, *pioneer*, 673
   precursor, 64
Avant-garde, *go-ahead*, 282
Avarice, *parsimony*, 819
Avast, *quiescence*, 265
   cessation, 142
Avaunt, *disappear*, 449
   depart, 293
   repulse, 289
*Ave, *arrival*, 292
Avenge, *revenge*, 919
Avenue, *street*, 189
   method, 627
Aver, *affirmation*, 535
Average, *mean*, 29

Barricade, *obstacle,* 706
Barrier, *fence,* 232
  obstacle, 706
Barring, *except,* 83
  save, 38
Barrister, *lawyer,* 968
Barrow, *vehicle,* 272
  grave, 363
Barter, *exchange,* 794
*Bas bleu, *affectation,* 855
Bascule, *instrument,* 633
Base, *lowest part,* 211
  support, 215
  bad, 649
  dishonourable, 940
  shameful, 874
  vicious, 945
  cowardly, 862
  plebeian, 876
Base-minded, *improbity,* 940
Baseless, *unreal,* 2
  erroneous, 495
Basement, *base,* 211
Bashaw, *ruler,* 745
Bashful, *modesty,* 881
Basic, *support,* 215
Basic English, *language,* 560
Basilica, *temple,* 1000
Basilisk, *serpent,* 949
  monster, 83
  evil eye, 441
Basin, *hollow,* 252
  vessel, 191
  plain, 344
  dock, 189
Basis, *preparation,* 673
  foundation, 215
Bask, *warmth,* 382
  physical enjoyment, 377
  moral enjoyment, 827
  prosperity, 734
Basket, *receptacle,* 191
Basket-work, *plaiting,* 219
Basketry, *plaiting,* 219
Bas-relief, *convexity,* 250
Bass, *deep-sounding,* 408, 413
Bass-viol, *musical instrument,*
  417
Bassinette, *vehicle,* 272
*Basso rilievo, *convexity,* 250
  sculpture, 557
Bassoon, *musical instrument,*
  417
Bastard, *spurious,* 544, 925
  erroneous, 495
Bastardy, *illegitimacy,* 964
Baste, *beat,* 276
  punish, 972
Bastille, *prison,* 752
Bastinado, *punishment,* 972
Bastion, *defence,* 717
Bat, *club,* 727, 633
  spree, 840
Batch, *assemblage,* 72
  quantity, 25

Bate, *diminish,* 36, 38
  reduce price, 813
Bath, *immersion,* 300
  water, 337
Bath-chair, *vehicle,* 272
Bath-room, *room,* 191
Bathe, *immersion,* 300
  plunge, 310
Bathing-suit, *dress,* 225
Bathos, *depth,* 208
  anticlimax, 497
  ridiculous, 853
Bathymetry, *depth,* 208
Bathysphere, *depth,* 208
Baton, *sceptre,* 747
  impact, 276
Bats, *insane,* 503
Battalion, *troop,* 726
  assemblage, 72
Batten, *feed,* 296
Batter, *beat,* 276
  destroy, 162
Battered, *imperfect,* 651
Battering-ram, *weapon,* 276, 727
Battery, *instrument,* 633
Battle, *contention,* 720
Battle array, *warfare,* 722
  arrangement, 60
Battle-axe, *arms,* 727
Battle-bowler, *defence,* 717
Battle-cruiser, *ship,* 273
Battle-dress, *dress,* 225
Battle-field, *arena,* 728
Battlement, *bulwark,* 666
  defence, 717
  enclosure, 232
  embrasure, 257
Battleship, *ship,* 273
Battue, *pursuit,* 622
  killing, 361
Batty, *insane,* 503
Bauble, *trifle,* 643
  toy, 840
Baulk, *see* Balk
*Bavardage, *absurdity,* 497
Bawbee, *money,* 800
Bawd, *libertine,* 962
Bawdy, *impurity,* 961
Bawl, *cry,* 411, 839
Bay, *gulf,* 343
  brown, 433
  to howl, 412
Bay, at, *defence,* 717
Bayadère, *dancer,* 599
Bayard, *carrier,* 271
  perfection, 650
Bayonet, *arms,* 727
  attack, 716
  kill, 361
Bays, *trophy,* 733
  reward, 973
Bazaar, *mart,* 799
Bazooka, *gun,* 727
Be, *existence,* 1
Be of, *inclusion,* 76

Be off, *departure,* 293
  ejection, 297
Beach, *land,* 342
Beacon, *sign,* 423, 550
  warning, 668
Bead-roll, *list,* 86
Beadle, *janitor,* 263
  officer, 745
  law officer, 965
  church, 996
Beads, *rite,* 998
Beak, *front,* 234
  nose, 250
  judge, 967
Beaker, *receptacle,* 191
Beam, *support,* 215
  of a balance, 466
  of light, 420
  beauty, 845
Beamless, *darkness,* 421
Bean-feast, *pleasure,* 827, 840
  meal, 298
Bear, *sustain,* 215
  produce, 161
  carry, 270
  suffer, 821
  admit, 470
  brute, 895
Bear down upon, *attack,* 716
Bear-garden, *arena,* 728
  brawl, 713
Bear-leader, *teacher,* 540
Bear off, *taking,* 789
Bear out, *confirm,* 467
  vindicate, 937
Bear up, *cheerfulness,* 836
Bear upon, *influence,* 175
  evidence, 467
  to relate to, 9
Bear with, *indulge,* 740
Bearable, *tolerable,* 651
Beard, *spike,* 253
  rough, 256
  to defy, 715
  courage, 861
  insolence, 885
Beardless, *youth,* 127
Bearer, *carrier,* 271
Bearing, *support,* 215
  direction, 278
  meaning, 516
  appearance, 448
  demeanour, 692
  circumstance, 8
  situation, 183
Bearish, *discourtesy,* 895
Beast, *animal,* 366
  blackguard, 895
Beastly, *uncleanness,* 653
Beat, *strike,* 716, 972
  surpass, 33, 303
  periodic, 138
  oscillation, 314
  agitation, 315
  crush, 330; *sound,* 407

Bow, *ornament*, 847
　fore-part, 234
　shot, 284
　arms, 727
　to stoop, 308
　reverence, 894
　submission, 725
　obeisance, 743
　servility, 886
　respect, 928
　prominence, 250
Bow-legged, *curvature*, 245
　distortion, 243
Bowdlerize, *expurgate*, 652
Bowels, *interior*, 221
　of compassion, 914
Bower, *alcove*, 189
　chamber, 191
Bowie-knife, *arms*, 727
　sharpness, 253
Bowl, *vessel*, 191
　hollow, 252
　to propel, 284
Bowler, *hat*, 225
Bowling-green, *horizontality*, 213
Bowshot, *nearness*, 197
Bowstring, *scourge*, 975
Box, *chest*, 191
　house, 189
　theatre, 599
　to strike, 972
　to fight, 720
Boxer, *combatant*, 726
Boxing, *contention*, 720
Boy, *infant*, 129
Boy friend, *love*, 897
Boycott, *exclude*, 893
　eject, 297
Boyhood, *youth*, 127
Bra, *dress*, 225
Brace, *to tie*, 43
　fastening, 45
　two, 89
　to refresh, 689
　to strengthen, 159
Brace and bit, *perforator*, 262
Bracelet, *ornament*, 847
　circularity, 247
Bracer, *remedy*, 662
Brachygraphy, *writing*, 590
Bracing, *strengthening*, 159
　refreshing, 689
Bracket, *tie*, 43
　support, 215
　vinculum, 45
　couple, 89
Brackish, *pungent*, 392
Brad, *vinculum*, 45
Bradawl, *perforator*, 262
Brae, *height*, 206
Brag, *boasting*, 884
Braggadocio, *boasting*, 884
Braggart, *boasting*, 884
　bully, 887
Brahma, *god*, 979

Brahmin, *clergy*, 996
　religious, 984
Braid, *to tie*, 43
　ligature, 45
　intersection, 219
Braille, *printing*, 591
Brain, *intellect*, 450
　skill, 498
Brain-sick, *giddy*, 460
Brain-storm, *excitability*, 825
Brainless, *imbecile*, 499
Brains trust, *council*, 696
Brainwash, *teach*, 537
Brake, *copse*, 367
　curb, 752
　vehicle, 272
Bramble, *thorn*, 253
　painful, 830
Bran, *pulverulence*, 330
Bran-new, *see* Brand-new
Branch, *member*, 51
　plant, 367
　duality, 91
　posterity, 167
　ramification, 256
Branch off, *divergence*, 291
Branch out, *style*, 573
　divide, 91
Brand, *to burn*, 384
　fuel, 388
　to stigmatize, 932
　mark, 550
　to accuse, 938
　reproach, 874
Brand-new, *new*, 123
Brander, *roast*, 384
Brandish, *oscillate*, 314
　flourish, 315
*Bras croisés, *inactive*, 683
Brasier, *furnace*, 386
Brass, *insolence*, 885
　colour, 439
Brass up, *pay*, 809
Brassed off, *bored*, 641
　sated, 869
Brasserie, *food*, 298
Brassière, *dress*, 225
Brassy, *club*, 276
Brat, *infant*, 129
Bravado, *boasting*, 884
Brave, *courage*, 861
　to defy, 715
Bravery, *courage*, 861
　ornament, 847
Bravo, *assassin*, 361
　applause, 931
*Bravura, *music*, 415
Braw, *handsome*, 845
Brawl, *cry*, 411
　discord, 713
　contention, 720
Brawny, *strong*, 159
　stout, 192
Bray, *cry*, 412
　to grind, 330

Brazen-faced, *insolent*, 885
Breach, *crack*, 44
　quarrel, 713
　violation, 925
　exception, 83
Bread, *food*, 298
Breadstuffs, *food*, 298
Breadth, *thickness*, 202
　of mind, 498
Break, *fracture*, 44
　shatter, 162
　incompleteness, 53
　interval, 70, 106, 198
　opportunity, 134
　luck, 621, 731
　crumble, 328
　violation, 773
　bankruptcy, 808
　to infringe, 927
　to disclose, 529
　to tame, 749
　to decline, 659
　to swerve, 311
Break down, *fail*, 158, 732
Break ground, *undertaking*, 676
Break in, *teach*, 537
　train, 370, 673
Break loose, *escape*, 671
　liberate, 750
Break off, *a habit*, 614
　leave off, 142
　abrogate, 756
Break out, *fly out*, 825
Break the ranks, *derangement*, 61
Break the record, *superiority*, 33
Break up, *destroy*, 162
　deteriorate, 659
　decompose, 49
Break with, *discord*, 713
Breaker, *wave*, 348
　danger, 667
Breakfast, *food*, 298
Breakneck, *perilous*, 665
　precipitous, 217
Breakwater, *refuge*, 666
　enclosure, 232
Breast, *interior*, 221
　convexity, 250
　mind, 450
　will, 600
　soul, 820
　to oppose, 708
Breastplate, *defence*, 717
Breastwork, *defence*, 717
Breath, *air*, 349
　sound, 405
　life, 359, 364
Breathe, *exist*, 1
　live, 359
　blow, 349
　mean, 516
　utter, 580, 582
　repose, 687

Breather, *preparation*, 673
Breathing, *lifelike*, 17
Breathing-space, *time*, 106
   pause, 141, 265
   leisure, 685
Breathless, *calm*, 265
   out of breath, 688
   feeling, 821
Breech, *rear*, 235
Breeches, *dress*, 225
Breed, *kind*, 75
   to multiply, 161
   domesticate, 370
   progeny, 167
Breeding, *fashion*, 852
Breeze, *wind*, 349
Breezy, *lively*, 836
Bren, *gun*, 727
Brevet, *warrant*, 741
   commission, 755
   permission, 760
Breviary, *liturgy*, 998
Brevity, *space*, 201
Brew, *mix*, 41
   prepare, 673
   impend, 121
Briar, *tobacco*, 298A
Bribe, *buy*, 795
   offer, 763
   gift, 784
   fee, 809
   tempt, 615
Bric-à-brac, *trifle*, 643
   ornament, 847
Brick, *materials*, 635
   hardness, 323
   good man, 939, 946
Brickbat, *missile*, 284
Bride, *marriage*, 903
Bridegroom, *marriage*, 903
Bridewell, *prison*, 752
Bridge, *intermedium*, 45
   way, 627
   escape, 671
Bridge over, *junction*, 43
Bridle, *curb*, 752
   to restrain, 751
   to moderate, 174
   to swagger, 878
Bridle up, *resentment*, 900
Brief, *time*, 111
   space, 201
   style, 572
   compendium, 596
   direct, 693, 741
Brief-case, *receptacle*, 191
Briefly, *transientness*, 111
Briefs, *dress*, 225
Brier, *sharp*, 253
   painful, 830
Brig, *ship*, 273
   prison, 752
Brigade, *combatant*, 726
Brigadier, *master*, 745
Brigand, *thief*, 792

Brigantine, *ship*, 273
Bright, *shining*, 420
   colour, 428
   cheerful, 836
   auspicious, 858
   glorious, 873
Brilliant, *shining*, 420
   beautiful, 845
   glorious, 873
   perfect, 650
   gem, 847
Brilliantine, *ornament*, 847
Brim, *edge*, 230
Brimful, *sufficient*, 639
   fullness, 52
Brimmer, *fullness*, 52
Brindled, *variegated*, 440
Brine, *salt*, 392
   sea, 341
Bring, *transfer*, 270
   induce, 615
Bring about, *cause*, 153
   achieve, 729
   succeed, 731
Bring forth, *produce*, 161
Bring forward, *manifest*, 525
Bring home to, *convince*, 537
   adduce, 467
Bring in, *price*, 812
Bring into, *existence*, 1
Bring off, *deliver*, 672
   accomplish, 161, 729
Bring out, *manifest*, 525
   publish, 531
Bring over, *persuade*, 484, 615
Bring to, *restore*, 658
Bring under, *subdue*, 824
Bring up, *educate*, 537
Brink, *edge*, 230
Brio, vivacity, 682
Briquette, *fuel*, 388
Brisk, *quick*, 274
   energetic, 171
   active, 682
   prompt, 111
Bristle, *sharpness*, 253
Bristle up, *resentment*, 900
Bristle with, *abound*, 639
British warm, *dress*, 225
Brittle, *brittleness*, 328
Broach, *begin*, 66
   tap, 297
   put forth, 535
Broad, *space*, 292
   indelicate, 961
   meaning, 535
Broad-minded, *wisdom*, 498
Broadcast, *scattered*, 73
   shed, 291
   radio, 418, 599B
   publication, 531
Broadmoor, *prison*, 752
Broadside, *side*, 236
   cannonade, 716
Broadsword, *arms*, 727

Brobdingnagian, *size*, 192, 193
Brocade, *ornament*, 847
Brochure, *book*, 593
Brog, *perforator*, 262
Brogue, *language*, 560
   shoe, 225
Broidery, *ornament*, 847
Broil, *heat*, 382
   to fry, 384
   fray, 720
Broken, *weakness*, 160
Broken-hearted, *unhappy*, 828
Broken-winded, *fatigue*, 688
Broker, *agent*, 690, 758, 769
   merchant, 797
Brokerage, *pay*, 812
Bromide, *photograph*, 556
   dull, 843
Bronze, *brown*, 433
   sculpture, 557
Brooch, *fastening*, 45
   ornament, 847
Brood, *posterity*, 167
Brood over, *think*, 451
   mope, 837
Brook, *stream*, 348
   to bear, 821, 826
Broom, *cleanness*, 652
Broth, *food*, 298
   semiliquid, 352
Brothel, *impurity*, 961
Brother, *kin*, 11
   similar, 17
   equal, 27
   friend, 888
Brother-in-law, *kin*, 11
Brougham, *vehicle*, 272
Brouillerie, discord, 713
Brow, *summit*, 210
   edge, 230
Browbeat, *intimidate*, 860
   swagger, 885
   attack, 716
Brown, *colour*, 433
Brown-out, *dim*, 422
Brown study, *reverie*, 458
   thought, 451
Browned off, *bored*, 841
   sated, 869
Brownie, *imp*, 980
Browse, *feed*, 296
Bruise, *hurt*, 619
   to injure, 649
   pound, 330
Bruiser, *fighter*, 726
Bruit, *publication*, 531
   news, 532
Brumal, *cold*, 383
   evening, 126
Brummagem, *spurious*, 544
Brumous, *foggy*, 422
Brunette, *brown*, 433
Brunt, *impulse*, 276
   attack, 716
Brush, *rapid motion*, 274

Burgeon, *expansion*, 194
  increase, 35
Burgess, *citizen*, 188, 373
Burgher, *man*, 373
Burglar, *thief*, 792
Burglary, *stealing*, 791
Burgomaster, *master*, 745
Burgrave, *master*, 745
Burial, *corpse*, 362
Buried, *depth*, 208
Burin, *engraving*, 559
Burke, *kill*, 361
  destroy, 162
  suppress, 528
Burlesque, *imitation*, 19
  travesty, 21
  drama, 599
  ridicule, 856
  ridiculous, 853
Burletta, *the drama*, 599
Burly, *size*, 192
Burn, *heat*, 382
  consume, 384
  detection, 480
  passions, 821
  rivulet, 348
Burnish, *polish*, 255
  beautify, 845
  shine, 420
Burnous, *dress*, 225
Burp, *belch*, 297
Burrow, *excavate*, 252
  lodge, 186
Bursar, *treasurer*, 801
Bursary, *treasury*, 802
Burst, *explosion*, 173
  sound, 406
  of anger, 900
  paroxysm, 825
  spree, 840
  separate, 44
Burst forth, *appear*, 446
  sprout, 194
Burst out, *ejaculate*, 580
Burst upon, *inexpectation*, 508
Bury, *inter*, 363
  conceal, 528
Bus, *vehicle*, 272
Busby, *hat*, 225
Bush, *branch*, 51
  shrub, 367
Bushel, *receptacle*, 191
Bushy, *roughness*, 256
Business, *occupation*, 625
  event, 151
  topic, 454
  action, 680
  barter, 794
Business-like, *activity*, 682
  skilful, 698
  order, 58
Buskin, *dress*, 225
  drama, 599
Buss, *ship*, 272
  kiss, 902

Bustle, *activity*, 682
  agitation, 315
  haste, 684
  energy, 171
  earliness, 132
Busy, *activity*, 682
Busybody, *activity*, 682
  curiosity, 455
But, *exception*, 83, 179
  counter-evidence, 468
Butcher, *evildoer*, 913
Butchery, *killing*, 361
Butler, *servant*, 746
Butt, *aim*, 620
  laughing-stock, 857
  remnant, 40
  part, 51; *to push*, 276
  to attack, 716
Butt-end, *end*, 67
Butt in, *intervene*, 228
Butte, *height*, 206
Butter, *softness*, 324
  oiliness, 356
  to flatter, 933
Butter-fingers, *bungler*, 701
Butterfly, *beauty*, 845
  fickleness, 605
  fear, 860
Butterscotch, *sweet*, 396
Button, *knob*, 250
  to fasten, 43
  fastening, 45
  hanging, 214
  trifle, 643
Buttoned up, *reserved*, 528
  taciturn, 585
Buttonhole, *ornament*, 847
  accost, 586
Buttonholer, *weariness*, 841
Buttons, *servant*, 746
Buttress, *support*, 215
  defence, 717
  strengthen, 159
Buxom, *plump*, 192
  cheerful, 836
Buy, *purchase*, 795
Buzz, *sound*, 409, 412
  to publish, 531
  news, 532
Buzz-bomb, *arms*, 727
Buzz off, *depart*, 293
Buzzard, *fool*, 501
By and by, *transientness*, 111
By fits and starts, *disorder*, 59
  irregularity, 139
By jingo, *affirmation*, 535
By-law, *legality*, 963
By-name, *misnomer*, 565
By the by, *opportunity*, 134
Bye-bye, *departure*, 293
  sleep, 683
Bygone, *former*, 122
  forgotten, 506
Bypath, *road*, 627
Byplay, *gesture*, 550

Byssus, *roughness*, 256
Bystander, *spectator*, 444
  near, 197
Byway, *road*, 627
Byword, *maxim*, 496
  cant term, 563
  contempt, 930

C

C.A., *accounts*, 811
C.O.D., *payment*, 807
Ca' canny, *caution*, 864
Cab, *vehicle*, 272
  translation, 522
Cabal, *confederacy*, 712
  plan, 626
Cabbage, *purloin*, 791
Cabbala, *spell*, 993
Cabbalistic, *mysterious*, 528
Caber, *missile*, 284
Cabin, *room*, 189
  receptacle, 191
Cabin cruiser, *ship*, 273
Cabinet, *receptacle*, 191
  workshop, 691
  council, 696
Cable, *vinculum*, 45
Cabriolet, *vehicle*, 272
Cache, *hiding-place*, 530
  conceal, 528
  store, 636
Cachexy, *disease*, 655
  weakness, 160
Cachinnation, *rejoicing*, 838
Cachucha, *dance*, 840
Cacique, *master*, 745
Cackle, *of geese*, 412
  talk, 588
  laughter, 838
Cacodemon, *demon*, 980
Cacodyl, *fetor*, 401
*Cacoethes, *habit*, 613
  itch, 865
  writing, 590
*Cacoethes loquendi,
  loquacity, 584
*Cacoethes scribendi,
  writing, 590
Cacography, *writing*, 590
Cacophony, *stridor*, 410
  discord, 414
  style, 579
Cad, *vulgarity*, 851
Cadastre, *list*, 86
Cadaverous, *corpse*, 362
  pale, 429
  thin, 203
  hideous, 846
Caddish, *mean*, 940
Caddy, *receptacle*, 191
Cadence, *accent*, 580
  music, 415
  descent, 306
Cadenza, *music*, 415

Cannon, *arms*, 727
   collision, 276
Cannonade, *attack*, 716
Cannoneer, *combatant*, 726
Canny, *cautious*, 459, 864
   cunning, 702
   intelligent, 498
   thrifty, 817
Canoe, *ship*, 273
Canon, *rule*, 80
   music, 415
   precept, 697
   priest, 996
Canonical, *orthodox*, 983A
Canonicals, *holy orders*, 999
Canonize, *rites*, 995, 998
   honour, 873
Canoodle, *endearment*, 902
Canopy, *height*, 206
   roof, 210
   covering, 222
Canorous, *resonant*, 402
   melodious, 415
Cant, *neology*, 563
   language, 560
   oblique, 217
   hypocrisy, 544, 988
Cantankerous, *discourtesy*, 895
Cantata, *music*, 415
*Cantatrice, *musician*, 416
Canted, *obliquity*, 217
Canteen, *receptacle*, 191
   feeding, 298
Canter, *move*, 266
   gallop, 274
Canticle, *music*, 415
Cantilever, *support*, 215
Cantle, *part*, 51
Canto, *poetry*, 597
Canton, *region*, 181
Cantonment, *location*, 184
   abode, 189
Canty, *cheerfulness*, 836
Canvas, *sail*, 267
Canvass, *investigate*, 461
   treat of, 595
   solicit, 765
Canyon, *ravine*, 198
Canzonet, *song*, 415
   poem, 597
Caoutchouc, *elasticity*, 325
Cap, *hat*, 225
   height, 206
   to be superior, 33, 194
   counter, 718
   to salute, 894
Cap-à-pie, *preparation*, 673
   length, 200
Capability, *power*, 157
   strength, 159
   skill, 698
   facility, 705
   endowment, 5
Capacity, *space*, 180
   size, 192

Capacity, *endowment*, 5
   power, 157
   intellect, 450
   aptitude, 539
   talent, 698
   wisdom, 498
   utility, 644
   office, 625
Caparison, *vestment*, 225
Cape, *land*, 342
   projection, 250
   height, 206
   cloak, 225
Caper, *leap*, 309
   dance, 840
Capillary, *thinness*, 203, 205
Capital, *excellent*, 648
   important, 642
   summit, 210
   money, 800; *wealth*, 803
Capitalist, *wealth*, 803
Capitation, *numeration*, 85
Capitol, *defence*, 717
Capitular, *clergy*, 996
Capitulate, *submission*, 725
Capote, *vestment*, 224
*Capriccio, *caprice*, 608
Caprice, *chance*, 608
   irresolution, 605
   music, 415
Capricious, *irregular*, 139
   changeable, 149
   whimsical, 608
Capriole, *leap*, 309
Capsize, *inversion*, 218
   wreck, 731
Capsized, *failure*, 732
Capstan, *instrument*, 633
Capsule, *vessel*, 191
   tunicle, 222
Captain, *master*, 745
   of industry, 745
Caption, *indication*, 550
Captious, *capricious*, 608
   censorious, 932
   discourteous, 795
Captivated, *fascinated*, 827, 897
   induced, 615
Captivating, *pleasing*, 829
   lovely, 897
Captive, *prisoner*, 754
Captivity, *restraint*, 751
Capture, *taking*, 789
Capuchin, *clergy*, 996
*Caput mortuum, *remainder*, 40
   unclean, 653
Car, *vehicle*, 272
Carabineer, *combatant*, 726
Caracole, *leap*, 309
   journey, 266
Carafe, *receptacle*, 191
*Carambole, *impulse*, 276
Caramel, *sweet*, 396
Carapace, *covering*, 222

Caravan, *vehicle*, 272
Caravansary, *abode*, 189
Caravel, *ship*, 273
Carbine, *arms*, 727
Carbon, *copy*, 590
Carbon print, *photograph*, 556
Carbonize, *calefaction*, 384
Carborundum, *sharpener*, 253
Carboy, *receptacle*, 191
Carcass, *corpse*, 362
Card, *ticket*, 550
   plan, 626
   oddity, 857
   to unravel, 60
Cardiac, *remedy*, 662
Cardigan, *dress*, 225
Cardinal, *important*, 642
   excellent, 648
   red, 434
   dress, 225
   priest, 995, 996
Care, *attention*, 459
   fear, 860
   pain, 828, 830
   custody, 751
Care for, *desire*, 865
   love, 642, 897
Care-worn, *pain*, 828
Careen, *slant*, 217, 306
   repair, 658
Career, *business*, 625
   conduct, 692
Careful, *caution*, 864
Careless, *inattentive*, 458
   neglectful, 460
   insensible, 823
Caress, *endearment*, 902
*Caret, *incomplete*, 53
   to want, 640
Caretaker, *keeper*, 753
Cargo, *goods*, 798
   contents, 190
   property, 780
   materials, 635
   large quantity, 31
Caricature, *likeness*, 19
   misrepresentation, 555
   ridicule, 856
Caricaturist, *humorist*, 844
Caries, *disease*, 655
Carillon, *musical instrument*, 417
Carking, *painful*, 830
Carle, *boor*, 876
Carmelite, *clergy*, 996
Carminative, *remedy*, 662
Carmine, *redness*, 434
Carnage, *killing*, 361
Carnal, *impure*, 961
   animality, 364
   intemperate, 954
   irreligious, 989
   material, 316
Carnation, *redness*, 434
Carnival, *amusement*, 840

Catastrophe, *convulsion*, 146
Catch, *take*, 134, 789
 receive, 785
 learn, 539
 gather meaning, 518
 cheat, 545
 vinculum, 45
Catch at, *receiving*, 785
Catch on, *success*, 731
Catch up, *overtake*, 292
Catching, *infectious*, 657
Catchpenny, *trumpery*, 643
 cheap, 815
 false, 544
Catchpoll, *jurisprudence*, 965
Catchword, *formula*, 80
 maxim, 496
Catechetical, *inquiry*, 461
Catechize, *inquiry*, 461
Catechumen, *learner*, 541
Categorical, *true*, 494
 positive, 474
 demonstrative, 478
 affirmative, 535
Category, *class*, 75
 arrangement, 60
 state, 7
Catenary, *curve*, 245
Catenation, *continuity*, 69
Cater, *provision*, 637
Caterwauling, *cry*, 412
 discord, 414
Cates, *food*, 298
Cathedral, *temple*, 1000
Catholic, *universal*, 78
 Christian, 983A
 broad-minded, 498
Catholicity, *generality*, 78
 broad-mindedness, 498
Catholicon, *remedy*, 662
Cat's-cradle, *crossing*, 219
Cat's-paw, *instrument*, 631
 dupe, 547
Cattle-lifting, *stealing*, 791
Cattle-truck, *vehicle*, 272
Caucus, *assemblage*, 72
Caudal, *end*, 67
Caudate, *pendency*, 214
Cauldron, *mixture*, 41
 vessel, 191
 heating, 386
 laboratory, 691
Caulk, *repair*, 658
Causality, *cause*, 153
 power, 157
Causation, *cause*, 153
 agency, 170
Cause, *source*, 153
 final, 620
 lawsuit, 969
Causeless, *casual*, 156
 aimless, 621
Causerie, *chat*, 588
*Causeur, *talker*, 588
Causeway, *road*, 627

Causidical, *juridical*, 965
Caustic, *feeling*, 821
 painful, 830
 gruff, 895
 disapproving, 932
 malevolent, 907
Cautelous, *caution*, 864
Cauterize, *calefaction*, 384
Caution, *care*, 459
 warning, 668
 prudence, 864
 advice, 695
 security, 771
Cavalcade, *continuity*, 69
Cavalier, *horseman*, 268
 insolent, 885
 discourteous, 895
 contemptuous, 930
*Cavaliere servente, *lover*, 897
Cavalierly, *inattention*, 458
Cavalry, *combatant*, 726
*Cavatina, *music*, 415
Cave, *cavity*, 252
 cell, 191
 dwelling, 189
 warning, 668
 care, 459
Cave in, *submit*, 729
Caveat, *warning*, 668
Cavendish, *tobacco*, 298A
Cavern, *hollow*, 252
 cell, 191
 dwelling, 189
Cavernous, *hollow*, 252
 porous, 322
Caviare, *pungent*, 171, 392
Cavil, *censure*, 932
 dissent, 489
 split hairs, 477
Caviller, *detractor*, 936
Cavity, *concavity*, 252
Cavort, *prance*, 315
Caw, *animal cry*, 412
Cayenne, *condiment*, 393
 pungent, 171
Cease, *cessation*, 142
Ceaseless, *perpetuity*, 112
Cecity, *blindness*, 442
Cede, *relinquish*, 782
Ceiling, *height*, 206
 summit, 210
 covering, 222
*Cela va sans dire, *conformity*, 82
 effect, 154
Celebrant, *worship*, 990
Celebrate, *solemnize*, 883
 publish, 531
 praise, 931
Celebration, *fête*, 883
 rite, 998
. Celebrity, *repute*, 873
 nobility, 875
Celerity, *velocity*, 274
Celestial, *physical*, 318

Celestial, *moral*, 829
 religious, 976, 981
 angelic, 977
Celibacy, *bachelor*, 904
Cell, *cavity*, 252
 receptacle, 191
 abode, 189
 prison, 752
Cellar, *room*, 191
 store, 636
 lowness, 207
Cellaret, *receptacle*, 191
Cellular, *concavity*, 252
Cellule, *receptacle*, 191
Celsius, *thermometer*, 389
Cembalo, *musical instrument*, 417
Cement, *connective*, 45
 to unite, 46
 concord, 714
Cemetery, *interment*, 363
Cenobite, *recluse*, 893
 anchoret, 996
Cenotaph, *interment*, 363
Censer, *temple*, 1000
Censor, *detractor*, 936
 inhibit, 616
Censorious, *disapprobation*, 932
Censorship, *authority*, 737
 secret, 533
Censure, *disapprobation*, 932
Census, *counting*, 85
 list, 86
Centaur, *unconformity*, 83
Centenary, *numbers*, 98
 celebration, 883
Centennial, *numbers*, 98
 period, 108, 138
Centesimal, *hundred*, 98
Centigrade, *thermometer*, 389
Cento, *poetry*, 597
Central, *centrality*, 223
Centralize, *combine*, 48
 focus, 72
 concentrate, 223
Centre, *in order*, 68
 in space, 223
Centre in, *convergence*, 290
Centrifugal, *divergence*, 291
Centripetal, *convergence*, 290
Centuple, *number*, 98
Centurion, *master*, 745
Century, *period*, 108
 duration, 106
Ceramic, *sculpture*, 557
Cerberus, *janitor*, 263
 custodian, 664
Cerebration, *thought*, 451
Cerebrum, *intellect*, 450
Cerement, *interment*, 363
Ceremonious, *respect*, 928
Ceremony, *parade*, 882
 religious, 998
Ceres, *botany*, 369
Cerise, *red*, 434

Cerography, *engraving*, 558
Certain, *sure*, 474, 484
   special, 79
   indefinite number, 100
Certainly, *assent*, 488
Certificate, *voucher*, 551
   security, 771
   evidence, 467
Certify, *evince*, 467
   inform, 527
   vouch, 535
Certitude, *certainty*, 474
Cerulean, *blue*, 438
Cess, *tax*, 812
Cessation, *ceasing*, 142
Cession, *surrender*, 725, 782
   gift, 784
Cesspool, *uncleanness*, 633
Cestus, *girdle*, 225
   ligature, 45
   ring, 247
Chafe, *warm*, 384
   pain, 378
   irritate, 825, 828
   vex, 830
   incense, 900
Chaff, *trash*, 643
   wit, 842
   ridicule, 856
   vulgar, 876
Chaffer, *bargain*, 769
   sale, 794
Chafing-dish, *furnace*, 386
Chagrin, *pain*, 828
Chain, *series*, 69
   to fasten, 43
   vinculum, 45
   ornament, 847
   to imprison, 752
Chain-mail, *arms*, 727
Chain-shot, *arms*, 727
Chair, *support*, 215
   vehicle, 272
   direction, 693
   professorship, 542
   throne, 747
Chairman, *director*, 694, 745
Chairmanship, *direction*, 693
Chaise, *vehicle*, 272
Chaise longue, support, 215
Chalcography, *engraving*, 558
Chalet, *abode*, 189
Chalice, *cup*, 191
   hollow, 252
Chalk, *mark*, 550
   drawing, 556, 559
   soil, 342
Chalk out, *plan*, 626
Chalky, *white*, 430
Challenge, *defy*, 715
   accuse, 938
   claim, 924
Cham, *master*, 745
Chamber, *room*, 191
   council, 696

Chamber, *mart*, 799
Chamber music, *music*, 415
Chamberlain, *servant*, 746
Chambermaid, *servant*, 746
Chameleon, *variegation*, 440
   inconstancy, 149, 605
Chamfer, *furrow*, 259
Champ, *eat*, 296
Champaign, *plain*, 344
Champion, *auxiliary*, 711
   proficient, 700
   good, 648
   defence, 717
   combatant, 726
Championship, *aid*, 707
   superiority, 33
Chance, *absence of cause*, 156
   absence of aim, 621
   opportunity, 134
Chance-medley, *chance*, 156
Chancel, *temple*, 1000
Chancellor, *president*, 745
   judge, 967
Chancy, *risky*, 665
   uncertain, 475
Chandelier, *luminary*, 423
Chandler, *merchant*, 797
Change, *alteration*, 140
   mart, 799
   small coin, 800
Changeable, *mutable*, 149, 607
   irresolute, 605
Changeful, *mutable*, 149
   volition, 607
Changeling, *changed*, 147
   fool, 501
Channel, *opening*, 260
   conduit, 350
   instrumentality, 631
   way, 627
   passage, 302
   furrow, 259
Chant, *sing*, 415
   worship, 990
   rites, 998
*Chantage, *blackmail*, 791
Chanty, *music*, 415
Chaos, *disorder*, 59
   secret, 533
Chap, *man*, 373
   fissure, 198
Chap-book, *book*, 593
Chap-fallen, *dejected*, 837
   humiliated, 879
Chapel, *temple*, 1000
   council, 696
Chaperon, *safety*, 664, 753
   accompaniment, 88
Chaplain, *clergy*, 996
Chaplet, *circle*, 247
   dress, 225
   ornament, 847
   trophy, 733
Chapman, *merchant*, 797
Chaps, *orifice*, 66

Chapter, *part*, 51
   topic, 454
   book, 593
   church, 995
   council, 696
Char, *calefaction*, 384
Charabanc, *vehicle*, 272
Character, *nature*, 5
   disposition, 820
   state, 7
   letter, 561
   type, 591
   drama, 599
   class, 75
   unconformity, 83
Characteristic, *special*, 79
   feature, 550
   intrinsic, 5
Characterize, *name*, 564
   description, 594
Charade, *secret*, 533
   drama, 599
Charcoal, *fuel*, 388
   black, 431
   artist, 559
Charge, *business*, 625
   direction, 693
   advice, 695
   precept, 697
   commission, 755
   load, 52, 639
   order, 741
   accusation, 938
   attack, 716
   impact, 276
   price, 812
   custody, 751
Charge-hand, *director*, 694
*Chargé d'affaires, *deputy*, 759
Chargeable, *debt*, 806
Charger, *carrier*, 271
Chariot, *vehicle*, 272
Charioteer, *director*, 694
Charity, *giving*, 784
   benevolence, 906
   bounty, 816
Charivari, *loudness*, 404
   discordance, 413
Charlatan, *impostor*, 548
   ignoramus, 493
   boaster, 884
Charlatanism, *quackery*, 545, 855
   ignorance, 491
Charm, *to please*, 829
   love, 897
   beauty, 845
   motive, 615
   to conjure, 992
   spell, 993
   flock, 72
Charnel-house, *interment*, 363
Chart, *representation*, 554
Charter, *privilege*, 924
   legality, 963
   permit, 760

Chivalrous, *honourable*, 939
   bold, 861
    generous, 942
Chivy, *chase*, 622
Chloral, *anaesthetic*, 376
Chlorosis, *achromatism*, 429
Chlorotic, *achromatism*, 429
Chock-full, *sufficiency*, 639
   fullness, 52
Chocolate, *brown*, 433
   sweet, 396
Choice, *election*, 609
   excellent, 648
Choir, *music*, 415
   orchestra, 416
   church, 1000
Choke, *close*, 261
   hinder, 706
   surfeit, 641
   suffocate, 361
Choke off, *dissuade*, 616
Chokka, *bored*, 841
   sated, 869
Choky, *prison*, 752
Choler, *resentment*, 900
Choleric, *irascible*, 901
Choose, *choice*, 609
   will, 600
Choosy, *particular*, 868
Chop, *disjoin*, 44
   change, 140
   barter, 794
   wave, 348
   sign, 550
Chop logic, *reasoning*, 476
Chopping, *large*, 192
Chops, *orifice*, 66
Choral, *music*, 415
Chord, *harmony*, 413
Chore, *business*, 625
Choreography, *dance*, 840
Chorister, *musician*, 416
   clergy, 996
Chorography, *situation*, 183, 554
Chortle, *to laugh*, 838
Chorus, *sound*, 404
   voices, 411
   musicians, 416
   unanimity, 488
*Chose jugée, *judgment*, 480
*Chota hazri, *food*, 298
Chouse, *deception*, 545
Chrism, *rite*, 998
CHRIST, *Deity*, 976
Christen, *nomenclature*, 564
Christendom, *Christianity*, 983A
Christian, *piety*, 987
   Christianity, 983A
Christianity, *Christian religion*, 983A
Christmas box, *gift*, 784
Chromatic, *colour*, 428
   musical scale, 413
Chromatrope, *optical instrument*, 445

Chromolithograph, *engraving*, 558
Chronic, *diuturnity*, 110
Chronicle, *annals*, 551
   measure of time, 114
   account, 594
Chronicler, *recorder*, 553
*Chronique scandaleuse, *gossip*, 532, 588
Chronology, *time measurement*, 114
Chronometry, *time measurement*, 114
Chrysalis, *youth*, 127, 129
Chubby, *size*, 192
Chuck, *throw*, 284
   desist, 142
   cry, 412
   food, 298
Chuck out, *expel*, 297
Chuck up, *abandon*, 624
Chucker-out, *doorkeeper*, 263
Chuckle, *laugh*, 838
   exult, 884
Chuckle-head, *fool*, 501
Chum, *friend*, 890
Chummy, *friendly*, 888
Chunk, *size*, 192
   part, 51
Chunky, *short*, 201
   broad, 202
Church, *Christian religion*, 983A
   temple, 1000
Churchdom, *churchdom*, 995
Churchman, *clergy*, 996
Churchwarden, *clergy*, 996
   tobacco-pipe, 298A
Churchy, *bigoted*, 988
Churchyard, *interment*, 363
Churl, *boor*, 876
   rude, 895
   irascible, 901
   niggard, 819
Churn, *agitation*, 315, 352
Chute, *obliquity*, 217
Chutney, *condiment*, 393
Chyle, *fluid*, 333
Chyme, *semiliquid*, 352
Cicatrize, *improvement*, 658
Cicerone, *teacher*, 540
   director, 694
*Cicisbeo, *love*, 897
*Ci-devant, *preterition*, 122
Cigar, *tobacco*, 298A
Cigar-case, *receptacle*, 191
Cigar-shaped, *rotund*, 249
Cigarette, *tobacco*, 298A
Cigarette-case, *receptacle*, 191
Ciliated, *roughness*, 256
Cimmerian, *darkness*, 421
Cinch, *grip*, 781
   connection, 45
   easy, 705
Cincture, *circularity*, 247
Cinders, *remainder*, 40

Cine-camera, *lens*, 445
Cinema, *theatre*, 599A
   amusement, 840
Cinemaddict, *cinema*, 599A
Cinematograph, *show*, 448
Cinerary, *burial*, 363
Cineration, *calefaction*, 384
Cinerator, *furnace*, 386
Cinereous, *grey*, 432
Cingulum, *belt*, 229
Cinnabar, *red*, 434
Cinque, *numbers*, 98
Cipher, *zero*, 101
   number, 84
   to compute, 85
   secret, 533
   mark, 550
   writing, 590
   unimportant, 643
Circe, *seductor*, 615
   sensuality, 954
Circle, *form*, 247
   curvature, 245
   space, 181
   theatre, 599
   party, 712
   social, 892
Circuit, *deviation*, 279
   indirect path, 629
   winding, 248
   turn, 311
   tour, 266
   space, 181
Circuitous, *devious*, 279
   turning, 311
   indirect, 629
Circular, *round*, 247
   curved, 245
   advertisement, 531
   letter, 592
Circulate, *rotate*, 312
   publish, 531
Circumambient, *circumjacence*, 227
Circumambulate, *move*, 266
   wind, 311
Circumbendibus, *winding*, 248
   circuit, 629
   circuition, 311
Circumference, *outline*, 229
Circumfluent, *circuition*, 311
Circumfuse, *dispersion*, 73
Circumgyration, *rotation*, 312
Circumjacence, *surrounding*, 227
Circumlocution, *phrase*, 566, 573
Circumnavigation, *navigation*, 267
   circuition, 311
Circumrotation, *rotation*, 312
Circumscribe, *surround*, 231
   limit, 761
Circumspect, *attentive*, 457
   careful, 459
   cautious, 864
Circumstance, *phrase*, 8

Circumstance, *event*, 151
Circumstantial, *diffuse*, 573
  evidence, 472
Circumvallation, *enclosure*, 232
  defence, 717
Circumvent, *cheat*, 545
  defeat, 731
  cunning, 702
Circumvolution, *rotation*, 312
Circus, *arena*, 728
  amusement, 840
  edifice, 189
Cistern, *receptacle*, 191
  store, 636
Citadel, *fort*, 666
  defence, 717
Cite, *quote as example*, 82, 564
  as evidence, 467
  summon, 741
  accuse, 938
  arraign, 969
Cithern, *musical instrument*, 417
Citizen, *inhabitant*, 188
  man, 373
Citrine, *yellow*, 436
City, *abode*, 189
Civet, *fragrance*, 400
Civic, *urban*, 189
  public, 372
Civicism, *patriotism*, 910
Civil, *courteous*, 894
  laity, 997
Civilian, *lawyer*, 968
  non-combatant, 726A
Civilization, *courtesy*, 894
  mankind, 372
Civvies, *dress*, 225
Clachan, *village*, 189
Clack, *talk*, 588
  snap, 406
  animal cry, 412
Clad, *dressed*, 225
Claim, *demand*, 741, 765
  property, 780
  right, 924
Claimant, *dueness*, 924
  petitioner, 767
Clairvoyance, *occult arts*, 992
  insight, 490
  foresight, 510
Clam, *taciturn*, 585
Clamant, *cry*, 411
Clamber, *ascent*, 305
Clammy, *semiliquid*, 352
Clamour, *loudness*, 404, 411
Clamp, *to fasten*, 43
  fastening, 45
Clamp down, *restrict*, 751
Clan, *class*, 75; *kindred*, 11
  clique, 892
Clandestine, *concealment*, 528
  secret, 534
Clang, *loudness*, 404
  resonance, 408
Clanger, *error*, 495, 732

Clanger, *solecism*, 568
Clank, *harsh sound*, 410
Clannishness, *prejudice*, 481
  co-operation, 709
Clap, *explosion*, 406
  to applaud, 931
Clap on, *addition*, 37
Clap up, *restraint*, 751
Clapperclaw, *beat*, 972
Claptrap, *plea*, 617
  pretence, 546
  sophistry, 477
  nonsense, 492
*Claqueur, *flatterer*, 935
Clarence, *vehicle*, 272
Clarify, *cleanness*, 652
Clarinet, *musical instrument*,
  417
Clarion, *musical instrument*, 417
Clarity, *transparency*, 425
  perspicuity, 570
Clart, *mud*, 352
  dirt, 653
Clash, *oppose*, 708
  disagree, 24
  discord, 713
  contest, 720
  concussion, 276
  sound, 406
  chatter, 584
Clasp, *to unite*, 43
  fastening, 45
  entrance, 903
  come close, 197
Clasp-knife, *sharpness*, 253
Class, *category*, 75
  to arrange, 60
  learner, 541
Classic, *masterpiece*, 650
  symmetry, 242
  ancient, 124
Classical, *taste*, 578, 580
Classify, *arrangement*, 60
  class, 75
Clatter, *roll*, 407
  din, 404
Clause, *part*, 51
  passage, 593
  condition, 770
Claustral, *secluded*, 893
Claustrophobia, *dislike*, 867
  seclusion, 893
Clavichord, *musical*, 417
Claw, *hook*, 633
  to grasp, 789
Clay, *earth*, 342
  corpse, 362
  tobacco-pipe, 298A
Clay-cold, *cold*, 383
Claymore, *arms*, 727
Clean, *unstained*, 652
  entirely, 31
Clean-handed, *innocence*, 946
Cleanse, *purge*, 652
Clear, *transparent*, 425

Clear, *light*, 420
  visible, 446
  intelligible, 518
  perspicuous style, 570
  to prepare, 673
  to free, 750
  to vindicate, 937
  to acquit, 970
  innocent, 946
  simple, 42
  easy, 705
  to pay, 807
  to pass, 302
Clear decks, *prepare*, 673
Clear of, *distant*, 196
Clear out, *eject*, 297
  depart, 203
Clear-sighted, *vision*, 441
  shrewd, 498
Clear up, *interpret*, 518, 522
Clearance, *payment*, 807
Clearway, *way*, 627
Cleave, *adhere*, 46
  sunder, 44, 91
Cleek, *club*, 276
Clef, *music*, 413
Cleft, *chink*, 198
Clem, *starve*, 956
Clement, *lenient*, 740
  kind, 906
  pitiful, 914
Clench, *see* Clinch
Clepsydra, *chronometry*, 114
Clergy, *clergy*, 996
Clerical, *churchdom*, 995
Clerihew, *drollery*, 853
  absurdity, 497
Clerk, *scholar*, 492
  recorder, 553
  writer, 590
  servant, 746
  agent, 758; *church*, 996
Clerkship, *commission*, 755
Clever, *skill*, 698
Cliché, *platitude*, 497
Click, *snap*, 406
Client, *dependant*, 746
  buyer, 795
  frequenter, 136
Clientship, *subjection*, 749
Cliff, *height*, 206
  verticality, 212, 217
Cliff-hanging, *suspense*, 485
Climacteric, *age*, 128
Climate, *region*, 181
  weather, 338
Climax, *summit*, 210
  completion, 729
  increase, 35
  in degree, 33
Climb, *ascent*, 305
Clime, *region*, 181
Clinch, *snatch*, 789
  fasten, 43
  close, 261

*Cocotte, *prostitute*, 962
Coction, *calefaction*, 384
Cocytus, *hell*, 982
Coda, *end*, 67
Code, *law*, 963
   precept, 697
   secret, 533
   signal, 550
Codex, *book*, 593
Codger, *parsimony*, 819
Codicil, *adjunct*, 39
   sequel, 65
Codify, *legality*, 963
Codswallop, *nonsense*, 643
Coefficient, *co-operating*, 709
   accompanying, 88
   factor, 84
Coemption, *purchase*, 795
Coenobite, *seclusion*, 893
Coequal, *equality*, 27
Coerce, *restrain*, 751
   compel, 744
   dissuade, 616
Coessential, *identity*, 13
Coetaneous, *synchronism*, 120
Coeternal, *perpetuity*, 112
Coeval, *synchronism*, 120
Coexist, *synchronism*, 120
   accompany, 88
   contiguity, 199
Coextension, *equality*, 27
   parallelism, 216
Coffee-house, *food*, 298
Coffer, *chest*, 191
   money-chest, 802
   store, 636
Coffin, *interment*, 363
Coffin-nail, *tobacco*, 298A
Cog, *tooth*, 253; *ship*, 273
   deceive, 545
   flatter, 933
Cogent, *powerful*, 157
   argument, 467, 476
Cogitate, *thought*, 451
Cognate, *rule*, 80
   relation, 9
Cognation, *relation*, 9
Cognition, *knowledge*, 490
Cognizance, *knowledge*, 490
Cognomen, *nomenclature*, 564
Cognoscence, *knowledge*, 490
*Cognoscente, *taste*, 850
Cognoscible, *knowledge*, 490
Cohabitation, *marriage*, 903
Co-heir, *partner*, 778
Cohere, *unite*, 46
   dense, 321
Cohesive, *uniting*, 46
   dense, 321
   tenacious, 327
Cohibition, *restraint*, 751
Cohort, *combatant*, 726
Coif, *dress*, 225
Coiffure, *dress*, 225
Coil, *convolution*, 248

Coil, *circuition*, 311
   disorder, 59
Coin, *money*, 800
   to fabricate, 161
   to imagine, 515
Coincidence, *identity*, 13
   in time, 120
   in place, 199
   in opinion, 488
Coinstantaneity, *synchronism*, 120
Coke, *fuel*, 388
Colander, *opening*, 260
Cold, *frigidity*, 383
   style, 575
   insensible, 823
   indifferent, 866
Cold-blooded, *malevolent*, 907
   dispassionate, 823, 826
Cold-hearted, *enmity*, 889
Cold-shoulder, *exclusion*, 893
   repulsion, 289
Cold war, *truce*, 723
Coliseum, *arena*, 728
Collaborate, *accompany*, 88
   co-operate, 178, 709
Collapse, *contraction*, 195
   prostration, 160
   fatigue, 688
   incapacity, 158
   failure, 732
Collar, *dress*, 225
   shackle, 749, 752
   seize, 789
Collate, *compare*, 464
Collateral, *relation*, 11
   lateral, 236
   consequential, 467
Collation, *food*, 299
   comparison, 464
Colleague, *auxiliary*, 711
   co-operating, 709
Collect, *assemble*, 72
   take, 789
   acquire, 775
   learn, 539
   opine, 480
   understand, 518
   prayer, 990
Collectanea, *assemblage*, 72
   compendium, 596
Collected, *calm*, 826
Collection, *store*, 636
   offering, 990
   assemblage, 72
Collectiveness, *whole*, 50
Collectivism, *participation*, 780
   authority, 737
Collector, *assemblage*, 72
Colleen, *woman*, 374
   girl, 129
College, *school*, 542
Collide, *see* Collision
Collier, *ship*, 273
   man, 373

Colligate, *assemblage*, 72
Colligation, *junction*, 43
Collimation, *direction*, 278
Collimator, *optical instrument*, 445
Collision, *approach*, 286
   percussion, 276
   clashing, 179
   opposition, 708
   encounter, 720
Collocate, *arrange*, 60
   assemble, 72
Collocution, *interlocution*, 588
Collogue, *confer*, 588
Colloid, *semiliquid*, 352
Collop, *part*, 51
Colloquialism, *language*, 560
Colloquy, *interlocution*, 588
Collotype, *engraving*, 558
Collusion, *deceit*, 545
   concurrence, 178
   conspiring, 709
Colon, *stop*, 142
Colonel, *master*, 745
Colonize, *location*, 184, 188
Colonnade, *continuity*, 69
Colony, *region*, 181
   settlement, 184, 188
Colophon, *end*, 67
   sequel, 65
Coloration, *colour*, 428
*Coloratura, *music*, 415
Colossal, *size*, 192
   height, 206
Colour, *hue*, 428
   plea, 617
   disguise, 545
   qualify, 469
   to blush, 434
Colourable, *deceptive*, 545
   ostensible, 472
Colouring, *meaning*, 516
   exaggeration, 549
Colourless, *achromatism*, 429
Colours, *standard*, 550
   decoration, 877
Colporteur, *agent*, 758
Colt, *fool*, 501
   horse, 271
Column, *series*, 69
   height, 206
   monument, 551
   cylinder, 249
   procession, 266
   troop, 726
Colure, *universe*, 318
Coma, *insensibility*, 376, 823
   inactivity, 683
Comb, *sharpness*, 253
Combat, *contention*, 720, 722
Combatant, *contention*, 726
Comber, *wave*, 348
Combination, *union*, 48
Combinations, *arithmetical*, 84
   dress, 225

Conjure, *entreat*, 765
  exorcise, 992
Conjure up, *imagine*, 515
Conjurer, *sorcerer*, 994
  adept, 700
Connate, *cause*, 153
  intrinsic, 5
Connatural, *uniform*, 16
  similar, 17
Connect, *relate*, 9
  link, 43
Connection, *kindred*, 11
  link, 45
Connective, *link*, 45
Connive, *overlook*, 460
  concur, 178 :
  allow, 760
Connoisseur, *taste*, 850
  judge, 480
  proficient, 700
Connotation, *indication*, 550
Connubial, *marriage*, 903
Conquer, *success*, 731
Conquered, *failure*, 732
Conquest, *success*, 731
Consanguinity, *kindred*, 11
Conscience, *moral sense*, 926
  knowledge, 490
Conscience-smitten, *penitence*, 950
Conscientious, *virtuous*, 944
  scrupulous, 726A, 939
  true, 494
Consciousness, *intuition*, 450
  knowledge, 490
Conscript, *soldier*, 726
Conscription, *compulsion*, 744
Consecrate, *dedicate*, 873
  sanctify, 987, 995, 998
Consectary, *corollary*, 480
Consecution, *sequence*, 63
Consecutive, *following*, 63
  continuous, 69
Consecutively, *gradually*, 144
Consensus, *agreement*, 23
  assent, 488
Consent, *grant*, 762
  concur, 178
  assent, 488
  agreement, 23
Consentaneous, *agreeing*, 23
  expedient, 646
Consequence, *effect*, 154
  event, 151
  importance, 642
Consequent, *sequence*, 63
Consequential, *arrogant*, 878
  deducible, 467, 478
Consequently, *reasoning*, 154, 476
Conservation, *preservation*, 670
Conservative, *permanence*, 141
Conservatoire, *school*, 542
Conservatory, *store*, 636
  hothouse, 386

Conserve, *sweet*, 396
Consider, *think*, 451
  attend to, 457
  inquire, 461
Considerable, *in degree*, 31
  in size, 192
  important, 642
Considerate, *judicious*, 498
  benevolent, 906
  respectful, 928
Consideration, *motive*, 615
  qualification, 469
  importance, 642
  requital, 973
  respect, 928
Considering, *reasoning*, 476
Consign, *transfer*, 783
  commission, 755
  give, 784
  allot, 786
Consignee, *delegate*, 758
Consignment, *commission*, 755
Consist in, *existence*, 1
Consist of, *composition*, 54
Consistence, *density*, 321
Consistency, *uniformity*, 16
Consistent, *agreement*, 23
Consistory, *council*, 696
  church, 995
Consociation, *sociality*, 892
Console, *relieve*, 834
  pity, 914
  table, 215
  keyboard, 417
Consolidate, *unite*, 46, 48
  condense, 321
Consols, *treasury*, 802
Consonance, *agreement*, 23
  expedience, 646
  music, 413
Consonant, *letter*, 561
Consort, *accompany*, 88
  associate, 892
  spouse, 903
Consort with, *fit*, 646
Consortship, *sociality*, 892
Conspectus, *compendium*, 596
Conspicuous, *visible*, 446
  eminent, 873
Conspiracy, *plot*, 626
Conspire, *concur*, 178
Constable, *governor*, 745
  police, 664
  officer, 965
Constant, *uniformity*, 16
  immutable, 150
  regular, 80, 82
  continuous, 69
  resolute, 604
  true, 494
  faithful, 939
Constantly, *frequently*, 136
Constellation, *stars* 318, 423
  glory, 873
Consternation, *fear*, 860

Constipate, *density*, 321
Constituent, *component*, 54, 56
  voter, 609
Constitute, *compose*, 54, 56
  produce, 161
Constitution, *nature*, 5
  state, 7
  texture, 329
  charter, 924
  law, 963
Constrain, *power*, 157
  restrain, 751
  compel, 744
  abash, 881
Constrict, *narrow*, 203
  contract, 195
Constringe, *narrow*, 203
Construct, *production*, 161
Construction, *form*, 240
  structure, 329
  meaning, 522
Construe, *meaning*, 522
Consubstantiation, *rite*, 998
Consul, *diplomat*, 758
Consult, *advice*, 695
Consume, *destroy*, 162
  waste, 638
  use, 677
  ravage, 649
Consuming, *painful*, 830
Consummate, *great*, 31
  complete, 52, 729
  skill, 698
Consummation, *end*, 67
Consumption, *shrinking*, 195
  waste, 638
  disease, 655
  use, 677
Contact, *contiguity*, 199
  meet, 292
*Contadino, *peasant*, 876
Contagious, *insalubrious*, 657
Contain, *include*, 76
  be composed of, 54
Contaminate, *spoil*, 659
  soil, 653
Contango, *discount*, 813
Contemn, *contempt*, 930
Contemper, *moderation*, 174
Contemplate, *view*, 441
  think, 451
  purpose, 620
  expect, 507
Contemporaneous, *synchronism* 120
Contemporary, *synchronism*, 120
Contempt, *despise*, 930
Contemptible, *unimportant*, 643
Contend, *fight*, 720
  assert, 535
Content, *satisfied*, 827, 831
  calm, 826
  assentient, 488
  patience, 821
  will, 600

Cook, *falsify*, 544
  accounts, 811
Cool, *cold*, 383
  to *refrigerate*, 385
  judicious, 498
  to *moderate*, 174
  to *dissuade*, 616
  to *allay*, 826
  indifferent, 866
  torpid, 826
Cool-headed, *torpid*, 826
  judicious, 498
Cooler, *refrigerator*, 387
  prison, 752
Coolie, *carrier*, 271
Coombe, *valley*, 252
Coon, *black*, 431
Coop, *confine*, 752
  restrain, 751
  abode, 189
Co-operate, *physically*, 178
  voluntarily, 709
Co-operation, *agreement*, 23
Co-operator, *auxiliary*, 711
Co-ordinate, *equality*, 27
  arrange, 60
Cop, *police*, 664
Copal, *semiliquid*, 352
Copartner, *participator*, 778
  associate, 892
  accompanying, 88
Cope, *contend*, 720
  equal, 27
  canonicals, 999
Copia verborum, diffuseness,
      573
  speech, 582
Coping-stone, *completion*, 729
Copious, *abundant*, 639
  style, 573
Copper, *money*, 800
  colour, 439
  police, 664
Copperplate, *engraving*, 558
Coppice, *plant*, 367
Coprology, *impurity*, 653
Copse, *see* Coppice
Copula, *junction*, 45
Copy, *imitation*, 19, 21
  prototype, 22
  to *write*, 590
  represent, 554
Copyholder, *printing*, 591
Copying, *imitating*, 19
Copyist, *writing*, 590
Copyright, *privilege*, 924
Coquetry, *affectation*, 855
Coquette, *flirt*, 902
  vacillate, 605
Cor anglais, musical, 417
Coracle, *boat*, 273
Coral, *ornament*, 847
Coram judice, jurisdiction,
      965
Corbeille, receptacle, 191

Cord *tie*, 45
  filament, 205
  furrow, 259
Cordage, *junction*, 45
Cordial, *grateful*, 829
  warm, 821
  willing, 602
  friendly, 888
  remedy, 662
Cordite, *arms*, 727
Cordon, *outline*, 229, 232
  circular, 247
  badge, 550
Corduroy, *furrow*, 259
Core, *centrality*, 223
  importance, 642
Co-respondent, *divorce*, 905
Corgi, *vehicle*, 272
Coriaceous, *tenacity*, 327
Corinthian, *taste*, 850
Co-rival, *see* Corrival
Cork, *lighthouse*, 320
  plug, 263
Cork up, *closure*, 261
  restrain, 751
Corkscrew, *extractor*, 301
  perforator, 262
  spiral, 248
Cormorant, *gluttony*, 865, 957
Corn, *projection*, 250
Corncob, *tobacco-pipe*, 298A
Cornea, *eye*, 441
Corned, *drunk*, 959
Corneous, *hard*, 323
Corner, *place*, 182
  receptacle, 191
  angularity, 244
Corner-stone, *support*, 215
  to *engross*, 777
  syndicate, 778
Cornet, *music*, 417
  officer, 745
Cornice, *summit*, 210
Cornucopia, *sufficiency*, 639
Cornute, *sharp*, 253
Corollary, *deduction*, 480
  addition, 37, 39
Corona, *circularity*, 247
  light, 420
Coronach, *lamentation*, 839
  funeral, 363
Coronary, *height*, 206
  summit, 210
Coronation, *celebration*, 883
Coronet, *sceptre*, 747
  ornament, 847
Corporal, *officer*, 745
  animality, 364
Corporality, *materiality*, 316
Corporate, *junction*, 43
Corporation, *association*, 712
  convexity, 350
  bulk, 192
Corporeal, *materiality*, 316
Corporeity, *substantiality*, 3

Corps, *assemblage*, 72
Corps, *troops*, 726
Corps de reserve, store, 636
*Corps diplomatique, con-
  signee*, 758
Corpse, *body*, 362
Corpulent, *size*, 192
  broad, 202
Corpus delicti, guilt, 947
Corpuscle, *atom*, 193
  jot, 32
Corradiation, *focus*, 74
Corral, *enclosure*, 232, 752
Correct, *true*, 494
  reason, 476; *order*, 58
  virtuous, 939, 944
  due, 924, 926
  style, 570
  elegant, 578
  undeceive, 529
  to *improve*, 658
  to *censure*, 932
  to *punish*, 972
Corrective, *remedy*, 662
  counteraction, 179
Corregidor, master, 745
Correlation, *relation*, 9
  reciprocity, 12
Correspond, *agree*, 23
  concur, 178
  write, 592
Correspondent, *report*, 527
Corridor, *place*, 191
  passage, 627
Corrie, *hollow*, 252
Corrigible, *improvement*, 658
Corrival, *combatant*, 726
Corrivalry, *contention*, 720
Corrivation, *river*, 348
Corroborant, *remedy*, 662
  assent, 488
Corroborate, *evidence*, 467
Corroboree, *festivity*, 840
Corrode, *erode*, 659
  consume, 649
  afflict, 830
Corrosion, *evil*, 619
Corrosive, *destructive*, 649
Corrugate, *constrict*, 195
  narrow, 203
  rumple, 258
  derange, 61
Corrupt, *foul*, 653
  noxious, 649
  evil, 619
  to *spoil*, 659
  vicious, 945
Corruption, *decomposition*, 49
Corsage, *dress*, 225
Corsair, *thief*, 792
Corse, *corpse*, 362
Corset, *dress*, 225
Corse, arena, 728
Cortège, *suite*, 746
  procession, 266

Cortège, *continuity*, 39, 69
Cortes, *council*, 696
Cortex, *covering*, 222
Corundum, *hardness*, 323
Coruscate, *light*, 420
Corvée, *compulsion*, 744
Corvette, *ship*, 273
Corybantic, *insanity*, 503
Coryphaeus, *leader*, 745
Cosh, *impact*, 276
   arms, 727
Cosmetic, *ornament*, 847
Cosmic, *world*, 318
Cosmogony, *world*, 318
Cosmography, *world*, 318
Cosmonaut, *navigator*, 269
Cosmopolitan, *world-wide*, 78
Cosmopolite, *philanthropy*, 910
Cosmorama, *view*, 448
Cossack, *combatant*, 726
Cosset, *favourite*, 899
Cost, *price*, 812
Costermonger, *merchant*, 797
Costly, *dearness*, 814
Costume, *dress*, 225
Cosy, *comfortable*, 377, 827, 829
Cot, *abode*, 189
Cote, *hut*, 189
Co-tenant, *partner*, 778
Coterie, *party*, 712
   sociality, 892
Cotillion, *amusement*, 840
Cottage, *abode*, 189
Cottar, *inhabitant*, 188
   peasant, 876
Cotton-wool, *softness*, 324
Couch, *bed*, 215
   to lie, 213
   recline, 308
   lie in wait, 530
   express, 566
Couchant, *horizontal*, 213
*Couci-couci, *imperfection*, 651
Cough, *puff*, 349
Couloir, *gully*, 198
Coulter, *sharpness*, 253
Council, *senate*, 696
   ecclesiastical, 995
Counsel, *advice*, 695
Counsellor, *adviser*, 695
   lawyer, 968
Count, *compute*, 85
   expect, 507
   believe, 484
   estimate, 480
   signify, 642
   lord, 875
Countenance, *face*, 234
   favour, 707
   appearance, 448
   to approve, 931
Counter, *contrary*, 14
   against, 179, 708
   retort, 479
   number, 84

Counter, *token*, 550
   table, 215
   shopboard, 799
   to retaliate, 718
Counter-attraction, *dissuasion*,
   616
   avoidance, 623
Counter-claim, *lawsuit*, 969
Counter-evidence, *contrary*, 468
Counter-intelligence, *secret*, 533
Counter-irritant, *counteraction*,
   179
Counter-movement, *regression*,
   283
Counter-order, *abrogation*, 756
Counter-project, *retaliation*, 718
   plan, 626
Counter-revolution, *revolution*,
   146
Counter-stroke, *retaliation*, 718
Counter-subject, *music*, 415
Counter-tenor, *melody*, 413
   high note, 410
Counteract, *physically*, 179
   voluntarily, 708
   hinder, 706
   compensate, 30
Counterbalance, *compensation*,
   30
Counterblast, *counteraction*, 179
   retaliation, 718
Counterchange, *reciprocality*,
   12, 148
Countercharm, *spell*, 993
Countercheck, *hindrance*, 706
Counterfeit, *simulate*, 544, 545
   imitate, 19
   copy, 21
Counterfoil, *check*, 550
Countermand, *abrogation*, 756
Countermarch, *regression*, 283
   journey, 266
Countermark, *indication*, 550
Countermine, *opposition*, 708
Counterpane, *covering*, 222
Counterpart, *copy*, 21
   match, 17
Counterplot, *retaliation*, 718
   plan, 626
Counterpoint, *harmony*, 413
Counterpoise, *compensation*, 30
   weight, 319
Counterpoison, *remedy*, 662
Countersign, *indication*, 550
   assent, 488
Countervail, *compensate*, 28, 30
   oppose, 179, 708
   evidence, 468
Counterweight, *weight*, 319
Counterwork, *opposition*, 708
Countess, *noble*, 875
   chief, 745
Counting-house, *mart*, 799
Countless, *infinity*, 105
Countrified, *rural*, 185

Countrified, *low*, 876
Country, *definite region*, 181, 189
   agriculture, 371
Countryman, *inhabitant*, 185
Counts, *particulars*, 79
County, *region*, 181
   fashionable, 852
Coup, *action*, 680
*Coup de grâce, *death-blow*, 361
   destruction, 162
   completion, 729
   end, 67
   pity, 914
   punishment, 972
*Coup de main, *violence*, 173
   action, 680
*Coup de maître, *skill*, 698
   success, 731
*Coup d'essai, *essay*, 675
*Coup d'état, *action*, 680
   plan, 626
   revolt, 719, 742
*Coup de théâtre, *appearance*,
   448
   ostentation, 882
*Coup d'œil, *vision*, 441
   appearance, 448
Coupé, *vehicle*, 272
Couple, *two*, 89
   to unite, 43
Couplet, *poetry*, 597
Coupon, *money*, 800
   ticket, 550
Courage, *bravery*, 861
Courier, *messenger*, 534
   interpreter, 524
Course, *order*, 58
   continuity, 69
   of time, 109
   layer, 204
   direction, 278
   motion, 264
   locomotion, 266
   effect, 154
   rapidity, 274
   pursuit, 622
   teaching, 537
   plan, 626
   way, 627
   conduct, 692
   arena, 728
   dinner, 298
Courser, *carrier*, 271
   swift, 274
Court, *house*, 189
   hall, 191
   council, 696
   arena, 728
   to invite, 615
   to pursue, 622
   to solicit, 765
   to wish, 865
   to woo, 902
   to flatter, 933
   gentility, 852

Crucify, *painfulness*, 830
   execution, 972
Crude, *unprepared*, 674
   inelegant, 579
Cruel, *painful*, 830
   inhuman, 907
Cruet, *receptacle*, 191
Cruise, *navigation*, 267
Cruiser, *ship*, 273
Crumb, *small part*, 51
   grain, 193
   powder, 330
   bit, 32
Crumble, *pulverize*, 330
   destroy, 162
   diminish, 36
   spoil, 659
   brittleness, 328
Crumple, *ruffle*, 256
   crease, 258
   contract, 195
Crunch, *bruise*, 44
   masticate, 297
   pulverize, 330
Crupper, *rear*, 235
Crusade, *warfare*, 722
Cruse, *vessel*, 191
Crush, *pulverize*, 330
   destroy, 162
   injure, 649
   humiliate, 879
   pain, 828
   contract, 195
   love, 897
Crust, *covering*, 222
   insolence, 885
Crusty, *discourtesy*, 895
Crutch, *support*, 215
   angle, 244
   instrument, 633
Crux, *question*, 461
   mystery, 533
Cry, *animal*, 412
   human, 411
   loudness, 404
   voice, 580
   publish, 531
   weep, 839
Cry down, *disapprove*, 932
Cry for, *desire*, 865
Cry to, *beseech*, 765
Cry up, *praise*, 931
Crypt, *cell*, 191
   hide, 530
   grave, 363
   altar, 1000
Cryptic, *latent*, 526, 528
Cryptogram, *cipher*, 533
Cryptography, *writing*, 590
Crystal-gazing, *prediction*, 511
Crystalline, *dense*, 321
   transparent, 425
Cub, *young*, 129
   clown, 876
Cube, *triality*, 92

Cube, *angularity*, 244
Cubist, *artist*, 559
Cuckold, *divorce*, 905
Cuckoo, *repetition*, 104
   imitation, 19
   cry, 412
   fool, 501
   insane, 503
Cuddle, *caress*, 902
Cuddy, *carrier*, 271
Cudgel, *beat*, 975
   bludgeon, 276, 727
Cue, *hint*, 527
   watchword, 550
   plea, 617
Cuff, *beat*, 276, 972
   dress, 225
*Cui bono, *utility*, 644
Cuirass, *defence*, 717
Cuirassier, *combatant*, 726
Cuisine, *food*, 298
*Cul-de-lampe, *tail-piece*, 67
Cul-de-sac, *concavity*, 252
   closure, 261
   difficulty, 704
*Culbute, *inversion*, 218
   descent, 306
Culinary, *food*, 298
Cull, *choice*, 609
   take, 789
Cullender, *sieve*, 260
Cullion, *wretch*, 941, 949
Cully, *dupe*, 547
Culminate, *maximum*, 33
   height, 206, 210
Culmination, *completion*, 729
Culpability, *guilt*, 947
Culpable, *vice*, 945
Culprit, *sinner*, 949
Cult, *worship*, 990
   rite, 998
Cultivate, *improve*, 658
   sensitiveness, 375
   taste, 850
   till, 371
Culture, *tillage*, 371
   taste, 850
   teaching, 537
   knowledge, 490
Culverin, *arms*, 727
Culvert, *conduit*, 350
*Cum grano salis, *qualify*, 469
   unbelief, 485
Cumber, *load*, 319
   to incommode, 647
   to obstruct, 706
Cummer, *friend*, 891
Cummerbund, *girdle*, 247
Cumshaw, *gift*, 784
Cumulation, *assemblage*, 72
Cumulative, *increase*, 35
   addition, 37
Cumulus, *cloud*, 353
Cunctation, *delay*, 133
   inactivity, 683

Cuneiform, *angular*, 244
   writing, 590
Cunning, *art*, 702
   sagacity, 698
   well-planned, 626
Cup, *hollow*, 252
   vessel, 191
Cupboard, *receptacle*, 191
Cupid, *beauty*, 845
   love, 897
Cupidity, *avarice*, 819
   desire, 865
Cupola, *dome*, 250
   height, 206
Cur, *knave*, 949
Curable, *improvement*, 658
Curacy, *churchdom*, 995
Curate, *clergy*, 996
Curative, *remedial*, 834
Curator, *consignee*, 758
Curb, *restrain*, 751
   hinder, 706
   shackle, 752
   moderate, 174
   check, 826
   dissuade, 616
   counteract, 179
   slacken, 275
Curd, *mass*, 46
   density, 321
   pulp, 354
Curdle, *condense*, 321
   coagulate, 46, 352
Cure, *remedy*, 662, 834
   reinstate, 660
   religious, 995
   preserve, 670
   improve, 656
*Curé, *priest*, 996
Curfew, *evening*, 126
Curio, *toy*, 643
*Curiosa felicitas, *elegance*, 578
Curiosity, *curiosity*, 455
   phenomenon, 872
Curious, *true*, 494
   exceptional, 83
Curl, *bend*, 245, 248
   cockle up, 258
Curlicue, *convolution*, 248
Curliewurlie, *convolution*, 248
Curmudgeon, *parsimony*, 819
Currency, *publicity*, 531
   money, 800
Current, *existing*, 1
   present, 118
   happening, 151
   stream, 347
   river, 348
   wind, 349
   course, 109
   danger, 667
   opinion, 484
   public, 531
   prevailing, 82
*Currente calamo, *diffuseness*,
    573

Dam, *obstruct*, 348, 706
  trifle, 643
Damage, *evil*, 619
  to injure, 649
  to spoil, 659
  payment, 812
Damages, *penalty*, 974
Damascene, *variegate*, 440
Damask, *redness*, 434
Dame, *woman*, 374
  teacher, 540
Damn, *condemn*, 971
  expletive, 908
Damn-all, *nothing*, 4
Damnable, *execrable*, 830
  spoil, 659
Damnify, *damage*, 649
Damnosa hereditas, *burden*, 706
Damp, *moist*, 339
  cold, 386
  to moderate, 174
  to dissuade, 616
  depress, 837
  calm, 826
Damper, *silencer*, 417
Damsel, *youth*, 129
  lady, 374
Dance, *oscillate*, 314
  agitate, 315
  jump, 309
  sport, 840
Dander, *resentment*, 900
  journey, 266
Dandify, *adorn*, 845
  dress, 225
Dandle, *endearment*, 902
Dandruff, *uncleanness*, 653
Dandy, *fop*, 854
Dandyism, *affectation*, 855
Danger, *danger*, 665
Dangle, *hang*, 214
  swing, 314
Dank, *moist*, 339
Dapper, *thin*, 203
  elegant, 845
Dapple, *brown*, 433
Dappled, *variegation*, 440
Darbies, *fetter*, 752
Dare, *defy*, 715
  face danger, 861
Dare-devil, *rashness*, 863
  blusterer, 887
Darg, *work*, 625
Daring, *courage*, 861
Dark, *obscure*, 421
  dim, 422
  invisible, 447
  unintelligible, 519
  mysterious, 528
  ignorant, 491
  blind, 442
  latent, 526
Darkie, *black*, 431
Darling, *favourable*, 899

Darling, *beloved*, 897
Darn, *improve*, 658
Dart, *missile*, 727
  to propel, 284
  swift, 274
Darwinism, *causation*, 153
Dash, *sprinkling*, 32, 193
  to mix, 41
  throw down, 308
  display, 882
  depress, 837
  shine, 873
  mark, 550
  expletive, 908
  velocity, 274
  energy, 171
  vivacity, 682
  gift, 784
Dash off, *sketch*, 556
Dash out, *rush*, 274
  haste, 684
Dashing, *brave*, 861
  snarl, 845
  fashionable, 852
Dastard, *coward*, 862
Data, *evidence*, 467
  reasoning, 476
Date, *chronometry*, 114
  party, 892
Daub, *cover*, 222
  dirt, 653
  bad painting, 555
  to deform, 846
Daughter, *posterity*, 167
Daunt, *frighten*, 860
Dauntless, *courage*, 861
Davenport, *receptacle*, 191
  support, 215
Dawdle, *slow*, 275
  tardy, 133
  inactive, 683
Dawn, *morning*, 125
  precursor, 116
  to begin, 66
  dim, 422
  glimpse, 490
Day, *period*, 108
  light, 420
Day-book, *list*, 86
  record, 551
  accounts, 811
Day-dream, *imagination*, 515
  hope, 858
  inattention, 458
Day-labourer, *workman*, 690
Day of Judgment, *end*, 67
Daybreak, *morning*, 125
  dim, 422
  beginning, 66
Daylight, *light*, 420
  publicity, 531
Dayspring, *morning*, 125
Daze, *light*, 420
  confuse, 442
  stupefy, 823

Dazzle, *light*, 420
  confuse, 442
De bon cœur, *willingly*, 602
De facto, *existence*, 1
  truth, 494
De haut en bas, *contempt*, 930
De jure, *right*, 922
  legal, 963
  dueness, 924
De novo, *repetition*, 104
  frequency, 136
De omnibus rebus, *multiformity*, 81
De Profundis, *worship*, 990
De règle, *rule*, 80
De rigueur, *rule*, 80
De trop, *redundance*, 641
Deacon, *clergy*, 996
Dead, *lifeless*, 360
  inert, 172
  insensible, 376, 823
  colourless, 429
Dead-beat, *fatigue*, 688
  weak, 160
Dead-drunk, *drunkenness*, 959
Dead heat, *equality*, 27
Dead weight, *hindrance*, 706
Deaden, *weaken*, 158, 160
  moderate, 174, 826
  benumb, 823
Deadfall, *trap*, 667
Deadlock, *stoppage*, 265
  hindrance, 706
Deadly, *mortal*, 361, 657
  destructive, 162
  pernicious, 649
Deadness, *numbness*, 381
  inertness, 172, 823
Deaf, *deafness*, 419
Deafening, *loud*, 404
Deal, *quantity*, 31
  mingle, 41
  give, 784
  allot, 786
  barter, 794
Deal out, *distribute*, 73, 784
Dealer, *merchant*, 797
Dealings, *action*, 680
Dean, *clergy*, 996
Deanery, *office*, 995
  house, 1000
Dear, *loved*, 897, 899
  high-priced, 814
Dear-bought, *worthless*, 645
Dearth, *insufficiency*, 640
Death, *death*, 360
Death-blow, *end*, 67
  killing, 361
  failure, 732
Deathless, *perpetuity*, 112
  celebrated, 873
Deathlike, *hideous*, 846
  silence, 403
Debacle, *river*, 348
  descent, 306

Debacle, *destruction*, 162
Debag, *divest*, 226
Debar, *prohibit*, 761
   hinder, 751
   exclude, 77
Debark, *arrive*, 292
Debase, *depress*, 308
   deteriorate, 659
   foul, 653
   vicious, 945
Debatable, *uncertain*, 475
Debate, *reason*, 476
   dispute, 713, 720
   hesitate, 605
   talk, 508
Debauch, *spoil*, 659
   vice, 945
   intemperance, 954
   impurity, 961
Debenture, *certificate*, 551
   security, 771
   credit, 805
Debility, *weakness*, 160
Debit, *debt*, 806
   accounts, 811
Debonair, *cheerfulness*, 836
Debouch, *march out*, 292
   flow out, 295, 348
Debrett, *list*, 86
Debris, *part*, 51
   pulverulence, 330
   unimportance, 643
Debt, *debt*, 806
Debtor, *debt*, 806
Debus, *arrival*, 292
Début, *beginning*, 66
Decade, *number*, 98
   period, 108
   duration, 106
Decadence, *deterioration*, 659
Decadent, *feeble*, 575
Decagon, *number*, 98
   angularity, 244
Decahedron, *ten*, 98
Decalogue, *duty*, 926
Decamp, *move off*, 287, 293
   escape, 671
Decant, *transfer to*, 270
Decanter, *receptacle*, 191
Decapitate, *kill*, 361, 972
Decay, *spoil*, 659
   disease, 655
   shrivel, 195
   decrease, 36
Decayed, *imperfect*, 651
   old, 124
   adversity, 735
Decease, *death*, 360
Deceit, *deception*, 544, 545
Deceiver, *deceiver*, 548
Decent, *modest*, 960
   tolerable, 651
   seemly, 926
   right, 922
Decentralize, *disperse*, 73

Deception, *deception*, 545
   sophistry, 477
Decide, *judge*, 480
   choose, 609
   make certain, 474
   cause, 153
Decided, *resolved*, 604
   positive, 535
   certain, 475
   great, 31
Deciduous, *transitory*, 111
   falling, 306
   spoiled, 659
Decimal, *number*, 84, 98
Decimate, *subduct*, 38, 103
   kill, 361
Decipher, *interpret*, 522
   solve, 462
Decision, *intention*, 620
   conclusion, 480
   resolution, 604
   verdict, 969
Decisive, *final*, 67
   evidence, 467
   resolution, 604
   demonstration, 478
Decivilize, *brutalize*, 895
Deck, *floor*, 211
   to beautify, 845
Declaim, *speech*, 582
Declamatory, *florid*, 577
Declare, *assert*, 535
   inform, 516, 527
Declension, *descent*, 306
   deterioration, 659
   grammar, 567
   intrinsicality, 5
Decline, *decrease*, 36
   descent, 306
   weaken, 160
   decay, 735
   disease, 655
   become worse, 659
   reject, 610
   refuse, 764
   be unwilling, 603
   grammar, 567
Declivity, *obliquity*, 217
Decoction, *calefaction*, 384
Decode, *interpret*, 522
Decollate, *punishment*, 972
Decoloration, *achromatism*, 429
Decompose, *decomposition*,
               49, 653
Decomposite, *combination*, 48
Decompound, *combination*, 48
Deconsecrate, *cancel*, 756
Decontamination, *cleanness*,
               652
Decorate, *embellish*, 845, 847
Decoration, *repute*, 873
   title, 877
   insignia, 747
Decorous, *decent*, 960
   befitting, 922

Decorticate, *divest*, 226
Decorum, *politeness*, 852
   respect, 928
   purity, 960
Decoy, *entice*, 615
   deceive, 545
   deceiver, 548
Decrease, *in degree*, 36
   in size, 195
Decree, *law*, 963
   judgment, 969
   order, 741
Decrement, *deduction*, 38
Decrepit, *old*, 124, 128
   weak, 160
   frail, 651
Decrepitude, *age*, 128
   feebleness, 160
*Decrescendo, *decrease*, 36, 415
Decretal, *law*, 963
   order, 741
Decry, *depreciate*, 483
   censure, 932
   defame, 934
Decumbent, *horizontality*, 213
Decuple, *number*, 98
Decurrent, *descent*, 306
Decursive, *descent*, 306
Decussation, *crossing*, 219
Dedicate, *consecrate*, 873
Deduce, *infer*, 480
   retrench, 38
Deducible, *evidence*, 467,
             478, 480
Deduct, *retrench*, 38
   deprive, 789
Deduction, *abatement*, 813
   decrease, 36
   reasoning, 476
Deed, *act*, 680
   record, 467, 551
   security, 771
Deem, *belief*, 484
Deep, *profound*, 208, 451
   the sea, 341
   cunning, 702
   prudent, 498
   feeling, 821
   sound, 404; *colour*, 428
   greatness, 31
Deep-mouthed, *loud*, 404
Deep-rooted, *fixed*, 150
Deep-seated, *interior*, 221
   deep, 208
Deep-toned, *resonant*, 408
Deepie, *cinema*, 599A
Deface, *render ugly*, 846
   injure, 659
   destroy form, 241
Defacement, *blemish*, 848
Defalcation, *default*, 304
   contraction, 195
   incompleteness, 53
   insufficiency, 640
   non-payment, 808

Defame, *detract*, 934
  shame, 874; *censure*, 932
Defamer, *detractor*, 936
Default, *insufficiency*, 640
  shortcoming, 304
  non-payment, 806, 808
Defaulter, *debtor*, 806
Defeat, *to confute*, 479
  master, 731; *failure*, 732
Defecate, *clean*, 652
  improve, 658
Defect, *incomplete*, 53
  imperfect, 651
  failing, 945
  to desert, 124
Defection, *disobedience*, 742
  disloyalty, 940
Defective, *incomplete*, 53
  imperfect, 651
  insufficient, 640
Defence, *resistance*, 717
  vindication, 937
  safety, 664
Defenceless, *weak*, 158, 160
  exposed, 665
Defendant, *judge*, 967
  accusation, 938
Defer, *put off*, 133
Defer to, *respect*, 928
  assent, 488
Deference, *subordination*, 743
  submission, 725
  respect, 928
Defiance, *daring*, 715
  threat, 909
Deficiency, *inferiority*, 34
  blemish, 848
  frailty, 945
Deficient, *incomplete*, 53
  imperfect, 651
  insufficient, 640
  inferior, 34
  witless, 499
  insane, 502
Deficit, *debt*, 806
Defile, *ravine*, 198, 203
  march, 266
  dirt, 653
  spoil, 659
  shame, 874
  debauch, 961
Define, *name*, 564
  explain, 522
Definite, *exact*, 494
  special, 79
  visible, 446
  limited, 233
  intelligible, 518
Definitely, *assent*, 488
Definitive, *decided*, 535
  final, 67
Deflagration, *calefaction*, 384
Deflate, *contract*, 195
Deflection, *curvature*, 245
  deviation, 279

Defloration, *impurity*, 961
  soil, 653
Defluxion, *river*, 348
Deform, *deface*, 241, 846
Deformity, *blemish*, 848
Defraud, *cheat*, 545
  non-payment, 808
Defray, *pay*, 807
Defrost, *melt*, 384
Deft, *clever*, 698
  suitable, 23
Defunct, *dead*, 360
Defy, *dare*, 715
  disobey, 742
  threaten, 909
*Dégagé, *freedom*, 748
  fashion, 825
Degenerate, *deterioration*, 659
  vice, 945
Deglutition, *swallowing*, 296
Degradation, *shame*, 874
  dishonour, 940
  deterioration, 659
Degree, *quantity*, 26
  term, 71
  honour, 873
Degustation, *taste*, 390
Dehortation, *dissuasion*, 616
  advice, 695
  warning, 668
Dehumanize, *brutalize*, 895
Dehydrate, *dry*, 340
  preserve, 670
De-ice, *melt*, 384
*Dei gratiâ, *dueness*, 924
Deification, *heaven*, 981
  idolatory, 991
  honour, 873
Deign, *condescend*, 879
  consent, 762
Deiseal, *rotation*, 312
Deism, *irreligion*, 989
  heresy, 984A
Deity, *deity*, 976
  great spirit, 979
Dejection, *sadness*, 828, 837, 841
*Déjeuner, *food*, 298
Dekko, *look*, 441
*Délâbrement, *deterioration*, 659
Delation, *accusation*, 938
Delay, *lateness*, 133
  protraction, 110
  slowness, 275
Dele, *obliteration*, 552
Delectable, *savoury*, 394
  agreeable, 829
Delectation, *pleasure*, 827
Delegate, *consignee*, 758, 759
  to commission, 755
Deleterious, *pernicious*, 649
  unwholesome, 657
Deletion, *obliteration*, 552
Deliberate, *think*, 451
  cautious, 864

Deliberate, *slow*, 275
  leisurely, 685
  advised, 620, 695
Deliberately, *slowly*, 133
  designedly, 600, 611
Delicacy, *of texture*, 329
  slenderness, 203
  weak, 160
  sickly, 655
  savoury, 394
  dainty, 298
  of taste, 850
  fastidiousness, 868
  exactness, 494
  pleasing, 829
  beauty, 845
  honour, 939
  purity, 960
  difficulty, 704
  scruple, 603, 616
Delicatessen, *food*, 298
Delicious, *taste*, 394
  pleasing, 829
Delight, *pleasure*, 827
Delightful, *pleasureableness*, 829
Delilah, *temptress*, 615
Delimit, *circumscribe*, 231
Delineate, *describe*, 594
  represent, 554
*Delineavit, *painting*, 556
Delinquency, *guilt*, 947
Delinquent, *sinner*, 949
Deliquescent, *liquid*, 333
*Deliquium, *weakness*, 160
  fatigue, 688
Delirium, *raving*, 503
  passion, 825
Delirium tremens, *drunkenness*, 959
Delitescence, *latency*, 526
Deliver, *transfer*, 270
  give, 784
  liberate, 750
  relieve, 834
  utter, 582
  rescue, 672
  escape, 671
Dell, *concavity*, 252
Delouse, *disinfect*, 652
Delta, *land*, 342
Delude, *deceive*, 495, 545
Deluge, *flow*, 337, 348
  redundance, 641
  multitude, 72
Delusion, *error*, 495
  deceit, 545
Delve, *dig*, 252
  cultivate, 371
  depth, 208
Demagogue, *leader*, 745
  director, 694
  agitator, 742
Demagogy, *authority*, 737
Demand, *claim*, 924
  ask, 765

Depuratory, *remedy,* 662
Depute, *commission,* 755
Deputy, *substitute,* 147, 634, 759
  jurisdiction, 965
Derangement, *mental,* 503
  physical, 61
  disorder, 59
Derelict, *solitary,* 893
Dereliction, *relinquishment,*
  624, 782
  guilt, 947
Derequisition, *restore,* 790
Deride, *ridicule,* 856
  disrespect, 929
  contempt, 930
  trifle with, 643
  scoff, 483
Derisive, *ridiculous,* 853
Derivation, *origin,* 153
  verbal, 562
Derivative, *effect,* 154
Derive, *attribute,* 155
  receive, 785
  acquire, 775
  income, 810
Dermal, *covering,* 222
*Dernier cri, *fashion,* 852
  newness, 123
*Dernier ressort, *plan,* 626
Derogate, *detract,* 483, 934
  demean, 940
  shame, 874
Derrick, *raise,* 307
Derring-do, *courage,* 861
Derringer, *arms,* 727
Dervish, *clergy,* 996
Descale, *clean,* 652
Descant, *dissert,* 595
  dwell upon, 584
  diffuseness, 573
Descendant, *posterity,* 167
Descent, *slope,* 217
  motion downwards, 306
  order, 58
Describe, *set forth,* 594
Description, *kind,* 75
  narration, 594
Descry, *vision,* 441
Desecrate, *misuse,* 679
  profane, 988
Desert, *solitude,* 101, 893
  waste, 645
  merit, 944
  to relinquish, 624
  to escape, 671
Deserter, *apostate,* 607
  coward, 862
Desertless, *vice,* 945
Deserve, *merit,* 944
  right, 922, 924
*Déshabillé, see Dishabille
Desiccate, *dryness,* 340
Desiderate, *desire,* 865
  require, 630
Desideratum, *desire,* 865

Desideratum, *inquiry,* 461
  requirement, 630
Design, *intention,* 620
  cunning, 702
  plan, 626
  delineation, 554
  prototype, 22
Designate, *specify,* 79, 564
Designation, *kind,* 75
Designed, *intended,* 600
Designer, *artist,* 559, 626
Designing, *false,* 544
  artful, 702
Desirable, *expedient,* 646
Desire, *longing,* 865
Desist, *discontinue,* 142
  relinquish, 624
  inaction, 681
Desk, *support,* 215
  receptacle, 191
Desolate, *alone,* 87
  secluded, 893
  afflicted, 828
  to ravage, 162
Desolation, *evil,* 619
*Désorienté, *ignorance,* 491
Despair, *hopelessness,* 859
  dejection, 837
Despatch, *see* Dispatch
Desperado, *rashness,* 863
Desperate, *great,* 31
  violent, 173
  rash, 863
  difficult, 704
  impossible, 471
Desperation, *hopelessness,* 859
Despicable, *shameful,* 874
  contemptible, 930
  trifling, 643
Despise, *contemn,* 930
  deride, 483, 929
Despite, *notwithstanding,*
  179, 708
  malevolence, 907
Despoil, *take,* 789
  rob, 791
  hurt, 649
Despondency, *sadness,* 837
  fear, 860
  despair, 859
Despot, *master,* 745
Despotism, *arbitrariness,* 964
  authority, 737
  severity, 739
Desquamation, *divestment,* 226
Dessert, *food,* 298
Destination, *fate,* 152, 601
  arrival, 292
  intention, 620
Destiny, *fate,* 601
  chance, 152
Destitute, *insufficient,* 640
  poor, 804
Destrier, *carrier,* 271
Destroy, *demolish,* 162

Destroy, *injure,* 649
  deface, 241
Destroyed, *inexistence,* 2
Destroyer, *ship,* 273
Destruction, *demolition,*
  162, 732
  evil, 619
Destructive, *hurtful,* 649
Desuetude, *disuse,* 614, 678
Desultory, *discontinuous,* 70
  irregular in time, 139
  disordered, 59
  multiform, 81
  deviating, 149, 279
  agitated, 315
Detach, *separate,* 10, 44, 47
Detached, *irrelated,* 10, 47
  indifferent, 456
  unity, 87
Detachment, *part,* 51
  army, 726
Detail, *to describe,* 594
  special portion, 79
Detain, *retention,* 781
Detection, *discovery,* 480A
Detective, *inquiry,* 461
Detention, *retention,* 781
  imprisonment, 751
*Détenu, *prisoner,* 754
Deter, *dissuasion,* 616
  fear, 860
Detergent, *remedy,* 662
  remedial, 656
  cleanness, 652
Deteriorate, *deterioration,* 659
Determinate, *special,* 79
  exact, 474
  resolute, 604
Determination, *resolution,* 604
  will, 600
  judgment, 480
Determine, *find out,* 480A
  intend, 620
  direction, 278
  make certain, 474
  cause, 153
  resolve, 604
  designate, 79
Determinism, *necessity,* 601
Deterrent, *restraint,* 616
Detersive, *cleanness,* 652
Detest, *hate,* 867, 898
Detestable, *bad,* 649, 867
Dethrone, *abrogation,* 756
Dethronement, *anarchy,* 738
Detonate, *sound,* 406
  explode, 173
Detonator, *signal,* 550
Detour, *circuit,* 629
  curvature, 245
  deviation, 279
Detract, *subduct,* 38
  depreciate, 483
  censure, 932
  slander, 934

Detractor, *slanderer*, 936
Detrain, *arrival*, 292
Detriment, *evil*, 619
Detrimental, *hurtful*, 649
Detritus, *part*, 51
   pulverulence, 330
Detrude, *cast out*, 297
   cast down, 308
Detruncation, *subduction*, 38
   disjunction, 44
Deuce, *duality*, 89
   demon, 980
Deuced, *great*, 31
*Deus ex machina, *helper*,
          707, 711
   wonder-worker, 994
Deuterogamy, *marriage*, 903
Devastate, *destroy*, 162
   injure, 649
Devastation, *havoc*, 659
Develop, *cause*, 153
   produce, 161
   increase, 35
   expand, 194
   evolve, 313
Development, *effect*, 154
Deviate, *differ*, 15
   vary, 20
   change, 140
   turn, 279
   diverge, 291
   circuit, 629
   bend, 245
Deviationist, *revolutionary*, 146
   dissent, 489
Device, *expedient*, 626
   instrument, 633
   motto, 550
Devices, *inclination*, 602
Devil, *Satan*, 978
   maleficent being, 913
   mediate, 631
   culprit, 949
   seasoned food, 392
Devil-may-care, *rash*, 863
Devilish, *great*, 31
   bad, 649
   hell, 982
Devilry, (or Deviltry), *evil*, 619
   cruelty, 907
   wickedness, 945
   sorcery, 992
Devious, *deviating*, 245, 279
   different, 15
Devise, *plan*, 620, 626
   imagine, 515
   bequeath, 784
Devitalize, *empty*, 640
   absent, 187
   not having, 776
*Devoir, *courtesy*, 894
Devolution, *delegation*, 755
Devolve, *transfer*, 783
Devolve on, *duty*, 926
Devote, *attention*, 457

Devote, *curse*, 908
   employ, 677
   consecrate, 873
Devoted, *loving*, 897
   friendly, 888
   doomed, 152, 735, 828
Devotee, *pious*, 987
   resolute, 604
   enthusiast, 682, 840
Devotion, *piety*, 987
   worship, 990
   respect, 928
   love, 897
   obedience, 743
   disinterestedness, 942
Devour, *eat*, 296
   gluttony, 957
   destroy, 162
Devout, *pious*, 897
Dew, *moisture*, 339
Dew-pond, *lake*, 343
Dexter, *right*, 238
Dexterous, *skill*, 698
Dey, *master*, 745
Dhow, *ship*, 273
Diablerie, *sorcery*, 992
Diabolic, *malevolent*, 907
   wicked, 945
   bad, 649
   satanic, 978
Diacoustics, *sound*, 402
Diacritical, *distinctive*, 550
Diadem, *regalia*, 747
   ornament, 847
Diagnostic, *intrinsicality*, 5
   speciality, 79
   discrimination, 465
Diagonal, *oblique*, 217
Diagram, *representation*, 554
Diagraph, *imitation*, 19
Dial, *clock*, 114
   face, 234, 448
Dialect, *neology*, 563
Dialectic, *argumentation*, 476
   language, 560
Dialogue, *interlocution*, 588
Diameter, *breadth*, 202
Diamond, *lozenge*, 244
   arena, 728
   gem, 650
   ornament, 847
   hardness, 323
Diana, *goddess*, 979
Diapason, *melody*, 413
Diaper, *reticulation*, 219
Diaphanous, *transparent*, 425
Diaphoresis, *excretion*, 298
Diaphoretic, *remedy*, 662
Diaphragm, *partition*, 228
   middle, 68
Diarchy, *authority*, 737
Diary, *record*, 551
   journal, 114
Diastole, *expansion*, 194
   pulse, 314

Diathermancy, *calefaction*, 384
Diathesis, *state*, 7
   habit, 613
   affections, 820
Diatonic, *harmony*, 413
Diatribe, *disapprobation*, 932
Dibble, *perforator*, 262
   cultivate, 371
Dibs, *money*, 800
Dice, *chance*, 156
Dichotomy, *bisection*, 91
   angularity, 244
Dichroism, *variegation*, 440
Dick, *detective*, 461
   police, 664
Dicker, *barter*, 794
   interchange, 148
Dicky, *seat*, 215
Dictaphone, *hearing*, 418
Dictate, *command*, 741
   authority, 737
   enjoin, 615
   write, 590
Dictator, *master*, 745
Dictatorial, *severe*, 739
   insolent, 885
Dictatorship, *authority*, 737
Diction, *style*, 569
Dictionary, *word*, 562
Dictum, *maxim*, 496
   affirmation, 535
   command, 741
Didactic, *teaching*, 537
Diddle, *deception*, 545
   swindle, 791
Dido, *leap*, 309
   prank, 840
   foolery, 497
   caprice, 608
Die, *chance*, 156
   mould, 22
   expire, 2, 360
   cease, 142
Die for, *desire*, 865
Die-hard, *obstinacy*, 606
*Dies non, *never*, 107
   repose, 687
Diet, *food*, 298
   remedy, 662
   council, 696
Dietetics, *remedy*, 662
Differ, *dissent*, 489
Difference, *difference*, 15
   inequality, 28
   dissimilarity, 18
   discord, 713
   numerical, 84
Differential, *number*, 84
Differentiation, *numeration*, 85
   difference, 15
   discrimination, 465
   fastidiousness, 868
*Difficile, *troublesome*, 704
Difficult, *fastidious*, 868
Difficulty, *hardness*, 704

Disaster, *calamity*, 830
Disavow, *negation*, 536
  retract, 607
Disband, *disperse*, 73
  separate, 44
Disbar, *punish*, 972
  dismiss, 756
Disbelief, *doubt*, 485
  religious, 988
Disbench, *punish*, 972
  dismiss, 756
Disbranch, *disjunction*, 44
Disburden, *facilitate*, 705
  disclose, 529
Disburse, *expend*, 809
Disc, *see* Disk
Discard, *dismiss*, 624, 756
  disuse, 678
  refuse, 764
  thought, 452
  repudiate, 773
  relinquish, 782
Discern, *behold*, 441
Discernible, *visibility*, 446
Discerning, *wisdom*, 498
Discernment, *wisdom*, 498
  discrimination, 465
Discerption, *disjunction*, 44
Discharge, *emit*, 297
  sound, 406
  violence, 173
  propel, 284
  excrete, 299
  flow, 348
  duty, 926
  acquit oneself, 692
  observe, 772
  pay, 807
  exempt, 927A
  accomplish, 729
  liberate, 750
  forget, 506
  acquit, 970
Disciple, *learner*, 541
Disciplinarian, *master*, 540
  martinet, 739
Discipline, *order*, 58
  teaching, 537
  training, 673
  restraint, 751
  punishment, 972
  religious, 990
Disclaim, *deny*, 536
  refuse, 764
  repudiate, 756
  abjure, 757
Disclose, *disclosure*, 529
Discoid, *horizontally*, 213
Discolour, *achromatism*, 429
  to stain, 846
Discomfit, *success*, 731
Discomfiture, *failure*, 732
Discomfort, *pain*, 378, 828
Discommendation, *blame*, 932
Discommodious, *inutility*, 645

Discommodious, *hindrance*, 706
Discommodity, *inexpedience*,
                              647
Discompose, *derange*, 61
  hinder, 706
  put out, 458
  to vex, 830
  disconcert, 874
  provoke, 900
Discomposure, *pain*, 828
Disconcert, *hinder*, 706
  frustrate, 731
  disappoint, 509
  distract, 458
  confuse, 874
Disconcerted, *inattention*, 458
Disconformity, *disagreement*,
                              24
Discongruity, *disagreement*, 24
Disconnect, *disjunction*, 44
  irrelation, 10
Disconnected, *confused*, 519
Disconsolate, *sad*, 837
  grief, 828
Discontent, *dissatisfaction*, 832
Discontented, *pain*, 828
Discontinuance, *cessation*, 142
Discontinue, *interrupt*, 70
  relinquish, 624
Discord, *disagreement*, 24
  dissension, 713
  musical, 414
Discordance, *incongruity*, 24
  sound, 410
  dissent, 489
Discount, *abatement*, 813
  deduction, 38
  to anticipate, 673
  disregard, 460, 483
  qualify, 469
Discountenance, *refuse*, 764
  disfavour, 706
  rudeness, 895
Discourage, *dissuade*, 616
  sadden, 837
  disfavour, 706
  fear, 860
Discourse, *talk*, 588
  speech, 582
  dissert, 595
Discourtesy, *rudeness*, 895
Discover, *perceive*, 441
  find, 480A
  solve, 462
Discredit, *disbelief*, 485
  dishonour, 874
Discreditable, *vice*, 945
Discreet, *careful*, 459
  cautious, 864
  prudent, 498
  clever, 698
Discrepancy, *disagreement*, 24
  discord, 713
Discrete, *separate*, 44
  single, 87

Discretion, *wisdom*, 498
  foresight, 510
  caution, 864
  skill, 698
  courtesy, 894
  will, 600
  care, 459
  choice, 609
Discrimination, *distinction*, 465
  difference, 15
  taste, 850
  fastidiousness, 868
  wisdom, 498
Disculpate, *vindicate*, 937
Discursive, *moving*, 264
  migratory, 266
  wandering, 279
  style, 573
  chatty, 588
  dissertation, 595
Discus, *missile*, 284
Discuss, *reason*, 476
  inquire, 461
  reflect, 451
  treat of, 595
  eat, 296
Disdain, *contempt*, 930
  indifference, 866
  fastidiousness, 868
Disdainful, *proud*, 878
Disease, *illness*, 655
Disembark, *arrive*, 292
Disembarrass, *facilitate*, 705
Disembodied, *immaterial*, 317
Disembody, *decompose*, 49
  disperse, 73
Disembogue, *flow out*, 348
  emit, 295
Disembowel, *extraction*, 300
  disjunction, 44
Disenable, *impotence*, 158
Disenchant, *dissuade*, 616
Disencumber, *facility*, 705
Disendow, *taking*, 789
  cancel, 756
Disengage, *detach*, 44
  facilitate, 705
  liberate, 750, 768A
Disentangle, *separate*, 44
  arrange, 60
  facilitate, 705
  unfold, 313
  decipher, 522
Disenthral, *liberate*, 750
Disentitled, *undueness*, 925
Disestablish, *displace*, 185
  cancel, 756
Disesteem, *disrespect*, 929
  censure, 932
Disfavour, *hate*, 898
  disrepute, 874
  to oppose, 708
Disfeature, *deface*, 241
  deform, 846
Disfigure, *deface*, 241, 659

Disfigure, *deform*, 846
  blemish, 848
Disfranchise, *disentitle*, 925
Disgorge, *emit*, 297
  restore, 790
  flow out, 348
Disgrace, *shame*, 874
  dishonour, 940
Disguise, *conceal*, 528
  falsify, 544
  deceive, 545
  mask, 530
  untruth, 546
Disguised, *in liquor*, 959
Disgust, *dislike*, 867
  hatred, 898
  offensive, 830
  weary, 841
  taste, 395
Dish, *plate*, 191
  food, 299
  upset, 162
  to foil, 731
Dishabille, *undress*, 225
  unprepared, 674
  simplicity, 849
Dishearten, *dissuade*, 616
  deject, 837
Dished, *failure*, 732
Dishevelled, *loose*, 47
  disordered, 61
  intermixed, 219
  twisted, 248
Dishonest, *false*, 544
  faithless, 940
Dishonour, *baseness*, 940
  to repudiate a bill, 808
  disrespect, 929
  disrepute, 874
Disillusion, *dissuasion*, 616
Disimprove, *deteriorate*, 659
Disincentive, *check*, 616
Disincline, *dissuade*, 616
Disinclined, *unwilling*, 603
  disliking, 867
Disinfect, *purify*, 652
  improve, 658
Disinfectant, *remedy*, 662
Disingenuous, *false*, 544
  dishonourable, 940
Disinherit, *transfer*, 783
Disintegrate, *separate*, 44
  decompose, 49
  pulverize, 330
Disinter, *exhume*, 363
  discover, 480A, 525
Disinterested, *unselfish*, 942
Disjoin, *loosen*, 44
Disjointed, *loosened*, 44
  in disorder, 59
Disjunction, *incoherence*, 47
  decomposition, 49
Disk, *face*, 234
  exterior, 220
Dislike, *distaste*, 867

Dislike, *disapproval*, 932
  hate, 898
  enmity, 889
  reluctance, 603
Dislocate, *loosen*, 44
  derange, 61
Dislodge, *displace*, 185
Disloyal, *improbity*, 940
Dismal, *dejection*, 837
  dullness, 843
Dismantle, *destroy*, 162
  disuse, 678
  despoil, 649
  injure, 659
  divest, 226
Dismast, *disuse*, 678
  dismantle, 659, 674
Dismay, *fear*, 860
Dismember, *loosen*, 44
Dismiss, *discard*, 678, 756, 782
  eject, 297
  liberate, 750
Dismount, *descend*, 306
  arrive, 292
  disable, 674
Disobey, *disobedience*, 742
Disobliging, *malevolent*, 907
Disorder, *confusion*, 59
  to derange, 61
  disease, 655
Disorderly, *violent*, 173
Disorganize, *derange*, 61
  destroy, 162
  spoil, 659
Disown, *negation*, 536
Disparage, *depreciate*, 483
  disrespect, 929
  censure, 932
Disparate, *different*, 15
  dissimilar, 18
  single, 87
  disagreeing, 24
  unequal, 28
Disparity, *dissimilarity*, 18
Dispart, *disjoin*, 44
Dispassionate, *calm*, 826
Dispatch, *speed*, 274
  activity, 682
  haste, 684
  earliness, 132
  to conduct, 692
  complete, 729
  kill, 162, 361
  eat, 296
  epistle, 592
  intelligence, 532
Dispatch-box, *receptacle*, 191
Dispatch-case, *receptacle*, 191
Dispel, *destroy*, 162
  scatter, 73
Dispensable, *disuse*, 678
Dispensation, *licence*, 760
  calamity, 830
Dispense, *exempt*, 927A
  permit, 760

Dispense, *disuse*, 678
  relinquish, 624
  give, 784
  allot, 786
  disperse, 73
  retail, 796
Dispeople, *seclusion*, 893
Disperse, *scatter*, 73, 638
  separate, 44
  diverge, 291
Dispersion, *removal*, 270
Dispirit, *sadden*, 837
  discourage, 616
Displace, *remove*, 185
  transfer, 270
  derange, 61
Display, *show*, 525
  appear, 448
  parade, 882
Displease, *painfulness*, 830
Displeasure, *pain*, 828
  anger, 900
Displosion, *violence*, 173
Disport, *amusement*, 840
Dispose, *arrange*, 60
  prepare, 673
  tend, 176
  induce, 615
Dispose of, *sell*, 796
  give, 784
  relinquish, 782
  use, 677
Disposition, *order*, 58
  arrangement, 60
  inclination, 602
  mind, 820
Dispossess, *take away*, 789
  transfer, 783
Dispossessed, *deprived*, 776
Dispraise, *disapprove*, 932
Disprize, *depreciate*, 483
Disproof, *counter-evidence*, 468
  confutation, 479
Disproportion, *irrelation*, 10
  disagreement, 24
Disprove, *confute*, 479
Disputant, *debater*, 476
  combatant, 726
Disputatious, *irritable*, 901
Dispute, *discord*, 713
  denial, 485, 536
  discussion, 476
Disqualified, *incapacitated*, 158
  incompetent, 699
Disqualify, *incapacitate*, 158
  weaken, 160
  disentitle, 925
  unprepared, 674
Disquiet, *excitement*, 825
  uneasiness, 149, 828
  to give pain, 830
Disquietude, *apprehension*, 860
Disquisition, *dissertation*, 595
Disregard, *overlook*, 458
  neglect, 460, 927

Divorce, *separation,* 44
Divulge, *disclose,* 529
Divulsion, *disjoin,* 44
Dizzard, *fool,* 501
Dizzy, *confused,* 458
   vertigo, 503
   foolish, 499
Djinn, *demon,* 980
Do, *act,* 680
   fare, 7
   produce, 161
   suffice, 639
   complete, 729
   cheat, 545
Do away with, *remove,* 185, 678
   destroy, 162, 681
Do for, *injure,* 659
   defeat, 731
   kill, 361
   suit, 646
   punish, 972
Do in, *kill,* 361
Do into, *interpret,* 522
Do-nothing, *inactivity,* 683
Do over, *cover,* 222
Do up, *repair,* 658
   pack, 72
Doch-an-doris, *departure,* 293
   intoxicant, 959
Docile, *teachable,* 539
   tractable, 705
   willing, 602
   obedient, 743
   dutiful, 926
Dock, *cut off,* 38
   diminish, 36
   incompleteness, 53
   shorten, 201
   port, 189
   yard, 636, 691
   tribunal, 966
Docker, *workman,* 690
Docket, *indication,* 467, 550
   record, 551
   security, 771
Doctor, *sage,* 492
   physician, 695
   to restore, 660
   amend, 658
   remedy, 662
   falsify, 544
Doctrinaire, *ignoramus,* 493
Doctrinal, *teaching,* 537
Doctrine, *tenet,* 484
   knowledge, 490
Document, *record,* 551
Documentary, *film,* 599A
Dodecahedron, *angle,* 244
Dodge, *oscillate,* 314
   pursue, 461
   deceive, 545
   avoid, 623
   contrivance, 626
   cunning, 702
Doe, *swiftness,* 274

Doer, *agent,* 690
   originator, 164
Doff, *put off,* 226
Dog, *to pursue,* 622
   follow, 281
   affectation, 855
Dog-cart, *vehicle,* 272
Dog-days, *heat,* 382
Dog-ear, *fold,* 258
Dog Latin, *solecism,* 568
Dog-tired, *fatigue,* 688
Dog-trot, *slowness,* 275
Doge, *master,* 745
Dogfight, *contest,* 720
Dogged, *obstinate,* 606
   discourteous, 895
Dogger, *ship,* 273
Doggerel, *verse,* 597
   ridiculous, 853
Dogma, *tenet,* 484
   theological, 983
Dogmatic, *obstinate,* 606
   certainty, 474
   assertion, 535
   intolerant, 481
Dog's-eared, *fold,* 258
Doings, *actions,* 680
   events, 151
Doit, *trifle,* 643
   coin, 800
Doited, *insane,* 503
*Dolce far niente, *inactivity,*
                     638
Doldrums, *dejection,* 837
Dole, *small quantity,* 32
   to give, 784
   to allot, 786
   expenditure, 809
   grief, 828
Dole out, *parsimony,* 819
Doleful, *dejected,* 837
   lament, 839
Doll, *plaything,* 840
   image, 554
   small, 193
Doll up, *beautify,* 845
   adorn, 847
Dollar, *money,* 800
Dollop, *part,* 51
Dolman, *dress,* 225
Dolmen, *grave,* 363
Dolorous, *pain,* 830
Dolour, *physical,* 378
   moral, 828
Dolphin, *ocean,* 341
Dolt, *fool,* 501
Doltish, *folly,* 499
Domain, *region,* 181
   class, 75
   property, 780
Domdaniel, *hell,* 982
Dome, *convexity,* 250
Domesday Book, *list,* 86
Domestic, *interior,* 188, 221
   servant, 746

   secluded, 893
Domesticate, *tame,* 537
Domicile, *abode,* 189
Dominance, *influence,* 175
Dominant, *prevailing,* 737
   note in music, 413
Domination, *authority,* 737
Domineer, *tyrannize,* 739
   insolence, 885
Dominican, *clergy,* 996
Dominie, *teacher,* 540
Dominion, *region,* 181
   spirit, 977
Domino, *dress,* 225
   mask, 530
Don, *to put on,* 225
   noble, 875
   scholar, 492
Dona, *woman,* 374
   sweetheart, 897
Donation, *gift,* 784, 804
Done, *finished,* 729
   cheated, 547
Donee, *receive,* 785
Donjon, *defence,* 717
Donkey, *ass,* 271
   fool, 501
Donkey's breakfast, *bed,* 215
*Donna, *woman,* 374
Donnybrook, *disorder,* 59
   discord, 713
   contention, 720
Donor, *giver,* 784
Doodlebug, *bomb,* 727
Doom, *fate,* 152
   necessity, 601
   destruction, 162, 360
   to sentence, 969
   condemn, 971
   end, 67
Doomed, *undone,* 828
   fated, 152, 601
Doomsday, *futurity,* 121
   end, 67
Door, *opening,* 260
   passage, 627
   brink, 230
   entrance, 66, 294
   barrier, 232
Door-keeper, *janitor,* 263
Doorway, *opening,* 260
Dope, *semiliquid,* 352
   stupefy, 376
Dope fiend, *intemperance,* 954
Dopy, *sleepy,* 683
Dormant, *latent,* 526
   inert, 172, 683
Dormitory, *room,* 191
Dormouse, *inactivity,* 683
Dorsal, *rear,* 235
*Dorsum, *rear,* 235
   convexity, 250
Dose, *part,* 51
   mixture, 41

Dudgeon, *club*, 727
Duds, *clothes*, 225
Due, *proper*, 924, 926
   owing, 806
   effect, 154
   expedient, 646
Duel, *contention*, 720
Duellist, *combatant*, 726
Dueness, *right*, 924
Duenna, *teacher*, 540
   accompaniment, 88
   keeper, 753
Dues, *price*, 812
Duet, *music*, 815
Duff, *false*, 495
Duffer, *fool*, 501
   bungler, 700
Duffle coat, *dress*, 225
Dug, *convexity*, 250
Dug-out, *refuge*, 666, 717
   canoe, 273
Duke, *noble*, 875
   ruler, 745
Dukedom, *title*, 877
Dulcet, *sound*, 405
   melodious, 413
   agreeable, 829
Dulcify, *sweeten*, 396
Dulcimer, *musical instrument*,
        417
Dulcinea, *favourite*, 899
Dull, *inert*, 172
   insensible, 376
   tame, 575
   callous, 823
   blunt, 254
   weak, 160
   moderate, 174
   colourless, 429
   dejected, 837
   inexcitable, 826
   stolid, 699
   prosing, 843
   unapt, 499
Dull-brained, *folly*, 499
Dull-witted, *folly*, 499
Dullard, *fool*, 501
Duma, *council*, 696
Dumb, *aphony*, 581
   stupid, 499, 843
   unskilful, 699
Dumb-bell, *fool*, 501
Dumb show, *the drama*, 599
Dumbfound, *astonish*, 870
   disappoint, 509
Dummy, *aphony*, 581
   effigy, 554
Dump, *deposit*, 184
Dumps, *sadness*, 837
   mortification, 832
Dumpy, *broad*, 202
   short, 200
   ugly, 846
Dun, *colour*, 432
   to importune, 765

Dun, *creditor*, 805
Dunce, *ignoramus*, 493
   fool, 501
Dunderhead, *fool*, 501
Dundreary, *whisker*, 256
Dune, *hillock*, 206
Dung, *uncleanness*, 653
Dungarees, *dress*, 225
Dungeon, *prison*, 752
   hide, 530
Dunghill, *vulgar*, 876
Dunt, *blow*, 619
Duodecimal, *twelve*, 98
Duodecimo, *littleness*, 193
   book, 593
Duodenary, *numbers*, 98
Duologue, *interlocution*, 588
   drama, 599
Dupe, *to deceive*, 545
   deceived, 547
   credulous, 486
Duplex, *double*, 89, 90
Duplicate, *double*, 89, 90
   superfluous, 641
   copy, 21, 590
   pledge, 550, 805
Duplication, *imitation*, 19
Duplicity, false, 544, 702
Durable, *lasting*, 110
   stable, 150
Durance, *restraint*, 751
Duration, *period*, 106
Durbar, *tribunal*, 966
   assembly, 696
Duress, *restraint*, 751
   compulsion, 744
During, *lasting*, 106
During pleasure, *contingent*
   duration, 108A
Durity, *hardness*, 323
Dusk, *evening*, 126
   obscurity, 422
Dusky, *darkness*, 421
Dust, *powder*, 330
   corpse, 362
   levity, 320
   dirt, 653
   trash, 643
   to clean, 652
   contest, 720
   money, 800
Dustman, *cleaner*, 652
Duteous, *virtue*, 944
Dutiful, *virtue*, 944
   filial, 167
Duty, *obligation*, 926
   business, 625
   work, 686
   tax, 812
   rite, 990, 998
Duumvirate, *authority*, 737
Dwarf, *small*, 193
   low, 207
   to lessen, 36
Dwell, *tarry*, 265

Dwell, *reside*, 186
Dwell on, *descant*, 573, **584**
Dweller, *inhabitant*, 188
Dwelling, *location*, 189
   residence, 184
Dwindle, *diminish*, 32, 195
   lessen, 36
Dyad, *duality*, 89
Dyarchy, *authority*, 737
Dye, *colour*, 428
Dying, *death*, 360
Dyke, see Dike
Dynamic, *powerful*, 157
Dynamics, *force*, 159, 276
Dynamite, *arms*, 727
Dynams, *instrument*, 633
Dynasty, *authority*, 737
Dyslogistic, *disapproving*, 932

E

Each, *speciality*, 79
Eager, *ardent*, 507, 821
   desirous, 865
   active, 682
Eagle, *swift*, 274
   sight, 441
   standard, 550
Eagre, *tide*, 348
Ear, *hearing*, 418
Ear-deafening, *loudness*, 404
Ear-phone, *hearing*, 418
Ear-piercing, *loud*, 404
Ear-trumpet, *hearing*, 418
Ear-witness, *evidence*, 467
Earache, *pain*, 378
Earl, *nobility*, 875
   master, 745
Earldom, *title*, 877
Earless, *deaf*, 419
Early, *earliness*, 132
Earmark, *sign*, 550
Earn, *acquire*, 775
Earnest, *intention*, 620
   strenuous, 682
   emphatic, 642
   pledge, 771
   pay in advance, 809
   eager, 821
Earring, *pendant*, 214
   ornament, 847
Earshot, *nearness*, 197
Earth, *land*, 342
   ground, 211
   world, 318
   den, 189
Earth-born, *commonalty*, 876
Earthly-minded, *selfish*, 943
   worldly, 989
Earthquake, *violence*, 146, 173
Earwig, *to flatter*, 933
   flatterer, 935
Ease, *facility*, 705
   relief, 834
   content, 831

Ease, *pleasure*, 827
   in style, 578
Easel, *frame*, 215
   painter's, 559
East, *side*, 236
Easy, *slow*, 275
Easy-going, *inactive*, 683
   indulgent, 740
   calm, 826
   willing, 602
Eat, *swallow*, 296
Eatable, *food*, 298
Eaves, *projection*, 250
Eavesdropping, *hearing*, 418
   prying, 455
*Ebauche, *plan*, 626
Ebb, *regress*, 283
   decrease, 36
   contract, 195
   waste, 638
   spoil, 659
   oscillation, 314
Eblis, *demon*, 980
Ebony, *blackness*, 431
Ebriety, *drunkenness*, 959
Ebullition, *heat*, 384
   energy, 171
   violence, 173
   agitation, 315
   excitation, 825
*Ecce signum, *evidence*, 467
   indication, 550
Eccentric, *irregular*, 83
   peculiar, 79
   exterior, 220
   wrong-headed, 499
   oddity, 857
Ecclesiastic, *clergy*, 996
*Ecervelé, *insanity*, 503
Echelon, *series*, 69
Echo, *repeat*, 104
   assent, 488
   imitate, 19
   loudness, 404
   resonance, 408
   answer, 462
*Eclaircissement, *interpretation*,
          522
*Éclat, *repute*, 873
Eclectic, *choice*, 609
Eclipse, *hide*, 528
   invisible, 447
   darkness, 421, 422
   outshine, 33, 874
Ecliptic, *universe*, 318
Eclogue, *poetry*, 597
Ecology, *organization*, 357
Economy, *order*, 58
   plan, 626
   conduct, 692
   frugality, 817
Ecstasy, *fancy*, 515
   rapture, 821, 827
Ecumenical, *theology*, 983
Edacity, *gluttony*, 957

Eddy, *current*, 348
   whirlpool, 312
Eden, *heaven*, 981
Edge, *brink*, 230
   energy, 171
   to move forward, 282
   to move sideways, 236
   to instigate, 615
Edge-tool, *sharpness*, 253
Edging, *ornament*, 847
Edible, *food*, 298
Edict, *legality*, 963
   command, 741
Edifice, *abode*, 189
Edify, *build*, 161
   teach, 537
   piety, 987
Edit, *publish*, 531
   alter, 140
Editorial, *dissertation*, 595
Educate, *teach*, 537
   train, 673
Education, *learning*, 490
Educe, *elicit*, 525
Educt, *remainder*, 40
Edulcorate, *sweeten*, 396
   clean, 652
Eel, *convolution*, 248
Eerie, *unconformity*, 83
   supernatural, 980
Efface, *obliterate*, 552
   oblivion, 506
   disappear, 449
Effect, *consequence*, 154
   to produce, 161
   to complete, 729
Effective, *capable*, 157
   impressive, 821
   successful, 731
   real, 1
Effects, *property*, 780
   goods, 798
   materials, 635
Effectual, *useful*, 644
Effeminate, *weak*, 160
   womanish, 374
   sensual, 954
   timorous, 862
Effendi, *master*, 745
   noble, 875
Effervesce, *bubble up*, 353
   agitate, 315
   energy, 171
   violence, 173
   excited, 825
Effete, *old*, 124
   weak, 160
   useless, 645
   spoiled, 659
Efficacy, *power*, 157
Efficiency, *utility*, 644
   skill, 698
Effigy, *representation*, 554
   copy, 21
*Effleurer, *skim*, 267

*Effleurer, *slur over*, 458
Efflorescence, *pulverulence*, 330
Effluence, *egress*, 295
   river, 348
Effluvium, *odour*, 398
   vapour, 334
Efflux, *flow*, 348
Effort, *exertion*, 686
Effrontery, *insolence*, 885
Effulgence, *light*, 420
Effusion, *outpouring*, 295
   ejection, 297, 299
Effusiveness, *feeling*, 821
Eftsoons, *soon*, 111
   early, 132
Egg, *beginning*, 66
Egg on, *urge*, 615
Egg-shaped, *round*, 247, 249
Egghead, *sage*, 500
Ego, *self*, 13
Egocentric, *vanity*, 880
Egoism, *vanity*, 880
   selfishness, 911
Egomania, *vanity*, 880
Egotism, *vanity*, 880
   selfishness, 911, 943
Egregious, *exceptional*, 83
   important, 642
   extravagant, 499
Egregiously, *greatness*, 31
Egress, *emergence*, 295
Eiderdown, *covering*, 222
Eidolon, *idea*, 453
Eirenicon, *mediation*, 724
Eisteddfod, *assemblage*, 72
Either, *choice*, 609
Ejaculate, *propel*, 284
   utter, 580
Eject, *displace*, 185
   emit, 297
Eke, *addition*, 37
   to complete, 52
   spin out, 110
Elaborate, *preparation*, 673
   complete, 729
   detail, 594
*Elan, *ardour*, 821
   vigour, 574
   activity, 682
Elapse, *pass*, 122
   flow, 109
Elastic, *resilient*, 325
   strong, 159
Elate, *to cheer*, 836
   boast, 884
Elbow, *angle*, 244, 258
   projection, 250
   to push, 276
Elbow-grease, *rubbing*, 331
Elbow-room, *space*, 180
   freedom, 748
Eld, *oldness*, 124
Elder, *oldness*, 124
   age, 128

Extract, *choice*, 609
   quotation, 596
Extradite, *deport*, 55, 270
   displace, 185
   eject, 297
Extrajudicial, *illegal*, 964
Extramundane, *immateriality*,
               317
Extramural, *exterior*, 220
Extraneous, *extrinsic*, 6
   not related, 10
   foreign, 57
Extraordinary, *unconformity*, 83
   greatness, 31
Extravagant, *exaggerated*, 549
   irrational, 477
   absurd, 497
   ridiculous, 853
   foolish, 499
   redundant, 641
   high-priced, 814
   prodigal, 818
   vulgar, 851
   inordinate, 31
Extravaganza, *fanciful*, 515
   burlesque, 853
   the drama, 599
Extravasate, *excretion*, 299
Extreme, *greatness*, 31
   revolutionary, 146
Extremist, *zealot*, 604
Extremity, *end*, 67
   exterior, 220
Extricate, *take out*, 301
   liberate, 750
   deliver, 672
   facilitate, 705
Extrinsic, *extrinsicality*, 6
Extrude, *eject*, 297
Exuberant, *redundant*, 641
   style, 573
   feeling, 821
Exude, *excretion*, 299
   egress, 295
Exult, *crow*, 836
   rejoice, 838
   boast, 873, 884
*Exuviae, *remainder*, 40
Eye, *organ of sight*, 441
   opening, 260
   circle, 247
Eye-opener, *enlightenment*, 527
   portent, 870
Eye-shade, *mask*, 530
Eye-witness, *evidence*, 467
   spectator, 444
Eyeglass, *optical instrument*, 445
Eyeless, *blind*, 442
Eyelet, *opening*, 260
Eyelet, *opening*, 260
Eyesight, *vision*, 441
Eyesore, *ugliness*, 846
Eyewash, *deception*, 545
Eyot, *island*, 346
Eyre, *jurisprudence*, 965
Eyrie, *abode*, 189

F

Fabian policy, *inactivity*,
              681, 683
   delay, 133
Fable, *fiction*, 546
   error, 495
   description, 594
Fabric, *texture*, 329
   house, 189
   effect, 154
   state, 7
Fabricate, *make*, 161
   invent, 515
   forge, 544
   falsify, 546
Fabulous, *imagination*, 515
   mythical, 979
   exaggerated, 549
   greatness, 31
   non-existent, 2
Façade, *front*, 234
Face, *exterior*, 220
   front, 234
   lining, 224
   impudence, 885
   confront, 861
   aspect, 448
Face about, *deviation*, 279
Face-cloth, *wash*, 652
Face down, *withstand*, 719
Face to face, *manifestation*, 525
Facet, *exterior*, 220
Facetious, *wit*, 842
Facia, *indication*, 550
Facile, *irresolute*, 605
   persuasible, 602, 615
   easy, 705
   skilful, 698
*Facile princeps, *superiority*, 33
   goodness, 648
Facility, *ease*, 705
   aid, 707
   skill, 698
Facing, *lining*, 224
   covering, 222
*Façon de parler, *meaning*, 516
   metaphor, 521
   exaggeration, 549
   phrase, 566
Facsimile, *copy*, 21
   identity, 13
   representation, 554
Fact, *event*, 151
   truth, 494
   existence, 1, 2
Faction, *party*, 712
Factious, *discord*, 713
Factitious, *artificial*, 544
Factor, *numerical*, 84
   agent, 690
   director, 694
   consignee, 758
   merchant, 797
Factory, *workshop*, 691

Factotum, *manager*, 694
   employee, 758
Faculty, *power*, 157
   intellect, 450
   skill, 698
   profession, 625
Fad, *caprice*, 608
   prejudice, 481
   fashion, 852
Fade, *vanish*, 2, 4, 111, 449
   dim, 422; *expel*, 297
   lose colour, 429
   spoil, 659
   droop, 160
   change, 149
   become old, 124
*Fade, *insipid*, 391
Fade-out, *cinema*, 599A
Fadge, *agreement*, 23
Faeces, *excretion*, 298
   foulness, 653
Faery, *fabulous being*, 979
   imagination, 515
Fag, *labour*, 686
   activity, 682
   fatigue, 688, 841
   drudge, 690
Fag-end, *remainder*, 40
   end, 67
Faggot, *bundle*, 72
   fuel, 388
Fahrenheit, *thermometer*, 389
Fail, *incomplete*, 53, 651
   shortcoming, 304
   non-observance, 732
   non-payment, 808
   dereliction, 927
   droop, 160
   break down, 158
   reject, 610
   vice, 945
Fain, *wish*, 865
   willing, 602
   compulsive, 744
*Fainéant, *idler*, 683
Faint, *weak*, 160
   sound, 405
   colour, 429
   small in degree, 32
   swoon, 683, 688
Faint-hearted, *coward*, 862
   fear, 860
Fair, *in degree*, 31
   white, 430
   just, 922
   impartial, 498
   honourable, 939
   true, 543
   tolerable, 651
   pleasing, 829
   beautiful, 845
   mart, 799
   festivity, 840
Fair play, *justice*, 922
   honour, 939

Fair sex, *woman*, 374
Fair-spoken, *courteous*, 894
 flattering, 933
Fairing, *gift*, 784
Fairly, *great*, 31
Fairy, *fabulous being*, 979
Fairy-cycle, *bicycle*, 266
Fairy godmother, *friend*, 891
 benefactor, 912
Fairy-tale, *lie*, 546
*Fait accompli, *completion*, 729
Faith, *belief*, 484
 hope, 858
 honour, 939
 creed, 983
 piety, 987
Faithful, *likeness*, 17
 true, 494
 obedient, 743
 observant, 772·
 Christian, 983A
 godly, 987
Faithless, *false*, 544
 dishonourable, 940
 sceptical, 989
Fake, *imitation*, 19
 deception, 545
 to forge, 544
Fakir, *clergy*, 996
Falcated, *curved*, 245
 sharp, 244
Falchion, *arms*, 727
Falciform, *angularity*, 244
 curvature, 245
Fall, *descend*, 306
 destruction, 162
 slope, 217
 fail, 732
 die, 360
 adversity, 735
 decline, 659
 happen, 151
 vice, 945
 autumn, 126
Fall away, *decrease*, 36
 shrink, 195
Fall back, *recede*, 283, 287
 relapse, 661
Fall behind, *sequence*, 281
Fall down, *descend*, 306
 worship, 990
Fall for, *love*, 897
Fall foul of, *oppose*, 708
 encounter, 720
 reprimand, 932
Fall in, *marshal*, 58, 60
 happen, 151
Fall in with, *find*, 480A
 uniformity, 16
 agree, 23
Fall off, *deterioration*, 659
 decrease, 36
 disjunction, 44
Fall out, *happen*, 151
 drop, 297

Fall short, *shortcoming*, 304, 730
 fail, 53
 insufficiency, 640
Fall through, *failure*, 732
Fall to, *work*, 686
 devour, 296
 fight, 722
Fall to pieces, *disjunction*, 44
Fall under, *inclusion*, 76
Fall upon, *attack*, 716
 discover, 480A
 devise, 626
Fallacy, *error*, 495
 uncertainty, 475
 sophistry, 477
Fal-lal, *ornament*, 847
 rifle, 643
Fallible, *uncertain*, 475, 477
Fallow, *yellow*, 436
 unproductive, 169
 unready, 674
False, *untrue*, 544
 error, 495
 sophistry, 477
 spurious, 925
 dishonourable, 940
False-hearted, *improbity*, 940
Falsehood, *lie*, 546
Falsetto, *music*, 413
 affected, 577
Falsify, *misinterpret*, 523
 accounts, 811
 deceive, 495
 lie, 544
Falstaffian, *fat*, 192
Falter, *stammer*, 583
 hesitate, 605
 demur, 603
 slowness, 275
Fame, *renown*, 873
 rumour, 531
 news, 532
Familiar, *common*, 82
 habit, 613
 known, 490
 friendly, 888
 affable, 894, 892
 spirit, 979
Family, *class*, 75
 consanguinity, 11
 paternity, 166
 posterity, 167
Famine, *insufficiency*, 640
Famished, *fasting*, 956
Famous, *repute*, 873
 greatness, 31
Fan, *blow*, 349
 excite, 615
 enthusiast, 840, 865
 frequenter, 136
Fanatic, *extravagant*, 515
Fanatical, *feeling*, 821
Fanaticism, *folly*, 499
 obstinacy, 606
 religious, 984A

Fanciful, *capricious*, 608
 imaginative, 515
 mistaken, 495
 unreal, 2
Fancy, *think*, 451
 believe, 484
 wit, 842
 idea, 453
 suppose, 514
 imagine, 515
 caprice, 608
 choice, 609
 desire, 865
 like, 394
 love, 897
 pugilism, 726
Fandango, *dance*, 840
Fane, *temple*, 1000
Fanfare, *loudness*, 404
 ostentation, 882
Fanfaronade, *boasting*, 884
Fang, *bane*, 663
Fanlight, *opening*, 260
Fantasia, *music*, 415
 imagination, 515
Fantastic, *odd*, 83
 imaginary, 515
 capricious, 608
 ridiculous, 853
Fantasy, *caprice*, 608
 imagination, 515
 idea, 453
*Fantoccini, *marionettes*,
     554, 599
Far, *distant*, 196
Far-fetched, *irrelation*, 10
 irrelevant, 24
 irrational, 477
 obscure, 519
Far from it, *dissimilarity*, 18
Far-seeing, *foresight*, 510
Farce, *drama*, 599
 ridiculous, 856
*Farceur, *humorist*, 844
Farcical, *ridiculous*, 856
 witty, 842
 trifling, 643
Fardel, *assemblage*, 72
Fare, *circumstance*, 8
 event, 151
 to eat, 296
 food, 298
 price, 812
Farewell, *departure*, 293
Farm, *house*, 189
 property, 780
 to rent, 788, 795
Farrago, *mixture*, 41
 confusion, 59
Farthing, *coin*, 800
 worthless, 643
Farthingale, *dress*, 225
Fasces, *sceptre*, 747
Fascia, *band*, 205
 circle, 247

Fitful, *irresolute*, 605
    discontinuous, 70
    irregular, 139
Fitness, *agreement*, 23
Fitting, *expedient*, 646
    right, 922, 926
    due, 924
    instrument, 633
Five, *number*, 98
Fiver, *money*, 800
Fix, *place*, 150, 184
    rectify, 658, 660
    solidify, 321
    arrangement, 60
    situation, 8
    difficulty, 704
Fix together, *junction*, 43
Fix upon, *choose*, 609
Fixed, *determined*, 604
    permanent, 141, 150
    quiescent, 265
Fixture, *property*, 780
    stability, 150
Fizgig, *firework*, 423
Fizz, *sibilation*, 409
    bubble, 353
Fizzle, *hiss*, 409
Fizzle out, *failure*, 158, 732
Fjord, *see* Fiord
Flabbergast, *astound*, 870
Flabby, *soft*, 324
Flaccid, *shrivelled*, 172, 193
    soft, 324
    empty, 640
Flag, *streamer*, 550
    flat stone, 204
    weakness, 160
    floor, 211
    droop, 688
    inactive, 683
    infirm, 160, 655
    slowness, 275
Flagellation, *flogging*, 972
    atonement, 952
    asceticism, 955
Flageolet, *musical*, 417
Flagitious, *vice*, 945
Flagrant, *notorious*, 531
    manifest, 525
    great, 408
    atrocious, 945
Flagstaff, *sign*, 550
    high, 206
Flail, *impulse*, 276
Flair, *intelligence*, 498
Flake, *layer*, 204
Flam, *untruth*, 546
Flambeau, *luminary*, 423
Flamboyant, *vulgar*, 851
    ornamented, 577, 847
Flame, *light*, 420
    fire, 382
    luminary, 423
    passion, 825
    love, 897

Flame, *favourable*, 899
Flame-coloured, *orange*, 439
Flaming, *excited*, 821, 825
*Flâneur, *idler*, 683
Flange, *support*, 215
Flank, *side*, 236
    safety, 664
Flannel, *flattery*, 933
Flannels, *dress*, 225
Flap, *adjunct*, 39
    hanging, 214
    move about, 315
    beat, 972
    fear, 860
Flapdoodle, *deception*, 546
    nonsense, 497
Flapjack, *receptacle*, 191
Flapper, *girl*, 129, 374
Flapping, *loose*, 47
Flare, *glare*, 420
    violence, 173
Flare up, *kindle*, 825
    anger, 900
Flaring, *colour*, 428
Flash, *instant*, 113
    fire, 382
    light, 420
    thought, 451
    sudden act, 612
    violence, 173
Flash-lamp, *light*, 423
Flash note, *money,* 800
Flashback, *memory*, 505
    cinema, 599A
Flashy, *gaudy colour*, 428
    bad taste, 851
    ostentatious, 882
Flask, *receptacle*, 191
Flat, *level*, 251
    uniform, 16
    horizontal, 213
    novice, 701
    dupe, 547
    low, 207
    vapid, 391
    inert, 172, 823
    dull, 841, 843
    insipid, 575
    dejected, 837
    sound, 408
    indifferent, 866
    positive, 535
    abode, 189
    apartment, 191
Flatlet, *abode*, 189
Flatter, *pleasure*, 829
    encourage, 858
    adulation, 933
    servility, 886
Flatterer, *eulogist*, 935
Flattie, *detective*, 461
    cinema, 599A
Flatulent, *windy*, 338
    gaseous, 334
    style, 573

Flaunt, *display*, 873, 882
    gaudy, 428
    ornament, 847
Flautist, *musician*, 416
Flavour, *taste*, 390
Flavous, *yellow*, 436
Flaw, *crack*, 198
    error, 495
    imperfection, 651
    blemish, 848
    fault, 947
Flay, *divest*, 226
    punish, 972
Flea-bag, *bed*, 215
Flea-bite, *trifle*, 643
Flea-bitten, *variegated*, 440
Fleckered, *variegation*, 440
Fledged, *preparation*, 673
Flee, *escape*, 671
    avoid, 623
Fleece, *tegument*, 222
    to rob, 791
    to strip, 789
    impoverish, 804
Fleer, *ridicule*, 956
Fleet, *swift*, 274
    ships, 273
Fleeting, *transient*, 111
    changeful, 607
Flesh, *mankind*, 372
    carnality, 961
Flesh colour, *redness*, 434
Flesh-pots, *food*, 298
Fleshly, *sensual*, 954, 961
Fleshy, *corpulent*, 192
Flexible, *pliant*, 324
    tractable, 705
Flexion, *bending*, 245
    deviation, 279
    fold, 258
Flexuous, *convolution*, 248
Flexure, *bending*, 245
    fold, 258
Flibbertigibbet, *trifler*, 460
Flick, *propel*, 284
    cinema, 599A
Flicker, *flutter*, 315
    oscillate, 314
    waver, 149, 605
    shine, 420
Flickering, *irregular*, 139
Flight, *departure*, 287, 293
    escape, 671
    volitation, 267
    swiftness, 174
    multitude, 102
Flight-lieutenant, *master*, 745
Flight of Fancy, *imagination*, 515
    idea, 453
Flighty, *insane*, 503
    fickle, 605
Flim-flam, *lie*, 546
    caprice, 608
Flimsy, *texture*, 329

Forewarn, *warn*, 668
  advise, 695
  predict, 511
Foreword, *preamble*, 64
  front, 234
Forfeit, *lose*, 776
  fail, 773
  undueness, 925
  penalty, 974
Forfend, *guard*, 717
  hinder, 706
Forge, *produce*, 161
  furnace, 386
  workshop, 691
  trump up, 544
Forge ahead, *advance*, 282
Forgery, *untruth*, 546
  imitation, 19
Forget, *oblivion*, 506
Forgive, *forgiveness*, 918
Forgo, *relinquish*, 624, 782
  renounce, 757
Forgotten, *unremembered*, 506
  ingratitude, 917
Fork, *angularity*, 244
  bisection, 91
Fork out, *give*, 784
  expend, 809
Forlorn, *abandoned*, 893
  dejected, 837
  woebegone, 828
Forlorn hope, *hopeless*, 859
  danger, 665
Form, *shape*, 240
  state, 7
  arrange, 60
  rule, 80
  to make up, 54
  produce, 161
  educate, 537
  habituate, 613
  bench, 215
  part, 569
  fashion, 852
  etiquette, 882
  law, 963
  rite, 998
  fours, 58
  manner, 627
  beauty, 845
  likeness, 21
  pupils, 541
Formal, *regular*, 82
  affected, 855
  positive, 535
Formalism, *hypocrisy*, 988
Formality, *ceremony*, 852
  parade, 882
  law, 963
Format, *style*, 7
Formation, *production*, 161
  shape, 240
Former, *in order*, 62
  in time, 122
Formication, *itching*, 380

Formidable, *fear*, 860
  difficult, 704
  great, 31
Formless, *amorphism*, 241
Formula, *rule*, 80
  precept, 697
  law, 963
  number, 84
Fornication, *impurity*, 961
Fornicator, *libertine*, 962
Forsake, *relinquish*, 624
Forsooth, *truth*, 494
Forswear, *renounce*, 624
  retract, 607
  refuse, 764
  perjure, 544, 940
  violate, 927
Fort, *defence*, 717
  refuge, 666
Forte, *excellence*, 698
*Forte, *loudness*, 404
Forth, *progression*, 282
Forthcoming, *futurity*, 121, 673
Forthwith, *transient*, 111
Fortification, *defence*, 717
  refuge, 666
Fortify, *strength*, 159
Fortitude, *courage*, 861
  endurance, 826
Fortnight, *period*, 108, 138
Fortress, *defence*, 716
  prison, 752
Fortuitous, *chance*, 156, 621
Fortunate, *opportune*, 134
  prosperous, 734
Fortune, *chance*, 156
  accident, 621
  wealth, 803
Fortune-teller, *oracle*, 513
Fortune-telling, *prediction*, 511
Forum, *tribunal*, 966
  school, 542
Forward, *early*, 132
  to advance, 282
  to help, 707
  active, 682
  willing, 602
  vain, 880
  impertinent, 885
Fosse, *furrow*, 259
  gap, 198
  defence, 717
  enclosure, 232
Fossick, *inquiry*, 461
Fossil, *antiquated*, 851
  old, 124
  bore, 841
Foster, *aid*, 707
Fou, *drunken*, 959
Foul, *bad*, 649
  corrupt, 653
  odour, 401
  offensive, 830
  ugly, 846
  vicious, 945

Foul-mouthed, *malevolent*, 907
Foul-tongued, *scurrilous*, 934
Found, *cause*, 153
  prepare, 673
Foundation, *base*, 211
  support, 215
Founder, *originator*, 164
  sink, 310, 732
Foundling, *outcast*, 893
Fount, *origin*, 153
  spring, 348
  type, 591
Fountain, *cause*, 153
  river, 348
  store, 636
Fountain-pen, *writing*, 590
Four, *number*, 95
Four-square, *number*, 95
Fourfold, *number*, 96
Fourscore, *number*, 98
Fourth, *number*, 97
Fowl, *animal*, 366
Fowling-piece, *arms*, 727
Fox, *cunning*, 702
Fox-trot, *dance*, 840
Foxhole, *refuge*, 666
  defence, 717
Foxhound, *chase*, 622
Foyer, *room*, 191
Fracas, *contention*, 720
  brawl, 713
Fraction, *part*, 51
  numerical, 84
Fractious, *irascibility*, 901
Fracture, *disjunction*, 44
  discontinuity, 70, 198
  to break, 328
Fragile, *brittle*, 328
  frail, 149, 160
Fragment, *part*, 51
Fragrant, *fragrant*, 400
'Fraid-cat, *coward*, 862
Frail, *brittle*, 328
  mutable, 149
  weak, 160
  irresolute, 605
  imperfect, 651
  unchaste, 961
  failing, 945
Frame, *condition*, 7
  support, 215
  texture, 329
  form, 240
  substance, 316
  to construct, 161
  border, 230
*Franc-tireur, *fighter*, 726
Franchise, *right*, 924
  freedom, 748
  exemption, 927
Franciscan, *clergy*, 996
Frangible, *brittle*, 328
Frank, *artless*, 703
  open, 525
  sincere, 543

Frank, *honourable*, 939
Frankincense, *fragrant*, 400
Frantic, *delirious*, 503
   violent, 173
   excited, 825
Fraternal, *brotherly*, 11
   friendly, 888, 906
Fraternity, *assemblage*, 72
   company, 712, 892
Fraternize, *co-operate*, 709
   harmonize, 714
Fratricide, *killing*, 361
Fraud, *deception*, 544, 545
   dishonour, 940
Fraught, *having*, 777
   full of, 639
Fray, *contention*, 720
   to abrade, 331
Freak, *caprice*, 608
   unconformity, 83
Freakish, *irresolution*, 605
Freckle, *blemish*, 848
Freckled, *variegation*, 440
Free, *detached*, 44
   at liberty, 748
   spontaneous, 600, 602
   exempt, 927
   unobstructed, 705
   liberal, 816
   gratuitous, 815
   insolent, 885
Free-born, *freedom*, 748
Free gift, *giving*, 784
Free play, *freedom*, 748
Free-spoken, *veracity*, 543
Free-thinking, *religion*, 989
Free will, *will*, 600
Freebooter, *thief*, 792
Freedom, *liberty*, 748
   looseness, 47
   full play, 705
   exemption, 927
   space, 180
Freehold, *property*, 780
   freedom, 748
Freelance, *writer*, 590
Freemasonry, *secrecy*, 528
   sign, 550
   fraternity, 712
   co-operation, 709
Freeze, *frigefaction*, 385
   stop dead, 265
Freight, *contents*, 190
   cargo, 798
   transfer, 270
Freight train, *vehicle*, 272
Frenzy, *insanity*, 503
Frequency, *repetition*, 104
Frequent, *in time*, 136
   in number, 102
   in space, 186
Fresco, *painting*, 556
Fresh, *new*, 123
   cold, 383
   colour, 428

Fresh, *unforgotten*, 505
   healthy, 654
   good, 648
   cheeky, 885
   tipsy, 959
Freshet, *flood*, 348
Freshman, *learner*, 541
Fret, *suffer*, 378
   grieve, 828
   to gall, 830
   sadness, 837
   to irritate, 900
   adorn, 847
Fretful, *irascibility*, 901
Fretwork, *crossing*, 219
Freya, *love*, 897
Friable, *pulverulence*, 330
Friar, *clergy*, 996
Friar's lantern, *light*, 423
Fribble, *trifle*, 460, 643
   dawdle, 683
Friction, *rubbing*, 331
   obstacle, 179
   discord, 713
Friend, *well-wisher*, 890
   relation, 11
   auxiliary, 711
Friendless, *seclusion*, 893
Friendly, *amical*, 714, 888
   helping, 707
Friendship, *amical*, 714, 888
Frieze, *summit*, 210
Frig, *refrigerator*, 387
Frigate, *ship*, 273
Frigga, *goddess*, 979
Fright, *alarm*, 860
   ugliness, 846
Frightful, *great*, 31
   hideous, 846
   dreadful, 830
Frigid, *cold*, 383
   callous, 823
   reluctant, 603
   indifferent, 866
Frigorific, *refrigeration*, 385
Frill, *border*, 230
Frills, *affectation*, 855
Fringe, *lace*, 256
   ornament, 847
Frippery, *dress*, 225
   trifle, 643
   ornament, 847
   ridiculous, 853
Frisk, *brisk*, 682
   gay, 836
   amuse, 840
Frisky, *nimble*, 274
   leap, 309
   in spirits, 836
Frith, *strait*, 343
   chasm, 198
Fritter, *small part*, 51
   waste, 135, 638, 683
   misuse, 679
   diminish, 36

Frivol, *trifle*, 460
Frivolous, *unimportant*, 643
   silly, 499
   frisky, 836
Frizzle, *curl*, 248
   fold, 258
Frock, *dress*, 225
Frog, *ornament*, 847
Frogman, *depth*, 208
   dive, 310
Frolic, *amusement*, 840
Frolicsome, *cheerful*, 836
Front, *fore-part*, 234
   precession, 280
   beginning, 66
   exterior, 220
   resistance, 719
Frontal, *beginning*, 66
   exterior, 220
Frontier, *limit*, 233
   vicinity, 199
Fronting, *antiposition*, 237
Frontispiece, *prefix*, 64
   front, 234
Frost, *cold*, 383
   failure, 732
Froth, *bubble*, 353
   trifle, 643
   style, 577
Frounce, *fold*, 258
Froward, *irascible*, 901
   discourteous, 895
Frown, *disapprove*, 932
   anger, 900
   scowl, 839, 895
   lower, 837
Frowzy, *fetor*, 401
Fructify, *production*, 161
   productiveness, 168
   prosper, 734
Frugal, *temperate*, 953
   economical, 817
Fruit, *result*, 154
   acquisition, 775
Fruitful, *productive*, 168
Fruition, *pleasure*, 827
   fulfilment, 729
Fruitless, *useless*, 645
   unproductive, 169
   abortive, 732
Frump, *dowdy*, 851
   dirty, 653
Frustrate, *defeat*, 731
   prevent, 706
Frustration, *failure*, 732
Frustrum, *part*, 51
Fry, *young*, 129
   small, 193
   heat, 384
Frying-pan, *furnace*, 386
Fubsy, *short*, 201
   broad, 202
Fuddled, *drunk*, 959
Fudge, *nonsense*, 497
   trivial, 643

Gird, *enclose*, 231
  strengthen, 159
Girder, *bond*, 45
  beam, 215
Girdle, *circular*, 247
  outline, 229
  connection, 45
Girl, *young*, 129
  female, 374
Girl friend, *sweetheart*, 897
Girth, *band*, 45
  outline, 229
Gist, *essence*, 5
  important, 642
  leaning, 516
Gittern, *musical instrument*,
          417
Give, *giving*, 784
  regress, 283
  bend, 324
Give and take, *probity*, 939
Give back, *restitute*, 790
Give ear, *listen*, 418
Give entrance to, *reception*, 296
Give forth, *publish*, 531
Give in, *submit*, 725
  obey, 743
Give notice, *inform*, 527
  warn, 668
Give out, *emit*, 297
  bestow, 784
  publish, 531
  teach, 537
  end, 67
Give over, *relinquish*, 624
  cease, 142
  lose hope, 859
Give up, *relinquish*, 624
  resign, 757
  yield, 743
  cease, 142
  reject, 610
  property, 782
  despair, 859
Give way, *yield*, 725
  obey, 743
  despond, 837
Gizzard, *receptacle*, 191
Glabrous, *smooth*, 255
Glacial, *cold*, 383
Glaciate, *frigefaction*, 385
Glacier, *cold*, 383
Glacis, *defence*, 717
Glad, *pleasure*, 827, 829
  cheerful, 836
Glad eye, *ogle*, 441, 902
Glad hand, *conviviality*, 892
Glade, *opening*, 260
  hollow, 252
  thicket, 367
Gladiator, *combatant*, 726
Gladiatorial, *warfare*, 722
Gladsome, *pleasurable*, 829
Glairy, *semiliquid*, 352
Glamour, *sorcery*, 992

Glance, *look*, 441
  rapid motion, 274
  attend to, 457
  hint, 527, 550
Glare, *light*, 420
  visible, 446
  colour, 428
Glaring, *greatness*, 31
  manifest, 518, 525
Glass, *vessel*, 191
  brittle, 328
  smooth, 255
  spectacles, 445
Glasshouse, *prison*, 752
Glassy, *dim*, 422
  transparent, 425
  colourless, 429
Glaucous, *green*, 435
Glaur, *mud*, 352
  dirt, 653
Glazed, *smooth*, 255
Gleam, *ray*, 429
  smallness, 32
Glean, *choose*, 609
  take, 789
  acquire, 775
  learn, 539
Glebe, *land*, 342
Glee, *satisfaction*, 827
  merriment, 836
  music, 415
Gleeman, *musician*, 416
Glen, *concavity*, 252
Glengarry, *cap*, 225
Glib, *voluble*, 584
  facile, 705
Glide, *move*, 266
  aviation, 267
  slowly, 275
  course, 109
Glider, *aircraft*, 273 A
Glimmer, *light*, 420
  dimness, 422
Glimmering, *slight knowledge*,
        490, 491
Glimpse, *sight*, 441
  knowledge, 490
Glint, *shine*, 420
Glissade, *descent*, 306
* Glissando, *music*, 415
Glisten, *shine*, 420
Glitter, *shine*, 420, 873
  display, 882
Gloaming, *evening*, 126
  dimness, 422
Gloat, *look*, 441
  revel, 377, 827
  boast, 884
Global, *worldwide*, 318
Globe, *sphere*, 249
  world, 318
Globe-trotter, *traveller*, 268
Globule, *spherule*, 249
  minute, 32, 193
Glockenspiel, *musical*, 417

Glomeration, *assembly*, 72
Gloom, *darkness*, 421
  sadness, 837
Glorify, *approve*, 931
  worship, 990
Glory, *honour*, 873
  light, 420
  boast, 884
  pride, 878
Gloss, *light*, 420
  smoothness, 255
  beauty, 845
  plea, 617
  falsehood, 546
  interpretation, 522
Gloss over, *neglect*, 460
  inattention, 458
  sophistry, 477
  vindication, 937
  falsehood, 544
Glossary, *interpretation*, 522
  verbal, 562
Glossy, *smooth*, 255
Glove, *cartel*, 715
Glow, *shine*, 420
  colour, 428
  warmth, 382
  passion, 821
  style, 574
Glow-worm, *luminary*, 423
Glower, *scowl*, 895
Gloze, *flatter*, 933
  palliate, 937
Glucose, *sweetness*, 396
Glue, *cement*, 45
  to stick, 46
  viscosity, 352
Glum, *discontented*, 832
  dejected, 837
  sulky, 895
Glut, *redundance*, 641
  satiety, 869
Glutinous, *coherence*, 46
  semiliquid, 352
Gluttony, *excess*, 957
  desire, 865
Glycerine, *semiliquid*, 352
Glyptography, *engraving*, 558
Gnarled, *rough*, 256
Gnash, *anger*, 900
Gnat, *littleness*, 193
Gnaw, *eat*, 296
  corrode, 659
  pain, 378
  give pain, 830
Gnome, *demon*, 980
  maxim, 496
Gnomic, *sententious*, 572
Gnosis, *knowledge*, 490
Gnostic, *intellectual*, 450
  mystic, 528
Go, *move*, 264
  depart, 293
  vigour, 574
  energy, 171, 682

Grace, *piety*, 987
   worship, 990
   thanks, 916
   style, 578
Grace-note, *music*, 415
Grace-stroke, *killing*, 361
Graceless, *ungraceful*, 846
   vicious, 945
   impenitent, 951
Gracile, *slender*, 203
Gracious, *courteous*, 894
   good-natured, 906
*Gradatim, *degree*, 26
   order, 58
   conversion, 144
Gradation, *degree*, 26
   order, 58
   arrangement, 60
   continuity, 69
Grade, *degree*, 26
   term, 71
Gradely, *good*, 648
Gradient, *obliquity*, 217
Gradual, *degree*, 26
   continuity, 69
Graduate, *to arrange*, 60
   to adapt, 23
   to measure, 466
   scholar, 492
Gradus, *dictionary*, 562
*Graffito, *drawing*, 556
Graft, *join*, 43
   insert, 300
   cultivate, 371
   locate, 184
   teach, 537
   bribe, 615
   improbity, 940
Grain, *essence*, 5
   minute, 32
   particle, 193
   texture, 329
   roughness, 256
   disposition, 820
   adorn, 847
Graminivorous, *eat*, 296
Grammar, *grammar*, 567
Grammar school, *school*, 542
Grammarian, *scholar*, 492
Grammercy, *gratitude*, 916
Gramophone, *reproduction*, 19
   music, 417
   hearing, 418
Granary, *store*, 636
Grand, *important*, 642
   beautiful, 845
   glorious, 873
   money, 800
Grandam, *veteran*, 130
Grandchild, *posterity*, 167
Grandee, *master*, 875
Grandeur, *repute*, 873
Grandiloquence, *eloquence*, 582
   style, 577
Grandiose, *style*, 577

Grandsire, *old*, 130
   ancestor, 166
Grandson, *posterity*, 167
Grange, *abode*, 189
Grangerize, *addition*, 36
Granite, *hardness*, 323
Granivorous, *eat*, 296
Grant, *give*, 784
   allow, 760
   consent, 762
   disclose, 529
   assent, 488
Grantee, *receive*, 785
Grantor, *give*, 784
Granulate, *pulverulence*, 330
Granule, *littleness*, 193
Grape-shot, *arms*, 727
Grapevine, *news*, 532
Graphic, *painting*, 556
   description, 594
   intelligible, 518
Grapnel, *anchor*, 666
Grapple, *contend*, 720
   undertake, 676
   join, 43
Grappling-iron, *fastening*, 45
   safety, 666
Grasp, *seize*, 789
   retain, 781
   comprehend, 518
   power, 737
Grasping, *parsimony*, 819
Grass, *plant*, 367
   green, 435
Grass widow, *divorce*, 905
Grate, *rub*, 330
   friction, 331
   harsh, 410, 414
   furnace, 386
   pain, physical, 378
   pain, moral, 830
Grateful, *thanks*, 916
   agreeable, 377, 829
Gratification, *animal*, 377
   moral, 827
Gratify, *pleasure*, 829
Grating, *noise*, 410
   lattice, 219
Gratis, *cheap*, 815
Gratitude, *thanks*, 916
Gratuitous, *spontaneous*,
           600, 602
   cheap, 815
Gratuity, *giving*, 784
Gratulation, *rejoicing*, 836
Gravamen, *importance*, 642
   grievance, 619
Grave, *sad*, 836
   serious, 642
   distressing, 830
   heinous, 945
   great, 31
   engrave, 559
   impress, 505
   shape, 240

Grave, *tomb*, 363
   sound, 408
Gravel, *offend*, 830
   puzzle, 704
   soil, 342
Graveolent, *odour*, 398
Graver, *artist*, 559
Gravestone, *interment*, 363
Graveyard, *interment*, 363
Gravid, *pregnant*, 168
Gravitate, *descent*, 306
Gravitation, *attraction*, 288
Gravity, *weight*, 319
   attraction, 288
   dullness, 843
   seriousness, 837
   importance, 642
   composure, 826
Gravy, *liquid*, 333
Graze, *browse*, 296
   touch, 199
Grease, *oil*, 332, 356
   unctuous, 355
Great, *much*, 31
   big, 192
   importance, 642
   glorious, 873
   magnanimous, 942
   pregnant, 168
Great circle, *direction*, 278
Greatcoat, *garment*, 225
Greaten, *enlarge*, 35
Greaves, *garment*, 225
Greedy, *voracious*, 957
   desirous, 865
   avaricious, 819
Greek Church, *Christian
   religion*, 983A
Green, *colour*, 435
   meadow, 344
   new, 123
   unskilled, 699
   unprepared, 674
   unaccustomed, 614
   credulous, 484
   ignorant, 491
Green belt, *environs*, 227
Green-eyed, *jealousy*, 920
Green light, *signal*, 550
Greenback, *money*, 800
Greenhorn, *fool*, 501
   dupe, 547
   novice, 493, 674
   stranger, 57
   bungler, 701
Greenroom, *the drama*, 599
Greet, *hail*, 894
   weep, 839
Gregarious, *social*, 892
Gremlin, *demon*, 980
Grenade, *arms*, 727
Grenadier, *soldier*, 726
   tall, 206
Grey, *colour*, 432
   age, 128

Grey-headed, *age*, 128
 veteran, 130
Grey market, *illegality*, 964
Grey matter, *brain*, 450
Greybeard, *veteran*, 130
Greyhound, *swift*, 274
Grid, *lattice*, 219
Gridelin, *purple*, 437
Gridiron, *lattice*, 219
 arena, 728
Grief, *dejection*, 837
Grievance, *injury*, 619
 pain, 830
Grieve, *complain*, 828, 839
 afflict, 830
 injure, 649
Griffin, *unconformity*, 83
 keeper, 753
Grig, *cheerful*, 836
Grill, *calefaction*, 384
 question, 461
Grille, *lattice*, 219
Grim, *ugly*, 846
 frightful, 828
 discourteous, 895
 ferocious, 907
Grim-visaged, *grave*, 837
Grimace, *ridicule*, 856
Grime, *unclean*, 653
Grin, *laugh*, 838
 ridicule, 856
 scorn, 929
Grind, *pulverize*, 330
 an organ, 415
 oppress, 907
 learn, 539
 sharpen, 253
 scholar, 492
Grinder, *teacher*, 540
Grinding, *painful*, 831
Grip, *power*, 737
 bag, 191
Grip-sack, *bag*, 191
Gripe, *seize*, 789
 retain, 781
 pain, 378, 828
 to give pain, 830
 power, 737
Griping, *avaricious*, 819
*Grisette, *woman*, 374
Grisly, *ugliness*, 846
Grist, *provision*, 637
 materials, 635
Gristle, *toughness*, 327
Grit, *pulverulence*, 330
 determination, 604
 courage, 861
Gritty, *hard*, 323
Grizzled, *variegation*, 440
Grizzly, *grey*, 432
Groan, *cry*, 411
 lament, 839
Groggy, *drunk*, 959
 ill, 655
Groin, *angular*, 244

Grooly, *ugly*, 845
Groom, *servant*, 746
 marriage, 903
Groomsman, *marriage*, 903
Groove, *furrow*, 259
 habit, 613
Grope, *feel*, 379
 experience, 463
 inquire, 461
 try, 675
Gross, *whole*, 51
 greatness, 31
 vulgar, 851
 vicious, 945
 impure, 961
*Grossièreté, *rudeness*, 895
Grot, see Grotto
Grotesque, *deformed*, 846
 ridiculous, 851, 853
 outlandish, 83
Grotto, *alcove*, 189
 hollow, 252
Grouchy, *discourteous*, 895
 bad-tempered, 901
Ground, *land*, 342
 support, 215
 base, 211
 region, 181
 cause, 153
 motive, 615
 plea, 617
 property, 780
 arena, 728
 teach, 537
Ground swell, *surge*, 348
 agitation, 315
Grounded, *knowing*, 490
 wrecked, 732
Groundless, *erroneous*, 495
 sophistical, 477
Groundling, *commonalty*, 876
Grounds, *lees*, 653
Groundwork, *basis*, 211
 support, 215
 cause, 153
 precursor, 64
 preparation, 673
Group, *cluster*, 72
 troop, 726
 to marshal, 58
Group-captain, *master*, 745
Grouse, *grumble*, 832, 839
Grout, *vinculum*, 45
Grove, *wood*, 367
 house, 189
Grovel, *move slowly*, 275
 be low, 207
 cringe, 886
 base, 940
Grow, *increase*, 35
 expand, 194
Grow from, *effect*, 154
Growl, *cry*, 412
 complain, 839
 threaten, 909

Growl, *be rude*, 895
 anger, 900
Growler, *vehicle*, 272
Growth, *in degree*, 35
 in size, 194
Groyne, *refuge*, 666
Grub, *little*, 193
 food, 298
Grub up, *extract*, 301
 destroy, 162
 discover, 480A
Grudge, *hate*, 898
 stingy, 640, 819
 unwilling, 603
Gruelling, *punishment*, 972
Gruesome, *ugly*, 846
Gruff, *morose*, 895
 sound, 410
Grumble, *sound*, 411
 complain, 832, 839
Grumous, *dense*, 321
 pulpy, 354
Grumpy, *discourteous*, 895
 bad-tempered, 901
Grundyism, *prudery*, 855
Grunt, *cry*, 412
 complain, 839
Guano, *manure*, 653
Guarantee, *security*, 771
 evidence, 467
 promise, 768
Guard, *defend*, 717
 safety, 664
Guard-room, *prison*, 752
Guarded, *circumspect*, 459
 conditional, 770
Guardian, *safety*, 664, 717
 keeper, 753
Guardless, *danger*, 665
Guardsman, *combatant*, 726
Gubernatorial, *directing*, 693
 authority, 737
Gudgeon, *dupe*, 547
Guerdon, *reward*, 973
Guerrilla, *combatant*, 726
Guess, *suppose*, 514
Guest, *friend*, 890
 arrival, 292
*Guet-apens, *untruth*, 546
 ambush, 530
Guffaw, *laughter*, 834
Guggle, see Gurgle
Guide, *direct*, 693
 director, 694
 advice, 695
 teach, 537
 teacher, 540
 road-book, 266
Guide-post, *indicator*, 550
 warning, 668
Guideless, *danger*, 665
Guild, *corporation*, 712
 tribunal, 966
 partnership, 797
Guildhall, *mart*, 799

Guile, *cunning*, 702
  deceit, 545
Guileless, *artless*, 703
  sincere, 543
Guillotine, *engine*, 975
  to decapitate, 972
Guilt, *crime*, 947
  vice, 945
Guiltless, *innocence*, 946
*Guindé, *conciseness*, 572
Guise, *state*, 7
  appearance, 448
  manner, 627
  plea, 617
Guiser, *the drama*, 599
Guitar, *music*, 417
Gulch, *gap*, 198
Gules, *redness*, 434
Gulf, *sea*, 343
  depth, 208
Gull, *dupe*, 547
  credulous, 486
Gullet, *throat*, 260
  rivulet, 348
Gullible, *credulity*, 486
Gully, *conduit*, 350
  opening, 260
  hollow, 252
  ravine, 198
Gulosity, *gluttony*, 957
Gulp, *swallow*, 297
  believe, 484
Gum, *fastening*, 45
  coherence, 46
  semiliquid, 352
Gum-boot, *dress*, 225
Gumption, *capacity*, 498
Gumshoe, *prowl*, 528
Gun, *arms*, 727
  fighter, 726
Gun-cotton, *arms*, 727
Gunboat, *ship*, 273
Gunman, *bad man*, 949
Gunner, *combatant*, 726
Gurgitation, *rotation*, 312
Gurgle, *sound*, 405, 408
  bubble, 353
Gurkha, *soldier*, 726
Guru, *priest*, 996
Gush, *flow*, 295
  flood, 348
  feeling, 821
  affectation, 855
Gusset, *angularity*, 244
Gust, *wind*, 349
  physical taste, 390
  enjoyment, 826
  moral taste, 850
Gustatory, *taste*, 390
Gusto, *relish*, 827
  taste, 850
Gut, *opening*, 260
  to sack, 789
  vitals, 221
Guts, *courage*, 861

Guts, *resolution*, 604
Gutter, *conduit*, 350
  groove, 259
Guttersnipe, *commonalty*, 876
  vulgarity, 851
Guttle, *devour*, 296
Guttural, *stammer*, 583
  letter, 561
Guy, *rope*, 45
  ugliness, 846
  man, 373
  to ridicule, 842, 856
  deride, 929
Guzzle, *drink*, 296
  tipple, 959
  gluttony, 957
Gymkhana, *contention*, 720
Gymnasium, *school*, 542
  training, 673
Gymnast, *strength*, 159
Gymnastic, *exertion*, 686
  contention, 720
  teaching, 537
Gymnosophist, *heathen*, 984
  temperance, 953
Gynaecocracy, *rule*, 737
Gynaecology, *remedy*, 662
Gyp, *servant*, 746
Gypsy, *see Gipsy*
Gyration, *rotation*, 312
Gyre, *rotation*, 312
Gyroscope, *rotation*, 312
Gyve, *chain*, 45
  shackle, 752

H

Haberdashery, *dress*, 225
Habergeon, *defence*, 717
Habiliment, *dress*, 225
Habilitation, *skill*, 698
Habit, *intrinsic*, 5
  custom, 613
  coat, 225
Habitat, *abode*, 189
Habitation, *abode*, 189
  location, 184
Habitual, *regular*, 82, 613
Habituate, *accustom*, 613
  train, 673
Habitude, *state*, 7
  relation, 9
  habit, 613
*Habitué, *guest*, 891
  frequenter, 136
*Hacienda, *property*, 780
Hack, *cut*, 44
  shorten, 201
  horse, 271
  drudge, 690
  writer, 590
Hackle, *cut*, 44
Hackneyed, *regular*, 82
  trite, 496
  habitual, 613

Hackneyed, *experienced*, 698
Hades, *hell*, 982
Hadji, *clergy*, 996
  pilgrim, 268
Haecceity, *speciality*, 79
Haemorrhage, *excretion*, 299
Haft, *instrument*, 633
Hag, *ugly*, 846
  veteran, 130
  wretch, 913
  bad woman, 949
Haggard, *ugly*, 846
  wild, 824
  insane, 503
Haggle, *bargain*, 769, 794
Hagiography, *theology*, 983
Ha-ha, *ditch*, 198
  defence, 717
Haik, *dress*, 225
Hail, *call*, 586
  ice, 383
Hair, *thread*, 45
  filament, 205
  roughness, 256
Hair-oil, *ornament*, 847
Hair-raising, *fear*, 860
Hair's breadth, *thin*, 203
Halberd, *arms*, 727
Halberdier, *combatant*, 726
Halcyon, *prosperous*, 734, 829
  joyful, 827
  calm, 174
Hale, *health*, 654
Half, *bisection*, 91
Half a dozen, *six*, 98
Half and half, *mixture*, 41
Half-baked, *incomplete*, 53
  witless, 499
Half-blood, *unconformity*, 83
Half-breed, *unconformity*, 83
Half-caste, *mixture*, 41
  unconformity, 83
Half-hearted, *indifferent*, 866
  irresolute, 605
  timorous, 862
Half-moon, *curvature*, 245
Half-pint, *little*, 193
Half-seas-over, *drunk*, 959
Half-track, *vehicle*, 272
Half-way, *middle*, 68
Half-wit, *fool*, 501
Half-witted, *folly*, 499
Hall, *chamber*, 189
  receptacle, 191
  mart, 799
Hall-marked, *genuine*, 494
Hallelujah, *worship*, 990
Hallo! *call*, 586
  wonder, 870
  arrival, 292
Halloo, *cry*, 411
Hallow, *sanctify*, 987
Hallowed, *venerated*, 928
  Deity, 976
Hallucination, *error*, 495

Hallucination, *delusion*, 503

Halo, *light*, 420
 glory, 873

Halt, *stop*, 142, 265
 flag, 655
 rest, 685, 687
 limp, 275

Halter, *rope*, 45
 fetter, 752
 punishment, 975

Halting, *lame*, 160

Halve, *bisect*, 91

Halyard, *rope*, 45

Hamadryad, *nymph*, 979

Hamlet, *abode*, 189

*Hammal, *carrier*, 271

Hammam, *furnace*, 386

Hammer, *to knock*, 276
 instrument, 633
 auction, 796
 repetition, 104
 bankrupt, 808

Hammer at, *thought*, 583
 action, 682

Hammock, *support*, 215

Hamper, *basket*, 191
 obstruct, 706

Hamstring, *injure*, 649
 weaken, 160
 incapacitate, 158

Hand, *instrument*, 633
 indicator, 550
 agent, 690
 side, 236
 writing, 590
 to give, 784
 agency, 170

Hand-barrow, *vehicle*, 272

Hand-gallop, *velocity*, 274

Hand in hand, *accompaniment*, 88

Hand over, *transfer*, 270

Handbook, *advice*, 695

Handcuff, *tie together*, 43
 manacle, 751, 752

Handfast, *marriage*, 903

Handful, *quantity*, 25, 103
 smallness, 32

Handicap, *inequality*, 28
 disadvantage, 651

Handicraft, *action*, 680

Handicraftsman, *agent*, 690

Handiwork, *action*, 680
 effect, 154

Handkerchief, *dress*, 225
 clean, 652

Handle, *instrument*, 633
 plea, 617
 touch, 379
 use, 677
 describe, 594
 dissert, 595
 work, 680

Handling, *treatment*, 692

Handmaid, *servant*, 746

Handmaid, *instrumentality*, 631

Hands off! *resist*, 719
 prohibit, 761

Handsel, *security*, 771
 give, 784
 pay, 809
 begin, 66

Handsome, *beautiful*, 845
 liberal, 816
 disinterested, 942

Handspike, *instrument*, 633

Handwriting, *omen*, 512
 signature, 550
 autograph, 590

Handy, *near*, 197
 skilful, 698
 useful, 644
 attainable, 705

Hang, *pendency*, 214
 kill, 361
 execute, 972
 expletive, 908

Hang about, *loiter*, 275

Hang back, *hesitate*, 603

Hang fire, *reluctance*, 603
 vacillation, 605
 stop, 142
 refuse, 764
 lateness, 133
 slowness, 275
 inactivity, 683

Hang out, *reside*, 188

Hang over, *futurity*, 121
 destiny, 152
 height, 206

Hang together, *junction*, 43

Hang up, *defer*, 133

Hangar, *building*, 189

Hanger, *arms*, 727

Hanger-on, *servant*, 746
 accompany, 88
 follow, 281
 parasite, 886
 flatterer, 935

Hangings, *ornaments*, 847

Hangman, *executioner*, 975

Hank, *skein*, 219

Hanker, *desire*, 865

Hanky-panky, *fraud*, 545

Hansard, *record*, 551

Hansel, *see* Handsel

Hansom, *vehicle*, 272

Hap, *chance*, 156, 621

Haphazard, *chance*, 156, 621

Hapless, *hopeless*, 859
 miserable, 828

Haply, *chance*, 156
 possibly, 470

Happen, *event*, 151

Happy, *glad*, 827
 expedient, 646
 agreement, 23

Happy-go-lucky, *careless*, 460
 aimless, 621
 improvident, 674

Happy medium, *middle*, 68

Happy thought, *wit*, 842

Hara-kiri, *suicide*, 361
 execution, 972

Harangue, *speech*, 582
 preach, 998

Harass, *worry*, 907
 fatigue, 688
 vex, 830

Harbinger, *omen*, 512
 precursor, 64, 116

Harbour, *anchorage*, 189
 refuge, 666
 haven, 292
 to cherish, 821

Harbourless, *exposed*, 665

Hard, *dense*, 323
 difficult, 704
 grievous, 830
 strong, 159
 obdurate, 951
 sour, 397

Hard-and-fast, *exact*, 494
 strict, 739

Hard-boiled, *callous*, 823

Hard case, *bad man*, 949

Hard currency, *money*, 800

Hard-favoured, *ugly*, 846

Hard-headed, *skill*, 698
 wise, 498

Hard-hearted, *cruel*, 907

Hard lines, *adversity*, 735

Hard-mouthed, *obstinacy*, 606

Hard up, *poverty*, 804

Hard-working, *exertion*, 682, 68

Harden, *accustom*, 613
 train, 673
 render callous, 376, 823
 impious, 988
 impenitent, 951

Hardihood, *courage*, 861
 insolence, 885

Hardly, *scarcely*, 32
 infrequency, 137

Hardness of heart, *vice*, 945

Hardship, *pain*, 830
 adversity, 735

Hardy, *strong*, 159
 healthy, 654

Hare, *velocity*, 274

Hare-brained, *rash*, 460, 863

Harem, *apartment*, 191
 impurity, 961

Hark, *hearing*, 418

Hark back, *regression*, 283

Harlequin, *motley*, 440
 pantomimic, 599
 humorist, 844

Harlot, *libertine*, 962

Harlotry, *impurity*, 961

Harm, *evil*, 619
 badness, 649
 malevolence, 907

Harmattan, *wind*, 349

Harmless, *innocent*, 946

Heartburning, *resentment*, 900
  jealousy, 920
Hearten, *inspirit*, 824, 861
Hearth, *abode*, 189
  fire, 386
Heartiness, *feeling*, 821
  sociality, 892
Heartless, *malevolent*, 945
Hearty, *healthy*, 654
  willing, 602
  feeling, 821
  cheerful, 831, 836
Heat, *warmth*, 382
  calefaction, 384
  contest, 720
  violence, 173
  excitement, 825
Heath, *plain*, 344
Heathen, *pagan*, 984, 986
  irreligious, 988
Heathenish, *vulgar*, 851
Heave, *raise*, 307
  pant, 821
  throw, 284
Heave in sight, *visibility*, 446
Heave to, *stop*, 265
Heaven, *paradise*, 981
  bliss, 827
Heaven-born, *virtue*, 944
Heaven-directed, *wisdom*, 498
Heavenly, *divine*, 976
  rapturous, 829
  celestial, 318
  angelic, 977
Heavens, *world*, 318
Heaviness, *inertia*, 172
  dejection, 837
  dullness, 843
Heaviside layer, *air*, 338
Heavy, *weighty*, 319
  inert, 172, 682
  slow, 275
  stupid, 499
  rude, 851
  large, 31
Hebdomadal, *period*, 108, 138
Hebe, *beauty*, 845
Hebetate, *insensible*, 823
Hecate, *hag*, 846
Hecatomb, *killing*, 361
Heckle, *question*, 461
Hectic, *fever*, 382
  feeling, 821
Hector, *courage*, 861
  bully, 885
Hedge, *enclosure*, 232
  to *shuffle*, 544
  to *compensate*, 30
Hedge-hop, *fly*, 267
Hedge in, *enclose*, 231
  safe, 664
Hedgehog, *sharpness*, 253
  defence, 717
Hedonism, *intemperance*, 954
Heed, *attend*, 457

Heed, *care*, 459
  caution, 864
Heedless, *inattentive*, 458
  neglectful, 460
Heel, *slope*, 217
  rascal, 949
Heel-tap, *remainder*, 40
Heels, *rear*, 235
Heels over head, *reckless*, 460
Heft, *handle*, 633
  exertion, 686
Hefty, *heavy*, 319
Hegemony, *authority*, 737
Hegira, *departure*, 293
Heigh-ho! *lamentation*, 839
Height, *altitude*, 206
  degree, 26
  superiority, 33
Heighten, *increase*, 35
  exalt, 206
  exaggerate, 549
  aggravate, 835
Heinous, *vice*, 945
Heir, *possessor*, 779
  posterity, 167
  futurity, 121
Heirloom, *property*, 780
Heirship, *possess*, 777
Helen, *beauty*, 845
Helicon, *poetry*, 597
Helicopter, *aircraft*, 273A
Helidrome, *arrival*, 292
Heliograph, *signal*, 550
Heliotherapy, *remedy*, 662
Helix, *convolution*, 248
Hell, *gehenna*, 982
  abyss, 208
Hell-born, *vice*, 945
Hellcat, *bad woman*, 949
  fury, 173
Hellebore, *bane*, 663
Hellhag, *bad woman*, 949
Hellhound, *miscreant*, 949
  ruffian, 173, 913
Hellish, *bad*, 649
  malevolent, 907
  vicious, 945
Hello, see Hallo
Helm, *handle*, 633
  direction, 693
  authority, 737
Helmet, *dress*, 225
  defence, 717
Helot, *servant*, 746
Help, *aid*, 707
  auxiliary, 711
  utility, 644
  remedy, 662
  servant, 746
Helpless, *weak*, 160
  incapable, 158
  exposed, 665
Helpmate, *auxiliary*, 711
  wife, 903
Helter-skelter, *disorder*, 59

Helter-skelter, *haste*, 684
  slope, 217
Hem, *edge*, 230
  fold, 258
  to *stammer*, 583
Hem in, *enclose*, 231
  surround, 227
  restrain, 751
Hemlock, *bane*, 663
Henbane, *bane*, 663
Hence, *arising from*, 155
  deduction, 476
  motive, 615
Henceforth, *futurity*, 121
Henchman, *servant*, 746
Henpecked, *obedience*, 743
  subjection, 749
Hep, *knowing*, 490
  informed, 527
Hephaestus, *god*, 979
Heptad, *seven*, 98
Heptagon, *angularity*, 244
  seven, 98
Hera, *goddess*, 979
Herald, *messenger*, 534
  precursor, 64
  omen, 512
  lead, 280
  to *predict*, 511
  to *proclaim*, 531
Herb, *plant*, 367
Herbarium, *botany*, 369
Herbivorous, *eat*, 296
Herculean, *strength*, 159
  huge, 192
  difficulty, 704
Herd, *animal*, 366
  flock, 72, 102
Here, *present*, 186
Hereabouts, *nearness*, 197
Hereafter, *futurity*, 121
Hereditament, *property*, 780
Hereditary, *derivative*, 154
  posterity, 167
  habit, 613
  intrinsic, 5
Heredity, *paternity*, 166
Heresy, *error*, 495
  unbelief, 485
  religious, 984A
Heretic, *dissent*, 489
  heresy, 984A
Heretofore, *preterition*, 122
  priority, 116
Herewith, *accompaniment*, 88
Heritage, *futurity*, 121
  possession, 777
  property, 780
Heritor, *possessor*, 779
Hermaphrodite, *incongruity*, 83
Hermeneutic, *interpretation*,
            522
Hermes, *god*, 979
  messenger, 534
Hermetically, *closure*, 261

Hive, *dwelling*, 186

Hive-off, *distribute*, 73

Hoar, *white*, 430; *aged*, 128

Hoar-frost, *cold*, 383

Hoard, *store*, 636
  assemblage, 72

Hoarding, *screen*, 530

Hoarse, *sound*, 405, 410
  voice, 581

Hoary, *white*, 430
  aged, 128

Hoax, *deception*, 545

Hob, *support*, 215
  fire, 386

Hobble, *limp*, 275
  difficulty, 704
  lame, 732
  tether, 751
  bond, 752
  awkward, 699

Hobbledehoy, *youth*, 129

Hobby, *pursuit*, 622
  desire, 865

Hobgoblin, *demon*, 980

Hobnob, *courtesy*, 894

Hobo, *traveller*, 268
  tramp, 876

Hobson's choice, *necessity*, 601
  absence of choice, 610

Hock, *pawn*, 787

Hocus, *deceive*, 545
  stupefy, 376

Hocus-pocus, *cheat*, 545
  conjuration, 992

Hod, *receptacle*, 191
  vehicle, 272

Hodge, *clown*, 876

Hodge-podge, *mixture*, 41
  confusion, 59

Hog, *sensuality*, 954
  gluttony, 957
  selfishness, 943

Hog-wash, *uncleanness*, 653

Hoist, *elevate*, 307
  lift, 627

Hoity-toity! *wonder*, 870

Hokum, *humbug*, 497
  deception, 545

Hold, *possess*, 777
  believe, 484
  retain, 781
  cohere, 46
  fix, 150
  stop, 265
  discontinue, 142
  continue, 141, 143
  refrain, 623
  contain, 54
  influence, 175
  prison, 752
  in a ship, 207
  term, 71

Hold forth, *declaim*, 582
  teach, 537

Hold good, *truth*, 494

Hold in, *moderation*, 174

Hold on, *move*, 264
  continue, 141, 143
  determination, 604

Hold out, *resist*, 718
  offer, 763

Hold the tongue, *silence*,
                                    403, 585

Hold together, *junction*, 43

Hold up, *sustain*, 707
  continue, 143
  delay, 133; *plunder*, 791

Holder, *possessor*, 779

Holdfast, *vinculum*, 45

Holding, *property*, 780

Hole, *opening*, 260
  place, 182; *den*, 189
  receptacle, 191
  ambush, 530
  difficulty, 704

Hole-and-corner, *concealment*,
                                    528

Holiday, *amusement*, 840
  repose, 687
  leisure, 685; *time*, 134

Holiness, *Deity*, 976

Hollow, *concavity*, 252
  depth, 208
  incomplete, 53
  false, 544; *sound*, 408
  specious, 477
  unsubstantial, 4

Holm, *island*, 346

Holocaust, *idolatry*, 991
  killing, 361

Holograph, *writing*, 590

Holt, *plant*, 367

Holy, *Deity*, 976
  piety, 987

HOLY GHOST, *Deity*, 976

Holy Writ, *revelation*, 985
  truth, 494

Homage, *reverence*, 928
  submission, 725
  approbation, 931
  fealty, 743
  worship, 990

Home, *habitation*, 189
  interior, 221
  focus, 74; *near*, 197
  arrival, 292

Home and dry, *successful*, 731

Home-felt, *feeling*, 821

Home Guard, *combatant*, 726

Homeless, *outcast*, 893
  displaced, 185

Homeliness, *ugliness*, 846
  simplicity, 849
  style, 576

Homeric, *poetry*, 597

Homespun, *simple*, 849
  ugly, 846
  vulgar, 851
  low, 876
  coarse, 329

Homespun, *style*, 576

Homestead, *abode*, 189

Homicide, *killing*, 361

Homily, *advice*, 595
  speech, 582
  sermon, 998

Homoeopathic, *littleness*, 32, 193

Homogeneity, *relation*, 9
  uniformity, 16
  simplicity, 42

Homologate, *concede*, 467, 762

Homology, *relation*, 9
  uniformity, 16

Homonym, *word*, 562
  equivocal, 520

*Homunculus, *littleness*, 193

Hone, *sharpener*, 253
  grind, 331

Honest, *pure*, 960
  true, 543
  candid, 703
  honour, 939

Honey, *sweetness*, 396
  darling, 899

Honeycomb, *concavity*, 252
  opening, 260

Honeydew, *tobacco*, 298A

Honeyed, *flattering*, 933

Honeymoon, *wedding*, 903
  happiness, 827

Honorarium, *expenditure*, 809

Honorary, *gratuitous*, 815

Honour, *probity*, 939
  glory, 873
  title, 877
  respect, 928
  to pay, 807

Hood, *cowl*, 999
  cap, 225

Hoodlum, *evildoer*, 913, 949

Hoodoo, *sorcery*, 992
  spell, 993

Hoodwink, *blind*, 442
  conceal, 528
  ignore, 491

Hooey, *nonsense*, 497
  trash, 643

Hoof, *to kick*, 276

Hoof it, *walking*, 266

Hoof out, *eject*, 297

Hook, *to fasten*, 43
  fastening, 45
  grip, 781
  hang, 214
  curvature, 245
  deviation, 279
  take, 789

Hook-up, *junction*, 43

Hookah, *tobacco-pipe*, 298A

Hooker, *ship*, 273

Hooligan, *ruffian*, 913, 949

Hooliganism, *brutality*, 907

Hoop, *circle*, 247

Hoot, *cry*, 411
  deride, 929, 930, 932

Hullabaloo, *noise*, 404
　　cry, 411
Hullo, *see* Hallo
Hum, *faint sound*, 405
　　continued sound, 407, 412
　　to sing, 415
　　deceive, 545
　　stink, 401
Hum and ha, *hesitate*, 583
　　demur, 605
Hum-note, *melody*, 413
Human, *mankind*, 372
Humane, *benevolent*, 906
　　philanthropic, 910
Humanism, *knowledge*, 490
Humanist, *scholar*, 492
Humanitarian, *philanthropist*,
　　　　　　　　　　906
Humanities, *letters*, 560
Humanity, *human nature*, 372
　　benevolence, 906
Humanize, *courtesy*, 894
Humble, *meek*, 879
　　modest, 881
　　to abash, 874
　　pious, 987
Humbug, *deception*, 545
　　falsehood, 544
Humdrum, *dull*, 843
Humectate, *moisten*, 339
Humid, *moist*, 339
Humiliate, *humble*, 879
　　shame, 874
　　worship, 990
Humility, *piety*, 987
Humming-top, *musical*, 417
Hummock, *height*, 206, 250
Humoresque, *music*, 415
Humorist, *humorist*, 844
Humour, *essence*, 5
　　liquid, 333
　　disposition, 602
　　tendency, 176
　　caprice, 608
　　indulge, 760
　　affections, 820
　　to please, 829
　　wit, 842
Humoursome, *capricious*, 608
　　discourteous, 895
Hump, *convexity*, 250
Hump bluey, *journey*, 266
Hump yourself, *activity*, 682
Humpbacked, *distortion*, 243
　　ugliness, 846
Humph! *wonder*, 870
Humus, *soil*, 342
Hun, *evildoer*, 913
Hunch, *convexity*, 250
Hundred, *number*, 99
　　region, 181
Hunger, *desire*, 865
Hunks, *parsimony*, 819
Hunnish, *malevolent*, 907
Hunt, *follow*, 281

Hunt, *pursue*, 622
　　inquire, 461
Hunter, *carrier*, 271
Hunting grounds, *heaven*, 981
Hurdle, *fence*, 232
Hurdy-gurdy, *musical*, 417
Hurl, *propel*, 284
Hurly-burly, *confusion*, 59
　　turmoil, 315
Hurrah! *cheerfulness*, 836
　　rejoicing, 838
Hurricane, *tempest*, 349
　　violence, 173
Hurried, *excitability*, 825
Hurry, *haste*, 684
　　swiftness, 274
　　earliness, 132
　　to urge, 615
　　to excite, 824
Hurst, *plant*, 367
Hurt, *evil*, 619
　　physical pain, 378
　　moral pain, 828
　　to injure, 649, 907
　　to molest, 830
Hurtful, *badness*, 649
Hurtle, *impulse*, 276
Husband, *spouse*, 903
　　to store, 636
Husbandman, *agriculture*, 371
Husbandry, *agriculture*, 371
　　conduct, 692
　　economy, 817
Hush, *silence*, 403
　　latent, 526
　　moderate, 174
　　assuage, 723
　　pacify, 723
Hush-hush, *secret*, 534
Hush-money, *bribe*, 809
　　compensation, 30
Hush up, *conceal*, 526, 528
Husk, *covering*, 222
　　to strip, 226
Husky, *dry*, 340
　　big, 192
　　strong, 159
　　faint sound, 405, 501
Hussar, *combatant*, 726
Hussy, *libertine*, 962
　　bad woman, 949
　　impertinent, 887
Hustings, *tribunal*, 966
　　platform, 542
Hustle, *push*, 276
　　disarrange, 61
　　agitate, 315
　　bustle, 171, 682
　　haste, 684
Hut, *abode*, 189
Hutch, *abode*, 189
Huzza! *cheerfulness*, 836
Hyaline, *transparency*, 425
Hybrid, *mixture*, 41
　　nondescript, 83

Hydra, *unconformity*, 83
Hydra-headed, *reproduction*,
　　　　　　　　　　163
Hydrant, *spray*, 348
Hydraulics, *fluids*, 348
Hydrogen bomb, *arms*, 727
Hydrographic, *sea*, 341
Hydrology, *water*, 333
Hydromel, *sweetness*, 396
Hydrometer, *density*, 321
Hydropathic, *salubrity*, 656
　　remedy, 662
Hydropathy, *remedy*, 662
Hydrophobia, *dislike*, 867
Hydroplane, *aircraft*, 273A
Hydroponics, *agriculture*, 371
Hydrostatics, *water*, 333
Hydrotherapy, *remedy*, 662
Hyena, *evildoer*, 913
Hygiene, *salubrity*, 656
Hygrology, *moisture*, 339
Hygrometer, *moisture*, 339
Hylotheism, *heathen*, 984
Hymen, *marriage*, 903
Hymn, *worship*, 990
Hymnal, *rite*, 998
Hyperaesthesia, *excitability*, 825
　　sensibility, 376, 822
Hyperbole, *exaggeration*, 549
Hyperborean, *cold*, 383
Hypercritical, *disapprobation*,
　　　　　　　　　　932
　　fastidious, 868
Hyperion, *beauty*, 845
Hypermetropia, *vision*, 443
Hyperpyrexia, *heat*, 382
Hypersensitive, *sensitive*, 375,
　　　　　　　　　　825
Hypertrophy, *expansion*, 194
Hyphen, *vinculum*, 45
Hypnology, *inactivity*, 683
Hypnosis, *inactivity*, 683
Hypnotic, *remedy*, 662
　　sedative, 683
Hypnotize, *occult*, 992, 994
Hypocaust, *furnace*, 386
Hypochondriac, *dejection*, 837
　　insanity, 503, 504
Hypocrisy, *deception*, 545
　　religious, 988
Hyprocite, *deceiver*, 548
Hypocritical, *falsehood*, 544
Hypostasis, *substantiality*, 3
Hypostatic, *Deity*, 976
Hypothecation, *lending*, 787
Hypothesis, *supposition*, 514
Hysterical, *violence*, 173
　　excitement, 825
Hysteron proteron, *inversion*,
　　　　　　　　　　218

I

Imbue, *tinge*, 428
  impregnate, 300
  moisten, 339
  teach, 537
  feel, 821
Imitate, *to copy*, 19
  repetition, 104
  to represent, 554
Imitation, *copy*, 21
Immaculate, *excellent*, 648
  spotless, 652
  faultless, 650
  innocent, 946
  pure, 960
Immanent, *inherent*, 5
Immanity, *malevolence*, 907
Immaterial, *unsubstantial*, 4
  spiritual, 317
  mental, 450
  trifling, 643
Immature, *new*, 123
  unprepared, 674
Immeasurable, *infinite*, 105
  great, 31
Immediate, *transient*, 111
Immedicable, *incurable*, 655, 659
Immemorial, *old*, 124
Immense, *in degree*, 31
  in size, 192
Immerse, *introduce*, 300
  dip, 337
  baptism, 998
Immethodical, *disorder*, 59
Immigrant, *stranger*, 57
Immigration, *migration*, 266
  entrance, 294
Imminent, *futurity*, 121
  destiny, 152
Immiscibility, *incoherence*, 47
Immission, *reception*, 296
Immitigable, *ire*, 900
  violence, 173
Immobility, *immutability*, 150
  quiescence, 265
  resolution, 604
Immoderately, *greatness*, 31
Immoderation, *intemperance*, 954
Immodest, *impurity*, 961
Immolate, *destroy*, 162
  kill, 361
  offer, 763
Immolation, *sacrifice*, 991
Immoral, *vicious*, 945
  wrong, 923
Immortal, *perpetual*, 112
  glorious, 873
  celebrated, 883
Immovable, *unchangeable*, 150
  resolved, 604
  obstinate, 606
Immunity, *exemption*, 927A
  right, 924
  freedom, 748
Immure, *enclose*, 231

Immure, *imprison*, 751
Immutable, *immutability*, 150
Imp, *demon*, 980
  ruffian, 913
  wretch, 943
Impact, *contact*, 43
  impulse, 276
  insertion, 300
Impair, *deterioration*, 659
Impale, *transfix*, 260
  pierce, 302
  execute, 972
Impalpable, *small*, 193
  powder, 330
  immaterial, 317
  intangible, 381
Impanation, *rite*, 998
Imparity, *inequality*, 28
Impart, *give*, 784
  inform, 527
Impartial, *just*, 922
  wise, 498
  indifferent, 866
  honourable, 939
Impassable, *closed*, 261, 704
Impasse, *hindrance*, 706
  situation, 8
  difficulty, 704
Impassible, *insensible*, 376, 823
Impassion, *excite*, 824
Impassive, *insensible*, 823
Impasto, *painting*, 556
Impatient, *excitable*, 825
Impawn, *lending*, 787
Impeach, *accuse*, 938
Impeccability, *perfection*, 650
Impecunious, *adversity*, 735
  poverty, 804
Impede, *hindrance*, 706
Impedimenta, *hindrance*, 706
  baggage, 635
Impel, *push*, 276, 284
  move, 264
  induce, 615
Impend, *future*, 121
  expectation, 507
  height, 206
  destiny, 152
Impenetrable, *latent*, 526
  hidden, 528
Impenitence, *impenitence*, 951
Imperative, *authority*, 737
  duty, 926
  requirement, 630
*Imperator, *master*, 745
Imperceptible, *invisible*, 447
  minute, 193
Impercipient, *insensibility*, 376
Imperfect, *incomplete*, 53
  failing, 651
  shortcoming, 304
  vicious, 945
  small, 32
Imperforate, *closure*, 261
Imperial, *authority*, 737

Imperial, *beard*, 256
Imperil, *endanger*, 665
Imperious, *stern*, 739
  insolent, 885
Imperishable, *external*, 112, 150
  glorious, 873
Impermanent, *transitory*, 111
Impermeable, *closed*, 261
  dense, 321
Impersonal, *generality*, 78
  material, 316
Impersonate, *represent*, 554
  imitate, 19
Impertinence, *inexpedience*, 647
Impertinent, *irrelevant*, 10
  disagreeing, 24
  insolent, 885
  discourteous, 895
Imperturbable, *unruffled*, 823, 826
Impervious, *closure*, 261
Impetrate, *beseech*, 765
Impetuous, *boisterous*, 173
  hot, 825
  hasty, 684
  rash, 863
  eager, 865
Impetus, *impulse*, 276
Impiety, *impiety*, 988
  irreligion, 989
Impignorate, *lending*, 787
Impinge, *impulse*, 276
Impish, *supernatural*, 980
Implacable, *hatred*, 898
  wrath, 900
  unforgiving, 919
Implant, *insert*, 300
  teach, 537
Implanted, *adventitious*, 6
  inborn, 5
Implement, *instrument*, 633
Impletion, *sufficiency*, 639
  fullness, 52
Implicate, *accuse*, 938
  involve, 54
Implication, *inference*, 521
Implicit, *understood*, 516
  metaphorical, 521
  untold, 526
Implore, *beseech*, 765
  pray, 990
  pity, 914
Imply, *mean*, 516
  latent, 526
  evidence, 467
  metaphor, 521
Impolite, *rude*, 895
  vulgar, 851
Impolitic, *folly*, 499
  inexpedient, 647
Imponderable, *light*, 320
  immaterial, 317
Import, *ingress*, 294
  transfer, 270

Inborn, *intrinsic*, 5, 820
   habitual, 613
Inbred, *intrinsic*, 5, 820
Inca, *master*, 745
Incalculable, *infinite*, 105
   much, 31
Incalescence, *heat*, 382
Incandescence, *heat*, 382
   light, 420
Incantation, *invocation*, 765
   spell, 993
Incapable, *weak*, 160
   unable, 158
Incapacity, *impotence*, 158
   weakness, 160
   stupidity, 499
   indocility, 538
Incarcerate, *imprison*, 751
   surround, 231
Incarnadine, *red*, 434
Incarnate, *materialize*, 316
Incarnation, *intrinsic*, 5
   Deity, 976
Incautious, *neglectful*, 460
   rash, 863
Incendiary, *evildoer*, 913
   destructive, 162
Incense, *fragrance*, 400
   to provoke, 900
   hatred, 898
   flattery, 933
   worship, 990
Incentive, *motive*, 615
Inception, *beginning*, 66
Inceptor, *learner*, 541
Incertitude, *uncertain*, 475
Incessant, *perpetual*, 112
   frequency, 136
Incest, *impurity*, 961
Inch, *littleness*, 193
   slowness, 275
   island, 346
Inch by inch, *degree*, 26
Inchoate, *amorphous*, 241
Inchoation, *beginning*, 66
Incidence, *direction*, 278
Incident, *event*, 151
Incidental, *extrinsic*, 6, 8
   irrelative, 10
   liable, 177
   casual, 156, 621
Incinerate, *calefaction*, 384
Incipient, *beginning*, 66
   style, 574
Incision, *cut*, 44
Incisive, *style*, 574
   feeling, 821
Incite, *urge*, 615
   exasperate, 173
Incivility, *rudeness*, 895
Incivism, *misanthropy*, 911
Inclement, *cold*, 383
   severe, 739
Incline, *slope*, 217
   direction, 278

Incline, *tendency*, 176
   willing, 602
   desire, 865
   love, 897
   induce, 615
Inclusive, *in a compound*, 4
   in a class, 76
Incogitable, *incogitancy*, 452
Incognito, *concealment*, 528
Incognizable, *unknowable*, 519
Incognizance, *ignorance*, 491
Incoherent, *physical*, 47
   mental, 503
   meaning, 519
Incombustible, *fire-proof*, 385
Income, *receipt*, 810
   wealth, 803
Incomer, *stranger*, 57
Incoming, *ingress*, 294
Incommensurable, *quantity*,
      84, 85
   irrelation, 10
   disagreeing, 24
Incommode, *to hinder*, 706
   annoy, 830
Incommodious, *inconvenient*,
      647
Incommunicable, *retention*, 781
   unintelligible, 519
Incommunicado, *concealed*,
      528
Incommutable, *unchangeable*,
      150
Incomparable, *goodness*, 648
Incompatible, *disagree*, 24
Incompetence, *inability*, 158
   incapacity, 499
   insufficiency, 640
   unskilfulness, 699
Incomplete, *defective*, 53
   not completed, 730
Incomprehensible, *unintel-
ligible*, 519
Incomprehension, *ignorance*,
      491
Incompressible, *density*, 321
Inconceivable, *unintelligible*,
      519
   incredible, 485
Inconcinnity, *ugliness*, 846
Inconclusive, *sophistry*, 477
Incondite, *inelegant*, 579
Incongruous, *disagreement*, 24
Inconsecutive, *discontinuous*,
      70
Inconsequential, *unreason-
ble*, 477
Inconsiderable, *in size*, 193
   in degree, 32
   unimportant, 643
Inconsiderate, *thoughtless*, 452
   heedless, 460
   foolish, 699
Inconsistent, *contrary*, 14
   unreasonable, 477

Inconsistent, *disagreeing*, 24
   multiform, 16A
   absurd, 497
   capricious, 608
Inconsolable, *pain*, 828
   dejection, 837
Inconsonance, *disagreement*,
      24
Inconspicuous, *invisible*, 447
   latent, 526
Inconstant, *irresolution*, 605
Incontestable, *certainty*, 474
Incontinent, *impurity*, 961
Incontinently, *transient*, 111
Incontrovertible, *certainty*, 474
   unchangeable, 150
Inconvenient, *inexpedient*, 647
Inconvincible, *incredulity*, 487
Incorporate, *combination*, 48
Incorporeal, *immaterial*, 317
Incorrect, *erroneous*, 495, 568
   sophistical, 477
Incorrigible, *vicious*, 945
   impenitent, 951
   irremediable, 649
   hopeless, 859
Incorruptible, *honourable*, 939
   pure, 942
Incorruption, *health*, 654
   innocence, 946
Incrassate, *thickness*, 202
   density, 321
Increase, *in degree*, 35
   in size, 194
Incredible, *impossible*, 471
   improbable, 473, 485
   much, 31
   wonderful, 870
Incredulity, *unbelief*, 487, 485
   religious, 989
Increment, *increase, in degree*,
      35
   in size, 194
   addition, 37, 39
Incrustation, *covering*, 222
Incubation, *preparation*, 673
Incubus, *hindrance*, 706
Inculcate, *teach*, 537
Inculpate, *accuse*, 938
Incumbent, *height*, 206
   weight, 319
   duty, 926
   clergyman, 996
Incunabula, *beginning*, 66
   book, 591
Incur, *liable*, 177
Incurable, *disease*, 655
Incuriosity, *incurious*, 456
Incursion, *ingress*, 294
   attack, 716
Incurvation, *curvature*, 245
Indaba, *council*, 696
Indebted, *owing*, 806
   duty, 926
   gratitude, 916

1

Inexplicable, *unintelligible*, 519
  wonderful, 870
Inexpressible, *unmeaning*, 517
  wonder, 870
  great degree, 31
Inexpressive, *unmeaning*, 517,
    510
Inexpugnable, *safety*, 664
Inextinguishable, *immutable*,
    150
  uncontrollable, 825
  energetic, 157
Inextricable, *difficult*, 704
  impossible, 471
  disorder, 59
  coherence, 46
Infallible, *certainty*, 474
  perfect, 650
Infamy, *dishonour*, 940
  shame, 874
  vice, 945
Infancy, *beginning*, 66
  youth, 127
Infant, *infant*, 129
Infanta, *master*, 745
Infanticide, *killing*, 361
Infantile, *puerile*, 643
  foolish, 499
Infantry, *combatant*, 726
Infatuation, *folly*, 499
  misjudgment, 481
  obstinacy, 606
  credulity, 486
  passion, 825
  love, 897
Infeasible, *impossible*, 471
  difficult, 704
Infect, *mix*, 41
Infection, *disease*, 655
  contamination, 659
  excitation, 824
Infectious, *insalubrity*, 657
Infecund, *unproductiveness*, 169
Infelicity, *unhappiness*, 828
  inexpertness, 699
Infer, *judgment*, 480
Inference, *judgment*, 480
  interpretation, 522
Inferential, *deducible*, 478
Inferior, *less*, 34
  imperfect, 651
Infernal, *bad*, 649
  wicked, 945
  malevolent, 907
Infertility, *unproductiveness*,
    169
Infest, *annoy*, 649, 830
  frequent, 136
Infibulation, *junction*, 43
Infidel, *heathen*, 984
Infidelity, *dishonour*, 940
  irreligion, 989
Infiltrate, *intervene*, 228
  influence, 175
  imbue, 339

Infiltrate, *teach*, 537
  mixture, 41
Infiltration, *ingress*, 294
  passage, 302
  presence, 186
Infinite, *in quantity*, 105
  in degree, 31
  in size, 192
Infinitesimal, *in degree*, 32
  in quantity, 193
Infinity, *infinitude*, 105
  space, 180
Infirm, *weak*, 160
  irresolute, 605
  vicious, 945
Infirmary, *remedy*, 662
Infirmity, *weakness*, 160
  disease, 655
  failing, 945
Infix, *teaching*, 537
Inflame, *burn*, 384
  stir up, 173
  incense, 900
  incite, 615
Inflammation, *disease*, 655
Inflate, *expend*, 194
  rarefy, 322
  blow, 349
  style, 573, 577
  ridiculous, 853
  vanity, 880
Inflect, *curvature*, 245
  grammar, 567
Inflexible, *hard*, 323
  resolved, 604
  obstinate, 606
  stern, 739
Inflexion, *curvature*, 245
  change, 140
  appendage, 39
  grammar, 567
Inflict, *condemn*, 971
  act upon, 680
  give pain, 830
Infliction, *pain*, 828
Influence, *physical*, 175
  authority, 737
  inducement, 615
  importance, 642
Influential, *important*, 642
Influx, *ingress*, 294
Inform, *information*, 527
Inform against, *accusation*, 938
Informal, *irregular*, 83
  lawless, 964
Information, *knowledge*, 490
  communication, 527
Informer, *witness*, 467
*Infra, *posterior*, 117
*Infra dignitatem, *disrepute*,
    874
Infra-microscopic, *little*, 193
Infraction, *non-observance*, 773
  unconformity, 83
  exemption, 927

Infraction, *disobedience*, 742
  violation, 614
Infrangible, *coherence*, 46, 321
Infrastructure, *base*, 211
Infrequency, *infrequency*, 137
  fewness, 103
Infringe, *transgress*, 303
  violate, 742, 773, 925, 927
  break through, 614
Infundibular, *concavity*, 252
Infuriate, *wrathful*, 900
  excite, 824
  violent, 173
Infuse, *mix*, 41
  insert, 300
  teach, 537
Infusible, *solid*, 321
Ingeminate, *duplication*, 90
Ingenious, *skill*, 698
*Ingénue, *actress*, 599
Ingenuous, *artless*, 703
  sincere, 543
  guileless, 939
Ingest, *absorb*, 296
Ingle, *fuel*, 388
Inglorious, *disrepute*, 874
  base, 940
Ingoing, *ingress*, 294
Ingot, *money*, 800
Ingraft, *see* Engraft
Ingrate, *ingratitude*, 917
Ingratiate, *love*, 897
Ingratitude, *ingratitude*, 917
Ingredient, *component*, 56
Ingress, *ingress*, 294
Ingrowing, *insertion*, 300
Ingurgitate, *reception*, 296
Inhabile, *unskilfulness*, 699
Inhabit, *presence*, 186
Inhabitant, *inhabitant*, 188
Inhale, *reception*, 296
  sniff, 398
Inharmonious, *discordant*, 414
  incongruity, 24
Inherence, *intrinsicality*, 5
Inherit, *acquire*, 775
  possess, 777
Inheritance, *property*, 780
Inhesion, *intrinsicality*, 5
Inhibit, *prohibit*, 761
  not think of, 452
  dissuade, 616
  hinder, 706
Inhospitable, *seclusion*, 893
Inhuman, *malevolence*, 907
Inhume, *interment*, 363
Inimical, *hostile*, 708, 889
  unfavourable, 706
Inimitable, *perfect*, 650
  good, 648
Iniquitous, *bad*, 649
Iniquity, *wrong*, 923
  vice, 945
Initiate, *begin*, 66
  teach, 537

Initiated, *skilful*, 698
Initiative, *enterprise*, 676
   beginning, 66
Inject, *insertion*, 300
Injudicious, *folly*, 499
   inexpedient, 647
Injunction, *command*, 741
   prohibition, 761
   advice, 695
   decree, 963
Injure, *to damage*, 659
   malevolence, 907
Injury, *harm*, 649
Injustice, *wrong*, 923
Ink, *blackness*, 431
Ink-slinger, *writer*, 590
Inkle, *connection*, 45
Inkling, *information*, 527
   supposition, 514
   knowledge, 490
Inlaid, *variegation*, 440
Inland, *interiority*, 221
Inlay, *variegation*, 440
Inlet, *opening*, 260
   way, 627
   beginning, 66
   of the sea, 343
Inly, *interiority*, 221
Inmate, *inhabitant*, 188
Inmost, *interiority*, 221
Inn, *abode*, 189
Innate, *intrinsicality*, 5
Innavigable, *difficulty*, 704
Inner, *interiority*, 221
Innocence, *innocence*, 946
   probity, 939
   virtue, 944
Innocuous, *harmless*, 648
   wholesome, 656
Innominate, *misnomer*, 565
Innovation, *newness*, 123
   change, 140
Innoxious, *innocent*, 946
   salubrious, 656
   harmless, 648
Innuendo, *information*, 527
   insinuation, 932
Innumerable, *infinity*, 105
Inobservance, *non-observance*, 773
Inoculate, *insert*, 300
   teach, 537
Inodorous, *inodorousness*, 399
Inoffensive, *harmless*, 648, 946
Inofficious, *malevolence*, 907
Inoperative, *unproductive*, 169
   useless, 645
Inopportune, *untimely*, 135
   inexpedient, 647
Inordinate, *size*, 192
   superfluous, 641
   excessive, 31
Inorganic, *inorganization*, 358
Inosculate, *intersect*, 219
   convoluted, 248

Inosculate, *joined*, 43
Inquest, *inquiry*, 461
   jurisdiction, 965
Inquietude, *uneasiness*, 828
   apprehension, 860
   discontent, 832
   restlessness, 264
   disorder, 59
Inquiry, *search*, 461
   curiosity, 455
Inquisition, *inquiry*, 461
   jurisdiction, 965
Inroad, *ingress*, 294
   invasion, 716
   devastation, 619
Insalubrity, *insalubrity*, 657
Insane, *mad*, 503
   rash, 863
Insanitary, *insalubrious*, 657
Insatiable, *desire*, 865
Inscribe, *write*, 590
   label, 551
   represent, 554
Inscrutable, *unintelligibility*, 519
Insculpture, *sculpture*, 557
Insect, *animal*, 366
   minute, 193
Insecure, *danger*, 665
Insensate, *foolish*, 499
   mad, 503
Insensibility, *physical*, 376
   moral, 823
Inseparable, *cohering*, 46
   attached, 43
Insert, *put in*, 300
   locate, 184
   interpose, 228
   enter, 294
Inseverable, *junction*, 43
   unity, 87
Inside, *interiority*, 221
Insidious, *false*, 544
   cunning, 702
   dishonourable, 940
Insight, *knowledge*, 490
   intuition, 477
Insignia, *indication*, 550
Insignificance, *smallness*, 32
Insignificant, *unimportance*, 643
Insincere, *falsehood*, 544
Insinuate, *intervene*, 228
   ingress, 294
   mean, 516
   suppose, 514
   hint, 527
   blame, 932
   insert, 300
Insipid, *tasteless*, 391
   dull, 575
   indifferent, 866
Insist, *command*, 741
Insistent, *importunate*, 830
Insobriety, *drunkenness*, 959
Insolence, *insolence*, 885

Insoluble, *dense*, 321
   unintelligible, 519
Insolvent, *non-payment*, 808
Insomnia, *wakefulness*, 680
Insomuch, *greatness*, 31
Insouciance, *thoughtlessness*, 458
   supineness, 823
   indifference, 866
Inspan, *harness*, 43
   depart, 293
Inspect, *look*, 441
   attend to, 457
Inspector, *spectator*, 444
   director, 694
   inquirer, 461
Inspiration, *breathing*, 349
   impulse, 612
   excitation, 824
   prompting, 615
   imagination, 515
   wisdom, 498
   piety, 987
Inspire, *prompt*, 615
   animate, 824
Inspirit, *urge*, 615
   animate, 824
   cheer, 836
   courage, 861
Inspissation, *semiliquidity*, 352
Instability, *mutability*, 149
Install, *locate*, 184
   commission, 755
   celebrate, 883
   ordain, 995
Instalment, *portion*, 51
   payment, 807
Instance, *example*, 82
   solicitation, 765
   motive, 615
Instancy, *urgency*, 642
Instant, *moment*, 113
   present, 118
   future, 121
Instanter, *earlier*, 132
   instantaneity, 113
Instauration, *restoration*, 600
Instead, *substitution*, 147
Instigate, *motive*, 615
Instil, *insert*, 300
   teach, 537
   mix, 41
Instinct, *intellect*, 450
   intuition, 477
   impulse, 601
   innate, 5
Instinctive, *habitual*, 613
   impulsive, 612
Institute, *school*, 542
   beginning, 66
   cause, 153
   organize, 161
Institution, *legality*, 963
   poorhouse, 804
Institutor, *teacher*, 540

Instruct, *teach*, 537
  advise, 695
  precept, 697
  command, 741
Instructor, *teacher*, 540
Instrument, *implement*, 633
  record, 551
  security, 771
Instrumental, *means*, 632
  music, 415
  subservient, 631
Instrumentality, *medium*, 631
Insubordinate, *disobedience*, 742
  anarchy, 738
Insubstantiality, *nothingness*, 4
Insufferable, *painfulness*, 830
Insufficient, *insufficiency*, 640
  shortcoming, 304
Insufflation, *wind*, 349
Insular, *island*, 346
  detach, 44
  single, 87
Insulate, *separate*, 44
Insult, *rudeness*, 895
  disrespect, 929
  offence, 900
Insuperable, *difficulty*, 704
  impossible, 471
Insupportable, *painfulness*, 830
Insuppressible, *violence*, 173
Insurance, *promise*, 768
  security, 771
  precaution, 664
Insurgent, *disobedience*, 742
Insurmountable, *difficulty*, 704
  impossible, 471
Insurrection, *disobedience*, 742
  resistance, 719
Insusceptible, *insensibility*, 823
Intact, *permanence*, 141
  preserve, 669
Intaglio, *concavity*, 252
  sculpture, 557
Intake, *inlet*, 260
Intangible, *numbness*, 381
  immaterial, 317
Integer, *whole*, 50
Integral calculus, *number*, 84
Integral part, *component*, 56
Integrate, *consolidate*, 50
  complete, 52
Integration, *number*, 84
Integrity, *whole*, 50
  virtue, 944
  probity, 939
Integument, *covering*, 222
Intellect, *intellect*, 450
Intelligence, *mind*, 450
  news, 532
  wisdom, 498
Intelligible, *intelligibility*, 518, 570
Intemperate, *intemperance*, 954
  drunkenness, 957

Intempestivity, *unseasonableness*, 135
Intend, *design*, 620
Intendant, *director*, 694
Intended, *will*, 600
Intensify, *energize*, 171
  aggravate, 835
Intensity, *degree*, 26
  greatness, 31
  energy, 171
Intent, *active*, 682
  thoughtful, 451, 457
Intention, *design*, 620
Intentional, *will*, 600
Intentness, *attention*, 457
  thought, 451
Inter, *bury*, 363
  insert, 300
*Inter alia, *conformity*, 82
Interaction, *reciprocal*, 12
Interblend, *mix*, 41
Interbreed, *mix*, 41
Intercalate, *insert*, 300
  intervene, 228
Intercede, *mediate*, 724
  deprecate, 766
Intercept, *hinder*, 706
  take, 789
Intercession, *deprecation*, 766
Interchange, *interchange*, 148
  reciprocate, 12
  barter, 794
  transfer, 783
Intercipient, *hinder*, 706
Interclude, *hindrance*, 706
Intercom, *hearing*, 418
Intercommunicate, *interlocution*, 588
  information, 527
Intercommunion, *society*, 892
Intercostal, *interiority*, 221
Intercourse, *converse*, 588
Intercross, *mix*, 41
Intercurrence, *passage*, 302
Interdict, *prohibition*, 761
Interdigitate, *intervene*, 228
  intersect, 219
Interest, *advantage*, 618
  concern, 9
  importance, 642
  curiosity, 455
  attention, 457
  aid, 707
  to please, 829; *debt*, 806
Interested, *selfish*, 943
Interesting, *style*, 574
Interfere, *intervene*, 228
  meddle, 682
  disagree, 24
  counteract, 179
  thwart, 706
  mediate, 724
  activity, 682
Interglossa, *language*, 560
Interim, *duration*, 106

Interim, *synchronism*, 120
Interior, *interiority*, 221
Interjacence, *coming between*, 228
  middle, 68
Interject, *insert*, 300
  interpose, 228
Interlace, *twine*, 219
  join, 43
Interlard, *interpose*, 228
  mix, 41
  insert, 300
Interleave, *interjacence*, 228
  addition, 37
Interline, *insert*, 228
  write, 590
Interlink, *junction*, 43
Interlocation, *interjacence*, 228
Interlock, *cross*, 219
  join, 43
Interlocution, *interlocution*, 588
Interloper, *intervene*, 228
  obstruct, 706
  extraneous, 57
Interlude, *dramatic*, 599
  time, 106
  interjacence, 228
  interruption, 70
Intermarriage, *marriage*, 903
Intermeddle, *hinder*, 706
  interfere, 682
Intermeddling, *mediation*, 724
Intermediary, *messenger*, 534
Intermediate, *mean*, 29
  middle, 68
  intervening, 228
Intermedium, *link*, 45
  instrument, 631
  intervention, 228
Interment, *interment*, 300, 363
Intermezzo, *interlude*, 106
  music, 415
Interminable, *infinite*, 105
  eternal, 112
  long, 200
Intermingle, *mixture*, 41
Intermission, *discontinuance*, 142
Intermit, *interrupt*, 70
  discontinue, 142
  recur, 138
  suspend, 265
  in time, 106
Intermix, *mixture*, 41
Intermutation, *interchange*, 148
Intern, *restrain*, 751
Internal, *interior*, 221
  intrinsic, 5
International, *reciprocal*, 12
  law, 963
Internecine, *slaughter*, 361
  war, 722
Internuncio, *messenger*, 534
  consignee, 758
Interpellation, *inquiry*, 461

Interpellation, *address*, 586
 appeal, 765
 summons, 741
Interpenetration, *passage*, 302
 interjacence, 228
 presence, 186
 ingress, 294
Interpolate, *intervene*, 228
 mix, 41
 analytical, 85
Interpose, *intervene*, 228
 mediate, 724; *mix*, 41
 act, 682; *hinder*, 706
Interpret, *explain*, 522
 answer, 462
Interpreter, *interpretation*, 524
Interregnum, *laxity*, 738
 intermission, 106
 transient, 111
 cessation, 142
 discontinuity, 70
Interrogate, *inquiry*, 461
Interrupt, *discontinuity*, 70
 hindrance, 706
 cessation, 142
 pause, 265
Intersect, *crossing*, 219
Interspace, *interval*, 198
 interior, 221
Intersperse, *diffuse*, 73
 mix, 41
 intervene, 228
Interstice, *interval*, 198
Interstitial, *interjacent*, 228
 internal, 221
Intertexture, *tissue*, 329
 intersection, 219
Intertwine, *cross*, 219
 intervene, 228
Intertwist, *unite*, 43, 219
Interval, *of space*, 198
 of order, 70
 of time, 106
Intervene, *in space*, 228, 300
 in time, 106
 in order, 68
Intervention, *mediation*, 724
 instrumentality, 170, 631
Interview, *conference*, 588
 society, 892
Intervolved, *junction*, 43
Interweave, *crossing*, 219
Intestate, *obliteration*, 552
Intestine, *interiority*, 221
Intimate, *to tell*, 527
 friendly, 888
 close, 197
Intimidate, *frighten*, 860
 insolence, 885
 threat, 909
Intolerable, *painfulness*, 830
Intolerant, *impatient*, 825
 insolent, 885
 prejudice, 481
Intonation, *sound*, 402

Intonation, *voice*, 580
Intone, *recite*, 582
Intoxicate, *excite*, 824, 825
 inebriate, 959
Intractable, *difficult*, 704
 obstinate, 606
 discourteous, 895
Intramural, *interiority*, 221
Intransient, *diuturnity*, 110
Intransigent, *discordant*, 24
 revolutionary, 146
Intransitive, *diuturnity*, 110
Intransmutable, *diuturnity*, 110
Intraregarding, *interiority*, 221
Intrepid, *courage*, 861
Intricate, *difficult*, 704
 confused, 59
 perplexed, 519
Intriguant, *activity*, 682
 libertine, 962
Intrigue, *plot*, 626
 cunning, 702
 activity, 682
 licentiousness, 961
Intrinsic, *intrinsicality*, 5
 interior, 221
Introduction, *addition*, 37
 ingress, 294
 admission, 296
 insertion, 300
 precursor, 64
 precession, 280
 acquaintance, 888
 presentation, 894
 musical, 415
Introductory, *preceding*, 62
 precursory, 116
 beginning, 66
Introgression, *ingress*, 294
Introit, *music*, 415
Intromit, *receive*, 294, 296
 insert, 300
 discontinue, 142
Introspection, *look into*, 441
 thought, 451
 attend to, 457
Introvert, *invert*, 140, 218
 evolve, 313
Intrude, *intervene*, 228
 enter, 294
 inopportune, 135
 interfere, 24
Intruder, *extraneous*, 57, 228
Intrusion, *mixture*, 41
Intuition, *mind*, 450
 instinct, 477
 knowledge, 490
Intuitive, *instinctive*, 477
Intumescence, *expansion*, 194
 convexity, 250
Inunction, *covering*, 222
Inundate, *effusion*, 337
 flow, 348
 redundance, 641
Inurbanity, *discourteous*, 895

Inure, *habituate*, 613
 train, 673
 harden, 823
Inutility, *inutility*, 645
Invade, *ingress*, 294
 attack, 716
Invalid, *disease*, 655
Invalidate, *disable*, 158
 disentitle, 925
 illegalize, 964
 confute, 479
 rebut, 468
Invalidity, *confutation*, 479
Invaluable, *goodness*, 648
Invariable, *intrinsic*, 5
 immutability, 150
Invasion, *ingress*, 294
 attack, 716
Invective, *accusation*, 938
 malediction, 908
 abuse, 932
Inveigh, *blame*, 932
Inveigle, *deceive*, 546
 seduce, 615
Invent, *imagine*, 515
 devise, 626
 falsehood, 544
Inventive, *skilful*, 698
 productive, 168
 original, 20
Inventory, *list*, 86
 record, 551
Inversion, *reversion*, 145
 of position, 218, 237
 of relation, 14
 of order, 59, 61
Invertebrate, *feeble*, 160, 575
 vicious, 945
 irresolute, 605
Invest, *give*, 784
 lend, 787
 empower, 157, 755
 ascribe, 155
 clothe, 225
 besiege, 716
Investigate, *inquiry*, 461
Investiture, *see* Invest
Investment, *see* Invest
Inveterate, *habit*, 613
 old, 124
Invidious, *envy*, 921
 hatred, 898
 unfair, 923
Invigorate, *stimulate*, 171
Invigoration, *strength*, 159
Invincible, *strength*, 159
Inviolable, *right*, 924
 honour, 939
 concealment, 528
Inviolate, *unchanged*, 141
 concealed, 528
Invisible, *not to be seen*, 447
 small, 193
 latent, 526
Invite, *ask*, 765

Invite, *offer*, 763
  induce, 615
Inviting, *pleasing*, 899
  alluring, 615
Invoice, *list*, 86
  record, 551
Invoke, *implore*, 765
  pray, 990
  address, 586
  curse, 908
Involuntary, *compulsory*, 601
  unintentional, 621
Involution, *disorder*, 59
  convolution, 248
  numerical, 85
  style, 571
Involve, *derange*, 61
  include, 54
  wrap, 225
  evidence, 467
  meaning, 516
Involved, *disorder*, 59
  in debt, 806
Invulnerable, *safety*, 664
Inward, *interiority*, 221
Inweave, *crossing*, 219
Ionosphere, *air*, 338
Iota, *particle*, 32
  minute, 193
*Ipse dixit, *certainty*, 474
*Ipsissimis verbis, *word*, 562
*Ipso facto, *being*, 1
  truth, 494
Irascible, *anger*, 901
Irate, *resentment*, 900
Ire, *resentment*, 900
Iridescent, *variegation*, 440
  changeable, 149
Iris, *variegation*, 440
  eye, 441
Irish bull, *ridiculousness*, 853
  error, 495
Irishism, *absurdity*, 497
  error, 495
Irk, *oppress*, 830
  tire, 688
Irksome, *tiresome*, 688
  tedious, 841
  oppressive, 830
Iron, *strength*, 159
  hardness, 323
  club, 276
  to smooth, 255
Iron age, *adversity*, 735
Iron curtain, *secret*, 533
Iron-hearted, *malevolence*, 907
Ironclad, *ship*, 273
  covering, 222
  defence, 717
Irons, *fetters*, 752
Irony, *ridicule*, 856
  untruth, 544, 546
Irradiate, *light*, 420
Irrational, *number*, 84
  silly, 477, 499

Irrational, *ridiculous*, 853
Irreclaimable, *vile*, 945
  impenitent, 951
Irreconcilable, *discordant*, 24
  unrelated, 10
  hostile, 889
Irrecoverable, *lost*, 776
  past, 122
Irredeemable, *impenitent*, 951
Irreducible, *out of order*, 59
  discordant, 24
  fixed, 150
Irrefragable, *certain*, 475
  proved, 478
Irrefutable, *certain*, 475
  proved, 467, 478
Irregular, *out of order*, 59
  against rule, 83
  in time, 139
  distorted, 243
  multiform, 16A, 81
  fighter, 726
Irrelation, *unrelated*, 10
  disagreement, 24
Irrelevant, *unrelated*, 10
  unaccordant, 24
  sophistical, 477
Irreligion, *atheism*, 989
Irremediable, *lost*, 776
  hopeless, 859
  bad, 649
Irremissible, *vice*, 945
Irremovable, *immutable*, 150
  quiescence, 265
Irreparable, *loss*, 776
  bad, 649
  hopeless, 859
Irrepentance, *impenitence*, 951
Irreplaceable, *indispensable*, 630
Irrepressible, *violent*, 173
  excitement, 825
  free, 778
Irreproachable, *innocence*, 946
Irresistible, *strength*, 159
  compulsory, 601
  evidence, 467
Irresolute, *irresolution*, 149, 605
Irresolvable, *unity*, 87
Irrespective, *irrelation*, 10
Irresponsible, *exempt*, 927A
  arbitrary, 964
  silly, 499
Irretrievable, *lost*, 776
Irreverence, *disrespect*, 929
  impiety, 988
Irreversible, *past*, 122
  immutable, 150
Irrevocable, *immutable*, 150, 601, 604
  hopeless, 859
Irrigate, *water*, 337
Irritable, *excitable*, 825
  irascible, 901
Irritate, *provoke*, 898

Irritate, *incense*, 900
  fret, 828
  pain, 830
Irruption, *ingress*, 294
  invasion, 716
Ishmael, *enemy*, 891
Isis, *deity*, 979
Islam, *religions*, 984
Island, *island*, 346
Isobar, *air*, 338
Isocheimal, *cold*, 383
Isochimenal, *cold*, 383
Isochronous, *synchronism*, 120
Isolation, *singleness*, 87
  seclusion, 893
  safety, 644
  detachment, 44
  irrelation, 10
Isomeric, *part*, 51
Isomorphism, *form*, 240
Isothermal, *heat*, 382
Issue, *effect*, 154
  event, 151
  end, 67
  posterity, 121, 167
  disease, 655
  kindred, 11
  depart, 293
  egress, 295
  stream, 347
  distribute, 73
  money, 800
Issueless, *unproductive*, 169
Isthmus, *narrowness*, 203
  land, 342
  connection, 45
It, *charm*, 829
Italicize, *emphasize*, 642
Italics, *indication*, 550
  type, 591
Itch, *desire*, 865
  titillation, 380
Item, *addition*, 37
  speciality, 79
  adjunct, 39
  part, 51
Iteration, *repetition*, 90, 104
Itinerant, *moving*, 266
  traveller, 268
Itinerary, *description*, 594
  guide, 695
Ivory, *whiteness*, 430
Ivory-skulled, *stupid*, 499
Ivory tower, *retirement*, 893

J

Jab, *stab*, 260
  poke, 276
Jabber, *chatter*, 584
  nonsense, 517
  stammer, 583
Jabot, *frill*, 230
Jacent, *horizontal*, 213
Jack, *instrument*, 633

L

L.S.D., *money*, 800
Laager, *defence*, 717
Labarum, *flag*, 550
Label, *indication*, 550
Labial, *letter*, 561
Laboratory, *workshop*, 691
Labour, *exertion*, 686
  work, 680
  difficulty, 704
Labourer, *agent*, 690
Labyrinth, *secret*, 533
  difficulty, 704
  disorder, 59
  convolution, 248
Lace, *tie*, 43
  net, 219
  to beat, 972
Lacerable, *fragile*, 328
Lacerate, *disjunction*, 44
  pain, 830
Laches, *neglect*, 460
  omission, 773
Lachrymation, *lamentation*, 839
Lack, *insufficiency*, 640
  destitution, 804
  requisition, 630
  number, 98
Lack-brain, *fool*, 501
Lack-lustre, *dim*, 423
  discoloured, 429
Lackadaisical, *affected*, 855
  indifferent, 866
Lacker, *see* Lacquer
Lackey, *servant*, 746
Laconic, *conciseness*, 572
  shortness, 201
Lacquer, *varnish*, 22
  adorn, 845, 847
Lacteal, *semiliquid*, 352
Lacuna, *orifice*, 260
  pit, 252
  deficiency, 53
  interval, 198
  break, 70
Lacuscular, *lake*, 343
Lacustrine, *lake*, 343
Lad, *infant*, 129
Ladder, *method*, 627
Lade, *transfer*, 270
Laden, *charged*, 639
La-di-da, *foppish*, 855
Lading, *cargo*, 190, 635
  baggage, 780
Ladle, *spoon*, 272
  vessel, 191
Lady, *woman*, 374
  wife, 903
  noble, 875
Lady help, *servant*, 746
Lady-killer, *fop*, 854
  philanderer, 902
Lady-love, *sweetheart*, 897
Ladylike, *fashion*, 852

Ladylike, *courteous*, 894
  noble, 875
Lag, *linger*, 275
  follow, 281
  dawdle, 683
  lateness, 133
  imprison, 751
  prisoner, 754
Laggard, *slack*, 603, 683
Lagoon, *lake*, 343
Laical, *laity*, 997
Lair, *den*, 189
  sty, 653
Laird, *nobility*, 875
  possessor, 779
*Laissez aller, *inactivity*, 683
*Laissez faire, *laxity*, 738
  inactivity, 683
  permanence, 141
Laity, *laity*, 997
Lake, *lake*, 343
Lama, *priest*, 996
  master, 745
Lamarckism, *causation*, 153
Lamb, *innocent*, 946
  nursling, 129
  Saviour, 976
  saint, 948
Lambent flame, *light*, 420
Lamblike, *innocent*, 946
Lame, *weak*, 160
  bad, 649
  imperfect, 650
  failing, 732
  laxity, 738
Lamella, *layer*, 204
Lament, *complain*, 839
  regret, 833
  funeral, 363
  pity, 914
Lamentable, *greatness*, 31
  painful, 830
  regret, 833
Lamia, *demon*, 980
Lamina, *layer*, 204
  part, 51
Lamp, *luminary*, 423
Lampoon, *disparage*, 932
  libel, 934
Lance, *perforate*, 260
  javelin, 727
Lancer, *combatant*, 726
Lancet, *perforator*, 262
  sharpness, 253
Lancinate, *pain*, 378
Land, *ground*, 342
  to arrive, 292
  to stop, 265
  estate, 780
Land girl, *agriculture*, 371
Land-mine, *arms*, 727
Landau, *vehicle*, 272
Landaulette, *vehicle*, 272
Landgrave, *master*, 745
Landing-ground, *arrival*, 292

Landing-place, *support*, 215
  destination, 292
Landing-stage, *arrival*, 292
Landlocked, *circumscribed*, 231
Landlord, *possessor*, 779
Landlubber, *bungler*, 701
Landmark, *indicate*, 550
Landowner, *possessor*, 779
Landscape, *view*, 448
  delineation, 556
Landslide, *fall*, 306
Landslip, *fall*, 306
Lane, *street*, 189
  way, 627
Language, *words*, 560
Languid, *weak*, 160
  slow, 275
  torpid, 683, 823
  style, 575
Languish, *desire*, 865
  illness, 655
  decline, 36
Languor, *weakness*, 160
  inactivity, 683
Lank, *little*, 193
Lanolin, *oil*, 356
Lantern, *light*, 423
Lantern-jawed, *lean*, 193
Lao-Tsze, *religious founder*, 986
Lap, *support*, 215
  interior, 221
  to wrap, 222
  encompass, 227
  speed, 274
  surpass, 303
  drink, 296
Lapel, *fold*, 258
Lapidary, *concise*, 572
Lapidate, *kill*, 361
Lapis lazuli, *blue*, 438
Lappet, *adjunct*, 39
Lapse, *of time*, 109, 135
  past time, 122
  fall, 306
  be lost, 776
  degeneracy, 659
  guilt, 947
  error, 495
*Lapsus linguae, *solecism*, 568
  ridicule, 856
  error, 495
  equivocal, 520
Larboard, *left*, 239
Larcener, *thief*, 792
Larceny, *theft*, 791
Lard, *unctuousness*, 353, 256
Larder, *store*, 636
  food, 298
Lares and Penates, *abode*, 189
Large, *in quantity*, 31
  in size, 192
Largess, *giving*, 784, 809
*Largo, *slowness*, 275, 415
Lariat, *vinculum*, 45
Lark, *mount*, 305

Linear, *length*, 200
Linger, *loiter*, 275
   delay, 133
   protract, 110
Lingo, *language*, 560
Lingua franca, *neology*, 563
Linguist, *scholar*, 492
   language, 560
Liniment, *unctuous*, 355
   remedy, 662
Lining, *lining*, 224
Link, *relation*, 9
   connecting, 45
   to connect, 43
   part, 51
   term, 71
   flambeau, 423
Links, *arena*, 728
Linn, *lake*, 343
Linocut, *engraving*, 558
Linoleum, *covering*, 222
Linotype, *printing*, 591
Linsey-woolsey, *mixed*, 41
Lion, *courage*, 861
   prodigy, 872
   celebrity, 873
Lip, *edge*, 230
   beginning, 66
   prominence, 250
   impudence, 885
Lip-devotion, *impiety*, 988
Lip-service, *insincerity*, 544
   flattery, 933
   impiety, 988
Lip-wisdom, *folly*, 499
Lipogram, *misnomer*, 565
Lippitude, *dim sight*, 443
Lipstick, *ornament*, 847
Liquation, *calefaction*, 384
Liquefaction, *soluble*, 335
   calefaction, 384
Liquescence, *calefaction*, 384
Liquescent, *soluble*, 335
Liquid, *fluid*, 333
   letter, 561
   sound, 405
Liquidate, *pay*, 807
   destroy, 162
Liquor, *liquid*, 333
   intoxicant, 959
   potable, 299
Liquorice, *sweet*, 396
Lisp, *stammering*, 583
Lissom, *soft*, 324
List, *catalogue*, 86
   record, 551
   strip, 205
   fringe, 230
   obliquity, 217
   hear, 418
   will, 600
   choose, 609
Listed, *variegation*, 440
Listen, *hearing*, 418
Listen in, *radio*, 599B

Listless, *inattentive*, 458
   inactive, 683
   impassive, 823
   indifferent, 866
Lists, *arena*, 728
Lit up, *drunk*, 959
Litany, *rite*, 998
*Literae humaniores, *language*, 560
Literal, *exact*, 19, 494
   meaning, 516
   unimaginative, 843
Literate, *knowledge*, 491
Literati, *scholar*, 492
*Literatim, *imitation*, 19
   word, 562
Literature, *learning*, 490
   language, 560
Lithe, *softness*, 324
Lithograph, *engraving*, 558
Litigant, *combatant*, 726
   lawsuit, 969
Litigate, *discord*, 713
   contention, 720
Litigious, *discord*, 713
   lawsuit, 969
Litter, *disorder*, 59
   to derange, 61
   trash, 643
   useless, 645
   vehicle, 272
   offspring, 167
Little, *in degree*, 32
   in size, 193
Littoral, *land*, 342
Liturgy, *rite*, 998
Live, *exist*, 1
   continue, 141
   dwell, 186
   fame, 873
Livelihood, *wealth*, 803
Livelong, *perpetuity*, 110
Lively, *sprightly*, 836
   acute, 821
   sensitive, 375, 822
   active, 682
   style, 574
Liver-coloured, *brown*, 433
Livery, *badge*, 550, 877
   colour, 428
   suit, 225
Livid, *dark*, 431
   purple, 437
Living, *life*, 359
   benefice, 995
Lixiviate, *cleanness*, 652
   liquefaction, 335
Lixivium, *liquidity*, 333
Llama, *carrier*, 271
Llano, *plain*, 344
Lo! *see*, 441
   wonder, 870
Load, *weight*, 319
   cargo, 190
   quantity, 31

Load, *redundance*, 641
   hindrance, 706
   anxiety, 828
   fill up, 52
   to oppress, 830
Loadstone, *attraction*, 289, 865
   motive, 615
Loaf, *head*, 450
Loafer, *idler*, 683
Loam, *soil*, 342
Loan, *lending*, 787
Loathe, *dislike*, 867
   hate, 898
Loathing, *nausea*, 841
Loathsome, *hateful*, 649, 898
   abhorrent, 867
   nauseous, 395
Lob, *toss*, 284
Lobby, *room*, 191
   passage, 627
Lobe, *part*, 51
Lobster, *red*, 434
Local, *situation*, 183
   regional, 180
Locality, *situation*, 183
Localize, *location*, 184
   limit, 231
Locate, *location*, 184
Loch, *lake*, 343
Lock, *fasten*, 43
   confine, 229
   rest, 265
   enclose, 232
   barrier, 706
   canal, 350
   tuft, 256
Lock up, *concealment*, 528
   restraint, 751
Lock-up, *jail*, 752
Locker, *receptacle*, 191
Locket, *ornament*, 847
Lockout, *resistance*, 719
Loco, *insane*, 503
Locomotion, *motion*, 264
Locomotive, *traction*, 285
Locum tenens, *deputy*, 759
   substitute, 634
*Locus standi, *influence*, 175
   support, 215
   repute, 873
Lode, *conduit*, 350
   mine, 636
Lodestar, *beacon*, 289, 550
Lodestone, *see* Loadstone
Lodge, *presence*, 186
   dwelling, 189
   receptacle, 191
   place, 184
Lodger, *inhabitant*, 188
Loft, *garret*, 191
   toss, 184
Lofty, *high*, 206
   proud, 878
   sublime, 574
   magnanimous, 942

Lubber, *fool,* 501
  big, 192
Lubricate, *smooth,* 255, 332
  facilitate, 705
Lubricity, *slippery,* 255
  impurity, 961
Lucid, *luminous,* 420
  intelligible, 518
  style, 570
  sane, 502
Lucifer, *Satan,* 978
  match, 388
Luck, *chance,* 156, 621
  good, 618
  success, 731
  prosperity, 734
Luckless, *failure,* 732
  adversity, 735
  distressed, 828
Lucky, *prosper,* 134, 734
Lucrative, *receipt,* 810
  useful, 644
  profitable, 775
Lucre, *gain,* 775
  wealth, 803
Lucubration, *thought,* 451
Luculent, *light,* 420
Ludicrous, *laughable,* 838
  ridiculous, 853
  witty, 842
Lug, *traction,* 285
Luggage, *baggage,* 635, 780
Lugger, *ship,* 273
Lugubrious, *dejection,* 837
Lukewarm, *temperate,* 382
  unwilling, 603
  indifferent, 866
  torpid, 823
Lull, *assuage,* 174
  mitigate, 826
  silence, 403
  quiescence, 142, 265
Lullaby, *soothing,* 174
  sleep, 683
  song, 415
  relief, 834
Lum, *funnel, chimney,* 351
Lumber, *useless,* 645
  slow, 275
  trash,

  hindrance, 647, 706
Lumber-room, *receptacle,*
                191, 636
Lumbering, *ugly,* 846
Lumberjacket, *dress,* 225
Luminary, *light,* 423
  sage, 500
Luminous, *light,* 420
Lump, *mass,* 192
  density, 321
  concrete, 46
  totality, 50
  to amass, 72
Lumpish, *heavy,* 319

Lumpish, *massive,* 192
  sluggish, 683
  awkward, 853
Lunacy, *insanity,* 503
Lunar, *world,* 318
Lunatic, *madman,* 504
Lunation, *period,* 108
Luncheon, *food,* 298
Lunette, *curvature,* 245
Lunge, *impulse,* 276
  attack, 716
Lunik, *space ship,* 273A
Lurch, *sink,* 306
  difficulty, 704
  deception, 545
  oscillation, 314
  slope, 217
Lure, *entice,* 615
  allurement, 865
  deception, 545
Lurid, *dim,* 422
  dark, 421
  yellow, 436
  sensational, 549
Lurk, *latent,* 526
  concealed, 528
  hide, 530
  unseen, 447
Luscious, *savoury,* 394, 396
  grateful, 829
  style, 577
Lush, *succulent,* 333
  vegetation, 365
  luxuriant, 639
Lushy, *drunkenness,* 959
Lust, *desire,* 865
  concupiscence, 961
Lustily, *exertion,* 686
Lustration, *purification,* 652
  atonement, 952
Lustre, *brightness,* 420
  chandelier, 423
Lustrum, *period,* 108
Lusty, *size,* 192
  strong, 159
*Lusus naturae, *uncon-
  formity,* 83
Lute, *cement,* 45
  to cement, 46
  guitar, 417
Luxation, *disjunction,* 44
Luxuriant, *sufficiency,* 639
  vegetation, 365
Luxuriate, *pleasure,* 827
Luxurious, *pleasurableness,*
                829
Luxury, *physical,* 377
  enjoyment, 827
  sensuality, 954
Lyceum, *school,* 542
Lych-gate, *opening,* 260
Lyddite, *arms,* 727
Lying, *decumbent,* 213
  deceptive, 546
Lyke-wake, *interment,* 363

Lymph, *water,* 337
Lymphatic, *inert,* 172
  soft, 324
Lynch, *punish,* 972
  kill, 361
Lynch law, *illegality,* 964
Lynx-eyed, *vision,* 441
Lyre, *musical instrument,* 417
Lyrics, *poetry,* 597

M

M.C., *director,* 694
Ma, *mother,* 166
Mab, *fairy,* 979
Macabre, *gruesome,* 846
Macadam, *smoothness,* 255
Macaroni, *fop,* 854
Macaronic, *poetry,* 597
Mace, *club,* 633
  weapon, 727
  sceptre, 747
Mace-bearer, *jurisprudence,*
                965
Macerate, *water,* 337
Maceration, *asceticism,* 995
  atonement, 952
Machiavellian, *falsehood,* 544
Machiavellism, *cunning,* 702
Machicolation, *embrasure,* 257
Machination, *plan,* 626
Machine, *instrument,* 633
Machinist, *agent,* 690
Mackerel sky, *cloud,* 353
Mackintosh, *dress,* 225
Macrobiotic, *lasting,* 110
Macrocosm, *world,* 318
  greatness, 31
Macrology, *diffuseness,* 573
Mactation, *idolatry,* 991
Macula, *blemish,* 848
Maculated, *variegation,* 440
Maculation, *ugliness,* 846
Mad, *insane,* 503
  violent, 173
Madcap, *caprice,* 608
  rash, 863
  excitable, 825
Madden, *excite,* 824
Madder, *red,* 434
Made of, *composition,* 54
Madefaction, *moisture,* 339
Madhouse, *hospital,* 662
Madman, *madman,* 504
Madness, *insanity,* 503
Madrigal, *poetry,* 597
Maelstrom, *whirlpool,* 312, 348
  turmoil, 59
Maenad, *violence,* 173
Maffick, *make merry,* 836
Magazine, *store,* 636
  record, 551
  book, 593
Magdalen, *penitent,* 950
Mage, *sorcerer,* 994

INDEX

INDEX

Mind, *to attend to,* 457
   believe, 484
   remember, 505
Minded, *willing,* 602
Mindful, *attentive,* 457
   remembering, 505
Mindless, *inattentive,* 458
   forgetful, 506
Mine, *store,* 636
   abundance, 639
   to hollow, 252
   open, 260; *snare,* 545
   sap, 162
   damage, 659
Mine-layer, *ship,* 273
Mine-sweeper, *ship,* 273
Mineral, *inorganic,* 358
Mineralogy, *inorganic,* 358
Minerva, *goddess,* 979
Mingle, *mix,* 41
Mingy, *parsimony,* 819
Mini, *small,* 193
Miniature, *portrait,* 556
   small, 193
Minikin, *small,* 193
Minim, *small,* 32, 193
Minimize, *moderate,* 174
   underestimate, 483
Minimum, *small,* 32, 193
Mining, *opening,* 260
Minion, *favourite,* 899
Minister, *deputy,* 759
   instrumentality, 631
   director, 694
   to aid, 707
   rites, 998
Ministry, *direction,* 693
   church, 995
Minnow, *littleness,* 193
Minor, *inferior,* 34
   infant, 129
Minority, *fewness,* 103
Minotaur, *unconformity,* 83
Minster, *temple,* 1000
Minstrel, *music,* 416
Minstrelsy, *musician,* 415
Mint, *workshop,* 691
   mould, 22
   wealth, 180
Minuend, *deduction,* 38
Minuet, *dance,* 840
   music, 415
Minus, *less,* 38
   in debt, 806
   deficient, 304
Minuscules, *printing,* 591
Minute, *in quantity,* 32
   in size, 193
   of time, 108
   instant, 113
   compendium, 596
   record, 551
   in style, 573
Minutest, *inferior,* 34
Minutiae, *small,* 32

Minutiae, *little,* 193
   unimportant, 643
Minx, *impertinent,* 887
   bad woman, 949
Mirabile dictu, wonder, 870
Miracle, *prodigy,* 872
Miraculous, *wonder,* 870
Mirage, *dim sight,* 443
   appearance, 448
   shadow, 4
Mire, *uncleanness,* 653
Mirk, *darkness,* 421
Mirror, *reflector,* 445
   perfection, 650
   saint, 948
   imitate, 19
Mirth, *cheerful,* 836
Mirthless, *dejected,* 837
Misadventure, *failure,* 732
   adversity, 735
   misfortune, 830
Misalliance, *marriage,* 903
Misanthrope, *recluse,* 893, 911
Misapply, *misuse,* 679
   misinterpret, 523
   mismanage, 699
Misapprehend, *mistake,* 495
   misinterpret, 523
Misappropriate, *misuse,* 679
Misarrange, *derange,* 61
Misbecome, *vice,* 945
Misbegotten, *vice,* 945
Misbehaviour, *discourtesy,* 895
   vulgarity, 852
   guilt, 947
Misbelief, *doubt,* 495
Miscalculate, *sophistry,* 477
   disappoint, 509
Miscall, *misnomer,* 565
Miscarriage, *failure,* 732
Miscegenation, *mixture,* 41
Miscellany, *mixture,* 41
   collection, 72
   generality, 78
Mischance, *misfortune,* 830
   adversity, 735
   failure, 732
Mischief, *evil,* 619
Mischievous, *badness,* 649
Miscible, *mix,* 41
Miscompute, *mistake,* 495
Misconceive, *mistake,* 495
   misinterpret, 481, 523
Misconduct, *guilt,* 947
   bungling, 699
Misconstrue, *misinterpret,* 523
Miscount, *error,* 495
Miscreant, *wretch,* 949
   apostate, 941
Miscreated, *vice,* 945
Miscue, *unskilfulness,* 699
Misdate, *anachronism,* 115
Misdeed, *guilt,* 947
Misdeem, *misinterpret,* 523
Misdemean, *vice,* 945

Misdevotion, *impiety,* 988
Misdirect, *misteaching,* 538
   bungle, 699
Misdoing, *guilt,* 947
Mise en scène, appearance, 448
Misemploy, *misuse,* 679
Miser, *parsimony,* 819
Miserable, *contemptible,* 643
   happy, 828
   pitiable, 914
   small, 32
Miserly, *parsimony,* 819
Misery, *pain,* 828
Misestimate, *error,* 495
Misfit, *disparity,* 24
Misfortune, *evil,* 619
   failure, 732
   adversity, 735
   unhappiness, 830
Misgiving, *fear,* 860
   doubt, 485
Misgovern, *unskilful,* 699
Misguide, *misteaching,* 538
Misguided, *foolish,* 699
Mishandle, *maltreat,* 649
Mishap, *evil,* 619
   failure, 732
   adversity, 735
   disaster, 830
Mishmash, *mixture,* 41
Misinform, *misteach,* 538
   ignorance, 491
   error, 495
Misintelligence, *misteach,* 538
Misinterpret, *misinterpret,* 523
Misjoined, *disagreement,* 24
Misjudge, *err,* 495
   sophistry, 477
Mislay, *lose,* 776
   derange, 61
Mislead, *deceive,* 477, 545
   misteach, 538
   error, 495
Mislike, *dislike,* 867
Mismanage, *unskilful,* 699
Mismatch, *difference,* 15
Mismatched, *disagreement,* 24
Misname, *misnomer,* 565
Misnomer, *misnomer,* 565
Misogamy, *celibacy,* 904
Misogynist, *celibacy,* 904
Misplace, *disorder,* 59
   unconformity, 83
Misplaced, *unsuitable,* 24
Mispronounce, *speech,* 583
Misproportioned, *ugliness,* 846
Misquote, *misinterpret,* 523
   false, 544
Misreckon, *error,* 495
Misrelate, *error,* 495
Misremember, *error,* 495
Misreport, *err,* 495
   falsify, 544
Misrepresent, *untruth,* 546

Misrepresentation, *perversion*, 523
  falsehood, 544
  caricature, 555
Misrule, *misconduct*, 699
  laxity, 738
Miss, *lose*, 776
  fail, 732
  inattention, 458, 460
  want, 865
  girl, 374
Missal, *rite*, 998
Missay, *stammer*, 583
  misnomer, 565
Misshapen, *ugliness*, 846
  distortion, 243
Missile, *thing thrown*, 284
  arms, 727
Missing, *absence*, 187
Mission, *commission*, 755
  undertaking, 676
  business, 625
  warfare, 722
Missionary, *clergy*, 996
Missive, *correspond*, 592
Misspell, *misinterpret*, 523
Misspend, *prodigal*, 818
Misstate, *misinterpret*, 523
  falsify, 544
Misstatement, *error*, 495
  falsehood, 544
  untruth, 546
  perversion, 523
Mist, *dimness*, 422
Mistake, *error*, 495
  failure, 732
  mismanagement, 699
  misconstrue, 523
Misteach, *misteach*, 538
Misterm, *misnomer*, 565
Misthink, *error*, 495
Mistime, *intempestivity*, 135
Mistral, *wind*, 349
Mistranslate, *misinterpret*, 523
Mistress, *lady*, 374
  sweetheart, 897
  concubine, 962
Mistrust, *doubt*, 485
Misty, *opaque*, 426
  dim, 422
  invisible, 447
Misunderstanding, *error*, 495
  misinterpretation, 523
  discord, 713
Misuse, *misuse*, 679
  waste, 638
Mite, *small*, 193
  bit, 32
  money, 800
Mitigate, *abate*, 36, 174
  relieve, 834
  calm, 826
  improve, 658
  extenuate, 937
*Mitrailleuse, *gun*, 727

Mitre, *canonicals*, 999
  joint, 43
Mitten, *dress*, 225
Mittimus, *command*, 741
Mix, *mix*, 41
Mixed, *disorder*, 59
Mixture, *mix*, 41
Mizzle, *rain*, 348
Mnemonics, *memory*, 505
Mnemosyne, *memory*, 505
Moan, *lamentation*, 839, 411
Moat, *enclosure*, 232
  ditch, 350
  defence, 717
Mob, *crowd*, 72, 31
  multitude, 102
  troop, 726
  plenty, 639
  vulgar, 876
  to scold, 932
Mob law, *illegal*, 964
Mobile, *movable*, 264
  sensible, 822
  inconstant, 607
Mobilization, *warfare*, 722
  move, 264
Mobility, *commonalty*, 876
Mobocracy, *authority*, 737
Mobsman, *thief*, 792
Moccasin, *dress*, 225
Mock, *imitate*, 17
  repeat, 104
  erroneous, 495
  false, 544
  to ridicule, 483, 856
  laugh at, 838
Mock-heroic, *ridiculous*, 853
Modal, *extrinsic*, 6
  state, 7
  circumstance, 8
Mode, *fashion*, 852
  method, 627
Model, *prototype*, 22
  to change, 140, 144
  rule, 80
  example, 82
  to copy, 19
  sculpture, 557
  perfection, 650
  saint, 948
Modeller, *artist*, 559
Moderate, *small*, 32
  allay, 174
  to assuage, 826
  temperate, 953
  cheap, 815
Moderation, *temperateness*, 174
  mediocrity, 736
*Moderato, *music*, 415
Moderator, *master*, 745
  director, 694
Modern, *newness*, 123
Modernize, *change*, 140
Modesty, *humility*, 881
  purity, 960

Modicum, *little*, 33
  allotment, 786
Modification, *difference*, 15
  variation, 20
  change, 140
  qualification, 469
Modify, *convert*, 144
Modish, *fashion*, 852
Modulation, *change*, 140
  harmony, 413
*Modus operandi, *method*, 627
  conduct, 692
*Modus vivendi, *arrangement*, 723
  compromise, 774
Mogul, *master*, 745
Mohammed, *religious founder*, 986
Mohammedanism, *religions*, 984
Mohock, *roisterer*, 949
Moider, *bewilder*, 475
  inattention, 458
Moiety, *bisection*, 91
Moil, *action*, 680
  work, 686
Moist, *wet*, 337
  humid, 339
Moke, *carrier*, 271
Molasses, *sweetness*, 396
Mole, *mound*, 206
  defence, 717
  refuge, 666
Molecule, *small*, 32, 193
Molehill, *lowness*, 207
  trifling, 643
Molestation, *evil*, 619
  .damage, 649
  malevolence, 907
Mollify, *allay*, 174
  soften, 324
  conciliate, 918
  assuage, 826
Mollusc, *animal*, 366
Mollycoddle, *cowardice*, 862
Moloch, *tyranny*, 739
  divinity, 979
  idol, 986
Molten, *liquid*, 335
Moment, *of time*, 113
  importance, 642
Momentary, *transient*, 111
Momentum, *impulse*, 276
Momus, *rejoicing*, 838
Monachism, *church*, 995
Monad, *littleness*, 193
  unity, 87
Monarch, *master*, 745
Monarchy, *authority*, 737
Monastery, *temple*, 1000
Monastic, *churchdom*, 995
Monetary, *money*, 800
Money, *money*, 800
Money-bag, *treasury*, 802
Money-changer, *merchant*, 797

Mortify, *to humiliate*, 874, 879
  disease, 655
  asceticism, 955
Mortise, *unite*, 43
  insert, 300
  intersect, 219
Mortuary, *interment*, 363
Mosaic, *mixture*, 41
  variegation, 440
  painting, 556
Moslem, *religions*, 984
Mosque, *temple*, 1000
Moss, *marsh*, 345
  tuft, 256
Moss-grown, *deterioration*, 659
Moss-trooper, *thief*, 792
Most, *greatness*, 31
Most part, for the, *general*, 78
  conformity, 82
*Mot, *maxim*, 496
Mote, *particle*, 193
  smallness, 32
  blemish, 848
  light, 320
Motel, *inn*, 189
Motet, *music*, 415
  worship, 990
Moth, *decay*, 659
Moth-eaten, *imperfect*, 651
Mother, *parent*, 166
  mould, 653
  nun, 997
Mother-of-pearl, *variegation*,
                        440
Mother tongue, *language*, 560
Mother wit, *wisdom*, 498
Motherland, *abode*, 189
Motherly, *love*, 897
Motif, *music*, 415
  theme, 454
Motion, *change of place*, 264
  proposition, 514
  topic, 454
  request, 765
  offer, 763
Motion picture, *drama*, 599
Motionless, *quiescence*, 265
Motive, *reason*, 615
  music, 415
Motiveless, *absence of motive*,
                        616
Motley, *multiform*, 81
  mixed, 41
  variegated, 440
Motor, *machine*, 633
  vehicle, 272
Motor-boat, *ship*, 273
Motor-bus, *vehicle*, 272
Motor-car, *vehicle*, 272
Motor-coach, *vehicle*, 272
Motor-cycle, *vehicle*, 272
Motor-van, *vehicle*, 272
Motorize, *move*, 264
Motorman, *director*, 694
Mottled, *variegated*, 440

Motto, *device*, 550
  maxim, 496
  phrase, 566
Mouch, *inactivity*, 688
Mould, *form*, 240, 329
  condition, 7
  earth, 342
  mildew, 653
  to model, 554
  carve, 557
  matrix, 22
Moulder, *deterioration*, 659
Moulding, *ornament*, 847
Mouldy, *decayed*, 653
  fetid, 401
Moult, *divestment*, 226
Mound, *defence*, 717
  hillock, 206
Mount, *to rise*, 305
  hill, 206, 250
  support, 215
  to prepare, 673
Mountain, *hill*, 206
  size, 192
  weight, 319
Mountaineer, *climber*, 305
Mountebank, *quack*, 548
  ignoramus, 493
  buffoon, 844, 857
Mourn, *grieve*, 828
  lament, 839
Mournful, *sad*, 837
  afflicting, 830
Mouse, *little*, 193
  to search, 461
Mouse-coloured, *grey*, 432
Mouse-hole, *opening*, 260
*Mousseux, *bubble*, 353
Moustache, *hair*, 256
Mouth, *entrance*, 66
  opening, 260
  brink, 230
  voice, 580
  stammer, 583
Mouth-honour, *flattery*, 933
Mouth-watering, *desire*, 865
Mouthful, *portion*, 51, 193
Mouthpiece, *speaker*, 524, 540
  speech, 582
Mouthy, *style*, 577
Movable, *transference*, 270
Movables, *property*, 780
Move, *be in motion*, 264
  induce, 615
  excite, 824
  act, 680
  undertaking, 676
  propose, 514
Move off, *recede*, 287
  depart, 293
Move on, *progression*, 282
Moved, *impressed*, 827
Moveless, *quiescence*, 265
Movement, *motion*, 264
  stir, 682

Movie, *cinema*, 599A
Mow, *cultivate*, 371
  destruction, 162
Mr., *title*, 877
Much, *greatness*, 31
Mucilage, *semiliquid*, 352
  adhesive, 45
Muck, *uncleanness*, 653
Muckle, *greatness*, 31
Muckworm, *miser*, 819
  baseborn, 876
Mucronate, *sharpness*, 253
Mucus, *semiliquid*, 352
Mud, *unclean*, 653
Muddle, *disorder*, 59
  derange, 61
  bungle, 699
Muddled, *confused*, 458
  tipsy, 959
  foolish, 499
Muddy, *opaque*, 426
Mudlark, *commonalty*, 876
Muezzin, *clergy*, 996
Muff, *bungler*, 701
  to bungle, 699
Muffle, *silent*, 403, 581
  conceal, 528
  taciturn, 585
  wrap, 225
Muffler, *dress*, 225
Mufti, *clergy*, 996
  judge, 966
  dress, 225
Mug, *receptacle*, 191
  fool, 501
  face, 448
  to study, 539
Muggy, *dim*, 422
  moist, 339
Mulatto, *unconformity*, 83
  mixture, 41
Mulct, *penalty*, 974
Mule, *beast*, 271
  mongrel, 83
  obstinate, 606
  fool, 499
  slipper, 225
Muleteer, *director*, 694
Muliebrity, *woman*, 374
Mull, *cape*, 250
  sweeten, 396
Mull over, *think*, 451
Mullah, *judge*, 967
  priest, 996
Mulligrubs, *depression*, 837
Mullion, *support*, 215
Multifarious, *multiform*, 81
  various, 15
Multifid, *divided*, 51
Multifold, *multiform*, 16A, 81
Multiform, *diversified*, 16A, 81
Multigenerous, *multiform*, 81
Multilateral, *side*, 236
Multipartite, *disjunction*, 44
Multiple, *numerous*, 102

Multiple, *product*, 84
Multiplicand, *number*, 84
Multiplication, *arithmetical*, 85
   reproduction, 163
Multiplicator, *number*, 84
Multiplicity, *multitude*, 102
Multiplier, *number*, 84
Multisonous, *loud*, 404
Multitude, *number*, 102
   greatness, 31; *mob*, 876
   assemblage, 72
Multitudinous, *multitude*, 102
*Multum in parvo, *contraction*, 195
   conciseness, 572
Mum, *silence*, 403
   aphony, 581
   mother, 166
Mumble, *eat*, 296
   mutter, 405, 583
Mumbo Jumbo, *idol*, 991
   spell, 993
Mumchance, *silent*, 403
   mute, 581
Mummer, *the drama*, 599
Mummery, *absurdity*, 497
   ridicule, 856
   parade, 882
   imposture, 545
   masquerade, 840
Mummify, *preserve*, 670
   bury, 363
Mummy, *corpse*, 362
   dryness, 340
   mother, 166
Mump, *dejection*, 837
Mumper, *beggar*, 767
Mumps, *sullenness*, 895
Munch, *eat*, 296
Munchausen, *exaggerate*, 549
Mundane, *world*, 318
   selfishness, 943
   irreligion, 989
Munerary, *reward*, 973
Municipal, *law*, 965
   distinct, 189
Munificent, *liberality*, 816
   giving, 784
Muniment, *record*, 551
   defence, 717
   refuge, 666
Munition, *material*, 635
Murder, *killing*, 361
   to bungle, 699
Murex, *purple*, 437
Muricate, *sharpness*, 253
Murky, *darkness*, 421
Murmur, *sound*, 405
   complaint, 839
   flow, 348
Murrain, *disease*, 655
Murrey, *redness*, 434
Muscle, *strength*, 159
Muse, *to reflect*, 451

Muse, *poetry*, 597
   language, 560
Musette, *musical instrument*, 415
Museum, *store*, 636
   collection, 72
   focus, 74
Mushroom, *small*, 193
   newness, 123
   low-born, 876
   upstart, 734; *increase*, 35
Music, *music*, 415
Music-hall, *theatre*, 599
   amusement, 840
Musical, *melodious*, 413
Musician, *musician*, 416
Musk, *fragrance*, 400
Musket, *arms*, 727
Musketeer, *combatant*, 726
Muslin, *semitransparent*, 427
Muss, *dishevel*, 61
Mussulman, *religions*, 984
Must, *mucor*, 653
   necessity, 152
   obligation, 926
   compulsion, 744
   essential, 630
Mustard, *condiment*, 393
   yellow, 436
Mustard-seed, *little*, 193
Muster, *collect*, 72
   numeration, 85
Muster-roll, *record*, 551
   list, 86
Musty, *foul*, 653
   rank, 401
Mutable, *changeable*, 149
   irresolute, 605
Mutation, *change*, 140
*Mutatis mutandis, *reciprocalness*, 12
   substitution, 147
*Mutato nomine, *substitution*, 147
Mute, *silent*, 403
   letter, 561
   silencer, 417
   speechless, 581
   taciturn, 585
   interment, 363
Mutilate, *retrench*, 38
   deform, 241
   garble, 651
   incomplete, 53
   injure, 649, 659
   spoliation, 619
Mutineer, *disobey*, 742
Mutiny, *disobey*, 742
   misrule, 738
   revolt, 719
Mutt, *fool*, 501
Mutter, *speak*, 583
   murmur, 405
   threaten, 909
Mutual, *reciprocal*, 12, 148

Muzzle, *opening*, 260
   edge, 230
   to silence, 403, 581
   taciturn, 585
   to incapacitate, 158
   restrain, 751
   imprison, 752
Muzzle-loader, *gun*, 727
Muzzy, *confused*, 458
   in liquor, 959
Myopic, *dim sight*, 443
Myriad, *number*, 98
   multitude, 102
Myrmidon, *troop*, 726
Myrrh, *fragrance*, 400
Myrtle, *love*, 897
Mysterious, *concealed*, 528
   obscure, 519
Mystery, *secret*, 533
   latency, 526
   concealment, 528
   craft, 625
   drama, 599
Mystery-ship, *deception*, 545
Mystic, *concealed*, 528
   obscure, 519
Mystify, *to deceive*, 545
   hide, 528
   falsify, 477
   misteach, 538
Myth, *imagination*, 515
Mythological, *god*, 979
   imaginary, 515

N

N.B., *attention*, 457
N or M, *generality*, 78
Na, *dissent*, 489
Nab, *seize*, 789
Nabob, *wealth*, 803
Nacreous, *variegation*, 440
Nadir, *base*, 211
Naffy, *food*, 298
Nag, *carrier*, 271
   be rude, 895
   discord, 713
   to scold, 932
Naiad, *mythological*, 979
Nail, *to fasten*, 43
   fastening, 45
Nail-brush, *clean*, 652
Nailing, *good*, 648
Naïveté, *artless*, 703
Naked, *denuded*, 226
   visible, 446
Namby-pamby, *affected*, 855
   insipid, 866
   trifling, 643
   style, 575
Name, *appellation*, 564
   fame, 873
   to appoint, 755
Nameless, *anonymous*, 565
   obscure, 874

Nest-egg, *store*, 636
Nested, *layer*, 204
Nestle, *lodge*, 186
   safety, 664
   endearment, 902
Nestling, *infant*, 129
Nestor, *veteran*, 130
Net, *intersection*, 219
   snare, 667, 702
   to capture, 789
   difficulty, 704
   remainder, 40
Nether, *lowness*, 207
Nettle, *to sting*, 830
   incense, 900
Network, *crossing*, 219
   disorder, 59
Neurasthenia, *weakness*, 160
Neurosis, *insanity*, 503
Neurotic, *sensitive physically*,
              375
   morally, 822
Neutral, *mean*, 29, 628
   indifferent, 610, 866
   non-interference, 681
Neutral tint, *grey*, 432
Neutralize, *counteract*, 179
   compensate, 30
Never, *neverness*, 107
Never-ending, *long*, 200
Never-never, *purchase*, 795
   debt, 806
Nevertheless, *counter*, 179
   compensation, 30
New, *newness*, 123
New-born, *newness*, 123
New-fashioned, *new*, 123
Newcomer, *extraneous*, 57
Newfangled, *new*, 123
   strange, 83
   barbarous, 851
News, *news*, 532
Newscast, *radio*, 599B
Newspaper, *record*, 551
Next, *after*, 63, 117
Nib, *point*, 253
   summit, 210
   disjunction, 44
   end, 67
Nibble, *carp at*, 932
   eat, 296
Niblick, *club*, 276
Nice, *savoury*, 394
   good, 648
   exact, 494
   pleasing, 829
   honourable, 939
   fastidious, 868
Nicely, *greatness*, 31
Nicety, *taste*, 850, 868
   discrimination, 465
   exactness, 494
Niche, *recess*, 182
   receptacle, 191
*Nichevo, *indifference*, 460, 823

Nick, *notch*, 257
   mark, 550
   deceive, 545
   of time, 134
   prison, 752
Nickelodeon, *juke box*, 417
Nicker, *animal sound*, 412
Nickname, *misnomer*, 565
Nicotian, *tobacco*, 298A
Nictitate, *blind*, 442
   dim sight, 443
Nidification, *abode*, 189
Nidus, *nest*, 189
   cradle, 153
Niff, *stink*, 401
Niggard, *parsimony*, 819
Nigger, *blackness*, 431
Niggle, *trifle*, 643
   depreciate, 483
Nigh, *nearness*, 197
Night, *darkness*, 421
Night-glass, *lens*, 445
Nightfall, *evening*, 126
Nightgown, *dress*, 225
Nightingale, *music*, 416
Nightmare, *pain*, 378, 828
   imagination, 515
   hindrance, 706
Nightshade, *bane*, 663
Nightshirt, *dress*, 225
Nigrification, *black*, 431
Nihilism, *non-existence*, 1
   scepticism, 487
   anarchism, 738
Nihilist, *evildoer*, 913
Nihility, *unsubstantiality*, 4
Nimble, *swift*, 274
   active, 682; *skilful*, 698
Nimbus, *cloud*, 353
   light, 420
Nimiety, *redundance*, 641
Niminy-piminy, *affectation*, 855
*N'importe, *unimportance*, 643
Nimrod, *chase*, 622
Nincompoop, *fool*, 501
Nine, *number*, 98
Nine days' wonder, *transient-*
   ness, 111
Ninny, *fool*, 501
Ninnyhammer, *fool*, 501
Niobe, *lament*, 839
Nip, *cut*, 44
   destroy, 162
   smallness, 32
Nip up, *taking*, 789
Nipper, *youngster*, 129
Nipping, *cold*, 383
Nipple, *convexity*, 250
Nirvana, *extinction*, 2
   happiness, 827
   heaven, 979
Nit, *dissent*, 489

Nitrous oxide, *anaesthetic*, 379
Niveous, *white*, 430
Nix, *nothing*, 4
Nixie, *fairy*, 980
Nizam, *master*, 745
No, *dissent*, 489
   negation, 536
No go, *impossible*, 471
Nob, *summit*, 210
   nobility, 875
Nobble, *deceive*, 545
   tamper with, 682
   circumvent, 702
Nobility, *nobleness*, 875
Noble, *rank*, 873
   greatness, 31
   generous, 942
   virtue, 944
Nobleman, *nobleness*, 875
Noblesse, *nobility*, 875
Nobody, *absence*, 187
   zero, 101
   unimportant, 643
   ignoble, 876
Noctivagant, *darkness*, 421
Nocturnal, *dark*, 421
   black, 431
Nocturne, *music*, 415
   picture, 556
Nod, *sleep*, 683
   signal, 550
   assent, 488; *order*, 741
   information, 527
   bow, 894; *to wag*, 314
Noddle, *head*, 450
   summit, 210
Noddy, *fool*, 501
Node, *convexity*, 250
Nodosity, *roughness*, 256
   convexity, 250
Nodule, *convexity*, 250
Noetic, *intellect*, 450
Noggin, *receptacle*, 191
Nohow, *negation*, 536
Noise, *sound*, 402
Noiseless, *silence*, 403
Noisome, *fetor*, 401
Noisy, *loud*, 404
   showy, 428
*Nolens volens, *compulsion*,
             744;
   necessity, 601
*Nom de guerre, *misnomer*, 565
*Nom de plume, *misnomer*, 565
Nomad, *vagrant*, 264
   traveller, 268
   locomotive, 266
No-man's-land, *interjacence*,
            228
Nomenclature, *name*, 564
Nominate, *commission*, 755
   name, 564
Nominee, *consignee*, 758
*Non constat, *sophistry*, 477
*Non est, *non-existence*, 2

*Non nobis Domine, *worship*, 990
*Non possumus, *impossible*, 471
  obstinacy, 606
*Non sequitur, *sophistry*, 477
Non-adhesion, *incoherence*, 47
Non-admission, *exclusion*, 55
Nonage, *youth*, 127
Nonagon, *angularity*, 244
  nine, 98
Non-appearance, *invisible*, 447
Non-attendance, *absence*, 187
Nonce, *present time*, 118
Nonce word, *neologism*, 563
Nonchalance, *neglect*, 460
  indifference, 456, 823, 866
  unwillingness, 603
Non-coincidence, *contrariety*, 14
Non-combatant, *non-combatant*, 726A
Non-committal, *cautious*, 864
Non-completion, *non-complete*, 730
Non-compliance, *disobey*, 742
Nonconformity, *dissent*, 489
  unconformity, 81
  sectarianism, 984A
Non-content, *dissent*, 489
Nondescript, *unconformity*, 83
None, *zero*, 101
Non-effective, *non-combatant*, 726A
Nonentity, *inexistence*, 2
  unimportance, 643
Nones, *worship*, 990
Non-essential, *unimportance*, 643
Nonesuch, *see* Nonsuch
Non-existence, *inexistence*, 2
Non-expectance, *inexpectation*, 508
Non-fulfilment, *incomplete*, 730
Non-inflammable, *fireproof*, 385
Non-intervention, *inaction*, 681
Nonjuror, *dissent*, 489
Non-observance, *non-observance*, 773
*Nonpareil, *perfection*, 650
Non-payment, *non-payment*, 808
Non-performance, *non-completion*, 730
Nonplus, *difficulty*, 704
  failure, 732
Non-preparation, *non-preparation*, 674
Non-residence, *absence*, 187
Non-resistance, *submission*, 725
  obedience, 743
Nonsense, *unmeaningness*, 517
  absurdity, 497

Nonsense, *ridiculousness*, 853
  folly, 499; *trash*, 643
Nonsuch, *perfection*, 650
  unconformity, 83
Nonsuit, *to cast*, 731
  to fail, 732
  condemn, 971
Non-uniformity, *variety*, 16A
Noodle, *fool*, 501
Nook, *place*, 182
  receptacle, 191
Noon, *midday*, 125
  light, 420
Noose, *ligature*, 45
  loop, 247; *snare*, 667
Nope, *dissent*, 489
Norm, *type*, 80
  mean, 29
Normal, *regular*, 82
  vertical, 212
North, *opposite*, 237
Northern lights, *light*, 423
Nose, *smell*, 398
  informer, 527, 529
  prominence, 250
Nose out, *detect*, 480A
Nosegay, *fragrance*, 400
  ornament, 847
Nosology, *disease*, 655
Nostalgia, *discontent*, 832
Nostril, *air-pipe*, 351
Nostrum, *remedy*, 662
Nosy, *curiosity*, 455
Not, *dissent*, 489
Not on your nelly, *dissent*, 489
Not-being, *inexistence*, 2
*Nota bene, *care*, 457
Notability, *personage*, 642, 875
  repute, 873
Notable, *visible*, 446
  manifest, 525
  important, 642
  famous, 873
Notably, *greatness*, 31
Notary, *recorder*, 553
  lawyer, 968
Notch, *nick*, 257
  mark, 550
Note, *sign*, 550
  record, 551
  letter, 592
  precursor, 64
  music, 413
  fame, 873
  notice, 450, 457
  minute, 596
  money, 800
Note-book, *compendium*, 596
Note-case, *purse*, 802
Noted, *known*, 490
Noteworthy, *greatness*, 31
Nothing, *nihility*, 4
  zero, 101
  trifle, 643
Notice, *observe*, 457

Notice, *mark*, 450, 550
  criticism, 480
  warning, 668
Notify, *inform*, 527
  publish, 531
Notion, *idea*, 453
  belief, 484
  knowledge, 490
Notoriety, *disrepute*, 874
  publication, 531
Notorious, *known*, 490
  seen, 446
Notwithstanding, *counter-action*, 179
  compensation, 30
Nought, *zero*, 101
Noumenal, *intellect*, 450
Noun, *nomenclature*, 564
Nourish, *aid*, 707
Nourishment, *food*, 298
Nous, *intellect*, 450
  wisdom, 498
*Nous verrons, *expectation*, 507
*Nouveau riche, *newness*, 123
  prosperity, 734
Novel, *new*, 18, 123
  fiction, 515
  description, 594
  unknown, 491
  false, 546
Novena, *nine*, 98
Novice, *learner*, 541, 674
  ignoramus, 493
  bungler, 701
  religious, 996
Novitiate, *learner*, 541
  training, 674
*Novus homo, *extraneous*, 57
  commonalty, 876
Now, *present time*, 118
Now or never, *occasion*, 134
Nowadays, *present time*, 118
Nowhere, *absence*, 187
Nowise, *in no degree*, 32
  dissent, 489
Noxious, *badness*, 649
*Noyade, *killing*, 361
  execution, 972
Nozzle, *projection*, 250
  air-pipe, 351
  opening, 260
Nuance, *difference*, 15
Nub, *importance*, 642
Nubble, *lump*, 150
Nubile, *adolescence*, 131
Nucleus, *centre*, 223
  middle, 68
  cause, 153
Nudge, *indication*, 550
Nudity, *divestment*, 226
*Nugae, *unmeaning*, 517
  unimportant, 643
Nugatory, *inexistence*, 2
  useless, 645
  inoperative, 158

Nugget, *lump*, 321
Nuisance, *annoyance*, 830
   evil, 619
Null, *unsubstantiality*, 4
Nullah, *gap*, 198
*Nulli secundus, *superiority*,
        33
   goodness, 648
Nullifidian, *atheist*, 988
Nullify, *counteract*, 179
   repudiate, 773
   invalidate, 964
   compensate, 30
Numb, *morally*, 823
   physically, 376, 381
Number, *abstract*, 84
   plurality, 100
   grammar, 568
   publication, 593
   to count, 85
Numberless, *infinity*, 105
Numbers, *poetry*, 597
Numbness, *physical*, 381
   moral, 823
Numen, *great spirit*, 979
Numeral, *number*, 84
Numeration, *numeration*, 85
Numerator, *number*, 84
Numerous, *multitude*, 102
Numismatics, *money*, 800
Numskull, *fool*, 501
Nun, *clergy*, 996
*Nunc dimittis, *worship*, 990
Nuncio, *messenger*, 534
   consignee, 758
Nuncupatory, *naming*, 564
   informing, 527
Nunnery, *temple*, 1000
   seclusion, 893
Nuptials, *marriage*, 903
Nurse, *servant*, 746
   treat, 662
   to help, 707
   preserve, 670
Nursery, *room*, 191
   school, 542
   workshop, 691
   for plants, 367
Nurseryman, *horticulture*, 371
Nursling, *infant*, 129
Nurture, *food*, 298
   to support, 707
   prepare, 673
Nut, *head*, 450
   fop, 854
   madman, 504
Nut-brown, *brown*, 433
Nutation, *oscillation*, 314
Nutmeg-grater, *rough*, 256
Nutriment, *food*, 298
Nutrition, *aid*, 707
Nuts, *insane*, 503
   rubbish, 643
Nutshell, *littleness*, 193
   compendium, 596

Nuzzle, *endearment*, 902
Nyctalopia, *dim-sighted*, 443
Nylons, *dress*, 225
Nymph, *woman*, 374
   goddess, 979
Nystagmus, *dim-sighted*, 443

O

O.K., *assent*, 488
   consent, 762
Oaf, *fool*, 501
Oak, *strength*, 159
Oar, *instrument*, 633
   paddle, 267
Oasis, *land*, 342
Oath, *promise*, 768
   assertion, 535
   expletive, 908
*Obbligato, *music*, 415
Obduracy, *sin*, 945
   impenitence, 931
   obstinacy, 606
   severity, 739
   malevolence, 907
Obeah, *occult arts*, 992
Obedience, *obedience*, 743
   duty, 926
Obeisance, *bow*, 894
   reverence, 928
   submission, 725
   worship, 990
   fealty, 743
Obelisk, *monument*, 551
   tall, 206
Obelize, *indicate*, 550
Oberon, *sprite*, 980
Obesity, *size*, 192
Obey, *obedience*, 743, 749
Obfuscate, *darken*, 421, 426
   bewilder, 458
Obit, *death*, 360
*Obiter dictum, *irrelation*, 10
Obituary, *description*, 594
   death, 360
Object, *thing*, 3, 316
   intention, 620
   ugly, 846
   to disapprove, 932
Object lesson, *explanation*, 522
Object to, *dislike*, 867
Objectify, *existence*, 1
Objective, *extrinsic*, 6
   material, 316, 450A
Objurgate, *disapprobation*, 932
Oblate, *shortness*, 201
   monk, 996
Oblation, *gift*, 789
   proffer, 763
   worship, 990
Obligation, *duty*, 926
   promise, 768
   conditions, 770
   debt, 806
   gratitude, 916

Oblige, *compel*, 744
   benefit, 707
Obliging, *kind*, 906
   courteous, 894
Oblique, *obliquity*, 217
Obliquity, *vice*, 945
Obliterate, *efface*, 552
Oblivion, *oblivion*, 506
Oblong, *length*, 200
Obloquy, *censure*, 932
   disgrace, 874
Obmutescence, *aphony*, 581
Obnoxious, *hateful*, 898
   unpleasing, 830
   pernicious, 649
Oboe, *musical instrument*, 417
Obscene, *impurity*, 961
Obscurantist, *ignoramus*, 493
Obscure, *dark*, 421
   unseen, 447
   unintelligible, 519
   style, 571
   to eclipse, 874
*Obscurum per obscurius,
   unintelligibility, 519
   misteaching, 538
Obsecration, *request*, 765
Obsequies, *interment*, 363
Obsequious, *respectful*, 928
   courteous, 894
   servile, 886
Observance, *fulfilment*, 772
   rule, 82
   habit, 613
   practice, 692
   rites, 998
Observatory, *universe*, 318
Observe, *note*, 457
   conform, 926
   remark, 535
Observer, *spectator*, 444
   fighter, 726
Obsess, *preoccupy*, 457
   worry, 830
   haunt, 860
Obsession, *misjudgment*, 481
   fixed idea, 606
Obsolete, *old*, 124
   effete, 645
   vulgar, 851
Obstacle, *physical*, 179
   moral, 706
Obstetrician, *instrumentality*,
        631
Obstinate, *stubborn*, 606
   resolute, 604
   prejudiced, 481
Obstreperous, *violent*, 173
   loud, 404
Obstruct, *hinder*, 706
   close, 261
Obtain, *exist*, 1
   acquire, 775
Obtainable, *possibility*, 470
Obtestation, *entreaty*, 765

INDEX

INDEX

Palsy, *incapacity*, 158
    insensibility, 376, 823
Palter, *falsehood*, 544
    shift, 605
    elude, 773
Paltry, *mean*, 940
    despicable, 643, 930
    little, 32
Paludal, *marsh*, 345
Pampas, *plain*, 344
Pamper, *indulge*, 954
    gorge, 957
Pampero, *wind*, 349
Pamphlet, *book*, 593
Pamphleteer, *writing*, 590
    dissertation, 595
Pan, *receptacle*, 191
    face, 234, 448
Panacea, *remedy*, 662
*Panache, *plume*, 256
    ornament, 847
Pandect, *code*, 963
    compendium, 596
    erudition, 490
Pandemic, *insalubrity*, 657
Pandemonium, *hell*, 982
    disorder, 59
Pander, *flatter*, 933
    indulge, 954
    mediate, 631
    help, 707
Pandora, *evil*, 619
Paned, *variegation*, 440
Panegyric, *approbation*, 931
Panel, *list*, 86
    partition, 228
    accused, 938
    legal, 967
*Panem et circenses, *giving*,
    784
Pang, *physical*, 378
    moral, 828
Panhandler, *tramp*, 876
Panic, *fear*, 860
Pannier, *receptacle*, 191
Panoply, *defence*, 717
Panopticon, *prison*, 752
Panorama, *view*, 448
    painting, 556
Panoramic, *general*, 78
Pansophy, *knowledge*, 490
Pansy, *effeminate*, 374
Pant, *breathless*, 688
    desire, 865
    agitation, 821
Pantaloon, *buffoon*, 844
    dress, 225
Pantechnicon, *vehicle*, 272
Pantheism, *heathen*, 984
Pantheon, *temple*, 1000
Pantograph, *imitation*, 19
Pantomime, *sign*, 550
    language, 560
    drama, 599
Pantry, *receptacle*, 191

Pap, *pulp*, 354
Pap, *teat*, 250
Papa, *father*, 166
Papacy, *churchdom*, 995
Paper, *writing*, 590
    book, 593
    record, 551
    white, 430
Paperback, *book*, 593
Papilla, *convexity*, 250
Papoose, *infant*, 129
Pappy, *semiliquidity*, 352
Par, *equality*, 27
Parable, *metaphor*, 521
    analogy, 464
    story, 594
Parabolic, *metaphor*, 521
    curve, 245
Parachronism, *anachronism*,
    115
Parachute, *refuge*, 666
Paraclete, *Deity*, 976
Parade, *walk*, 189
    ostentation, 882
Paradigm, *prototype*, 22
    example, 80
Paradise, *heaven*, 981
    bliss, 827
Paradox, *obscurity*, 519
    absurdity, 497
    mystery, 528
    enigma, 533
Paragon, *perfection*, 650
    saint, 948
    glory, 873
Paragraph, *phrase*, 566
    part, 51
    article, 593
Paralipsis, *neglect*, 460
Parallax, *distance*, 196
Parallel, *position*, 216
    similarity, 17
    to imitate, 19
    agreement, 23
    comparison, 464
Parallelepiped, *angularity*, 244
Parallelogram, *angularity*, 244
Paralogism, *sophistry*, 477
Paralyse, *weaken*, 160
    benumb, 381
    deaden, 823
    insensibility, 376
    impassivity, 823
    stillness, 265
    disqualify, 158
    disease, 655
Paramount, *essential*, 642
    in degree, 33
    authority, 737
Paramour, *love*, 897
Paranoia, *insanity*, 503, 504
Parapet, *defence*, 717
Paraph, *writing*, 590
Paraphernalia, *machinery*, 633
    materials, 635

Paraphernalia, *property*, 780
Paraphrase, *interpretation*,
    522, 524
    phrase, 566
    imitation, 19, 21
Paraplectic, *disease*, 655
Parapsychology, *occult*, 992
Parasite, *flatterer*, 935
    servile, 886
    follow, 88
Parasol, *shade*, 424
Paratrooper, *fighter*, 726
Paravane, *defence*, 717
Parboil, *calefaction*, 384
Parcel, *group*, 72
    portion, 51
Parcel out, *arrange*, 60
    allot, 786
Parch, *dry*, 340
    heat, 382
    bake, 384
Parchment, *manuscript*, 590
    record, 551
Pardon, *forgiveness*, 918
Pardonable, *vindication*, 937
Pare, *scrape*, 38, 226, 331
    shorten, 201
    decrease, 36
Paregoric, *salubrity*, 656
Parenchyma, *texture*, 329
Parent, *paternity*, 166
Parentage, *kindred*, 11
Parenthesis, *interjacence*, 228
    discontinue, 70
Parenthetical, *irrelation*, 10
    occasion, 134
*Par excellence, *greatness*, 31
    superiority, 33
*Pari passu, *equality*, 27
Pariah, *commonalty*, 876
    outcast, 892
Paring, *part*, 51
    smallness, 32
Parish, *region*, 181
Parishioner, *laity*, 997
Parity, *equality*, 27
Park, *plain*, 344
    vegetation, 367
    amusement, 840
    artillery, 727
    locate, 184
Parlance, *speech*, 582
*Parlementaire, *messenger*,
    534
Parley, *talk*, 588
    mediation, 724
Parliament, *council*, 696
Parlour, *room*, 191
Parlour-car, *vehicle*, 272
Parlourmaid, *servant*, 746
Parnassus, *poetry*, 597
Parochial, *regional*, 181
    ignoble, 876
Parody, *imitation*, 19
    copy, 21

Pelf, *materials*, 635
   gain, 775
Pellet, *rotundity*, 249
   remedy, 662
Pellicle, *film*, 205
   skin, 222
Pell-mell, *disorder*, 59
Pellucid, *transparency*, 425
Pelt, *skin*, 222
   throw, 276
   attack, 716
   beat, 972
Pen, *surround*, 231
   enclose, 232
   restrain, 751
   imprison, 752
   draw, 559
   write, 590
Pen-and-ink, *drawing*, 556
Pen-name, *misnomer*, 565
Penal, *punishment*, 972
Penalty, *penalty*, 974
Penance, *atonement*, 952
   rite, 998
   penalty, 974
*Penchant, *inclination*, 865
   love, 897
Pencil, *bundle*, 72
   of light, 420
   artist, 556, 559, 590
Pencraft, *writing*, 590
Pendant, *adjunct*, 39
   flag, 550
   pendency, 214
   match, 17
Pendent, *during*, 106
   hanging, 214
   uncertain, 485
*Pendente lite, *warfare*, 722
   lawsuit, 969
Pending, *duration*, 106
   lateness, 133
   uncertain, 475
Pendulous, *pendency*, 214
Pendulum, *clock*, 114
   oscillation, 314
Penetralia, *interiority*, 221
   secret, 533
Penetrate, *fill*, 186
   influence, 175
Penetrating, *affecting*, 821
Penetration, *ingress*, 294
   passage, 302
   discernment, 441
   sagacity, 498
Penfold, *enclosure*, 232
Peninsula, *land*, 342
Penitent, *penitence*, 950
Penitentiary, *prison*, 752
Penmanship, *writing*, 590
Penniless, *poverty*, 804
Pennon, *indication*, 550
Penny-a-liner, *writer*, 590
Penny-farthing, *bicycle*, 266
Pennyworth, *price*, 812

*Penseroso, *dejection*, 837
Pensile, *pendency*, 214
Pension, *wealth*, 803, 810
Pensioner, *servant*, 746
   recipient, 785
Pensive, *thoughtful*, 451
   sad, 837
Pent, *imprisoned*, 754
Pentad, *five*, 98
Pentagon, *angularity*, 244
   five, 98
Pentahedron, *angularity*, 244
   five, 98
Pentatonic, *melody*, 413
Penthouse, *building*, 189
Penultimate, *end*, 67
Penumbra, *darkness*, 421, 424
Penurious, *parsimony*, 819
Penury, *poverty*, 804
   scantiness, 640
People, *man*, 373
   inhabitant, 188
   commonalty, 876
   to colonize, 184
Pep, *energy*, 171, 682
   vigour, 574
Pep-talk, *speech*, 582
Pepper, *hot*, 171
   pungent, 392
   condiment, 393
   attack, 716
Peppercorn, *unimportance*, 643
Peppery, *irascibility*, 901
Peptic, *remedy*, 662
*Per contra, *contrariety*, 14
   opposition, 708
*Per procurationem, *commission*, 755
*Per saltum, *discontinuity*, 70
   transientness, 111
   instantaneity, 113
*Per se, *unity*, 87
Peradventure, *change*, 156
   possibly, 470
   uncertainty, 475
Perambulate, *journey*, 266
Perceivable, *visible*, 446
Percentage, *proportion*, 84
   discount, 813
Perceptible, *visibility*, 446
Perception, *idea*, 453
   of touch, 380
Perceptivity, *sensibility*, 375
Perch, *support*, 215
   to alight, 186
   tall, 206
   habitation, 189
Perchance, *chance*, 156
   possibly, 470
Percipience, *intellect*, 450
Percolate, *distil*, 295
Percolation, *passage*, 302
Percussion, *impulse*, 276
Perdition, *ruin*, 732
   loss, 776

Perdu, *concealment*, 528
Perdurable, *permanence*, 141
Peregrination, *journey*, 266
Peremptory, *assertion*, 535
   denial, 536
   firm, 604
   rigorous, 739
   authoritative, 737
   compulsory, 744
   obligatory, 926
   order, 740, 741
Perennial, *diuturnity*, 110, 150
Perfect, *entire*, 52
   complete, 729
   excellent, 650
Perfectly, *greatness*, 31
Perfidy, *improbity*, 940
Perforate, *opening*, 260
Perforator, *perforator*, 263
Perforce, *compulsion*, 744
Perform, *do*, 170, 680
   achieve, 729
   produce, 161
   act, 599
   fulfil, 772
   duty, 926
Performable, *facility*, 705
   possible, 470
Performance, *effect*, 154
Performer, *musician*, 416
   actor, 599
   workman, 164
   agent, 690
Perfume, *fragrance*, 400
Perfunctory, *neglect*, 460
   incomplete, 53
Perhaps, *possibly*, 470
   chance, 156
   supposition, 514
Peri, *fairy*, 979
Periapt, *spell*, 993
Perigee, *nearness*, 197
Perihelion, *nearness*, 197
Peril, *danger*, 665
Perimeter, *outline*, 229
Period, *end*, 67
   of time, 106, 108
   stop, 142
   point, 71
   recurrence, 138
Periodical, *book*, 593
   publication, 531
Peripatetic, *traveller*, 268
   ambulatory, 266
Periphery, *outline*, 229
Periphrasis, *phrase*, 566
   diffuseness, 573
Perique, *tobacco*, 298A
Periscope, *vision*, 441
   optical instrument, 445
Perish, *vanish*, 2
   be destroyed, 162
   die, 360; *decay*, 659
Peristaltic, *convolution*, 248
Periwig, *dress*, 225

Phantom, *imaginary*, 515
Pharisaical, *falsehood*, 544
Pharmacology, *remedy*, 662
Pharmacy, *remedy*, 662
Pharos, *warning*, 668
   indication, 550
Phase, *aspect*, 8
   appearance, 448
   change, 144
   form, 240
Phenomenal, *great*, 31
   apparent, 448
   wonderful, 870
Phenomenon, *appearance*, 448
   event, 151
   prodigy, 872
Phial, *receptacle*, 191
Phidias, *artist*, 559
Philanderer, *flirt*, 902
Philanthropy, *philanthropy*,
   910
Philatelist, *collector*, 775
Philibeg, *dress*, 225
Philippic, *disapproval*, 932
Philistine, *uncultured*, 491, 493
Phillumenist, *collector*, 775
Philology, *grammar*, 567
Philomath, *scholar*, 492
   sage, 500
Philomel, *musician*, 416
Philosopher, *scholar*, 492
Philosophy, *calmness*, 826
   thought, 451
   knowledge, 490
Philtre, *charm*, 993
Phiz, *appearance*, 448
Phlebotomy, *ejection*, 297
Phlegethon, *hell*, 982
Phlegm, *insensibility*, 823
   semiliquid, 352
Phoenix, *prodigy*, 872
   exception, 83
   paragon, 650
   saint, 948
   renovation, 163, 660
Phonetics, *sound*, 402
   speech, 580
Phoney, *false*, 495, 544
Phonic, *sound*, 402
Phonograph, *musical
   instrument*, 417
   hearing, 418
Phonography, *shorthand*, 590
Phosphorescent, *light*, 420, 423
Photo-lithograph, *engraving*,
   558
Photogenic, *beauty*, 845
Photograph, *copy*, 21
   representation, 554
Photography, *painting*, 556
Photogravure, *engraving*, 558
Photology, *light*, 420
Photometer, *optical
   instrument*, 445
Photostat, *copy*, 21

Phrase, *phrase*, 566
Phrase-monger, *floridity*, 577
Phraseology, *style*, 569
Phratry, *class*, 75
Phrenetic, *see* Frantic
Phrenitis, *insanity*, 503
Phrenology, *intellect*, 450
Phrontistery, *room*, 191
Phylactery, *spell*, 993
Phylum, *class*, 75
Physic, *remedy*, 662
   to cure, 660
Physical, *materiality*, 316
Physician, *advice*, 695
Physics, *materiality*, 316
Physiognomy, *appearance*, 448
   face, 234
Physiology, *life*, 359
Physique, *substance*, 3
   animality, 364
Phytography, *botany*, 369
Phytology, *botany*, 369
Piacular, *atonement*, 952
*Pianissimo, *faint*, 405
Pianist, *musician*, 416
Piano, *instrument*, 417
   slowly, 275
   faint sound, 405
Pianola, *instrument*, 417
Piazza, *street*, 189
   veranda, 191
Pibroch, *music*, 415
Picaroon, *thief*, 792
Piccaninny, *child*, 129
Piccolo, *musical instrument*, 417
Pick, *select*, 609
   goodness, 648
   extract, 301
   eat, 296
   clean, 652
   sharpness, 253
Pick-me-up, *stimulant*, 615
   remedy, 662
Pick-thank, *flatterer*, 935
Pick up, *learn*, 539
   improve, 658
   acquire, 775
Pickaxe, *sharpness*, 253
Picket, *join*, 43
   tether, 265
   fence, 231
   defence, 717
   guard, 664
   imprison, 752
Pickings, *part*, 51
   booty, 793
Pickle, *difficulty*, 704
   preserve, 670
   pungent, 392
   condiment, 393
   macerate, 337
Pickpocket, *thief*, 792
Picnic, *food*, 298
   party, 892
Picture, *painting*, 556

Picture, *representation*, 554
   fancy, 515
Picturesque, *beautiful*, 845
   graphic, 556
Piddling, *paltry*, 643
Pidgin English, *language*, 560
Pie, *type*, 591
   disorder, 59
Piebald, *variegation*, 440
Piece, *bit*, 51
   cannon, 727
   drama, 599
Piece out, *completeness*, 42
Piecemeal, *part*, 51
Pied, *variegation*, 440
*Pied à terre, *abode*, 189
Pier, *refuge*, 666
Pier-glass, *optical instru-
   ment*, 445
Pierce, *perforate*, 260, 302
   pain, 378, 830
   affect, 824
Piercing, *cold*, 383
   sound, 404
   sagacious, 498
   feeling, 821
   sight, 441
Pierian spring, *poetry*, 597
Pierrot, *actor*, 599
Pietism, *impiety*, 988
Piety, *piety*, 987
Piffle, *absurdity*, 497
Pig, *gluttony*, 957
Pig-headed, *prejudiced*, 481
   obstinate, 606
   stupid, 499
Pigeon-chested, *distorted*, 243
Pigeon-hole, *receptacle*, 191
   aperture, 260
   arrange, 60
   discard, 624
   reject, 610
Piggish, *intemperance*, 954
   gluttony, 957
Pigment, *colour*, 428
Pigmy, *see* Pygmy
Pigsty, *uncleanness*, 653
Pigtail, *pendant*, 214
Pi-jaw, *speech*, 582
Pike, *arms*, 727
   sharpness, 253
   hill, 206
Pikestaff, *height*, 206
Pilaster, *height*, 206
Pile, *heap*, 72
   nap, 256
   building, 189
   store, 636
   wealth, 803
Pile-driver, *hammer*, 276
Pilfer, *stealing*, 791, 792
Pilgrim, *traveller*, 268
Pilgrimage, *journey*, 266
Pill, *rotundity*, 249
   remedy, 662

Pill-box, *defence*, 717
Pillage, *rob*, 971
 rapine, 619
 devastation, 649
Pillar, *support*, 150, 215
 monument, 551
 lofty, 206
Pillar-box, *red*, 434
Pillion, *support*, 215
Pillory, *scourge*, 975
 to ridicule, 856
Pillow, *support*, 215, 265
 soft, 324
 ease, 831
Pilot, *director*, 694
 mariner, 269
 to guide, 693
 balloon, 273
 fighter, 726
 trial, 463
Pilous, *roughness*, 256
Pimp, *libertine*, 962
Pimple, *tumour*, 250
 blemish, 848
Pin, *fastening*, 45
 to fasten, 43
 axis, 312
 sharp, 253
 trifle, 643
Pin down, *restrain*, 751
 compel, 744
Pin-prick, *annoyance*, 830
Pinafore, *dress*, 225
Pincers, *extraction*, 301
 grip, 781
Pinch, *emergency*, 8
 difficulty, 704
 to contract, 195
 narrow, 203
 chill, 385
 pain, 378
 stint, 640, 819
 to hurt, 830
 to steal, 791
Pinch-hitter, *substitute*, 147, 634
 deputy, 759
Pinchbeck, *spurious*, 544
Pinched, *chilled*, 383
 thin, 203
 indigent, 804
Pinching, *miserly*, 819
Pine, *desire*, 865
 grieve, 828
 droop, 837
Ping, *sound*, 406
Pinguid, *unctuousness*, 355
Pinhole, *opening*, 260
Pinion, *instrument*, 633
 wing, 267
 fetter, 752
 to fasten, 43
 to restrain, 751
Pink, *colour*, 434
 perfection, 650
 beauty, 845

Pink, *glory*, 873
 to pierce, 260
Pinnace, *ship*, 273
Pinnacle, *summit*, 210
*Pinxit, *painting*, 556
Pioneer, *precursor*, 64
 preparer, 673
 teacher, 540
Pious, *piety*, 987
Pip-pip, *departure*, 293
Pipe, *conduit*, 350
 passage, 302
 vent, 351
 tobacco, 298A
 tube, 160
 sound, 510
 cry, 411
 music, 415
 instrument, 417
 observe, 457
Pipe down, *subside*, 826
Pipe-dream, *hope*, 858
 imagination, 515
Piper, *musician*, 416
Piping, *sound*, 410
 hot, 382
Pipkin, *receptacle*, 191
Piquant, *pungent*, 392
 style, 574
 motive, 615
 feeling, 821
 exciting, 824
Pique, *enmity*, 889
 hate, 898
 anger, 900
 irritate, 830
 stimulate, 615, 824
Pique oneself, *pride*, 878
Pirate, *thief*, 792
 to steal, 791
Pirouette, *rotation*, 312
*Pis aller, *substitute*, 634
 necessity, 601
 plan, 626
Piscatory, *animal*, 366
Pisciculture, *taming*, 370
Piscina, *church*, 1000
Pistol, *arms*, 727
Pistol-shot, *nearness*, 197
Piston, *stopper*, 264
Pit, *hole*, 252
 opening, 260
 deep, 208
 grave, 363
 hell, 982
 theatre, 599
Pit against, *opposition*, 708
Pit-a-pat, *feeling*, 821
Pitch, *degree*, 26
 term, 51
 station, 182
 arena, 728
 height, 206
 descent, 306
 summit, 210

Pitch, *musical note*, 413
 dark, 421
 black, 431
 semiliquid, 352
 to throw, 294
 to reel, 314
 to place, 184
Pitch-and-toss, *gambling*, 621
Pitch into, *contention*, 720
Pitch-pipe, *musical*, 417
Pitch tent, *settle*, 265
Pitch upon, *choose*, 609
 reach, 292
Pitcher, *receptacle*, 191
Pitchfork, *propel*, 284
Piteous, *painfulness*, 830
 greatness, 31
Pitfall, *pitfall*, 667
Pith, *gist*, 5, 516
 strength, 159
 interior, 221
 central, 223
 important, 642
Pithy, *significant*, 516
 concise, 572
Pitiable, *unimportance*, 643
Pitiful, *unimportant*, 643
 compassionate, 914
 paltry, 940
Pitiless, *malevolent*, 907
 revengeful, 900, 919
Pittance, *allotment*, 786
Pitted, *blemished*, 848
Pity, *compassion*, 914
 regret, 833
Pivot, *cause*, 153
 axis, 312
Pix, *cinema*, 599A
Pixillated, *mad*, 503
Pixy, *sprite*, 980
*Pizzicato, *music*, 415
Placable, *forgiveness*, 918
Placard, *notice*, 550
 to publish, 531
Placate, *pacify*, 826
Place, *situation*, 182, 183
 circumstances, 8
 rank, 873
 term, 71
 in order, 58
 abode, 189
 to locate, 184
 substitution, 147
 office, 625
Placebo, *remedy*, 662
Placeman, *consignee*, 758
*Placet, *command*, 741
Placid, *calm*, 826
Placket, *dress*, 225
Plagiarism, *stealing*, 791
 borrowing, 788
 imitation, 19
Plagiarist, *thief*, 792
Plagioclastic, *oblique*, 217
Plague, *disease*, 655

Posthumous, *subsequent*, 117
Postiche, *artificial*, 544
Postilion, *director*, 694
Postlude, *music*, 415
   posterior, 117
Postman, *messenger*, 534
Postpone, *lateness*, 133
Postscript, *sequel*, 65
   appendix, 39
Postulant, *petitioner*, 767
   request, 765
   nun, 997
Postulate, *supposition*, 514
   evidence, 467
   reasoning, 476
Postulation, *request*, 765
Posture, *circumstance*, 8
   attitude, 240
   display, 882
Posy, *motto*, 550
   poem, 597
   flowers, 847
Pot, *mug*, 191
   stove, 386
   greatness, 31
   ruin, 732
Pot-companion, *friend*, 890
Pot-hooks, *writing*, 590
Pot-hunting, *acquisition*, 775
Pot-luck, *food*, 298
Pot-pourri, *mixture*, 41
   fragrance, 400
   music, 415
Pot-valiant, *drunk*, 959
Potable, *drinkable*, 298
Potation, *drink*, 296
Potency, *power*, 157
Potentate, *master*, 745
Potential, *virtual*, 2
   possible, 470
   power, 157
Pother, *to worry*, 830
   fuss, 682
   confusion, 59
Pottage, *food*, 298
Potter, *idle*, 683
Pottle, *receptacle*, 191
Potty, *mad*, 503
*Pou sto, *influence*, 175
Pouch, *receptacle*, 191
   insert, 184
   receive, 785
   take, 789
   acquire, 775
Pouffe, *support*, 215
Poultice, *soft* , 354
   remedy, 662
Pounce upon, *taking*, 789
Pound, *bruise*, 330
   mix, 41
   enclose, 232
   imprison, 752
Poundage, *discount*, 813
Pounds, *money*, 800
Pour, *egress*, 295

Pour out, *eject*, 185, 297, 248
*Pour rire, *ridicule*, 853
*Pourboire, *giving*, 784
   expenditure, 809
*Pourparler, *discussion*, 476
Pout, *sullen*, 895
   sad, 837
Poverty, *indigence*, 804
   scantiness, 640
   trifle, 643
Powder, *pulverulence*, 330
   ornament, 845, 847
Powder-box, *receptacle*, 191
Power, *efficacy*, 157
   physical energy, 171
   authority, 737
   spirit, 977
   much, 31
   multitude, 102
   numerical, 84
   of style, 574
Powerful, *strength*, 159
Powerless, *weakness*, 160
Pow-wow, *conference*, 588
Pox, *disease*, 655
   expletive, 908
Praam, *ship*, 273
Practicable, *possible*, 470
   easy, 705
Practical, *activity*, 672
   agency, 170
Practice, *act*, 680
   conduct, 692
   use, 677; *habit*, 613
   teaching, 537; *rule*, 80
   proceeding, 626
Practise, *deceive*, 645
Practised, *skill*, 698
Practitioner, *agent*, 690
*Praecognita, *evidence*, 467
Praenomen, *name*, 564
Praetor, *master*, 745
Pragmatical, *pedantic*, 855
   vain, 880
Prairie, *plain*, 344
   plaint, 367
Praise, *commendation*, 931
   thanks, 916
   worship, 990
Praiseworthy, *commendable*, 931
   virtuous, 944
Prance, *dance*, 315
   swagger, 878
   move, 266
Prang, *bomb*, 162, 716, 732
Prank, *caprice*, 608
   amusement, 840
   vagary, 856
   to adorn, 845
Prate, *babble*, 584, 588
Prattle, *talk*, 582, 588
Pravity, *badness*, 649
Pray, *request*, 765
Prayer, *request*, 765
   worship, 990

Preach, *teach*, 537
   speech, 582
   predication, 998
Preacher, *clergy*, 996
Preachify, *speech*, 582
Preamble, *precursor*, 64
   speech, 582
Preapprehension, *misjudgment*,
      481
Prebendary, *clergy*, 996
Prebendaryship, *churchdom*,
      995
Precarious, *uncertain*, 475
   perilous, 665
Precatory, *request*, 764
Precaution, *care*, 459
   expedient, 626
   preparation, 673
Precede, *in order*, 62
   in time, 116
   lead, 280
Precedence, *rank*, 873
Precedent, *rule*, 80
   verdict, 969
Precentor, *clergy*, 996
   director, 694
Precept, *maxim*, 697
   order, 741
   rule, 80
   permit, 760
   decree, 963
Preceptor, *teacher*, 540
Precession, *in order*, 62
   in motion, 280
*Précieuse ridicule, *affecta-*
tion, 855
   style, 577
Precincts, *environs*, 227
   boundary, 233
   region, 181
   place, 182
Preciosity, *affectation*, 855
Precious, *excellent*, 648
   valuable, 814
   beloved, 897
Precipice, *slope*, 217
   vertical, 212
   danger, 667
Precipitancy, *haste*, 274, 684
Precipitate, *rash*, 863
   impulse, 612
   early, 132
   transient, 111
   to sink, 308
   refuse, 653
   consolidate, 321
   swift, 274
Precipitous, *obliquity*, 217
Précis, *compendium*, 596
Precise, *exact*, 494
   definite, 518
Precisely, *assent*, 488
Precisian, *formalist*, 855
   taste, 850
Preclude, *hindrance*, 706

Prize, *love*, 897
  approve, 931
Prize-fighter, *combatant*, 726
Pro and con, *reasoning*, 476
*Pro bono publico, *utility*, 644
  philanthropy, 910
*Pro forma, *habit*, 613
*Pro hac vice, *present*, 118
*Pro more, *conformity*, 62
  habit, 613
*Pro rata, *relation*, 9
*Pro re nata, *circumstance*, 8
  occasion, 134
*Pro tanto, *greatness*, 31
  smallness, 32
Proa, *ship*, 273
Probable, *probability*, 472
  chance, 156
Probate, *evidence*, 467
Probation, *trial*, 463
  essay, 675
  demonstration, 478
Probationer, *learner*, 541
Probe, *stiletto*, 262
  measure, 466
  depth, 208
  investigate, 461
Probity, *virtue*, 944
  right, 922
  integrity, 939
Problem, *enigma*, 533
  inquiry, 461
Problematical, *uncertain*, 475
  hidden, 528
Proboscis, *convexity*, 250
Procedure, *conduct*, 692
  action, 680
  plan, 626
Proceed, *advance*, 282
  from, 154
  elapse, 109
  happen, 151
Proceeding, *action*, 680
  event, 151
  plan, 626
  incomplete, 53
Proceeds, *money*, 800
  receipts, 810
  gain, 775
Procerity, *height*, 206
*Procès-verbal, *compendium*, 596
Process, *projection*, 250
  plan, 626
  action, 680
  conduct, 692
  engraving, 558
  time, 109
Procession, *train*, 69
  ceremony, 882
Prochronism, *anachronism*, 115
Proclaim, *publication*, 531
Proclivity, *disposition*, 602
  proneness, 176, 820
Proconsul, *deputy*, 759

Proconsul, *master*, 745
Proconsulship, *authority*, 737
Procrastination, *delay*, 133, 683
Procreant, *productiveness*, 168
Procreate, *production*, 161
Procreator, *paternity*, 166
Proctor, *officer*, 694
  law, 968
Proctorship, *direction*, 693
Procumbent, *horizontality*, 213
Procuration, *commission*, 755
  pimping, 961
Procurator, *director*, 694
Procure, *get*, 775
  cause, 153
  buy, 795
  pimp, 962
Prod, *poke*, 276
Prodigal, *extravagant*, 818
  lavish, 641
  penitent, 950
Prodigious, *wonderful*, 870
  much, 31
Prodigy, *prodigy*, 872
Prodromal, *precedence*, 62
Prodrome, *precursor*, 64
Produce, *cause*, 153
  create, 161; *prolong*, 200
  show, 525, 599
  evidence, 467
  result, 154
  fruit, 775; *ware*, 798
Product, *effect*, 154
  acquisition, 775
  multiple, 84
Productive, *productiveness*, 168
Proem, *precursor*, 64
Proemial, *preceding, in order*, 62
  in time, 106
  beginning, 66
Profane, *impious*, 988
  pagan, 986
  desecrate, 679
  laical, 997
Profess, *affirmation*, 535
Profession, *business*, 625
  promise, 768
Professor, *teacher*, 540
Proffer, *offer*, 763
Proficiency, *skill*, 698
Proficient, *adept*, 700
  knowledge, 490
  skilful, 698
Profile, *lateral*, 236
  outline, 229
  appearance, 448
Profit, *acquisition*, 775
  advantage, 618
Profitable, *useful*, 644
  gainful, 810
Profiteer, *acquisition*, 775
  upstart, 734
Profitless, *inutility*, 645
Profligacy, *vice*, 945
Profligate, *vice*, 945
Profluent, *advancing*, 282

Profluent, *flowing*, 348
Profound, *deep*, 208
  sagacity, 702
  feeling, 821
  thought, 451
Profoundly, *great*, 31
Profuse, *prodigal*, 818
  lavish, 641
Prog, *food*, 298
Progenitor, *paternity*, 166
Progeny, *posterity*, 121, 167
Prognostic, *omen*, 512
Prognosticate, *prediction*, 511
Programme, *catalogue*, 86
  announcement, 510
  plan, 626
Progress, *advance*, 282
  speed, 274
  of time, 109
  improvement, 658
  success, 731
Progression, *series*, 69
  gradation, 58
  numerical, 84
  motion, 282
Prohibit, *forbid*, 761
Prohibition, *sobriety*, 953, 958
Project, *bulge*, 250
  propel, 284
  eject, 297
  move, 264
  plan, 626
  intend, 620
Projectile, *missile*, 284
  weapon, 727
Projection, *map*, 554
Prolegomena, *precursor*, 64
Prolepsis, *anachronism*, 115
*Prolétaire, *commonalty*, 876
Proletarian, *commonalty*, 876
Proliferate, *reproduction*, 161
Prolific, *productive*, 168
Prolix, *diffuse*, 573
Prolocuter, *teacher*, 540
  speaker, 582
Prologue, *precursor*, 64
  drama, 599
Prolong, *lengthen*, 200
  protract, 110, 133
Prolusion, *beginning*, 64
  lesson, 537
  dissertation, 595
Promenade, *journey*, 266
  causeway, 627
  display, 882
Promethean, *life*, 359
Prominent, *convex*, 250, 252
  conspicuous, 446, 525
  important, 642
  famous, 873
Prominently, *great*, 31
Promiscuous, *irregular*, 59
  casual, 621
Promise, *engage*, 768
  augur, 507

Pun, *wit*, 842
  similarity, 17
Punch, *to perforate*, 260
  perforator, 262
  to strike, 276
  punish, 972
  energy, 171
  vigour, 574
  buffoon, 857
  humorist, 844
  puppet, 599
  horse, 271
Punctate, *spotted*, 440
Punctilio, *ostentation*, 882
Punctilious, *correct*, 494
  fashionable, 852
  observant, 772
  fastidious, 868
  scrupulous, 939
Punctual, *early*, 132
  periodical, 138
  scrupulous, 939
Punctuation, *grammar*, 567
Puncture, *opening*, 260
Pundit, *scholar*, 462
  sage, 500
  clergy, 996
Pungent, *taste*, 392
  caustic, 171
  feeling, 821
Punic faith, *improbity*, 940
Punish, *punishment*, 972
Punk, *prostitute*, 962
  trash, 645
Punka, *fan*, 349
Punnet, *receptacle*, 191
Punster, *humorist*, 844
Punt, *ship*, 273
  propel, 267, 284
  gamble, 621
Puny, *in degree*, 32
  in size, 193
  weak, 160
Pup, *infant*, 129
Pupil, *learner*, 541
  eye, 441
Puppet, *subjection*, 749
  effigy, 554
  plaything, 840
  dupe, 547
  little, 193
Puppet-show, *the drama*, 599
  amusement, 840
Puppy, *fop*, 854
  blusterer, 887
Puranas, *sacred books*, 986
Purblind, *dim-sighted*, 443
  undiscerning, 499
Purchase, *buy*, 795
  leverage, 175
Pure, *simple*, 42
  true, 494
  good taste, 850
  clean, 652
  innocent, 946

Pure, *virtuous*, 944
Purely, *smallness*, 32
  greatness, 31
Purgation, *cleansing*, 652
  atonement, 952
Purgative, *remedy*, 662
Purgatory, *suffering*, 828
  atonement, 952
  hell, 982
Purge, *clean*, 652
  improve, 658
  atone, 952
  subduction, 38
Purify, *cleanse*, 652
  improve, 658
Purist, *style*, 578
  taste, 850
Puritanical, *ascetic*, 955
  pedantic, 855
Puritanism, *heterodoxy*, 984A
Purity, *purity*, 960
  of style, 578
Purl, *gargle*, 405
  flow, 348
Purler, *fall*, 306
Purlieus, *suburbs*, 197, 227
Purloin, *steal*, 791
Purple, *purple*, 437
  insignia, 747
Purport, *meaning*, 516
  intent, 620
Purpose, *intention*, 620
Purposeless, *chance*, 621
  motiveless, 616
Purposely, *will*, 600, 620
Purr, *animal sound*, 412
Purse, *money-bag*, 802
  wealth, 803
  to shrivel, 195
  prize, 973
Purse-bearer, *treasurer*, 801
Purse-proud, *pride*, 878
Purse-strings, *treasury*, 802
Purser, *treasurer*, 801
Pursuant to, *intention*, 620
Pursue, *follow*, 281
  continue, 143; *aim*, 622
  inquire, 461
Pursuer, *prosecutor*, 938, 967
Pursuit, *hobby*, 865
  business, 625
Pursuivant, *messenger*, 534
Pursy, *size*, 192
Purulent, *unclean*, 653
Purvey, *provision*, 637
Purview, *extent*, 180
  intention, 620
Pus, *dirt*, 653
Push, *exigency*, 8
  accelerate, 274
  impel, 276
  propel, 284
  repel, 289
  activity, 682
  dismissal, 756

Push on, *progress*, 282, 684
Push-button, *instant*, 113
Pusher, *girl*, 374
Pushover, *dupe*, 547
Pusillanimity, *cowardice*, 862
Puss, *face*, 234, 448
Pustule, *pimple*, 250
  blemish, 848
Put, *place*, 184
  a question, 461; *fool*, 501
Put about, *turn back*, 283
  circuition, 311
Put away, *relinquish*, 624
Put by, *economy*, 817
Put down, *destroy*, 162
  confute, 479
  coerce, 744; *baffle*, 731
  humiliate, 874
Put forth, *assert*, 535
  suggest, 514
Put in, *interject*, 228
Put into, *insert*, 300
  arrive, 292
Put off, *delay*, 133
  deter, 616
Put on, *clothe*, 225
  deceive, 544
Put out, *quench*, 385
  darken, 421
  perplex, 458
  difficulty, 704
Put up to, *teach*, 537
Put up with, *feeling*, 821
Put upon, *deception*, 545
Putative, *attribution*, 155, 514
Putid, *improbity*, 940
Putrefy, *unclean*, 653
Putrid, *unclean*, 653
*Putsch, *revolt*, 719, 742
Putt, *impel*, 276
Puttee, *dress*, 225
Putty, *vinculum*, 45
Puzzle, *enigma*, 533
  obscurity, 519
  mystify, 528
  stagger, 485
  bewilder, 491
Puzzle-headed, *fool*, 499
Puzzling, *uncertain*, 475
Pygmy, *little*, 193
  low, 207
Pylades, *friend*, 890
Pyramid, *point*, 253
  heap, 72
Pyre, *interment*, 363
Pyretic, *hot*, 382
Pyrexia, *heat*, 382
Pyrometer, *thermometer*, 389
Pyrotechny, *heat*, 382
Pyrrhonism, *incredulity*, 487
Pythagorean, *temperance*, 953
Python, *oracle*, 513
Pyx, *receptacle*, 191
  assay, 463
  ritual, 998

Q

Q-boat, *ship*, 273
    deception, 545
Q.C., *lawyer*, 968
Q.E.D., *answer*, 462
Quack, *impostor*, 548
    ignoramus, 493
    cry, 412
Quackery, *deception*, 545
    ignorance, 491
    affectation, 855
Quacksalver, *deceiver*, 548
Quadragesima, *fasting*, 956
Quadragesimal, *forty*, 98
Quadrangular, *angularity*, 244
Quadrant, *measure*, 466
    angularity, 244
Quadrate with, *agreement*, 23
Quadratic, *number*, 95
Quadrifid, *number*, 97
Quadrilateral, *side*, 236
Quadrille, *dance*, 840
Quadripartition, *number*, 97
Quadrireme, *ship*, 273
Quadrisection, *number*, 97
Quadruped, *animal*, 366
Quadruple, *number*, 96
*Quaere, *inquiry*, 461
Quaestor, *master*, 745
Quaff, *reception*, 296
Quag, *bog*, 345
Quagmire, *bog*, 345
    mire, 653
    difficulty, 704
Quaich, *bowl*, 191
Quail, *fear*, 800, 862
Quaint, *odd*, 83
    ridiculous, 853
    pretty, 845
Quake, *shake*, 315
    fear, 860
    cold, 383
Qualification, *modification*, 469
    accomplishment, 698
    change, 140
    retractation, 536
    training, 673
    right, 924
Qualify, *train*, 673
    modify, 469
    change, 140
    teach, 537
Quality, *power*, 157
    nature, 5
    tendency, 176
    character, 820
    nobility, 875
Qualm, *fear*, 860
    scruple, 603, 616
    disbelief, 485
    penitence, 950
Quandary, *difficulty*, 704
*Quand même, *opposition*, 708

Quantitative, *amount*, 25
    allotment, 786
Quantity, *amount*, 25
Quantum, *amount*, 25
    apportionment, 786
*Quantum sufficit, *sufficiency*,
         639
*Quaquaversum, *direction*, 278
Quarantine, *safety*, 664
    confinement, 751
Quarrel, *discord*, 713
Quarrelsome, *enemy*, 901
Quarry, *mine*, 636
    object, 620
Quarter, *forth*, 97
    region, 181
    side, 236
    direction, 278
    to place, 184
    mercy, 914
Quartering, *number*, 97
Quartermaster, *provision*, 637
    master, 745
Quarters, *abode*, 189
Quartet, *number*, 95
Quarto, *book*, 593
Quash, *destroy*, 162
    annul, 756, 964
Quasi, *similarity*, 17
Quatercentenary, *celebration*,
         883
Quaternal, *number*, 95
Quaternity, *number*, 95
Quatrain, *poetry*, 597
Quaver, *oscillate*, 314
    shake, 315
    sound, 407
    music, 413
    hesitate, 605
    fear, 860
    shiver, 383
Quay, *abode*, 189
Quean, *libertine*, 962
Queasiness, *dislike*, 867
    fastidious, 868
Queen, *master*, 745
Queenly, *majestic*, 873
Queer, *unconformity*, 83
    sick, 655
    whimsical, 853
Quell, *destroy*, 162
    hush, 265
    calm, 826
    moderate, 174
    subdue, 732
Quench, *cool*, 385
    dissuade, 616
    extinguish, 162
    satiate, 869
Querimonious, *lament*, 839
Querist, *inquiry*, 461
Quern, *mill*, 330
Querulous, *complaining*, 839
    quarrelsome, 901
Query, *inquiry*, 461

Query, *to doubt*, 485
Quest, *inquiry*, 461
    pursuit, 622
    undertaking, 676
Question, *inquiry*, 461
    topic, 454
    to doubt, 485
    to deny, 536
Questionable, *uncertainty*,
         475, 485
Questionless, *certainty*, 474
Questor, *treasurer*, 801
Queue, *appendix*, 39, 214
    sequel, 65
    row, 69
Quibble, *sophistry*, 477
    equivocate, 544
    absurdity, 497
    wit, 842
Quick, *rapid*, 274
    transient, 111
    active, 682
    haste, 684
    early, 132
    skilful, 698
    irascible, 901
    feeling, 821, 822
Quick-sighted, *quick-eyed*, 441
    sagacious, 498
Quick-witted, *wit*, 842
    clever, 498
Quicken, *hasten*, 132
    animate, 163
    vivify, 359
    operate, 170
    urge, 615
    excite, 824
    promote, 907
    violence, 173
Quicksand, *pitfall*, 667
Quicksilver, *velocity*, 274
Quid, *tobacco*, 298A
    money, 800
*Quid pro quo, *compensation*,
         30
    payment, 807
    exchange, 794
    interchange, 148
Quiddity, *essence*, 1, 5
    quibble, 477
    wit, 842
Quidnunc, *curiosity*, 455
Quiescence, *cessation*, 142
    inertness, 172
    inactivity, 683
    rest, 265
Quiet, *rest*, 265
    silent, 403
    calm, 174, 826
    dissuade, 616
    peace, 714
Quietism, *piety*, 987
    heresy, 984A
Quietus, *death*, 360
    downfall, 732

Quill, *writing*, 590
Quill-driver, *writing*, 590
Quinary, *number*, 98
Quincentenary, *see* Quin-
  gentenary
Quincunx, *number*, 98
Quingentenary, *celebration*,
  883
Quinquagesimal, *fifty*, 98
Quinquefid, *number*, 99
Quinquereme, *ship*, 273
Quinquesection, *number*, 99
Quint, *number*, 98
Quintessence, *essence*, 5
  importance, 642
Quintet, *five*, 98
Quintuple, *number*, 98
Quip, *wit*, 842
  amusement, 840
  ridicule, 856
  satire, 932
Quirites, *non-combatant*, 726A
Quirk, *caprice*, 608
  evasion, 617
  wit, 842
Quisling, *traitor*, 742
Quit, *depart*, 293
  relinquish, 624
  loss, 776
  neglect, 927
  pay, 807
Quite, *greatness*, 31
Quits, *equality*, 27
  atonement, 952
Quittance, *forgiveness*, 918
  atonement, 952
  reward, 973
  payment, 807
  observance, 772
Quitter, *cowardice*, 862
  shirker, 623
Quiver, *agitate*, 315
  vibrate, 314
  shiver, 383
  fear, 860
  affect, 821
  store, 636
  arm, 727
Quixotic, *imaginary*, 515
  rash, 863
  enthusiastic, 825
Quiz, *to ridicule*, 856
  inquiry, 461
Quizzical, *ridiculous*, 853
*Quocumque modo, *means*,
  632
Quod, *prison*, 752
Quodlibet, *sophism*, 477
  subtle point, 454
  enigma, 461
  wit, 842
Quondam, *preterition*, 122
Quorum, *assembly*, 72
Quota, *apportionment*, 786
Quotation, *imitation*, 19

Quotation, *citation*, 82
  price, 812
Quote, *cite*, 82, 467
  bargain, 794
Quotidian, *period*, 108, 138
Quotient, *number*, 84

R

R.A., *artist*, 559
R.I.P., *burial*, 363
Rabbet, *junction*, 43
Rabbi, *clergy*, 996
Rabble, *mob*, 876
  bad man, 949
  assemblage, 72
Rabelaisian, *coarse*, 961
Rabid, *insanity*, 503
  headstrong, 606
  angry, 900
  feeling, 821
Race, *to run*, 274
  contest, 720
  course, 622
  career, 625
  torrent, 348
  lineage, 11, 69
  kind, 75
  people, 372
Racehorse, *horse*, 271
  fleetness, 274
Racer, *horse*, 271
  fleetness, 274
Racial, *ethnic*, 372
Rack, *frame*, 215
  physical pain, 378
  moral pain, 828
  to torture, 830
  punish, 975
  purify, 652
  refine, 58
  cloud, 353
Racket, *noise*, 402, 404
  brawl, 713
  roll, 407
  bat, 633
  plan, 626
*Raconteur, *narrator*, 594
Racy, *strong*, 171
  pungent, 392
  feeling, 821
  style, 574
Radar, *direction*, 693
Raddle, *weave*, 219
  red, 434
Radiant, *diverging*, 291
  light, 420, 423
  beauty, 845
  glory, 873
Radiator, *fire*, 386
Radical, *cause* ,153
  algebraic root, 84
  complete, 52
  intrinsic, 5
  reformer, 658

Radical, *revolution*, 146
Radically, *thorough*, 31
Radio, *hearing*, 418
  publication, 531
  news, 532
  wireless, 599B
Radioactivity, *light*, 420
Radiogram, *hearing*, 418
  news, 532
Radioscopy, *light*, 420
Radiotherapy, *light*, 420
Radius, *length*, 200
  degree, 26
Radix, *cause*, 153
Raff, *refuse*, 653
  rabble, 876
Raffia, *tape*, 45
Raffish, *vulgar*, 851
Raffle, *chance*, 156, 621
Raft, *ship*, 273
Rafter, *support*, 215
Rag, *shred*, 51
  clothes, 225
  escapade, 497
  to tease, 830
  joke, 842
  deride, 929
  revile, 932
Ragamuffin, *rabble*, 876
Rage, *violence*, 173
  fury, 825
  wrath, 900
  desire, 865
  fashion, 852
Ragged, *bare*, 226
Ragout, *food*, 298
Ragtag, *commonalty*, 876
  bad man, 949
Raid, *attack*, 716
  robbery, 791
Rail, *enclosure*, 232
  fence, 666
  imprison, 752
Rail at, *disapprove*, 932
Rail-car, *vehicle*, 272
Rail in, *circumscribe*, 231
Raillery, *ridicule*, 856
Railroad, *way*, 627
Railway, *road*, 627
Raiment, *dress*, 225
Rain, *river*, 348
Rainbow, *variegation*, 440
Raise, *elevate*, 307
  increase, 35
  produce, 161
  excite, 824
*Raison d'être, *cause*, 153
  motive, 615, 620
Raj, *authority*, 737
Rajah, *master*, 745
Rake, *cultivate*, 371
Rake-off, *payment*, 809
Rake up, *collect*, 72
  extract, 301
  recall, 504

Raze, *level*, 308
    obliterate, 552
    demolish, 649
Razor, *sharp*, 253
Razz, *ridicule*, 856
Razzle-dazzle, *frolic*, 840
*Re, *concerning*, 454
Reabsorb, *reception*, 296
Reach, *length*, 200
    river, 348
    degree, 26
    distance, 196
    fetch, 270
    arrive at, 292
    grasp, 737
React, *recoil*, 277
    revert, 145
    counteract, 179
    sensibility, 375
    relapse, 661
Reactionary, *mulish*, 499
    reversion, 145
Read, *interpret*, 522
    learn, 539
Readable, *intelligible*, 518
Reader, *teacher*, 492, 540
    clergy, 996
Reading, *meaning*, 516
Reading-glass, *lens*, 445
Readjust, *equality*, 27
Readmit, *reception*, 296
Ready, *prepared*, 673
    capable, 157
    willing, 602
    useful, 644
    eager, 682
    dexterous, 698
    early, 132
    cash, 800
Ready money, *payment*, 807
Reagent, *criterion*, 467
    test, 463
Real, *existing*, 1
    substantial, 3
    true, 494
Realism, *truth*, 494
Realistic, *description*, 594
Reality, *existence*, 1
Realize, *attribute*, 155
    produce, 161
    substantiate, 494
    be aware of, 450
    imagine, 515
    price, 812
Really, *very*, 31
    indeed, 870
Realm, *region*, 181
    property, 780
    land, 372
Reanimate, *revivify*, 163
    refresh, 689
    reinstate, 660
Reap, *cultivate*, 371
    acquire, 775
    succeed, 731

Reap, *take*, 789
Reaping-hook, *sharpness*, 253
Reappear, *repetition*, 104, 163
    frequency, 136
Rear, *back*, 67, 235
    erect, 161, 307
    sequel, 65
    bring up, 537
    room, 191
    privy, 653
Rearrange, *arrangement*, 60
Reason, *cause*, 153
    motive, 615
    intellect, 450
    evidence, 467
    argue, 476
    wisdom, 498
    moderation, 174
Reasonable, *judicious*, 498
    right, 922
    equitable, 924
    probable, 472
    sane, 502
    moderate, 174
    cheap, 815
Reasoning, *logic*, 476
Reasonless, *fool*, 499
Reassemble, *gather*, 72
Reassure, *hope*, 858
Reasty, *foul*, 653
    fetid, 401
Réaumur, *thermometer*, 389
Rebate, *moderate*, 174, 813
Rebeck, *musical instrument*,
    417
Rebel, *disobey*, 742
Rebellion, *resistance*, 719
    revolution, 146
Rebellow, *ululation*, 412
Rebound, *recoil*, 277, 283
    revert, 144
    react, 179
*Rebours, *regression*, 283
Rebuff, *refuse*, 764
    repulse, 732
    resist, 719
    recoil, 277, 325
Rebuild, *reconstruct*, 163
    restore, 660
Rebuke, *disapprove*, 932
Rebus, *secret*, 533
Rebut, *answer*, 462
    confute, 479
    deny, 536
    counter-evidence, 468
Rebutter, *lawsuit*, 969
Recalcitrant, *disobedient*, 742
Recalcitrate, *resist*, 276, 719
    counteract, 179
Recall, *recollect*, 505
    cancel, 756
Recant, *retract*, 607
    repent, 950
    deny, 536
    resign, 757

Recapitulate, *summary*, 596
    describe, 594
    repeat, 104
    enumerate, 85
Recast, *plan*, 626, 660
    refashion, 146
Recede, *move back*, 283
    move from, 287
    decline, 659
Receipt, *money*, 810
    recipe, 697
Receive, *admit*, 296
    take in, 785
    include, 76
    acquire, 775
    learn, 539
    believe, 484
    welcome, 892, 894
    money, 810
Received, *ordinary*, 82
    habitual, 613
Recension, *revision*, 457
    improvement, 658
Recent, *past*, 122
    new, 123
Receptacle, *recipient*, 191
    store, 636
Reception, *arrival*, 292
    comprehension, 54
    inclusion, 76
    ingestion, 296
    conference, 588
    admission, 785
    visit, 892, 894
Receptive, *intelligent*, 498
Recess, *place*, 182
    regression, 283
    ambush, 530
    holiday, 685
    interval, 106
    retirement, 893
Recession, *motion from*, 287
    motion backwards, 283
*Réchauffé, *copy*, 21
    improve, 658
*Recherché, *goodness*, 648
Recidivism, *relapse*, 661
    reversion, 145
    vice, 945
Recidivist, *criminal*, 949
    turncoat, 607
Recipe, *remedy*, 662
    precept, 697
Recipient, *receptacle*, 191
    receiving, 785
Reciprocal, *mutual*, 12
    quantity, 84
    interchange, 148
Reciprocation, *retaliation*, 718
Recital, *music*, 415
Recitative, *music*, 415
Recite, *narrate*, 594
    speak, 582
    enumerate, 85
Reck, *care*, 459

Reckless, *rash,* 863
  excitable, 825
  careless, 460
Reckon, *count,* 85
  measure, 466
  believe, 484
Reckon upon, *expect,* 507
Reckoning, *accounts,* 811
  price, 812
Reclaim, *restoration,* 660
*Réclame, *advertisement,* 531
  self-advertisement, 884
Recline, *lie flat,* 213
  rest upon, 215
  repose, 687
  lowering, 308
Recluse, *seclusion,* 893, 955
Recognizable, *visible,* 446
Recognizance, *security,* 771
Recognize, *see,* 441
  know, 490
  assent, 488
  remember, 505
  discover, 480A
  acknowledge, 535
Recognized, *received,* 82
  habitual, 613
Recoil, *repercussion,* 277, 325
  revert, 145
  shun, 623
  reluctance, 603
  dislike, 867
  hate, 898
  reaction, 179
Recollect, *remember,* 505
Recommence, *repetition,* 104
Recommend, *advise,* 695
  approve, 931
  induce, 615
Recompense, *reward,* 973
  payment, 809
Reconcile, *agree,* 23
  content, 831
  pacify, 723
  forgive, 918
Recondite, *obscure,* 519
  hidden, 529
Reconnaissance, *survey,* 441
Reconnoitre, *see,* 441
  inquire, 461
Reconsideration, *thought,* 451
Reconstitute, *restore,* 660
Reconstruct, *reproduce,* 164
  remodel, 146
  restore, 660
Reconvert, *restore,* 660
Record, *note,* 551
  list, 86
Recorder, *recorder,* 553
  judge, 967
Recording, *copy,* 21
Recount, *description,* 594
Recoup, *restore,* 660, 790
  reward, 973
Recourse, *use,* 677

Recovery, *reinstatement,* 660
  improvement, 658
  recruit, 689
Recreant, *coward,* 862
  base, 940, 945
  apostate, 941
  wretch, 949
Recreation, *amusement,* 840
Recrement, *unclean,* 653
Recrimination, *accusation,* 938
  reprobation, 932
  retaliation, 718
Recrudescence, *recurrence,* 104, 136
Recruit, *refresh,* 689
  reinstate, 660
  health, 654
  repair, 658
  aid, 707
  provide, 637
  strengthen, 159
  beginner, 674
  fighter, 726
Rectangle, *angularity,* 244
Rectify, *straighten,* 246
  improve, 658
  re-establish, 660
Rectilinear, *straightness,* 246
Rectitude, *virtue,* 944
  right, 922
  probity, 939
Recto, *dextrality,* 228
Rector, *clergy,* 996
  director, 694
Rectory, *office,* 995
  house, 1000
*Reculons, *regression,* 283
Recumbent, *horizontal,* 213
  oblique, 217
Recuperation, *restitution,* 790
  improvement, 658
  restore, 660
  refresh, 689
Recur, *repeat,* 104
  frequent, 136
  periodic, 138
Recurvation, *curvature,* 245
Recurvature, *curvature,* 245
Recusant, *denying,* 536
  dissenting, 489
  disobedient, 742
  unwilling, 603
  refusing, 764
  heterodox, 984A
  impenitent, 951
Red, *redness,* 434
Red book, *list,* 86
Red cent, *trifle,* 643
Red-handed, *murderous,* 361
  action, 681
Red-hot, *heat,* 382
Red lamp, *brothel,* 961
Red letter, *indication,* 550
Red light, *signal,* 550
Red tape, *custom,* 613
Red-tapist, *director,* 695

Redaction, *publication,* 531
  improvement, 658
Redargue, *confute,* 479
Redcoat, *combatant,* 726
Redden, *flush,* 821
Reddition, *restoration,* 790
Redeem, *reinstate,* 660
  deliver, 672
  liberate, 750
  fulfil, 772
  atone, 952
  compensate, 30
  restore, 790
Redemption, *salvation,* 976
Redintegrate, *reinstate,* 660
  renovate, 658
Redolence, *odour,* 398
  fragrance, 400
Redouble, *duplication,* 90
  repeat, 104
  increase, 35
Redoubt, *defence,* 717
Redoubtable, *fear,* 860
Redound, *conduce,* 176
Redress, *remedy,* 662
  rectify, 658
  restore, 660
  reward, 873
Reduce, *lessen,* 36
  contract, 195
  shorten, 201
  lower, 308
  weaken, 160
  convert, 144
  subdue, 731
  impoverish, 804
  in number, 103
*Reductio ad absurdum,
  confutation, 479
Reduction, *arithmetical,* 85
Redundant, *ample,* 641
  diffuse, 573
  remaining, 40
Reduplication, *imitation,* 19
  doubling, 90
Re-echo, *imitate,* 19
  repeat, 104
  reduplication, 90
  sound, 404, 408
Reechy, *uncleanness,* 653
Reed, *musical instrument,* 417
Re-educate, *teach,* 537
Reef, *slacken,* 275
  shoal, 346
  danger, 667
Reek, *hot,* 382
  fume, 334
Reel, *rock,* 314
  agitate, 315
  rotate, 312
  cinema, 599
  dance, 840
Re-embody, *combine,* 43
  junction, 48
Re-entrant, *angle,* 244

Relax, *repose*, 687
  leisure, 685
  amuse, 840
  lounge, 683
  loose, 47
  misrule, 738
  relent, 914
Relaxing, *unhealthy*, 657
Relay, *materials*, 635
Release, *liberate*, 750
  deliver, 672
  discharge, 970
  restore, 790
  exempt, 927A
  repay, 807
  death, 360
Relegate, *transfer*, 270
  remove, 185
  banish, 55
Relent, *moderate*, 174
  pity, 914
  relax, 324
Relentless, *malevolent*, 907
  wrathful, 900
  revengeful, 919
  flagitious, 945
  impenitent, 951
Relevancy, *pertinence*, 9
  congruity, 23
Reliable, *believable*, 484
  trustworthy, 939
Reliance, *confidence*, 484
  hope, 858
Relic, *remainder*, 40
  reminiscence, 505
  token, 551
  sacred, 998
Relict, *widow*, 905
Relief, *sculpture*, 557
  convexity, 250
  aid, 707
Relieve, *comfort*, 834
  refresh, 689
  help, 707
  improve, 658
Religion, *theology*, 983
  belief, 484
  piety, 987
Religiosity, *sanctimony*, 988
Religious, *exact*, 494
  pious, 987
Relinquish, *a purpose*, 607, 624
  property, 782
  to discontinue, 142
Reliquary, *rite*, 998
Relish, *like*, 377, 827
  taste, 390
  savoury, 394
  desire, 865
Relucent, *luminous*, 420
  transparent, 425
Reluct, *resist*, 719
Reluctance, *dislike*, 867
  unwillingness, 603
  dissuasion, 616

Reluctation, *resistance*, 719
Relume, *light*, 384
Rely, *confidence*, 484
  expectation, 507
  hope, 858
Remain, *endure*, 106, 110
  exist, 1
  to be left, 40
  rest, 265
  continue, 141
Remainder, *left*, 40
  property, 780
Remains, *corpse*, 362
  vestige, 551
Remand, *restraint*, 751
  delay, 133
Remark, *observe*, 457
  assert, 535
Remarkable, *important*, 642
Remarkably, *greatness*, 31
Remedy, *cure*, 662
  salubrious, 656
  to restore, 660, 834
Remember, *recollect*, 505
Remembrance, *compliment*, 894
Remembrancer, *recorder*, 553
Remigration, *egress*, 295
Remind, *recollect*, 505
Reminiscence, *remember*, 505
Remiss, *neglectful*, 460
  idle, 683
  reluctant, 603
  laxity, 738
Remission, *see* Remit
Remit, *relax*, 174
  forgive, 918
  restore, 790
  discontinue, 142
  pay, 807
Remnant, *remainder*, 40
Remodel, *conversion*, 140, 144
  improve, 658
Remonstrate, *dissuade*, 616
  expostulate, 932
Remorse, *penitence*, 950
Remorseless, *resentment*, 900
  revenge, 919
Remote, *distant*, 196
  not related, 10
Remotion, *see* Remove
Remove, *displace*, 185
  retrench, 38
  depart, 293
  recede, 287
  transfer, 270
  extract, 301
  term, 71
Removed, *distant*, 196
Remunerate, *reward*, 973
  pay, 810
Renaissance, *revival*, 660
Renascent, *reproduction*, 163
Rencontre, *see* Rencounter
Rencounter, *fight*, 720
  meeting, 197, 292

Rend, *disjoin*, 44
Render, *give*, 784
  restore, 790
  interpret, 522
  music, 415
Rendezvous, *focus*, 74
  assemblage, 72
Rending, *loud*, 404
  painful, 830
Rendition, *surrender*, 782
  interpretation, 522
Renegade, *apostate*, 742, 941
  turncoat, 144, 607
Renew, *repeat*, 104
  reproduce, 163
  frequent, 136
  newness, 123
  repair, 658
  restore, 660
Reniform, *curvature*, 245
Renounce, *relinquish*, 624
  property, 782
  recant, 607
  resign, 757
  deny, 536
  repudiate, 927
  exempt, 927A
Renovate, *reproduce*, 163
  newness, 123
  restore, 660
Renown, *repute*, 873
Rent, *fissure*, 44, 198
  hire, 788, 794
  receipt, 810
Renter, *possessor*, 779
*Rentier, *wealth*, 803
Renunciation, *see* Renounce
Reorganize, *conversion*, 144
  restore, 660
Repair, *mend*, 658
  refresh, 689
  restore, 660, 790
  atone, 952
Repair to, *journey*, 266
Reparation, *compensation*, 973
Repartee, *wit*, 842
  answer, 462
Repast, *food*, 298
Repatriation, *egress*, 295
Repay, *payment*, 807
  recompense, 973
Repeal, *abrogation*, 756
Repeat, *iterate*, 104, 143
  imitate, 19
  duplication, 90
  frequent, 136
  multiplied, 102
Repeater, *watch*, 114
Repel, *repulse*, 289
  defend, 717
  resist, 719
  disincline, 867
  shock, 898
  refuse, 764
  deter, 616

Reverberatory, *fire*, 386
Reverence, *respect*, 928
   salutation, 894
   piety, 987
   worship, 990
   title, 877
Reverend, *clergy*, 996
Reverie, *train of thought*, 451
   imagination, 515
Reversal, *inversion*, 218
Reverse, *antiposition*, 237
   contrary, 14
   change, 140
   cancel, 756
   evolution, 313
   inversion, 218
   misfortune, 830
   adversity, 735
Reversion, *possession*, 777
   property, 780
   transfer, 783
Revert, *recur*, 104, 136
   go back, 283
   deteriorate, 659
Review, *consider*, 457
   memory, 505
   judge, 480
   criticism, 595
   rectify, 658
   display, 882
Reviewer, *writer*, 590
Revile, *abuse*, 932
   blaspheme, 988
Revise, *consider*, 457
   improve, 658
   restore, 660
   proof, 21, 591
Revisit, *presence*, 186
Revitalize, *restore*, 660
Revival, *worship*, 990
Revivalist, *clergy*, 996
Revive, *live*, 359
   restore, 660
   refresh, 689
Revivify, *reproduction*, 163
   restore, 660
Revoke, *recant*, 607
   deny, 536
   cancel, 756
   refuse, 754
Revolt, *resist*, 719
   revolution, 146
   disobey, 742
   shock, 830, 932
Revolting, *vulgar*, 851
Revolution, *rotation*, 312
   change, 140, 146
   periodicity, 138
Revolve, *meditate*, 451
Revolver, *arms*, 727
Revue, *drama*, 599
Revulsion, *recoil*, 277
Reward, *reward*, 973
Rhadamanthine, *severe*, 739
Rhapsody, *discontinuity*, 70

Rhapsody, *nonsense*, 497
   fancy, 515
   music, 415
Rhetoric, *speech*, 582
Rhetorical, *ornament*, 577
Rheum, *humour*, 333
   water, 337
Rhine, *ditch*, 350
Rhino, *money*, 800
Rhomb, *angularity*, 244
Rhombohedron, *angularity*, 244
Rhomboid, *angularity*, 244
Rhombus, *angularity*, 244
Rhumb, *direction*, 278
Rhyme, *poetry*, 597
   similarity, 17
Rhymeless, *prose*, 598
Rhythm, *harmony*, 413
   regularity, 138
   poetry, 597
Rib, *ridge*, 250
   banter, 256
   wife, 903
Ribald, *vile*, 874, 961
   vulgar, 851
   maledictory, 908
   impious, 988
   abuse, 932
Ribbed, *furrow*, 259
Ribbon, *filament*, 205
   tie, 45
   trophy, 733
   decoration, 877
Rich, *wealthy*, 803
   abundant, 639
   savoury, 394
   adorned, 847
   style, 577
Richly, *great*, 31
Rick, *store*, 636
   accumulation, 72
Rickety, *weak*, 160
   imperfect, 651
   ugly, 846
Rickshaw, *vehicle*, 272
Ricochet, *recoil*, 277
   reversion, 145
Rid, *loss*, 776
   relinquish, 782
   abandon, 624
   deliver, 672
Riddle, *enigma*, 533
   obscurity, 519
   question, 461
   confute, 479
   sieve, 260
   arrange, 60
Ride, *move*, 266
   get above, 206
   road, 627
Rider, *equestrian*, 268
   corollary, 480
   appendix, 39
Ridge, *narrowness*, 203
   projection, 250

Ridicule, *deride*, 856
   depreciate, 483
   disrespect, 929
Ridiculous, *grotesque*, 853
   vulgar, 851
   absurd, 497
   silly, 499
   trifling, 643
Riding, *region*, 181
*Ridotto, *gala*, 840
   rout, 892
*Rifacimento, *recast*, 660
Rife, *ordinary*, 82
   frequent, 136
   prevailing, 175
Riff-raff, *rabble*, 876, 949
   dirt, 653
Rifle, *to plunder*, 791
   arms, 727
Rifleman, *combatant*, 726
Rift, *separation*, 44
   fissure, 198
Rig, *dress*, 225
   prepare, 673
   frolic, 840
   deception, 545
   adorn, 845
Rigadoon, *dance*, 840
Rigescence, *hardness*, 323
Rigging, *gear*, 225
   cordage, 45
Right, *just*, 922
   privilege, 924
   duty, 926
   honour, 939
   straight, 246
   true, 494
   suitable, 646
Righteous, *virtuous*, 944
   just, 922
Rigid, *hard*, 323
   exact, 494
   strict, 772
   severe, 739
   stubborn, 606
   regular, 82
Rigmarole, *nonsense*, 497, 517
   unintelligible, 519
Rigour, *severity*, 739
   compulsion, 744
   exactness, 494
Rile, *irritate*, 830, 900
   alienate, 898
Rill, *river*, 348
Rim, *edge*, 230
Rime, *cold*, 383
Rind, *covering*, 222
Ring, *circle*, 247
   sound, 408
   arena, 728
   party, 712
   syndicate, 778
Ring-fence, *enclosure*, 232
Ringleader, *master*, 745
   director, 694

Scintilla, *small*, 32
   spark, 420
Sciolism, *smattering*, 491
Sciolist, *smatterer*, 493
Scion, *child*, 129
   posterity, 167
*Scire facias, *inquiry*, 641
Scission, *cut*, 44
Scissors, *sharpness*, 253
Sclerosis, *hardness*, 323
Scobs, *pulverulence*, 330
Scoff, *ridicule*, 856
   deride, 929
   impiety, 988
Scold, *abuse*, 932
   vixen, 936, 901
Scollop, *see* Scallop
Sconce, *summit*, 210
   mulct, 974
   candlestick, 423
Scoop, *depth*, 208
   depression, 252
   performer, 262
   profit, 775
   news, 532
Scoot, *hurry*, 274, 684
   escape, 671
Scooter, *locomotion*, 266
Scope, *degree*, 26
   extent, 180
   intention, 620
   freedom, 748
Scorch, *burn*, 384
   hurry, 684
Score, *mark*, 550, 842
   furrow, 259
   motive, 615
   price, 812
   accounts, 805, 811
   record, 551
   twenty, 98
   musical, 415
   to count, 85
   to succeed, 731
Scoriae, *unimportance*, 643
   uncleanness, 653
Scorify, *calefaction*, 384
Scorn, *contempt*, 930
Scorpion, *bane*, 663, 913
   painful, 830
Scot-free, *gratuitous*, 815
   deliverance, 672
   exemption, 927A
Scotch, *maltreat*, 649
   stop, 706
   notch, 257
Scotch mist, *rain*, 348
Scotomy, *dim-sightedness*, 443
Scotticism, *language*, 560
Scoundrel, *vice*, 949
   evildoer, 913
Scour, *rub*, 331
   run, 274
   clean, 652
Scourge, *whip*, 972, 975

Scourge, *bane*, 663
   painful, 830
   bad, 649
Scourings, *refuse*, 643
Scout, *messenger*, 534
   servant, 746
   watch, 664
   to disdain , 930
   deride, 643
Scowl, *frown*, 895
   complain, 839
   anger, 900
Scrabble, *fumble*, 379
   nonsense, 517
Scraggy, *narrow*, 203
   ugly, 846
Scram, *go away*, 293, 287
   escape, 671
   repel, 289
   ejection, 297
Scramble, *confusion*, 59
   haste, 684
   difficulty, 704
   mount, 305
Scrannel, *stridulous*, 410
   meagre, 643
Scrap, *piece*, 51
   small portion, 32, 193
   disuse, 678
   contention, 720
   to fight, 722
Scrap-book, *collection*, 596
Scrape, *difficulty*, 704
   mischance, 732
   abrade, 330, 331
   bow, 894
   save, 817
Scrape together, *collect*, 72
   get, 775
Scratch, *groove*, 259
   mark, 550
   write, 590
   daub, 555
   abrade, 331
   hurt, 619
   to wound, 649
Scratch out, *obliteration*, 552
Scrawl, *write*, 590
Scrawny, *lean*, 193, 203
Scream, *cry*, 410
   complain, 839
Screech, *cry*, 410
   complain, 839
Screech-owl, *noise*, 412
Screed, *speech*, 582
Screen, *concealment*, 528
   asylum, 666, 717
   ambush, 530
   to shield, 664
   sieve, 260
   sift, 652
   inquire, 461
   discriminate, 465
   sort, 42, 60
   exclude, 55

Screen, *shade*, 424
   cinema, 599A
Screened, *safe*, 664
   invisible, 447
Screever, *artist*, 559
Screw, *fasten*, 43
   joining, 45
   instrument, 367, 633
   rotation, 312
   salary, 809
   miser, 819
Screw-steamer, *ship*, 273
Screw up, *strengthen*, 159
Screwball, *madman*, 504
Screwed, *drunk*, 959
Scribble, *write*, 590
   unmeaning, 517
Scribe, *writer*, 553, 590
   priest, 996
Scrimp, *shorten*, 201
   stint, 640
   save, 817
Scrip, *receptacle*, 191
Script, *writing*, 590
   radio, 599B
Scriptural, *Christian*, 983A
Scripture, *revelation*, 985
   certain, 474
Scrivener, *writing*, 590
Scroll, *record*, 551
   convolution, 248
Scrounge, *steal*, 791
Scrub, *clean*, 652
   plant, 367
Scrubby, *vulgar*, 876
   shabby, 940
   bad, 649
   trifling, 643
   small, 193
   rough, 256
Scrumptious, *pleasing*, 829
Scrunch, *pulverulence*, 330
Scruple, *doubt*, 485
   dissuasion, 616
   smallness, 32
Scrupulous, *careful*, 459
   incredulous, 487
   exact, 494
   reluctant, 603
   punctilious,939
   virtuous, 944
Scrutator, *inquiry*, 461
Scrutinize, *examine*, 457, 461
Scud, *speed*, 274
   sail, 267
   shower, 348
   haze, 353
Scuffle, *contention*, 720
Scull, *navigation*, 267
Scullery, *room*, 191
Scullion, *servant*, 746
Sculp, *produce*, 161
Sculptor, *artist*, 559
Sculpture, *carving*, 557
   form, 240

INDEX

Scum, *dregs*, 643, 653
Scunner, *disgust*, 395
Scupper, *conduit*, 350
Scurf, *uncleanness*, 653
Scurrility, *ridicule*, 856
  malediction, 908
  detraction, 934
  disrespect, 929
Scurry, *hasten*, 274, 684
Scurvy, *bad*, 649
  base, 940, 945
Scut, *tail*, 235
Scutcheon, *standard*, 550
  honour, 877
Scuttle, *tray*, 191
  opening, 260
  to destroy, 162
  hasten, 274, 684
Scythe, *angularity*, 244
  sharpness, 253
Sea, *water*, 341
  blue, 438
Sea-nymph, *sea*, 341
Seaboard, *edge*, 342
Seal, *to close*, 67, 261
  sigil, 550
  mould, 22
  evidence, 467
  record, 551
  compact, 769
  security, 771
  authority, 747
Seal up, *shut up*, 231, 751
Seam, *junction*, 43
Seaman, *mariner*, 269
Seamanship, *conduct*, 603
Seamstress, *see* Sempstress
Séance, *council*, 696
Seaplane, *aircraft*, 273A
Sear, *burn*, 384
  deaden, 823
Search, *seek*, 461
  pursuit, 622
Searching, *thorough*, 52
Searchless, *unintelligible*, 519
Seared, *impenitent*, 951
Seascape, *spectacle*, 448
Seaside, *edge*, 342
Season, *time*, 106
  opportunity, 134
  pungent, 392, 393
  to preserve, 670
  prepare, 673
  accustom, 613
Seasonable, *opportune*, 134
  expedient, 646
  agreement, 23
Seasonal, *period*, 108
Seasoning, *mixture*, 41
  pungency, 171, 393
Seat, *abode*, 189
  position, 183
  to place, 184
  support, 215
Seaworthy, *useful*, 644

Seaworthy, *fit*, 673
Sebaceous, *unctuous*, 355
Secateurs, *sharpness*, 253
Secede, *dissent*, 489
  disobedience, 742
Seclude, *restrain*, 751
Seclusion, *retirement*, 526, 893
Second, *of time*, 108
  instant, 113
  abet, 707
  auxiliary, 711
  duplication, 90
Second-best, *imperfection*, 651
  inferiority, 34
Second-hand, *borrowed*, 788
  indifferent, 651
  imitated, 19
Second-rate, *imperfection*, 651
  inferiority, 34
Second sight, *prediction*, 510
  intuition, 477
  witchcraft, 992
Secondary, *following*, 63
  consignee, 758
  deputy, 759
  inferior, 34, 643
  imperfect, 651
Secondly, *bisection*, 91
Secret, *latent*, 526
  hidden, 528
  riddle, 533
Secretary, *recorder*, 553
  writer, 590
Secrete, *hide*, 528
Secretive, *reserved*, 528
Sect, *division*, 75
Sectarian, *dissenter*, 984A
  theology, 983
Section, *part*, 51
  division, 44
  class, 75
  chapter, 593
Sector, *part*, 51
  circularity, 247
Secular, *number*, 99
  laity, 997
Secularism, *heterodoxy*, 984A
Secure, *fasten*, 43
  safe, 664
  engage, 768
  gain, 775
  retain, 781
  confident, 858
Security, *pledge*, 771
  warranty, 924
Sedan, *vehicle*, 272
Sedan chair, *vehicle*, 272
Sedate, *thoughtful*, 451
  calm, 826
  grave, 837
Sedative, *calming*, 174
  sleep, 683
  remedy, 662
Sedentary, *quiescence*, 265
Sederunt, *council*, 696

Sediment, *dregs*, 653
  remainder, 40
Sedition, *disobedience*, 742
Seduce, *entice*, 615
  vice, 945
  impurity, 961
  love, 897
Seducer, *libertine*, 962
Seducing, *charming*, 829
Seduction, *impurity*, 961
Seductive, *attractive*,
                829, 845, 897
Sedulous, *active*, 682
See, *view*, 441
  look, 457
  bishopric, 995
See to, *manage*, 693
Seed, *cause*, 153
  posterity, 167
Seedling, *youth*, 129
Seedy, *weak*, 160
  ailing, 655
  worn, 651
Seek, *inquire*, 461
  pursue, 622
Seem, *appear*, 448
Seeming, *semblance*, 448
Seemly, *expedient*, 646
  proper, 927
  handsome, 845
Seepage, *egress*, 295
Seer, *veteran*, 130
  oracle, 513
  sorcerer, 994
Seesaw, *oscillation*, 314
Seethe, *boil*, 382, 384
Segar, *tobacco*, 298A
Segment, *part*, 51
  circularity, 247
Segnitude, *inactivity*, 683
Segregate, *exclude*, 55
  separate, 44
  safety, 664
  not related, 10
  incoherent, 47
Seignior, *master*, 745
Seisin, *possession*, 777
Seismometer, *impulse*, 276
Seize, *take*, 789
  rob, 791
  possess, 777
Seizure, *weakness*, 160
  disease, 655
Seldom, *infrequency*, 137
Select, *choose*, 609
  good, 648
Selection, *part*, 51
Self, *special*, 13
Self-abasement, *humility*, 879
Self-accusation, *penitence*, 950
Self-admiration, *pride*, 880
Self-advertisement,
  boasting, 884
Self-applause, *vanity*, 880
Self-assertion, *effrontery*, 885

Shady, *dishonest*, 544
   disreputable, 945
Shaft, *pit*, 260
   air-pipe, 351
   deep, 208
   frame, 215
   missile, 284
   shank, 633
   weapon, 727
Shag, *roughness*, 256
   tobacco, 298A
Shaggy, *hirsute*, 256
Shah, *master*, 745
Shake, *agitate*, 315
   fluctuate, 149
   trill, 314, 407
   musical, 415
   dissuade, 616
   injure, 659
   impress, 821
   flutter, 824
   shiver, 383
Shake-down, *bed*, 215
Shake off, *ejection*, 297
Shake up, *agitation*, 315
Shaken, *weak*, 160
Shakespearian, *poetry*, 597
Shaky, *in danger*, 665
   frail, 149
Shallop, *ship*, 273
Shallow, *not deep*, 209
   ignorant, 491
   foolish, 499
Shallow-brained, *foolish*, 499
Shallow-pated, *foolish*, 499
Shallows, *dangers*, 667
Sham, *humbug*, 544
   deceive, 545
Shamble, *shuffle*, 275, 315
Shambles, *butchery*, 361
Shame, *disgrace*, 874
   humiliation, 879
Shamefaced, *abashed*, 881
Shameful, *disgraceful*, 874
   profligate, 945
Shameless, *profligate*, 945
   impudent, 885
Shampoo, *friction*, 331
   cleanness, 652
Shandrydan, *vehicle*, 272
Shanghai, *kidnap*, 789
Shangri-la, *fancy*, 515
   retirement, 893
Shank, *shaft*, 633
Shape, *form*, 240
   condition, 7
   to fashion, 144
   aspect, 448
Shape well, *hopeful*, 858
Shapeless, *amorphous*, 241
   ugly, 846
Shapely, *comely*, 845
   symmetrical, 242
Share, *part*, 51
   participate, 778

Share, *allotted portion*, 786
Shark, *thief*, 792
   cheat, 548
Sharp, *acute*, 253, 376
   musical tone, 410
   pungent, 392, 821
   energetic, 171
   violent, 173
   intelligent, 498
   clever, 698
   cunning, 702
   active, 682
   rude, 895
   censorious, 932
Sharper, *cheat*, 548
   thief, 792
   knave, 941
Sharp-sighted, *vision*, 441
Sharpshooter, *combatant*, 726
Shatter, *destroy*, 162
   weaken, 160
Shave, *cut*, 203
Shaving, *layer*, 204
   filament, 205
   small part, 32, 51
Shawl, *dress*, 225
Sheaf, *assemblage*, 72
Shear, *subduction*, 38
   take, 789
Shears, *sharpness*, 253
Sheath, *receptacle*, 191
   envelope, 222
Shed, *building*, 189
   to emit, 297
   scatter, 73
   diverge, 291
Shed tears, *weep*, 839
Sheen, *light*, 420
Sheepfold, *enclosure*, 232
Sheepish, *foolish*, 881
Sheep's eyes, *ogle*, 902
Sheer, *vertical*, 212
   simple, 42
   complete, 52
   smallness, 32
Sheer off, *departure*, 293
Sheet, *layer*, 204
   paper, 593
Sheet-anchor, *refuge*, 666
Sheik, *ruler*, 745
   priest, 996
   philanderer, 902
Shelf, *support*, 215
Shell, *cover*, 222
   arms, 727; *attack*, 716
Shell out, *expend*, 809
Shelter, *refuge*, 666, 717
   safety, 664
Shenanigans, *caprice*, 608
Shelty, *horse*, 271
Shelve, *slope*, 217
   locate, 184
   neglect, 460
   relinquish, 624
   disuse, 678

Shemozzle, *row*, 713
   contention, 720
Shepherd, *director*, 694
   pastor, 996
Sheriff, *jurisdiction*, 965
Sherlock Holmes, *inquiry*, 461
Shibboleth, *indication*, 550
   criterion, 467
Shield, *defend*, 717
   safety, 664
   buckler, 666
Shift, *move*, 264
   change, 140, 144
   substitute, 147
   transfer, 270
   expedient, 626, 634
   evasion, 546
   plea, 617
   difficulty, 704
   dress, 225
Shifting, *transient*, 111
   moving, 270
Shiftless, *unprepared*, 674
   inhabile, 699, 951
Shifty, *dishonest*, 544
Shikar, *pursuit*, 622
Shillelagh, *club*, 727
   impact, 276
Shilly-shally, *irresolution*, 605
Shilpit, *weak*, 160
Shimmer, *lustre*, 420
Shin, *climb*, 305
   kick, 276
Shindig, *prank*, 840
Shindy, *violence*, 173
   contention, 720
   din, 404
Shine, *to emit light*, 420
   glory, 873
   beauty, 845
Shintoism, *religions*, 984
Ship, *vessel*, 273
   to deliver, 270
Shipload, *cargo*, 31
   abundance, 639
Shipment, *transference*, 270
Shipshape, *order*, 58
   conformity, 82
Shipwreck, *failure*, 732
   to defeat, 731
Shire, *county*, 181
Shirk, *avoid*, 623
   disobey, 742
Shirt, *dress*, 225
Shirt-waist, *dress*, 225
Shirty, *angry*, 900
Shivaree, *uproar*, 404
Shiver, *shake*, 315
   cold, 385; *layer*, 204
   fragment, 51
   filament, 205
   to divide, 44
   destroy, 162
Shoal, *shallow*, 209
   assemblage, 72, 102

/

Stable, *immutable*, 150
   resolute, 604
Stable-boy, *servant*, 746
*Staccato, *music*, 415
Stack, *assembly*, 72
Stadtholder, *master*, 745
Staff, *support*, 215
   instrument, 633
   weapon, 727
   impact, 276
   sceptre, 747
   retinue, 746
   party, 712
   hope, 858
Stage, *degree*, 26
   term, 71
   step, 58
   layer, 204
   forum, 542
   vehicle, 272
   arena, 728
   drama, 599
Stage effect, *drama*, 599
   ostentation, 882
Stage-play, *the drama*, 599
Stager, old, *proficient*, 700
Stagger, *totter*, 314
   slow, 275
   agitate, 315
   doubt, 485
   dissuade, 616
   affect, 824
   astonish, 508, 870
Stagnant, *quiescent*, 265
   unchanging, 141
   inert, 172
   inactive, 683
Stagy, *affected*, 855
   ostentatious, 882
Staid, *steady*, 604
   calm, 826
   wise, 498
   grave, 837
Stain, *colour*, 428
   adorn, 847
   deface, 846
   blemish, 848
   spoil, 659
   disgrace, 874
   dishonour, 940
Stainless, *clean*, 652
   innocent, 946
Stair, *way*, 627
Stake, *wager*, 621
   payment, 807
   danger, 665
   security, 771
   property, 780
   execution, 975
Stalactite, *lining*, 224
Stalagmite, *lining*, 224
Stale, *old*, 124
   vapid, 866
   weary, 841
Stalemate, *non-compliance*, 730

Stalk, *follow*, 266
   pursue, 622
Stalking-horse, *plea*, 617
   deception, 545
Stall, *lodge*, 189
   mart, 799
   theatre, 599
   cathedral, 1000
   delay, 133
Stallion, *horse*, 271
Stalwart, *strong*, 159
   large, 192
Stamina, *strength*, 159
   resolution, 604
Stammel, *redness*, 434
Stammer, *stutter*, 583
Stamp, *character*, 7
   form, 240
   mould, 22
   to impress, 505
   mark, 550
   record, 551
   complete, 729
   security, 771
Stampede, *flight*, 287
   fear, 860, 862
Stance, *footing*, 175
Stanch, *dam up*, 348
   stop, 658
Stanchion, *support*, 215
Stand, *to be*, 1
   rest, 265
   be present, 186
   to continue, 141, 143
   endure, 110
   station, 58
   rank, 71
   support, 215
   resistance, 719
Stand against, *resist*, 719
Stand by, *near*, 197
   be firm, 604
   befriend, 707
   auxiliary, 711
Stand for, *represent*, 550
   signify, 516
Stand-in, *substitute*, 147, 634
   deputy, 759
   assistant, 711
Stand in with, *participation*, 778
Stand off, *distance*, 196, 287
Stand-offish, *unsociable*, 893
Stand on, *support*, 215
Stand out, *project*, 250
   appear, 446
   opposition, 708
Stand still, *stop*, 265
   remain, 141
Stand over, *lateness*, 133
Stand up, *vertical*, 212
   elevation, 307
   disappoint, 509
Stand up for, *vindicate*, 937
Stand up to, *courage*, 861
Standard, *rule*, 80

Standard, *measure*, 466
   degree, 26
   pupil, 541
   colours, 550
   good, 648
   prototype, 22
Standard-bearer, *combatant*, 726
Standardize, *conformity*, 82
Standing, *footing*, 8
   term, 71
   situation, 183
   degree, 26
   repute, 873
   vertical, 212
Standpoint, *aspect*, 453
Stanza, *poetry*, 597
Staple, *whole*, 50
   peg, 214
   mart, 799
Star, *luminary*, 423
   decoration, 877
   ornament, 847
   glory, 873
   actor, 599, 599A
Star Chamber, *jurisprudence*,
                  966
Star-gazer, *astronomer*, 318
Starbeam, *light*, 420
   dimness, 422
Starboard, *dextrality*, 238
Starch, *viscidity*, 352
Starchy, *stiff*, 323
   proud, 878
   affected, 855
Stare, *look*, 441
   curiosity, 455
   wonder, 870
Staring, *visible*, 446
Stark, *stiff*, 323
   stubborn, 606
Starless, *dark*, 421
Starlight, *light*, 420
   dimness, 422
Stars, *celestial*, 318
   necessity, 601
Stars and Stripes, *flag*, 550
Start, *depart*, 293
   begin, 66
   desultory, 139
   jump, 139; *arise*, 151
   suggest, 514
   from surprise, 508
   from fear, 860
   from wonder, 870
Start up, *project*, 250
   appear, 446
Starting-point, *beginning*, 66
   departure, 293
Startle, *unexpected*, 508
   wonder, 870
   fear, 860
   doubt, 485
Starve, *fast*, 956
   with cold, 383, 385
   want, 804

Submerge, *sink*, 162, 208
  plunge, 310
Submission, *surrender*, 725, 879
Submissive, *humble*, 725, 879
  enduring, 826
Submit, *surrender*, 725
  obey, 743
Subordinate, *inferior*, 34
  unimportant, 643
  servant, 746
  subjection, 749
Subordination, *order*, 58
Suborn, *hire*, 795
  bribe, 784
Subpoena, *mandate*, 741
Subscribe, *assent*, 488
  agree to, 762, 769
  give, 707, 784
Subscription, *donation*, 809
Subsequent, *in time*, 117
  in order, 63, 65
Subservient, *utility*, 644
  intermediate, 631
  aiding, 707
  servility, 886
Subside, *sink*, 306
  cave in, 252
  decrease, 36
  calm down, 826
Subsidiary, *tending*, 176
  means, 632
  auxiliary, 707
Subsidy, *pay*, 809
  gift, 784
  aid, 707
Subsist, *existence*, 1
  life, 359
  continuance, 141
Subsistence, *food*, 298
  livelihood, 803
Subsistence money, *loan*, 787
  advance, 809
Subsoil, *earth*, 342
  interior, 221
*Substance, *thing*, 3
  matter, 316
  interior, 221
  quantity, 25
  texture, 329
  compendium, 596
  meaning, 516
  important, 642
  wealth, 803
Substantial, *dense*, 321
  existence, 1
  true, 494
Substantially, *intrinsically*, 5
Substantiate, *demonstrate*, 478
  make good, 494, 924
Substantive, *substance*, 3
Substitute, *means*, 634
  deputy, 759
Substitution, *change*, 147
Substratum, *substance*, 3
  interior, 221

Substratum, *layer*, 204
  base, 211
  support, 215
  materiality, 316
Subsumption, *inclusion*, 76
Subterfuge, *lie*, 546
  sophistry, 477
  cunning, 702
Subterranean, *underground*, 208
Subtilize, *sophistry*, 477
Subtle, *cunning*, 702
  wise, 498
  rare, 322
  light, 320
  texture, 329
Subtract, *retrench*, 38
  diminish, 36
  arithmetical, 84
  to take, 789
Subtrahend, *deduction*, 38
  number, 84
Suburban, *environs*, 227
  distance, 197
Subvention, *aid*, 707
  gift, 784
Subvert, *invert*, 218
  depress, 308
  change, 140
  destroy, 162
Subway, *road*, 627
Succedaneum, *substitute*,
    147, 634
Succeed, *answer*, 731
  follow, 63
*Succès d'estime, *approbation*,
    931
Success, *success*, 731
Succession, *sequence*, 63
  transfer, 783
  continuity, 69
  of time, 109
  lateness, 117
Successor, *sequel*, 65
  posterior, 117
Succinct, *concise*, 572
Succour, *help*, 707
Succubus, *demon*, 980
Succulent, *juicy*, 333
  edible, 298
  semiliquid, 352
Succumb, *yield*, 725
  obey, 743
  fatigue, 688
Such, *similarity*, 17
Suck, *imbibe*, 296
  deprive, 789
Sucker, *dupe*, 547
Suckling, *youth*, 129
Suction, *imbibition*, 296
Sudatorium, *furnace*, 386
Sudden, *early*, 132
  abrupt, 508
  transient, 111
Suds, *froth*, 353
Sue, *demand*, 765

Sue, *at law*, 969
Suet, *fat*, 356
Suffer, *physical pain*, 378
  moral pain, 828
  to endure, 821
  to allow, 760
  disease, 655
  experience, 151
Sufferance, *permission*, 760
Sufficient, *enough*, 639
Suffix, *sequel*, 65
  adjunct, 39
Sufflation, *wind*, 349
Suffocate, *choke*, 361
Suffragan, *church*, 996
Suffrage, *vote*, 609
  prayer, 990
Suffragist, *dueness*, 924
Suffuse, *mix*, 41
  feel, 821
  blush, 874
Sufism, *religions*, 984
Sugar, *sweet*, 396
  to flatter, 933
Sugarloaf, *convexity*, 250
Suggest, *suppose*, 514
  advise, 695
  inform, 527
  recall, 505
  occur, 451
*Suggestio falsi, *equivocalness*,
    520
  falsehood, 544
Suggestion, *plan*, 626
Suggestive, *impure*, 961
*Sui generis, *special*, 79
  unconformity, 83
*Sui juris, *freedom*, 748
Suicide, *kill*, 361
Suit, *accord*, 23
  class, 75
  expedient, 646
  series, 69
  clothes, 225
  courtship, 902
  at law, 969
Suit-case, *receptacle*, 191
Suite, *series*, 69
  adjunct, 39
  sequel, 65
  retinue, 746
Suiting, *accord*, 23
Suitor, *love*, 897
Sulcated, *furrow*, 259
Sulky, *discourteous*, 895
  bad-tempered, 901
  gloomy, 837
Sullen, *discourteous*, 895
  bad-tempered, 901
  gloomy, 837
  misanthropical, 911
Sully, *deface*, 846
  dirty, 653
  dishonour, 874, 940
Sulphur, *colour*, 436

Trade, *traffic,* 794
Trade mark, *indication,* 550
Trader, *merchant,* 797
Tradition, *record,* 551
  description, 594
Traditional, *old,* 124
Traduce, *detract,* 934, 932
Traffic, *barter,* 794
  business, 625
Traffic warden, *police,* 965
Tragedy, *drama,* 599
  disaster, 830
Tragelaph, *unconformity,* 83
Tragic, *distressing,* 830
Tragi-comedy, *ridicule,* 856
Tragi-comic, *the drama,* 599
Trail, *sequel,* 65
  pendent, 214
  slow, 275
  drag, 285
  odour, 398
  indication, 551
  pursue, 622
  to track, 281, 461
Trailer, *cinema,* 599A
Train, *series,* 69
  sequel, 65
  sequence, 281
  retinue, 746
  appendix, 39
  traction, 285
  vehicle, 272
  teach, 537, 540
  cultivate, 375
  tame, 370
  accustom, 613
  drill, 673
Train-bearer, *servant,* 746
Train oil, *oil,* 356
Trained, *skill,* 698
Trait, *appearance,* 448
  lineament, 550
Traitor, *knave,* 941
  disobedient, 742
Trajectory, *path,* 627
Tram, *vehicle,* 272
Tram-car, *vehicle,* 272
Trammel, *fetter,* 752
  restrain, 751
  hinder, 706
*Tramontana, *wind,* 349
Tramontane, *distant,* 196
  alien, 57
Tramp, *to stroll,* 266
  stroller, 268
  commonalty, 876
  ship, 273
Trample, *violate,* 927
  bully, 885
  spurn, 930
Tramway, *way,* 627
Trance, *lethargy,* 823
  insensibility, 376
  inactivity, 683
Tranquil, *calm,* 174, 826

Tranquil, *peaceful,* 721
  quiet, 165
  to pacify, 723
Tranquillizer, *drug,* 662
Transact, *conduct,* 692
  traffic, 794
Transaction, *event,* 151
Transalpine, *distance,* 196
Transatlantic, *distance,* 196
Transcend, *go beyond,* 303
Transcendent, *great,* 31, 33
  spiritual, 317
  perfect, 650
  good, 648
  glorious, 873
Transcendental, *recondite,* 519
  spiritual, 317, 450
Transcribe, *write,* 590
  copy, 21
Transcript, *write,* 590
  copy, 21
Transcursion, *trespass,* 303
Transept, *of church,* 1000
  crossing, 219
Transfer, *things,* 270
  property, 783
  remove, 185
Transfiguration, *change,* 140
  divine, 998
Transfix, *perforate,* 260
Transform, *change,* 140
Transformation, *wig,* 225
Transfuse, *transfer,* 270
  mix, 41
  translate, 522
Transgress, *go beyond,* 303
  infringe, 773
  violate, 927
  sins, 947
Tranship, *transfer,* 270
Transient, *passing,* 111
Transilient, *transcursion,* 303
Transistor, *radio,* 599
Transit, *conversion,* 144
  motion, 264
  transference, 270
Transition, *motion,* 264
  conversion, 144
  transference, 270
Transitive, *passing,* 111
Transitory, *passing,* 111
Translate, *interpret,* 522
  transfer, 270
  promote, 995
Translucent, *transparent,* 425
Transmigration, *change,* 140
  conversion, 144
Transmission, *moving,* 270
  of property, 783
  passage, 302
Transmitter, *hearing,* 418
Transmogrify, *change,* 140, 144
Transmute, *change,* 140
  conversion, 144
Transparent, *pellucid,* 425

Transparent, *obvious,* 518
  perspicuous, 570
Transpicuous, *transparent,* 425
Transpierce, *pierce,* 260
Transpire, *appear,* 525
  disclose, 529
Transplant, *displace,* 185
  transfer, 270
Transpontine, *drama,* 599
Transport, *transfer,* 185, 270
  punish, 972
  ship, 272
  feeling, 821, 824
  please, 827, 829
Transpose, *displace,* 185
  invert, 218
  transfer, 270
  exchange, 148
Transubstantiation, *rite,* 998
Transude, *ooze,* 295
  pass through, 302
  exude, 348
Transverse, *oblique,* 217
Trap, *snare,* 667
  vehicle, 272
Trap-door, *escape,* 671
  pitfall, 667
Trapes, *journey,* 266
Trappings, *clothes,* 39, 225
  gear, 633
  ornament, 847
  property, 780
Trash, *absurdity,* 497
  nonsense, 517
  trifle, 643
Travail, *work,* 686
Travel, *journey,* 266
  motion, 264
Traveller, *traveller,* 268
Traverse, *move,* 266
  pass, 302
  investigate, 461
  obstruct, 706
Travesty, *copy,* 21
  to imitate, 19
  misinterpret, 523
  burlesque, 856
Travolator, *way,* 627
Tray, *receptacle,* 191
Treachery, *deceit,* 940
Treacle, *sweet,* 396
  semiliquid, 352
Tread, *journey,* 266
  motion, 264
Treadle, *instrument,* 633
Treadmill, *punishment,* 975
  wearisome, 841
Treason, *revolt,* 742
  treachery, 940
Treasure, *money,* 800
  goodness, 648
  perfection, 650
  windfall, 618
Treasurer, *treasurer,* 801
Treasury, *treasury,* 802

Treasury, *store*, 636
Treat, *manage*, 692
 bargain, 769
 amuse, 840
 please, 827
Treatise, *book*, 595
Treatment, *action*, 692
 remedy, 662
 painting, 556
Treaty, *agreement*, 769
Treble, *number*, 93
 music, 413
Tree, *plant*, 367
 execution, 975
Trefoil, *three*, 92
Trek, *journey*, 266
Trellis, *cross*, 219
Tremble, *agitate*, 315
 waver, 149
 with cold, 385
 with fear, 860
 with emotion, 821
Tremendous, *great*, 31
 fearful, 860
Tremolo, *quaver*, 407
Tremor, *agitation*, 315
 feeling, 827; *fear*, 860
Tremulous, *stammer*, 583
Trench, *furrow*, 259
 defence, 717
Trench on, *nearness*, 197
 encroach, 303, 925
Trenchant, *keen*, 171
 sharp, 253
 disapproving, 932
 style, 574
Trencher, *plate*, 191
 layer, 204
Trend, *direction*, 278
 curve, 245; *tendency*, 176
Trendy, *fashion*, 852
Trepan, *deceive*, 545
 perforator, 262
Trepidation, *agitation*, 315
 emotion, 821
 excitability, 825
 fear, 860
Trespass, *go beyond*, 303
 sin, 947
Tress, *hair*, 256
Trestle, *support*, 215
Trey, *number*, 92
Triad, *number*, 92
Trial, *experiment*, 463
 essay, 675
 difficulty, 704
 suffering, 828
 lawsuit, 969
Triality, *number*, 92
Triangle, *angularity*, 244
 triality, 92
 musical instrument, 417
Triangulate, *measurement*, 466
Tribe, *class*, 75
 kindred, 11

Tribe, *assemblage*, 72
Tribrach, *verse*, 597
Tribulation, *pain*, 828
Tribunal, *tribunal*, 966
Tribune, *officer*, 745
Tributary, *giving*, 784
 river, 348
Tribute, *donation*, 784
 reward, 973
 approbation, 931
Tricar, *vehicle*, 272
Trice, *instantaneous*, 113
Trichotomy, *trisection*, 94
Trick, *deception*, 545
 contrivance, 626
 skill, 698
 cunning, 702
 speciality, 79
 to dress, 225
 adorn, 845
Trickery, *artifice*, 702
Trickle, *ooze*, 295
 drip, 348
Trickster, *deceiver*, 548, 702
 thief, 792
Tricksy, *sportive*, 840
Tricolour, *variegation*, 440
 flag, 550
Trident, *ocean*, 341
Tried, *employed*, 677
 trusty, 939
Triennial, *periodical*, 138
Trifid, *number*, 94
Trifle, *unimportant*, 643
 small, 32
 loaf, 683
Trifle away, *idle*, 683
Trifle with, *neglect*, 460
 disparage, 483
Triform, *number*, 92
Trig, *beauty*, 845
Trigeminal, *triple*, 93
Trigger, *instrument*, 633
Trigonal, *angularity*, 244
Trilateral, *side*, 236
Trilby, *hat*, 225
Trill, *sound*, 407
 resonance, 408
 music, 415
Trilogy, *triality*, 92
Trim, *state*, 7
 form, 240
 dress, 225
 ornamental, 845, 847
 order, 58
 to adjust, 27
 prepare, 673
 beat, 731
 scold, 932
 change sides, 607
Trimmer, *fickle*, 605, 607
 apostate, 941
Trimming, *edge*, 230
 ornament, 847
Trinal, *number*, 92

Trine, *triplication*, 93
Trinity, *Deity*, 976
Trinket, *ornament*, 847
Trinkgeld, *gift*, 784
Trinomial, *triality*, 92
 triplication, 93
Trio, *number*, 92
Triolet, *poetry*, 597
Trip, *jaunt*, 266
 to fall, 306
 hasten, 274
 mistake, 495
 fail, 945
 guilt, 947
Trip up, *overthrow*, 731
 deceive, 545
Tripartition, *trisection*, 94
Triphthong, *letter*, 561
Triple, *triplication*, 93
Triplet, *triality*, 92
 poetry, 597
Triplicate, *triplication*, 93
Tripod, *support*, 215
Tripper, *traveller*, 268
Tripping, *nimble*, 682
 failing, 495
Triquetra, *triality*, 92
Trireme, *ship*, 273
Trisect, *tripartition*, 94
*Triste, *dejected*, 837
Tristful, *dejected*, 837
Trisulcate, *tripartition*, 94
 furrow, 259
Trisyllable, *letter*, 561
Trite, *old*, 82
 hackneyed, 496
 unimportant, 643
Tritheism, *heathen*, 984
Triturate, *pulverulence*, 330
Triumph, *success*, 731
 trophy, 733
 exult, 838
 boast, 884
 celebrate, 883
Triumphant, *elated*, 836
Trivet, *support*, 215
Trivial, *trifling*, 643
 useless, 645
 flimsy, 477
 smallness, 32
Trochee, *verse*, 597
Troglodyte, *seclusion*, 893
Troll, *roll*, 312
 sing, 415
 fairy, 980
Trolley, *vehicle*, 272
Trolley-bus, *vehicle*, 272
Trollop, *libertine*, 962
Trombone, *musical instrument*,
      417
Troop, *army*, 726
 assemblage, 72
Troop-ship, *ship*, 273
Trooper, *combatant*, 726
 ship, 273

Untinged, *simple*, 42
   uncoloured, 429
Untired, *refreshed*, 689
Untiring, *active*, 682
Untitled, *commonalty*, 876
Untold, *secret*, 526, 528
   countless, 105
Untouched, *disused*, 678
   insensible, 376, 823
Untoward, *bad*, 649
   inopportune, 135
   unprosperous, 735
   unpleasant, 830
Untraced, *latency*, 526
Untracked, *latency*, 526
Untrained, *unskilled*, 699
   unprepared, 674
   unaccustomed, 614
Untrammelled, *free*, 705, 748
Untranslated, *misinterpre-*
   tation, 523
Untravelled, *quiescent*, 265
   unknown, 491
Untreasured, *unstored*, 640
Untried, *undetermined*, 461
Untrimmed, *simple*, 849
   unprepared, 674
Untrodden, *new*, 123
   not used, 678
   impervious, 261
Untroubled, *calm*, 174, 721
Untrue, *false*, 544
Untrustworthy, *dishonest*, 940
   erroneous, 495
   uncertain, 475
   dangerous, 665
Untruth, *falsehood*, 544, 546
Untunable, *discord*, 414
Unturned, *straight*, 246
Untutored, *ignorant*, 491
Untwine, *unfold*, 313
Untwist, *straighten*, 246
   evolve, 313
   separate, 44, 47
Unurged, *spontaneous*, 600
Unused, *unaccustomed*,
            614, 699
   untouched, 678
Unusual, *unconformity*, 83
   greatness, 31
Unutilized, *disuse*, 678
Unutterable, *wonderful*, 870
   great, 31
Unvalued, *depreciated*, 483
   undesired, 866
   disliked, 898
Unvanquished, *free*, 748
Unvaried, *permanent*, 141
   continued, 143
   monotonous, 576
Unvarnished, *truth*, 494
Unvarying, *uniform*, 16
Unveil, *manifest*, 525
   disclose, 529
Unventilated, *close*, 261

Unveracious, *false*, 544
Unverified, *indiscrimination*,
            465A
Unversed, *unconversant*, 491
   unskilled, 699
Unvexed, *content*, 831
Unviolated, *probity*, 939
Unvisited, *exclusion*, 893
Unvitiated, *unspoiled*, 648
Unvouched-for, *unattested*, 468
Unwakened, *dormant*, 683
Unwanted, *unnecessary*, 645
Unwarlike, *cowardly*, 862
Unwarmed, *cold*, 383
Unwarned, *danger*, 665
Unwarped, *unprejudiced*, 480
Unwarranted, *unjustifiable*,
            923, 925
   inconclusive, 477
Unwary, *heedless*, 460
Unwashed, *unclean*, 653
   vulgar, 851
Unwasted, *unexhausted*, 639
Unwatched, *neglected*, 460
Unwatchful, *inattentive*, 458
Unwatered, *dry*, 340
   undiluted, 159
Unwavering, *resolute*, 604
Unweakened, *strong*, 159
Unwearied, *indefatigable*, 682
   refreshed, 689
Unwedded, *celibacy*, 904
Unweeded, *neglected*, 460
Unweighed, *neglected*, 460
Unwelcome, *disagreeable*, 830
Unwell, *ill*, 655
Unwept, *hate*, 898
Unwholesome, *insalubrious*,
            657
Unwieldy, *large*, 192
   heavy, 319
   difficult, 704
   cumbersome, 647
Unwilling, *unwillingness*, 603
   dissent, 489
Unwind, *evolve*, 313
   straighten, 246
Unwinking, *vigilant*, 457
Unwiped, *unclean*, 653
Unwise, *fool*, 499
Unwished, *undesirable*, 866
Unwithered, *strong*, 159
Unwitnessed, *unseen*, 526
Unwitting, *ignorant*, 491
   involuntary, 601
Unwomanly, *unbecoming*, 940
Unwonted, *unaccustomed*, 624
   unusual, 83
Unworkmanlike, *unskilful*, 699
Unworldly, *disinterested*, 943
   pious, 987
Unworn, *unused*, 159
Unworthy, *vicious*, 945
   base, 940
   shameful, 874

Unwrap, *straighten*, 246
Unwreathe, *straighten*, 246
Unwrinkled, *smooth*, 255
Unwritten, *untold*, 526
Unwrought, *unprepared*, 674
Unyielding, *tough*, 323
   resolute, 604
   severe, 739
   obstinate, 606
   resisting, 719
Unyoke, *disjoin*, 44
Up, *fizzy*, 353
Up in arms, *resist*, 719
Up-country, *interiority*, 221
Upanishads, *sacred books*, 986
Upbear, *support*, 215
Upbraid, *disapprove*, 932
Upbringing, *teaching*, 537
Upcast, *elevation*, 307
Upgrow, *height*, 206
Upgrowth, *ascent*, 305
Upheave, *elevation*, 307
Uphill, *activity*, 217
   ascent, 305
   difficulty, 704
Uphold, *support*, 215
   evidence, 467
   aid, 707
   continue, 143
Upholster, *cover*, 222
   furnish, 637
Upkeep, *preservation*, 670
Uplands, *height*, 206
Uplift, *elevation*, 307
Upper, *height*, 206
Upper hand, *authority*, 737
   success, 731
Upper storey, *brain*, 450
Uppermost, *height*, 206, 210
Uppish, *self-assertive*, 885
Upraise, *elevation*, 307
Uprear, *elevation*, 307
Upright, *vertical*, 212
   honest, 939
   virtuous, 944
Uprise, *ascent*, 305
Uproar, *noise*, 404
   turmoil, 173
   disorder, 59
Uproot, *destruction*, 162
   extraction, 301
Upset, *throw down*, 308
   disorder, 59
   derange, 61
   change, 140
   invert, 218
   destroy, 162
Upshot, *end*, 66
   total, 50
Upside-down, *inversion*, 218
Upstage, *affected*, 855
   supercilious, 930
   proud, 878
Upstairs, *height*, 207
Upstart, *plebeian*, 876

Visage, *front*, 234
   appearance, 448
Vis-à-vis, *front*, 234
   opposite, 237
Viscera, *interior*, 221
Viscid, *semiliquid*, 352
Viscount, *noble*, 875
   master, 745
Viscounty, *title*, 877
Viscous, *semiliquid*, 352
*Visé, *indication*, 550
Vishnu, *deity*, 979
Visible, *visibility*, 446
Vision, *sight*, 441
   imagination, 515
   apparition, 980
Visionary, *erroneous*, 495
   imaginary, 515
   impossible, 471
   heterodox, 984A
Visit, *sociality*, 892
   frequent, 136
   arrival, 292
Visitation, *pain*, 828
   disease, 655
   calamity, 830
Visiting-card, *indication*, 560
Visitor, *arrival*, 292
   director, 694
Visor, *concealment*, 528
Vista, *point of view*, 441
   prospect, 448, 507
Visual, *vision*, 441
Vital, *importance*, 642
Vitality, *life*, 359
   strength, 159
Vitals, *interior*, 221
Vitiate, *deteriorate*, 659
   debase, 945
Vitreous, *density*, 321
Vitrify, *density*, 321
   harden, 323
Vitriolic, *malevolent*, 907
Vituperate, *disapprove*, 932
   scold, 908
*Viva, *honour*, 873
Viva voce, *speech*, 582
Vivacious, *active*, 682
   sensitive, 822
   cheerful, 836
Vivarium, *taming*, 370
*Vive, *honour*, 873
Vivid, *light*, 420
   colour, 428
   lively, 375
   energetic, 171
   style, 574
Vivify, *life*, 359
Vivisect, *anatomize*, 44
Vixen, *scold*, 901
   fury, 173
Viz., *meaning*, 516
Vizier, *deputy*, 759
Vizor, *see* Visor
Vocable, *word*, 562

Vocabulary, *word*, 562
Vocal, *voice*, 580
   loudness, 404
   music, 415
Vocalist, *musician*, 416
Vocalize, *speech*, 580
Vocation, *business*, 625
Vociferate, *cry*, 411
   loudness, 404
   voice, 580
Vogue, *fashion*, 852
   custom, 613
   repute, 873
Vogue word, *neology*, 563
Voice, *speech*, 580
   grammar, 567
   sound, 402
   cry, 411
   choice, 609
   affirmation, 535
   opinion, 484
Void, *vacuum*, 2, 4
   absence, 187
   to emit, 297
   invalidate, 964
Voivode, *master*, 745
Volant, *flight*, 267
Volapük, *language*, 560
Volatile, *vaporizable*, 336
   changeable, 149
   irresolute, 605
Volatility, *caprice*, 608
Volcanic, *violence*, 173
   excitable, 825
Volitation, *flight*, 267
Volition, *will*, 600
Volley, *impulse*, 276
   attack, 716
   violence, 173
   collection, 72
Volplane, *descent*, 306
Volte-face, *recantation*, 607
Voluble, *loquacity*, 584
Volume, *bulk*, 192
   quantity, 25
   greatness, 31
   book, 593
Voluntary, *willing*, 600, 602
   music, 415
Volunteer, *endeavour*, 676
   offer, 600, 763
Voluptuary, *libertine*, 962
Voluptuous, *sensual*, 954
   pleasure, 377
   joy, 827
   delight, 829
Volute, *convolution*, 248
Vomit, *ejection*, 297
Vomitory, *opening*, 260
Voodooism, *occult arts*, 992
Voracity, *appetite*, 865
   gluttony, 957
Vortex, *rotation*, 312
   whirlpool, 348
Votary, *devotee*, 840, 865

Vote, *choice*, 609
   affirmation, 535
Vote for, *assent*, 488
Votive, *promise*, 768
Vouch, *testify*, 467
   assert, 535
Voucher, *evidence*, 467
   record, 551
   security, 771
Vouchsafe, *permit*, 760
   consent, 762
   ask, 765; *deign*, 879
Vow, *promise*, 768
   assert, 535
   worship, 990
Voyage, *journey*, 267
   motion, 264
Voyageur, *boatman*, 269
Voyeur, *curiosity*, 455
*Vraisemblance, *probability*, 472
Vulcan, *god*, 979
Vulgar, *unrefined*, 851
   discourteous, 895
   commonalty, 876
Vulgarism, *solecism*, 568
   language, 560
Vulgate, *revelation*, 985
Vulnerable, *danger*, 665
Vulpine, *cunning*, 702
Vulture, *bane*, 663

W

W.C., *lavatory*, 653
Wabble, *oscillation*, 314
Wacky, *mad*, 503
Wadding, *lining*, 224
   softness, 324
   stopping, 263
Waddle, *slowness*, 275
   oscillation, 314
Wade, *swim*, 267
Wafer, *layer*, 204
Waft, *transfer*, 270
   blow, 267, 349
Wag, *oscillate*, 214
   agitate, 315
   wit, 844
Wage war, *contention*, 720
Wager, *chance*, 621
Wages, *expenditure*, 809
Waggery, *wit*, 842
Waggish, *merry*, 836
Waggle, *oscillation*, 314
   agitation, 315
Wagon, *vehicle*, 272
Wagonette, *vehicle*, 272
Waif, *outcast*, 893
Wail, *lamentation*, 839
Wain, *vehicle*, 272
Wainscot, *lining*, 224
   base, 211
Waist, *narrow*, 203
Waistcoat, *dress*, 225

ORIGINAL INTRODUCTION

By Peter Roget

The present work is intended to supply, with respect to the English language, a desideratum hitherto unsupplied in any language; namely, a collection of the words it contains and of the idiomatic combinations peculiar to it, arranged, not in alphabetical order, as they are in a dictionary. but according to the *ideas* which they express.[1] The purpose of an ordinary dictionary is simply to explain the meaning of words; and the problem of which it professes to furnish the solution may be stated thus: The word being given, to find its signification, or the idea it is intended to convey. The object aimed at in the present undertaking is exactly the converse of this; namely, the idea being given, to find the word, or words, by which that idea may be most fitly and aptly expressed. For this purpose, the words and phrases of the language are here classed, not according to their sound or their orthography, but strictly according to their *signification*.

The communication of our thoughts by means of language, whether spoken or written, like every other object of mental exertion, constitutes a peculiar art, which, like other parts, cannot be acquired in any perfection but by long and continued practice. Some, indeed, there are, more highly gifted than others with a facility of expression, and naturally endowed with the power of eloquence; but to none is it at all times an easy process to embody in exact and appropriate language the various trains of ideas that are passing through the mind, or to depict in their true colours and proportions the diversified and nicer shades of feeling which accompany them. To those who are unpractised in the art of composition, or unused to extempore speaking, these difficulties present themselves in their most formidable aspect. However distinct may be our views, however vivid our conceptions, or however fervent our emotions, we cannot but be often

[1]See note on p.555

conscious that the phraseology we have at our command is inadequate to do them justice. We seek in vain the words we need, and strive ineffectually to devise forms of expression which shall faithfully portray our thoughts and sentiments. The appropriate terms, notwithstanding our utmost efforts, cannot be conjured up at will. Like 'spirits from the vasty deep,' they come not when we call; and we are driven to the employment of a set of words and phrases either too general or too limited, too strong or too feeble, which suit not the occasion, which hit not the mark we aim at; and the result of our prolonged exertion is a style at once laboured and obscure, vapid and redundant, or vitiated by the still graver faults of affectation or ambiguity.

It is to those who are thus painfully groping their way and struggling with the difficulties of composition, that this work professes to hold out a helping hand. The assistance it gives is that of furnishing on every topic a copious store of words and phrases, adapted to express all the recognizable shades and modifications of the general idea under which those words and phrases are arranged. The inquirer can readily select, out of the ample collection spread out before his eyes in the following pages, those expressions which are best suited to his purpose, and which might not have occurred to him without such assistance. In order to make this selection, he scarcely ever need engage in any elaborate or critical study of the subtle distinctions existing between synonymous terms; for if the materials set before him be sufficiently abundant, an instinctive tact will rarely fail to lead him to the proper choice. Even while glancing over the columns of this work, his eye may chance to light upon a particular term, which may save the cost of a clumsy paraphrase, or spare the labour of a tortuous circumlocution. Some felicitous turn of expression thus introduced will frequently open to the mind of the reader a whole vista of collateral ideas, which could not, without an extended and obtrusive episode, have been unfolded to his view; and often will the judicious insertion of a happy epithet, like a beam of sunshine in a landscape, illumine and adorn the subject which touches it, imparting new grace, and giving life and spirit to the picture.

Every workman in the exercise of his art should be provided with proper implements. For the fabrication of complicated and curious pieces of mechanism the artisan requires a corresponding assortment of various tools and instruments. For giving proper effect to the fictions of the drama, the actor should have at his disposal a well-furnished wardrobe, supplying the costumes best suited to the personage he is to represent. For the perfect delineation of the beauties of nature, the painter should have within reach of his pencil every variety and combination of hues and tints. Now the writer, as well as the orator, employs for the accomplishment of his purposes the instrumentality of words; it is in words that he clothes his thoughts; it is by means of words that he depicts his feelings. It is therefore essential to his success that he be provided with a copious vocabulary, and that he possess an entire command of all the resources and appliances of his language. To the acquisition of this power no procedure appears more directly conducive than the study of a methodized system such as that now offered to his use.

The utility of the present work will be appreciated more especially by those who are engaged in the arduous process of translating into English a work written in another language. Simple as the operation may appear, on a superficial view, of rendering into English each of its sentences, the task of transfusing, with perfect exactness, the sense of the original, preserving at the same time the style and character of its composition, and reflecting with fidelity the mind and the spirit of the author, is a task of extreme difficulty. The cultivation of this useful department of literature was in ancient times strongly recommended both by Cicero and by Quintilian as essential to the formation of a good writer and accomplished orator. Regarded simply as a mental exercise, the practice of translation is the best training for the attainment of that mastery of language and felicity of diction which are the sources of the highest oratory and are requisite for the possession of a graceful and persuasive eloquence. By rendering ourselves the faithful interpreters of the thoughts and feelings of others, we are rewarded with the acquisition of greater readiness and facility in correctly expressing our own; as he who has best learned to execute the orders of a commander becomes himself best qualified to command.

In the earliest periods of civilization, translations have been the agents for propagating knowledge from nation to nation, and the value of their labours has been inestimable; but, in the present age, when so many different languages have become the depositories of the vast treasures of literature and of science which have been accumulating for centuries, the utility of accurate translations has greatly increased, and it has become a more important object to attain perfection in the art.

The use of language is not confined to its being the medium through which we communicate our ideas to one another; it fulfils a no less important function as an *instrument of thought*, not being merely its vehicle, but giving it wings for flight. Metaphysicians are agreed that scarcely any of our intellectual operations could be carried on to any considerable extent without the agency of words. None but those who are conversant with the philosophy of mental phenomena can be aware of the immense influence that is exercised by language in promoting the development of our ideas, in fixing them in the mind, and detaining them for steady contemplation. In every process of reasoning, language enters as an essential element. Words are the instruments by which we form all our abstractions, by which we fashion and embody our ideas, and by which we are enabled to glide along a series of premises and conclusions with a rapidity so great as to leave in the memory no trace of the successive steps of the process; and we remain unconscious how much we owe to this potent auxiliary of the reasoning faculty. It is on this ground, also, that the present work founds a claim to utility. The review of a catalogue of words of analogous signification will often suggest by association other trains of thought, which, presenting the subject under new and varied aspects, will vastly expand the sphere of our mental vision. Amidst the many objects thus brought within the range of our contemplation, some striking similitude or appropriate image, some excursive flight or brilliant conception, may flash on the mind, giving point and force to our arguments, awakening a responsive chord in the imagination or sensibility of the reader, and procuring for our reasonings a more ready access both to his understanding and to his heart.

It is of the utmost consequence that strict accuracy should regulate our use of language, and that every one should acquire the power and the habit of expressing his thoughts with perspicuity and correctness. Few, indeed, can appreciate the real extent and importance of that influence which language has always exercised on human affairs, or can be aware how often these are determined by causes much slighter than are apparent to a superficial observer. False logic, disguised under specious phraseology, too often gains the assent of the unthinking multitude, disseminating far and wide the seeds of prejudice and error. Truisms pass current, and wear the semblance of profound wisdom, when dressed up in the tinsel garb of antithetical phrases, or set off by an imposing pomp of paradox. By a confused jargon of involved and mystical sentences, the imagination is easily inveigled into a transcendental region of clouds, and the understanding beguiled into the belief that it is acquiring knowledge and approaching truth. A misapplied or misapprehended term is sufficient to give rise to fierce and interminable disputes: a misnomer has turned the tide of popular opinion; a verbal sophism has decided a party question; an artful watchword, thrown among combustible materials, has kindled the flames of deadly warfare, and changed the destiny of an empire.

In constructing the following system of classification of the ideas which are expressible by language, my chief aim has been to obtain the greatest amount of practical utility. I have accordingly adopted such principles of arrangement as appeared to me to be the simplest and most natural, and which would not require, either for their comprehension or application, any disciplined acumen, or depth of metaphysical or antiquarian lore. Eschewing all needless refinements and subtleties, I have taken as my guide the more obvious characters of the ideas for which expressions were to be tabulated, arranging them under such classes and categories as reflection and experience had taught me would conduct the inquirer most readily and quickly to the object of his search. Commencing with the ideas expressing mere abstract relations, I proceed to those which relate to the phenomena of the material world, and lastly to those in which the mind is concerned, and which comprehend intellect, volition, and feeling; thus establishing six primary Classes of Categories.

1. The first of these classes comprehends ideas derived from the more general and ABSTRACT RELATIONS among things, such as *Existence, Resemblance, Quantity, Order, Number, Time, Power.*

2. The second class refers to SPACE and its various relations, including *Motion*, or change of place.

3. The third class includes all ideas that relate to the MATERIAL WORLD, namely, the *Properties of Matter*, such as *Solidity, Fluidity, Heat, Sound, Light,* and the *Phenomena* they present, as well as the simple *Perceptions* to which they give rise.

4. The fourth class embraces all ideas of phenomena relating to the INTELLECT and its operations, comprising the *Acquisition*, the *Retention*, and the *Communication of Ideas*.

5. The fifth class includes the ideas derived from the exercise of VOLITION, embracing the phenomena and results of our *Voluntary and Active Powers*, such as *Choice, Intention, Utility, Action, Antagonism, Authority, Compact, Property*, etc.

6. The sixth and last class comprehends all ideas derived from the operation of our SENTIENT AND MORAL POWERS, including our *Feelings, Emotions, Passions*, and *Moral and Religious Sentiments*.[1]

The object I have proposed to myself in this work would have been but imperfectly attained if I had confined myself to a mere

---

[1] It must necessarily happen in every system of classification framed with this view, that ideas and expressions arranged under one class must include also ideas relating to another class; for the operations of the *Intellect* generally involve also those of the *Will* and vice versa; and our *affections* and *emotions*, in like manner, generally imply the agency both of the *Intellect* and the *Will*. All that can be effected, therefore, is to arrange the words according to the principal or dominant idea they convey. *Teaching*, for example, although a Voluntary act, relates primarily to the Communication of Ideas, and is accordingly placed at No 537, under Class IV, Division II. On the other hand, *Choice, Conduct, Skill*, etc., although implying the co-operation of Voluntary with Intellectual acts, relate principally to the former, and are therefore arranged under Class V.

It often happens that the same word admits of various applications, or may be used in different senses. In consulting the Index the reader will be guided to the number of the heading under which that word, in each particular acceptation, will be found, by means of *supplementary words*, printed in italics; which words, however, are not to be understood as explaining the meaning of the word to which they are annexed, but only assisting in the required reference. I have also, for shortness' sake, generally omitted words immediately derived from the primary one inserted, which sufficiently represents the whole group of correlative words referable to the same heading. Thus the number affixed to *Beauty* applies to all its derivatives, such as *Beautiful, Beauteous, Beautify, Beautifulness, Beautifully*, etc., the insertion of which was therefore needless.

catalogue of words, and had omitted the numerous phrases and forms of expression, composed of several words, which are of such frequent use as to entitle them to rank among the constituent parts of the language.[1] Very few of these verbal combinations, so essential to the knowledge of our native tongue, and so profusely abounding in its daily use, are to be met with in ordinary dictionaries. These phrases and forms of expression I have endeavoured diligently to collect and to insert in their proper places, under the general ideas they are designed to convey. Some of these conventional forms, indeed, partake of the nature of proverbial expressions; but actual proverbs, as such, being wholly of a didactic character, do not come within the scope of the present work, and the reader must therefore not expect to find them here inserted.

For the purpose of exhibiting with greater distinctness the relations between words expressing opposite and correlative ideas, I have, whenever the subject admitted of such an arrangement, placed them in two parallel columns on the same page, so that each group of expressions may be readily contrasted with those which occupy the adjacent column, and constitute their antitheses. By carrying the eye from the one to the other, the inquirer may often discover forms of expression of which he may avail himself advantageously to diversify and infuse vigour into his phraseology. Rhetoricians, indeed, are well aware of the power derived from the skilful introduction of antitheses in giving point to an argument, and imparting force and brilliancy to the diction. A too frequent and indiscreet employment of this figure of rhetoric may, it is true, give rise to a vicious and affected style; but it is unreasonable to condemn indiscriminately the occasional and moderate use of a practice on account of its possible abuse.

The study of correlative terms existing in a particular language may often throw valuable light on the manners and customs of the nations using it. Thus Hume has drawn important inferences with regard to the state of society among the ancient Romans, from

---

[1] For example: To take time by the forelock; to turn over a new leaf; to show the white feather; to have a finger in the pie; to let the cat out of the bag; to take care of number one; to kill two birds with one stone, etc.

certain deficiencies which he remarked in the Latin language.[1]

In many cases, two ideas, which are completely opposed to each other, admit of an intermediate or neutral idea, equidistant from both: all these being expressible by corresponding definite terms. Thus, in the following examples, the words in the first and third columns, which express opposite ideas, admit of the intermediate terms contained in the middle column having a neutral sense with reference to the former.

Identity	Difference	Contrariety
Beginning	Middle	End
Past	Present	Future

In other cases, the intermediate word is simply the negative to each of the two opposite positions; as, for example:

| Convexity | Flatness | Concavity |
| Desire | Indifference | Aversion |

[1] 'It is an universal observation,' he remarks, 'which we may form upon language, that where two related parts of a whole bear any proportion to each other, in numbers, rank, or consideration, there are always correlative terms invented which answer to both the parts and express their mutual relation. If they bear no proportion to each other, the term is only invented for the less, and marks its distinction from the whole. Thus *man* and *woman, master* and *servant, father* and *son, prince* and *subject, stranger* and *citizen,* are correlative terms. But the words *seaman, carpenter, smith, tailor,* etc., have no correspondent terms which express those who are no seamen, no carpenters, etc. Languages differ very much with regard to the particular words where this distinction obtains; and may thence afford very strong inferences concerning the manners and customs of different nations. The military government of the Roman emperors had exalted the soldiery so high, that they balanced all the other orders of the state: hence *miles* and *paganus* became relative terms; a thing, till then, unknown to ancient, and still so to modern, languages.' 'The term for a slave, born and bred in the family, was *verna.* As *servus* was the name of the genus, and *verna* of the species without any correlative, this forms a strong presumption that the latter were by far the least numerous: and from the same principles I infer that if the number of slaves brought by the Romans from foreign countries had not extremely exceeded those which were bred at home, *verna* would have had a correlative, which would have expressed the former species of slaves. But these, it would seem, composed the main body of the ancient slaves, and the latter were but a few exceptions.'—HUME, *Essay on the Populousness of Ancient Nations.*

The warlike propensity of the same nation may in a like manner be inferred from the use of the word *hostis* to denote both a *foreigner* and an *enemy.*

Sometimes the intermediate word is properly the standard with which each of the extremes is compared; as in the case of:

Insufficiency   Sufficiency   Redundance

For here the middle term, *Sufficiency*, is equally opposed on the one hand to *Insufficiency* and on the other to *Redundance*.

The forms of correlative expressions would suggest the use of triple, instead of double, columns for tabulating this threefold order of words; but the practical inconvenience attending such an arrangement would probably overbalance its advantages.

It often happens that the same word has several correlative terms, according to the different relations in which it is considered. Thus to the word *Giving* are opposed both *Receiving* and *Taking*; the former correlation having reference to the *persons* concerned in the transfer, while the latter relates to the *mode* of transfer. *Old* has for opposite both *New* and *Young*, according as it is applied to *things* or to *living beings*. *Attack* and *Defence* are correlative terms, as are also *Attack* and *Resistance*. *Resistance*, again, has for its other correlative *Submission*. *Truth in the abstract* is opposed to *Error*, but the opposite of *Truth communicated* is *Falsehood*. *Acquisition* is contrasted both with *Deprivation* and with *Loss*. *Refusal* is the counterpart both of *Offer* and of *Consent*. *Disuse* and *Misuse* may either of them be considered as the correlative of *Use*. *Teaching*, with reference to what is taught, is opposed to *Misteaching*, but with reference to the act itself, its proper reciprocal is *Learning*.

Words contrasted in form do not always bear the same contrast in their meaning. The word *Malefactor*, for example, would, from its derivation, appear to be exactly the opposite of *Benefactor*, but the ideas attached to these two words are far from being directly opposed; for while the latter expresses one who confers a benefit, the former denotes one who has violated the laws.

Independently of the immediate practical uses derivable from the arrangement of words in double columns, many considerations, interesting in a philosophical point of view, are presented by the study of correlative expressions. It will be found, on strict examination, that there seldom exists an exact opposition between two words which may at first sight appear to be the counterparts of one another;

for, in general, the one will be found to possess in reality more force or extent of meaning than the other with which it is contrasted. The correlative term sometimes assumes the form of a mere negative, although it is really endowed with a considerable positive force. Thus *Disrespect* is not merely the absence of *Respect*; its signification trenches on the opposite idea, namely, *Contempt*. In like manner, *Untruth* is not merely the negative of *Truth*; it involves a degree of *Falsehood*. *Irreligion*, which is properly *the want of Religion*, is understood as being nearly synonymous with *Impiety*. For these reasons, the reader must not expect that all the words which stand side by side in the two columns shall be the precise correlatives of each other; for the nature of the subject, as well as the imperfections of language, renders it impossible always to preserve such an exactness of correlation.

There exist comparatively few words of a general character to which no correlative term, either of negation or of opposition, can be assigned, and which therefore require no corresponding second column. The correlative idea, especially that which constitutes a sense negative to the primary one, may, indeed, be formed or conceived; but, from its occurring rarely, no word has been framed to represent it; for in language, as in other matters, the supply fails when there is no probability of a demand. Occasionally we find this deficiency provided for by the contrivance of prefixing the syllable *non*; as, for instance, the negatives of *existence, performance, payment,* etc., are expressed by the compound words, *non-existence, non-performance, non-payment,* etc. Functions of a similar kind are performed by the prefixes *dis-*,[1] *anti-, contra-, mis-, in-,* and *un*[2]. With respect to all these, and especially the last, great latitude is allowed according to the necessities of the case, a latitude which is limited only by the taste and discretion of the author.

On the other hand, it is hardly possible to find two words having in all respects the same meaning, and being therefore interchangeable; that is admitted of being employed indiscriminately, the one or the

---

[1] The word *disannul*, however, had the same meaning as *annul*.

[2] In the case of adjectives, the addition to a substantive of the terminal syllable *less*, gives it a negative meaning : as *taste, tasteless; care, careless; hope, hopeless; friend, friendless; fault, faultless,* etc.

other, in all their applications. The investigation of the distinctions to be drawn between words apparently synonymous forms a separate branch of inquiry which I have not presumed here to enter upon; for the subject has already occupied the attention of much abler critics than myself, and its complete exhaustion would require the devotion of a whole life. The purpose of this work, it must be borne in mind, is not to explain the signification of words, but simply to classify and arrange them according to the sense in which they are now used, and which I presume to be already known to the reader. I enter into no inquiry into the changes of meaning they may have undergone in the course of time.[1] I am content to accept them at the value of their present currency, and have no concern with their etymologies, or with the history of their transformations; far less do I venture to thrid the mazes of the vast labyrinth into which I should be led by any attempt at a general discrimination of synonyms. The difficulties I have had to contend with have already been sufficiently great without this addition to my labours.

The most cursory glance over the pages of a dictionary will show that a great number of words are used in various senses, sometimes distinguished by slight shades of difference, but often diverging widely from their primary signification, and even, in some cases, bearing to it no perceptible relation. It may even happen that the very same word has two significations quite opposite to one another. This is the case with the verb *to cleave*, which means *to adhere tenaciously*, and also *to separate by a blow*. *To propugn* sometimes expresses *to attack*; at other times, *to defend*. *To ravel* means both *to entangle* and *to disentangle*. The alphabetical index at the end of this work sufficiently shows the multiplicity of uses to which, by the elasticity of language, the meaning of words has been stretched so as to adapt them to a great

---

[1] Such changes are innumerable; for instance, the words *tyrant, parasite, sophist, churl, knave, villain,* anciently conveyed no opprobrious meaning. *Impertinent* merely expressed *irrelative*, and implied neither *rudeness* nor *intrusion*, as it does at present. *Indifferent* originally meant *impartial*; *extravagant* was simply *digressive*; and *to prevent* was properly to *precede* and *assist*. The old translations of the Scriptures furnish many striking examples of the alterations which time has brought in the signification of words. Much curious information on this subject is contained in Trench's *Lectures on the Study of Words.*

variety of modified significations in subservience to the nicer shades of thought which, under peculiarity of circumstances, require corresponding expression. Words thus admitting of different meanings have therefore to be arranged under each of the respective heads corresponding to these various acceptations. There are many words, again, which express ideas compounded of two elementary ideas belonging to different classes. It is therefore necessary to place these words respectively under each of the generic heads to which they relate. The necessity of these repetitions is increased by the circumstance that ideas included under one class are often connected by relations of the same kind as the ideas which belong to another class. Thus we find the same relations of *order* and of *quantity* existing among the ideas of *Time* as well as those of *Space*. Sequence in the one is denoted by the same terms as sequence in the other, and the measures of time also express the measures of space. The cause and the effect are often designated by the same word. The word *Sound,* for instance, denotes both the impression made upon the ear by sonorous vibrations, and also the vibrations themselves, which are the cause or source of that impression. *Mixture* is used for the act of mixing, as well as for the product of that operation. *Taste* and *smell* express both the sensations and the qualities of material bodies giving rise to them. *Thought* is the act of thinking, but the same word denotes also the idea resulting from that act. *Judgment* is the act of deciding, and also the decision come to. *Purchase* is the acquisition of a thing by payment, as well as the thing itself so acquired. *Speech* is both the act of speaking and the words spoken; and so on with regard to an endless multiplicity of words. Mind is essentially distinct from Matter, and yet, in all languages, the attributes of the one are metaphorically transferred to those of the other. Matter, in all its forms, is endowed by the figurative genius of every language with the functions which pertain to intellect; and we perpetually talk of its phenomena and of its powers as if they resulted from the voluntary influence of one body on another, acting and reacting, impelling and being impelled, controlling and being controlled, as if animated by spontaneous energies and guided by specific intentions. On the other hand, expressions of which the primary signification refers exclusively to the properties and actions of matter are metaphorically applied to the phenomena of thought and volition, and even to the feelings and passions of the soul; and in speaking of a *ray of hope*, a *shade of doubt*, a *flight of fancy*, a *flash of wit*, the *warmth of emotion*, or the *ebullitions of anger,* we are scarcely conscious that we are employing metaphors which have this material origin.

As a general rule, I have deemed it incumbent on me to place words and phrases which appertain more especially to one head also under the other heads to which they have a relation, whenever it appeared to me that this repetition would suit the convenience of the inquirer, and spare him the trouble of turning to other parts of the work; for I have always preferred to subject myself to the imputation of redundance, rather than incur the reproach of insufficiency.[1] When, however, the divergence of the associated from the primary idea is sufficiently marked, I have contented myself with making a reference to the place where the modified signification will be found. But in order to prevent needless extension, I have, in general, omitted *conjugate words*[2] which are so obviously derivable from those that are given in the same place, that the reader may safely be left to form them for himself. This is the case with adverbs derived from adjectives by the simple addition of the terminal syllable *-ly,* such as *closely, carefully, safely,* etc., from *close, careful, safe,* etc., and also with adjectives or participles immediately derived from the verbs which are already given. In all such cases, an 'etc.' indicates that reference is understood to be made to these roots. I have observed the same rule in compiling the index, retaining only the primary or more simple word, and omitting the conjugate words

[1] Frequent repetitions of the same series of expressions, accordingly, will be met with under various headings. For example, the word *Relinquishment*, with its synonyms, occurs as a heading at No. 624, where it applies to *intention*, and also at No. 782, where it refers to *property*. The word *Chance* has two significations, distinct from one another: the one implying the *absence of an assignable* cause, in which case it comes under the category of the relation of Causation, and occupies the place No. 156; the other, the *absence of design*, in which latter sense it ranks under the operations of the Will, and has assigned to it the place No. 621. I have, in like manner, distinguished *Sensibility, Pleasure, Pain, Taste,* etc., according as they relate to *Physical* or to *Moral Affections*; the former being found at Nos. 375, 377, 378, 390, etc., and the latter at Nos. 822, 827, 828, 850, etc.

[2] By '*conjugate* or *paronymous* words is meant, correctly speaking, different parts of speech from the same root, which exactly correspond in point of meaning' – *A Selection of English Synonyms*, edited by Archbishop Whately.

obviously derived from them. Thus I assume the word *short* as the representative of its immediate derivatives *shortness, shorten, shortening, shortened, shorter, shortly,* which would have had the same references, and which the reader can readily supply.

The same verb is frequently used indiscriminately either in the active or transitive, or in the neuter or intransitive sense. In these cases I have generally not thought it worth while to increase the bulk of the work by the needless repetition of that word, for the reader, whom I suppose to understand the use of the words, must also be presumed to be competent to apply them correctly.

There are a multitude of words of a specific character, which although they properly occupy places in the columns of a dictionary, yet, having no relation to general ideas, do not come within the scope of this compilation, and are consequently omitted. The names of objects in Natural History, and technical terms belonging exclusively to Science or to Art, or relating to particular operations, and of which the signification is restricted to those specific objects, come under this category. Exceptions must, however, be made in favour of such words as admit of metaphorical application to general subjects with which custom has associated them and of which they may be cited as being typical or illustrative. Thus the word *Lion* will find a place under the head of *Courage,* of which it is regarded as the type. *Anchor*, being emblematic of *Hope*, is introduced among the words expressing that emotion; and, in like manner, *butterfly* and *weathercock*, which are suggestive of fickleness, are included in the category of *Irresolution.*

With regard to the admission of many words and expressions which the classical reader might be disposed to condemn as vulgarisms, or which he, perhaps, might stigmatize as pertaining rather to the slang than to the legitimate language of the day, I would beg to observe that, having due regard to the uses to which this work was to be adapted, I did not feel myself justified in excluding them solely on that ground, if they possessed an acknowledged currency in general intercourse. It is obvious that, with respect to degrees of conventionality, I could not have attempted to draw any strict lines of demarcation, and far less could I have presumed to erect any absolute standard of purity. My object, be it remembered, is not to regulate the use of words, but simply to supply and to suggest such as may be wanted on occasion, leaving the proper selection entirely to the discretion and taste of the employer. If a novelist or a dramatist, for example, proposed to delineate some vulgar personage, he would wish to have the power of putting into the mouth of the speaker expressions that would accord with his character, just as the actor, to revert to a former comparison, who had to personate a peasant, would choose for his attire the most homely garb, and would have just reason to complain if the theatrical wardrobe furnished him with no suitable costume.

Words which have, in process of time, become obsolete, are, of course, rejected from this collection. On the other hand, I have admitted a considerable number of words and phrases borrowed from other languages, chiefly the French and Latin, some of which may be considered as already naturalized; while others, though avowedly foreign, are frequently introduced in English composition, particularly in familiar style, on account of their being peculiarly expressive, and because we have no corresponding words of equal force in our own language.[1] The rapid advances which are being made in scientific knowledge, and consequent improvement in all the arts of life, and the extension of those arts and sciences to so many new purposes and objects, create a continual demand for the formation of new terms to express new agencies, new wants, and new combinations. Such terms, from being at first merely technical, are rendered, by more general use, familiar to the multitude, and having a well-defined acceptation, are eventually incorporated into the language, which they contribute to enlarge and to enrich. *Neologies* of this kind are perfectly legitimate, and highly advantageous; and they necessarily introduce those gradual and progressive changes which every language is destined to undergo.[2] Some modern writers,

[1] All these words and phrases are printed in italics.

[2] Thus in framing the present classification I have frequently felt the want of substantive terms corresponding to abstract qualities or ideas denoted by certain adjectives, and have been tempted to invent words that might express these abstractions; but I have yielded to this temptation only in the four following instances: having framed from the adjectives *irrelative, amorphous, sinistral,* amd *gaseous* the abstract nouns *irrelation, amorphism, sinistrality,* and *gaseity.* I have ventured also to introduce the adjective *intersocial* to express the active voluntary relations between man and man.

however, have indulged in a habit of arbitrarily fabricating new words and a new-fangled phraseology without any necessity, and with manifest injury to the purity of the language. This vicious practice, the offspring of indolence or conceit, implies an ignorance or neglect of the riches in which the English language already abounds, and which would have supplied them with words of recognized legitimacy, conveying precisely the same meaning as those they so recklessly coin in the illegal mint of their own fancy.

A work constructed on the plan of classification I have proposed might, if ably executed, be of great value in tending to limit the fluctuations to which language has always been subject, by establishing an authoritative standard for its regulation. Future historians, philologists, and lexicographers, when investigating the period when new words were introduced, or discussing the import given at the present time to the old, might find their labours lightened by being enabled to appeal to such a standard, instead of having to search for data among the scattered writings of the age. Nor would its utility be confined to a single language, for the principles of its construction are universally applicable to all languages, whether living or dead. On the same plan of classification there might be formed a French, a German, a Latin, or a Greek Thesaurus, possessing, in their respective spheres, the same advantages as those of the English model. Still more useful would be a conjunction of these methodized compilations in two languages, the French and the English, for instance; the columns of each being placed in parallel juxtaposition. No means yet devised would so greatly facilitate the acquisition of the one language by those who are acquainted with the other: none would afford such ample assistance to the translator in either language; and none would supply such ready and effectual means of instituting an accurate comparison between them and of fairly appreciating their respective merits and defects. In a still higher degree would all those advantages be combined and multiplied in a *Polyglot Lexicon* constructed on this system.

Metaphysicians engaged in the more profound investigation of the Philosophy of Language will be materially assisted by having the ground thus prepared for them in a previous analysis and classification of our ideas, for such classification of ideas is the true basis on which words, which are their symbols, should be classified.[1] It is by such analysis alone that we can arrive at a clear perception of the relation which these symbols bear to their corresponding ideas, or can obtain a correct knowledge of the elements which enter into the formation of compound ideas, and of the exclusions by which we arrive at the abstractions so perpetually resorted to in the process of reasoning and in the communication of our thoughts.

Lastly, such analyses alone can determine the principles on which a

---

[1] The principle by which I have been guided in framing my verbal classification is the same as that which is employed in the various departments of natural history. Thus the sectional divisions I have formed correspond to natural families in botany and zoology, and the filiation of words presents a network analogous to the natural filiation of plants or animals.

The following are the only publications that have come to my knowledge in which any attempt has been made to construct a systematic arrangement of Ideas with a view to their expression. The earliest of these, supposed to be at at least nine hundred years old, is the AMERA CÓSHA, or *Vocabulary of the Sanscrit Language*, by Amera Sinha, of which an English translation, by the late Henry T. Colebrooke, was printed at Serampoor in the year 1808. The classification of words is there, as might be expected, exceedingly imperfect and confused, especially in all that relates to abstract Ideas or mental operations. This will be apparent from the very title of the first section, which comprehends '*Heaven, Gods, Demons, Fire, Air, Velocity, Eternity, Much*'; while *Sin, Virtue, Happiness, Destiny, Cause, Nature, Intellect, Reasoning, Knowledge, Senses, Tastes, Odours, Colours*, are all included and jumbled together in the fourth section. A more logical order, however, pervades the sections relating to natural objects, such as *Seas, Earth, Towns, Plants*, and *Animals*, which form separate classes, exhibiting a remarkable effort at analysis at so remote a period of Indian literature.

The well-known work of Bishop Wilkins, entitled *An Essay towards a Real Character and a Philosophical Language*, published in 1668, had for its object the formation of a system of symbols which might serve as a universal language. It professed to be founded on a 'scheme of analysis of the things or notions to which names were to be assigned'; but notwithstanding the immense labour and ingenuity expended in the construction of this system, it was soon found to be far too abstruse and recondite for practical application.

In the year 1797 there appeared in Paris an anonymous work, entitled *Pasigraphie, ou Premiers Éléments du nouvel Art-Science d'écrire et d'im...* *une langue de manière à être lu et entendu dans toute autre langue sans...* of which an edition in German was also published. It contains... tabular schemes of categories, all of which appear to be ex... artificial, and extremely difficult of application, as well...

strictly *Philosophical Language* might be constructed. The probable result of the construction of such a language would be its eventual adoption by every civilized nation, thus realizing that splendid aspiration of philanthropists – the establishment of a Universal Language. However Utopian such a project may appear to the present generation, and however abortive may have been the former endeavours of Bishop Wilkins and others to realize it,[1] its accomplishment is surely not beset with greater difficulties than have impeded the progress to many other beneficial objects which in former times appeared to be no less visionary, and which yet were successfully achieved, in later ages, by the continued and persevering exertions of the human intellect. Is there at the present day, then, any ground for despair that, at some future stage of that higher civilization to which we trust the world is gradually tending, some new and bolder effort of genius towards the solution of this great problem may be crowned with success, and compass an object of such vast and paramount utility? Nothing, indeed, would conduce more directly to bring about a golden age of union and harmony among the several nations and races of mankind than the removal of that barrier to the interchange of thought and mutual good understanding between man and man which is now interposed by the diversity of their respective languages.

[1] 'The languages,' observes Horne Tooke, 'which are commonly used throughout the world, are much more simple and easy, convenient and philosophical, than Wilkins's scheme for a *real character*; or than any other scheme that has been at any other time imagined or proposed for the purpose.' – ''Επεα Πτερόεντα, p. 125.

Sphere Reference

THE STUDENT'S CONTEMPORARY ENGLISH DICTIONARY

A dictionary for all students.
Straightforward definitions are supplemented with examples to
show the word defined, in context. A simple pronunciation system
is used. Idiomatic expressions and contemporary meanings are
included.

Sphere Reference

GUIDE TO CONTEMPORARY ENGLISH USAGE

A clear guide to take you through the maze of English grammar.
Technical terms are avoided and explanations illustrated by
quotations taken from such well-known writers as Iris Murdoch,
Graham Greene and Frederic Raphael.

Sphere Reference

HANDBOOK OF 20th CENTURY QUOTATIONS

DEATH ('on the plus side, death is one of the few things that can be done as easily lying down'), **CELIBACY** ('is not an inherited characteristic'), **CHILDREN** ('It is no wonder people are so horrible when they start life as children'), **GERTRUDE STEIN** ('the mama of dada'), **POETRY** ('the stuff in books that doesn't quite reach the margins'), **VIRGINIA WOOLF** ('a beautiful little knitter'), **LONGEVITY** ('the revenge of talent upon genius'), **BOGNOR** ('Bugger Bognor!') . . . .

Sphere Reference

DICTIONARY OF BIOGRAPHICAL QUOTATIONS

GLADSTONE ('They told me Gladstone read Homer for fun, which I thought served him right'), **HENRY JAMES** ('was one of the nicest old ladies I ever met'), **LORD MACAULAY** ('good sort of fellow, made of oatmeal'), **RONALD FIRBANK** ('as orchidaceous as his fictional fantasies'), **QUEEN ANNE** ('one of the smallest people ever set in a great place'), **BEAUMONT AND FLETCHER** ('had one wench in the house between them'), **CAMUS** ('The Humphrey Bogart of Absurdism'), **NAPOLEON** ('ought not to be confused with Nelson, in spite of their hats being so alike') . . . .